Re

MW00449410

Domain-Specific
Application Frameworks
Frameworks Experience by Industry

Mohamed E. Fayad
Ralph E. Johnson

Wiley Computer Publishing

John Wiley & Sons, Inc.
NEW YORK · CHICHESTER · WEINHEIM · BRISBANE · SINGAPORE · TORONTO

Publisher: Robert Ipsen
Editor: Marjorie Spencer
Assistant Editor: Margaret Hendrey
Managing Editor: Marnie Wielage
Text Design & Composition: North Market Street Graphics

Designations used by companies to distinguish their products are often claimed as trademarks. In all instances where John Wiley & Sons, Inc., is aware of a claim, the product names appear in initial capital or ALL CAPITAL LETTERS. Readers, however, should contact the appropriate companies for more complete information regarding trademarks and registration.

This book is printed on acid-free paper. ⊚

This publication is designed to provide accurate and authoritative information in regard to the subject matter covered. It is sold with the understanding that the publisher is not engaged in professional services. If professional advice or other expert assistance is required, the services of a competent professional person should be sought.

Chapter 25, "The Amulet Prototype-Instance Framework," is based on "The Amulet Environment: New Models for Effective User Interface Software Development," by Brad A. Myers, Richard G. McDaniel, Robert C. Miller, Alan Ferrency, Andrew Faulring, Bruce D. Kyle, Andrew Mickish, Alex Klimovitski, and Patrick Doane, which appeared in *IEEE Transactions on Sotfware Engineering*, Volume 23, Issue 6. pp. 347–365; June 1997.

Chapter 28, "A Multimodeling Simulation Framework," was originally published as, "OOPM: An Object-Oriented Multimodeling and Simulation Framework," Copyright 1998 by Simulation Councils, Inc. Reprinted by permission.

Library of Congress Cataloging-in-Publication Data:
Domain-specific application frameworks : frameworks experience by
   industry / editors, Mohamed Fayad, Ralph Johnson
        p.   cm.
   Includes bibliographical references.
   ISBN 0-471-33280-1
   1. Application software—Development.   2. Computer software—
Reusability.   3. Object-oriented programming (Computer science)
I. Fayad, Mohamed, 1950–   . II. Johnson, Ralph.
QA76.76.D47D66   1999
005.1—dc21   99-26920
                                                          CIP

Printed in the United States of America.

10 9 8 7 6 5 4 3 2 1

*To the memory of my mom and dad,
to my lovely wife Raefa, to my beautiful
daughters Rodina and Rawan, and to my
handsome son Ahmad.*

—Mohamed E. Fayad

*To the creators of Simula and Smalltalk,
who were the first to see the vision.*

—Ralph E. Johnson

Contents

Dedication   iii

Preface   xv

Acknowledgments   xix

Chapter 1   **Introduction**   1
                Mohamed E. Fayad

                1.1 Application Framework Classifications   2

                1.2 Organization of This Book   2

                1.3 Summary   4

                1.4 References   4

Part One: **Computer-Integrated Manufacturing Frameworks**   5
                Mohamed E. Fayad

Chapter 2   **SEMATECH CIM Framework**   7
                David Doscher and Robert Hodges

                2.1 Background   7

                2.2 Why Use a Framework?   10

                2.3 Structure of the CIM Framework   11

                2.4 Infrastructure Support for the CIM Framework   14

                2.5 CIM Framework Documentation   16

                2.6 Lessons from Framework Specification and Development   17

                2.7 Future Directions   18

                2.8 Summary   18

                2.9 References   18

Chapter 3   **A CIM Framework and Pattern Language**   **21**
         Amund Aarsten, Davide Brugali, and Giuseppe Menga

         3.1   Patterns and Pattern Languages   21
         3.2   The FMS Example   23
         3.3   The Pattern Language   23
         3.4   Summary   41
         3.5   References   41

Chapter 4   **OSEFA: Framework for Manufacturing**   **43**
         Hans Albrecht Schmid

         4.1   Domain-Specific Blackbox Frameworks   44
         4.2   Manufacturing Subdomain with Frozen Spots   45
         4.3   Variability of a Manufacturing Cell Configuration
               and Hot Spots   49
         4.4   Layered Framework Architecture   52
         4.5   Processing Control Layer   53
         4.6   Processing Command Hot Spot   56
         4.7   Domain Object Layer   57
         4.8   Standardized Machine and Device Layer   59
         4.9   Concrete Machine and Device Layer   60
         4.10   Application Creation   61
         4.11   Interface Configurator   63
         4.12   Experiences   63
         4.13   Summary   65
         4.14   Selected References   65

Chapter 5   **Framework Reuse over Different CIM Subdomains**   **67**
         Hans Albrecht Schmid

         5.1   Manufacturing Subdomains   68
         5.2   Framework Architecture   71
         5.3   Common Subdomain Properties and Basic Framework
               Architecure   72
         5.4   Store-Centered Framework OSEFA   74
         5.5   Extending OSEFA for Decentral Data Storage   77
         5.6   Flow-Centered Manufacturing Framework   78
         5.7   Intelligent Assembly Line Framework   79
         5.8   General Results   82

	5.9 Summary	83
	5.10 References	84

Chapter 6 | **A Case Study for Flexible Manufacturing Systems** | **85**
Davide Brugali, Giuseppe Menga, and Amund Aarsten

6.1 Frameworks and Pattern Languages	86
6.2 The Application Domain	87
6.3 The Framework	89
6.4 Summary	97
6.5 References	98

Sidebar 1 | **Theory Meets Practice: Lessons Learned Using SEMATECH's CIM Framework** | **100**
Pete Whelan

Part Two: | **More Manufacturing Frameworks** | **103**
Mohamed E. Fayad

Chapter 7 | **CEF: A Concurrent Engineering Framework** | **105**
Der Shung Yang and Uday Mehta

7.1 Customization Process	106
7.2 Dynamic Domain Modeling	109
7.3 Architectural Design	113
7.4 Lessons Learned	117
7.5 Summary	118
7.6 References	119

Chapter 8 | **Distributed Manufacturing Execution Systems Framework** | **121**
William Boyle

8.1 Architecture	122
8.2 Framework Implementation	129
8.3 Summary	137

Chapter 9 | **Production Resource Manager (PRM) Framework** | **139**
Walter C. Dietrich, Jr., Goodwin R. Chin, Brenda L. Dietrich, Thomas Robert Ervolina, J.P. Fasano, Robin Lougee-Heimer, Elizabeth J. Poole, Jung-Mu Tang, Robert H. Wang, Robert J. Wittrock, and Danny C. Wong

| 9.1 Domain Background and Framework Design Objectives | 140 |
| 9.2 Framework Architecture | 143 |

9.3 Scenario Framework   146

9.4 Data Interface Framework   151

9.5 User Interface Framework   154

9.6 Two PRM Applications   155

9.7 Summary   157

9.8 References   158

Chapter 10 Developing Domain Frameworks   **159**

Sally M. Chan and Terence L. Lammers

10.1 Object-Oriented Domain Engineering (OODE) Method   159

10.2 Case Study: Process Monitoring and Diagnosis Domain 167

10.3 Summary   175

10.4 References   175

Chapter 11 Measurement Systems Framework   **177**

Jan Bosch

11.1 Measurement Systems: Requirements   178

11.2 Measurement System Framework Design   181

11.3 Simulating Framework Applications   189

11.4 Example: Beer Can System   193

11.5 Evaluation   199

11.6 Related Work   204

11.7 Summary   204

11.8 References   205

Part Three: Distributed Systems Frameworks   **207**

Mohamed E. Fayad

Chapter 12 Compound Active Documents   **211**

Peter Wegner

12.1 CORBA Component-Based Software Architecture   212

12.2 CORBA System and Application Services   215

12.3 OpenDoc: A CORBA Framework for Compound
      Active Documents   216

12.4 Microsoft's Compound Document Architecture:
      COM/OLE/ActiveX   219

12.5 Java Interfaces, Applets, and Beans   221

12.6 The Event Model of Component Interaction   224

12.7 Modes of Interaction   226

12.8 Specifying Frameworks by Constraints on Component
       Behavior   228

12.9 Summary   230

12.10 References   230

Chapter 13 Supervision and Control Systems Framework Architecture   231
*Riccardo Capobianchi, Denis Carcagno, Alberto Coen-Porisini,
Dino Mandrioli, and Angelo Motzenti*

13.1 The OpenDREAMS Architecture and Methodology   233

13.2 The CORBA/OpenDREAMS Services   235

13.3 S&C CORBA/OpenDREAMS Domain   236

13.4 The TRIO-Based Development Method   239

13.5 State of the Art and Future Development   247

13.6 Summary   248

13.7 References   248

Chapter 14 EPEE: A Framework for Supercomputing   251
Jean-Marc Jezequel and Jean-Lin Pacherie

14.1 The EPEE Framework   252

14.2 Using EPEE to Build a Parallel Linear Algebra Library 265

14.3 Writing Applications with Paladin   272

14.4 Related Work   275

14.5 Summary   276

14.6 References   277

Sidebar 2   Frameworks in the Healthcare Domain   280
Yasser alSafadi

Chapter 15 The Bast Framework for Reliable Distributed Computing   283
Benoit Garbinato and Rachid Guerraoui

15.1 Chapter Overview   283

15.2 The Need for Reliability   284

15.3 The Bast Framework   287

15.4 Reliable Distributed Programming   288

15.5 Bast Overview   291

15.6 Using Bast   294

15.7 In-Depth View of Bast   296

15.8   Protocol Composition and Tuning   302

15.9   Applying the DTM Agreement Pattern   305

15.10   Implementation Issues   313

15.11   Summary   323

15.12   References   324

Chapter 16   **Object-Oriented Realtime System Framework**   **327**
Win-Bin See and Sao-Jie Chen

16.1   High-Level Reuse Techniques   328

16.2   Class Hierarchy in OORTSF   330

16.3   Scenario of Object Collaboration in OORTSF   332

16.4   Framework-Oriented Development of Application Systems   334

16.5   Extending OORTSF   336

16.6   Summary   337

16.7   References   337

Chapter 17   **JAWS: A Framework for High-Performance Web Servers**   **339**
James Hu and Douglas Schmidt

17.1   Applying Patterns and Frameworks to Web Servers   340

17.2   The JAWS Adaptive Web Server   345

17.3   Web Server Benchmarking Testbed and Empirical Results   365

17.4   Summary   375

17.5   References   376

Sidebar 3   **The Five-Module Framework for Internet Application Development**   **379**
Wei-Tek Tsai

Part Four: Network and Telecommunication Frameworks   **383**
Mohamed E. Fayad

Chapter 18   **A Framework for Network Management Agents**   **385**
Hartmut Kocher and Joerg Schabernack

18.1   MIB Framework   387

18.2   Summary   395

18.3   References   396

Chapter 19 Telecommunication Network Planning Framework   **397**
Bruno Messmer, Kateel Vijayananda, and Beat Liver

19.1 The Framework NETPLAN   399

19.2 Example Application   414

19.3 Summary   415

19.4 References   417

**Chapter 20 FIONA: A Framework for Integrating Distributed
C³I Applications**   **419**
Per Spilling, Chris Dee, and Peter Beijderwellen

20.1 The GRACE System Architecture   421

20.2 The FIONA Framework   423

20.3 Design Patterns Used in FIONA   425

20.4 The Applet Framework   431

20.5 Lessons Learned   433

20.6 Summary   434

20.7 References   434

**Chapter 21 MultiTel: Multimedia Telecommunication
Services Framework**   **437**
Lidia Fuentes and Jose M. Troya

21.1 Component-Oriented Model   439

21.2 The Compositional Architecture of MultiTEL   443

21.3 MultiTEL: An MTS Framework in Java   450

21.4 Middleware Platform   457

21.5 Framework Deployment   459

21.6 Summary   465

21.7 References   466

Chapter 22 Event Filter Framework and Applications   **469**
Mohamed Fayad and Jingkun Hu

22.1 Event-Filtering Framework Components   470

22.2 Event-Filtering Framework Design   471

22.3 Implementation of the Event-Filtering Framework   474

22.4 Event-Filtering Framework Applications   479

22.5 Experiences and Lessons Learned   483

22.6 Summary   486

22.7 References   487

Sidebar 4   Layla: Network Management Interfaces Framework   489
Rudolf K. Keller and Jean Tessier

Part Five: Environments   491
Mohamed E. Fayad

Chapter 23 Beyond-Sniff: A Framework-Based Component   495
Walter Bischofberger and Kai-Uwe Maetzel

23.1 From Sniff to Beyond-Sniff   497

23.2 Beyond-Sniff's Architecture   498

23.3 The Tool Integration Framework: A Component-
Collaboration Framework   503

23.4 Architectural Support for Iterative Development
and Evolution   505

23.5 Case Study: Boar   508

23.6 Lessons Learned   509

23.7 Summary   510

23.8 References   511

Chapter 24 Extensible Computational Chemistry Environment (ECCE) 513
Donald R. Jones, Deborah K. Gracio, Karen L. Schuchardt,
Thomas L. Keller, and Hugh L. Taylor

24.1 What Is Ecce?   513

24.2 Design Objectives   514

24.3 Data-Centered Design   515

24.4 Why an Object-Oriented Framework?   516

24.5 Problem Domain: Computational Chemistry   517

24.6 Ecce Architecture   518

24.7 Framework Components   519

24.8 Chemistry Data Model Framework   520

24.9 Experiences   525

24.10 Future Work   526

24.11 Summary   526

24.12 References   527

Chapter 25 The Amulet Prototype-Instance Framework   **529**
          Brad A. Myers, Richard G. McDaniel, and Robert C. Miller

          25.1 Layered Design   530

          25.2 Outline of Typical Applications   542

          25.3 Debugging Tools   543

          25.4 Status and Future Work   544

          25.5 Related Work   544

          25.6 Summary   545

          25.7 References   545

Chapter 26 Jadve: Graph-Based Data Visualization Framework   **547**
          Wenke Lee and Naser S. Barghouti

          26.1 The Design and Implementation of Jadve   549

          26.2 The Jadve API   555

          26.3 Jadve Applications   556

          26.4 Related Work   560

          26.5 Future Work   561

          26.6 Summary   561

          26.7 References   562

Chapter 27 Object Environments   **565**
          James C. Stafford

          27.1 Framework for Building an Object Environment   566

          27.2 Package Overview   567

          27.3 Summary   590

          27.4 References   590

Chapter 28 A Multimodeling Simulation Framework   **591**
          Robert M. Cubert and Paul A. Fishwick

          28.1 An Overview   594

          28.2 Object-Oriented Approach to Modeling Geometry
                and Dynamics   595

          28.3 Model Refinement   598

          28.4 Visual Elements of OOPM   600

          28.5 Nonvisual Elements of OOPM   609

28.6 Summary   612

28.7 References   612

Chapter 29 Application Frameworks: A Survey   615
Amr Yassin and Mohamed Fayad

29.1 Framework Classification   616

29.2 Framework Documentation   619

29.3 Framework Comparisons   621

29.4 Frameworks Facts   623

29.5 Problems and Lessons Learned   625

29.6 Summary   632

29.7 References   632

Appendix A Glossary   633
Mohamed E. Fayad

Appendix B Index of Authors   643
Mohamed E. Fayad

Appendix C About the CD-ROM   661

Index   665

Preface

This book is for anyone who wants to implement large-scale software reuse through object-oriented (OO) application frameworks. Its purpose is to help the reader understand one of the hottest technologies related to software reuse—*frameworks*—and provide guidelines for making decisions about this technology. Decision makers such as corporate presidents and vice presidents, as well as software project managers and project leaders, will benefit from the experiences and lessons learned in this book. It illustrates the development and use of framework technology in several domains, such as manufacturing, communication and networking, distributed systems, and software development environments. In 29 chapters, we describe application frameworks in diverse domains and discuss our real-world experiences.

Domain-Specific Application Frameworks follows three central themes:

How to build and adapt domain-specific application frameworks through examples

How to overcome problems with application frameworks

What we can learn from our experiences with domain-specific application frameworks

Outstanding Features

This book provides valuable insight into successful OO application framework examples. All the material has been derived from actual experiences and is presented in a practical, easy-to-understand manner. We explain in detail the philosophy behind the frameworks and how to apply them to different domains. After reading this book you will:

- Understand how to build OO application frameworks (through extensive examples)
- Be prepared to utilize frameworks

- Understand diverse domain-specific application framework architectures
- Be ready to face problems with frameworks, by learning from our experiences
- Be familiar with the design of more than 25 domain-specific application frameworks
- Be ready to explore new areas of domain-specific framework technology

Who Should Read This Book

This book draws on the experience and collective wisdom of its numerous contributors to explore problems and present insights into the design, development, and deployment of specific application and enterprise frameworks. It will prove invaluable to software vendors in building frameworks that are both robust and flexible; to managers in identifying the most appropriate frameworks for the specific enterprise they are engaged in; and to application developers in effectively exploiting frameworks to construct complete applications quickly and efficiently.

This book is intended for a broad community of computer and software professionals involved in the management and development of domain-specific application framework projects, including company executives, project managers, engineering staff, technologists, software managers, object-oriented business owners, presidents, and CEOs. Software engineers, system engineers, system analysts, software developers, software process groups, contract administrators, customers, technologists, software methodologists, and enterprise program developers will greatly benefit from this book.

Supplemental Materials

Supplemental materials can be found at the contributors' URLs, which are included in the Index of Authors at the end of this book. Updates, news, question–and-answer sessions, and comments for the authors can be found on www.cs.unr.edu/~fayad and the Wiley Web page for this book at **www.wiley.com/compbooks/fayad.**

The Wiley Web page for this book includes the following:

Extended preface

Extended acknowledgments that recognize the work of the contributors to and reviewers of this book

Brief table of contents

Detailed table of contents

Chapter abstracts

Complete chapter references

Miscellaneous listings of theme issues, special interest groups, conferences, and so on

Extended index of authors

Annotated references

Question-and-answer session

FAQ: application and enterprise frameworks

CD-ROM Contents

The CD-ROM that accompanies this book contains several complete or partial application frameworks that are mostly described in this book. The CD-ROM contains several items, such as complete application frameworks, demos, framework code, sample models, manuals, documentation, presentations, design patterns, freeware and shareware, and more. Appendix C provides more information about the CD-ROM contents.

Acknowledgments

This book would not have been possible without the help of many great people. I am grateful to all of the authors for their submissions and their patience, and to all of the reviewers for valuable and useful reviews and input.. I would like to take this opportunity to say that I am honored to have had a chance to work with the two editors for this book, Douglas Schmidt and Ralph Johnson, and with all of the authors and reviewers—this was a great and fun project because of your tremendous help and extensive patience. Thank you for believing in me.

I would also like to thank all of the people who have had a part in the production of this book. First, and foremost, all of the coauthors of this book and I owe our families our utmost gratitude for being so patient while we have turned their world in a whirlwind by injecting this writing activity into their already full lives. We also thank the various reviewers and editors that have helped in so many ways to get the book together. We thank our associates who have offered their advice and wisdom in defining the content of the book and we owe a special thanks to those who have worked on the various projects covered in the case studies and examples.

A special thanks to my wife Raefa, my lovely daughters Rodina and Rawan, and my son Ahmad for their great patience and understanding. Special thanks to my friend Mauri Laitinen for his encouragement and long discussions about the topics and the issues in this book. Thanks to all my students, in particular, Amr Yassin, Jinkun Hu, David Naney, Adam Altman; to my friends Jun Gu, Marshall Cline, W.T. Tsai, and Yasser alSafadi for their encouragement during this project; and to the *Communications of the ACM* staff—Diana Crawford, Tom Lambert, and Robert Fox —for their support.

We are very grateful to the editors at John Wiley & Sons. Thanks to Marjorie Spencer for her belief in and support of the book, to Margaret Hendrey for her patience while helping me to put this text together, and to Marnie Wielage for overseeing the production of such a gigantic project.

Contributor Acknowledgments

Thank you to all of the contributors for their tremendous effort and patience in making this volume a reality. Thanks also to all the many contributors who participated in the review process for their valuable comments and excellent reviews. This volume provides a unique source and a wide spectrum of knowledge to aid software vendors, managers, developers, and users in their journey to manage, develop, adapt, and utilize application and enterprise frameworks. It is an appropriate book for a variety of graduate courses in advanced software engineering and framework technology. It was a great honor to work with all of you. This volume was made possible only by your enormous efforts; we sincerely thank all of the contributors. (See www.wiley.com/compbooks/fayad for detailed contributor acknowledgments.)

Reviewer Acknowledgments

A special thanks to all the reviewers for their useful reviews, helpful critiques, and great insights, which have resulted in a clearer presentation and more integrated book than anything I could have done alone. This book is part of a three-volume publication and has been thoroughly reviewed by more than 500 reviewers. Your comments and reviews were invaluable contributions to the making of this book. I have been honored to work with all of you and I believe that your valuable comments have led to improvements in the overall content and presentation of this book. Thank you all. Please see www.wiley.com/compbooks/fayad on the Wiley Web page for a complete list of acknowledgments.

Special Acknowledgments

The authors of Chapter 3 (A. Aarsten, D. Brugali, and G. Menga) would like to note that the work presented in that chapter has been supported by the project "Tecnologie di elaborazione distribuita nei servizi multimediali per l'azienda virtuale e il commercio elettronico" in collaboration with CSELT, Turin, Italy.

The author of Chapters 4 and 5 (Hans A. Schmid) would like to thank Clemens Ballarin, Franco Indolfo, Frank Mueller, and Jochen Peters for their help in building the framework OSEFA, Juergen Roeder for helping him prepare the chapters, and the Deutsche Forschungsgemeinschaft (DFG) for their support.

The author of Chapter 11 (Jan Bosch) would like to thank Anders Kambrin, Anders Dackehed, and Sven-Ove Olsson from EC-Gruppen, and Martin Walfisz, Jonas Matton, and Magnus Robertsson, master students at the University of Karlskrona/Ronneby, for their help.

The authors of Chapter 13 (R. Capobianchi, D. Carcagno, A. Coen-Porisini, D. Mandrioli, and A. Motzenti) would like to thank Virginie Watine and Alexandre Feray for their contributions to the definition of the OpenDREAMS domains. The present work is partially funded by the ESPRIT project OpenDREAMS (Ep 20843).

The authors of Chapter 14 (J. Jezequel and J. Pacherie) would like to thank all of the people who have been involved in this project. Special thanks to Frédéric Guidec for his work on the design, development, and testing of the PALADIN library.

The authors of Sidebar 4 (R.K. Keller and J. Tessier) acknowledge that this work was in part funded by the Ministry of Industry, Commerce, Science, and Technology, Quebec, under the IGLOO project organized by the Centre de Recherche Informatique de Montreal, by Teleglobe Canada Inc., and by the National Sciences and Research Council of Canada.

The authors of Chapter 23 (W. Bischofberger and K. Maetzel) would like to thank all of the former members of the Beyond-Sniff team (Bruno Schäffer, Brad Edelman, Thomas Kofler, Marcel Neuhäusler, Arno Vrtacnik, and Jürgen Wothke), Erich Gamma, Dirk Riehle, Peter Schnorf, and André Weinand.

The authors of Chapter 25 (B.A. Myers, R.G. McDaniel, and R.C. Miller) would like to thank Bernita Myers, Alan Ferrency, Andrew Faulring, Bruce D. Kyle, Andrew Mickish, Alex Klimovitski, and Patrick Doane for helping in the preparation of this chapter.

The authors of Chapter 26 (W. Lee and N.S. Barghouti) would like to thank Eleftherios (Lefty) Koutsofios, Stephen North, John Mocenigo, and Robin Chen of AT&T Labs–Research, and Jeff Korn of Princeton University, for their helpful discussions.

The authors of Chapter 28 (R.M. Cubert and P.A. Fishwick) would like to thank the following funding sources: Rome Laboratory, Griffiss Air Force Base under contract F30602-95-C-0267 and under grant F30602-95-1-0031; U.S. Department of the Interior under grant 14-45-0009-1544-154; National Science Foundation Engineering Research Center (ERC) under grant EEC-94-02989; and University of Florida College of Engineering for providing a fellowship to the first author. The authors acknowledge those who have authored some of the OOPM software, including Tolga Goktekin (conceptual modeler and FSM editor), Youngsup Kim (FBM and SDM editors), Gyooseok Kim (RBM editor), Kangsun Lee and Dean Norris (EQN editor), and Andrew Reddish (VRML geometry). The authors also thank Phil Darby for being our model author and domain expert on snails, and Kangsun Lee for additional work as model author.

Introduction

Application frameworks are generally domain-specific applications, such as user interfaces, computer-integrated manufacturing frameworks, distributed systems, networking and telecommunications, or multimedia collaborative work environments [Fayad 1999a]. A framework is more than a class hierarchy [Lewis 1995]. It is a semicomplete application containing dynamic and static components that can be customized to produce user-specific applications [Fayad 1999b]. Due to the generic nature of framework components, mature frameworks can be reused as the basis for many other applications [Fayad 1999b]. This book consists of 28 chapters and 4 sidebars that describe several size application frameworks in multiple and different domains, and discusses experiences related to object-oriented (OO) application frameworks.

This book helps framework developers and application developer organizations apply framework technology effectively by citing examples from the real world. It combines the actual experiences and lessons learned from developing and/or adapting different application frameworks. It illustrates how framework technology is used in application development, providing valuable and real insights drawn from successful OO application framework examples. Most of the application frameworks in this book are derived from actual experiences and are presented in a practical, easy-to-understand manner. This book provides several distinguished framework architectures and discusses in detail the philosophy behind the frameworks and how to apply it to different domains. This book covers the following domains:

Computer-integrated manufacturing frameworks. These include SEMATECH CIM, OSEFA, and production resource manager (PRM).

Distributed system frameworks. These include EPEE, BAST, and JAWS.

Networking and telecommunication application frameworks. These include the Telecommunication Network Planning framework, FIONA, MultiTEL, Event Filters, and Layla.

System development environment frameworks. These include Beyond Sniff, the Extensible Computational Chemistry Environment (ECCE), the Amulet Prototype-Instance framework, Jadve, and the Multimodeling Simulation framework.

1.1 Application Frameworks Classifications

The application frameworks in this book map well to the application framework classifications based on their scope [Fayad 1999a; Fayad-Schmidt 1997; Fayad-Laitinen 1998], which are classified into three categories:

- System infrastructure frameworks
- Middleware integration frameworks
- Enterprise application frameworks

The majority of application frameworks in this book are middleware integration frameworks, such as BEST and JAWS, and enterprise application frameworks, such as SEMATECH CIM, OSEFA, and PRM.

1.2 Organization of This Book

This book is organized into five major parts: Part One, "Computer-Integrated Manufacturing Frameworks," Part Two, "More Manufacturing Frameworks," Part Three, "Distributed Systems Frameworks," Part Four, "Networking and Telecommunication Frameworks," and Part Five, "Environments."

Part One contains Chapters 2 through 6 and Sidebar 1. This part discusses computer-integrated manufacturing (CIM) and OSEFA frameworks. Chapter 2 describes the background, key goals, and structure of the SEMATECH CIM framework. Chapter 3 discusses the G++ framework, which supports the evolutionary development of computer-integrated manufacturing systems; its main contribution is to document the framework by means of the corresponding pattern language. Chapter 4 describes the OSEFA framework and shows how to generate applications from OSEFA by calling first configuration services of the framework class Manufacturing Cell and then its Run method. Chapter 5 discusses framework reuse over different CIM subdomains. Chapter 6 presents the G++ application framework for computer-integrated manufacturing. Sidebar 1 presents lessons learned from working with the SEMATECH CIM framework.

Part Two contains Chapters 7 through 11 and describes several manufacturing frameworks. Chapter 7 introduces a framework for building concurrent engineering applications. Chapter 8 describes the technology utilized by FACTORYworks, a next-generation manufacturing execution system (MES). Chapter 9 describes a production resource manager framework. Chapter 10 discusses the object-oriented domain engineering (OODE) process. Chapter 11 discusses the design and implementation of an object-oriented framework for the domain of measurement systems that can be used as a functional core.

Part Three contains Chapters 12 through 17 and Sidebars 2 and 3. Chapter 12 discusses CORBA/OpenDoc, COM/OLE/ActiveX, and Java/JavaBeans, which concretely illustrate emerging principles of component and document design, such as the events-properties-methods model. Chapter 13 describes a framework architecture to support the development of supervision and control systems based on Common Object Request Broker Architecture (CORBA). Chapter 14 proposes a framework whereby the parallel codes can be encapsulated in object-oriented software components that can be reused, combined, and customized with confidence by library designers to offer application programmers easy-to-use programming models. Sidebar 2 discusses the frameworks in the health care domain. Chapter 15 describes BAST, an open object-oriented framework for building reliable distributed applications and middleware. Chapter 16 shows how to exploit the key issues of the design and application of an object-oriented realtime system framework (OORTSF) for the development of realtime applications in embedded systems. Chapter 17 illustrates how to use frameworks and patterns for communication software to develop a high-performance web server called JAWS. Sidebar 3 presents the five-module architecture of a framework for Internet application development.

Part Four contains Chapters 18 through 22 and Sidebar 4. This part introduces network management and telecommunication frameworks, such as FIONA and Multi-TEL. Chapter 18 discusses the design of an object-oriented framework dedicated to the implementation of the network management interfaces in telecommunication networks. Chapter 19 proposes a flexible, object-oriented software framework for the development of integrated network planning and design tools. Chapter 20 allows distributed C^3I application components to share a common presentation facility. Chapter 21 presents a compositional framework (MultiTEL) that encapsulates the architecture of multimedia telecommunication services (MTSs) as a collection of computational components controlled by connectors that abstract coordination patterns. Chapter 22 describes the main components of the event-filtering framework. Sidebar 4 defines a network management interface (NMI) as the middle layer of a network management system, situated between the high-level control processes and the low-level components of the system.

Part Five contains Chapters 23 through 28. This part introduces environments frameworks, such as Beyond Sniff (Chapter 23), ECCE (Chapter 24), Amulet (Chapter 25), Jadve (Chapter 26), Object Environments (Chapter 27), and object-oriented physical multimodeling (OOPM) (Chapter 28). Chapter 23 presents the framework-specific experience gained in developing Sniff and Beyond Sniff from the architecture's perspective as well as the development process's perspective. Chapter 24 introduces ECCE, which is a comprehensive, object-oriented environment for molecular modeling, analysis, and simulation. Chapter 25 discusses the Amulet framework. Chapter 26 presents the design and implementation, as well as example applications, of Jadve, a framework for graph-based data visualization applications written in Java. Chapter 27 describes an object environment as a set of useful interfaces required by most objects, which should come under the management of the targeted application. Chapter 28 discusses the Multimodeling Simulation framework.

1.3 Summary

This book contains real samples of computer-integration manufacturing frameworks (Part One and Part Two), distributed systems frameworks (Part Three), networking and telecommunication application frameworks (Part Four), and system development environment frameworks (Part Five). This indicates that enterprise and application frameworks are becoming mainstream and accepted technology in developing software applications. These enterprise and application frameworks samples are just the beginning of widespread use of framework technology in major domains. We encourage you to get involved with others working on enterprise and application frameworks by attending conferences, participating in online mailing lists and newsgroups, and contributing your insights and experience.

1.4 References

[Fayad 1999a] Fayad, M.E., D. Schmidt, and R. Johnson. *Building Application Frameworks: Object-Oriented Foundations of Framework Design.* New York: John Wiley & Sons, 1999.

[Fayad 1999b] Fayad, M.E., D. Schmidt, and R. Johnson. *Implementing Application Frameworks: Object-Oriented Frameworks at Work.* New York: John Wiley & Sons, 1999.

[Fayad-Laitinen 1998] Fayad, M.E. and M. Laitinen. *Transition to Object-Oriented Software Development.* New York: John Wiley & Sons, August 1998.

[Fayad-Schmidt 1997] Fayad, M.E., and D. Schmidt. Object-oriented application frameworks. *Communications of the ACM* 40(10), October 1997.

[Lewis 1995] Lewis, Ted. *Object-Oriented Application Frameworks.* Greenwich, CT: Manning, 1995.

Computer-Integrated Manufacturing Frameworks

Part One discusses computer-integrated manufacturing (CIM) and OSEFA frameworks. The CIM framework defines a component-based architecture for a next generation of agile manufacturing execution systems (MESs). For the first time, suppliers of semiconductor MESs and users of those systems have collaborated to specify the standard partitioning and capabilities for a marketplace of commercial MES solutions. The need for rapid information systems changes has resulted in a requirement that applications be broken into smaller pieces for manageability and implemented across distributed networks for cost and performance reasons. Interoperability between individual applications in this environment has also become of paramount importance. Independent applications, each of which performs separate enterprise information systems functions, must interoperate to be effective because most have complex dependencies and relationships with each other. The requirements for rapid change and interoperability in the face of increased applications complexity led SEMATECH to conclude that a CIM framework architecture is a necessity. A framework architecture will become an essential part of using information systems for competitive advantage in the semiconductor industry.

In OSEFA, software cell controllers for manufacturing cells are created from the blackbox framework OSEFA without programming, by selecting, parameterizing, and configuring blackbox components. Different kinds of blackbox components, ranging from ones that represent the manufacturing processing logic, through others that represent abstract entities from the manufacturing domain, to those representing concrete machines and devices, cover the complete manufacturing subdomain.

Part One of this volume contains Chapters 2 through 6 and Sidebar 1.

Chapter 2, "The SEMATECH CIM Framework," describes the background, key goals, and structure of the CIM framework. This experience and the results SEMATECH and its member companies achieved offer practical lessons on standardizing object-oriented frameworks for specific business domains.

Chapter 3, "A CIM Framework and Pattern Languages," discusses the G++ framework, which supports the evolutionary development of computer-integrated manufacturing systems, and its main contribution is to document the framework by means of the corresponding pattern language.

Chapter 4, "OSEFA: Framework for Manufacturing," describes the OSEFA framework, providing an overview of the frozen spots of the manufacturing domain and its hot spots. The different abstraction levels of the hot spots correspond to a layered implementation of the framework. The hot-spot subsystems that implement the hot spots on the different layers transform an abstract, domain-related service request, step by step, in different ways, depending on the configuration of the manufacturing cell, into service requests to concrete machines and devices. An application is created from OSEFA by calling first configuration services of the framework class Manufacturing Cell and then its Run method. An interactive configurator, comparable to a graphical user interface (GUI) configurator, simplifies the task of application creation even more. Experiences with OSEFA show that the application creation effort and time to market may be reduced by an order of magnitude or more.

Chapter 5, "Framework Reuse over Different CIM Subdomains," addresses a central problem for the development of a domain-specific framework: Which properties of a domain allow a statement to be made if it can be covered by a single framework? Based on real-life experience with the CIM manufacturing domain, the chapter presents the approach: Use orthogonal characteristics of a domain to partition it into subdomains, make a rough design of the architecture of the frameworks for the subdomains, and analyze and compare the subdomain architectures for conclusions. This chapter presents experiences from a CIM manufacturing domain and generalizes them. Since this domain is too large to be covered by a single framework, it is partitioned into 24 subdomains. The architecture of three frameworks designed and developed for altogether six subdomains is presented and compared. The chapter demonstrates why one framework cannot cover the whole domain, as well as which sets of subdomains can be covered by a single framework. The chapter also shows which framework artifacts can be reused among different frameworks when integration into a single framework is not possible.

Chapter 6, "A Case Study for Flexible Manufacturing Systems," presents the G++ application framework for computer-integrated manufacturing and illustrates how its design is derived from the G++ pattern language, highlighting the relationships between application frameworks, patterns, and pattern languages.

Sidebar 1, "Theory Meets Practice: Lessons Learned Using SEMATECH's CIM Framework," presents lessons learned from working with the SEMATECH CIM framework. It discusses benefits and shortcomings of the CIM framework and identifies several general issues. It also provides graphical representations of the CIM framework components and an overall architecture.

CHAPTER 2

Sematech CIM Framework

SEMATECH is the semiconductor manufacturing technology consortium, whose member companies are AMD, Digital, Hewlett-Packard, IBM, Intel, Lucent, Motorola, National Semiconductor, Rockwell, and Texas Instruments. SEMATECH has worked with major U.S. semiconductor companies to develop a software framework for computer-integrated manufacturing (CIM). This chapter describes the background, key goals, and structure of the CIM framework [Sematech 1997] and offers practical lessons for standardizing object-oriented frameworks for specific business domains.

2.1 Background

The history and the goals of the CIM framework are discussed in this section.

2.1.1 History

SEMATECH initiated the CIM framework project in 1991, anticipating the following future manufacturing needs:

- Commercial alternatives to proprietary internal software
- Solutions assembled from multiple suppliers' offerings
- Use of existing systems while evolving new capabilities

SEMATECH first partnered with Texas Instruments to build on the object-oriented foundation provided by the Microelectronics Manufacturing Science and Technology (MMST) project [Baudoin 1996]. SEMATECH member companies helped validate, evolve, and broaden support for the CIM framework specification. CIM software suppliers, including the Texas Instruments WORKS project, the IBM SuperPOSEIDON project, and the Promis Encore! Group, provided key improvements based on implementation experience.

2.1.2 Business Case

The complexity of the information systems that support the execution of semiconductor manufacturing increases with the complexity of the manufacturing processes. Manufacturing execution systems (MESs) are a fundamental resource that is essential to the success of semiconductor manufacturing operations. The MES interfaces with the manufacturing, equipment, and process technologies, as well as the factory architecture, software, and hardware platforms. The investment required to develop MESs is huge and the rate of change adds an even larger burden of software maintenance to the cost of ownership.

To help manage this growing software complexity, SEMATECH has developed a semiconductor manufacturing framework specification, called the SEMATECH CIM framework. The CIM framework defines a component-based architecture that forms the basis for a next generation of agile MESs. For the first time, suppliers of semiconductor MESs and users of those systems have collaborated to specify the standard partitioning and capabilities for a marketplace of commercial MES solutions.

Rapid information systems changes require applications that can be separated into smaller pieces and managed independently. These smaller software components can then be deployed across distributed networks to reduce cost and improve performance. Interoperability between individual applications in this environment has also become more important. Independent applications that perform separate functions must work well together because of complex dependencies and relationships with each other.

The requirements for rapid change and interoperability in the face of increased applications complexity led SEMATECH to conclude that a CIM framework architecture was a necessity. A framework architecture will become an essential part of using information systems for competitive advantage in the semiconductor industry.

2.1.3 Goals of the CIM Framework

Flexibility, interoperability, substitutability, integration, reuse, and a healthy supplier marketplace are some of the goals of CIM framework, which are discussed in this section.

Flexibility

The CIM framework makes information systems more flexible in adapting to changes in requirements. Just as the manufacturing environment exists in a constant state of change, the information systems that support the factories must also be engineered for change. The most flexible and cost-effective means of change is small, manageable increments. New CIM framework–compliant components may need to be added to extend functionality or be substituted for previous implementations to achieve better alignment with business needs, improved performance, or reduced cost of ownership.

Interoperability

The CIM framework allows separate software components to interoperate in providing a complete solution. The move toward cost-effective open distributed computing environments is a fundamental force in most enterprises. This change brings with it increased risks associated with heterogeneous software components that must communicate across local and wide area networks. The CIM framework specifications help ensure that these diverse, distributed software components will interoperate with one another in a production environment.

The CIM framework provides a guarantee of interoperability by specifying verifiable contracts between software components in terms of services exchanged, events recognized, data passed, and constraints enforced. Further, it provides a common architectural foundation to ensure that the implementers will realize their contracts in a consistent fashion. This results in interoperability between interacting software components at both a technology level and, more important, at a semantic level, which defines the common understanding of the behavior of each component.

Substitutability

The CIM framework establishes the basis for replaceability of software components by establishing standard boundaries for the units of change. Framework-compliant components will have well-defined specifications for each interconnection or dependency on other components. Any new component that adheres to the same specification can be expected to work with minimal impact on the unchanged components.

Integration

The CIM framework enables integration of legacy systems that were not developed to work as part of a framework. Use of techniques that wrap the functionality of existing software allows those capabilities to coexist and integrate with new framework components. Through encapsulation of the implementation details, a wrapped component may be used in a framework solution along with those that are built for framework compliance.

This degree of integration can be achieved only with rigorous specifications of the dependencies between parts. The goal of integration can be in conflict with the other goals of flexibility and substitutability. This conflict is minimized with the CIM framework through a behavioral focus that makes the interactions between components an integral part of the specifications.

Reuse

The SEMATECH CIM framework facilitates the reuse of a growing collection of proven design patterns as well as implemented components. The specification of the framework provides a well-documented model defining the abstraction of the components' design while still allowing implementation choices that offer suppliers the opportunity to differentiate their products. This abstract level of reuse complements the more concrete potential for factoring common services that can be reused by different components.

Reuse of framework components depends on the ability first to locate and select the reusable resource and then to specialize it for the new usage context. The CIM framework supports specialization of reusable components through the mechanisms of object-oriented inheritance and delegation of responsibility to tailored lower-level components.

A Healthy Supplier Marketplace

The CIM framework, along with complementary external framework efforts such as the Object Management Group's Domain Technology Committee, provides a basis for competition among software suppliers to provide the common components needed by many enterprises. To respond to this opportunity, the software industry is moving en masse toward a component-based packaging of commercial software. Today's commercial systems are being rearchitected to allow migration toward a vital marketplace of software components in the not-too-distant future.

As semiconductor manufacturers struggle to reduce operating costs wherever possible to enhance profits and shareholder value, internal information technology (IT) budgets for custom software development must be focused on key areas for competitive advantage. There is no room for redundant efforts to create software components that have little differentiating value. The suppliers of CIM framework–compliant components will fill this need by offering components that can be used effectively across the semiconductor industry.

2.2 Why Use a Framework?

SEMATECH uses the term *framework* to refer to a collection of specifications of interacting software components that comprise a solution for a particular domain. A framework embodies generalized expertise in the domain based on analysis and synthesis of a wide range of specific solutions. Framework technology also supports the assembly of these solutions from multiple supplier offerings.

The CIM framework is an instance of a *callable* framework [Sparks 1996]. A callable framework allows the application to retain the thread of control and provides services when the application calls the framework. By contrast, a *calling* framework provides a control loop that calls application-provided code at appropriate times.

Frameworks are an evolutionary step up from traditional software class libraries. By utilizing object-oriented techniques, such as inheritance and polymorphism, interfaces can be specialized and extended by software developers. Traditional software class library interfaces are limited to using the interface as provided, composing new interfaces from existing ones, or simply ignoring provided interfaces.

2.3 Structure of the CIM Framework

The CIM framework is based on the Object Management Group's Object Management Architecture (OMG's OMA) [OMG 1996; Siegel 1996]. OMG's OMA enables distributed-location transparent and language-independent communication between objects. It also supplies a set of common services needed by distributed object applications. Interfaces between service requesters and service providers are specified using OMG Interface Definition Language (IDL). Clients are isolated from server implementation details such as internal data representations and algorithms.

Behavior specifications supplement interfaces through an object-oriented analysis of the CIM domain [Baudoin 1996]. Interfaces representing object types map real-world semiconductor manufacturing objects and concepts to their software equivalents. Components package these interfaces and behavior specifications as the building blocks of the framework. CIM suppliers develop executable code called *application objects* based on one or more of the CIM framework components. Suppliers have flexibility in grouping component implementations into product packages and provide added value through extensions or optimizations. Components that have an open specification support the integration of application objects from multiple suppliers.

Figure 2.1 shows a sample application object implementing a specialized software ProcessMachine interface to a specific type of equipment. The executable code contains the CIM framework–specified interfaces, supplier-defined interfaces, and translation layer code to convert the CIM-level instructions into instructions executed by the tool control software. The executable would then be registered as the interface module to the XYZ equipment.

2.3.1 Interfaces

Interfaces in the CIM framework are collections of externally visible features that belong to a particular type of domain object such as a Lot or Machine, mapping a real-world object into its software equivalent. The most important features of interfaces are operation signatures that define the names and parameters of the methods the interface provides. Interfaces also offer the specification of anticipated abnormal outcomes in the form of declared exceptions. Finally, interfaces include the specification of events that are occurrences detected by the object, usually based on real-world state changes of the corresponding domain object, which are published for notification to any other object that may subscribe to the Event. The producer of an Event does not have knowledge of the consumers of its event notifications.

Interfaces may be abstract or concrete. Abstract interfaces are not meant to be directly instantiated and are defined for interface inheritance purposes. Concrete interfaces are intended to be implemented as executable software. An interface may be implemented in various ways depending on the target platform and programming language. In a language such as C++, an interface would typically map to a class. Some examples of CIM framework interfaces are:

Resource. Abstract class for entities that plays an active role in the factory.

NamedEntity. Abstract class that supports the concept of a named item.

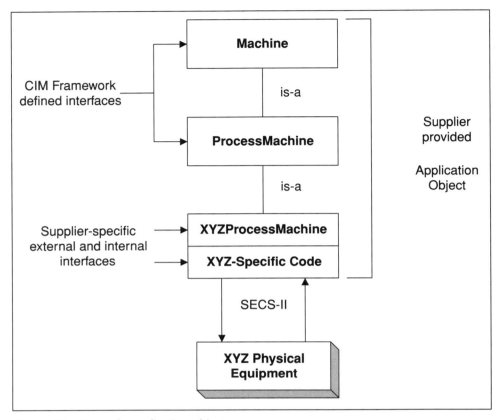

Figure 2.1   Example application object.

OwnedEntity. Abstract class that supports the concept of an owned item.

ComponentManager. Manages the resources in its domain.

JobSupervisor. Creates and tracks system-level operations (jobs).

MaterialManager. Manages materials in the factory.

Material. Products, consumables, and durables used in manufacturing.

2.3.2 Components

CIM framework components are collections of related interfaces that form a coherent unit. The CIM framework deals with the specification of components, not their actual implementations. Though implementation details are beyond the scope of the CIM framework, conformant systems must provide an implementation for each interface of any supported component. The component is the smallest unit of functionality that can be added, deleted, enabled, or disabled in a CIM framework–compliant application.

2.3.3 Application Objects

Application objects that conform to the CIM framework are collections of components that can be considered subsystems. Collections of components may be packaged together into deployable pieces of software that provide the units of installation and substitutability. Suppliers have flexibility in grouping component implementations into product packages and provide added value through extensions or optimizations. The CIM framework has not specified the application object level, although it is likely that the component groupings that have been informally defined under the designation *Functional Group* will become the basis for implemented application objects.

2.3.4 Scope of the CIM Framework

Figure 2.2 represents the scope of the CIM framework and illustrates its context. Note that application objects can use one or more CIM framework components, as illustrated by the dotted lines. Each CIM framework component is, in turn, composed of one or more interfaces. The core of the distributed computing infrastructure is an Object Request Broker (ORB) that conforms to the OMG's Common Object Request Broker Architecture (CORBA) [OMG 1996]. The ORB is responsible for managing the communications between requesters of services (clients) and providers of services (servers).

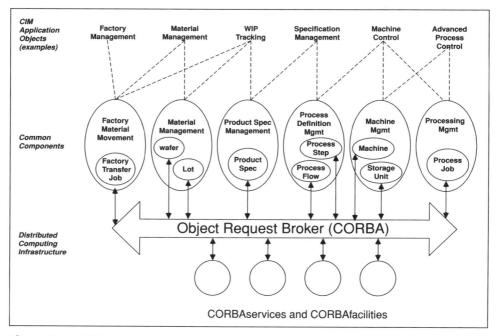

Figure 2.2   CIM framework architecture context.

2.4 Infrastructure Support for the CIM Framework

The CIM framework depends upon a set of services, facilities, and communications mechanisms that support collaboration between distributed CIM domain objects. OMG's OMA provides standard specifications for most of those mechanisms. The OMA specifies a services architecture that includes the Object Request Broker, Common Object Services (CORBAServices), Common Facilities (CORBAfacilities), Domain Interfaces and non-standard interfaces for application objects. Figure 2.3 depicts the OMA Reference Model.

Each element of the OMA Reference Model is summarized subsequently. For further information, the reader is encouraged to see [OMG 1996]. The approach taken by the CIM framework is to leverage existing (and anticipated) OMG specifications through selective composition of defined CORBAServices and CORBAfacilities, with minimal specialization.

2.4.1 Object Request Broker

The Object Request Broker is the backbone of the OMA in that it is the mechanism that supports communications between distributed objects. That is, it enables client objects

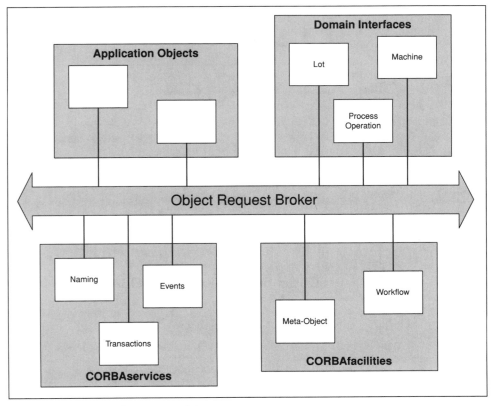

Figure 2.3   OMA Reference Model.

to send requests and receive responses from server objects. (Note that an object may be both a client and a server.)

The Common Object Request Broker Architecture "defines a framework for different ORB implementations to provide common ORB services and interfaces to support portable clients and implementation of objects" [OMG 1995]. It is an open specification for a global message bus (the ORB) that provides communications between distributed objects. CORBA specifies the mechanisms by which components within an implementation of a CIM framework communicate with one another.

2.4.2 CORBAServices

CORBAServices provide basic functionality to support distributed object applications. CORBAServices are a collection of specifications that support basic functions for using and implementing objects. These basic services are necessary to construct any distributed application and should be defined independently of application domains.

CIM framework–conformant applications will need the support of the following object services:

- Persistent object service
- Transaction service
- Life-cycle service
- Event service
- Naming service

2.4.3 CORBAFacilities

CORBAFacilities provide functionality at a higher level and are intended to support distributed applications. CORBAFacilities represent those interfaces and uniform sequencing semantics that reduce the effort required to develop or improve interoperability between OMA-compliant applications. CORBAFacilities are just now beginning to be specified by the OMG in the area of metadata management and Internet support. These should play an increasing role in the CIM framework as they mature.

2.4.4 Domain Interfaces

The CIM framework is itself an example of the type of domain interfaces that are being specified by the OMG Domain Technical Committee. These specifications provide the standard interfaces that form a precompetitive foundation for the development of interoperable applications in specific industry domains.

2.4.5 Application Objects

Application objects correspond to the traditional notion of an application and represent functionality within a specific vertical market. An application object is coarse-grained and usually is a self-contained executable entity. The OMG notion of application object is the same as the concept employed in the CIM framework.

2.5 CIM Framework Documentation

The SEMATECH CIM framework is documented through SEMATECH Technology Transfer documents, which are available through the SEMATECH home page on the Internet [Sematech 1997]. The main documents are the SEMATECH CIM Framework Specification and the companion Sematech CIM Framework Architecture Guide.

The SEMATECH CIM Framework Specification provides a description of the functional groups, components, and classes of the CIM framework. Each functional group has the following:

- A descriptive summary of capabilities
- A list of components in the group
- A brief description of each component
- A component relationship diagram

Each Component within a functional group provides the following:

- A summary of provided services
- A component information model
- A component interaction diagram, if relevant

Interfaces are documented using a standard template and fully compilable OMG Interface Definition Language (IDL). The standard format includes the following:

- The interface name
- The interface inheritance
- A description of the interface
- Operation signatures
- Exceptions
- Events

The notation used to describe the CIM framework includes the following:

Component relationship model. This shows the logical combination of components within a functional group and interactions among the component parts.

Component information model. This shows the object types (interfaces) along with their interobject relationships and cardinalities.

Component interaction diagram. This expresses framework dynamics by describing the sequence of collaborations between objects.

Object dynamic model. This shows object behavior as changes in state that result from specific events.

Object state tables. A set of tables that provide supplementary state information. The tables provide descriptive state definitions and identify state query mechanisms, the triggers effecting state transition, and the actions resulting from state transitions.

The notations used for the CIM framework documentation are derived from leading second-generation object-oriented methodologies. The OMG is adopting a standard object analysis and design metamodel and notation based on these same foundations that will provide a solid basis for future documentation of frameworks.

The entire SEMATECH CIM framework is also described using the OMG Interface Definition Language (IDL), which provides a rigorous textual description of the defined interfaces. IDL can be compiled into any of several programming languages, as provided by the OMG CORBA specification language mappings.

2.6 Lessons from Framework Specification and Development

SEMATECH's experience with the CIM framework highlighted several challenges that face developers of domain framework specifications.

2.6.1 Implementation Experience Is Essential

A stable framework specification must be based on experience from several different implementations. Industry acceptance is enhanced when key suppliers influence the specification based on product development experience.

2.6.2 Frameworks Increase Initial Cost

Specifying a framework involves significant cost beyond that needed for single-use software development. Costly framework skills, added education, validation, and conformance testing further increase the initial cost of specification and implementation. Generalizing and refining the specification multiplies cost with iterations through the development process.

2.6.3 Infrastructure Coupling Is Hard to Avoid

The framework specification tends to become coupled to the architecture of the underlying infrastructure. Separating domain and technology concerns and keeping implementation details out of the framework specifications require great diligence.

2.6.4 Frameworks Overlap

As domain frameworks become more common, the specifications of multiple frameworks will need to be integrated. Independent frameworks will overlap and intersect in ways that require reconciliation and alignment.

2.6.5 Technology Is Immature

The CIM framework is based on technology that is still maturing in fundamental ways. The OMA does not yet provide all of the capabilities needed for framework specification and component-based development. Stronger specification techniques such as pre- and postconditions are needed to ensure semantic interoperability. Additional object model features such as operation overloading or multiple interfaces will be required for larger-scale integration of components.

2.7 Future Directions

The future of the CIM framework lies in broadening the marketplace of compliant implementations and achieving formal standardization. Standardization of the CIM framework was started by the Semiconductor Materials and Equipment International (SEMI) organization in early 1997. In 1998, the SEMI Global CIM Framework Task Force initiated two successful letter ballots, resulting in adoption of the first two parts of the CIM framework standard. The first part, the Provisional Specification for CIM Framework Domain Architecture, establishes the architectural foundation for the component structure and partitioning, and identifies the responsibilities of each major component of the framework. The second document, Guide for CIM Framework Technical Architecture, defines required infrastructure technologies needed to support framework implementations and provides guidance on the technical choices system implementers and their customers must be prepared to make. These first standards will be followed by a series of ballots to adopt each of the component specifications that together will form the complete CIM framework standard.

Other groups have also started work to evolve the CIM framework and apply it to other manufacturing industries. The National Institute for Standards and Technology (NIST) has established projects based on the CIM framework. The Object Management Group Manufacturing Domain Task Force is also expected to specify related areas of manufacturing execution systems functionality in future OMG technology adoptions.

2.8 Summary

SEMATECH provided an extendible framework specification designed to meet the semiconductor industry's needs for flexible, cost-effective applications. CIM suppliers are learning to use the CIM Framework Specification and are exploring the implications of open, framework-based products. The CIM framework will achieve its goals as these compliant commercial solutions become available.

Framework technology signifies the beginning of a new era in software development that will challenge developers and greatly benefit users of information technology solutions.

2.9 References

[Baudoin 1996] Baudoin, C., and G. Hollowell. *Realizing the Object-Oriented Lifecycle*. Upper Saddle River, NJ: Prentice Hall, 1996.

[OMG 1995] Object Management Group. *The Common Object Request Broker: Architecture and Specification, Revision 2.0.* Framingham, MA: Object Management Group, 1995.

[OMG 1996] Object Management Group World Wide Web Site, www.omg.org, 1996.

[Sematech 1997] SEMATECH. *Computer Integrated Manufacturing (CIM) Framework Specification, Version 1.5.* Austin, TX: SEMATECH. Available from www.sematech.org; INTERNET, 1997.

[Siegel 1996] Siegel, J. *CORBA Fundamentals and Programming.* New York: John Wiley & Sons, 1996.

[Sparks 1996] Sparks, S., K. Benner, and C. Faris. Managing object-oriented framework reuse. *IEEE Computer*, Theme Issue on Managing Object-Oriented Development, M.E. Fayad and M. Cline, editors, pp. 52–61, 29(9), September 1996.

CHAPTER 3

A CIM Framework
and Pattern Language

Computer integrated manufacturing (CIM) systems build on large client-server control architectures and factory-wide information systems. They are created by integrating multivendor, heterogeneous, and ad hoc subsystems, and their development spans a relatively long period of time. Because of their size and complexity, CIM systems are a challenging environment for the definition of standard architectures and the development of reusable application frameworks.

This chapter describes G++, a framework for developing CIM systems. The framework solves the basic architectural and design problems of CIM systems and provides classes that implement building blocks for new applications. Using the framework, a specific CIM control system will be developed by adopting the architecture embedded in the framework, by reusing elemental building blocks, and by extending the basic design components.

As described in [Brugali 1997], the G++ framework has followed a life span that is strictly interlaced with the development of the corresponding G++ pattern language. This chapter describes the G++ framework in detail and emphasizes how the pattern language supports the evolutionary development of CIM applications that build on the framework.

Examples of G++ CIM applications can be found in [Menga 1993].

3.1 Patterns and Pattern Languages

Traditionally, object-oriented reuse was conceived as class or component reuse. Recently, as also evidenced by the growing interest in application frameworks, more importance has been given to reuse of structures of components. An important role in this development has been played by *design patterns*, a literary form introduced by the architect Christopher Alexander [Alexander 1979], which has been adopted in object-oriented development as a technique for design reuse [Gamma 1995]. Design patterns focus attention on the fundamental role that patterns of relationships between the elements of an architecture have in any design.

Alexander suggests that each design pattern ". . . is a rule, which establishes a relationship between a context, a system of forces which arises in that context, and a configuration which allows these forces to resolve themselves in that context" [Alexander 1977]. Moreover, all of these rules—or patterns—are part of a larger system, a pattern language, which embodies the experience gained by generations of designers in solving a class of similar problems. In order that the knowledge represented by a pattern language can be shared and become part of the collective knowledge in a certain application domain, it has to be structured, and the structure of the language is created by the network of connections among individual patterns.

The whole set of patterns for a specific application domain, together with their structuring principles, becomes a high-level language and is a design method for the domain that accompanies the software life cycle from the analysis to the final implementation.

In order to describe the patterns, we use the generally accepted structure, which has the following fields. Each component within a group is detailed with:

- The *pattern name*

- The *context* in which the pattern is applicable

- The design *problem* raised by the context

- The conflicting *forces* that must be resolved

- The *solution* offered by the pattern

- An *example* of the pattern in the case study; the set of all the examples for a pattern language defines a whole application from the analysis phase to the final implementation

- References to *related patterns* at lower levels of the language, when applicable

Design patterns have been proposed as a technique to document frameworks [Johnson 1992]. In our opinion, a pattern language is even better suited for framework documentation than a collection of individual patterns. Just as a framework is not just a collection of classes, a pattern language is not just a collection of patterns. The pattern language provides an organization of the sequence of decisions that generated the framework design, and these must be understood in their proper context by the developer when making new decisions regarding which classes and collaboration structures to add to the framework. The pattern language therefore makes it easier for the developer to reach the level of understanding required to extend the framework. We believe that the framework user also benefits from a better understanding of the architecture and design behind the framework.

For further consideration of the relationships between frameworks and pattern languages, see [Brugali 1999].

3.2 The FMS Example

Throughout this chapter, a simple flexible manufacturing system (FMS), the most dynamic subsystem of a CIM application, will be used as an example. An FMS is a control system at the shop-floor level of a factory. It is made up of a certain number of production cells composed of machine tools, stores, and automatic transportation systems, which concurrently execute the manufacture of lots composed of different types of pieces. (A *lot* is an administrative entity, representing a group of identical pieces manufactured together.)

   The FMS used as an example is a production shop made up of two cells—one for machining and the other for assembling. Each cell is made up of a set of numerically controlled machines, an automatic inventory system for raw and finished pieces, and an automatic guided vehicle (AGV) system to move pieces. Integration is achieved through a network, which encompasses shop and cell computers, along with computerized numerical controls (CNCs) for the machines and programmable logic controllers (PLCs) for the inventory and the AGV systems. The production is characterized, in any period of time, by the presence in the cells of several concurrent small lots of different piece types. Each piece of a lot undergoes a sequence of operations, each one on a different machine, according to the piece type. The cell, with a realtime dispatcher, assigns pieces to the machines as soon as they become idle and issues requests for missions to the AGV system, monitoring the shop-floor (lot production) all the time. A database is present and contains the technological data (operation, piece type, machine type) and the management data (order, piece, lot), which allow the shop and the cells to control the production.

3.3 The Pattern Language

The G++ pattern language is structured, following Alexander, as in the tree shown in Figure 3.1; each oval denotes a pattern, with arcs representing the relationship between pat-

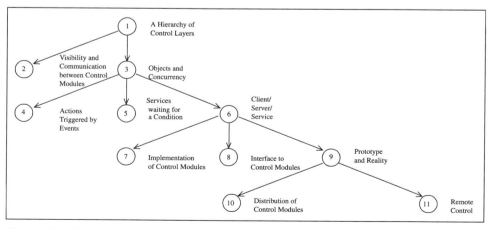

Figure 3.1   The G++ pattern language.

terns. The network of these relationships creates the pattern language. The pattern language guides the developer through the evolutionary development process from overall architecture analysis, through the transformations that map the analysis into a logical design to be locally prototyped, and then map the logical design into a physical design for final implementation. In fact, the design of an application is the result of following the network from the root to the leaves. The framework provides mechanisms, abstract classes, and customizable building blocks for the solutions documented by the pattern language.

3.3.1 Pattern 1: A Hierarchy of Control Layers

The Hierarchy of Control Layers pattern is discussed in this section.

Context

Large, distributed control systems are difficult to design and manage. The presence of multiple concurrent activities increases the difficulty further.

Problem

How can the system be organized and divided into parts in order to cope with its complexity? Which is the best architecture for such systems?

Forces

Even though the systems are complex, the architecture should not be. If an architecture is not simple, it will not be used.

The different functionalities of the systems should be encapsulated into modules or components that can be reused for similar projects. It should also be easy to extend the system by accommodating new functional modules.

Solution

It is necessary to organize the control system following a *hierarchical decentralized architecture*. A *control module* with precise responsibilities should be made for each component of the system, and they should be assigned to the different levels in the hierarchy so that a higher-level control module coordinates the control modules below it.

The analysis phase should indicate the types of control modules needed and their place in the hierarchy. Concerns between control modules should be separated so that control can be decentralized.

The representation of control modules has to be standardized in order to facilitate reuse and architectural unity. Generally, a control module has the following characteristics:

- Autonomous decision-making capabilities
- A series of available services that are offered to the outside (such as production planning and executing a machine operation)
- A pool of controlled resources

In G++, the class Server provides a unitary representation for the control modules.

Example

For CIM application, the USA-NBS reference model [McLean 1983] provides an excellent starting point for analysis, as it describes the hierarchy levels Facility, Shop, Cell, Workstation, and Equipment, along with the general control responsibilities of each level.

Figure 3.2 shows an analysis of the example FMS described in the introduction. The control modules in the system are the Shop, the Cell, and at the lowest level, Store, Transport, and Machine.

Other than G++, the SEMATECH framework [Dosher-Hodges 1997] is based on the same hierarchical, decentralized architecture.

Related Patterns

The hierarchical nature of the architecture is enforced by the visibility constraints in Pattern 2.

The control module base class Server is described in Pattern 6. The implementation of the decentralized nature of the architecture is supported by Patterns 9 to 12.

3.3.2 Pattern 2: Visibility and Communication between Control Modules

The Visibility and Communication between Control Modules pattern is discussed in this section.

Context

The control modules in the hierarchy need to communicate with each other, and in order to communicate they must have visibility [Booch 1991].

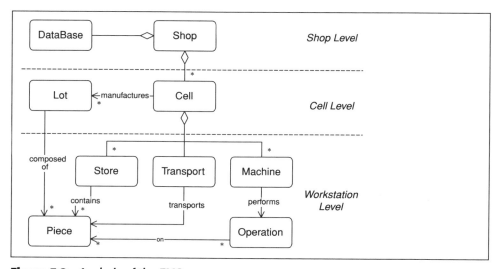

Figure 3.2 Analysis of the FMS.

Problem

How can the right visibility relationships between the control modules be established?

Forces

Visibility implies dependency, so if wrong decisions are made about the visibility relationships, the flexibility, reusability, and maintainability of the system can be seriously compromised. For instance, when building new modules for an existing system, the new modules could potentially have visibility of all of the environment in which they will operate. However, if they depend on the specific system in which they will be used, they will not be easily reusable.

In CIM systems, the evolution is usually bottom-up. A higher-layer control module (such as a shop controller or a cell controller) acts as an integration environment for lower-level controllers (like machines, transports, and buffers), which act as servers. Such subsystems have often been developed by different vendors without prior knowledge of the specific environment in which the system integrator will embed them.

Solution

The less stable modules, whose interfaces might change, have to have visibility of the stable modules, whose interfaces do not change. This way, the changing parts of the system depend on the stable parts, and not vice versa.

In client-server systems, clients should have visibility of the server. In the hierarchical architecture described in Pattern 1, this means that a higher-level control module should have visibility of the control modules on the lower level that it coordinates. This is due to the bottom-up nature of CIM systems integration. For instance, a cell controller must change in order to adapt to a new machine in the cell; the machine should definitely not depend upon the specific cell controller that will use it. The cell acts as the client and the machine as the server.

When a client initiates a communication with the server, it does so having visibility of the server and uses the normal object-oriented method call mechanism, which we term *Caller/Provider.* Sometimes, however, the server must inform the client that something has happened (for example, the machine is broken), and the communication must be initiated by the server. This means that the communication must be initiated in the opposite direction to the visibility relationship. This reversal is accomplished through a mechanism that we call *Broadcaster/Listener* (B/L) (see Figure 3.3), which allows objects to broadcast (publish) and listen (subscribe) to events.

In the G++ framework, all objects have the ability to broadcast and listen to events. An event is identified by a symbolic name and has some data associated with it. The mechanism is implemented by three methods in the top-level class Object: attachTo( ) and detachFrom( ), to subscribe to and unsubscribe from events, and callCbacks( ), which notifies all subscribers of an event. When an object raises an event, each listener receives and stores a copy of the event data in a private queue. The method registered for each event is executed in first in, first out (FIFO) order.

Generally, in a hierarchical architecture, due to the principle of information hiding, a control module at a higher layer should always encapsulate all the lower-level modules that it controls, thus creating layers of virtual machines. Control modules in the same layer of the hierarchy should not be entitled to communicate directly with each other. This ensures that there are no visibility loops and that the design minimizes the dependencies, which compromise the system's flexibility and reusability. There may, however, be exceptions to this, such as a centralized database server, which is used (shared) by several modules.

Example

The cell for machining, detailed in Figure 3.3, asks for services directly from the machines (calling the methods execPieceOperation( ), waitRemovePiece( ), and so on) and from the transport (execMission( )), but the evolution of the cell production has to be driven by the events broadcast by its components, such as MAC_OUT_FULL when a piece enters the output buffer of a machine.

The Broadcaster/Listener event mechanism is similar to Smalltalk dependencies [Goldberg 1983], X-Windows callbacks [Young 1989], and the Observer pattern from [Gamma 1995].

3.3.3 Pattern 3: Objects and Concurrency

The Objects and Concurrency pattern is discussed in this section.

Context

A complex control system is characterized by the presence of many different activities being executed concurrently. Concurrency assumes different scales of granularity.

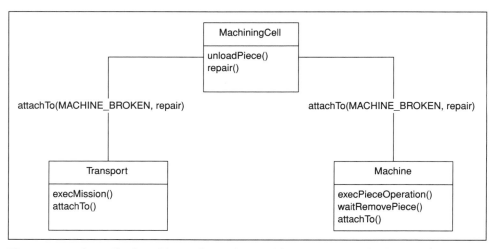

Figure 3.3 The Caller/Provider and Broadcaster/Listener communication mechanisms.

Problem

How should concurrency at the different levels of granularity be modeled?

Forces

A too complex model is difficult to understand and apply correctly. On the other hand, a too simple model might not offer the flexibility needed by real control systems. Concurrency often implies resource sharing and contention, so the model that is adopted must be able to deal with such aspects.

Solution

Classify the concurrent activities into the three commonly accepted [Chin 1991] levels of granularity:

- Simple actions without a predefined order (we also say with a weak cohesion), as in a multiwindow graphical interface

- Operations composed of an ordered sequence of actions, which have a stronger cohesion, such as the production processes of different (logically concurrent) lots of pieces processed by a cell controller

- Control modules operating in parallel, such as the distinct machine controllers executing independent operations

These are referred to as *fine, medium,* and *large* levels of granularity.

Fine-level activities are usually atomic and are implemented by normal (or *sequential*) objects whose semantics are defined only in the presence of a single thread of control. Medium-level activities are implemented by services, which are supported by their own sequential process or thread within a control module. When several services access the resources of the control module in which they are contained, there is a possibility of conflict; the resources should therefore be implemented as *blocking objects,* which allow only a single thread to access them at a time, while the other services are kept waiting. Large-level activities (the control modules) should be implemented as *active objects,* which possess, create, and internally manage one or more independent threads of control that govern the execution of their services.

Sequential objects offered by the G++ framework include basic value types (for example, String) and collection classes such as OrderedCltn and Dictionary. Medium-level activities are implemented by using the class ThreadOfControl. Control modules are implemented from the active object base class Server.

Example: Active Objects in the FMS

In the FMS example, the following control modules—that is, active objects—are identified in Figure 3.4:

- The shop: shop

- The cells: machiningCell for piece machining and assemblingCell for piece assembly

- The machines: a collection of machines called machines

- The transport system: transport

The different activities managed simultaneously are:

- For the cells, management of different lots of pieces
- For the machines, handling multiple pieces in the input, working, and output buffers
- For the transport, handling as many different missions as the number of available carts

Instead, stores for semiworked and finished pieces (named storeIn and storeOut) are modeled as blocking objects. This is because they act as shared resources between different lot production services.

Related Patterns

The next patterns (Patterns 4 through 6) discuss the use and implementation of the three levels of granularity.

3.3.4 Pattern 4: Actions Triggered by Events

The Actions Triggered by Events pattern is discussed in this section.

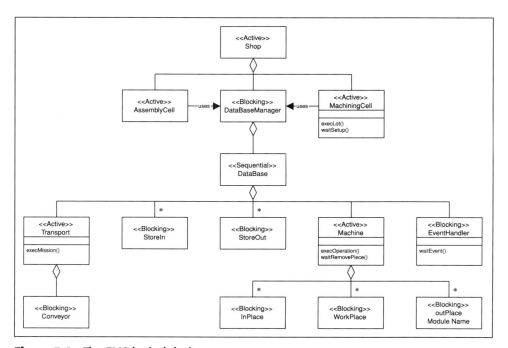

Figure 3.4 The FMS logical design.

Context

The Broadcaster/Listener mechanism can be used in two different contexts.

Object exchanging events intraservice. The most typical cases are offered by activating rules in a rule-based decision-making system (for example, rules are used for scheduling production) or by executing callback functions in a multiwindow graphical interface. In both examples the participating objects are in the scope of a unique service.

Object exchanging events interservice. A different situation is when the participating object belongs to distinct concurrent processes. In the FMS, for example, when the *piece machining* service of a workstation raises a failure event that is listened to by the *lot production* service of the cell, which is waiting for it.

Problem

How should intraservice events be handled?

Forces

Since all objects in the framework possess the capability to raise and react to events, a discipline for their use is needed; otherwise, the design and implementation will be unstructured and difficult to understand, maintain, and reuse.

Solution

A service can be composed of actions executed in response to events by sequential objects in one service scope. The result is fine-grain concurrency, as in the XtMainLoop of the X-Windows system [Young 1989]. Alternatively, interaction between objects within the scope of different services involves a larger grain of concurrency because there is the need to release waiting services.

The Broadcaster/Listener mechanism is used to model fine-grained concurrency by triggering actions executed by sequential objects that are bounded to one service.

Example

Fine-grained concurrency is present, for instance, in the dispatching algorithms, which execute (one for each lot) inside the cell: When activated by the cell controller, each dispatcher sets off the execution of a certain number of rules, which are carried out concurrently by different decision-making sequential objects.

Related Patterns

The case of interaction through events between objects belonging to different services is discussed in Pattern 5.

3.3.5 Pattern 5: Services Waiting for a Condition

The Services Waiting for a Condition pattern is discussed in this section.

Context

The Broadcaster/Listener mechanism can also be used between different services. An example of this is when the service pieceMachining of a workstation raises a failure event captured by the cell's service lotProduction.

Problem

How should interservice events be handled?

Forces

The need for a discipline discussed in the previous pattern applies here, too. Most interservice events are waited for by the listening services; the listening service does not do any processing unless one of the events occurs.

Solution

The handling of events external to the service with blocking objects is encapsulated by exploiting the «wait» functionality these objects offer to threads.

The services waiting for an event can be seen as a specialized case of waiting for a condition to become true. The framework offers the class Condition as a base class for these condition objects. Interservice events are handled by the EventHandler class, which is derived from Condition and which blocks the calling thread until one of a set of events occurs.

The blocking objects in the framework, such as Semaphore and CondCltn are also implemented using the Broadcaster/Listener mechanism encapsulated in a blocking method call. While the EventHandler maintains a queue of events for a service, the CondCltn maintains a queue of services waiting for an event. The basic blocking objects offered by the framework are shown in Figure 3.5.

Example: Blocking Objects in the FMS Cell

In the FMS example, there are different blocking objects (see Figure 3.4):

- The storeIn and storeOut buffers are CondCltn and belong to the MachiningCell class. They act as a bounded buffer: The cell service automatically stops if it tries to remove a piece when storeIn is empty or to add a new piece when storeOut is full.

- Similarly, inPlace, workPlace, and outPlace are CondCltn objects and act as blocking objects of the Machine services.

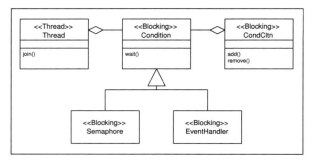

Figure 3.5   Blocking objects.

- Because it is a shared resource between the cells, database is modeled as a blocking object.

- The MachiningCell has an EventHandler, which is used to block its services while waiting for the events from transport, machines, and stores. Here the cell controller uses an event handler to monitor its resources (for example, MAC_OUT_FULL or WAIT_NOT_FULL) and to take the appropriate actions.

Related Patterns

The synchronous request of a service to an active object, as will be seen in Pattern 6, is one example that shows the presence of a condition inside a ThreadOfControl.

3.3.6 Pattern 6: Client/Server/Service

The Client/Server/Service pattern is discussed in this section.

Context

As explained in Pattern 1, the domain is perceived as consisting of a hierarchy of control modules; hence, most development work is going to deal with their design and implementation. Control modules deal with different topics: concurrency, abstraction, and encapsulation.

Problem

The first requirement of a control module is to be able to create and internally manage one or more independent threads that govern the execution of the services (in other words, operations that develop over time). A second requirement of a control module is to offer concurrency: It should be able to offer more than a single service at any one moment to its clients (for example, a cell may be producing more than one single lot of pieces at the same time). Another requirement is that control modules should have the capability of encapsulating the resources and the services that manipulate them. Finally, a common representation of the control modules at the different levels of the hierarchy is required for standardization purposes, so as to enforce reusability and facilitate the task of distributing the application.

Forces

The control module model should facilitate the development of complex real control systems. The model should also be flexible enough to facilitate the development of modules at every level of the control hierarchy.

Solution

These requirements are satisfied by the Client/Server/Service model proposed in this pattern and derived from the programming paradigm of the language synchronizing Resources SR [Andrews 1988]. The framework offers two classes to support the model: the Service and the Server (see Figure 3.6).

Service is a subclass of Thread, so that its instances represent independent sequential execution processes. A Service object always belongs to a unique Server owner, it has internal data, it maintains a symbolic state value, and it broadcasts events with the incoming state name every time a state transition occurs. Each Service object embeds the dynamic specification of its activity and it is started by the default method doService(). The Service has to be redefined for every concrete specification. The pattern Implementation of Control Modules suggests that the behavior of the different services should be specified in terms of finite state machines, extended by the necessary sequential objects, and implemented by the Service.

Server is the base class of every control module. It encapsulates a collection of Service objects and has to be redefined in order to encapsulate specific resources or other subservers. The Server class offers three concrete public methods: execService(), waitService(), and joinService(). They represent asynchronous, synchronous, and deferred-synchronous service requests, respectively, and accept as a parameter an instance of a Service subclass. When a client calls one of these methods, a new Service is created and added to the list of services and is then set up to use the private resources of the server. Server also subscribes to state transition events generated by its services and relays them externally using the B/L mechanism.

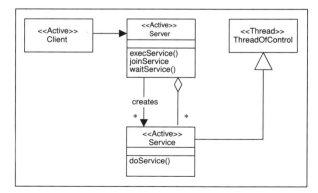

Figure 3.6   The Client/Server/Service model.

Example

The Client/Server/Service pattern gives the standard representation of control modules that is applied throughout the entire CIM reference model. In this model, therefore, each server becomes a client of the servers it coordinates on the level below.

3.3.7 Pattern 7: Implementation of Control Modules

The Implementation of Control Modules pattern is discussed in this section.

Context

A control module manages different pools of resources—for example, a manufacturing cell has machines, transport systems, and workers. These resources are often shared between the different concurrent services offered by the control module.

Problem

How do we implement concrete control modules? How do we synchronize the access to the shared resources?

Forces

Usually, services manage concurrent activities at the lowest level of granularity internally (discussed in Pattern 3: Objects and Concurrency). Their execution is conveniently driven and synchronized by events. It should be noted here that like most object-oriented languages, event-driven concurrent algorithms are difficult to implement.

Solution

The resources needed by the control module must be identified. In hierarchical decentralized control architectures, shared resources should always be hidden by one control module. The resources shared by the services of a Server object can only be blocking objects (Condition or CondCltn) or other Server objects. In this way, the service access to the shared resources is mutually exclusive. There should not be any sequential objects inside the Server; they should be encapsulated into blocking objects or into each service. The different types of services offered by a Server object have to be identified and implemented inside concrete subclasses of Service (for example, for the class MachiningCell, the services LotProduction and MachineSetup). Due to the difficulties of event-driven concurrent programming in most object-oriented languages, the behavior of a concrete service should be specified in terms of finite-state machines using a special-purpose language (such as SDL, the Specification and Description Language standardized by CCITT [CCITT 1986]). A graphical notation aimed at specifying service behaviors will add expressiveness to the formalism and, as it can be animated, debugging will be easier.

Example

Figure 3.7 shows an example of a Service behavior specification. At this point it is possible to consider the design of the FMS machining cell, defined by the class MachiningCellImpl. It inherits from Server and its member data (see Figure 3.4) are the AGV system transport, an instance of class Transport, the collection of machines, and the stores of semiworked and finished pieces (storeIn and storeOut, of class CondCltn). The service of routing pieces between machines and stores is expressed by the class LotProduction(), which specializes the class Service.

3.3.8 Pattern 8: Interface to Control Modules

The Interface to Control Modules pattern is discussed in this section.

Context

Different clients can exploit the functionalities of a server in different ways. For instance, one client might want to invoke a service synchronously, while another client invokes the same service asynchronously. The ways the services are accessed may also change over time.

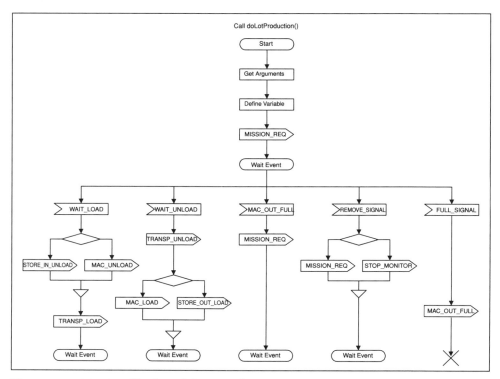

Figure 3.7   SDL Specification of doLotProduction().

Problem

The classes derived by inheritance from the Server in Pattern Implementation of Control Modules are heavyweight objects, which may have to encapsulate many shared resources and offer a variety of different functionalities. Therefore, it is desirable to reduce dependencies between a server and its clients.

Forces

The Client/Server/Service model gives a client the flexibility to customize the services provided by a server. Each new service is defined by specializing the class Service. When a client requests a server to execute a specific service, it has to create an instance of the corresponding Service subclass and provide it with a reference to the server resources. This means that the client has to have knowledge of the server definition.

Solution

The definition of a control module is separated into two distinct interface and implementation classes, which offer the model a great deal of flexibility, as is shown here in relation to distribution. When a control module with the services it offers has been conceived, one or more Interface classes are generated. They offer public methods, which create instances of concrete services and pass them to the three standard Server methods, according to the three synchronization semantics of the specification. Figure 3.8 presents an example, where the Cell control module is split into an interface class (CellInterf}) and an implementation class (CellImpl). CellImpl is a subclass of Server and encapsulates instances of class LotProduction (a subclass of Service). CellInterf is a subclass of Interface and offers the method execLotProduction(): It creates an instance of class LotProduction and passes it to the method execService() of CellImp. When the instance of class LotProduction has been created, it receives a reference to CellImpl because it has to be able to access its shared resources. Figure 3.9 shows the code that implements this method.

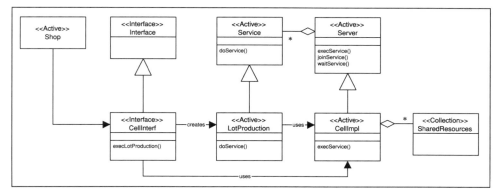

Figure 3.8   Interface and implementation of a Cell.

```
Void CellInterf::execLotProduction(Lot *lot)
{
    cellImpl -> execService(new LotProduction(cellImpl, lot));
}
```

Figure 3.9   Implementation of execLotProduction().

3.3.9 Pattern 9: Prototype and Reality

The Prototype and Reality pattern is discussed in this section.

Context

All complex applications require prototyping and simulation of the different elements, which have to be integrated before they can be implemented. So far, patterns have been used to deal with the evolution from analysis to logical design, and the result of the logical design is a prototype of the final application. The program, which is used to implement the prototype, is an executable specification on a single processor of the naturally concurrent reality, that is, a discrete event simulation where the dynamic specifications represented by a graphical notation are animated.

Problem

How can a seamless evolution from the simulation to the final implementation be ensured?

Forces

A prototype of the logical design and its physical implementation are two distinct aspects of the same concept; often both are present at the same time during development, as when prototypes are used to emulate parts of the physical process when certain critical software systems are installed.

Solution

In order to guarantee a seamless evolution from prototype to reality, it is convenient to maintain two coexisting implementations for any physical element: 1) the *prototype*, which simulates or emulates the object behavior, and 2) the *reality*, which embeds the physical object.

The reality may assume two distinct forms in a client program: Either it can be a surrogate or a reference to an external object, as in CORBA, or it can be a wrapper of an external functionality, such as the libraries of a graphical user interface. The former is an example of the Proxy of [Gamma 1995] pattern; the latter, of the Adaptor of [Gamma 1995] pattern. In order to be able to switch from one prototype implementation to another with the minimum change in the surrounding code, the distinction of objects between *interface* and *implementation* from Pattern Interface to Control Modules is again useful. Whereas for control modules the interface objects are a way of specifying their functionality, they can be applied more generally as a way of approaching the design in a prototyping situation.

In order to maintain two distinct implementations of a certain conceptual entity and to switch from one to the other, it is necessary to use the pattern Bridge of [Gamma 1995]. Consistency in the transition is guaranteed, as in Pattern Interface to Control Modules, either by exploiting polymorphism by inheriting from a common base class, or by assigning to the same object different implementations through the use relationship. Switching from prototype to physical implementation in the same program can speed up installation. This is achieved by using a suitable design pattern such as the Abstract Factory of [Gamma 1995], which allows the user to decide at runtime which specific class he or she needs.

3.3.10 Pattern 10: Distribution of Control Modules

The Distribution of Control Modules pattern is discussed in this section.

Context

Control modules usually reside on remote computers or peripheral devices, interconnected through a common communication network. These modules define the physical architecture, which must be created by the final distributed system.

Problem

How can we exploit an evolutionary approach to the transformation of a local control module prototype into a distributed module, which controls a physical device?

Forces

When passing from a nondistributed simulation to the distributed reality, the objects that are moved to the remote nodes are no longer part of the original program; they must become independent programs in their own right. The rest of the system, however, should not be affected when some objects are moved to a remote node. Further, moving objects to remote nodes should be relatively easy so that the system can change with the physical architecture.

Solution

This is the situation when a control module is not local to the application, but resides, instead, on a remote computer. Let us consider the example of the Cell in Figure 3.8. The framework provides an abstract class Network, whose concrete implementations hide the physical characteristic of the communication medium. In particular, the framework provides subclasses of Network for TCP/IP sockets and for a CORBA platform.

The class CellInterface is substituted by the class CellProxy (a subclass of Interface), which offers the same public methods and encapsulates a concrete specialization of Network to forward messages over the communication medium. The class CellImpl is substituted by a Server object, the DistributedCell, which resides on the remote platform. It encapsulates an object of class Network, which is used to unwrap and address the messages it receives from the corresponding CellProxy. Figure 3.10 shows the structure of the prototype and of the final distributed reality for the Cell example.

Example

In complex and changing environments, the distributed program components must avoid dependencies on the physical location of other control modules. This *location transparency* is achieved through the use of a Router, which is a special kind of control module. Server applications register themselves with the Router. When a client application needs to connect to a server, it queries the Router to find the server's location. The DistributedProxy offers the class method bind() for this purpose; it takes as parameter the server name and returns a new DistributedProxy object representing the remote server.

3.3.11 Pattern 11: Remote Control

The Remote Control pattern is discussed in this section.

Context

Reality can be a remote device, and it might be part of a reactive, event-driven system.

Problem

CIM control software often must interface *reactive* and *event-driven* systems [Aarsten 1996). A reactive system receives stimuli from the outside world and responds to them by updating its state and giving feedback. An event-driven system is a special kind of reactive system, where the interaction with the external world (stimuli and feedback) takes place through events. In addition, the control software must be able to access the

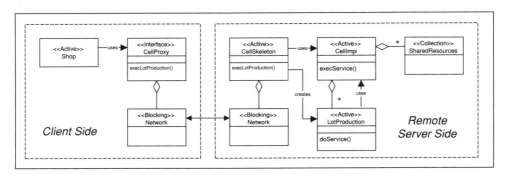

Figure 3.10 Distribution of the Cell control module.

system's state in order to perform monitoring and control activities. A common characteristic of an event-driven system is the presence of active data [Minoura 1993], variables that generate events when their values change. This is, among other things, useful to implement constraints between related values.

Forces

Developing object-oriented software for event-driven systems presents some particular difficulties, especially with regard to moving smoothly from the simulated prototype to the final implementation. In the simulation, the control of a peripheral device is achieved by using variables to represent the state of the device, such as the control registers of a programmable logic controller (PLC). In the real system, the device does not have variables in the program's address space. The G++ logical events used in the simulation are just a communication mechanism; they are not first-class objects as in the external system. Therefore, it is necessary to create external event objects for the relevant logical events. Also, program objects that subscribe to events from simulated controlled devices must continue to receive those logical events in the final system. This means a bridge is needed between the logical and the external events.

Solution

Virtualize the data used by the component simulation to access the peripheral's state variables via a proxy class. In C++, this can be done transparently by defining the methods operator T( )and operator=(T&) for each relevant data type T. The simulation variable is replaced by a proxy for the same type, as shown in Figure 3.11.

A class Event is made to encapsulate external events, as shown in Figure 3.11. Event knows the external event that it encapsulates, the logical event to which it corresponds (called the *name* and represented by a Symbol), and the program object (called the *owner*), which should raise the logical event when the external event occurs. It offers a method to raise the event in the external system, and it also has the task of intercepting external events. When an external event occurs, the Event object makes its owner raise the corresponding logical event.

The method used to broadcast logical events (in G++ called *callCbacks*) is overloaded with a new method taking an Event as a parameter, as shown in the lower part of Fig-

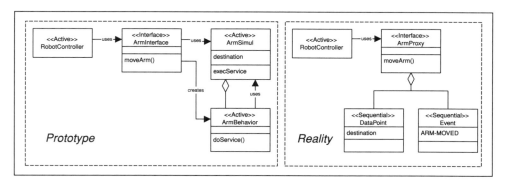

Figure 3.11 Control of a robot arm.

ure 3.11. For each external event that must be translated to and from logical events, an Event object is declared with the same identifier as the desired logical event, within the scope of the owner class. The Event is then associated with the logical event by setting its name attribute. The Event translates from external events into logical events. Calls to callCbacks will now bind to the new method, since the global event identifier is hidden by the Event object declared in the class scope. This ensures that the logical event is relayed as an external event.

Example

As an example, we consider the control of a robot arm, which interacts with the control system through events. The robot arm has a control register containing the current position of the arm and another register for the destination of the moves. To move the robot arm, the control program writes the desired coordinates in the destination register and raises a MOVE_ARM event in the external system. The robot then raises an ARM_MOVED event when the destination is reached.

This scenario results in the object structure shown in Figure 3.11. In the simulation, each control register is a public data member of the robot prototype object and the events are logical events used by the Broadcaster/Listener mechanism, as explained in Pattern 2: Visibility and Communication.

In the final implementation, the robot's data members are replaced by proxies, which read and write the control registers, and there is an associated Event object for the MOVE_ARM and ARM_MOVED events.

3.4 Summary

We have presented G++, a framework and pattern language for the evolutionary development of CIM systems. Many of the problems raised by the CIM domain are similar to problems in other application domains. The G++ framework has demonstrated its appropriateness for diverse projects for several of these other fields, including process control [VASME 1996], telecommunications [Bosco 1996], and computer-telephone integration [Billi 1996] systems.

Many of the solutions in the pattern language indicate that a CASE tool, which can be used to automate some of the development, would be useful, and a CASE tool with special provisions to support the framework has in fact been developed. A trial version of the G++ CASE tool and framework can be downloaded from www.syco.it.

3.5 References

[Aarsten 1996] Aarsten, A., G. Menga, and L. Mosconi. Object oriented design patterns in reactive systems. In *Pattern Languages of Program Design 2*. Reading, MA: Addison-Wesley, 1996.

[Alexander 1977] Alexander, C. *A Pattern Language: Towns, Buildings, Construction*. New York: Oxford University Press, 1977.

[Alexander 1979] Alexander, C. *The Timeless Way of Building*. New York: Oxford University Press, 1979.

[Andrews 1988] Andrews, G.R. An overview of the SR language and implementation. *ACM Transaction on Programming Languages and Systems* 10(1): 51–86, 1988.

[Billi 1996] Billi, R., et al. Field trial evaluations of two different information inquiry systems. *IEEE Third Workshop on Interactive Voice Technology for Telecommunications Applications*, Basking Ridge, NJ, September 30–October 1, 1996.

[Booch 1991] Booch, G. *Object Oriented Design with Applications*. Redwood City, CA: Benjamin/Cummings, 1991.

[Bosco 1996] Bosco, P.G., D. LoGiudice, G. Martini, and C. Moiso. ACE: an environment for specifying, developing and generating TINA services. *Proceedings IFIP/IEEE IM 1996*, 1996.

[Brugali 1997] Brugali, D., G. Menga, and A. Aarsten. The framework life span. *Communication of the ACM*, Theme Issue on Object-Oriented Application Frameworks, Mohamed E. Fayad and Douglas Schmidt, editors, 40(10):65–68, October 1997.

[Brugali 1999] Brugali, D., and G. Menga. Frameworks and pattern languages: An intriguing relationship. *ACM Computing Surveys*, *Application Framework Symposium*, Mohamed E. Fayad, editor, September 1999. New York: ACM Press.

[CCITT 1986] CCITT. *Specification and Description Language.* Recommendation Z.100, 1986.

[Chin 1991] Chin, R.S., and S.T. Chanson. Distributed object-based programming system. *ACM Computing Surveys* 23: 91–124, March 1991.

[Dosher-Hodges 1997] Dosher, D., and R. Hodges. SEMATECH's experiences with the CIM framework. *Communications of the ACM*, Theme Issue on Object-Oriented Application Frameworks, Mohamed E. Fayad and Douglas Schmidt, editors, 40(10): 65–68, October 1997.

[Gamma 1995] Gamma, E., R. Helm, R. Johnson, J. Vlissides. *Design Patterns: Elements of Reusable Object Oriented Software*. Reading, MA: Addison-Wesley, 1995.

[Goldberg 1983] Goldberg, A., and D. Robson. *Smalltalk80: The Language and Its Implementation*. Reading, MA: Addison-Wesley, 1983.

[Johnson 1992] Johnson, R. Documenting frameworks using patterns. *Proceedings of OOPSLA 1992*, Vancouver, BC, Canada, October 1992.

[McLean 1983] McLean, C., M. Mitchel, and E. Barkmeyer. A computer architecture for small-batch manufacturing. *IEEE Spectrum*,20(5):59–64, 1983.

[Menga 1993] Menga, G., G. Elia, and M. Mancin. G++: An environment for object oriented design and prototyping of manufacturing systems. In *Intelligent Manufacturing: Programming Environments for CIM*, W. Gruver and G. Boudreaux, editors. New York: Springer-Verlag, 1993.

[Minoura 1993] Minoura, T., S. Pargaonkar, K. Rehfuss. Structural active object systems for simulation. *Proceedings of OOPSLA 1993*,Washington DC, USA, October 1993.

[VASME 1996] VASME. Value-added services for maritime environments. *European Union Framework Program IV*, project no. WA-95-SC.010, document no. 960628/D1.12.1996.

[Young 1989] Young, D.A. *The X Window System Programming and Application with Xt*. Englewood Cliffs, NJ: Prentice Hall, 1989.

OSEFA: Framework for Manufacturing

The development of the cell control software for a specific manufacturing cell by an individual project is quite expensive and requires a long development time. The software development cost is an important part of the overall cost of a ready-to-run manufacturing cell. The software development time has a major influence on its time to market. Both the development cost and time may be decreased substantially, according to our experience, by an order of magnitude or more, by investing in an object-oriented framework.

OSEFA (German: Objektorientierter SoftwarebaukastEn für FertigungsAnlagen) is a blackbox framework, from which software cell controllers are created without programming for a great variety of manufacturing cells. The created cell control applications are identical with regard to some aspects, called *frozen spots*. An example of a frozen spot is the organization of the production flow. Frozen spots are variable with regard to other aspects, called *hot spots* [Pree 1995, Fayad 1999, Chapters 9, 15, and 16]. Examples of hot spots are the variability of the material flow and part processing, the variability of the systems and devices that are used to move pallets, and the variability of concrete machines and devices that manufacture the parts. For each hot spot, a set of blackbox components is provided with the framework.

An application developer creates an application from OSEFA by selecting the blackbox components that represent both the technical components and the organizational concepts of the real manufacturing cell, and by parametrizing and configuring them according to the characteristics and the connectivity of the real manufacturing cell. This is done in a configuration program by calling first configuration services (methods) of the framework class manufacturing cell and then its Run method. An interactive configurator, comparable to a graphical user interface (GUI) configurator, simplifies the task of application creation even more. Experiences with OSEFA show that the application creation effort and time to market may be reduced by an order of magnitude or more. OSEFA has been developed in C++ for Windows or OS/2-based PC platforms at the Fachhochschule Konstanz from 1993 to early 1996. Different aspects of its design are described in [Schmid 1995; Schmid 1996a; Schmid 1996b; Schmid-Mueller 1998].

After explaining the concept of domain-specific blackbox frameworks in *Section 4.1*, we will define the manufacturing subdomain covered by the OSEFA and the fixed aspects of all control applications created from it in *Section 4.2*. *Section 4.3* presents the variable aspects and the configuration flexibility of the framework subdomain, and gives an overview of the hot spots. *Section 4.4* shows that the required variability and flexibility lead to a layered framework architecture, each layer embodying hot spots on the same abstraction level. *Section 4.5* through *Section 4.9* each describes a layer and a hot spot in some detail. *Section 4.10* and *Section 4.11* describe how to create an application, while *Section 4.12* and *Section 4.13* present our experiences and conclusions.

4.1 Domain-Specific Blackbox Frameworks

A framework [Johnson 1988] is a generic application with certain aspects, called frozen spots, that are fixed and cannot be changed, and with other aspects, called hot spots, that are variable and are intended to be changed. Different applications from a family of applications, called the *framework domain,* may be created from a framework depending on how its variable aspects are filled out.

When creating an application from a framework, a hot spot (see Figure 4.1, left) allows you to plug in application-specific occurrences of the variable aspect. A responsibility, named R in Figure 4.1, is common to the different alternatives. It generalizes them and abstracts from their differences, such that you can exchange one alternative for another. The common responsibility characterizes, together with other characteristics, the requirements for a hot spot [Schmid 1999].

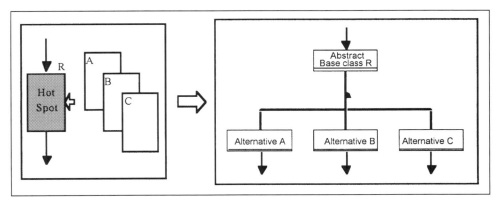

Figure 4.1   Hot spot and hot-spot subsystem in a blackbox framework.

A hot spot is implemented by a hot-spot subsystem [Schmid 1996a; Schmid 1999]. A hot-spot subsystem (see Figure 4.1, right) contains an abstract base class, concrete derived classes, and, possibly, additional classes and relationships. The abstract base class defines the common responsibility R; that means it represents a generalized and abstract concept. Each derived class (which may be the facade [Gamma 1995] of a subsystem) represents a different alternative of the variability. In a domain-specific framework, derived classes represent, depending on the level of abstraction of the hot spot, either concepts, or entities, or machines and devices from the domain.

A hot-spot subsystem is usually structured according to a design pattern. Design patterns [Gamma 1995] describe typical, common, and frequently observed relationships among classes; most of them (that is 19 out of 23 from [Gamma 1995]) provide for variability and flexibility. The kinds of variability and flexibility required from a hot spot are built into a hot-spot subsystem by structuring it according to the design pattern that provides the required kind of variability and flexibility (for a detailed discussion, see [Schmid 1999]).

The variability introduced by a hot-spot subsystem is usually transparent to the subsystem's outside. An object of the framework requests a service from the hot-spot subsystem via a polymorphic reference typed with the subsystem base class (that is dynamically bound). Binding a hot spot means to set the polymorphic reference to one (or several) subclass objects. You bind a hot spot, which means you set this reference, either when configuring an application from the framework or at runtime.

In a blackbox framework, an application developer selects, for a hot spot bound at application development time, a subclass (object) from the set of subclasses provided by the framework as blackbox components and binds it to the hot spot. Thus, the developer may create an application without programming, merely by selecting, configuring, and parameterizing framework components. The relative ease and minimal effort required from the application developer were the reasons that we decided to develop OSEFA as a blackbox framework. On the other hand, it is quite an effort to develop a blackbox framework (compare [Schmid 1996a]).

4.2 Manufacturing Subdomain with Frozen Spots

A control framework can cover only a subdomain of an application domain like manufacturing. To build a framework successfully, the subdomain should not be too large. Our experience is that even a subdomain of manufacturing—for example, control of flexible manufacturing cells that process metal parts—needs to be partitioned further.

Defining the boundaries of a subdomain is an iterative process. A first rough cut done when framework development is started is refined during the subsequent development steps. We restricted the subdomain to be covered by OSEFA to machines with a restricted intelligence such as CNC machines, to a cell-store-centered topology of the machines and devices in cell, as well as to a corresponding organization of the production flow to centrally store all data about parts and pallets and their production status in the cell computer (alternative: decentralized storage with each pallet) and to administrate and store no product data that describe the production of a specific part (alternative: document each production step of each part).

Let us explain what we call machines with restricted intelligence: They know to perform autonomously single, repetitive activities when told. For example, a CNC machine is a computerized, numerically controlled (CNC) machine containing a computer as a controller; an RC-controlled (robot control) robot or a PLC-controlled (programmed logical control) device contains a different kind of controller. During the manufacturing process, a cell control program (in the cell computer) may request from the controller of a machine or robot that different manufacturing programs (called CNC, RC, or PLC programs, respectively, which undergo a preparatory process) be loaded into its storage and start the execution of such a program. A manufacturing program controls the sequence of movements required to perform a manufacturing activity—for example, the movements that a machine makes to lathe an axis, or those a robot makes to move a pallet.

For example, a manufacturing cell controlled by an OSEFA application may produce an axis in three processing steps: lathing a bar of metal on a CNC lathe machine, milling the lathed bar on a CNC milling machine, and drilling holes in it on a CNC processing center. For each processing step, a separate manufacturing program is prepared to process the axis.

After preliminarily defining the subdomain boundaries, we have to determine the frozen spots that are common to all applications in the subdomain. There are structural frozen spots and processing-logic-related frozen spots.

The main structural frozen spot of a store-centered manufacturing cell (see Figure 4.2) is that it is composed of one or several (concurrently working) machining stations consisting of:

- A machine or device for the machining, assembly, or measurement of parts of a buffer, and of one or several handling units that load and unload a part from the buffer into the machine or device and back.

- A cell store that contains the pallets between the processing steps.

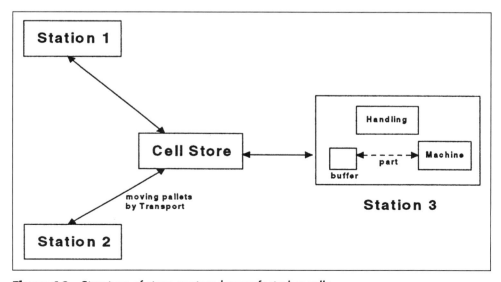

Figure 4.2 Structure of store-centered manufacturing cells.

■ A (topologically) star-structured transport system that moves pallets among the cell store and the buffer of machining stations.

We will see that this topology includes a very large variety of different physical cell configurations (see *Section 4.4*). For a configuration example, consider the (extremely simplified) CIM model manufacturing cell of the Fachhochschule Konstanz (see Figure 4.3). It contains one machining station with a CNC lathe machine. The portal robot is used both for the handling within the machining station (that is, loading and unloading parts in the machine with a part gripper) and for moving pallets from the cell store to the buffer store and back with a pallet gripper. It is equipped with a gripper exchange system so that a part gripper or a pallet gripper can be used as required. Note that the physical transport possibilities of the portal robot are not limited to the star-structured topology that we presuppose as a logical structural frozen spot.

The store-centered cell structure is paralleled by the processing organization, which is a processing-related frozen spot. A machine order schedule, prescheduled by an external system, allocates to each machine a list of machine orders to be processed (giving their sequence and start and finishing time). A machine order describes a single processing step—the kind and number of parts to be processed—and it refers to a worksheet entry that describes the required resources (such as the parts in the store, the CNC or robot program that performs the machining or assembly, and tools and equipment). For example, when a part X undergoes three subsequent machining steps on machining stations 1, 2, and 3, the machine order schedule may contain three machine order entries among other ones, as shown in Table 4.1.

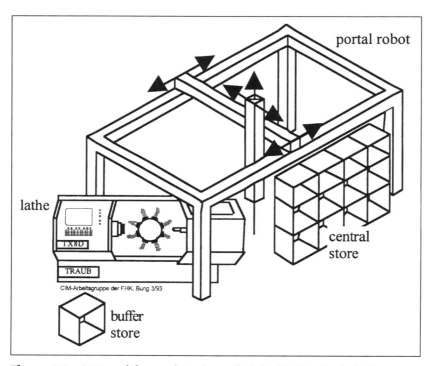

Figure 4.3 CIM model manufacturing cell of the Fachhochschule Konstanz.

Table 4.1   Machine Order Schedule for Three Machines

STATION 1, MILLING MACHINE	STATION 2, LATHE	STATION 3, PROCESSING CENTER
–	8.00–9.00: order Y, part X step 1	–
11.00–13.00: order Y, part X step 2	–	–
–	–	15.30–17.00: order Y, part X step 3

A machine order is processed by performing first the setup (for example, providing and fixing the equipment and loading the manufacturing programs required) and then a sequence of material flow and part-processing steps. The pallets with the parts required for the order are moved, one after another, from the cell store to the machining station, processed, and moved back. Details are presented in the following list. However, with different tools and equipment, the details of the part-processing sequence may differ slightly (see [Schmid 1995]). The description of Figure 4.4 is simplified for easier understanding; for example, the processing sequence is, in reality, optimized such that the pallets are moved, when possible, in parallel with and not between machining steps. The point is that one tries to keep the rather expensive machines busy.

Another frozen spot is that the cell control software performs the described processing sequence concurrently for all machining stations. The overall processing sequence is not tailored to a particular machine configuration and a particular mix and schedule of machine orders, but is flexible. This means the processing sequence is different for differing machine configurations and machine order mixes and schedules. This is achieved by providing, for each machining station, a dedicated processing control object in the cell control framework. Each processing control

0. Read next entry of machine order list, read corresponding worksheet entry, set up the machining station with tools and other resources such as NC programs.

Repeat steps 1 through 5 until all pallets of a machine order are processed.

1. Move pallet with raw parts from the central store (position x) to the buffer (with number y) of the machining station.

Repeat steps 2 to 4 until all parts on the pallet are processed.

2. Load a raw part from the pallet on the buffer into the machine.
3. Process the part by the machine.
4. Unload the machined part from the machine into the pallet.
5. Move the pallet with machined parts from the buffer to the central store.

Figure 4.4   Part processing sequence, or subdomain-specific application logic.

works, as an active object, concurrently with the other ones and is in competition with them for shared resources such as buffers, the cell store, or the transport system that moves pallets among the buffers and the store. In addition, machining, handling, and moving pallets are also active objects that receive work requests from processing control.

To support the concurrent execution of different processing control objects, we provided mechanisms for concurrency and concurrency control, which are quite similar to some patterns described by G++ [Aarsten 1995]. The framework provides active objects (compare Pattern 3 of G++) by multithreading; concurrency control mechanisms (compare Pattern 5 of G++) like the locking of shared resources and signaling semaphores for communication among concurrent processing controls; and an event mechanism (compare Patterns 2 and 4 of G++) that connects the synchronous execution of a processing control to the asynchronous execution of machining, handling, and move requests.

The visualization of the manufacturing cell and of the processing is done in a visualization subframework and is not described here (compare [Schmid-Mueller 1998]).

4.3 Variability of a Manufacturing Cell Configuration and Hot Spots

Manufacturing cells from the OSEFA framework domain can be integrated into different manufacturing environments and may have completely different physical and technical structures and configurations. The framework must provide hot spots that cover the required configuration flexibility, as described in the following.

The integration into different manufacturing environments requires that the framework can access a list of machine orders and a worksheet from different sources—from a fine-grain scheduling material request processing (MRP) system, from a Leitstand, or from interactive input by a cell operator in the shop floor, in order to allow for manual shop floor planning with group-centered work organization (see Figure 4.5).

The (global) variability requirements for different configurations of manufacturing cells are presented in the following list. There is a lot of configuration variability to work with. For example, contrast the CIM cell, described in *Section 4.2*, with a cell that has a conveyor belt ring for moving pallets. Along this ring are different machining stations and the cell store. Each of them has a device or robot associated that lifts a pallet from the conveyor belt to the buffer store of a machining station, or of the cell store, and back. Handling is done with the same robot or with a separate robot or device.

The structural variability of the manufacturing subdomain is as follows:

- The number, variety, and kind of machines. This includes different CNC machines, different RC-controlled assembly stations, and different PLC-controlled machines or assembly stations.

- The number, variety, and kind of handling devices. Handling may be performed by robots or PLC-controlled devices.

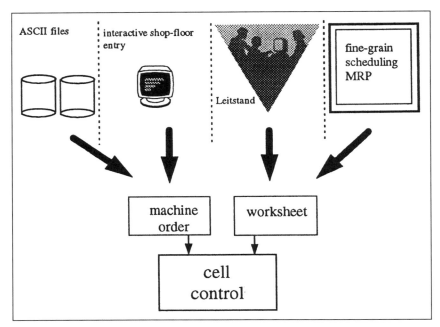

Figure 4.5   Different possible sources for machine order list and worksheet.

- The association of handling devices to machining stations. For example, one portal robot may serve all machines, or one or even two smaller robots or devices may each serve a machine.

- The geometry, topology, and kind of system that moves the pallets. This transport system may be, for example, a portal robot or a PLC-controlled conveyor belt.

- The combination of the transport and the handling system. The handling devices and the system for moving pallets may be either separate or combined, as by a portal robot.

- The geometry, topology, and kind of cell store.

- The kind and geometry of pallets and inlays.

The automated processing may include only the part processing, as described in this chapter, or also the setup and preparation of tools.

Once a manufacturing cell is built, the global variability is fixed and does not change. In contrast, the local configuration may change dynamically during the manufacturing cycle, depending on the machine order to be processed. For example, a machine order may require the use of either one kind of pallet to carry both the unmachined and the machined parts or two different kinds of pallets (with different inlays) for each of them. Another example is that either a single gripper or a double gripper may be used for the loading and unloading of parts. With different local configurations, the required part processing sequences differ slightly from the one shown in Figure 4.4.

4.3.1 Overview on Hot Spots

We have to analyze and structure the variability described in the list of structural variables of the manufacturing subdomain and identify the elementary variable aspects [Schmid 1999] that form the hot spots. A hot-spot diagram (see Figure 4.6) collects all hot spots and orders them according to their level of abstraction. Some hot spots correspond directly to a subdomain variability item, whereas others cover parts of one item or several items.

Let us give a summarizing description of the hot-spot diagram from the bottom up; more details on selected hot spots and their implementation are presented in *Section 4.5* through *Section 4.9*. The CNC-machine, RC-robot, PLC-device, and pallet hot spot each embodies the variability of a kind of machine or device. For example, it should be possible to use different CNC machines in different manufacturing cells. The machines, robots, and devices may be connected to a cell computer over a communication line with different protocols (transmission protocol hot spot, not shown in Figure 4.6) and on different platforms, which use different operating system commands to access a communication line via a serial input/output (I/O) port (communication line access hot spot, not shown in Figure 4.6).

The pallet transport, handling, and machining hot spot each allow a domain-related responsibility, such as moving a pallet, to be performed by completely different kinds of machines or devices—for example, by a robot or a conveyor belt. The material flow optimization hot spot allows different optimization strategies to be used for different kinds of machines or devices. The cell store and buffer hot spots allow the use of different technical components.

The processing sequence variability hot spot allows different material flow and part processing sequences to be used with different local configurations. The processing command hot spot allows internal commands that constitute a request for manufacturing-related services to vary with framework evolution and permits better software structuring (see [Schmid 1996a]).

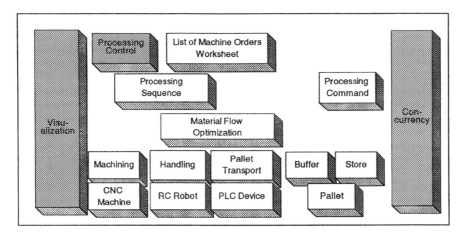

Figure 4.6 Hot-spot diagram, structured according to the abstraction level.

4.4 Layered Framework Architecture

A framework has more layers than a specialized application that is tailored to a manufacturing cell with a fixed configuration. The reason is that the hot spots introduce classes for new, generalized concepts, and with them, new layers in the class structure. Let us consider first the class structure of a specialized application (for details, see [Schmid 1996b]). It consists essentially of two layers:

An upper processing control layer. This contains classes that implement a concrete material flow and part processing sequence as manufacturing logic (that is, a concrete application logic). They request services from the machines, robots, and devices on the lower layer. For example, to move a pallet from the store to a buffer, a ProcessingControl class requests from the robot the following services: loading the robot program that moves the pallet, parameterizing this robot program with the position of the pallet and the number of the buffer, and starting its execution. To machine a part in a lathe CNC machine, it requests from the lathe the following services: loading the CNC program that performs the specific machining and starting its execution.

The lower machine and device layer. This is subdivided into two sublayers. The upper sublayer contains classes modeling machines, robots, and PLC-controlled devices. They provide services such as load CNC program. Different kinds of CNC machines offer slightly different services, even though they are, in principle, identical. The lower sublayer couples the machine object (in the cell computer) to the controller of the real machine via communication lines. This holds also for robots and PLC-controlled devices.

With the two-layer architecture, the manufacturing logic is not abstract, but very concrete. It consists of a sequence of machine-specific requests. Therefore, it is bound to specific machines and devices. When they change, the logic needs to be modified, too.

The manufacturing logic becomes independent on the machines and devices in a manufacturing cell when it requests more abstract, manufacturing-related services, as were presented in Figure 4.4. The abstract service requests are mapped in concrete machine- and device-related service requests by the hot spots described in *Section 4.3*. For each layer of hot spots, we introduce a corresponding layer in the framework class structure (see Figure 4.7). The new layers are a processing strategy sublayer, a domain object layer, and a generalized machine and device layer. An original abstract request is passed through one layer after another and transformed into a more concrete request each time, until it is, eventually, a concrete request for the service of a concrete machine or device.

We have subdivided the ProcessingControl layer, which contains the hot spots for machine order and worksheet access variability, and have split off (as a lower sublayer) the ProcessingStrategy sublayer. It contains the processing sequence variability hot spot.

The next lower layer, the domain object layer, contains the material flow optimization hot spot, pallet transport hot spot, handling hot spot, and machining hot spot. It receives requests for abstract services, such as moving a pallet, and maps them to service requests to standardized machines or devices.

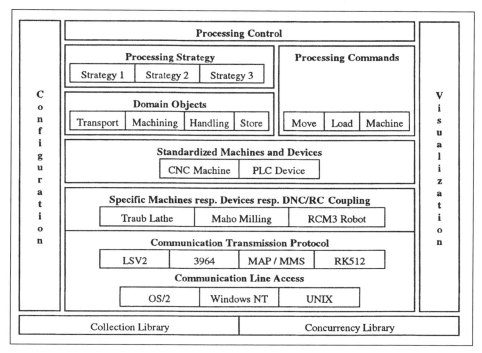

Figure 4.7 Layer structure of the framework.

The next lower layer, the standardized machine and device layer, contains the CNC machine hot spot, RC-robot hot spot, PLC device hot spot, and pallet hot spot. It receives requests for standardized services, such as loading a robot program, that are specific for a kind of machine, such as robots. It maps a standardized service request into a specialized request for a concrete machine.

The next lower layer, the specific machine and device layer, contains concrete machines and devices. In the communication sublayer, it contains the communication-related transmission protocol hot spots and communication line access hot spot. It receives requests for specific services, such as load robot program on a RCM3 robot control, that relate to a specific machine, such as a RCM3-controlled Mannesmann/Demag robot. It sends a request via the communication sublayer and a communication line to the controller of the machine or device, such as a robot-controller.

4.5 Processing Control Layer

The processing control layer contains classes that control the manufacturing process (that is, the application logic or business procedure of the manufacturing subdomain). It embeds two hot spots, found on the top row of Figure 4.7: the machine order and worksheet access hot spot allows transparent access to the list of machine orders and the worksheet from different sources, and the processing sequence variability hot spot allows the material flow and part processing sequence to vary slightly. In the following, we describe the implementation of the latter in detail.

ProcessingControl performs the coarse-grained processing of machine orders, which is identical for all manufacturing cells from the framework domain. It fetches (via the machine order and worksheet access hot spot) the information concerning which machine order is to be performed next and which resources, such as NC programs and tools, are required, and performs the setup with these resources. It fetches other required information from store, buffer, and pallets. It is important that it implements, in collaboration with other classes (not described), the reaction to technical events, and the locking of concurrent access to shared resources such as buffers or pallets.

4.5.1 Hot-Spot Variability

Though the manufacturing process is, in principle, a frozen spot, the moving of pallets and loading/unloading of parts, called the *material flow and part processing,* is to be done in slightly different sequences for different local configurations. Consider, for example, the part processing sequence, in other words, the application logic (as described in Figure 4.4), when using a single part gripper. The action to machine a part is followed by the action to unload the machine and to put the machined part in the pallet, and then by the action to fetch the next raw part from the pallet and to load the machine again. With a double grippper (that can grip both a raw part and a machined part), loading and unloading is a combined action that fetches the raw part from the pallet, unloads, and loads the machine before putting the completed part into the pallet.

It would be too expensive to provide a ProcessingControl class for every different material flow and part processing sequence. Therefore, we need to separate the control of the variable material flow and part processing from that of the coarse-grained processing that is invariant to local configuration changes.

4.5.2 Hot-Spot Subsystem

The Strategy pattern [Gamma 1995] shows how to meet this requirement. Following it, we split off the material flow and part processing from the class ProcessingControl and objectify it (see Figure 4.8). An abstract hot-spot subsystem base class, ProcessingStrategy, defines the interface, which consists of an operation, called Process, that executes the material flow and part processing.

Different subclasses, ProcessingStrategyX, are derived. Each subclass implements the operation Process with a different material flow and part processing sequence. ProcessingControl requests the Process service via a reference (typed with the base class ProcessingStrategy) when everything is prepared to produce the parts. ProcessingControl selects the appropriate ProcessingStrategy and sets the reference to it. It does this when preparing the execution of a machine order, during the runtime of the framework, since the local configuration may differ for each subsequent machine order.

The ProcessingStrategy subclasses request manufacturing-logic-related (not device-related) services from the domain objects on the domain object layer, like moving a pallet from the cell store, position x, to a buffer y, or loading a part from position z of a

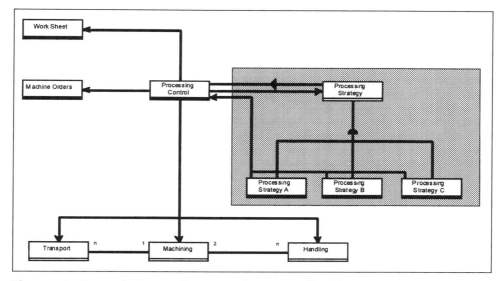

Figure 4.8   ProcessingStrategy hot-spot subsystem, split off from ProcessingControl.

pallet into a machine n. However, we want to make a ProcessingStrategy as simple as possible; it should not have to know the pallet position x, the buffer number y, and so on, since these items are independent from the strategy. A ProcessingStrategy should describe only the sequencing of the service requests for material flow and part processing, but should not have to provide all parameters for these requests.

Therefore, we split off this responsibility from the ProcessingStrategy. Instead of giving it, as an additional responsibility, to ProcessingControl, we use the Mediator design pattern [Gamma 1995] to achieve a clearer structuring (see Figure 4.9). A Processing-Mediator object, attached to each ProcessingControl object, collects the information about all machines and devices with which a ProcessingControl object works. It provides parameterless services as, for example, UnloadMachine, ExchangePallet, DoMachining, and IsCompletedPartPalletFull. ProcessingStrategy requests these services in the right sequence of time from the ProcessingMediator. The ProcessingMediator adds the missing parameter values to these service requests and forwards the requests to the domain objects serving them.

Consider, for example, the request UnloadMachine. When ProcessingMediator receives this request from a ProcessingStrategy, it adds, as parameters, the number of the machine to be unloaded, the number of the buffer into which the part is put, and the position of the part in the pallet on the buffer. It forwards the completed request to the associated handling object.

The advantage gained by introducing the ProcessingStrategy hot-spot subsystem is that the framework contains only one class ProcessingControl. Furthermore, a ProcessingStrategy is coded nearly as easily as writing the pseudocode presented in Figure 4.4. It takes one to a few hours to write a new processing strategy, if a suitable one is not available in the framework. A quite universally usable strategy and several other ones are blackbox components of the framework.

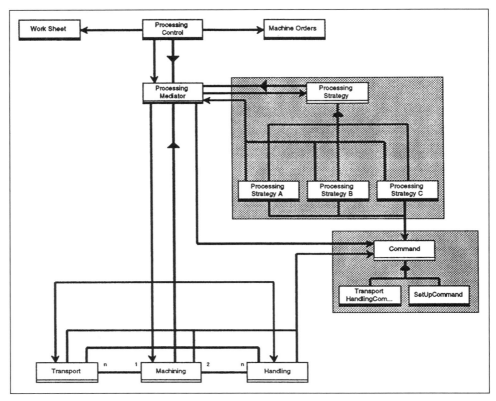

Figure 4.9 The command hot-spot subsystem and its use by other classes.

4.6 Processing Command Hot Spot

ProcessingStrategy and ProcessingControl request services from the domain layer objects. These service requests are forwarded over classes such as ProcessingMediator to the service providing classes such as Transport and Handling. Each of the classes that forwards service requests has to provide a method for each service, such as load, unload, and move pallet, even though it handles different services in a similar way. Further, classes not described in this chapter (see [Schmid 1995]) queue service requests and forward one request after another.

4.6.1 Hot-Spot Variability

During the life cycle of the framework, when extending its functionality, the flexibility to add new services might be required. For example, when automated tool processing would be added to automated part processing as a framework functionality, service requests related to the setup of machines with tools would have to be supplemented. One framework evolution problem is that if a new kind of service is defined, the interfaces of all participating classes have to be modified. In addition, there are structuring deficiencies: Different methods are required to forward, in the same way, similar services, and service requests cannot be passed over thread boundaries (refer to *Section 4.2*) and be queued easily.

It is required that the forwarding classes provide a service interface that may evolve easily, that the forwarding classes be simplified, and that there be a simple possibility for the queuing of service requests.

4.6.2 Hot-Spot Subsystem

The Command pattern [Gamma 1995] allows these requirements to be met. Its essential idea is to objectify a service request in a command object. However, our motivation to introduce commands contains aspects, such as the forwarding and queuing of requests, that are missing with the original Command pattern. Consequently, the hot-spot subsystem design is a variation of the Command pattern (for details, see [Schmid 1995]).

There is an abstract base class called Command, which has as subclasses concrete commands such as TransportCommand, HandlingCommand, and SetUpCommand. A command subclass describes the kind of the requested service(for example, Move Pallet from Store to Buffer) and has parameters giving the service details (for example, Store Position x and Buffer Number y). Since the detail parameters vary with the kind of service, they are described in subclass-specific methods. These methods allow the parameters of a service to be incrementally defined and to query commands for them.

A command object is created by the ProcessingStrategy as invoker. The details are added by the ProcessingMediator, before it forwards the commands, possibly via intermediate objects, to the respective provider of the service.

The command hot-spot subsystem differs from the hot-spot subsystems shown in the preceding sections with respect to the transparency of its variability. When we add a new Command subclass during the framework life cycle, it will probably provide new, specialized services not defined in the base class. They are used by newly added classes that process this command. Whereas when we add a new subclass to the hot-spot subsystems defined in the preceding sections, it will only provide a different implementation of the abstract services defined in the base class. As a consequence, the variability of the processing command hot spot is not completely transparent to the other framework classes (for a comparison, see [Schmid 1996a]).

4.7 Domain Object Layer

A domain object, such as transport, provides machine- and device-independent, domain-related services, like the moving of a pallet. The material flow optimization, machining, pallet transport, handling, buffer, and store hot spots, found in the medium rows in Figure 4.7, let the implementation of these services vary in different manufacturing cell configurations. These hot spots map domain-related responsibilities to different kinds of standardized machines and devices. We use the pallet transport hot spot as an example.

4.7.1 Hot-Spot Variability

In two differently configured manufacturing cells, either a robot or a conveyor belt may move pallets. That means different kinds of devices, with completely different interfaces, are used to perform domain-related services (as an analogy, compare the sending of a message, which may be performed by: a fax, a letter, or a messenger).

A domain object, such as pallet transport, maps the domain-related service request into a service request to a machine or device, incorporating the knowledge of how a transport service is performed by the robot. For example, it has to know which robot program performs a certain kind of transport task and how this robot program is to be parameterized with the position of the pallet. The problem is that different kinds of devices as, for example, a portal robot or a conveyor belt method, require completely different mappings.

4.7.2 Hot-Spot Subsystem

The (object) Adapter pattern [Gamma 1995], with the participants target, adapter, and adaptee, meets this requirement.

The domain-related services defined by the hot-spot subsystem base class Transport, the target, are adapted by a hot-spot subsystem subclass, like CNC-Transport, to a standardized machine, robot, or device that moves pallets, as an adaptee (see Figure 4.10). An adapter subclass is parameterizable to be itself adapted to different cell configurations: It contains a reference to the generalized machine or device that implements the service (in Figure 4.10, see the CNC-Machine), as well as mapping tables. These tables contain a configuration-specific description of which service (moving a pallet between a cell store

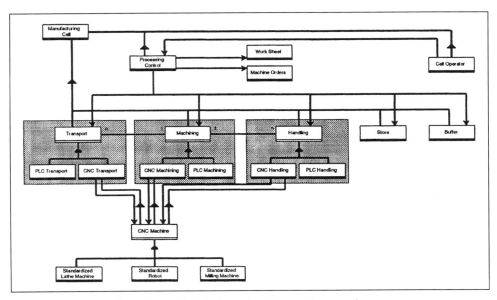

Figure 4.10   Manufacturing cell with domain object hot-spot subsystems.

position and a buffer store) with which parameter values is mapped to which robot program, and how the parameters of the transport service (which describe, for example, the position of a pallet) are mapped to the concrete parameters of the robot program.

When an adapter like CNC-Transport receives a request for a transport service, it transforms this request, using the mapping tables, into one or several requests to a CNC machine and forwards these requests to the referenced machine.

The same considerations apply to the handling hot spot and the machining hot spot. Introducing Transport, Handling, and Machining hot-spot subsystems results in the class diagram shown in Figure 4.11. The relations among Machining and Transport, respectively, and Handling in Figure 4.11 show that one Transport object and maximally two Handling objects provide services for a Machining object.

4.8 Standardized Machine and Device Layer

The standardized machine and device layer provides standardized machines and devices for use by the domain objects. The machine variability hot spot, the robot variability hot spot, and the PLC-controlled device variability hot spot, found on the third row from the bottom in Figure 4.7, map the standardized objects to concrete machines and devices. This layer makes the variability of devices, which is quite common, transparent to the other objects of the framework.

4.8.1 Hot-Spot Variability

Different manufacturing cell configurations may contain different machines and robots from different classes with a similar responsibility. CNC-Transport should be able to request services from any robot. Exchanging a robot of a manufacturing cell for another one should be possible without modifying CNC-Transport. The problem is that different robot classes have different interfaces.

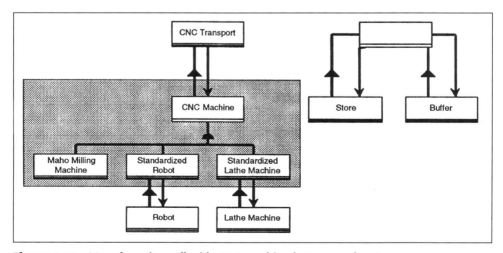

Figure 4.11 Manufacturing cell with CNC machine hot-spot subsystem.

4.8.2 Hot-Spot Subsystem

The (object) Adapter pattern [Gamma 1995] meets this requirement. The client, CNC-Transport, requests services that the target, CNC-Machine, the base class of the hot-spot subsystem, defines. An adapter class, such as StandardizedRobot, derived from CNC-Machine, adapts the common interface to a concrete machine class, such as Robot (see Figure 4.11).

CNC-Machine, an abstract class, defines the standardized interface and provides some common internal data and services. Standardizing the interfaces of different CNC machines and robots by generalizing them and by abstracting from their differing details is a difficult and lengthy domain-related process. In practice, we included indus-trial robots in this class, though we conceptually distinguished them from machines, since they have similar behavior with regard to RC programs, as CNC machines with regard to NC programs.

For an existing concrete machine class, we derive an adapter class, such as StandardizedRobot, from the base class. It contains (a reference to) the concrete machine it adapts. StandardizedRobot transforms a standardized service request into a request, or a sequence of requests, to a concrete Robot, and forwards them to it.

In case a machine class does not yet exist but is newly developed, we use interface inheritance and do not follow the Adapter pattern. That means a subclass, such as Maho Milling Machine, derived from the base class CNC-Machine, directly imple-ments the required functionality, using the communication classes on the communica-tion sublayer.

The hot spots for machines or devices controlled by a programmable logic control (PLC), and other kinds of machines and devices, are standardized with separate base classes, such as PLC-Device, in the same way as described.

4.9 Concrete Machine and Device Layer

The concrete machine and device layer provides concrete machines and devices for use by the standardized machine and device layer. Concrete CNC machines are all coupled mainly in the same way as the controller of a real CNC machine via communication lines. However, the transmission protocol may vary, as well as the access to a commu-nication line (this access differs with different platforms like Windows, Windows/NT, OS/2, and Unix). The transmission protocol hot spot and the communication line access hot spot, contained in the communication sublayer, cope with this variability.

A specific machine class exchanges specific telegrams with its machine controller. A telegram passed to Transmission-Protocol is packed in a transmission protocol. The resulting byte sequences are passed to CommunicationlineAccess and put by it on the communication line. Both the transmission protocol and the communication line access form a hot-spot subsystem (see Figure 4.12), which is structured following inter-face inheritance. Each hot-spot subsystem base class, TransmissionProtocol and Com-municationlineAccess, defines a common interface, which is implemented differently by different subclasses, such as LSV2, with respect to OS/2 (Communication-lineAccess).

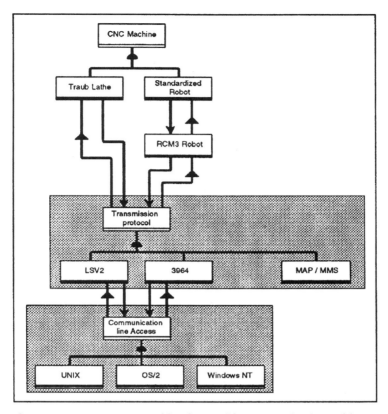

Figure 4.12   Concrete machine layer with communication sublayer.

The machine layer forms a subframework together with the transmission protocol and CommunicationlineAccess sublayers. Machines can be and have been used in other applications, independent from the main part of the framework. Figure 4.13 shows how we put together a machine by selecting the blackbox components from the different layers and configuring them together. The required parameterization (for example, with the number of the I/O-port to which a communication line is attached) is not shown. The same considerations apply to PLC-controlled devices.

4.10 Application Creation

We have put much emphasis on making the configuration easy. That means we provided with the framework a class called ManufacturingCell with configuration services like the following:

>   **AddMachiningCluster.** This adds a new machining station to a manufacturing cell (which will run as a thread).

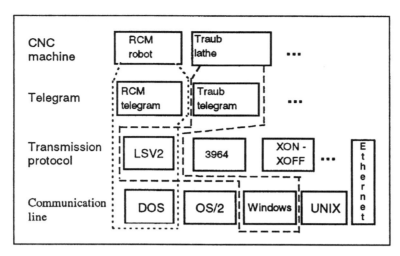

Figure 4.13   Blackbox subframework for CNC machines.

AddMachineToAMachiningCluster. This associates a machine to a machining station.

AddMaterialFlowCluster. This adds a transport or handling robot or device to a manufacturing cell (which will run as a thread).

AddMachineToAMaterialFlowCluster. This associates a robot or device machine to a material flow cluster.

ConnectMaterialFlowClusterToAMachiningCluster. This lets a machining cluster use a material flow cluster, either as a handling unit as a transport unit, or as a combined handling and transport unit.

To develop a manufacturing cell control application from the framework, an application developer writes a configuration program that defines a manufacturing cell object and machine and device objects, and calls the configuration services of the manufacturing cell object to add the machines and devices to it.

Depending on the knowledge of the framework, it takes a few hours to a few days to write the configuration program. The tables used to parameterize hot-spot subsystems are supplied in the form of files, and it may take from a day to a few days to write them. Both activities together create a new cell control application, under the assumption that all required blackbox components are provided with the framework.

When required components such as a given CNC machine or a part processing strategy are missing, they are to be programmed and supplemented to the framework. The required effort and time depend on the kind of component. It takes a few hours to write and test a new strategy. On the other hand, it may take a week or more to develop a new machine with a CNC coupling.

4.11 Interactive Configurator

We developed an interactive configurator (prototype) to obviate the need for programming when creating an application from OSEFA. Similar to working with a GUI configurator, the application developer does the following:

1. Creates the structure of the manufacturing cell with machining stations and material flow stations for handling and pallet transport
2. Selects the technical components that form a part of the machining stations and material flow stations
3. Parameterizes them when required
4. Adds them to the corresponding stations

During all these steps, the interactive configurator performs a lot of consistency checks (which are not done by the configuration services). Using an interactive configurator has twofold advantages. On one hand, the time and effort required to create a cell control application are reduced even more (in comparison to writing a configuration program), which is compounded by the fact that no erroneous configuration programs are written. On the other hand (what seems to be more important), an application developer needs little or no programming skill. Mainly, a good knowledge of the application domain and of the framework is required to create a manufacturing application.

4.12 Experiences

Our experiences related to framework development, testing, application creation effort, and costs are described in the following sections.

4.12.1 Development

A framework prototype with very limited flexibility (it contained only the CNC-machine and the RC-controlled robot hot-spot subsystems and very restricted concurrency) was built in 1993. It supported a manufacturing cell configuration similar to the one described in *Section 4.2* (which was at that time the configuration of a joint CIM laboratory of the Fachhochschule Konstanz). A full version of the framework supporting all described hot-spot subsystems became operational in early 1996.

4.12.2 Testing

In a first test stage, we used the framework configuration features to replace all real machines and devices by simulated machine and device classes, and the visualization to observe if the system ran correctly. Thus, we could find principal and smaller logical errors with relatively little effort. In a subsequent test stage, we replaced the simulated classes with the real classes and attached simulated machines and devices via communication lines to the cell computer. Eventually, we performed the test in the manufacturing cell, with real machines and devices. In this way, we could save considerable testing effort and cost.

4.12.3 Application Creation Effort

It takes roughly a day—maybe a few days when we include testing—to create an application from the framework. By adding a few more days for the analysis of a manufacturing cell, and some time for complementing not-yet-existing framework components, the overall effort and elapsed time is still very small compared to the time it usually takes to develop the control software through an individual project, which is in the range of some person-months to a person-year.

For example, shortly after Version 1 of OSEFA was completed, we were asked, on a relatively short term before a demonstration, for a considerable modification of the cell configuration, requiring another machining station, a laser scanner for measuring, and the production program. In other words, the parts to be produced were exchanged completely. Two new processing strategies were quite different from those known and considered in planning the framework (which were similar to those shown in Figure 4.4).

The part processing sequence to process a new part in the lathe machine was different, since the part had to be machined from both sides (with two different CNC programs) and turned between the two machining steps by the handling device. The part processing sequence to do the measurement in the laser scanner was unanticipated, since the handling device robot moves the part through the laser scanner such that the loading, machining, and unloading were melded into one combined handling and machining step.

It took less than a week to create a cell control application for the new manufacturing cell configuration and part processing sequences and to test it—less time than the mechanical and equipment changes took. For changed configuration and production requirements to react with such a short time to market would have been impossible without the framework.

However, when doing these changes, we also were confronted with the problem of unplanned variability. We had not anticipated part-processing sequences (in a ProcessingStrategy subclass) with characteristics that the newly developed ones had, such as two machining steps or the absence of a loading and unloading step. Only because the architecture of OSEFA was sufficiently general could we use some features of it in a way that was different from the planned one, in order to accommodate the unplanned variability.

Before starting the project we had expected that, in developing an application for a given domain configuration, a domain-specific blackbox framework would reduce both development cost and time to market by a factor of 3 to 4. Our expectations were exceeded by the results, which indicate rather a factor 10 or more. This is a very substantial saving of development effort and time, on the order of a magnitude, compared to the development of cell control software through a typical development project.

4.12.4 Framework Costs

Developing a blackbox framework for a selected domain requires considerable investment. Our experience indicates that developing a framework takes around two to three times as much effort as developing a fixed application from the domain. This number may vary with the domain; it includes the costs of analyzing the domain and sufficiently generalizing the class structure, but not the cost to acquire knowledge of framework structuring and design. We also suppose that, initially, mainly the components required for the first application are provided. When creating more applications, you can incrementally increase the number of application components.

4.13 Summary

Our experience strongly indicates that developing a framework is worth the effort. The investment will pay off after the creation of about the third application from the framework. Another advantage, which is very important in today's markets, is the short time span required for the creation of a customer-specific or product-specific application from a framework.

The concept of hot spots and of their implementation by hot-spot subsystems, according to the hot-spot requirements, makes framework development much easier. A systematic approach to framework design and development, based on proven software engineering principles [Schmid 1998], reduces the effort and is the only sound way to develop a framework.

4.14 References

[Aarsten 1995] Aarsten, A., G. Elia, and G. Menga: G++: A pattern language for computer integrated manufacturing. In *Pattern Languages of Program Design,* J. Coplien and D. Schmidt, editors. Reading, MA: Addison-Wesley, 1995.

[Fayad 1999] Fayad, M.E., D. Schmidt, R. Johnson. *Building Application Frameworks: Object-Oriented Foundations of Framework Design.* New York: John Wiley & Sons, 1999.

[Gamma 1995] Gamma, E., R. Helm, R. Johnson, and J. Vlissides. *Design Patterns: Elements of Reusable Object-Oriented Software.* Reading, MA: Addison-Wesley, 1995.

[Johnson 1988)] Johnson, R.E., and B. Foote. Designing reusable classes. *Journal of Object-Oriented Programming* 2:22–35, June 1988.

[Pree 1995] Pree, W. *Design Patterns for Object-Oriented Software Development.* Reading, MA: Addison-Wesley, 1994.

[Schmid 1995] Schmid, H.A. Creating the architecture of a manufacturing framework by design patterns. *Proceedings OOPSLA 1995,* ACM SIGPLAN Notices 30(10):370–384, October 1995.

[Schmid 1996a] Schmid, H.A. Design patterns for constructing the hot spots of a manufacturing framework. *Journal of Object-Oriented Programming* 9(3):25–37, June 1996.

[Schmid 1996b] Schmid, H.A. Creating applications from components: A manufacturing framework design. *IEEE Software* 13(6):67–75, November, 1996.

[Schmid 1999] Schmid, H.A. Framework design by systematic generalization. In *Building Application Frameworks: Object-Oriented Foundations of Framework Design,* M.E. Fayad, R. Johnson, and D. Schmidt, editors. New York: John Wiley & Sons, 1999.

[Schmid-Mueller 1998] Schmid, H.A., and F. Mueller. Patterns for extending black-box frameworks—with a GUI and visualization example. *Journal of Object-Oriented Programming* 11(3):38–47, June 1998.

CHAPTER 5

Framework Reuse over Different CIM Subdomains

When starting to develop a domain-specific framework an important question is this: How large a framework domain should one choose? The larger it is, the more variable aspects and the fewer fixed aspects the domain will have, making it more difficult to build the framework. On the other hand, the larger the framework domain, the greater the opportunities to make use of the framework.

For a given domain the question is whether a framework can successfully cover it or whether the domain is too large. For example, is it a reasonable objective to build a framework for the computer-integrated manufacturing (CIM) domain? If this domain is too large, how can we determine a subdomain that can be covered successfully?

And suppose you have built a framework covering a subdomain and require a framework for a related subdomain. Can the existing framework be extended or modified to cover the related subdomain? If not, can we reuse artifacts as, for example, complete layers, or components such as hot-spot subsystems, or at least architectural principles, from the existing framework to build the new one? In addition to application creation, the extension, modification, or reuse of an existing framework is a second way to get a return on the investment in the original framework.

One would like to get some support in making these decisions. Based on our experience with the CIM domain, we propose the approach of partitioning a domain into subdomains according to orthogonal characteristics that vary over the domain. An analysis of the framework architectures for the subdomains of interest gives hard evidence for the required decisions.

We will not discuss this approach from a theoretical point of view, but we will use, as a real-life example, the CIM domain. Since it is too large to be covered by one framework, we partitioned it into 36 smaller subdomains that are described by four orthogonal characteristics. Presenting and comparing the architecture of several frameworks we have designed and developed for altogether six subdomains, we demonstrate why one framework could not cover all subdomains, which subdomains could be covered by single frameworks, and which artifacts could be reused over the subdomains.

5.1 Manufacturing Subdomains

Let us consider a subdomain of manufacturing: metal part-processing manufacturing, which is a typical CIM domain. In this domain, a manufacturing cell consists of machining stations that process parts; a cell store or first in, first out (FIFO) buffer stores that store pallets, each with one or more parts, between processing steps; and a transport system that moves pallets among the machining stations and the store. Typically, several processing steps at different machining stations are required to complete the processing of a part. For example, an axis might be produced after having entered a pallet with raw metal cylinders in the cell by lathing a cylinder in a lathing station and, subsequently, drilling holes in it in a drilling station.

Though the metal part-processing manufacturing domain looks very uniform at first glance, a more detailed analysis shows that manufacturing cells from it may have quite different characteristics. The processing of work may be organized in different ways; the machining stations may be dumb, of restricted intelligence, or very intelligent and autonomous; data may be stored centrally or decentrally; and an elaborate storing of production data may or may not be required. However, building a framework successfully is possible only when the domain to be covered is uniform enough. If it is too varied, one should consider partitioning the domain according to important characteristics that vary over it. Let us consider the varying characteristics of the metal part-processing manufacturing domain.

5.1.1 Work Organization and Cell Topology

In a *store-centered subdomain* (see Figure 5.1, left), the time at which a machining station performs a given machining step with given parts is prescheduled. For example, when a part X undergoes three subsequent machining steps on machines A, B, and C, the machine order schedule may contain three entries: machine A, order part X step 1, 8.00–9.00; machine B, order part X step 2, 11.00–13.00; machine C, order part X step 3, 15.30–17.00. When scheduled, a station fetches the pallets with the required parts from the cell store for processing and returns it afterwards.

In the *flow-centered subdomain* (see Figure 5.1, middle), parts flow from one machining station to another in the required sequence of processing. A machining station processes pallets in the sequence in which they arrive. For example, when a pallet with part X is entered into the cell, it is sent to machining station A and waits until it is free. After machining, station A sends the pallet to station B, and this sends it, after machining, in turn to station C. The (cell central) store is replaced by a FIFO store at each station.

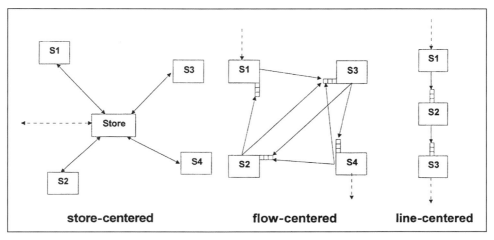

Figure 5.1 Different cell topologies and work organizations.

The *line-centered subdomain* (see Figure 5.1, right) is similar to the flow-centered subdomain except that all stations are in a linear sequence. The transport line may be formed, for example, by a circular conveyor belt. A pallet is moved from one station to the next station, but can skip stations. This means that the processing steps are done for all parts in the same sequence, but steps may be skipped.

Intelligence of a Station

We distinguish three degrees of intelligence: dumb stations, stations with restricted intelligence, and intelligent stations. Dumb stations have all, even minor, movements controlled by the cell computer [Lewerentz 1995]. Stations with restricted intelligence are, for example, computerized numerical control (CNC) machines, robot control (RC) controlled robots, or programmable logic control (PLC) machines and devices. They know how to machine a part or move a part from a pallet into a machine when they are told to do it. Intelligent stations understand and control the manufacturing process; for example, they know autonomously how to react on the arrival of a pallet with parts.

Central or (Partially) Decentral Data Storage

Data describing the content of a pallet and its production status, as well as the required processing steps (with production parameters and result data), may be stored centrally in the cell computer or decentrally on a mobile data carrier fixed at a pallet.

Production Data Administration

Different machining stations may use differently structured records of production data describing the production parameters and result data of each production step, which are possibly dynamically changing over time. The framework has to access these changing data structures in a database, and a tool for the administration of these data structures is required. We call this *production data administration.* There are also cases where no production data administration is required.

These characteristics are orthogonal to each other and vary over the domain. The first one, work organization and cell topology, characterizes the domain logic (also called *domain processes*), whereas the second one, intelligence of a station, characterizes the technical components of the domain. The third characteristic, central or decentral data storage, describes a property of the data processing system, which is the same as the last characteristic, production data administration. Note also that the first three characteristics give alternative selections, whereas the fourth one gives an add-on selection. We may partition the metal part-processing manufacturing domain by means of these orthogonal characteristics into 36 subdomains, which are presented in Figure 5.2. A few combinations of characteristics may be rarely found in the real world, though theoretically they are possible.

With knowledge of these subdomains, the question for the size of the framework domain may be put more precisely as follows: Is it reasonable to develop a framework for the total domain, or just for a single subdomain, or for a set of neighboring subdomains? An answer cannot come from educated conjecture or guessing; it must stem from practical experience. Our experience is based on developing a first framework, called OSEFA, for one subdomain, and later extending it and developing frameworks for other subdomains.

OSEFA [Schmid 1995, 1996] covers the subdomain marked in Figure 5.2 with the following characteristics: store centered topology and organization, stations with re-

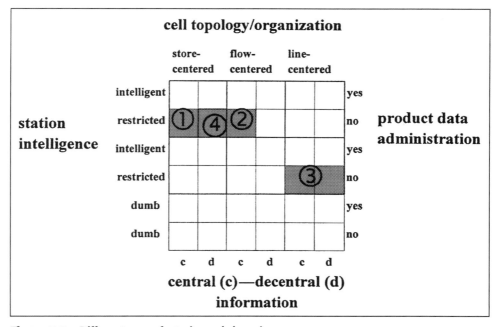

Figure 5.2   Different manufacturing subdomains.

stricted intelligence, central data storage, and no product data administration. At the time of developing the framework, we had the subdomain well defined, but we could not have demarcated it in terms of these characteristics from the other subdomains. This understanding grew gradually at a later time when we explored the other subdomains.

After completion and use of OSEFA, we explored four more subdomains with the objective to extend or modify OSEFA to cover them, or if this was not possible, to build a new framework reusing as much as possible from OSEFA:

- A subdomain with all characteristics being identical to the OSEFA subdomain with the exception of decentral data storage (marked with 4)

- Flow-centered manufacturing subdomain with all other characteristics being identical to the OSEFA subdomain (marked with 2)

- Assembly lines (line-centered) with intelligent stations, product data administration, and both central and decentral data storage (marked with 3) in cooperation with the Robert Bosch GmbH, Stuttgart.

These subdomains seem to be a good sample since the flow-centered one and the one with decentral data storage are both closely related to the OSEFA subdomain, and the assembly line subdomain is as different from it as possible.

5.2 Framework Architecture

Class diagrams would present too much detail for the description and comparison of the different frameworks. For this reason, we describe and compare the architecture of the considered frameworks. A framework architecture is defined as a specialization of a software architecture. A software architecture is described, following [Garlan-Perry 1995], by the structure of the components of a system, their interrelationships (also called *connectors*), and the principles and guidelines governing their design and evolution over time.

A framework architecture distinguishes between two kinds of components: components that model the fixed aspects, called *frozen spots,* and components that model the variable aspects, called *hot spots,* of the framework domain. A hot-spot subsystem [Schmid 1997, 1999] implements a hot spot by a base class and subclasses and, possibly, by additional classes and relationships that realize a design pattern [Gamma 1995].

The logical view [Kruchten 1995] of an architecture (also called *conceptual architecture*) describes the components and connectors in terms of an object model. Other views describe, for example, the module and code structure (called *module* and *code architecture,* respectively [Soni 1995]) or the concurrency and synchronization aspects (called the *process view*).

We introduce a framework architecture diagram to represent the logical view of a framework architecture. It contains as components frozen spots, denoted by boxes; hot-spot subsystems; and use relationships (called also *messagerelationships*). A hot-spot subsystem (see Figure 5.3) is denoted by a box with an inscribed symbolized class hierarchy. The symbol contains the names of the design pattern and of the generalized concept that is modeled by the base class. A service request is denoted by an arrow. A dashed arrow indicates a potential service request that is configured when creating an application from a framework.

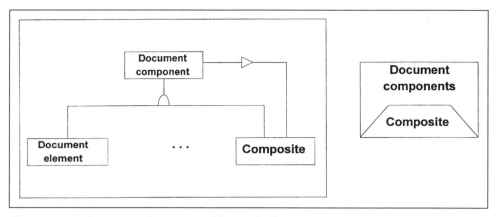

Figure 5.3   A hot-spot subsystem and its symbolic representation.

Boehm et al. [Gacek 1995] extend the definition of a software architecture by stakeholders' need statements and by a rationale that demonstrates that the components and so on, if implemented, would satisfy the collection of stakeholders' need statements. An extended framework architecture includes, along these lines, a description of the domain variability as the central part of the need statements, and, as a central part of the rationale, how the hot-spot subsystems of the framework architecture satisfy the domain variability.

In the following, we will use extended framework architectures, that is, framework architecture diagrams and the rationale for how the framework covers the domain variability, to describe the frameworks to be presented.

5.3 Common Subdomain Properties and Basic Framework Architecture

All manufacturing cells of the metal part-processing domain contain technical (processing) components such as machines, robots, and conveyor belts, that are connected to a cell computer. We model such a component by a machine or device object that has the same responsibilities as the component. A machine or device object hides its implementation; in particular, it encapsulates its coupling to the technical component over communication lines. The knowledge about the flow of processing in a manufacturing cell is not modeled within the machine or device objects, but by separate processing control objects.

5.3.1 Basic Framework Architecture Logical View

The basic structuring of a manufacturing framework is abstracted into the layers presented in Figure 5.4. (We use the notion of a layer both in the sense of abstraction and of the use-relation: A more concrete lower layer may not request services from a more abstract higher layer.) The layers that make up the manufacturing framework are as follows:

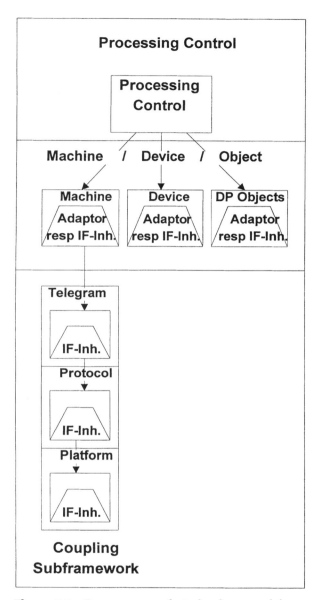

Figure 5.4 Common manufacturing framework layer architecture.

- A processing control layer that contains Processing Control objects.
- A machine/device layer that contains the technical component objects from the application domain, and, as we will see, technical objects from the DP (data processing) domain, such as a production data server. To cope with the variability (over different manufacturing cells) of machines, devices, and DP objects, we generalize them each in the form of a hot-spot subsystem, thus achieving device generalization.

- A subframework for the coupling of a machine or device object to the technical (processing) component. The subframework typically consists of a telegram layer (also called *communication layer*), a protocol layer, and a communication line access layer.

Since the telegram, the protocol, and the platform for communication line access may vary, we include for each a hot-spot subsystem for varying telegrams, protocols, and platforms into them. The hot-spot subsystems in the generalized machine layer, telegram layer, protocol layer, and communication line access layer are structured following either the Adaptor design pattern or interface inheritance if no adaptation to an existing module is required [Schmid 1995, Chapter 4].

5.3.2 Basic Framework Architecture Process View

Since all objects modeling technical processing components and the processing control objects work concurrently, the framework requires subsystems or services that support threads and thread communication/synchronization.

In addition, there are usually subsystems that provide the visualization of the processing in the manufacturing cell, as well as the configuration.

5.4 Store-Centered Framework OSEFA

The manufacturing framework OSEFA was developed by the author and a project group at the Computer Science Department of the Fachhochschule Konstanz from late 1993 through 1995 and was evaluated in cooperation with the Mechanical Engineering Department in the CIM model factory. The subdomain covered is characterized by a store-centered topology and organization, machines such as CNCmachines with restricted intelligence, central data storage, and no product data administration. To derive the framework architecture and its central concepts from the subdomain characteristics, we expand on the short subdomain description given in *Section 5.1*.

5.4.1 OSEFA Subdomain Characteristics

Store-centered cells (compare Figure 5.1 left) are topologically star-structured: A transport system moves each pallet from the cell store to (the buffer store of) each of the machining stations. A machining station consists of a processing machine or device, which machines, assembles, or measures a part, and a handling device, which loads a part into the machine and unloads it after processing. The processing is CNC-, RC-, or PLC-controlled, handling machine, robot, or device, respectively. Note that this topology includes a very large variety of different cell configurations [Schmid 1995, Chapter 4].

The structure is paralleled by the processing organization. The machine order schedule contains, for each machining station, the sequence of machine orders to be executed. A machine order refers to a worksheet entry that describes the resources required (such as the parts in the store, the CNC or robot program that performs the machining or assembly, and tools and equipment). A machine order is processed by performing first the setup and then a sequence of part-processing steps: A pallet with parts to be machined is moved from the cell store to a buffer store of the machining station. A part is loaded from the pallet into the machine, machined, and unloaded back into the pallet until all parts of the pallet are processed. The pallet is moved back to the store, and the described processing steps are repeated until all pallets of the machine order are processed. However, with different tools and equipment, the details of this part-processing sequence may differ slightly (see [Schmid 1995]).

5.4.2 Framework Architecture

Since the CNC and similar machines have restricted intelligence, they cannot process a machine order. To control this processing, we introduce for each machining station a Processing Control object (see Figure 5.5). Processing Control accesses the Machine Order and related WorkSheet entries, performs the setup, and then requests, service by service, the objects on the machine/device layer to execute the steps of the part-processing sequence.

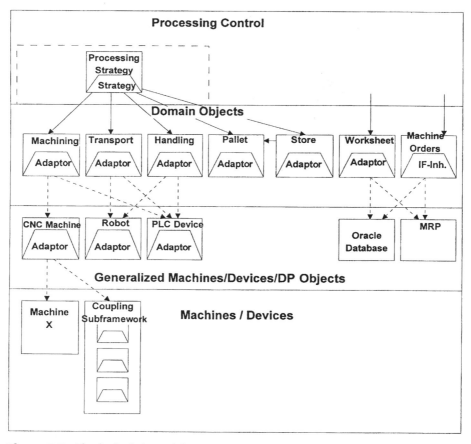

Figure 5.5 The logical view of the OSEFA framework architecture.

Since the details of the part-processing sequence may differ slightly, we split them off from Processing Control into a Processing Strategy hot-spot subsystem. It is structured following the Strategy design pattern and bound at runtime [Gamma 1995]). In this way, a part-processing Strategy may be exchanged, when required, for another one. As a consequence, the Processing Control becomes a frozen spot of the framework.

However, the semantic gap between the processing strategy layer and the machine/device layer, as described in *Section 5.3*, would be very great; for example, machines do not understand a service request such as "move pallet." We reduce this gap by introducing a domain object layer. It contains domain-related concepts and entities that provide services that are typical for the domain and requested by processing control and strategy. For example, a Transport domain object provides the service to move a pallet and transform these services into machine-specific requests. We obtain the required variability by realizing a domain object as an adaptor-structured hot-spot subsystem, thus obtaining device independence (see [Schmid 1996]). For example, a Transport hot-spot subsystem hides if a robot or a conveyor belt performs a transport service; a Machine Order hot-spot subsystem provides the service to get a machine order entry, without the requester having to know if this information comes from a material request planning (MRP) system or has been entered interactively on the shop floor.

The domain objects store all information about the state of the manufacturing cell. For example, a Store object has the information concerning which (domain objects) Pallets it contains, and Pallet object has the information concerning which parts it contains at which position and what their processing status is. Thus, all data are stored centrally in the cell computer.

5.4.3 Framework Architecture
Process View

Each Processing Control (including a Processing Strategy) object and each technical processing component object, such as a CNC machine, is an *active* object running in its own thread. Asynchronous service requests are passed from Processing Control over thread boundaries as command objects (a variation [Schmid 1995] of the Command design pattern [Gamma 1995]), and notifications on the termination of the services are received as events (compare [Aarsten 1995]). Shared passive domain objects such as Store and Buffer Store need to be locked (compare [Aarsten 1995]).

5.4.4 Experiences and Results

When we developed a first framework in the CIM domain, we selected one of the 36 subdomains as framework domain. During development, we had to solve many quite complex detail problems, some of them stemming from the interaction between the framework architecture logical view and the process view, others being domain-specific such as the optimization of the sequence of transport command execution or the realization of two different domain entities by one machine/device (compare [Schmid 1995]). Adding another degree of complexity by additional inclusion of a neighbor subdomain would have jeopardized the success of the project.

Development of OSEFA was done in about two years, with an effort of about four person-years (including the time to understand frameworks). We invested quite a considerable effort in a sound design (which paid off directly and when extending the framework). The framework met our expectations completely; for example, for application generation from the framework we experienced a reduction of the effort and elapsed time by up to an order of magnitude, compared to software development through an individual project [Schmid 1996]. From this experience and later experiences with neighbor subdomains, we conclude that selecting one subdomain for development of a first framework in a domain is a sound decision.

5.5 Extending OSEFA for Decentral Data Storage

After the completion of the first version of OSEFA, the requirement for partially decentral data storage in the CIM model factory was raised from our Mechanical Engineering Department. The reason is that a manual exchange of pallets in the cell store goes unnoticed by cell control software that stores information about the pallets and their position in the store centrally. However, an exchange might cause errors or even damage to the machines. After an analysis we determined that we could extend OSEFA to include the closely related subdomain (marked with 4 in Figure 5.2) of decentral data storage.

5.5.1 Decentral Data Storage

Mobile data carriers attached to a pallet store detail information about the pallet and the parts. However, some minimal information about a pallet in the cell-store, such as its position and the machine order to which it belongs, needs to be kept centrally in a store-centered subdomain. The reason is that when (the Processing Control of) a machining station prepares to execute a machine order, it has to find out (by asking the cell-store object) the position of the pallets that it has to process.

After a pallet has been moved by the transport system to the machining station, a data carrier reader at the buffer store reads the detail information into the software system, which also keeps it centrally during the machining of the parts on the pallet. After the machining of each part, both the central and the decentral information on the pallet is updated such that the latter contains, in the case of a system breakdown, the valid information. After processing, the pallet is moved back to the central store. The central detail information is no longer required and dropped. Please note that with flow-centered work organization, no information (not even some minimal information) needs to be kept centrally when a pallet is not being machined.

5.5.2 Framework Architecture

Two already existing hot-spot subsystems, Pallet and Strategy, could be used to extend OSEFA for decentral data storage. The Pallet hot-spot subsystem (see Figure 5.5) is used in OSEFA to include different kinds of pallets, for example, with different geometries. As a new kind of pallet, one containing only minimal information was added. The Store (object) contains minimal-information Pallets when a pallet is in the cell store. The Strategy hot-spot subsystem (see Figure 5.5) contains slightly varying part-processing sequences. A new kind of part-processing sequence for decentral data storage that extends the existing ones was added. A Decentral Strategy adds three actions to those of an existing (central) Strategy: After a pallet has been moved from the cell store to the buffer store of a machining station, it reads the detail information from the data carrier into a full-information Pallet object; after processing of each part, it updates both the full-information Pallet object and the mobile data carrier; and after completing the processing of a pallet, it updates the mobile data carrier and the minimal-information Pallet object and drops the full-information Pallet object.

A reader/writer for mobile data carriers was modeled by introducing objects on the domain object and the machine/device layer: A reader/writer of mobile data carriers with device-independent services is a new domain object (class) and a hot-spot subsystem; a reader/writer of mobile data carriers with device-dependent services is a new device object (class). The reader/writer domain object transforms the device-independent services, which a Strategy requests, into device-dependent services, which it requests from the reader/writer device object.

5.5.3 Experience

The design and implementation of this extension to OSEFA took a little more than a person-month. It was possible in this smooth way without modification of the existing framework only because it already contained hot-spot subsystems that could be used to integrate the additional functionality. To use the existing hot-spot subsystems in this way was not preplanned.

5.6 Flow-Centered Manufacturing Framework

After the completion of the first version of OSEFA, we analyzed the closely related flow-centered manufacturing subdomain (marked with 2 in Figure 5.2). Its characteristics are the same as those of the OSEFA subdomain, except for the work organization/topology characteristic. The objective of the analysis and subsequent design was to determine if it would be reasonable to extend OSEFA to also cover this subdomain, or if a separate framework had to be designed.

5.6.1 Flow-Centered Topology and Organization

The processing in a flow-centered manufacturing cell is organized: by pallets flowing from one machining station to the next one in the sequence required by the processing steps of a part and by machining stations processing pallets in the sequence of their arrival. A route sheet attached to a pallet describes, for each of the subsequent processing steps of a part, which machine has to perform it and which resources are required. The (cell central) store is replaced by a FIFO store at each machining station.

When a machining station is not busy and the FIFO-store is not empty, a pallet is fetched from the FIFO store into the machining station buffer store. Then, the machine is set up according to the route sheet information. From the buffer, the parts are processed in a flow-centered part-processing sequence that is similar to the inner loop (of handling and machining steps, but without moving of pallet steps) of the store-centered sequence. After processing, the machining station requests the transport system to move the processed pallet to the FIFO store of the machining station that is to process the subsequent step.

5.6.2 Framework Architecture

Proceeding from the OSEFA architecture we analyze the modifications required for the flow-centered domain. Since the flow-centered processing is completely different from the store-centered one, the objects from the processing control and strategy layer need to be exchanged. A flow-centered Processing Control controls a machining station. When a pallet is in the FIFO store, it moves it to the buffer, sets up the machine, and performs the flow-centered part-processing sequence as described. As in the store-centered domain, the sequence may vary with equipment and tools such that it is realized by a Processing Strategy hot-spot subsystem. It is nearly identical to that of a store-centered framework, though the strategy content differs.

The changes to the domain object layer are not as great. New domain object hot-spot subsystems are added, such as a FIFO-Store and a Route Sheet that describes the sequence of stations that a part visits; and others not required in this subdomain, such as Store and Machine Orders, might be removed. Other domain object hot-spot subsystems have slightly different responsibilities. For example, Transport provides services to move a pallet from a machining station to (the FIFO store of) another machining station, instead of between a machining station and the store.

The lower layers remain unchanged. As a consequence, the resulting architecture logical view is similar to that of the OSEFA architecture, except for one layer being exchanged and another one being slightly modified.

5.6.3 Experiences

The design took only a few person-months, though the change to the organization is a major modification. One reason is that OSEFA encapsulates the changed aspect: work organization within a layer of the framework. In principle, one might be able to build one framework that embodies both the store-centered and flow-centered subdomains. This might be done by including a super-hot-spot subsystem that provides a choice between the two work organizations in the processing layer. However, our judgment was that the resulting framework would become too complex. Our decision was to separate the two frameworks, but to reuse the common layers.

5.7 Intelligent Assembly Line Framework

In a joint project with the Robert Bosch GmbH, Stuttgart, we designed and developed the prototype of an assembly line framework. Bosch factories at different locations quite often build new production assembly lines for new electronic-mechanical automotive products. Different assembly lines are similar, but never identical. An assembly line is attached to a cell computer. In the past, the cell computer software was produced individually, but with reuse of experience and code for each new assembly line.

Bosch assembly lines belong to the line-centered subdomain with intelligent and autonomous stations, production data administration, and both central and decentral data storage. We present the characteristics of this subdomain, which are all different from those of the OSEFA subdomain.

5.7.1 Line-Centered Topology

Since all assembly stations are attached sequentially to the transport line, there is no choice about where a pallet has to go when it leaves a station and is put on the line. The line between two stations serves as a FIFO buffer. When it is ready, the subsequent station takes the first part from the line. As a consequence, moving pallets is an implicit functionality; there is no transport domain object and hot-spot subsystem (as in the OSEFA architecture—see Figure 5.5).

5.7.2 Intelligent Stations

An intelligent assembly station performs a complex assembly subtask (including the handling of pallets and parts) at a complex automotive subsystem such as a fuel injection pump. It is developed and built individually for the purpose, both from mechanical and control points of view. It contains an individually programmed intelligent controller, often based on a realtime computer. The controller interacts with the cell computer in domain-specific terms (which are encoded in telegrams); there is no semantic gap between a station and the processing control layer. Assembly stations are domain objects that provide and request domain-related services. Consequently, the framework architecture has a combined machine/device object and domain object layer that contains as technical domain objects only assembly stations (see Figure 5.6).

Based on its intelligence, a station is autonomous. It decides if an arriving part should be processed or passed on, what kind of processing and which production parameters are required, and whether the processing was successful. This means that the control of the pallet flow among stations and of the processing within a station are done autonomously by an assembly station. In the OSEFA subdomain, this control is the primary task of the cell computer.

In the intelligent assembly line subdomain, the control task of the cell computer falls away. It is primarily replaced by the functionality of a production data server: procuring the production parameters and storing the production result data. Consequently, the intelligent assembly line framework architecture replaces the processing control and strategy layer of the OSEFA architecture by a production data server layer. An assembly station object requests services from a data server object. This means that the use-hierarchy is partially inverted; one might consider it as a callback structure. The domain object and device layer requests services from the data server layer.

5.7.3 Production Data Administration

Different assembly stations use differently structured production parameters and production results that are stored in a database. The data structures are not fixed when the assembly line is configured; they may be changed dynamically in the course of the run-

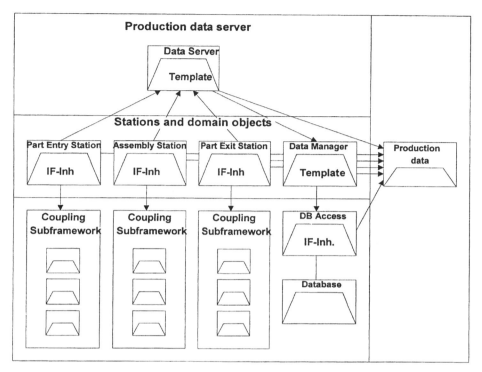

Figure 5.6   Architecture of an intelligent assembly station line framework.

ning production (mainly for providing a fast response to production problems): New production parameters or results may be added or existing ones dropped. Thus, the production data structure is a hot spot (bound during the runtime of the application created from the framework). Production data administration allows the data structures to be defined and the data in a database to be accessed without programming and recompilation.

The production data administration is subdivided into production data managers and production data servers. Each assembly station has an associated production data server, from which it requests production parameters and, possibly, the storing of result data. A data server caches data and, when required, passes requests to a production data manager. Only one shared production data manager exists for each kind of production data; it accesses the production data in a relational database. The relational tables may vary slightly with different assembly lines, though their structure is, in principle, identical. The differences in table structures are made transparent by hot-spot subsystems for accessing production parameters and storing production results. The database management system used is also a hot spot of the framework. Production data managers are introduced as domain objects on the domain object/station layer, and as production data servers on the data server layer.

A data server object cooperates with only one station, but with no other technical domain objects. This simplifies the process view of the architecture considerably. It has a common thread for each station and server object with synchronous service requests between them, and a thread for each production data manager. The process view of the OSEFA architecture has a separate thread for each processing control and each active technical domain object with asynchronous communication, which is much more complex.

5.7.4 Central or Decentral Data Storage

Bosch assembly lines use central as well as decentral data storage. With decentral data storage, the cell computer provides the production parameters related to a part to the part entry station, which stores them on a mobile data carrier with the part. The other assembly stations access the data carrier, until the cell computer fetches the production result data at the part exit station. With central data storage, each station obtains the production parameters directly from the cell computer and delivers production results to it. The framework supports both different functionalities with a hot spot on the data server layer.

5.7.5 Architecture Summary

The assembly line framework architecture differs completely from the OSEFA architecture. The data server layer is completely different from the OSEFA processing control and strategy layer. The domain object layer and the machine/device layer are melded into one new, different domain object and station layer. Only the bottom subframework layers are very similar (telegram) or even identical (protocol and communication line access).

5.7.6 Experiences and Results

Due to the very large differences between the intelligent assembly line subdomain and the OSEFA subdomain, a completely new framework had to be designed and developed. A team consisting of the author (a small part of his time), a graduate student, and two students with no framework experience developed a prototype (including the requirements analysis) in around six months and tested it successfully in a Bosch factory. Direct reuse of OSEFA design and code was possible only for the bottom layers (telegram, protocol, and communication line access). In spite of the small architectural similarity with OSEFA, the OSEFA experience contributed much to the fast progress. Our approach to the design was to start from the OSEFA architecture and modify it where required, similar to what was described here.

5.8 General Results

When it is questionable whether a larger domain can be covered by a single framework, the domain should be partitioned into subdomains according to orthogonal characteristics. Proposed characteristics for the partitioning of a domain are important properties of domain entities, of the domain logic, and of the information system. One should select the properties in such a way as to ensure confidence in the ability to cover a subdomain by a single framework.

The properties of a characteristic may change either quantitatively or qualitatively. Consider, for example, the characteristic intelligence and autonomy of a machining station. The change of property from dumb to restricted intelligent is of a quantitative nature. In both cases, a machining station needs to be told what to do, either on a very low level (for example, on this signal open that valve) or on a level that encompasses complete machining sequences (for example, execute a CNC-program). The change to the property of being intelligent and autonomous is of a qualitative nature. In this case, a machining station itself knows what to do.

Our experience is—and we conjecture that it is a generally valid statement—that qualitative changes of the characteristics of domain entities and of the domain logic cause such great changes in the framework architecture that it is impossible or unreasonable to integrate subdomains differing in this way in a framework. Quantitative changes of the characteristics of domain entities and of the domain logic do not disturb a well-chosen framework architecture. As a consequence, it is possible to integrate subdomains differing in this way in a framework.

Another conjecture based on our experience is that qualitative changes of characteristics of the information system (such as central versus decentral storage of data, or production data administration versus none) do not, in general, disturb a well-chosen framework architecture. As a consequence, it may be possible to integrate subdomains with these differing characteristics in a framework.

Our recommendation is that when developing the first framework in a domain, one should cover only one elementary subdomain. From a design point of view, it is too difficult to try to cope with principal differences between subdomains when even the smaller differences within a subdomain are not yet resolved. From a project point of view, it is better to deliver the first result faster and gain practical experience with it, than to postpone the first delivery.

If one anticipates the need for the inclusion of a neighbor subdomain with one changed characteristic in the framework (such as central and decentral data storage), one should check, after the rough design of the framework architecture, what consequences the inclusion of the neighbor subdomain would have, and change the framework architecture, if required and possible, to make the inclusion easier.

5.9 Summary

We have introduced the notion of a framework architecture and proven its value for comparing frameworks from different subdomains of a single domain. We have used orthogonal domain characteristics to partition a domain into subdomains. They can be used in two ways: When a domain is given, but it is not clear whether it should be covered by one framework, you should use them for partitioning into subdomains and analyze and compare the framework architectures for the resulting subdomains. If they are too different, you should not try to cover the domain with a single framework. On the other hand, when a subdomain is given that can be clearly covered by one framework, you should look for differing characteristics that define neighbor subdomains. A comparison of the framework architectures might suggest a change of the architecture for the selected subdomain to make future extension easier.

When the architecture of frameworks for different subdomains differs too much—for example, when a framework layer has to be exchanged completely (such as from a store-centered to a flow-centered subdomain)—it is usually more reasonable to develop separate frameworks and to reuse parts of a framework than to try to build one integrated framework, which might become overly complex. Reusing artifacts from a framework in another subdomain is easier if a framework is structured into layers.

However, when all characteristics are changed between two subdomains, such as the OSEFA and the assembly line, almost no layers may be reused. But even in these cases there are a few tangible artifacts that may be reused. One of them is a familiarity with and understanding of the domain. This extends even over subdomains that have very little direct commonality. Another is the reuse of a framework architectural style that is extremely valuable. Had we not had the experiences with the development of OSEFA, the development of the intelligent assembly line framework prototype would easily have taken two or three times the effort and time.

5.10 References

[Aarsten 1995] Aarsten, A., G. Elia, and G. Menga. G++: A Pattern Language for Computer Integrated Manufacturing. *Proceedings PLOPS 1994,* J. Coplien and D. Schmidt, editors. Reading, MA: Addison Wesley, 1995.

[Gacek 1995] Gacek, C., A. Abd-Allah, B.K. Clark, and B. Boehm. On the definition of software system architecture. *Proceedings 1st Workshop on Software Architecture 1995,* pp. 85–95, D. Garlan, editor. April 1995.

[Gamma 1995] Gamma, E., R. Helm, R. Johnson, and J. Vlissides. *Design Patterns: Elements of Reusable Object-Oriented Software.* Reading, MA: Addison-Wesley, 1994.

[Garlan-Perry 1995] Garlan, D., and F. Perry. Introduction to the Special Issue on Software Architecture. *IEEE Transactions on Software Engineering,* April 1995.

[Johnson 1988] Johnson, R.E., and B. Foote. Designing reusable classes. *Journal of Object-Oriented Programming* 2:22–35, June 1988.

[Kruchten 1995] Kruchten, P.B. The 4+1 view model of architecture. *IEEE Software,* November 1995, pp. 42–50.

[Lewerentz 1995] Lewerentz, C., and T. Lindner, editors. *Formal Development of Reactive Systems.* Springer LNCS 891, Berlin: Springer-Verlag, 1995.

[Schmid 1995] Schmid, H.A. Creating the architecture of a manufacturing framework by design patterns. *Proceedings OOPSLA 1995,* ACM SIGPLAN Notices 30(10):370–384, October 1995.

[Schmid 1996] Schmid, H.A. Creating applications from components: A manufacturing framework design. *IEEE Software* 13(6):67–75, November 1996.

[Schmid 1997] Schmid, H.A. Systematic framework design by generalization. *Communications of the ACM,* Theme Issue on Object-Oriented Application Frameworks, M.E. Fayad and D. Schmidt, editors, 40(10):48–51, October 1997.

[Schmid 1999] Schmid, H.A. Framework design by systematic generalization: From hot spot specification to hot spot subsystem implementation. In *Building Application Frameworks: Object-Oriented Foundations of Framework Design,* M.E Fayad, D.C. Schmidt, and R.E Johnson, editors. New York: John Wiley & Sons, 1999.

[Soni 1995] Soni, D., R. Nord, and C. Hofmeister. Software architecture in industrial applications. *Proceedings 17th International Conference on Software Engineering,* April 1995, pp. 196–207. New York: ACM Press, 1995.

A Case Study for Flexible Manufacturing Systems

In the software community, a framework indicates an integrated set of domain-specific software components [Coplien 1995a, 1995b], which can be reused to create applications, the most common examples being graphical user interfaces [Weinand 1994]. Frameworks have acquired popularity in object-oriented (OO) programming [Coplien 1995a, 1995b]. Here, the interpretation of *framework* ranges from structures of classes of cooperating objects that provide, through extension, reusable basic designs for a family of similar applications [Johnson 1988], to the more restrictive view [Schmid 1995] of complete high-level modules, which, through customization, directly result in specific applications for a certain domain. Customization is done through parameterization or by writing some functional specifications.

Frequently, the two views of frameworks, referred to as *whitebox* and *blackbox* approaches to reuse, may be simultaneously present in one framework [Johnson 1988]. In fact, features that are likely to be common to most applications can be offered, and therefore reused, as blackboxes with minor changes. On the other hand, the class library accompanying the framework usually provides base classes (seen as whiteboxes) that can be specialized, by adding subclasses as needed, and easily integrated with the rest of the framework.

An intriguing relationship exists between frameworks and patterns [Gamma 1995] or, more generally, pattern languages [Aarsten 1996]. Patterns and pattern languages are another concept, in addition to frameworks, proposed in the OO literature [Coplien 1995a, 1995b; Gamma 1995; Vlissides 1996] for capturing unifying aspects in software development and raising reusability from the basic level of components to the higher level of complete architectures. In a pioneering paper [Johnson 1992] Johnson argues that patterns document frameworks and help to ensure the correct use of framework functionalities. We take a more radical position: A pattern language—the organized collection of patterns for a certain application domain [Alexander 1977] in our view generates the framework that, thereafter, offers the elements for the pattern implementations, and accompanies the framework through its life. Any application framework, in fact, follows an evolution in time, which we call the *framework life span*. In this life span, the basic architectural elements, which are independent from any specific application, are implemented first. Then by generalizing from concrete applications, as stated in [Roberts 1997], the framework evolves. This evolution means that in its early stages, the framework is mainly conceived as a whitebox framework [Johnson 1988]. However, through its adoption in an increasing number of applications, the framework matures: More concrete components that provide blackbox solutions for the difficult problems, as well as high-level objects that represent the major abstractions found in the problem domain, become available within the framework.

The aim of this chapter is to support these views by using as an example the evolution of the framework related to the G++ pattern language [Aarsten 1996], conceived for the design and development of concurrent and distributed control systems in the realm of computer integrated manufacturing (CIM). *Section 6.1* reviews patterns and pattern language concepts, and highlights the relationships between patterns, pattern languages, and application frameworks. *Section 6.2* introduces the application domain for which the G++ pattern language and its framework have been conceived. *Section 6.3* illustrates the components of the framework, highlighting their evolution in the framework life span and their use in the development of a concrete application. *Section 6.4* draws some conclusions.

6.1 Frameworks and Pattern Languages

A *design pattern* is a three-part rule, which expresses a relation between a certain context, a design problem, and a solution [Alexander 1977]. In an object-oriented environment, a pattern [Gamma 1995] indicates a cluster of cooperating objects linked by certain relationships found repeatedly in a design.

While each pattern describes a decision point in the development of an application, groups of related patterns can be organized as a tree or graph where each pattern leads to a series of other patterns. Such a structure is called a *pattern language* [Alexander 1977] and represents the sequence of decisions in time leading to the complete design, so that a pattern language becomes a method that guides the development process. This method does not conflict with general development methods such as Booch [Booch 1991] or Object Modeling Technique (OMT) [Rumbaugh 1991]; instead, it complements them by bringing domain-specific, concrete advice to their general guidelines.

While a pattern language represents the essential design knowledge of a specific application domain, the solutions indicated by each pattern are general enough to be applied in many different contexts of concrete applications. Alexander wrote [Alexander 1977]: "Each pattern describes a problem which occurs over and over in our environment, and then describes the core of the solution to that problem, in such a way that you can use this solution a million times over, without ever doing in the same way twice."

All the specific implementations of a design pattern, however, will have some things in common, which can be captured as reusable elements to generate a framework.

These elements therefore represent common design solutions in a domain along with reusable implementations, so that the developer in most cases need not even be aware of the design problems behind that part of the application.

Frameworks and pattern languages for a specific application domain are therefore inextricably connected to each other. In our experience we note that this relationship is bidirectional. On one hand, a framework enables the implementation of an application designed following a pattern language. On the other hand, a pattern language offers the rules for the use of the framework elements [Gamma 1995] and for its extension.

6.2 The Application Domain

The framework described here has been derived as the implementation support of the G++ pattern language [Aarsten 1996], which builds on the generally accepted reference model for CIM systems [McLean 1983] from the U.S. National Bureau of Standards (NBS), shown in Figure 6.1. A factory is organized in a hierarchy of controls, with different responsibilities allocated to each level. A Facility represents one complete production system or a factory and performs long-term, strategic planning. The Shop is a shop-floor module that schedules production *lots* (a lot is an administrative entity indicating a group of identical pieces to be manufactured together), which coordinates production cells.

A Cell is a production unit that performs realtime dispatching, sequencing, and routing pieces on the machines and manages the necessary setup of equipment to process the pieces. A Workstation is a machine or transport resource of a Cell and is capable of performing distinct operations. Equipment represents the smallest component with independent control, such as a robot arm or a conveyor cart.

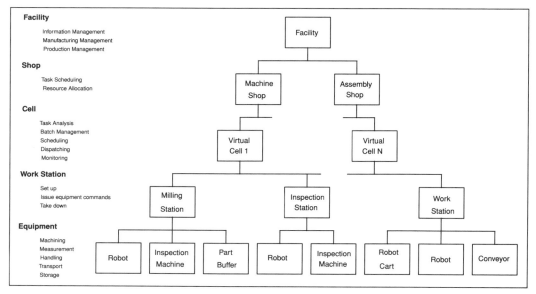

Figure 6.1   The USA-NBS reference model for flexible manufacturing systems.

6.2.1 The Production Problem

The production, in the current trend of small-batch manufacturing, is represented by small lots of pieces assigned to each cell. Several lots of different types of pieces can be in production at the same time in a given cell. This has led to the name *flexible manufacturing systems* (FMS) given to modern production systems.

Each type of piece requires a specific ordered sequence of operations, where a machine can perform one or more of those operations. A hierarchical computer network represents the factory information system: the facility computer communicates through a factory backbone to the shop computers, which coordinate production through the production cells. These are usually FMS, fully automated units whose controllers receive orders from the shop and communicate through low-level networks known as *field buses* (such as BASEstar Open [DEC 1993]) with the machine, inventory, and transport controllers. A realtime dispatcher of the cell assigns pieces to the machines as soon as they become idle, issues requests of missions to the transport system, and monitors the shop floor.

Pieces are taken one at a time from the input store and transported to the machine where the first operation is performed. As soon as one operation is finished, the piece is evacuated from the machine and transported elsewhere; either to another machine so that the next operation can be performed or to the output stores at the completion of the production cycle.

The applications covered by the G++ framework focus on the whole architecture of control layers of a CIM system; however, for simplicity, the case study presented here covers the Cell, Workstation, and Equipment layers, while interacting with Shop and Facility in order to obtain production orders and to return monitoring data to the higher levels.

6.2.2 The Software Control Architecture

There is an important aspect in the control architecture emphasized by the reference model previously described. Modules at one layer of the hierarchy are the servers to a higher-level client, and in turn are the clients of lower-level subservers. Different grains of concurrency [Chin 1991] naturally unfold from the behavior of the requests of services from clients to servers that uniformly repeat themselves at the different layers of the control hierarchy.

The G++ pattern language captures this aspect of the architecture, distinguishing and integrating three different models of concurrency, based on the granularity of the actions and the lifetime of the data being processed.

The finest grain comprises short-lived actions in response to events. Each action processes small amounts of data and the life span of the data typically coincides with that of the action itself. Groups of these actions that are triggered by events are present inside a sequential process (thread) and the event-driven nature of the resulting model answers more to modularity and to the convenience and clarity offered by a declarative specification of requirements than to real concurrency (parallelization) needs.

In the FMS the finest grain is found inside the implementation of the services offered by Workstation or Cell control modules, and typical events include the arrival of a new piece at a Workstation or a machine failure at the Cell level.

A medium grain of concurrency is identified between sequential processes. Here, each process offers the protected environment to fine-grain concurrency previously described and hides local data that are fragile *sequential objects* from other processes. The processes communicate with each other through shared resources, which are more robust *blocking objects*. In the FMS, medium-grain concurrency is found between the different services executed in parallel by the control modules, as in the case of each of the threads dispatching pieces of one lot in a Cell.

The largest grain is between the control modules, which are *active objects* [Minoura 1993], providing the environment for the concurrent processes they support and encapsulating the shared resources, which can be blocking objects or other active objects, in turn. (The encapsulation by an active object of other active objects exactly mirrors the logical control hierarchy envisioned for the whole system.) In the control architecture of the logical design, control modules represent either different programs running on different computers, such as the Cell and the Shop, or peripheral devices, such as computerized numerically controlled machines (CNCs), robots, and programmable logical controllers (PLCs).

6.3 The Framework

The framework provides mechanisms, abstract classes, and customizable building blocks for most of the solutions proposed by the G++ pattern language, such as logical mechanisms for communication between modules, a uniform representation of control modules through a hierarchy of layers of controls, support for different grains of concurrency, and a smooth transition from simulation to final implementation.

The components of the framework offer different levels of abstraction to the design needs found in the application domain. They are classified as elemental, basic design, and domain-dependent components. The classification also reflects the different stages of the framework life span in which they have been introduced.

Elemental components, such as mechanisms for logical communication and concurrency, and classification of the objects as *Sequential, Blocking, Active,* and *Thread* objects, determine the language (elements of the architecture) in which the whole application has to be written.

Basic components are intermediary classes, which by their very nature are fairly application-independent, although they have been conceived bearing in mind a specific application domain. They are written using the elemental components of the framework, and they have to be specialized for each concrete application.

The other components are domain-dependent and are usually specializations of the basic elements. They are the result of the adoption of the framework for the development of more and more applications and in some cases they become pluggable blackboxes.

In the following, the low-level (elemental and basic) components, which appear early in the framework life span, are described first. Subsequently, more specific components such as Shop, Cell, and Machine, will be introduced by exemplifying the development of the architecture of an FMS; finally the relevance of the G++ pattern language is emphasized.

6.3.1 Low-Level Components

Communication and concurrency low-level components are discussed in the following sections.

Communication

Control modules of the architecture have to communicate with each other in order to cooperate. The fundamental issue in communicating is that some sort of visibility [Booch 1991] must exist among the parties. Visibility implies dependency with respect to changes; hence, it has consequences for the reusability of a design. In order to avoid the propagation of local changes to the entire architecture, visibility relationships have to be designed taking into account the possible evolution of the application. In CIM systems the evolution is traditionally bottom-up. A higher-level control module (such as a shop controller or a cell controller), acting as a client, integrates lower-level controllers, which act as servers (for example, machines, transports, and buffers). Such subsystems have been developed by different vendors without any prior knowledge of the environment in which they will have to be embedded. Following the pattern Communication and Visibility Between Control Modules, it is better that modules at the same layer are not designed to communicate with each other directly and that visibility loops must be avoided between different layers.

This is achieved by offering the framework two communication mechanisms where visibility and flow of information move in the same direction, and in the opposite direction, with respect to the communicating parties, for the two cases.

The first mechanism, indicated here as Caller/Provider (C/P), is involved when an object invokes another object method and is deeply rooted in OO programming, so it will not be discussed further. In CIM application, it is convenient that higher-level control modules have visibility of and ask for services from lower-level modules by invoking their interface methods.

The second, the Broadcaster/Listener (B/L) mechanism, is achieved by giving all the objects of the framework the capability of broadcasting and listening to events. In CIM applications, it is convenient that lower-level control modules communicate with the higher-level ones by broadcasting events. This capability is offered by three basic methods (see Figure 6.2) of the class Object, the basic abstract class of the framework, from which all the other components are derived.

A listener object establishes a communication session at a certain instant of time with a broadcaster object by calling the broadcaster's method addCback( ). This method takes as parameters the event of interest (ev) and an action object. The latter must be of a subclass of the abstract class Action, and must implement the method handleEvent( ), which embodies the required behavior in response to the event, according to the specifications. The Action object is typically created by the listener, passing, when necessary, references to its internal resources. When the event is raised (by the broadcaster calling callCbacks( )), the action specified in the call to addCback( ) is executed for all listeners. The method removeCback( )of the broadcaster is called to stop listening to its events. The implementation offered to this communication mechanism is similar to the callback functions in X-Windows [Young 1989] objectified according to the pattern Command [Gamma 1995].

```
Object& addCback(const Symbol& ev, Action& action,
                 Object& userData = nil)
```

Attach action to the event ev with optional userData, a listener-supplied object made available to action when handling the event.

```
Object& removeCback(const Symbol& ev, Action& action,
                    Object& userData = nil)
```

Detach action from the even ev with optional userdData.

```
void callCbacks(Symbol& ev, Object& calldata = nil)
```

Calls all the callbacks attached to the event ev of this object, with optional event parameter callData.

Figure 6.2 Principal methods implementing the B/L mechanism.

Concurrency

In order to cope with concurrency, the framework must first of all offer the class Thread, each instance of which represents an independent sequential execution process. In light of this requirement, the framework must then distinguish among its components—that is, between *sequential*, *blocking*, and *active* objects—which are used to model fine-grain, medium-grain, and large-grain concurrency, respectively.

Fine-Grain Concurrency

The pattern Actions Triggered by Events, which uses the B/L mechanism, specifies the way to model fine-grain concurrency: The relevant Action objects, which have to be triggered when an event is raised, are themselves the *sequential* objects defined in the scope of a single thread of execution. (A sequential object may in turn raise events, in response to which other actions are executed, which originate the classical event-driven programming structure.) Sequential objects behave as a procedure call in a sequential program and represent the kernel of any OO framework. Fine-grain concurrency is present, for instance, in the dispatching algorithms, which execute (one for each lot) inside the cell. When activated by the cell controller, each dispatcher sets off the execution of a certain number of rules, which are carried out concurrently by different decision-making sequential objects.

Medium-Grain Concurrency

Several independent instances of Thread may execute concurrently inside a control module, each one carrying out a service. The pattern Services Waiting For shows that Blocking Objects are needed for synchronizing the concurrent execution threads. Blocking Objects offer the wait primitive, which suspends any calling process until a specified condition is verified. Condition is the abstract class offered by the framework to model Blocking Objects. The specializations of this class are basically of two kinds: synchronization conditions and shared resources. The former are essentially a few concrete implementations offered by the environment, such as Semaphore and Event-Handler. EventHandler, in an event-driven control environment, is the most commonly used concrete implementation of Condition. It blocks the current thread until an event is received from one of the objects it monitors. Every time a process calls the waitEvent(Symbol& filter) method of the EventHandler, it is suspended until the event named filter is raised. When one of the events to which the EventHandler is attached is raised, the processes waiting for this event are awakened in turn and continue their execution. EventHandler integrates fine-grain with medium-grain concurrency, thus extending the B/L model from intrathread to interthread communication. A typical use of an EventHandler is monitoring all concurrent activities evolving inside the cell. The latter are Condition-Collection (CondCltn in the framework), which offer blocking capabilities to the read-write primitives of a Collection and can be customized in various ways. In Figure 6.3, the stores storeIn and storeOut are examples of CondCltn; the Database is an example of a customized blocking collection.

Large-Grain Concurrency

Control modules usually are modeled as active objects, that is, objects that create and internally manage one or more independent threads governing the execution of their services (operations that develop over time). Following the pattern Client/Server/Service, the framework provides two classes in order to implement control modules: the Service and the Server. Service extends the Thread in the following ways: It always belongs to a unique Server owner, it has internal data (sequential objects, such as the Action objects in response to events), it maintains a symbolic state value, and it broadcasts events with the incoming state name every time a state transition occurs. The Service, which embeds the dynamic specification of its activity, has to be redefined for any concrete specifications. It is started by the default method doService(). Server is the base

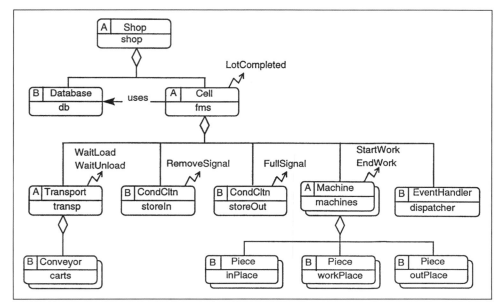

Figure 6.3   Class hierarchy of the framework.

class of every module of control. It encapsulates a collection of Service objects and shared resources as implementations of Condition, or other sub-Servers. In order to be accessed, the Server offers the concrete public methods: execService( ), waitService( ), and joinService( ), which represent asynchronous, synchronous, and deferred-synchronous service requests, respectively. They accept a Service as a parameter, which will be an instance of a concrete subclass of Service. Whenever one of these methods is invoked, the Service's thread of execution is activated.

Object, Thread, Condition, EventHandler, CondCltn, Action, Server, and Service are the low-level components offered by the framework in its early stages, which allow a developer to implement software control architectures for concurrent systems. Concrete components for implementing specific FMS applications, which are provided by the framework in its more mature stages, build on these, as will be described in the next section.

6.3.2 Building an FMS Application

As for all living beings, frameworks can also be considered in terms of age. When the framework has been used repeatedly for several similar applications, it grows in the following ways:

- By adding more concrete higher-level modules that can be customized by replacing service behaviors and in turn action objects (these are called *hot spots* by [Pree 1994] and are an example of a separation between fixed and variable code theorized by [Roberts 1997])

- By offering different implementations of the same basic mechanisms according to different computer platforms and communication protocols for distributed systems

In the case of the FMS (see Figure 6.3), the Shop, Cell, Machine, and Transport classes are concrete high-level control modules that are specializations of the class Server. As an example, the Cell encapsulates specific resources, such as the collection of *Machines*, the *Transport*, and the *Stores*. The reuse of these concrete components in a specific application simply requires the customization of their hot spot. This is a three-step problem:

At the level of fine-grain concurrency, the action objects that respond to events must be built. The task is simplified by the support offered by the event mechanisms of the framework at the basic level and by a superimposed event-driven programming environment, which automatically generates the Action subclasses from the specifications.

At the level of medium-grain concurrency, for each kind of service of the control module a subclass of Service must be implemented. For example, the Cell can perform LotProduction, MachineSetup, and Maintenance, which are represented here as the LotProduction, MachineSetup, and Maintenance subclasses of Service. The pattern Implementation of Modules of Control suggests that the behavior of the different services should be specified in terms of finite state machines, extended by the necessary sequential objects, and implemented by the Service. The framework achieves this through an ad hoc graphical language (for example, Specification Description Language [CCITT 1986]).

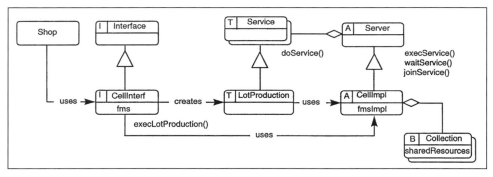

Figure 6.4   Interface and implementation of the Cell control module.

At the level of large-grain concurrency, following the pattern Interface to Modules of Control, the definition of a control module is separated into two distinct interface and implementation classes, which offer a great deal of flexibility to the model, as shown in relation to distribution. When a control module with the service it offers has been conceived, one or more Interface classes are generated. They offer public methods, which create instances of concrete services and pass them to the standard Server methods, according to the three synchronization semantics of the specification. Figure 6.4 shows an example, where the interface of the Cell control module (CellInterf) offers the method execLotProduction( ): It creates an instance of class LotProduction and passes it to the method execService( ) of the Cell implementation (CellImp). Figure 6.5 shows the code that implements this method. Figure 6.6 illustrates an example of interactions between a Shop, a Cell, and their Services.

The result, at the conclusion of this stage of development, is a prototype of the logical design of the application. The development of a real CIM application, in fact, requires a simulation or emulation of the application at the prototyping stage, which is mandatory as it would be impracticable to test and debug it in the factory itself.

In order to guarantee a seamless evolution to the physical system, the pattern Prototype and Reality suggests that two existing implementations should be maintained for any physical element, and these should offer the same interface to their clients (implemented following the pattern Interface to Modules of Control): One is the *prototype*, which simulates or emulates the object behavior (implemented following the pattern Implementation of Modules of Control), while the other is the *reality*, which embeds the physical object.

```
void CellInterf: :execLotProduction(Lot *lot)
{
     cellImpl -> execservice(new LotProduction(cellImpl, lot);
}
```

Figure 6.5   Implementation of execLotProduction().

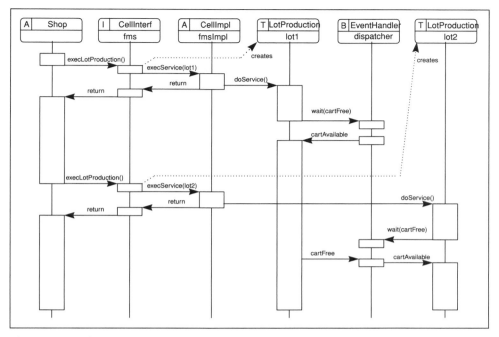

Figure 6.6   Object interaction diagram.

The transformation from prototype to reality—that is, from logical to physical design—is achieved by identifying those Server objects (that, in the logical design, represent remote software or physical elements), and changing their class declaration. Two distinct situations may occur:

- The control (the Server) is a remote software module, such as in the case of the Shop or the Cell, which reside on a different computer connected through a LAN (TCP/IP, CORBA [OMG 1992]).

- The software module is driven by a remote control hardware, such as in the case of a Server representing a machine controlled by a CNC or a transportation system controlled by a PLC.

These situations characterize two concrete instances of the pattern.

Remote Control Module

This is the situation when a control module is not local to the application, but resides, instead, on a remote computer. Let us consider the example of the Cell shown in Figure 6.4. The framework provides an abstract class Network, whose concrete implementation hides the physical characteristics of the communication medium. In particular, the framework provides subclasses of Network for TCP/IP sockets and for a CORBA platform. The class CellInterf is substituted by the class CellProxy (a subclass of Interface), which offers the same public methods and encapsulates a concrete specialization of Network to forward messages through the communication medium. The

CellProxy class can be automatically generated by a CASE tool [Menga 1993] from the Server prototype of the logical design. The class CellImpl is substituted by a Server object, the DistributedCell, which resides on the remote platform: It listens for incoming requests over the network by delegating the communication once again to a Network object. Figure 6.7 shows the object structure of the simulated and final distributed implementation classes involved in the simulated and final system for a Cell.

Modules with a Remote Control

The second practical instance of the Prototype and Reality occurs when the prototype control module referred to by the application represents a physical device such as a machine, a robot, an inventory, or a transportation system. These are special remote hardware control units (PLCs, CNCs) evolving as finite state machines and communicating with the central computer through field buses by transmitting state values and notifying events. In this case, it is not the control module that is remote, but some of its data and the logic of its behavior. The pattern Remote Control suggests that the data and the events that it broadcasts or listens to should be virtualized inside the Server. For this virtualization, the framework provides the classes DataPoint and Event, which embed the application programmer interface (API) of the communication system. DataPoint is an abstract class, which raises an event each time the remote data it represents changes value, and has to be specialized by redefining the assignment and casting operators for each data type needed. Event is a concrete class, which relays the event locally, from/to the network, and must only be instantiated for each distinct event name.

The implementation of the common structure of the Server class for all control modules enables a CASE tool to generate the final implementation automatically from the prototype. The flexibility of the solution has been proved by offering a transparent interface to two distinct field buses, specifically the DEC-BASEstar Open [DEC 1993] and WorldFip [Leterrier 1997].

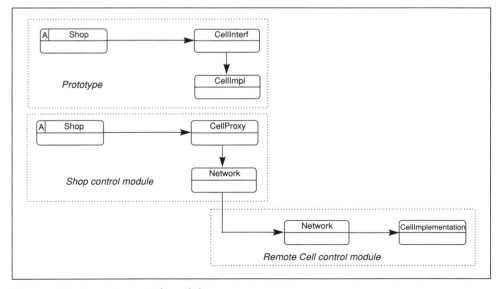

Figure 6.7 Remote control module.

Figure 6.8 shows the classes involved in the simulated and final system for the control of a robot arm. The robot arm is moved by writing the destination into the control register of the external controller. In the prototype, this control register is represented by a simple member variable of the RobotArmSim class. In the final implementation (the class RobotArmImpl), this member variable is replaced with a DataPoint of the same name, which encapsulates the access to the external control register. In a similar way, we operate for the events returned from the field bus to notify the action performed.

6.4 Summary

We have shown the strict interrelationship between a pattern language and a framework for a specific application domain. The domain considered was computer-integrated manufacturing, which is characterized by hierarchical layers of control, events, concurrency, and distribution, and the pattern language was the G++ pattern language, which has been described elsewhere in the literature [Aarsten 1996; Menga 1990, 1991]. The analysis of the resulting framework evidences an interesting hierarchy in the structure of its elements, which is linked to the framework life span. In fact, at an early stage of the framework life, the originator pattern language first determines the language and then the basic design components of the architecture. These result fairly independent from any specific application and turn out to be used mostly as whitebox elements. With the help of the pattern language, new applications are developed from

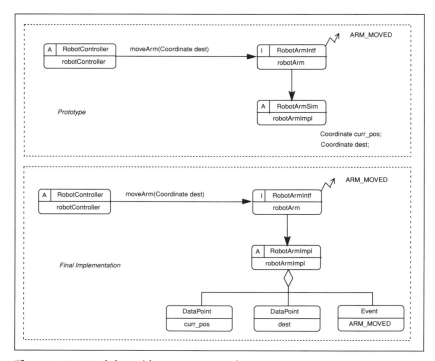

Figure 6.8 Modules with remote control.

the framework. These evolve into new blackbox components and support elements that enrich the framework as it reaches maturity. The former are concrete high-level artifacts, which have to be customized from application to application, and this is done simply by changing their internal behavior (by exploiting the Command pattern [Gamma 1995]). The latter, in an integration environment, are mostly the classes within the framework architecture, which wrap drivers to different communication protocols, database management systems, and peripheral devices.

As added value, the uniformity of the architecture that results from the framework facilitates the construction of CASE tools for the automatic code generation and the automatic transformations needed at several stages of the software development life cycle [Menga 1990].

The validity of our approach is demonstrated by the fact that, although originally conceived for the CIM domain, it has recently found applications in process control [VASME 1996], telecommunications [Bosco 1996], and computer-telephone integration [Billi 1996] systems. Interestingly, in this respect, the experience with both the G++ pattern language and its framework confirm characteristic issues regarding frameworks that have recently been discussed in the literature by [Roberts 1997; Schmid 1995].

6.5 References

[Aarsten 1996] Aarsten, A., D. Brugali, and G. Menga. 1996. Designing concurrent and distributed control architectures. *Communications of the ACM*, Theme Issue on Software Patterns, D. Schmidt, M.E. Fayad, and R. Johnson, editors, October 1996.

[Alexander 1977] Alexander, C. *The Timeless Way of Building*. New York: Oxford University Press, 1977.

[Andrews 1988] Andrews, G.R. An overview of the SR language and implementation. *ACM Transaction on Programming Languages and Systems* 10(1):51–86, 1988.

[Billi 1996] Billi, R., et. al. Field trial evaluations of two different information inquiry systems. *IEEE Third Workshop on Interactive Voice Technology for Telecommunications Applications*, Basking Ridge, NJ, September 30–October 1, 1996.

[Booch 1991] Booch, G. *Object Oriented Design with Applications*. Redwood City, CA: Benjamin/Cummings, 1991.

[Bosco 1996] Bosco, P.G., D. LoGiudice, G. Martini, and C. Moiso. ACE: An environment for specifying, developing, and generating TINA services. *Proceedings IFIP/ IEEE IM 1996*.

[CCITT 1986] CCITT. *Specification and Description Language*. Recommendation Z.100, 1986.

[Chin 1991] Chin, R.S., and S.T. Chanson. Distributed object-based programming system. *ACM Computing Surveys* 23: 91–124, March 1991.

[Coplien 1995a] Coplien, J.O., and D.C. Schmidt. Frameworks and components. In *Pattern Languages of Program Design*, pp. 1–5. Reading, MA: Addison-Wesley, 1995.

[Coplien 1995b] Coplien, J., and D. Schmidt. *Pattern Languages of Program Design*. Reading, MA: Addison-Wesley, 1995.

[DEC 1993] Digital Equipment Corporation. *BASEstar Open Reference Guide*. Order number AA-PQVRB-TE, November 1993.

[Gamma 1995] Gamma, E., R. Helm, R. Johnson, and J. Vlissides. *Design Patterns: Elements of Reusable Object Oriented Software*. Reading, MA: Addison-Wesley, 1995.

[Johnson 1988] Johnson, R.E., and B. Foote. Designing reusable classes. *Journal of Object-Oriented Programming*, June 1988.

[Johnson 1992] Johnson, R. Documenting frameworks using patterns. *Proceedings of OOPSLA 1992*, Vancouver, BC, Canada, October 1992.

[Leterrier 1997] Leterrier, P. *The FIP Protocol*. Centre de Competénce FIP, 54000 Nancy, France.

[McLean 1983] McLean, C., M. Mitchel, and E. Barkmeyer. A computer architecture for small-batch manufacturing. *IEEE Spectrum* 20(5):59–64.

[Menga 1990] Menga, G., and G. Lo Russo. G++: An environment for object oriented design and prototyping. *Proceedings of TOOLS 2*, Paris, France, 1990.

[Menga 1991] Menga, G., M. Morisio, P. Picchiottino, P. Gallo, and G. Lo Russo. Framework for object-oriented design and prototyping of manufacturing systems. *Journal of Object-Oriented Programming*, 1991.

[Menga 1993] Menga, G., G. Elia, and M. Mancin. G++: An environment for object oriented design and prototyping of manufacturing systems. In *Intelligent Manufacturing: Programming Environments for CIM*, W. Gruver and G. Boudreaux, editors. New York: Springer-Verlag, 1993.

[Minoura 1993] Minoura, T., S. Pargaonkar, and K. Rehfuss. Structural active object systems for simulation. *Proceedings of OOPSLA 1993*, Washington, DC, USA, October 1993.

[OMG 1992] Object Management Group. *The Common Object Request Broker: Architecture and Specification*, September 1992.

[Pree 1994] Pree, W. *Design Patterns for Object-Oriented Software Development*. Reading, MA: Addison-Wesley, 1994.

[Roberts 1997] Roberts, D., and R. Johnson. Evolve frameworks into domain-specific languages. *Pattern Languages of Program Design 3*. Reading, MA: Addison-Wesley, 1997.

[Rumbaugh 1991] Rumbaugh, J., M. Blaha, W. Premerlani, F. Eddy, and W. Lorensen. *Object-Oriented Modeling and Design*. Englewood Cliffs, NJ: Prentice Hall, 1991.

[Schmid 1995] Schmid, H.A. Creating the architecture of a manufacturing framework by design patterns. *Proceedings of OOPSLA 1995*, SIGPLAN, ACM, 1995.

[VASME 1996] VASME. Value-added services for maritime environments. *European Union Framework Program IV*. Project no. WA-95-SC.010, document no. 960628/ D1.12.1996.

[Vlissides 1996] Vlissides, J., J. Coplien, and N. Kerth. *Pattern Languages of Program Design 2*. Reading, MA: Addison-Wesley, 1996.

[Weinand 1994] Weinand, A., and E. Gamma. ET++: A portable, homogeneous class library and application framework. *Proceedings of the UBILAB 1994 Conference*, Zurich, Switzerland, September 1994.

[Young 1989] Young, D.A. *The X Window System Programming and Application with Xt*. Englewood Cliffs, NJ: Prentice Hall, 1989.

SIDEBAR 1
THEORY MEETS PRACTICE:
LESSONS LEARNED USING SEMATECH'S CIM FRAMEWORK

Semiconductor and other types of manufacturing businesses have become much more reliant on integrated software applications across multiple functional areas, such as customer order fulfillment, product design, and shop-floor control. Constructing such applications requires knowledge that spans multiple domains. In a complex environment, such as computer-integrated manufacturing (CIM), a divide-and-conquer approach is being used to break down the problem into manageable pieces. A framework-based approach is particularly useful; such an approach can provide well-organized templates for domain-specific applications. SEMATECH's CIM framework specification provides such a template for semiconductor and precision electronic parts manufacturing [SEMATECH 1998, Whelan 1995].

The benefits of using the CIM framework for developing manufacturing system software include (1) a predefined set of components with well-defined interfaces and, where appropriate, state models, (2) a set of basic object services based on the Object Management Architecture (OMA) from the Object Management Group (OMG) [OMG 1995], (3) a logical starting point for creating modular applications, and (4) the ability to extend the framework [Whelan 1995]. Figure SB1.1 depicts the major components of the CIM framework.

From a practical perspective, the biggest advantage of using the CIM framework is the ability for a software development organization to partition the manufacturing system domain space into manageable pieces—material management, material movement, job management, equipment management, and so on. A design team can focus on its particular module and not have to be concerned with other design teams unless changes to the interfaces or basic object services are required.

A good framework captures the essence of a particular domain and provides enough detail to allow a software developer to build an application or a system [Fayad 1997]. The documentation supporting the framework is as important as the framework itself. Usage scenarios help to reduce the learning time required to understand a framework design.

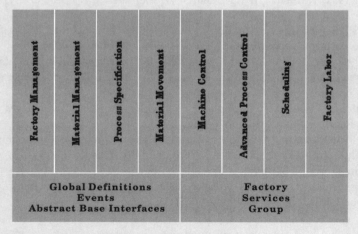

Figure SB1.1 CIM framework components.

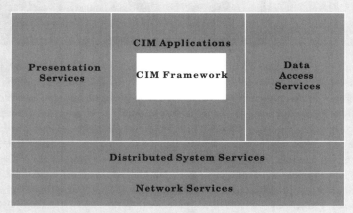

Figure SB1.2   CIM framework-based architecture.

Capturing and documenting the framework developer's thinking process gives a software developer valuable insights [Schmidt-Fayad 1997]. Figure SB1.2 represents an architecture based on the CIM framework.

SB1.1 Lessons Learned

Shortcomings of using frameworks in general [Fayad 1997; Schmidt 1996] and the CIM framework in particular include (1) insufficient supporting documentation that provides usage scenarios; (2) insufficient robustness of the interface and component definition languages, specifically, more support is needed for pre- and postconditions; (3) insufficient definition of state model(s); (4) a lack of consensus on the appropriate level of detail to be included; and (5) disagreement on the level of component granularity.

The most elegant and concise framework will not be used unless it can be understood and implemented by others. Semantic, as well as syntactic, definitions of components and objects must be supplied with a framework. Framework developers must define the specific meanings and behaviors of their components and objects.

The OMG's Interface Definition Language (IDL) provides a good base for interface definitions, but needs additional support for pre- and postconditions [OMG 1995]. Framework developers must provide such information to ensure that software developers understand the conditions under which the framework will properly perform.

State models are required in some cases. In the CIM framework, equipment management acts as a proxy for processing equipment on the factory floor. The proxy must be able to assume the various equipment states, such as running, idle, and out of service; and to provide appropriate behaviors. For example, a piece of equipment that is in an out-of-service state should not be available to a scheduler or dispatcher to process material.

Much discussion has occurred over the amount of detail to be included in a framework. The CIM framework is fairly sparse, but contains the basic elements required of a set of software applications to run a semiconductor factory. The trade-off is flexibility and reusability versus completeness for a specific implementation.

Continues

SIDEBAR 1
THEORY MEETS PRACTICE:
LESSONS LEARNED USING SEMATECH'S CIM FRAMEWORK *(Continued)*

The granularity of the CIM framework's components has been a significant issue. One of the goals of the CIM framework is for it to enable component substitutability. Having a large number of small-grained components exposes a greater number of interfaces and provides more flexibility than does having a small number of large-grained components. However, commercial software suppliers have not been willing to support standardized small-grained components, but have been willing to support standardized large-grained components, even though a system composed of these is less flexible, especially where components are composed of multiple related but distinct functions. To change any one function requires a substitution of the entire component, even if no changes were made to the remaining functions.

SB1.2 Summary

The CIM framework provides a useful set of component templates that supports the creation of a system of integrated manufacturing applications. Several commercial software suppliers are using the CIM framework as the foundation for their next-generation CIM systems. As with any new approach, shortcomings have been identified and improvements have been recommended. A SEMI (Semiconductor Equipment and Materials International) Task Force has been established to establish the CIM framework as a standard to be used for the development of manufacturing system software.

SB1.3 References

[Fayad 1997] Fayad, M., and D. Schmidt. Object-oriented application frameworks. *Communications of the ACM* 40(10), October 1997.

[OMG 1995] *The Common Object Request Broker: Architecture and Specification, Revision 2.0.* Framingham, MA: Object Management Group, 1995. Object Management Group World Wide Web site: www.omg.org.

[Schmidt 1996] Schmidt, D., M. Fayad, and R. Johnson. Software Patterns. *Communications of the ACM* 39(10), October 1996.

[Schmidt-Fayad 1997] Schmidt, D., and M. Fayad. Lessons learned building reusable OO frameworks for distributed software. *Communications of the ACM* 40(10), October 1997.

[SEMATECH 1998] *Computer Integrated Manufacturing (CIM) Framework Specification-Version 2.0,* SEMATECH Technology Transfer #93061697J-ENG. Austin, TX: SEMATECH, 1998. www.sematech.org

[Whelan 1995] Whelan, P. SEMATECH's CIM application framework: A new paradigm for manufacturing systems. *Proceedings for the International Conference on Improving Manufacturing Performance in a Distributed Enterprise: Advanced Systems and Tools, ESPRIT Project 9245—New Planning and Scheduling Software and Systems for Europe (PASSE),* Edinburgh, Scotland, July 13–14, 1995, pp. 43–52.

PART Two

More Manufacturing Frameworks

Part Two describes several manufacturing frameworks. Manufacturing systems must be flexible, reliable, and scalable in order to meet the rapidly changing needs of today's enterprise. Each manufacturing facility has specific processing requirements (business rules) that need to be accommodated in order to successfully operate. Therefore, application framework technology is the perfect approach to building such systems. Part Two contains Chapters 7 through 11.

Chapter 7, "CEF: A Concurrent Engineering Framework," has two purposes: First, it introduces a framework for building concurrent engineering applications, wherein traditional sequential product development phases are transformed into concurrent activities to allow early detection and resolution of design flaws and conflicts; second, it discusses an alternative domain modeling approach that allows the construction and evolution of a domain model from domain experts alone without the assistance of software developers.

Chapter 8, "Distributed Manufacturing Execution Systems Framework," describes the technology utilized by FACTORYworks, a next-generation manufacturing execution system (MES). The challenges faced and overcome by this framework included: (1) the ability to survive process, central processing unit (CPU), and network failures in order to provide 7×24×365 service; (2) the scale to handle very large systems in terms of users as well as data sets; (3) recovery from database and other system failures without compromise of data integrity; and (4) the ability to extend the system and modify its behavior without making source code changes.

Chapter 9, "Production Resource Manager (PRM) Framework," describes a framework that provides reusable design and implementation components for decision support applications, built around a specific set of mathematical solvers.

Chapter 10, "Developing Domain Frameworks," discusses the object-oriented domain engineering (OODE) process. This process, its subprocesses, and their deliverables have been described in this chapter with respect to the process monitoring and diagnosis (PM&D) domain. OODE has taken a step beyond defining a process and executed the process in the PM&D domain. The result is a set of documented processes, deliverables, and domain architecture. The architecture is a tool for developing a PM&D framework and it is a tool in its own right for defining a domain. In addition, a physical framework has been produced from the PM&D architecture. This framework has supported two applications, RMS and CMS.

Chapter 11, "Measurement Systems Framework," discusses the design and implementation of an object-oriented framework for the domain of measurement systems that can be used as a functional core. Evaluations of the framework show that it captures the main concepts in the domain and that the required extensions for individual applications are limited.

CHAPTER 7

CEF: A Concurrent Engineering Framework

Concurrent engineering refers to the practice of *simultaneous* participation in product design from people working on different phases of the entire product life cycle. This differs drastically from the traditional sequential approach where activities in different phases are completely isolated and disjoint. The lack of communication between phases often leaves major design flaws undetected until late in the production cycle, and the fix can be extremely costly. A concurrent engineering environment fosters active communication among participants and allows early detection and resolution of design conflicts, hence reducing product cycle time and cost [Dean 1997]. CEF is a framework for building such concurrent engineering applications.

CEF addresses many issues in concurrent engineering. In this chapter, we focus on only two of these issues. First, *engineering* is a broad term covering many disciplines. We have to determine how to handle domain modeling for all these different disciplines in one framework. In fact, even if we concentrate on a single discipline, we still must face the challenge that hardly any engineering discipline has a static domain model. The design of CEF must be flexible enough to allow constant and smooth evolution of a domain model.

The second issue centers on the *concurrent* aspect. By definition, all participants in a concurrent engineering environment are working simultaneously on the same product. This translates into concurrent access to the same computational resources. System architectural issues such as concurrency control and security checking must be designed into the framework to ensure system and data integrity. And yet, different environments often call for different system configuration requirements. CEF should allow these system-level components to be customizable.

To address both of these issues, we employ a novel customization process when implementing a domain-specific application with CEF. We will first explain the entire customization process to give an overview of the functionality of CEF. Then we will discuss the architecture design of CEF.

7.1 Customization Process

An application framework can be typically categorized as either vertical or horizontal. Vertical frameworks are domain-specific and already encompass a good wealth of knowledge about the particular domain. Horizontal frameworks are technology-centric, providing the infrastructure to build applications of similar types, and do not host any information related to any domain. It is common to build a vertical framework based on a horizontal framework.

CEF can be best categorized as a horizontal framework that can be extended into a vertical framework. CEF differs from other frameworks primarily in its ability to allow domain experts, not software developers, to implement such an extension. In essence, this approach empowers domain experts to actively participate in the customization process. This section discusses our rationale for such a design.

7.1.1 Traditional Approach

Typical customization of a framework involves the completion of the domain model and must be implemented by software developers. These developers have to abstract the domain model from a series of interviews with domain experts and then code it into the system; this is a process commonly referred to as *knowledge engineering*. Knowledge engineering is iterative in nature and requires strong interpersonal and communication skills in addition to technical competence and experience. The most serious challenge for knowledge engineering is the communication gap between domain experts and software developers due to their background differences. Object-oriented technologies certainly alleviate such a problem by offering a common language with which both parties feel comfortable.

However, for most engineering domains, the domain model is hardly static. New technologies, new business structures, or new regulations can all make the current domain model obsolete. The main drawback of coding the domain model into the software is the inability to evolve the domain model without software modification. Software development is rarely a specialty for most engineering firms, which means the evolution of a domain model often translates into a significant commitment to outside resources.

The evolution of a domain model does not involve just software modification, but also modification to persistent data structure, also known as *schema evolution*. Schema evolution can become quite difficult, especially for object-oriented databases (OODBs) due to the intimate dependencies among objects. For example, in a typical OODB, objects refer to each other by pointers. Schema evolution entails the change of object sizes, hence their addresses as well. A great challenge to schema evolution for an OODB is thus how to maintain referential integrity.

Schema evolution is also a nightmare for database administrators. Since the database schema is tied closely to software, we must evolve *all* production databases at once when delivering a new version of the software that uses a new schema. Otherwise, any databases that are not evolved will not function with the new software. For a real-world database application, the total size of all production databases can easily reach several hundred gigabytes. Evolving such a huge amount of data is certainly not trivial and requires careful planning.

To avoid the difficulties of evolving a domain model, we offer an alternative customization process that will enable domain experts to build and evolve their own domain models without the participation from software developers.

7.1.2 Design Philosophy

Our customization process was designed based on two philosophies. First, we believe that ordinary engineers can absorb and utilize basic object-oriented modeling concepts, such as objects and inheritance. We contend that engineers can formalize their domain models without having to rely on software developers if they are provided with an appropriate expression tool.

Second, we believe each person should perform the tasks in which he or she is specialized. In the case of customizing CEF, we let domain experts develop their own domain models and leave infrastructural customization to software developers. Our primary departure from the traditional knowledge engineering approach is the elimination of the translation process that a knowledge engineer uses to make an abstract domain model into concrete software code.

7.1.3 Three-Phase Customization

Figure 7.1 illustrates our three-phase customization process: Infrastructure and graphical user interface (GUI) customization, domain modeling, and case modeling delivered by software developers, domain specialists, and end users, respectively. Notice that both domain specialists and end users are engineers, but have slightly different roles in the customization process. Also notice that the third phase is completely optional.

Before any customization takes place, CEF is not an executable but a group of libraries, header files, and template definitions, hence the notation "CEF.lib" in Figure 7.1.

Infrastructure and GUI Customization

Software developers accomplish this phase by using typical object-oriented language features such as class inheritance and polymorphism. Examples of infrastructural components include concurrency control, security control, command dispatch, and event notification. GUI components include organizational environments, navigational tools, object viewers and editors, and so on. CEF provides a rich set of architectural objects that fully exploit modern distributed computing technologies and yet shield developers from implementation details with appropriate encapsulation.

The deliverable of this phase is already an executable program ("CEF.exe" in Figure 7.1). However, it is still not a complete application in the sense that it cannot yet per-

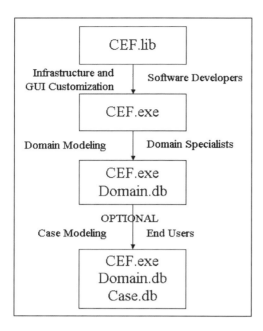

Figure 7.1   Three-phase customization.

form any domain-specific functionality. In essence, the executable generated from this phase is yet another horizontal framework to be completed with a domain model.

Domain Modeling

A group of domain specialists then uses this executable as a modeling tool to conduct the domain modeling phase, including defining domain objects and specifying information flow. These specialists should be senior engineers who are intimately familiar with the typical engineering principles and processes in that domain. However, they do not need to have any software development experience. To facilitate easy understanding and utilization of this modeling tool, we have chosen a hybrid representation scheme that incorporates basic object-oriented concepts, such as inheritance and encapsulation, and a spreadsheet-like computational paradigm.

The end product of this customization phase is a repository of prototypical domain objects whose definitions are stored in a database ("Domain.db" in Figure 7.1), but not in software. Together with the executable built from the first phase, this domain model constitutes a vertical framework especially tailored to this domain.

Case Modeling

This vertical framework is what is delivered to real end users. In their day-to-day use of this vertical framework, end users clone prototype objects from the repository and make minor modifications to suit their individual *cases* if necessary, hence the term *case modeling*. Of course, if the end user is dealing with a typical engineering case covered by the domain model developed in the previous phase, he or she may not need any modifications and this customization phase will be bypassed. The main point is that even end users can have the ability to customize the system to their needs.

7.2 Dynamic Domain Modeling

Allowing domain experts to construct and evolve their own domain models is what distinguishes CEF from other frameworks. In this section, we will explain the technical approach and the usage of this dynamic modeling feature. In the next section, we will provide an architectural description of CEF, which forms the foundation in which the infrastructure and GUI customization is conducted.

7.2.1 Prototype-Based Object System

The dynamic modeling feature offered in CEF is based on the concept of *prototype-based* object systems. One of the most significant strengths of a prototype-based object system is that it allows users to avoid the permanent commitment to a single object hierarchy in software [Hallman 1997].

Basic Concepts

The concept of *prototype* objects is introduced in prototype-based languages such as Self [Ungar 1994]. *Prototype* refers to the fact that new objects can be created dynamically by cloning existing objects, serving as prototypes. The key point that makes these prototype-based objects special is that they are complete, self-contained entities that can exist by themselves, whereas objects in class-based languages, such as C++, cannot exist without their class definitions. Prototype-based objects are typically composed of *slots* or *attributes*—essentially name-value pairs.

In class-based languages, the definition of a class determines the structures of all objects instantiated from this class. These class definitions are maintained separately from the object instances. An object cannot be created, deleted, or modified without its class definition. When the class definition changes, the existing instances of the class must also have their structures changed.

This problem increases when these instances are stored persistently. Evolving the definition of a class thus must involve modifications not only to software components but also to object sizes and locations in production databases. The latter can often cause major technical and/or logistical problems. Objects in prototype-based languages do not suffer from the same problem since each of them has its own definition stored within itself.

Our prototype-based object system is implemented using C++, a class-based language. Figure 7.2 is a simple example to illustrate how this approach can help avoid the object evolution problem. Figure 7.2 has two parts; the top portion showing the class-based approach and the bottom the prototype-based approach. The task is to add the field *height* to the definition of Table.

In Figure 7.2a, adding one field to the Table class definition changes the size of the class. As explained earlier, the size change of a class entails software modification and

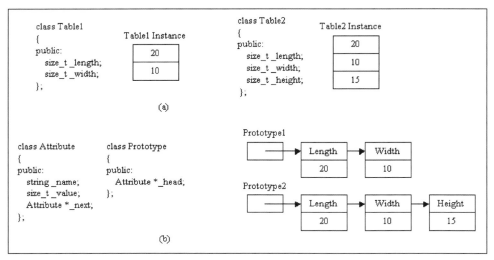

Figure 7.2   *(a)* Class-based and *(b)* prototype-based objects.

the evolution of all existing instances of the original class. In Figure 7.2b, the Prototype class simply maintains a pointer to its first attribute. Therefore, the definition of Table has no effect on the size of the Prototype class; in other words, Prototype1 and Prototype2 have exactly the same size. Although this is an oversimplified implementation, it illustrates the principle that prototype-based objects can dynamically change their definitions without affecting existing objects and without code modifications.

Object Inheritance

Cloning prototype objects is a form of object inheritance. Two basic types of relationships can exist between a child object and a parent object [Hallman 1994] and are illustrated in Figure 7.3. A child can maintain a link back to the parent and delegate unknown messages to the parent, as depicted in Figure 7.3a. Or a child can simply concatenate the parent's definition into its own definition and become totally independent of the parent, shown in Figure 7.3b.

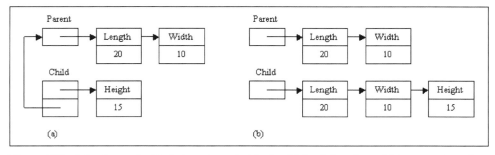

Figure 7.3   Inheritance for Prototype-based objects: *(a)* by delegation; *(b)* by concatenation.

Inheritance by delegation allows the change to the behaviors of a child object by changing its parent's behaviors or by reassigning it to a different parent. Inheritance by concatenation makes the child and the parent objects totally independent of each other, maximizing information locality. Both approaches have their legitimate uses and both are offered in CEF.

CEF does not implement a full-fledged prototype-based language like Self, but rather capitalizes on the idea of constructing self-contained objects without classes dynamically. Independent work from Gamma, Helm, and Vlissides [Gamma 1996] has also reached a similar approach called the Instance Type pattern, which is essentially a prototype-based inheritance-by-delegation object system. What CEF adds to this instance type pattern are the abilities to model the aggregation relationship among objects via the concept of *packages* and to allow the specification of information flow via *function* attributes.

7.2.2 Packages and Dictionaries

Design objects are modeled as packages in CEF. A *package* is composed of *attributes* of a rich set of data types. An attribute in CEF is actually an *expression* containing constants, functions, and/or other attributes. For example, a table object could be defined with the following attributes: dimension, unit price, and price, where the price attribute is a function of the dimension and the unit price attributes.

Modularity is an indispensable concept for both engineering design and software design. An engineering design task can be subtasked in a hierarchical and structural fashion, akin to the concept of procedures and libraries in software practice. Modularity is supported in CEF by nested packages, an application of the composite pattern [Gamma 1995] that describes the aggregation relationship among objects. Whether a package contains subpackages is known to the package itself only. A package is thus the only interface between its contained subpackages and the outside world, enforcing system encapsulation and modularity.

The fact that engineers can construct their own object models does not imply that they must do so. As mentioned earlier, a group of domain specialists can construct libraries or *dictionaries* of prototype design objects during the domain modeling customization phase. Other engineers who are less experienced with the system can simply clone these prototype objects into their working areas and start using or modifying them. The concept of a dictionary achieves the same effect as a catalog of types in the Instance Type pattern.

Recall that both inheritance by delegation and inheritance by concatenation are utilized in CEF. Objects in dictionaries are maintained with the delegation approach to allow sharing of object definitions. When an object is cloned out of a dictionary, the concatenation approach is used to create a completely self-contained object.

7.2.3 Change Propagation

Attribute references constitute the foundation of the change propagation scheme in CEF, which is essentially how information flow among design objects is specified. When the value of an attribute is changed, all attributes that reference this attribute will have their values updated automatically. For instance, suppose that package A contains attributes A1 and A2, package B contains B1 and B2, and B1 has the value A1+A2/B2. When the value of A2 is changed, B1 will be updated accordingly. Qualifiers can be used in expressions to resolve name conflicts.

The visibility of one attribute to another is determined by scope rules, similar to the lexical scope found in most languages. In essence, all sibling packages share the same scope so that they can cross-reference each other's attributes. All descendants from the same parent package share the same scope with the parent. This means that a package can reference all packages up the containment hierarchy, similar to the concept of global variables, but can reference only its immediate contained subpackages, akin to the notion of return values. Circular references are prohibited. A topological ordering of all attributes in the system is maintained at all times to detect circular references and determine the path of calculation.

Figure 7.4 illustrates how information is propagated among sibling and nested packages, with arrows showing the calculation path. Package C0 consists of packages C1, C3, and C2, which is in turn an aggregate of packages C4 and C5. A change of value to 10 for attribute A will eventually lead to the change of value to 2.5 for attribute Z. Notice that attribute S is a special type of attribute, called a *signal*, that will be turned on when Z < 10. Therefore, the change of A will turn on S, signaling the engineer that a significant change has occurred. This is the basic approach of our change notification.

Completely automatic change propagation can sometimes cause problems. Engineers may sometimes need temporary isolation from interference to concentrate on their own design. Or, occasionally, they may feel that their design is still immature and not ready to be shared by others. Engineers should be able to control when information

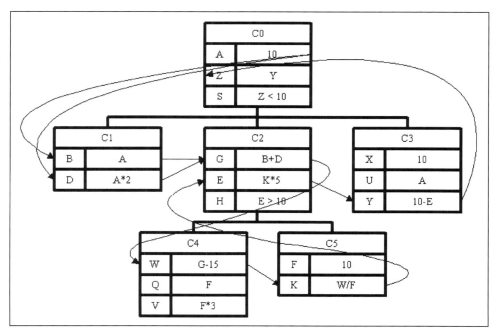

Figure 7.4 Example of change propagation.

can flow into or out of their design objects. To accomplish this, a conceptual valve is placed on either side of every attribute. When an input valve to an attribute is closed, this attribute cannot receive any propagated changes. Conversely, when an output valve is closed, the attribute cannot export its changes.

The similarity between the change propagation scheme in CEF and the popular spreadsheet calculation model is by design. Most engineering works involve extensive mathematical calculations and can be well described by a spreadsheet model. CEF extends the conventional spreadsheet model with the notion of objects, offering the concept of aggregation and inheritance. CEF also supports concurrent usage from multiple users and allows users to control when the information can flow into or out of an object.

7.3 Architectural Design

Three principles guide our design of the CEF architecture. First, the framework should mandate minimal system behaviors to allow a high degree of customization. Second, the responsibility of each customizable element should be simple and specific to reduce customization effort. And last, the logic pertaining to specific development tools should be isolated to facilitate easier adaptation to different development environments. Several design patterns are utilized to implement these principles.

It should be noted that these architectural issues are of no concern to domain specialists and end users. Customization to any infrastructure or GUI components is conducted solely by software developers in the first phase of the customization process.

7.3.1 Architecture Overview

Figure 7.5 illustrates the major architectural components in CEF. A user action is first received by the View object and then delegated to the Command object for execution. To ensure the integrity of the system in a distributed concurrent environment, the Command class enforces the following execution sequence. First, the Security Manager

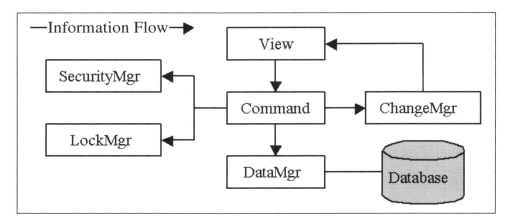

Figure 7.5 Framework architecture.

checks if the user has the privilege to perform such an action on the object. Second, the Lock Manager uses locks to guarantee that this action will not conflict with actions from other users. Third, the Data Manager performs database transactions to manipulate the object. And last, the Change Manager broadcasts the changes to interested parties.

Only the View must reside on a client machine. The placements of other components are configurable during the customization phase to suit different system requirements in different environments. For instance, in a local area network (LAN) environment with a centralized database server, the DataMgr can be spawned on a local machine to better utilize that machine's computation power. In a web-based environment, however, the DataMgr is most appropriate to reside on a web server because maintaining live transactions across Internet connections can be prohibitively expensive.

Command

Figure 7.5 demonstrates that the Command class is the real center of control in CEF. It dispatches tasks to the DataMgr, the SecurityMgr, the LockMgr, and the ChangeMgr classes. Most commands take similar bookkeeping steps before and after the operation. For instance, each concurrent operation must acquire an appropriate lock before its execution and release the lock after it completes. To enforce these rules and free developers from related programming details, we encapsulate them with the Command and the Template Method patterns [Gamma 1995].

Figure 7.6 depicts the class diagram for the Command class. All operations are implemented as concrete Command classes derived from the base Command class, which implements an execute function called by a view object. The execute function calls five major functions: checking the user's privilege, requesting a lock, executing

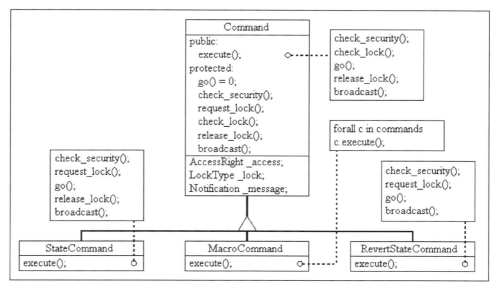

Figure 7.6   Command class diagram.

the operation (go), releasing the lock, and, finally, broadcasting the change. This is an application of the Template Method pattern that defines a skeleton algorithm.

The Command class encapsulates the details of the interaction among these manager objects and at the same time enforces the correctness of a command execution. Two tasks are required to implement a concrete Command class. First, a concrete derived Command class must implement the pure virtual go function. Also, a concrete Command class must initialize the data members of its base class, namely, the minimal access right required to execute the command, the necessary lock type on the target object, and the notification to be sent after the execution. In this way, developers can concentrate on implementing the main logic of a command without worrying about bookkeeping details.

Some variants of the Command class exist regarding the implementation of the execute function. For instance, the RevertStateCommand class represents commands using locks as the state information and does not release the lock after the command completes. Developers can define their own execute functions to enforce certain execution steps.

Data Manager

A data manager hides from its views the data representation of the object that it manages. Definitions of objects are not directly accessed by views and can hence be modified without affecting the rest of the system. All database transaction boundaries are specified in data managers. This ensures that database-dependent transaction logic can be well encapsulated.

Another important functionality of a data manager is the determination of the placement policy for an object. Ideally, objects referenced in one transaction should be clustered in the database as closely as possible to optimize database access. Due to the limitation on communication bandwidth and the quantity of transaction data, database access is often the major performance bottleneck for a database application. This object placement policy is made explicit in CEF to force developers to consider this issue beforehand.

Change Manager

Change propagation is an important feature of CEF and is implemented primarily via change managers. As discussed earlier, the implementation of the base Command class forces the broadcast of a notification upon the completion of an operation. The ChangeMgr class is designed to perform this task so that the change made by a user can be broadcast to all interested parties.

The relationship among View, DataMgr, and ChangeMgr is conceptually similar to the classic Model/View/Controller architecture. The difference is at the implementation level where CEF architectural components encapsulate much of the distributed computing technologies. For instance, CEF utilizes Common Object Request Broker Architecture (CORBA)–compliant implementation to ensure cross-platform operability.

Security Manager

The need for security in a concurrent application is to keep an unauthorized user from tampering with other users' contents and to grant certain privileges to individual users or groups. Figure 7.7 depicts the class diagram for the SecurityMgr class. A Security-Mgr object uses two permission objects, user and group permissions, to maintain the access rights for users and groups. The base AccessRight class can be derived to construct application-specific access rights.

The permission objects cannot determine the access right of a given user with a given group on the object, which is the responsibility of the AccessPolicy object. This separation of algorithm (AccessPolicy) and data structure objects (Permission) facilitates the customization of security features. For instance, an AccessPolicy object can dictate the order in which permission objects are traversed, or the default access right when neither permission object includes the user. The concept of policy classes is a direct application of the Strategy pattern [Gamma 1995].

The security manager is not intended to replace the security features offered by the underlying operating system, but simply an interface that guides the customization of such features. In fact, we encourage the use of native security system application programmer interfaces (APIs) to implement the security manager because this approach saves development costs and provides a uniform treatment to objects and files residing in the operating system, allowing easier administrative functions.

Lock Manager

Locking is the mechanism used to resolve concurrent access conflicts on an object. An object type determines the validity of coexistence of various lock types on the same object of this type. For instance, some objects can support multiple concurrent writers, whereas some cannot. Hence, the locking subsystem in our framework is designed to offer developers the flexibility to implement their own strategies for lock compatibility check.

Virtually all commercial databases offer locking in one form or another. However, these locking mechanisms protect data integrity from the viewpoint of transaction seri-

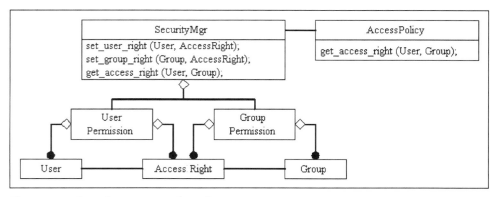

Figure 7.7 Security manager class diagram.

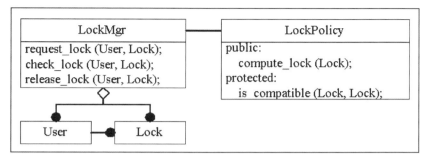

Figure 7.8   Lock manager class diagram.

alization, which may not guarantee the semantic correctness of concurrent operations. For instance, when an object is being edited by a user, we can either use a long transaction to protect the entire editing duration or use a short transaction to retrieve the data and have the user work on the local copy of the data. The former can cause serious database contention issues and the latter cannot protect the object after the retrieval transaction completes. Also, most databases extend only two lock types, read and write, and do not allow addition of new lock types. In CEF, the locking subsystem provides application-level locking semantics and is much more flexible.

Figure 7.8 illustrates the class diagram for the LockMgr class, which exhibits a parallel design philosophy to the SecurityMgr class, namely, the separation of data structure and algorithm objects. More specifically, a LockMgr object maintains a data structure mapping a user to the locks held for that user on the object, similar to the Permission object for security. The LockMgr object delegates to a LockPolicy object to determine if a new lock request can be granted based on the current locks on the same object, akin to the AccessPolicy class.

The LockMgr offers several lock-related interfaces. Only the request_lock function is delegated to the LockPolicy object via the function compute_lock, whose default implementation iterates through all locks currently held on the object and calls is_compatible to determine if each of them is compatible with the requested lock. A lock can be granted if all existing locks are compatible with the desired lock.

To customize the lock mechanism, developers can define new lock types by deriving from the base Lock class, which necessitates the implementation of the virtual is_compatible functions for all object types that can accept such lock types. The compute_lock is also a virtual function, which can be useful in automatic downgrading of the request lock in the case in which that lock cannot be granted.

7.4 Lessons Learned

Framework development is a long, iterative process, just as any other software development process. Our strategy was to convert an existing application directly into a general framework. The original application from which CEF was converted is in the domain of chemical engineering and has been deployed for over 18 months, as of the time of this writing. The current user population is over 100 engineers and is projected to grow to 400 by the end of 1999.

In retrospect, we attribute the success of this application largely to the concept of prototype-based object systems. Since we deployed this application for our client about 18 months ago, we have not been requested to help the construction or evolution of any domain or case models. Our client now has a team of about 15 specialists, who continue to improve their domain models and assist other engineers to adapt their own case models. This demonstrates the ease of use of our prototype-based object system and confirms our assertion that ordinary engineers can construct and evolve their own models by themselves when given an appropriate expression language.

This observation also illustrates an economic advantage of this prototype-based approach. Had we chosen to adopt the traditional approach of coding the domain model into the software, our client would have to constantly rely on our consultants to perform domain evolution tasks for them. This could amount to significant budget and resource commitment.

Since the delivery of this system, we have conducted two episodes of schema evolution: once for performance improvement and another time for adding new functionality. Both times, significant technical and logistical difficulties were encountered. Currently, the production databases have reached over 20 gigabytes of data and are projected to grow at the rate of 50 gigabytes annually. Technical difficulties aside, evolving this huge set of data is extremely time-consuming and requires careful planning.

This logistical problem exists because when we deliver a new version of the application with a new database schema, we have to evolve *all* production databases at once. Otherwise, the databases not evolved will not be functional with the new version of the application. And worse yet, during the time of evolving databases, the entire system has to be nonoperational. In order not to disturb the normal business operations, the evolution process must be completed in one weekend. To achieve this goal, several high-end servers and a massive number of client machines were used to perform such a task.

The moral of the story is that schema evolution is nontrivial and we should avoid it at all costs. Again, had we coded the domain model in the software, schema evolution would have occurred much more frequently, causing more system downtime and more administrative problems.

We anticipate continuous evolution of this framework as more and more applications are built from it. Our goal is to reduce the application development effort each time by carefully balancing among the framework's extensibility, functionality, simplicity, and encapsulation. Our future clients will benefit most from this framework development endeavor because we will be able to deliver similar systems with better quality in a shorter duration with lower budget.

7.5 Summary

We introduced a framework for building concurrent engineering applications, wherein traditional sequential product development phases are transformed into concurrent activities to allow early detection and resolution of design flaws and conflicts. We also advocated an alternative domain modeling approach that allows the construction and evolution of a domain model from domain experts alone without the assistance of software developers.

The principal contribution of this chapter comes from this novel domain modeling approach, although the field of concurrent engineering itself also deserves attention. We contend that our domain modeling approach is of both theoretical and practical importance. Theoretically, this is an alternative paradigm to the traditional knowledge engineering process. Instead of having software developers abstract the domain model from domain experts and then translate it into software components, we eliminate such a translation step and have domain experts build their own models by themselves. Practically, this approach alleviates the technical and logistical hurdles of model evolution and allows engineering firms to take full control of their own domain models.

Our technical approach is based on the concept of prototype-based languages. For class-based languages, such as C++ and Java, the definition of a class is maintained in software, separate from its object instances. An object cannot be created, deleted, or modified without referring to its class definition in software. For prototype-based languages, all objects contain within themselves their own definitions and can thus be manipulated directly without referring to software. This breaks the dependency on software developers to code the domain model into software and empowers domain experts to build and maintain their own models.

7.6 References

[Dean 1997] Dean, Edwin B. *Concurrent Engineering from the Perspective of Competitive Advantage.* http://dfca.larc.nasa.gov/dfc/ce.html, NASA Langley Research Center, January1997.

[Gamma 1995] Gamma, E., R. Helm, R. Johnson, and J. Vlissides. *Design Patterns: Elements of Reusable Object-Oriented Software.* Reading, MA: Addison-Wesley, 1995.

[Gamma 1996] Gamma, E., R. Helm, and J. Vlissides. Tutorial 29: Design Patterns Applied. *OOPSLA 1996,* San Jose, CA, October 1996. New York: ACM/SIGPLAN, 1996.

[Hallman 1997] Hallman, B. Are classes necessary? *Journal of Object-Oriented Programming* 10(5):16–21, September 1997.

[Ungar 1994] Ungar, D., and R.B. Smith. *Self: The Power of Simplicity.* SMLI-TR-94-30, Mountain View, CA: Sun Microsystems Laboratories Inc., 1994.

CHAPTER 8

Distributed Manufacturing Execution Systems Framework

Manufacturing execution systems (MESs) are shop-floor control and work-flow systems that control the flow of materials through the manufacturing process and coordinate the equipment needed to process these materials. Most MESs in use today give little thought to the needs of the enterprise with regard to changing manufacturing requirements, processes, and priorities. The resulting inflexible and monolithic systems are at best difficult and expensive to change. This is no longer an acceptable situation in today's highly competitive business environment. The survival of a manufacturing enterprise is dependent upon its ability to quickly adapt to changing requirements. The systems that support the enterprise must be able to adapt as quickly and as well.

FACTORYworks, a next-generation manufacturing execution system, is a design based upon the Semiconductor Generic Manufacturing Model (SGMM), which was the result of an object-oriented analysis of semiconductor manufacturing processes made by SEMATECH, the U.S. semiconductor manufacturing consortium. In 1992, after working with SEMATECH to develop manufacturing software control systems, FASTech Integration (FASTech Integration, Inc. Lincoln, MA. 01773) formed a private consortium with a number of first-tier semiconductor manufacturers, the objective of which was to design and implement a shop-floor control and manufacturing execution system that would support the complex and rapidly changing requirements of the semiconductor industry. Because of the dynamic and high-volume nature of semiconductor manufacturing, this system has to fulfill a number of essential requirements:

- Readily adapt to changing business rules and processes.
- Scale in size with the needs of the enterprise.
- Support popular development tools and methodologies.
- Run on common PCs or workstations.
- Allow existing applications and systems to be integrated without undue effort.

In addition, it must also exhibit these five characteristics:

Reliability. A 24x7 operational environment (continuous operations, 24 hours per day, 7 days per week) must be maintained while running on readily available and cost-effective computer/network hardware and standard operating system software.

Availability. The system should be resilient to single points of failure. The demise of a single processor, network segment, or application server should not cause the system as a whole to cease operation.

Scalability. The system must be able to add users and applications without significantly degrading performance. Concurrent access to data by many client applications must not cause deadlocks or excessive delays.

Integrity. Data validity must be maintained in the event of client, server, network, or database failure.

Extensibility. Means must be available to add additional features and components as needed, such as recipe management, equipment maintenance, or statistical process control, without modification of existing components.

The requirements analysis and system design were done with object-oriented methods in order to accommodate their complexity. A mixture of Object-Modeling Technique (OMT) [Rumbaugh 1991], Harel state charts [Harel 1988], use cases [Jacobson 1992], and Class Responsibility-Collaborator (CRC) [Beck 1993] modeling techniques were utilized. The complexity of the design led to the decision that FACTORYworks should be implemented with an object-oriented language as well. It was felt that traditional development tools and languages would make the primary goal of a highly adaptable system too difficult to achieve. After essential algorithms and processes were prototyped in SmallTalk, C++ was utilized for the delivered systems.

8.1 Architecture

The overview of the framework architecture and its components is discussed in the following sections.

8.1.1 Overview

The design philosophy of FACTORYworks is that a generalized architectural framework will encourage the development of industry-standard reusable software components from different suppliers, as well as simplify the integration of existing applications and systems. The cost of deploying custom manufacturing solutions has become so high that the ability to easily integrate different applications as required has become a requirement for new manufacturing software systems.

As Figure 8.1 illustrates, the fundamental design is a framework of application component servers that provides the application services and a message bus that provides the means of communication between clients and application servers. Client applications plug in to this framework (the Common Services shown in Figure 8.1) in order to interact with the application servers. These framework services can be provided by an Object Request Broker (ORB) such as implemented by vendors of CORBA (Common Object Request Broker Architecture—Object Management Group) [OMG 1995] compliant products, or by such means as message-oriented middleware (MOM) products like MQSeries from IBM. For FACTORYworks we chose the MOM approach, partly due to the immaturity of CORBA products at the time we were implementing the system and partly because we had extensive experience utilizing messaging systems to implement complex distributed applications. The application servers in turn communicate with a relational database for a persistent object repository. This implies a three-tier client-server model of user interface, application logic, and database, as shown in Figure 8.2.

In Figure 8.2, an interface appears between the application servers and clients called the Distributed Transaction Processing Framework (DTPF). This is the application-enabling framework of FACTORYworks, which makes possible rapid development of FACTORYworks applications and extensions. As such, it supports services such as interprocess communications, object migration, object persistence, and transactional integrity; however, it provides more than just a support foundation for distributed application development. Its implementation goal was to make application development, maintenance, and enhancement as natural and easy as possible by providing a

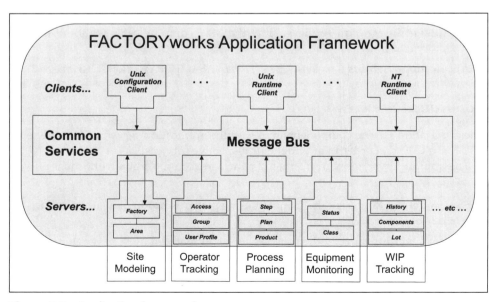

Figure 8.1 Application framework.

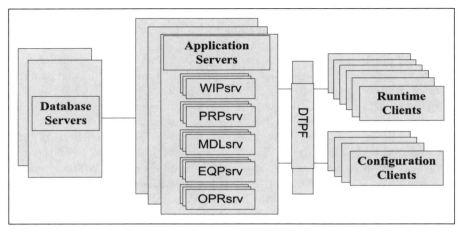

Figure 8.2 Three-tier model.

logical and consistent abstraction of the infrastructure and its operation. This is the key to a successful application-enabling framework, to provide application developers with the ability to program complex applications without distracting them from the domain that they are addressing [Fayad 1997].

8.1.2 Framework Components

During the specification and design process, a number of service components were identified:

Application services. The actual MES implementation.

Equipment integration services. How the MES communicates with and controls factory equipment.

Application-enabling services. The DTPF and FACTORYworks CORE classes.

Application Services

The application service components make up the application servers. They utilize the DTPF and CORE in order to provide their respective services.

The application services that a manufacturing execution framework must provide include:

Site modeling. Represent the manufacturing plant, its production areas, and associated equipment.

Process planning. Specify the process steps that material must undergo in order to produce finished goods.

Work-flow management. Execute the process plans, utilizing production resources defined in the site model.

Equipment monitoring. Dynamically determine the state of production equipment in order to dispatch work to functional units.

Engineering data collection. Collect production data for statistical process and quality control.

Operator tracking and access control. Track operator activities for production and quality statistics and limit access to those processes and operations they are authorized for.

These services were implemented as a set of C++ class libraries, compartmentalized into two layers: one that encapsulates the behavior of the domain and another that provides the application programming interface (API) that is utilized by the external world to communicate with a server. Each service domain is kept decoupled as much as possible from the others, although there is a limit to this. For example, the work-flow component must communicate with process planning in order to determine which process step is to be applied next to a particular lot or manufactured item.

Each application server has a dedicated connection to the database repository containing the instances of each class it controls. In order to provide fault resilience and enhance the performance and scalability of the system, multiple copies of each server can be run on any number of host systems. The distribution of work is handled by the DTPF and message bus, which will route service requests to the next available server. We decided to utilize this more coarse-grained parallel processing technique rather than in-process threading for several reasons:

- Using multiple executable images is much simpler to implement since thread-safe libraries with complex use of locking semaphores would not be required.

- Debugging is simplified.

- Thread-safe libraries were not supported on all required platforms when we were developing the system.

As a result, none of our code has to be explicitly thread-safe. We utilized instead the transactional capabilities provided by current relational database products in order to provide the level of isolation required to reliably manipulate persistent objects.

Site Modeling—MDLsrv

Site modeling provides a model of the factory and represents relationships between physical and logical areas in the factory as well as the resources required for production. It is used to hierarchically define areas and subareas of the shop floor, equipment resources that are associated with each area, and reason codes that are customized to explain why a manufactured item (lot or component) deviated from normal processing. Figure 8.3 shows how a site might be configured.

A graphical layout tool is utilized to design and view graphical representations of the model. Because the objects that represent the model are version controlled, whenever a new site model is rolled out the system automatically creates a new version. This allows changes to be made to the model concurrently with the operation of the factory. Changes will not take effect until the model is rolled out and the new version created.

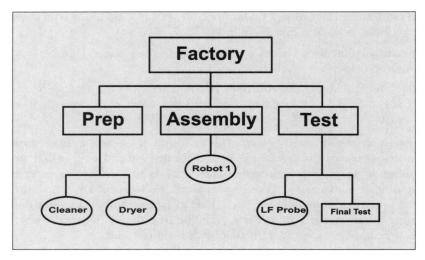

Figure 8.3   Site model example.

Process Planning—PRPsrv

Process planning provides step-by-step instructions that must be followed in order to manufacture a product or component. The components of a process plan can include manufacturing steps, rules to apply when the manufactured item is moved into or out of a step, subplans, and products associated with plans. All components of a process plan, including the plan itself, can be reused in other plans, which provides a great degree of reusability and consistency across an entire manufacturing product line.

As in site modeling, process planning utilizes a graphical layout tool in order to design and view process plans. Process plans are also version controlled, so that a plan may be altered concurrently with use of the plan in the manufacturing process. When the plan is rolled out, any production that requires it can utilize the new version.

Six fundamental constructs are used to model process flows:

Sequential steps. Where one step follows another.

Alternative steps. Where conditional logic specifies which of several paths should be traversed.

Iterative steps. Where a single step is repeated multiple times.

Composite steps. Where steps are nested within other steps.

Optional steps. Where any one of a set of steps may be traversed, depending on the results of a boolean operation.

Checklist. Where all of a number of steps must be traversed, but in any order.

These constructs allow virtually any type of process flow to be modeled and are utilized by the work-flow services in the actual manufacturing process.

Business rules can also be specified and applied to individual steps in order to tailor system behavior to site-specific requirements. A business rule can include:

- Tasks to be executed

- Calculations to be performed on engineering data collected

- Changes to make to equipment state

- Messages to be sent to external applications, such as the corporate Enterprise Resource Planning (ERP) or inventory systems

Work Flow—WIPsrv

Work-flow execution is the heart of a manufacturing execution system. This module tracks work in process through all stages of manufacturing from raw materials to finished goods, accumulating a history of work done at each step of the process. The work-flow engine executes the process plans, triggering business rules as specified in the plans.

WIPsrv maintains the following information about each lot or component:

- Product assignment

- Process data

- Current location

- History and sequence of process steps performed

- Holds and releases from holds

- Lot splits and merges (if appropriate)

- Rework performed

- Scrap generated

Additional site-specific, custom attributes can be defined and assigned to a lot or component, such as capacity, units of measurement, or priority. Some sites have defined hundreds of custom attributes, which can be utilized to trigger execution of specific business rules or process steps.

Equipment Monitoring—EQPsrv

The equipment monitoring server maintains a repository of information about types of equipment in the factory along with instances of that equipment and their status and other relevant information. Equipment groups can be defined, which provides support for situations where some processing equipment must be associated with others as a conceptual unit. This supports situations where a fault in one piece of equipment will affect the availability of the entire group.

Engineering Data Collection—EDCsrv

Data collection plans are devised that determine what data is to be collected from which equipment, as well as what analyses will be performed on that data. This is integrated with a statistical process control package for realtime quality control. Plans, rules, and collected data are all stored as persistent objects. The statistical process control functions support Western Electric as well as custom rules, providing a powerful means of keeping manufacturing processes under control and minimizing waste of time and materials.

Operator Tracking—OPRsrv

Operator tracking provides the ability to define operational groups and access privileges as well as to manage operators. It tracks the login/logout of operators on the system and enforces their access to permitted system modules and functions. Access privileges are attributes of the operational groups and operators can belong to zero or more groups.

Equipment Integration Services

Because this framework is primarily intended for the semiconductor manufacturing industry, the equipment integration services must provide support for the Semiconductor Equipment Communication Standard (SECS), Generic Equipment Model (GEM), and Virtual Factory Equipment Interface (VFEI) protocols. These protocols (SECS and GEM are international standards) are used extensively in semiconductor manufacturing. Besides these standards, support for other equipment communication interfaces, such as programmable controllers and tag and barcode readers, is required.

In order to assure the ability to utilize the widest possible variety of manufacturing devices, we decided to license existing software products to integrate with FACTORYworks. Because the design consortium members had extensive experience with it and because it supports a wide variety of manufacturing equipment and devices, the CELLworks manufacturing integration tool set from FASTech Integration was chosen to provide many of these services. CELLworks provides the ability to generate messages in any required format, allowing the integration with FACTORYworks of almost any manufacturing equipment. This is accomplished by mapping equipment output to the message format required by the FACTORYworks API. For example, if a particular piece of manufacturing equipment becomes disabled, the appropriate message will be generated for the equipment monitoring server (EQPsrv), thereby keeping the workflow engine from dispatching work to that resource.

Application-Enabling Services

The key to getting everything working together—client applications, application servers, databases, and manufacturing equipment—is a generalized application-enabling framework that provides a relatively simple abstraction of common services. The classes we needed to provide fell into two categories: low-level, which is the DTPF, and more complex application enabling, which is the FACTORYworks CORE.

Class libraries that support some of the DTPF services were purchased or licensed from Rogue-Wave (Rogue-Wave Software, Inc., Corvallis, Oregon) in order to speed up the development process. These enabled us to implement the framework in much less time than would be required for us to write everything ourselves. The Rogue-Wave classes we utilized included collections, strings, regular expressions, date, time, and database interfaces. Even though we were able to take advantage of these, our long-term goal was to remove our dependence upon any third-party code wherever feasible. In order to do that, we created a layer of abstraction so that any purchased components could be integrated while providing a consistent programming interface. At this time, all of the Rogue-Wave classes have been replaced, or are being replaced, with components written entirely in-house. By doing so, we have already experienced significant improvements in system performance, primarily due to the removal of unneeded features, the elimination of extra code to compensate for missing features, and the ability to optimize code to address specific performance issues where needed.

The DTPF consists of four class libraries and the CORE consists of two:

Utilities: strings, date/time, collections, environment, garbage collection, error handling.

Distribution: object marshaling, event notification, interprocess communication.

Presentation: interface to window manager, GUI callback handling.

Persistence: transaction processing services, database interface.

Application components: state machines, object versioning.

User interface: common dialogs, object browsers.

We have found that the DTPF and CORE classes provide all the general services required by a typical application. This allows application developers to concentrate on the structure and behavior of their application-specific classes. They do not need to concern themselves with how an object is made persistent or moved from process to process. They only need to invoke the interfaces defined by the abstract base classes. For example, to send an object to another process, application developers only need to ask the object distribution components to "Send" the object to a specified destination. To store a persistent object in the database, they only need to tell the object to "store" itself.

8.2 Framework Implementation

Just as the work-flow engine is the heart of the MES, so too are the DTPF and CORE the connective tissues of FACTORYworks applications. A manufacturing execution system is principally an online transaction processing system (OLTP). To function successfully in a 24x7 environment of a large manufacturing enterprise, where planned downtime is typically measured in hours per year, an MES must be built on a stable framework that makes efficient use of resources (central processing unit, database, network) and minimizes the complexity of developed applications by encapsulating the more difficult functions of a distributed system. Used to implement all application classes and the servers that manage them, the six class libraries of the DTPF and CORE provide a common interface for the rapid development of domain-level classes that have consistent and testable behavior. These libraries provide the abstractions necessary to encourage application class developers to focus on their area problems and issues instead of being distracted by the demands of communication protocols, database interfaces, or window programming techniques. The result of this infrastructure is an estimated 90 percent reduction in the amount of code required to achieve a specific degree of application functionality, as compared to more traditional structured programming methods.

8.2.1 Class Libraries

The DTPF encompasses such things as event notification, remote method invocation, and object persistence. The CORE encompasses net-list traversal, finite-state machines, Model/View/Controller abstractions, and business rule processing.

Utility Classes

The utility class library provides the lowest level of application development support. Some of these classes were derived from the Rogue-Wave Tools.h++ classes. Others were wholly developed in-house.

CLASSES AND SERVICES

Associations (key/value pairs for collections)

Date, time, and date+time

Strings (currently single-byte character sets only)

Timers

Binary (machine recipes, image processing)

Tokenizer (processing of input streams or strings for parsers)

Collections (ordered, set, identity set, dictionary, sorted)

Iterators (traverse collections)

Collectable primitives (to store integer, float, boolean types in collections)

Errors (C++ exceptions are not yet supported on all required platforms)

Diagnostic tracing

Environment variable handling

Garbage collection

Function interface to CELLworks message bus

Although it may appear as though many of these functions are commonly supported by the standard libraries provided by all Unix and PC platforms, there are generally enough differences in implementation and behavior to require the development of a function set that isolates these differences from the application developers. Since we run on a variety of platforms, we give the developers the advantage of needing to learn only one set of functions and classes that provides guaranteed consistent behavior instead of working around the plethora of differences from system to system.

Distribution Classes

The main purpose of the distribution class library is to support the distribution of objects around a local area network. It also provides interprocess communication support, event-management classes, and the registration of object/callback methods to handle the dispatch of asynchronous messages from external sources.

In order to move objects between processes, both the sender and the receiver application must know how an object is constructed so that the sender can decompose and send it and the receiver can read and reconstitute the object from a message buffer or input stream. The common term for this is *object marshaling and unmarshaling*. Since an object can be very complex, consisting of many connected pieces, this is not a trivial process and is difficult to do efficiently. Our implementation requires that each class whose instances are be distributed do two things:

- Be derived from a common base class that implements the code required to marshal and unmarshal an object from an input stream or memory buffer.

- Define its structure in the form of class metadata. The metadata will be used by an object to write itself to an output or to read itself from an input.

Because we must be able to send objects over any type of input/output (I/O) mechanism, we use an ASCII string in a form very similar to TCL (Tool Command Language), in which each object and attribute describes itself as to member and type. This provides an interchange format that can be translated with a simple parser in any programming language. Even though this is generally less efficient than utilizing binary data values, it significantly simplifies the logic required and makes debugging much easier. In practice, the overhead required is an insignificant portion of the total time taken by a typical service request or transaction.

CLASSES AND SERVICES

Distribution: abstract base for marshaling/unmarshaling objects.

Metadata: detailed class structure information.

Attributes: details about class structural components.

Communication adapters: abstract interface to network I/O.

Message publication: send to individual process or subscription list.

Subscription: asynchronously receive messages from possibly unknown sources.

Event handlers: register/dispatch events and messages.

Command processing: query/set parameters, modify runtime behavior, application shutdown.

Presentation Classes

There are two user interface environments to be addressed: X-Windows/Motif and Microsoft Windows-NT. For X-Motif, the CELLworks toolset provides user interface builders and runtime servers on Unix platforms, which interoperate well with the CELLworks message bus. A framework of VisualBasic (VB) and Object Linking and Embedding (OLE) controls was built for Windows-NT, which allows user interface customization with VB. As a result, customers can tailor their user interfaces using these common tools.

The presentation class library provides a high degree of abstraction to user interface components in the X-Windows environment. User interface objects are defined and controlled using the CELLworks window configuration tool and runtime server. The presentation library manages events from the runtime window server, and dispatches these events to the appropriate application widget callback function. In the Windows-NT environment, OLE custom controls and VisualBasic are used instead.

CLASSES AND SERVICES

Windows: titles, colors.

Window elements: buttons, sliders, menus, text editor, icons.

Access filters and context attributes: limit operator access to allowed functions.

Window event handlers: GUI callback registration and dispatch.

This library is used by the CORE user interface classes and is not typically accessed directly by the application developer. The interface to the application is via user interface objects and callback functions the developer writes, which are derived from classes provided by the CORE library. This allows client applications to contain no window-system-specific code.

Persistence Classes

Object persistence is vital to FACTORYworks. A manufacturing execution system is a high-volume OLTP application. Candidate classes for persistence include process plans, user profiles, site models, and equipment configurations. Requirements analysis, customer feedback, and the general consensus of the design team led us to utilize a standard relational database management system (RDBMS) instead of an object database. It was believed that it would be much easier for a customer to find people to administer a standard RDBMS and that there would be better tools to assist in data management and reporting.

We had the following options to interface an RDBMS to our object-oriented design:

- A hybrid object-relational database, such as UniSQL/M, which can integrate to a common RDBMS such as Oracle. Today, there are a number of other suitable candidates such as Oracle8, DB/2, and Informix.

- A relational to object mapping product such as Persistence.

- An object wrapper library such as Rogue-Wave's DBTools.h++.

- An interface class library of our own design.

We did not want to irreversibly tie FACTORYworks to any specific database product, and there was the feeling that eventually we may want the efficiencies of a true object database. This led us to choose a combination of options 3 and 4, to develop our own abstraction layer in conjunction with the Rogue-Wave database library. This allowed a more seamless coupling of the database to our object model, as well as the ability to replace the Rogue-Wave library with our own library or a pure object database if necessary. The Rogue-Wave library was recently replaced with our own RDBMS interface, achieving significant performance gains and reduction in database resource utilization as a result.

The persistence class library provides an abstracted interface to an object repository held in a relational database. Persistent classes are implemented in a manner very similar to distribution classes. In fact, they are also distribution classes, derived from a common base class that knows how to use the metadata to generate the SQL code required to insert, update, and delete instances of the class from a relational database as well as to transfer instances between processes as distribution objects.

CLASSES AND SERVICES

Object identifiers

Reference management and smart pointers

Containers and persistent collections

Storage adapters

Transactions

Database interface

Object Identifiers

It is possible (and common) for each application service module to utilize a totally different database. This requires the use of globally unique object identifiers as surrogate (primary) keys. The algorithm used to generate these identifiers guarantees that each is universally unique, not just within a single installation, but for any and all installations, networks, and systems. We investigated a number of algorithms in general use and found none that would provide the capabilities we required. Because a container object may hold references to objects of any class, the class of an object must be derivable from the reference identifier. This enables us to determine how to access the object at runtime. As a result, we structured our identifiers by class, host, creation time, process ID, and sequence number generated by the creating process. This provides enough information and flexibility so that any FACTORYworks object can be moved between systems unambiguously.

Reference Management and Smart Pointers

To ensure that only one copy of a persistent object can exist within an application memory space, persistent objects are accessed via reference objects that behave as *smart pointers.* These reference objects also behave as reference-counting garbage collectors, deleting the object from process memory when all references to it have been destroyed. The first time an object is accessed via a reference, it is fetched from the database into memory. If the application is a client process, it will be retrieved from the appropriate application server using the distribution library and message bus. If the application is connected to the appropriate database for the object, then it will be fetched from the database directly. When properly initialized, reference objects can connect complex networks of objects such as petri-nets and AVL trees, even in cases where there exist circular references between objects of the network. These networks can be fetched, stored, and deleted from the system (database and memory) as a unit without special handling by application code. Unfortunately, the possibility of nonterminating structures that must be manually removed from memory does exist if all back-references have not been properly initialized. In practice, however, we have not found this to be an issue, even with highly convoluted structures. Application testing with some of the more sophisticated memory leak detection software currently available will easily identify such situations when they do occur. Caveat programmer!

Persistent Containers and Collections

Persistent objects can be containers of other persistent objects. If a container is deleted from the database, all attached objects that it owns must be deleted along with it (referential integrity—cascade delete). Additionally, if an owned object is removed from its container, it must be deleted when the owner is stored unless it is transferred to another container. An example of a C++ persistent container class might be:

```
// This is a version of a container class – details removed for
// brevity.
class MyContainerClass : public FwPersistObject {
private:
  FwOwnRef(OwnedClass) Attribute;   // Owned subobject
  FwRef(UnownedClass)  Other;       // Unowned subobject
  FwPersistDictionary  Collection; // Collection of subobjects
public:
  MyContainerClass() :
    Attribute(this),                    // Sets attribute owner
    Collection(this, "myCollection") {} // Sets collection owner and
                                        // name
};
```

When an object of MyContainerClass is deleted from the database, the object referenced by Attribute will be deleted with it automatically. Also, if the object Attribute refers to is removed from the reference or replaced with another instance, then it will also be deleted from the database when the container is stored again. This operation can conceivably cascade down through a very deep and complex object hierarchy. One of the jobs of the persistence library is to minimize the amount of work that the database does in order to perform this cleanup. No database-specific triggers need to be written, nor does application code have to deal with these referential integrity issues. These integrity constraints do not need to be addressed by the application developer, except to specify that the contained reference or collection of references is owned in the container's constructor (as shown in the preceding example).

Persistent collections express one-to-many (1-M) or many-to-many (N-M) relationships between the container and other classes. Classes that contain collections will have ancillary tables associated with them that contain the collection references or primitive objects. When such a container object is stored to the database, any changes to its collections are stored along with it; however, when fetching a container object, the application can specify whether to fetch the collections and subcomponents at that time. If the collections and subcomponents are not fetched with the container (lazy fetch), then they will only be fetched from the database when the application references them. This enhances the ability to tune an application for performance, by fetching only that data that the application actually needs for processing.

Storage Adaptors

FACTORYworks persistent objects really have no notion of database. Each class or class hierarchy can be assigned an object that we call a *storage adaptor*. Consider it a socket into which you plug your class and put objects in or get objects out. Similar to an object broker, it is an abstract base class used by persistent objects to store themselves when required. As such, it provides some general transactional semantics and methods to fetch/store persistent objects. At this time we have two storage adaptor classes that are used by FACTORYworks C++ clients and servers:

Database storage adaptor: talks to any relational database that we support.

Bus storage adaptor: talks to the next available application server.

This decoupling of object from actual storage mechanism is the fundamental means by which we can easily use alternative distribution mechanisms as required, such as CORBA [Mowbray-Zahavi 1995; Siegel 1996] or the Distributed Common Object Model (DCOM) [Sessions 1998; Orfali-Harkey 1998]. As long as we can get the persistent and transaction objects from client to server, then all application code remains unchanged and maintenance becomes much simpler.

Transactions

The persistence class library defines a set of transaction classes that allows clients and servers to coordinate operations on persistent data. Although not implemented presently, these transaction classes have been designed to support the use of an XA (X/Open Distributed Transaction Processing: The XA Specification) compliant distributed transaction coordinator for two-phase commitments of transactions that may involve multiple application servers.

From the client perspective there are two interfaces to FACTORYworks objects and services. The most common is an application-level transactional API, which is used mostly by non-C++ clients. It does not give the client direct access to the persistent objects themselves. These transaction objects are sent in their entirety to the appropriate application server for data validation and execution. All transactions execute atomically and will leave the database unaltered if there is a failure. C++ clients (currently on Unix only) can use the same interface to persistent objects as do the application servers, by manipulating the objects directly. The only difference between the client and the server then, is that the client will utilize a bus storage adaptor whereas the application server will use a database storage adaptor for storing objects. All class behavior remains the same in either case, allowing clients to perform extensive processing on persistent objects and only communicate to a server when it is ready to commit those changes to the database.

This last point implies an optimistic locking strategy. We have found that in the typical manufacturing system, most resources are utilized by one operator or operation at a time. It is unlikely that more than one operator will try to process a specific lot or utilize a particular piece of equipment simultaneously. This means that the use of an optimistic locking procedure can significantly improve system throughput and resource utilization. If a conflict does occur, our detection strategy—to validate a transaction sequence number associated with the object—will determine that an object has been updated, forcing the failing client to take appropriate recovery measures. An example of this may be that an operator is tracking a lot into a processing station while at the same time a manager in another part of the building wants to place that lot on hold for some reason. If the operator tracks the lot in first, the manager will be informed that the lot's state has changed (is now being processed). If appropriate, the manager can retry the hold, which will remove that lot from the dispatch list, keeping it from further processing until the hold is released.

Database Interface and SQL Generation

When utilizing a relational database for an object repository, several technical issues conspire to keep the system from performing as well as it can and to keep maintenance costs too high. These issues are database optimization and the mapping of classes and attributes to database tables and columns. By use of the class metadata we are able to automatically generate proper code for insert, update, and delete operations, as well as to optimize database access in a variety of ways. These optimizations can include performing multirow insert, update, and delete operations on objects that are stored in a common table. By traversing the list of all objects to be modified within a transaction, we group the modified objects by class and operation required, and then process them with as little Structured Query Language (SQL) as possible. If the database API supports it, we are able to cache parsed statements for standard insert, update, delete, and select statements, binding the variable data for an object just before telling the database to execute the operation. Fetches can return as many rows as is efficient to cache, further reducing the traffic between the application server and database.

By removing the SQL generation from the application developer's domain, we have been able to eliminate a large portion of the cost associated with maintenance of the database code. By isolating the database-specific operations to a small set of concrete classes, we are easily able to support multiple RDBMS products in a highly optimized way.

Application Core Classes

The FACTORYworks CORE is composed of two class libraries. They contain higher-level abstractions for application development, encapsulating Model/View/Controller relationships for user interface control, finite-state machines for complex logic handling, object version control, business rule definitions, and tools to support the generation and traversal of complex networks of objects. These classes have proven exceptionally stable over time and are utilized extensively by the application libraries to implement domain-specific behavior.

Enabling Classes

Object versioning

Collectors (object caching)

Finite-state machines

Network nodes and links

Walkers and filters (process networks of objects)

Domain and business rules

Domain attributes

GUI Classes

Utilization of these classes, either as base or concrete classes, helps maintain a consistent look and feel of application user interfaces.

Generic dialogs (confirm, input, warn, choose, inform)

Error dialogs

Asynchronous event notification dialogs

Object browsers

Business Rule Processing

In a manufacturing execution system, business rules may be applied at each step of the manufacturing process to enforce manufacturing policies or to trigger communications with enterprise applications such as inventory control or scheduling. In order to quickly and easily adapt to changing business requirements, the ability to express and apply business rules is critical. Without this facility, complex configuration parameters or a great deal of custom programming would be required to tailor the system to the needs of a particular installation.

Currently there are two methods to write and process rules. One is using CELLman, a multithreaded rule processing language that is part of CELLworks and runs on Unix hosts. The other is to use VisualBasic on Windows NT. Future plans include the ability to write rules in Java, storing the class byte code in the database, then execute the rule in either the application server or client process, whichever would be appropriate for a given rule. In any case, it is by a large measure the ability to modify the behavior of the system in significant ways by the implementation of custom business rules that has propelled the success of FACTORYworks.

8.3 Summary

We have done nothing revolutionary in the design and development of FACTORYworks. What we have done is to take fundamentally sound object-oriented design principles and our experience in the implementation and integration of large-scale, distributed manufacturing systems to build this framework. After five years of design, development, and refinement, FACTORYworks systems have been deployed at dozens of sites. Some of these sites have 500+ users and have run continuously for over 100 days with no downtime. The result of this effort is that new applications can be developed in a matter of weeks, not months or years, and then deployed into running systems without stopping work. Complex manufacturing systems can be integrated and deployed in a matter of weeks or months instead of years. Our goal for the year 2000 is to provide an MES framework that can be deployed in any semiconductor manufacturing plant in as little as one week, including the integration with all the manufacturing and material handling equipment. Only time will tell how successful we will be, but we have made major progress toward that end.

8.4 References

[Beck 1993] Beck, K. CRC: Finding Objects the Easy Way, *Object Magazine*, 3(4): 42-44, November/December 1993.

[Fayad 1997] Fayad, M.E., and D. Schmidt. Object-Oriented Application Frameworks, *Communications of the ACM*, 40(10), October 1997.

[Harel 1988] Harel, D. On Visual Formalisms, *Communications of the ACM*, 31(5), May 1988.

[Jacobson 1992] Jacobson, I., M. Christerson, O. Jonsson, and G. Övergaard. *Object-Oriented Software Engineering: A Use Case-Driven Approach.* Reading, MA: ACM Press, 1992.

[Mobray-Zahavi 1995] Mowbray, T.J., and R. Zahavi. *The Essential CORBA: Systems Integration Using Distributed Objects,* New York: John Wiley & Sons, 1995.

[OMG 1995] Object Management Group (OMG), *CORBA Specification.* New York: John Wiley & Sons, 1995.

[Orfali-Harkey 1998] Orfali, R., and D. Harkey. *Client/Server Programming with JAVA and CORBA.* Second Edition, New York: John Wiley & Sons, 1998.

[Rumbaugh 1991] Rumbaugh, J., M. Blaha, W. Premerlani, F. Eddy, and W. Lorensen. *Object-Oriented Modeling and Design.* Englewood Cliffs, NJ: Prentice Hall, 1991.

[Sessions 1998] Sessions, R. *COM and DCOM: Microsoft's Vision for Distributed Objects.* New York: John Wiley & Sons, 1998.

[Siegel 1996] Siegel, J. *CORBA: Fundamentals and Programming.* New York: John Wiley & Sons, 1996.

CHAPTER 9

Production Resource Manager (PRM) Framework

Developing manufacturing logistics decision support software has been a labor-intensive and costly endeavor. Except for the underlying solver software (such as linear-programming libraries, search engines based on genetic algorithms or simulated annealing, and constraint-based solvers), many applications have been developed as one-off solutions, with custom-written software for preparing input data, specifying modeling methods, and presenting results to the users.

This chapter describes the Production Resource Manager (PRM) framework, which encapsulates the systemic similarities among manufacturers and allows software developers to readily extend framework components into applications that address specific manufacturing requirements. The PRM framework contains frameworks that provide (1) rapid graphical user interface (GUI) development, (2) access to a variety of manufacturing information system data, (3) objects for representing manufacturing logistics problems, and (4) transformation objects for mapping manufacturing logistics problems to mathematical solution methods. This chapter describes the overall framework architecture, with an emphasis on important use cases [Jacobson 1992], responsibilities [Wirfs-Brock 1990], design patterns [Gamma 1995], and object class hierarchies. The PRM framework objects represent the manufacturing logistics domain and provide a reusable architecture for new application development. This allows developers to quickly write new applications with a proven base design. As a demonstration of the framework, this chapter also briefly describes the construction of two PRM applications.

The organization of this chapter is as follows. *Section 9.1* describes the manufacturing logistics domain and summarizes the design objectives of the PRM framework.

Section 9.2 presents the PRM framework architecture in terms of its frameworks and their relationships. *Section 9.3* discusses the Scenario and Solver subsystems. The Scenario framework contains objects that can be combined and configured to solve different manufacturing logistics problems. In our development efforts, two solvers were used: one based on a search heuristic, the other based on a linear programming model of manufacturing resource allocation. However, other solvers could be used with appropriate mapping between solver structures and the manufacturing objects in the framework. The Factory and Strategy patterns are used to create objects that take data from a variety of sources [Gamma 1995]. The Core framework contains a set of objects for capturing inputs, specifying the working problem, and maintaining previously obtained solutions. *Section 9.4* describes the Data Interface (DIF) framework, which uses the Bridge pattern to implement a reusable data interface to a variety of manufacturing information systems, such as MAPICS XA [MAPICS 1993] and SAP R3 [SAP 1994]. *Section 9.5* describes the interaction between the User Interface framework and the Scenario framework. *Section 9.6* describes the construction of two PRM applications: TIA (The Implosion Application) and CMRP (Capacitated Material Requirements Planning).

9.1 Domain Background and Framework Design Objectives

Manufacturing firms compete on the basis of cost, quality, and delivery. They are under constant pressure to deliver better quality products more quickly at lower cost. Manufacturing companies use a variety of software tools to improve the quality and speed with which decisions are made. In this section we briefly discuss MRP/MRP II environments and the limitations of some current practices. We describe a situation within IBM that led us to develop new models and software tools for manufacturing resource allocation. For a discussion of the underlying mathematics and the solution methods in PRM, see [Dietrich 1996a]. For a discussion of modeling and optimization techniques in manufacturing, see [Dietrich 1995].

9.1.1 Current Practice

Manufacturing logistics planning typically begins with a master production schedule (MPS), which specifies the amount of each product to produce in each period [Vollmann 1992]. The MPS reflects product demand, from forecasts and/or customer orders, as well as a high-level aggregate view of manufacturing constraints, such as production capacity. Then the material requirements planning (MRP) process uses the MPS, together with inventory data and detailed manufacturing bill-of-material information, to determine the time-phased requirements for raw materials. A capacity requirements planning (CRP) process may be used to determine detailed capacity requirements. Both MRP and CRP use an *explode and net* iterative logic to determine detailed requirements. A full explanation of these processes, as well as examples, can be found in [Vollmann 1992]; however, for the reader's convenience, the basic ideas are presented here.

A product's *bill of material* (BOM) can be thought of as a recipe for producing that product. For each part (raw material or subassembly) that is directly required to produce the product, the BOM specifies the number of units of that part required to make one unit of the product (*quantity-per*). It also specifies a time offset, indicating the time between the usage of that part and the completion of the production of the product. It is important to note that the BOM of a product specifies usage of a subassembly, but not the usage of the parts for the subassembly itself. Each product also has a *bill of capacity* (BOC) that specifies the capacity resources required to produce the product. The BOC includes quantity-per and offset data.

In MRP explode and net logic, one starts with a demand for a part, which specifies the number of units of that product required in a specific time period. First, any available inventory that could be used to meet this requirement is applied, and both the inventory data and the requirement quantity are updated (the netting step). Note that only inventory that is projected to be available on or earlier than the requirement date can be applied. If the part is a raw material (that is, it has no BOM) or is otherwise not manufacturable (for example, the demand period is within the required manufacturing lead time), then the remaining requirement is recorded as a net requirement. Otherwise, for each item on the product's BOM, the remaining product requirement is multiplied by the quantity-per, the usage period is computed by subtracting the offset from the product demand period, and the resulting quantity–time period pair is recorded. In addition, for each BOC entry, the capacity requirements are computed. These two calculations are called the *explode step.* Each of the newly computed part requirements is then netted and exploded, and the process continues. The result is a schedule of net material requirements. Net capacity requirements are computed by collecting the requirements for a given capacity in a given period and subtracting from that sum the quantity of that capacity available in that period. Note that capacity available in an earlier period cannot be used to meet a requirement in a later period. In practice, various ordering schemes are used to reduce the number of computations required.

Although MRP logic and CRP logic are fairly simple, the number of calculations required can be enormous. For this reason, until the 1990s MRP was typically a batch process, run on a regular *regeneration* schedule. With the increased computing power available in today's desktop machines, MRP and CRP can be run much more frequently.

One commonly cited shortcoming of both MRP and CRP is that neither process considers the availability of resources (material, capacity) to be constrained. They simply subtract the quantity that is available from the quantity that is required and generate a list of net requirements. The consideration of constraints is relegated to the master production scheduling (MPS) process, which must take into account "backlog, availability of material, availability of capacity, management policy, and goals" [Cox 1995], and resolve competing demands for limited resources. The MPS has often been identified as a critical but poorly addressed issue in manufacturing planning. Several data analysis tools are available to aid in this process. These tools identify each plan inconsistency (such as shortage), trace the requirements for a scarce resource to the higher-level assemblies that use it, and, through the use of MRP/CRP emulation, allow the planner to evaluate the quality of alternative plans. These tools are not truly schedulers because they are only capable of evaluating a proposed schedule. They cannot generate a feasible MPS, let alone determine a schedule that is both feasible and optimal with respect to economic factors.

9.1.2 Experience within IBM

In the late 1980s IBM used a planning process in which the master production schedule was composed at the corporate level and the MRP was done monthly in a single corporate-wide run. The corporate MRP system did not consider the availability of materials or the limited capacity at some of IBM's semiconductor plants. The IBM printed circuit card plant in Austin was experiencing shortages of components for Personal System/2 (PS/2) personal computer cards. Each scarce component was used in several different cards and each card was used in one or more PS/2 models. IBM's worldwide material planning process required the card plant to determine an availability schedule for PS/2 cards within a few days of receiving card requirements and component availability projections. The card volume planners had no tools, other than simple spreadsheets, to aid them in allocating the scarce components to cards.

The Enterprise Shortfall Implosion Tool (ESIT), which provided allocation capability, was implemented for Austin in 1990 [Dietrich 1996a]. The term *implosion* was used to convey the idea that this tool provided bottom-up planning, rather than the traditional top-down explosion-based planning used in MRP. ESIT took as input data the availability of scarce components, the card BOMs, and the demand for finished cards. It produced a production schedule for cards that could be produced with the available components. Components were allocated based either on card priority and due date or on economic data such as revenue and manufacturing cost, using either a priority-based critical ratio method [Dietrich 1996b] or linear programming [Dietrich 1997]. ESIT was implemented in the PL/I programming language on the Multiple Virtual Storage (MVS, a System/370 and System/390 operating system) with data interfaces to IBM's corporate planning systems. In addition to the implosion module, ESIT included an explosion module. The output of ESIT's implosion, a feasible committed schedule for finished PS/2 cards, was used at a corporate planning meeting to finalize the PS/2 box plan.

The ESIT tool was intended to run once, or perhaps twice, in each monthly planning cycle; however, planners in Austin quickly began exploring other uses for ESIT. The explosion module was used frequently for what-if analyses of changes in supply or demand. New output reports were created to provide additional decision support capability, such as reports on short components that showed the affected card volumes. More implosion-like problems surfaced in areas such as outsourcing of production and use of substitute parts.

Despite ESIT's success in Austin, corporate-wide rollout of ESIT was made difficult by differences between the sites' information systems and manufacturing policies. Adapting ESIT to address plants with multilevel build processes (for example, components to cards to computers) required significant modifications of the interfaces, the underlying mathematical models, and the implosion and explosion logic.

With the increased availability of Reduced Instruction Set Computer (RISC) workstations and optimization libraries specifically developed for them, it became clear that a change in development philosophy was needed. To fully realize the benefits of implosion, we found that two issues must be addressed. Our software must be easy to integrate with a wide variety of manufacturing information systems. In addition, since many manufacturing companies have unique environments and philosophies, developing and customizing different implosion applications must be easy.

The entire software system was redesigned using object technology. This new generation of implosion technology is architected to permit rapid development of customized applications by manufacturing software experts with limited mathematical modeling expertise. Implosion applications, ranging from final assembly scheduling to worldwide allocation of scarce components, have been deployed throughout IBM manufacturing, and the PRM software has been used to develop applications for some of IBM's customers.

9.2 Framework Architecture

Figure 9.1 shows a very general way of solving real-world problems using mathematical solvers. Using a two-step refinement process, real-world problems are transformed into mathematical models that can be solved to find solutions for the real-world problems. In the first step, the real world is modeled using domain-specific concepts. In the second step, this domain-specific model is transformed into a specific mathematical model such as a linear program or a general search problem. Once the mathematical model is solved, the inverse of step two transforms the result into a solution in the domain model and the inverse of step one transforms it into a solution in the real world. Corresponding to steps one and two are two steps in which information in the

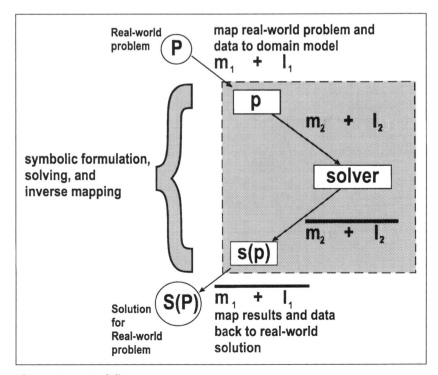

Figure 9.1 Modeling process.

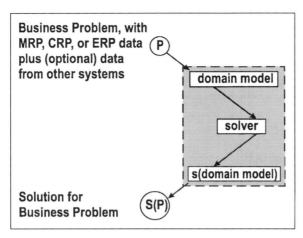

Figure 9.2 Manufacturing logistics modeling process.

real world is transformed into data in the domain-specific model and then transformed into data in the mathematical model, such as constraint coefficients or bounds on decision variables. The solver's result must also be transformed into information that can be used in the real world. These transformations can be quite complicated, depending on both the overall problem being solved and the manner in which the solver is used (for example, to solve a single problem or a series of related problems).

Figure 9.2 shows this metamodel applied to manufacturing logistics decision support. The data in the MRP, CRP, or ERP[1] is the real-world data,[2] the problem is a business problem that uses the MRP/CRP/ERP data and possibly other data, and the domain has been restricted to manufacturing logistics. The PRM framework supports this metamodel by providing frameworks for representing the manufacturing domain and for transforming data as it enters and leaves the framework. As Figure 9.3 shows, the PRM framework uses a solver subsystem and consists of several frameworks, some of which are nested. The PRM framework contains two top-level frameworks: the Data Interface framework and the Scenario framework. The Data Interface framework is responsible for providing an interface to the manufacturing information system that is the same regardless of which manufacturing information system is being used. It isolates the rest of the PRM framework from the peculiarities of a specific manufacturing information system.

The Scenario framework is a layered system that consists of three frameworks: the Core framework, the Application framework, and the User Interface framework. The Core framework provides the lowest-level domain-specific classes in the PRM framework. These consist of the fundamental objects in the domain, specialized collections of fundamental objects, objects that wrap [Dietrich 1993] the solver, and objects that

---

[1]ERP (enterprise resource planning) systems generally provide MRP and CRP functionality and also support many other business processes, such as payroll and accounting.

[2]Although the fidelity between the data in a manufacturing information system and the real world varies, our goal is to help manufacturers make the best decisions possible using the data they already maintain.

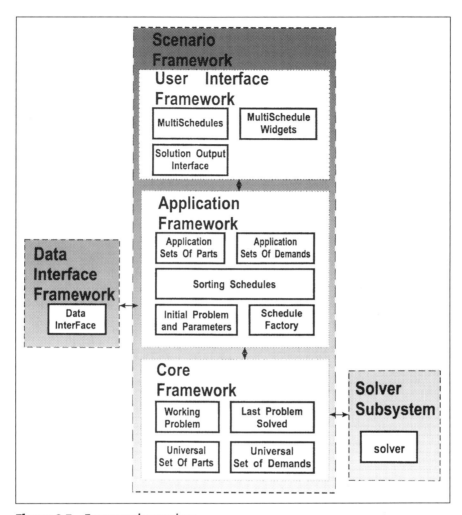

Figure 9.3 Framework overview.

cache data that will be sent to the solver. The fundamental objects in the domain include materials, capacities, and demands. Because of the multiperiod nature of the problems addressed by the framework, calendars are also fundamental, as are vectors that associate quantities with subperiods in the calendars. The Application framework is responsible for representing the domain-specific model of the problem being solved. It contains classes that represent attributes of the capacities, materials, and demands that are relevant to the problem being solved (such as quantity-required or quantity-available). It also contains classes that can be used to combine the attributes in various ways. Classes that transform these attributes to and from data in the solver are also part of the Application framework. This framework also contains classes that automate the construction of application-level algorithms (such as a state diagram class for applications that do multiple implosions to solve a problem). The User Interface framework supports the development of both interactive, graphical user interfaces and batch-, file-, or database-oriented user interfaces. It has facilities for combining, sorting, and filtering data in the Application framework so that the development of user interfaces is simpler. The User Interface framework is designed to be used in conjunction with GUI-builders for interactive applications.

The PRM framework depends on a solver subsystem. The current PRM solver subsystem, the PRM Implosion Engine, is a layered object-oriented system [Dietrich 1996a]. Because the Implosion Engine started out as a C program and continues to be used in non-object-oriented-systems, it is accessed through a procedural application programming interface (API).

9.3 Scenario Framework

The most important class in the PRM framework is the Scenario class. It provides the glue that makes everything else work together. As shown in Figure 9.2, for any tractable real-world problem there is a domain model that represents the problem and its solution. The Scenario classes are responsible for (1) representing the domain model, (2) populating the domain model with data from the real world, (3) transforming the domain model to and from the mathematical model and invoking a solver, and (4) providing a mapping back to the real world. These responsibilities are fulfilled with the help of other classes. Generally, each problem has its own Scenario subclass. Two very similar problems might use the same Scenario subclass, but that would be unusual. Generally, each problem should have its own Scenario subclass. Reuse is achieved because many of the classes that are used by Scenario subclasses apply to many different problems. Each Scenario instance represents one instance of a problem and its data. The Scenario framework contains a low-level framework called the Core framework and higher-level frameworks called the Application framework and the User Interface framework.

9.3.1 Core Framework

The Core framework contains fundamental classes in the manufacturing domain, such as Capacities, Materials, and Demands (sales orders and forecasts), and classes that wrap the solver and cache data that will be sent to the solver. Capacities and Materials are represented by objects called Parts. Customer orders and forecasts are represented by objects called Demands. Every instance of a Demand or Part, whether it is used by the solver or not, is in the UniversalSetOfDemands (USOD) or UniversalSetOfParts (USOP), respectively. The most interesting classes in the Core framework are the LastProblemSolved (LPS) and WorkingProblem (WIP) classes.

The LPS class provides a wrapper [Dietrich 1993] for the Solver subsystem. In other words, it provides an object-oriented interface to the Solver subsystem. It represents the last set of inputs that was given to the solver (the *problem instance*) and the last solution generated by the solver. Because it represents both the problem instance and the solution, it allows clients to see a consistent picture of the model. The WIP class allows new instances of problems to be created, generally by editing existing ones. This capability is particularly useful for what-if analysis in which, for example, supply of a raw material is increased. It represents the original input to the solver and all changes made to that input. The LPS and WIP classes work together. When a client of the WIP class asks for problem data that hasn't been changed, the WIP class gets it from the LPS class. When a new solution is needed, the LPS class gets all of the changes from the WIP class, puts them into the Solver subsystem, and invokes the solver to get a new solution. Because the WIP class is closely related to the LPS class, the WIP class provides the same level of abstraction that the LPS class provides.

Because of the multiperiod nature of manufacturing logistics problems, the Core framework also has Calendar and TimeVec classes. Calendar represents the time interval being considered and the number of subperiods in the problem. TimeVec represents a vector of floating-point numbers with one number for each subperiod in the problem. For example, an inventory TimeVec would represent the amount of inventory available in each time period.

9.3.2 Application Framework

The classes in the Application framework provide a higher level of abstraction than those in the Core framework. These classes help the Scenario class represent the domain model of the manufacturing logistics problem.

Many Scenario subclasses need proper subsets of the parts and demands contained in the UniversalSetOfParts and UniversalSetOfDemands instances, so there are ApplicationSetOfParts (ASOP) and ApplicationSetOfDemands (ASOD) classes that may be contained in each Scenario instance. For example, an ASOD instance might contain all of the demands from preferred customers.

When a Scenario instance is created, the domain model and the solver model must be populated. This is the responsibility of the InitialProblemAndParameters (IPP) class. The IPP uses the DIF framework to get data and put it into both the domain model and the solver model. IPP is designed as a base class. When writing an application to solve a manufacturing problem, an application developer derives from the IPP class an application-specific IPP class. Application-specific IPP classes interact with the DIF framework to populate LPS, USOD, and USOP objects with manufacturing data through a feedInto method. Besides populating objects in the Core framework, the IPP class is also responsible for initializing any other objects the Scenario object needs.

Schedule Framework

In the Manufacturing Logistics domain, a spreadsheet view of part and demand data is a very powerful mechanism for representing time-phased data and is preferred by many users. In this view, each column corresponds to one time period and each row corresponds to a part or demand. For example, the planned inventory in a factory is a table containing the volume of each part in each time period. See Table 9.1, which contains data representing supply volumes. Because this view of the data is powerful for users (such as planners, materials managers, and customer representatives) and is used in many manufacturing information systems and decision support algorithms, the PRM framework provides a flexible Schedule framework for manipulating and viewing part or demand attributes.

Table 9.1   Tabular Representation of Sample Schedule

PART #	VOLUMES/TIME PERIOD						
6042977	10	10	10	15	15	20	20
32G3917	5	15	10	15	10	0	0
92G7235	0	0	20	20	15	10	6
04H6922	50	75	40	50	80	95	100

The base class in the Schedule framework is the Schedule class, which consists of ItemTimeVec instances. Operations on schedules include insertion, array subscripting, and value retrieval based on Item. To support application development, the Schedule framework must provide more functionality. For instance, a PRM application might need a schedule called SortedPartInventorySchedule, which is sorted by part name and contains the supply quantity for each part that has nonzero inventories. To provide this functionality, the framework has a SortingSchedule (SortSchedule) class that contains a representation of the attribute definitions, the sorting criteria, and the filtering criteria for the schedule. See Figure 9.4. To make this representation flexible with respect to these definitions and criteria, the Schedule framework makes heavy use of the Strategy pattern [Gamma 1995]. The Schedule framework has an AttributeStrategy class hierarchy, which implements attribute definition strategies for accessing and updating a variety of attributes such as demand volume, shipment volume, backlog volume, supply volume, and shortage volume. The AttributeStrategy class hierarchy also contains classes that allow new schedules to be constructed from existing ones. For example, there are AttributeStrategy classes that allow one to subtract two schedules or to sum each row of a schedule. The framework also has a PairCompareStrategy class hierarchy, which provides sort criteria such as part name or TimeVec quantity. The framework also has a FilterStrategy class hierarchy, which provides a variety of selection criteria such as *nonzero* TimeVec objects and regular expression matching. The SortSchedule class contains optional references to instances of the aforementioned Strategy objects. To make a SortedPartInventorySchedule, one instantiates a SortSchedule object and associates the object with the SupplyVolumeAttributeStrategy, the NamePairCompareStrategy, and the NonZeroTimeVecFilterStrategy.

A wide variety of schedules can be created by combining instances of AttributeStrategy, PairCompareStrategy, and FilterStrategy. To encapsulate the knowledge needed to make schedules (and simplify the use of the Schedule framework), there is a ScheduleFactory class that has methods that take a ScheduleDescriptor and return a SortSchedule that uses the appropriate strategies. To make the aforementioned SortedPartInventorySchedule, one only has to call the ScheduleFactory's newPartSchedule method with the instance of ScheduleDescriptor named SortedPartInventorySchedule. When the SortedPartInventorySchedule is made, it is populated with supply volumes that are taken from the WIP object. If a supply volume in the WIP object changes, the data in the SortedPartInventorySchedule should change, too. The Subscription mechanism is used to do this.

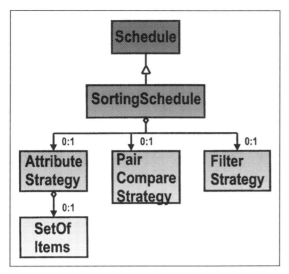

Figure 9.4 Schedule framework class diagram.

9.3.3 The Subscription Mechanism

The Subscription mechanism provides the dynamic update mechanisms necessary to keep schedule objects up to date when problem-related data changes (either the user changes an input quantity or the solver creates a new result). Any class in the framework that has values that may change dynamically (based on the values in other objects) inherits from the Subscription class. Figure 9.5 shows an example of a simulation triggered update. The object at the head of each arrow subscribes to the object at the tail of the arrow. After the LPS calls the Solver's implode function, a series of notifications occurs. These notifications cause the changes in the LPS to propagate through the objects on the left side of the figure all the way to the MultiSchedule object. After the LPS calls the solver to calculate a new implosion result, the following events occur: 1) The presence of new data in the LPS object triggers an update in the Implode object; 2) changes in the Implode object trigger an update in the AttributeStrategy object; 3) changes in the AttributeStrategy object trigger an update in the SortSchedule object; 4) changes in the SortSchedule object trigger an update in the MultiSchedule object. A similar sequence occurs after the LPS calls the Solver's explode function.

The Subscription base class is implemented using a modified Observer pattern [Gamma 1995], as shown in Figure 9.6. The modification is necessary to allow an object to act both as observer and subject. For example, a SortSchedule object can be an observer of an Implode object and the subject of a ScheduleSensitiveStrategy object.

When a subject's state changes, the observers must be informed. Doing this efficiently is a nontrivial problem because classes in the Schedule framework allow many-to-many relationships between subjects and observers. See [Alpern 1990] for a discussion of this problem and good solutions.

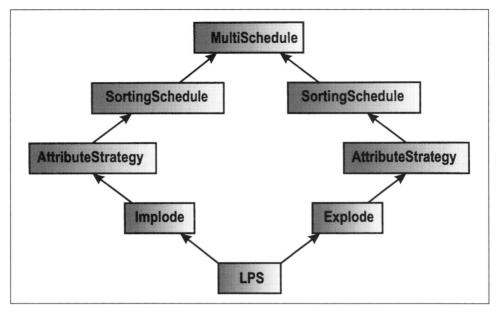

Figure 9.5   Subscription chain.

9.3.4 Class Hierarchy for Scenario and Related Classes

Each application is built by using some parts of the framework as components and by creating subclasses of other parts of the framework. The SortSchedule class is an example of a component, while the ScheduleFactory class is an example of a base class. As shown in Figure 9.7, each application (with the exception of TIA) has its own subclass of Scenario, InitialProblemAndParameters, and ScheduleFactory. (TIA uses Scenario, IniInitialProblemAndParameters, and ScheduleFactory without subclassing them.) Because it is difficult to create and initialize Scenario framework objects correctly using

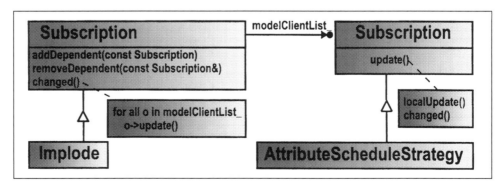

Figure 9.6   Modified Observer pattern.

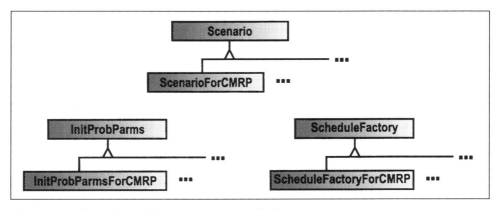

Figure 9.7 Class hierarchies that vary by application.

constructors alone, the Builder and Abstract Factory patterns are used to instantiate all of the objects in the Core framework and the Application framework, and to establish the relationship between these objects.

9.4 Data Interface Framework

As mentioned earlier, many different manufacturing applications can be developed using the PRM framework. Most manufacturing companies use either in-house or commercial MRP/CRP/ERP systems (hereafter referred to as *manufacturing information systems*) regularly to plan and track their production. These companies have made large investments in building or acquiring these systems and keeping the data in them up to date. PRM must access data in these systems and must sometimes access data from multiple systems for a single application.

9.4.1 Design Criteria

Because many different manufacturing information systems are in use, the Data Interface framework should allow the rest of PRM to access data the same way from any manufacturing information system. For example, the Application framework should be able to use exactly the same method and parameters to read in supply volumes whether the data is coming from R3 or Trident (two ERP systems). In addition, it should be easy to extend the DIF framework to support new manufacturing information systems. Since a wide variety of applications can be written using PRM and it is impossible to anticipate the information that will be required by a new application, it should be easy to extend the DIF framework to support new attributes.

In addition to the primary requirements previously described, there are two secondary requirements. It should be possible to use the DIF framework without using the rest of PRM (to maximize code reuse) and it should be possible to implement interfaces to manufacturing information systems without requiring a specific programming language. Using the DIF framework without the rest of PRM allows one to build manufacturing logistics applications that do not require solvers (for example, reporting and alerts) or that use solvers other than our implosion solvers. Permitting the use of different languages provides flexibility in the implementations and maximizes the pool of developers available.

9.4.2 Design Alternatives

There are many alternative approaches that could be used to implement the DIF framework. One straightforward approach is to use simple inheritance. With this approach, an abstract class is used to define the interface and a different concrete subclass interfaces to each manufacturing information system. This would be difficult to modify and extend. Another approach is to use double dispatching, but this is not extensible enough either.

Satisfying the design criteria requires a design that decouples interface from implementation, provides extensibility, and hides the details of the manufacturing information systems. The Bridge pattern does this, but it does not provide an obvious way to add new attributes and allow implementations to be written in any language [Gamma 1995]. Satisfying those requirements requires invention.

9.4.3 DIF Framework Design

Figure 9.8 shows the basic design. Two main classes are defined in this structure: DataInterface (DIF) and DataInterfaceImplementation (DifImp). The DIF class uses the DifImp class to access data. DIF is the abstract base class that provides the interface between manufacturing information systems and applications. The detailed implementation is defined in the DifImp class, which is hidden from application developers. DIF clients use the Attribute method to access data in the manufacturing information systems.

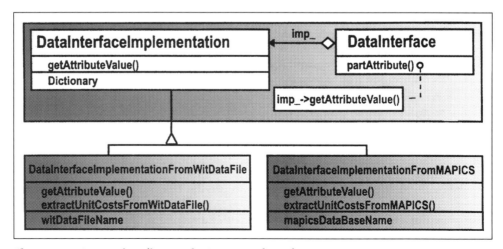

Figure 9.8   Interaction diagram for Data Interface classes.

Although the DIF framework is separated from its clients (for example, the Scenario framework), the DIF framework calls client methods to create parts and demands and to access calendar information. If the DIF framework called the Scenario framework methods directly, it would be impossible to use the DIF framework with non-PRM applications, limiting reusability. This problem can be solved by using the Bridge pattern a second time, but an important aspect of good pattern usage is to use them only when needed. Instead, we solve this problem by simply using inheritance. As shown in Figure 9.9, the DataInterfaceEssentials class provides all of the Scenario objects that the DIF framework needs.

As shown in Figure 9.8, the DIF instance uses a DifImp instance to access a manufacturing information system. The attribute the client is accessing is passed to the DIF instance and the DifImp instance uses a table (see Table 9.2) to look up a function that will access that attribute in the manufacturing information system.

This design provides significant flexibility in that: (1) New attributes can be added easily, (2) clients of DIF can find out what attributes are supported by a given DifImp, and (3) the DifImp programmers can write all of the access functions in any language that can be called from C. This last feature is important when accessing legacy systems. This design also provides a lot of reusability. (1) When writing PRM applications for a manufacturing information system that is only slightly different from a previously used system, most of the same functions can be reused. This situation occurs when a company installs a given manufacturing information system at several sites, with minor, unique customization at each site. (2) Access functions from multiple DifImps can be

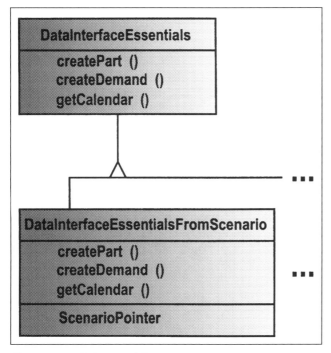

Figure 9.9   DIF essentials.

Table 9.2 Part of the DifImp Table for Demand Information

ATTRIBUTE	POINTER TO FUNCTION
Demand Quantity	GetDemandQuantity( )
Priority	GetDemandPriority( )
Revenue	GetDemandRevenue( )

mixed and matched to create DifImps for hybrid manufacturing information systems. Such hybrid information systems occur when manufacturers want to use best-of-breed systems or when they are moving from legacy information systems to new ones.

9.4.4 Data Interface Framework Summary

In general, application developers only need to instantiate the DIF and DifImp base classes. In addition, the general attribute table mechanism provided in the generic DifImp base class is flexible and powerful enough for most manufacturing information systems and most applications. When more flexibility is needed, subclasses can be derived for either or both of these classes.

Overall, the DIF framework is a flexible, modifiable, extendible, and reusable framework with the following features:

- It grants the customer total control to manage the data access methodology and allows easy integration with other parts of PRM.

- It allows the DIF framework design and implementation to be reused with both PRM and non-PRM applications.

- It allows one application to access a variety of manufacturing information systems without changing or recompiling the application code and even allows runtime substitution of data access functions using the flexible attribute table managing mechanism.

9.5 User Interface Framework

The User Interface framework supports the development and implementation of user interfaces for batch and interactive applications. Because the domain model and solver interface logic is implemented in the Scenario framework, user interface developers can concentrate on usability and human factors. The User Interface framework contains a class for saving data in flat files and a hierarchy of classes for displaying or saving attributes grouped by part or demand.

A MultiSchedule contains one or more sets of related schedules. For example, a Part-MultiSchedule might contain all parts needed by a specified assembly and for each part might include the attributes for quantity available per period and quantity consumed per period. See Table 9.3, which shows two parts' supply and usage volumes. The Multi-Schedule class makes it easier to use the information stored in schedules by combining

Table 9.3   Tabular Representation of Sample MultiSchedule

PART #	VOLUME ATTRIBUTES	QUANTITY AVAILABLE/ CONSUMED PER PERIOD						
6042977	Supply Volume	10	10	10	15	15	20	20
	Usage Volume	5	10	15	15	10	10	10
32G3917	Supply Volume	5	15	10	15	10	0	0
	Usage Volume	5	15	10	15	10	0	0

schedules in different ways. The MultiSchedule class contains a set of schedules. Due to the large volumes of data that planners must deal with, the MultiSchedule class supports sorted and filtered views of the data. Schedules in a MultiSchedule can be chosen to be *selection schedules* (used for filtering out uninteresting data) and *order schedules* (used for sorting by part name, demand name, quantity, shortage, and so on). Multi-Schedule provides iterators that can traverse by item (for each item, iterate over all the attributes) and by attribute (for each attribute, iterate over all the items).

The MultiScheduleWidget (MSWidget) collaborates with the MultiSchedule to provide GUI support for PRM applications. In this collaboration, the MSWidget is responsible for managing and updating the display of the data, and the MultiSchedule is responsible for sorting, filtering, and generally managing the schedules that are displayed.

9.6 Two PRM Applications

Several applications have been written using the PRM framework, and they interface to a variety of manufacturing information systems. The Implosion Application (TIA) is the simplest application and is used to demonstrate the Implosion Engine and prototype new models. Capacitated MRP (CMRP) is used by master production schedulers and materials managers to plan production and purchasing. Other applications have been written for scheduling daily production, reducing inventories, and giving customers optimal ship-date quotes [Dietrich 1996a].

9.6.1 The Implosion Application

TIA was written after two other applications, because analysts needed an easy way to experiment with Implosion Engine models and data. TIA solves the basic implosion problem described in *Section 9.1*; that is, it takes as input supply, demand, and BOM data and produces a feasible master production schedule using one of the two implosion solvers. The domain model (see Figure 9.2) in TIA is exactly the same as the solver model, which is not surprising considering that the solvers were designed to solve this basic implosion problem. Although most applications require subclasses of Scenario, IPP, and ScheduleFactory, TIA uses them directly.

Except for new subclasses for the Builder and Abstract Factory patterns that control Scenario initialization [Gamma 1995], most of the new code in TIA was GUI code. The MSWidget classes were reused without change. Most of the development effort was spent with users, deciding what Implosion Engine options to expose through the GUI, what schedules to display, how many MSWidgets to display, and how to subdivide the data. TIA development required less than two person-weeks.

9.6.2 The CMRP Application

The CMRP application is used by procurement planners when the availability of either manufacturing capacity or some purchased materials is constrained. Standard planning methods can generate purchase orders that exceed known availability limits. Furthermore, if the materials that are readily available are purchased without regard to the availability of the short materials, then large inventories of unusable parts can be created. By producing an MPS that respects capacity and material availability limits, the CMRP application generates purchase orders for unconstrained materials so that those materials arrive just in time for use.

Using either demand priorities or economic factors to drive the resource allocation decisions, CMRP quickly calculates a feasible, optimal MPS, which accounts for availability of constrained materials, procurement lead times of unconstrained materials, manufacturing capacity, and demand. It determines a procurement plan for each unconstrained material and identifies the most critical resources. This schedule can be viewed with CMRP's GUI, which allows the user to perform what-if analyses. Figure 9.10 shows the CMRP screen with two of the MultiSchedule widgets iconified (minimized).

Developing the Application

Once the initial requirements were known, a model of the problem was defined. A transformation was developed to map this model to and from the solver. The data elements that were not in traditional manufacturing information systems, such as the

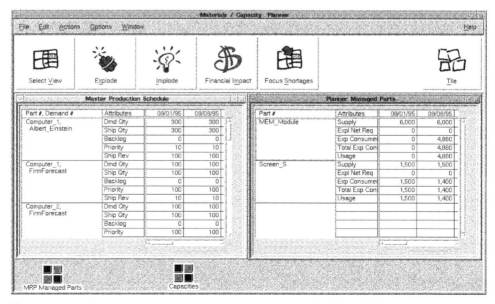

Figure 9.10   CMRP screen.

attribute *constrained* associated with parts, were defined. The general appearance of the GUI was described and the multischedules that would be used were specified.

The model of the problem was defined mathematically and was implemented by a new subclass of Scenario called ScenarioForCMRP. This subclass contained Application-SetOfParts (ASOP) instances for capacities, constrained parts, and unconstrained parts. A new subclass of InitialProblemAndParameters implemented the mapping to the solver. This subclass got data from the DIF framework. It used the LastProblemSolved class to populate the solver's internal model. It also initialized the ASOP instances.

A new subclass of ScheduleFactory implemented the mapping back to the domain model. ScheduleFactoryForCMRP reused many existing attribute, sort, and filter strategies (such as supply volume, part name pair-compare, and zero-time-vector filter). The reason so many strategies were reused was that ScheduleFactoryForCMRP associated the right instance of ASOP with each schedule. For example, the schedule for Constrained Part Supply Volume was constructed by reusing SupplyVolumeAttributeStrategy in a schedule that used the constrain*ed* ASOP.

The GUI used MSWidget instances for the MPS, Capacity, Constrained Parts, and Unconstrained Parts windows. The GUI used the ScheduleFactoryForCMRP class to insert CMRP-specific schedules into the appropriate MultiSchedule instances. For example, the GUI inserted the Constrained Part Supply Volume schedule into the Constrained Parts MSWidget.

The vast majority of the application logic was put into the Application framework and was simply triggered by the GUI. For example, when the user clicked on the Implode button (the light bulb button), the GUI called the ScenarioForCMRP class's implode method. The implode method caused the solver to compute a solution that took all constraints into account. Then the Subscription mechanism caused the output schedules and the multischedules to update themselves automatically. When the implode method returned, the GUI updated the data on the screen.

9.7 Summary

The design concepts that made the PRM framework successful are the following. The data interface classes separate the I/O from the problem being solved so that any application can be used at different sites by only replacing the data interface implementation classes. It also allows a site to use many applications via only one set of databases and one data interface implementation. The scenario architecture handles the transformation to and from the manufacturing logistics domain to the mathematical one. The spreadsheet/tabular GUI has proven to be flexible for developers and comfortable and intuitive for end users.

We made heavy use of use cases for analysis, responsibility-driven design for high-level design, and design patterns for detailed design. They aided both our thought processes and our intrateam communication. We found that using spiral development with heavy user involvement was essential.

A variety of applications have been written using the PRM framework. The framework's performance overhead is low. The DIF framework has allowed us to use data from a variety of sources. The Scenario structure supports the reuse of a fundamental design by many applications. The PRM framework has successfully met its objective.

9.8 References

[Alpern 1990] Alpern, B., R. Hoover, B. Rosen, P. Sweeny, and K. Zadeck. Incremental evaluation of computational circuits. *Proceedings of First Annual ACM-SIAM Symposium on Discrete Algorithms,* San Francisco, CA, January 22–24. Society for Industrial and Applied Mathematics, 1990, pp. 32–42.

[Cox 1995] Cox, James F., III, John H. Blackstone Jr., and Michael S. Spencer. *The APICS Dictionary, 8th edition.* Falls Church, VA: American Production and Inventory Control Society, 1995.

[Dietrich 1993] Dietrich, Walter C., Jr., Lee R. Nackman, and Franklin Gracer. Saving a legacy with objects. In *Software Reengineering,* Robert S. Arnold, editor. Los Alamitos, CA: IEEE Computer Society Press. Originally published in *Proceedings of OOPSLA 1989,* ACM Press, 1993, pp. 77–83.

[Dietrich 1995] Dietrich, Brenda, Tom Ervolina, and Robin Lougee-Heimer. Mathematical modeling and optimization techniques in manufacturing—it's not your father's computing environment. *APICS 1995 Conference Proceedings,* Orlando, FL. American Production and Inventory Control Society, 1995, pp. 56–61.

[Dietrich 1996a] Dietrich, Brenda. Applications of implosion in manufacturing. *IBM Technical Research Report RC 20389.* Yorktown Heights, NY: IBM TJ Watson Research Center, 1996. This can be found at http://domino.watson.ibm.com/library/CyberDig.nsf/Home/; search for the keyword *Dietrich.*

[Dietrich 1996b] Dietrich, Brenda L, and Robert J. Wittrock. *Allocation Method for Generating a Production Schedule.* U.S. patent number 5,548,518. Filed May 31, 1994, issued August 20, 1996. To see U.S. patents issued since January 5, 1971, go to www.patents.ibm.com.

[Dietrich 1997] Dietrich, Brenda L., and Robert J. Wittrock. *Optimization of Manufacturing Resource Planning.* U.S. patent number 5,630,070. Filed August 16, 1993, issued May 13, 1997.

[Gamma 1995] Gamma, Erich, Richard Helm, Ralph Johnson, and John Vlissides. *Design Patterns: Elements of Reusable Object-Oriented Software.* Reading, MA: Addison-Wesley, 1995.

[Jacobson 1992] Jacobson, Ivar, Magnus Christerson, Patrik Jonsson, and Gunnar Oevergaard. *Object-Oriented Software Engineering, A Use Case Driven Approach.* Wokingham, England: Addison-Wesley, 1992.

[MAPICS 1993] MAPICS. *AS/400 Manufacturing Accounting and Production Information Control System Extended Advantage (MAPICS XA) Master Production Schedule Planning User's Guide.* Atlanta, GA: MAPICS, Inc, 1993.

[SAP 1994] SAP. *SAP R/3 System Architecture (BC010).* Walldorf, Germany: SAP AG, 1994.

[Vollmann 1992] Vollmann, T.E., W.L. Berry, and D.C. Whybark. *Manufacturing Planning and Control Systems, 3rd edition.* Boston: Richard D. Irwin, Inc, 1992.

[Wirfs-Brock 1990] Wirfs-Brock, Rebecca, Brian Wilkerson, and Lauren Wiener. *Designing Object-Oriented Software.* Englewood Cliffs, NJ: Prentice Hall, 1990.

CHAPTER 10

Developing Domain Frameworks

The software industry recognizes the benefit of object-oriented technology [Fayad 1997; Gamma 1995; Izygon 1996] and domain engineering [Orfali 1996; Rumbaugh 1991; Wilkinson 1995]; however, current object-oriented technology methods do not aim at large-scale reuse, and domain engineering methods are not based on object advantages. It is a challenge for many software engineers to apply both technologies to develop reusable software effectively. A formal process needs to be defined. This chapter discusses extending formally defined object-oriented analysis and design methods with domain engineering concepts to define the object-oriented domain engineering (OODE) method [Chan 1998c; Coad 1995] for domain application framework development [Schmid 1996]. The OODE development cycle, processes, and deliverables will be discussed. The chapter also presents a case study of OODE [Chan 1997a, 1997b, 1998a, 1998b] for the Process Monitoring and Diagnosis (PM&D) domain.

10.1 Object-Oriented Domain Engineering (OODE) Method

OODE is one of the two life cycles in a dual life cycle software development method. The OODE life cycle consists of three phases: object-oriented domain analysis (OODA), object-oriented domain design (OODD), and object-oriented domain engineering delivery (OODED). These phases run in parallel with the application engineering life cycle. Figure 10.1 shows the interrelations, including feedback loops, between the OODE and application engineering life cycles.

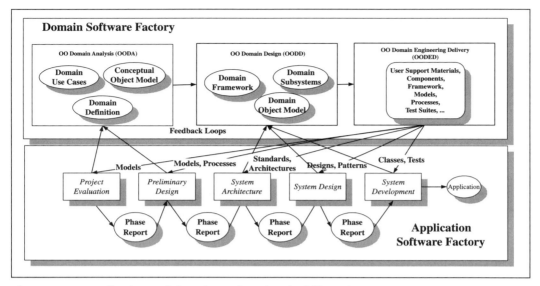

Figure 10.1   Application and domain engineering dual life cycles.

In reality, OODE is a spiral method (see Figure 10.2) because the same deliverables are improved throughout the life cycle. The OODE spiral carries out design and test tasks iteratively and incrementally. For example, the domain object model is created from the domain use cases and they are validated against each other. As the domain object model uncovers deficiencies, improvements to the domain use cases take place. Analysis and design patterns [Kang 1990] are used to generalize the model by replacing application-specific classes. The domain use cases are brought in again for validation. Triggers move the method from phase to phase.

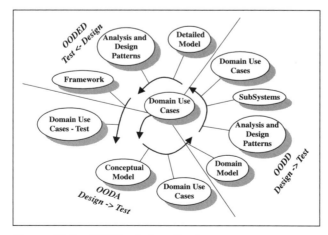

Figure 10.2   OODE spiral method.

10.1.1 Object-Oriented Domain Analysis (OODA) Phase

OODA is the first phase of OODE. OODE is derived from several object-oriented methodologies [Tansley 1993], but it differs from them in terms of the analysis deliverables produced. Object-oriented analysis creates use cases [Tansley 1993] and an object model, which span one application. OODA creates a generic domain object model and domain use cases, which span multiple domain applications as well as the domain through time. Figure 10.3 shows the OODA process in terms of its deliverables and information flow.

Selection Criteria

Selection of an appropriate domain is critical to the success of an OODE project. The key business criterion is whether multiple applications will be built in the domain. In this case, OODE confers strategic business advantages of decreased application development time, higher quality, and lower cost. For the Process Monitoring and Diagnosis (PM&D) domain, the main selection criterion was a business case for multiple applications in the domain.

Survey of Existing Domain Systems

The survey lays the foundation for acquisition of knowledge about the domain. In it, domain practitioners capture each domain system's external actors, business processes, and models. The practice of OODE relies on knowledge acquisition to define and document a domain. To improve knowledge acquisition, knowledge acquisition and design structure [Jacobson 1992] techniques were applied using cognitive models and problem-solving templates. Problem-solving templates illustrate the reasoning pattern that underlies a domain business process.

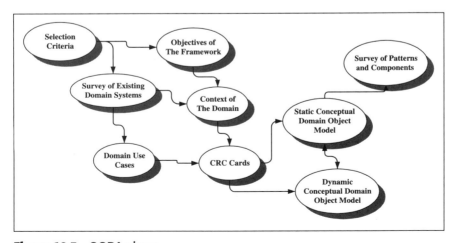

Figure 10.3 OODA phase.

Domain Definition

The domain definition scopes the domain in terms of its logical boundary, its actors, its events, and the interfaces between it and other domains. Figure 10.4 shows the PM&D domain boundary and its interfaces with two other domains. Actors and events may appear in several domains, but the combination of an event and an actor is unique. These define the domain's boundary.

Domain Use Cases

The domain use cases are one of the fundamental deliverables of the OODE life cycle. They are abstract business process descriptions that apply to an entire domain rather than to a specific application. They are developed from knowledge gathered from end users, domain subject matter experts, and domain developers. To supplement knowledge acquisition, application-specific use cases and other project documents are used. Once created, the domain use cases drive the production of the class responsibility collaborator (CRC) cards and then the conceptual domain object models. They are refined and updated during the OODE process to reflect new information and validate the models as they evolve.

Static and Dynamic Conceptual Domain Object Models

The static conceptual domain object model graphically shows inheritance and composition relations among the domain classes. Figure 10.5 is an example from the PM&D domain. The static conceptual domain object model is the basis for identifying patterns in the model and for aggregating classes into subsystems. For example, using structure

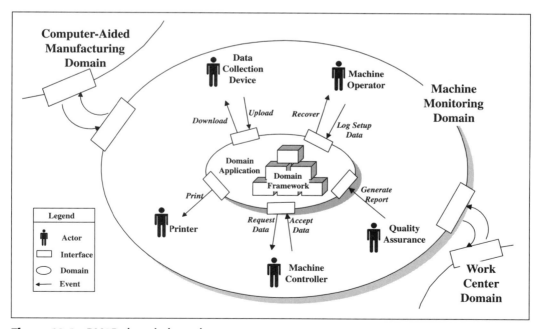

Figure 10.4   PM&D domain boundary.

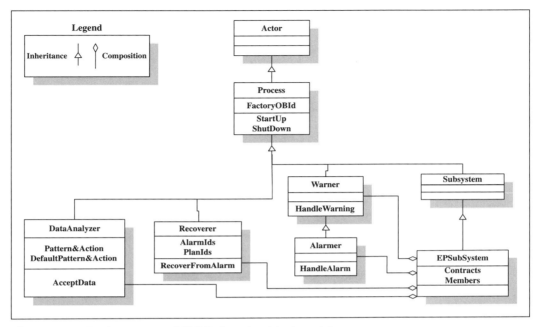

Figure 10.5   Static conceptual PM&D domain object model.

as Gamma [Kang 1990] defines the term, the Subsystem class in the model can be replaced with the generic Mediator pattern.

The dynamic conceptual object model shows events, collaboration, and time relationships among objects over the course of a domain use case. This model demonstrates whether all responsibilities have been allocated to classes and well distributed among them. If events flow repeatedly back and forth through a model, then responsibilities are poorly distributed. If there is very limited event flow then collaboration has not been well designed.

Summary of OODA Deliverables

The OODA phase has four key deliverables: (1) the domain use cases, (2) the definition of the domain, (3) the static conceptual domain object model, and (4) the dynamic conceptual domain object model. The domain use cases capture the domain requirements and validate the completeness of the model. The definition focuses the OODE process and constrains the project. The static and dynamic conceptual domain object models define the domain classes and their relationships and responsibilities.

10.1.2 Object-Oriented Domain Design (OODD) Phase

The OODD process and deliverables are built on the results of the OODA phase. This section discusses the major OODD phase processes and deliverables. Figure 10.6 depicts the overall OODD phase process, its subprocesses, and their deliverables.

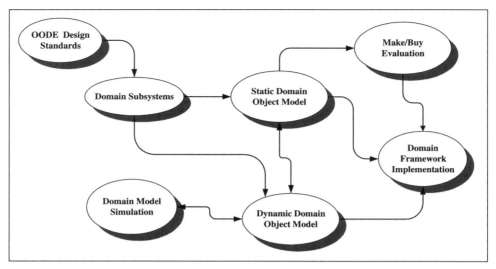

Figure 10.6 OODD phase.

Design Standards

Design standards provide guidelines on the definition of classes and the formation of inheritance hierarchies and guides the development of distributed object servers. A server is defined as a complex, large-scale domain framework component. A server is complex because it is composed of several classes and these classes collaborate to provide a set of related services. Collaboration takes place within servers and among servers.

Servers are designed and implemented to be fail-safe. They recover from their own errors and errors caused by their clients and collaborators. They continue to execute so long as they are able to provide even some of their services. They inform their clients of the capabilities they do have, even if they are not able to provide the full set.

Domain Subsystems

On the PM&D project, several benefits were realized by applying, in an iterative manner, the subsystem analysis process defined by Wirfs-Brock and extended for OODE. Communication and collaboration among objects were simplified. Functional encapsulation was improved through the use of subsystem contracts. The model was validated for completeness and correctness using subsystem cards, similar to CRC cards, to walk through the subsystems with respect to the domain use cases. This led to a better model, which was simpler and more coherent. Subsystems are critical for domain engineering because they lead to higher-level reuse and facilitate comparisons among domains, especially at the contract level.

Domain Object Model

The OODD domain object model is the elaboration of the OODA conceptual domain object model. It contains class signatures not defined at the conceptual level. On the

PM&D project, the domain object model benefited from further work on the domain use cases and the development of the subsystems.

Domain Object Model Simulation

On the PM&D project, simulations done by hand with class and subsystem CRC cards early and frequently in the OODA and OODD phases led to major benefits for the project. This work reduced the number of classes from 200 to 17. Simulation uncovered duplication and improved coherence in the model. It defined the role of an object bus as an essential middleware subsystem to broker service requests.

Domain Framework Implementation

In the OODE process, implementation focuses on creating large-scale distributed servers that integrate with an object bus. Details of the implementation of the PM&D framework with respect to this focus are discussed in the case study. The major OODD deliverables are the domain subsystems, the completed domain object model, and the domain framework.

10.1.3 OODE Delivery Phase

The ready-to-assemble model is the OODE approach to delivery. At delivery time the framework is not just an integrated set of software components, but an application ready to be assembled, complete with the needed tools, training, and instructions (see Figure 10.7).

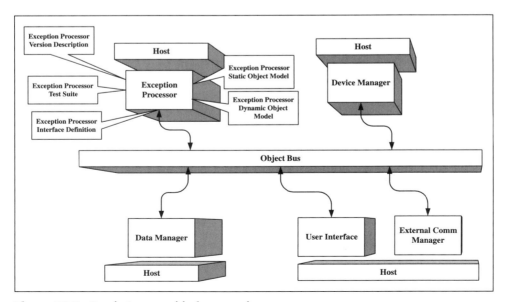

Figure 10.7   Ready-to-assemble framework.

10.1.4 Relationship of OODE to Other Methods

There are several other software engineering methods that deal with domains: feature-oriented domain analysis (FODA), organization domain modeling (ODM), Joint Integrated Avionics Working Group object-oriented domain analysis (JODA), and synthesis. The following paragraphs discuss their strengths, weaknesses, and relationships to OODE.

The FODA methodology identifies common features within a class of related software systems to define a domain. FODA consists of three phases of domain analysis: *Context analysis* defines the domain boundary, *domain modeling* identifies commonalities and variability in the domain, and *architecture modeling* develops a design model for the domain.

ODM models the variability of a business domain based on the organization and provides guidelines for tailoring the organizational process. ODM consists of three phases: *Planning* identifies a highly focused business domain, *modeling* describes the common and variant features of systems within the domain, and *engineering* produces and implements an architecture that covers a subset of the total range of variability.

JODA captures the domain structure and requirements within a domain model expressed with the Coad-Yourdon object-oriented analysis and design method. JODA's three process are *domain preparation* for identifying and gathering domain knowledge, *domain definition* for defining the scope of the domain and developing a high-level view of the domain, and *domain modeling*. JODA develops all object-oriented models using the Coad-Yourdon method.

Synthesis defined the first complete domain engineering/application engineering process for constructing software systems for reuse in a family of similar systems. The synthesis process has four phases. *Domain management* plans, monitors, and controls domain resources to achieve business goals. *Domain analysis* studies and formalizes the domain and specifies the appropriate application engineering process and product family. *Domain implementation* creates a set of adaptable components and standardized application engineering processes. *Project support* provides means for feedback to domain engineers from application engineers.

The synthesis domain engineering method is considered the most mature method, followed by FODA, ODM, and JODA. Synthesis is not based on object-oriented technology; therefore, it does not bring this advanced software engineering technique to domain engineering. JODA is the only domain engineering method that introduces the concept of object-oriented technology; however, this methodology only deals with domain analysis, not domain engineering. It is not a mature method. The FODA and ODM methods are at the medium maturity level. They also lack application engineering and object-oriented technology.

Advantages of OODE

A major advantage of OODE is that it defines a complete life-cycle process from domain analysis through framework delivery. Besides a life-cycle approach, OODE focuses on large-scale reuse on servers that are complex aggregations of classes. Moreover, these servers are designed and developed for distributed applications, which increases their potential for reuse.

OODE is directly based on object-oriented technology and brings the benefits of this approach to domain analysis and framework development. It incorporates well-known OO techniques such as use cases, the Unified Modeling Language, and responsibility-driven design, but applies those techniques not to the development of individual applications and small-scale reuse, but to generic frameworks and large-scale reuse.

10.2 Case Study: Process Monitoring and Diagnosis Domain

This section describes the use of OODE to develop and apply a framework for the Process Monitoring and Diagnosis (PM&D) domain. Three applications, Data Collection system (DCS), Rivet Monitoring system (RMS), and Hardware Variability Control system (HVCS), defined the domain and contributed to its architecture. From the domain architecture, a partial framework was built to support the Rivet Monitoring system's need to handle alarms. Another domain application, Chemical Monitoring system (CMS), has been developed with the framework. CMS benefited from the domain architecture and the partial framework. In turn, CMS contributed to the architecture and the completion of the framework. A further domain application, Overall Equipment Effectiveness, is planned for the framework. This application monitors equipment usage and reports on utilization and behavior trends.

10.2.1 PM&D Domain Analysis

The OODE process begins with the identification and definition of a domain. Three applications, Data Collection system, Rivet Monitoring system, and Hardware Variability Control system, contributed to the definition of the PM&D domain.

Data Collection System

The Data Collection system transports data from devices that collect information to applications that store and analyze the data. Along with transporting the data, DCS manages the transportation infrastructure.

Use cases are business processes that define an application's functionality. In OODE they are the foundation for the domain use cases, abstract processes that span the domain. The 13 use cases defined for DCS are listed in Table 10.1. The abstract PM&D domain use cases are discussed later (see Figure 10.11 later in this chapter).

An example of a part of an application static model, the DCS software subsystem is shown in Figure 10.8. The static model formalizes the inheritance and composition relationships and class signatures for the subsystem. In the OODE domain analysis phase, the application object models form the basis for the domain conceptual object model.

Rivet Monitoring System

The Rivet Monitoring system supports an automated riveting machine. It is typical of applications in the Process Monitoring and Diagnosis domain that interact directly

Table 10.1   Data Collection Use Cases

DCS USE CASES
Download software from a central location.
Update software from a local source.
Guarantee message delivery.
Validate user input.
Verify software configuration on a device.
Handle an error.
Handle a system point failure.
Synchronize time (unsolicited).
Synchronize time (solicited).
Monitor the network from a central point.
Respond to a call for service.
Manage a network device.
Drive the system by data entry events.

with intelligent machine tools and their operators. During the operation of the RMS, data is collected from the machine, analyzed, and stored. Analysis may indicate that an alarm condition exists. In this case, the alarm is logged, and the machine operator is advised and then offered a recovery plan.

A sample RMS use case is shown in Figure 10.9. This use case illustrates how RMS handles an alarm thrown by the machine it is monitoring. The use case contains the actor who initiates the process, the intent of the use case, its assumptions, and results. The base course is a step-by-step description of the process. It is one of the 20 RMS use cases.

The RMS object models were collected and incorporated into the conceptual PM&D domain object model in Figure 10.5. Only a part of the complete conceptual model is shown in the figure.

Hardware Variability Control System (HVCS) Application

The HVCS application supports the collection of part measurement data from the factory floor and provides reports on this data. It predicts how well a part will fit into its larger assembly from the measurement data. The application is defined by the six use cases in Table 10.2.

The HVCS object models are a subset of RMS. They were incorporated into the PM&D conceptual model along with the RMS models.

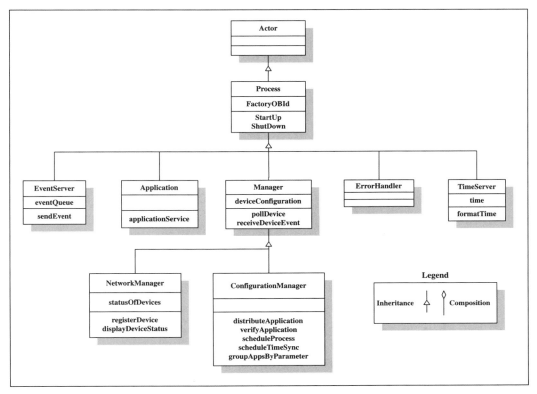

Figure 10.8   DCS static object model.

PM&D Domain Use Cases

From the application use cases that lie within the domain, domain use cases are derived. These abstract the application use cases. The PM&D domain use cases are shown in Table 10.3.

Table 10.2   HVCS Use Cases

HVCS USE CASES
SPC-O: Report process measurements for QA.
HVC-O: Report part measurements for mechanic.
Supplier upload: Import flat file of data into HVC.
Custom extract: Export data from HVC database.
Data collector: Mechanic enters data with a device.
Fit prediction: Analyze data against specifications.

Handle RMS alarm

Actors: Machine operator, RMS, EP.
Intent: Provide a recovery plan and exception reporting for an RMS alarm.
Assumptions: Some of the base course steps happen in parallel. EP provides its own GUI.
                   EP owns the recovery plans.
Limitations: Details of the recovery plans and exception reports are defined.
Uses/extends: N/A.
Results: Recovery plan is identified for an alarm.
Base course:
A. RMS throws an alarm to EP.
B. EP catches the alarm.
C. EP determines what recovery is needed.
D. EP adds to the current exception report for the alarm.
E. RMS displays the alarm to the user.
F. RMS logs raw data.
G. If the user requests to see the recovery plan, RMS tells EP to display it.
   EP prints the recovery plan on user request.

Figure 10.9   Use case: Handle RMS alarm.

10.2.2 PM&D Domain Design

The OODE domain design phase is concerned with refining the domain conceptual object model to a completely defined domain object model The PM&D domain object model contains the 14 core business classes in Table 10.4. The core classes exclude user interface and data management classes. The domain framework may be implemented during this phase or delayed until an application project is ready to receive it.

Table 10.3   PM&D Domain Use Cases

PM&D USE CASES
Set up job.
Collect data.
Analyze data.
Handle alarm.
Store data.
Generate report.
Administer system.
Synchronize time.
Manage network.
Respond to a service request.
Manage system configuration.

Table 10.4 PM&D Core Classes

PM&D CLASS	DESCRIPTION
Alarmer	Handles alarm from exception
Broker	Brokers a request for service
DataAnalyzer	Analyzes raw data for exceptions
Device	Manages output to a device
Interface	Defines a server's services
Logger	Logs events
Plotter	Specialized device
Printer	Specialized device
Proxy	Links a service to its provider
Recoverer	Recovers from exception
Reporter	Creates and displays reports
SubSystem	Manages a group of objects
Validator	Validates data
Warner	Handles warning from exception

In the OODE approach, a *domain subsystem* is a large-scale actor that aggregates a number of classes. The subsystem manages its members to fulfill the services exposed in the subsystem's public contract. Figure 10.10 is a detailed example of the Exception-Processor subsystem and its interactions. For example, an invocation of the SetAlarm interface method on the server side is accepted first by the ExceptionProcessor (EP). EP then requests the Alarmer component to handle the alarm. It collaborates with the Recoverer to recover from the alarm. The Recoverer requests services from the Data-Manager subsystem, another member of the PM&D framework, through its contract. The return from the method is sent back to the client by the ObjectBus.

The domain subsystems together form the *domain architecture*. The PM&D architecture, shown in Figure 10.11, is composed of 10 subsystems. The architecture is inherently distributed because communication among subsystems in the architecture is handled by a software object bus.

10.2.3 PM&D Domain Delivery

This section describes the third OODE phase: how the PM&D framework was developed and then applied to two applications in the Process Monitoring and Diagnosis domain. The first application was an implementation of the framework's Exception-Processor (EP) subsystem to support the Rivet Monitoring system. Experience quickly showed that there was a need to broaden the scope to include two additional subsys-

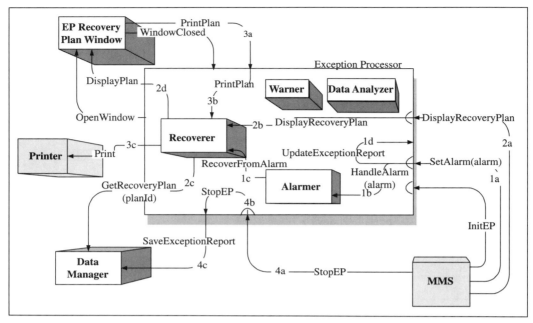

Figure 10.10 EP object interaction diagram.

tems, DataManager and DeviceManager. It was found that these three subsystems are the essential core of any PM&D application.

The second application of the framework was for a Chemical Monitoring system (CMS). This application brought out the need to enhance the analysis capability of the EP by adding a case-based reasoning (CBR) tool. CBR technology is a problem-solving paradigm that matches a current problem against problems solved successfully in the past. A case base can be augmented by adapting new solutions to closely match the current problem.

A CBR case consists of a problem description, questions related to the problem ,and solutions for the problem. Answers provided to the CBR tool narrow down the problem and lead to a specific solution. Figure 10.12 is an example of a case implemented for the Chemical Monitoring system.

Application of PM&D Domain Use Cases

To begin the application of the framework, the PM&D domain use cases are used to analyze the new system. These domain use cases are tailored to meet the business requirements of the new system. Tailoring the domain use cases reduces the time needed for analysis and identifies what part of the framework will be used to assemble the new system. Two PM&D domain use cases satisfied the requirements for the ExceptionProcessor extension of the RMS.

The ability of the PM&D use cases to support the CMS requirements was verified by analysis by the development team and subject matter experts. There were several sig-

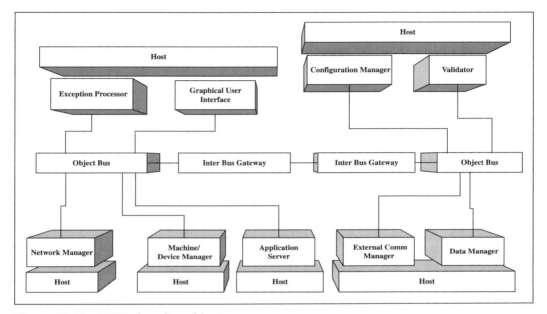

Figure 10.11   PM&D domain architecture.

nificant findings from this analysis. One was that the domain use cases did not define an application server, the main server that coordinates all other components in the architecture. While this server is specialized for each application, the framework was incomplete without it.

A second finding was that the original PM&D domain use cases were too specific in that they were based on machine input of data only. CMS required human input data. Collecting data from a human actor is more complex than from a machine, so a variant domain use case for data collection has been defined.

PROBLEM DESCRIPTION: BUILDING 23-05 TankID H-9	
Questions:	**Answers:**
What is the reading of nickel chloride ($NiCl_2$)? What is the reading of chloride (Cl)? What is the reading of boric acid (H_3Bo_3)?	1.5 16.6 25.6
Solution: Check history log on $NiCl_2$, retest. If result is the same, add 170 lb. $NiCl_2$. Add 150 lb. NH_4Cl. H_3Bo_3 is normal.	

Figure 10.12   Sample case in Chemical Monitoring system.

It was also found that several other PM&D use cases were too specific. For example, one of these documented a process to edit the warning and alarm limits used by the ExceptionProcessor subsystem. The CMS use case that best corresponded to this was a process to manage all the configuration data for the system. In other words, the original PM&D domain use case was a subset of the CMS case, not the other way around. The result from application of the domain use cases is that no new use cases have been added, but generalization has occurred.

Application of PM&D Object Model

To implement the ExceptionProcessor extension to the RMS, 8 of the 14 PM&D core classes in Table 10.4 were used. Thus, the PM&D model supported 100 percent of the core ExceptionProcessor business classes. Four user interface classes supplemented the 8 core classes. These classes were provided by a vendor framework. The vendor framework supplied an additional 8 infrastructure classes, such as a class that encapsulated character strings.

The CMS project added four classes to the core classes. One is AuthorizingDocument, a plan to recover from an exception. Another is InBox, which manages AuthorizingDocuments. The Sampler class manages data sampling done by a chemical lab technician and Archiver archives data for long-term storage. The total of 18 classes support all of the CMS requirements. Thus, the initial PM&D core classes supplied 78 percent of the CMS core business model.

There was significant code reuse from two of the ExceptionProcessor subsystems by the CMS. One of these was the DeviceManager, the subsystem that handles output devices such as printers. The other subsystem that contributed significant code reuse was the ObjectBus.

The physical implementation of the ObjectBus (see Figure 10.13) in both ExceptionProcessor and CMS is as a proxy on a client's side of the bus and an interface on the server's side. The proxy is a class on the client side whose methods and attributes map

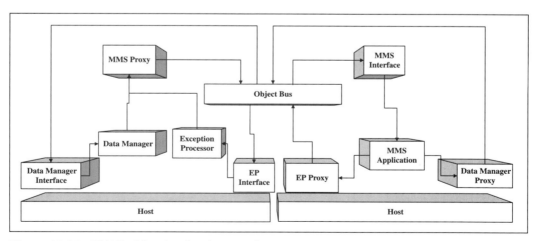

Figure 10.13   PM&D object bus implementation.

to the server's interface. The client invokes methods or accesses attributes on a proxy object as if they were local. These invocations are then mapped by the object bus to the server-side methods defined by a subsystem's interface.

Significant code reuse by CMS from the ExceptionProcessor was provided by reusing the proxies and interfaces. They were reused from the servers' subsystems that were common between the ExceptionProcessor and CMS. These common servers are ExceptionProcessor, DataManager, and DeviceManager.

10.3 Summary

The effort to create object-oriented domain engineering (OODE) has produced three results. First, it has defined a formal OODE process. This process, its subprocesses, and their deliverables have been described in the preceding sections with respect to the Process Monitoring and Diagnosis (PM&D) domain. This process has been improved with each use. The OODE process is a significant contribution to the field of domain engineering because it has created a domain engineering method with object technology as the central abstraction. OODE is also a contribution because it defines a domain engineering process that covers the complete software engineering life cycle. Many other approaches confine themselves only to domain analysis.

Second, OODE has taken a step beyond defining a process and executed the process in the PM&D domain. The result is a set of documented processes, deliverables, and a domain architecture. The architecture is a tool for developing a PM&D framework and it is a tool in its own right for defining a domain. Third, a physical framework has been produced from the PM&D architecture. This framework has supported two applications, RMS and CMS. It is planned that it will support several others.

One advantage of OODE is that analysis, design, and implementation time for complex manufacturing systems is greatly reduced. For example, the generic PM&D framework in Figure 10.11 contains 10 subsystems and 18 core classes, excluding user interface and infrastructure classes. On CMS, all 18 of the PM&D core classes were used and 4 new classes were defined. Thus, one can say that approximately 80 percent of the analysis and design time on CMS was saved by using the PM&D framework. This is not quite the case, because some analysis and design time was needed to tailor the PM&D classes to the specifics of the CMS application. It is significant that only 4 new classes were defined. This indicates that OODE does define a common domain architecture.

10.4 References

[Chan 1997a] Chan, S., and T. Lammers. Intelligent, distributed NC system. *Proceedings of the 4th International Conference on Computer Integrated Manufacturing (ICCIM 1997)*, vol. 2, pp. 1359–1368. Springer-Verlag Singapore Pte. Ltd., 1997.

[Chan 1997b] Chan, S., and T. Lammers. Creating a distributed factory object architecture. *Proceedings of the 1st Enterprise Distributed Object Computing (EDOC 1997) Workshop*, pp. 282–290. Los Alamitos, CA: IEEE Computer Society Press, 1997.

[Chan 1998a] Chan, S., and T. Lammers. Integrating AI with object technology for manufacturing. *Proceedings of the Artificial Intelligence and Soft Computing Conference (ASC 1998)*, pp. 261–264. IASTED, 1998.

[Chan 1998b] Chan, S., and T. Lammers. Reusing a distributed object domain framework. *Proceedings of the 5th International Conference on Software Reuse (ICSR5 1998)*, pp. 216–223. Los Alamitos, CA: IEEE Computer Society Press, 1998.

[Chan 1998c] Chan, S., and T. Lammers. Object-oriented domain engineering. *5th International Conference on Software Reuse (ICSR5 1998) Tutorial.* Los Alamitos, CA: IEEE Computer Society Press, 1998.

[Coad 1995] Coad, P., and E. Yourdon. *Object-Oriented Analysis.* Englewood Cliffs, New Jersey: Yourdon Press, 1991.

[Fayad 1997] Fayad, M.E., and D. Schmidt. Object-oriented application framework. *Communications of the ACM,* Theme Issue 40(10):32–87, October 1997.

[Gamma 1995] Gamma E., R. Helm, R. Johnson, and J. Vlissides. *Design Patterns: Elements of Reusable Object-Oriented Software.* Reading, MA: Addison Wesley, 1995.

[Izygon 1996] Izygon, Michel. Reuse engineering: Inserting a domain analysis method in an organization. *OOPSLA 1996 Tutorial 12,* San Jose, CA, October 1996.

[Jacobson 1992] Jacobson, I., M. Christerson, P. Jonsson, and G. Övergaard. *Object-Oriented Software Engineering: A Use Case Driven Approach.* Reading, MA: Addison-Wesley, 1992.

[Kang 1990] Kang, K., et al. *Feature-Oriented Domain Analysis (FODA) Feasibility Study.* Pittsburgh, PA: Carnegie Mellon University, 1990.

[Orfali 1996] Orfali, R., D. Harkey, and J. Edwards. *The Essential Distributed Objects Survival Guide.* New York: John Wiley & Sons, 1996.

[Rumbaugh 1991] Rumbaugh, J., M. Blaha, W. Premerlani, F. Eddy, and W. Lorensen. *Object-Oriented Modeling and Design.* Englewood Cliffs, NJ: Prentice Hall, 1991.

[Schmid 1996] Schmid, H.A. Creating applications from components: A manufacturing framework design. *IEEE Software* 13(6):67–75, November 1996.

[Tansley 1993] Tansley, D., and C. Hayball. *Knowledge-Based Systems Analysis and Design: A KADS Developer's Handbook.* Englewood Cliffs, NJ: Prentice Hall, 1993.

[Wilkinson 1995] Wilkinson, Nancy. *Using CRC Cards: An Informal Approach to Object-Oriented Development.* New York: SIGS Books, 1995.

CHAPTER 11

Measurement Systems Framework

The increasing automation of the production process has begun to address processes beyond the primary production activities. During the past decade, the need for automated tools that support the quality control processes surrounding the actual production has increased. The emergence of the ISO-9000 quality standards, quality-oriented thinking in general, and the increased productivity brought about by technology require quality control systems to improve their productivity as well. Whereas many factories traditionally used manual quality control performed by personnel, nowadays the need for automated support is obvious. This development has dramatically increased the need for automated measurement systems.

The advantages of measurement systems are generally improved performance/cost ratio and more consistent and accurate quality control, which underscore the imperative that existing measurement system software be reusable. Although conceptually these systems have a rather similar structure, in practice we found the implementation of them to be rather diverse. This is due to the fact that realtime constraints, concurrency, and requirements resulting from the underlying hardware strongly influence the actual implementation.

Despite these difficulties, we have, together with an industrial partner, EC-Gruppen, designed a framework for measurement systems that would decrease their software development cost by increasing the reuse of existing software and, as an important second requirement, increase the flexibility of running applications. Operators of these measurement systems often need to make some adjustments in the way the systems evaluate measurement items, and such systems should provide this flexibility. However, traditional systems constructed in C and assembly language often have difficulty doing so.

The contribution of this chapter is to describe the experiences resulting from the design of the measurement systems framework. For this design, we used the conventional object-oriented paradigm as expressed in C++ and Smalltalk. We believe a second contribution of this chapter is an evaluation of the object-oriented paradigm in itself and a determination of the expressiveness that could be considered as lacking in the conventional object-oriented (OO) paradigm.

The remainder of this chapter is organized as follows. In *Section 11.1,* measurement systems are described in more detail and the requirements of the object-oriented framework, as put forward by the software engineers actually building these systems, are described. *Section 11.2* presents the actual architecture design, using the conventional object-oriented paradigm. In *Section 11.3,* we describe the modeling problems that we identified during the framework design and implementation. *Section 11.4* presents an example measurement system, followed by *Section 11.5,* which provides an evaluation. *Section 11.6* discusses work related to the topics considered in this chapter, and *Section 11.7* is the conclusion.

11.1 Measurement Systems: Requirements

Measurement systems are a class of systems used to measure the relevant values of a process or product. These systems are different from the better known process control systems in that the measured values are not directly (that is, as part of the same system) used to control the production process that creates the product or process that is being measured. A measurement system is used for quality control of parts entering production or of produced products that can then be used to separate acceptable from unacceptable items or to categorize the products in quality categories. In some systems, the results from the measurement are stored in case a future need arises to refer to this information—for example, if customers complain about products that passed the measurement criteria.

Although a measurement system contains a considerable amount of software, a substantial part of such a system is hardware, since the system is connected to the real world through a number of sensors and actuators. The sensors provide information about the real world through the noticed impulses. However, whereas traditional sensors were primarily hardware and had a very low-level interface to the software system, new sensors provide increasing amounts of functionality that previously had to be implemented as part of the software. For instance, a conventional temperature sensor would provide only the A/D conversion, and the software would need to convert this A/D value into the actual temperature in Celsius or Kelvin, as well as calibrate the sensor. Modern temperature sensors perform their own calibration and immediately provide the actual temperature in the required format. The interface between the sensor and the system is becoming more high-level, but also more complex, since the degree of configurability of the sensors is increasing.

A similar development is taking place with respect to the actuators. Whereas previously the software had to be concerned with the actuation through the actuators, modern actuators often need only a set value expressed in application domain concepts such as angular speed or force. For example, to control the open angle of a valve in a traditional measurement system, one would have to generate a *duty cycle* in software.

A duty cycle is the periodic process of sending out a 1 for part of the cycle and a 0 for the rest. The ratio between the time the output is 1 and the time the output is 0 represents the *force* expressed through the actuator. Opening a valve 70 percent requires that the system output a 1 for 70 percent of the cyclic period and a 0 for the remaining 30 percent. The implementation of this is often achieved through an interrupt routine that changes the output signal when required. Modern actuators contain considerably more functionality and will generate the duty cycle themselves, requiring only the set value from the software.

These developments in the domain of sensors and actuators change measurement systems from small, single-processor systems that are developed very close to the hardware to distributed computing systems, since the more complex sensors and actuators often contain their own processors. However, although the increased functionality of the sensors and actuators reduces the complexity of constructing measurement systems, the increased demands on these systems and the resulting increase in size make the construction of measurement systems a complex activity. The languages and tools used to construct measurement systems should provide powerful means to deal with this complexity.

A measurement system, however, consists of more than sensors and actuators. A typical measurement cycle starts with a trigger, indicating that a product, or a measurement item, is entering the system. The first step after the trigger is the *data collection* phase performed by the sensors. The sensors measure the relevant variables of the measurement item. The second step is the *analysis* phase, during which the data from the sensors is collected in a central representation and transformed until it appears in a form in which it can be compared to the ideal values. Based on this comparison, certain discrepancies can be deduced, which, in turn, lead to a classification of the measurement item. In the third, *actuation,* phase, the classification of the measurement item is used to perform associated actions, such as rejecting the item, which causes the actuators to remove the item from the conveyer belt and put it in a separate store, or to print the classification on the item so that it can be automatically recognized at a later stage. One of the requirements for the analysis phase is that the way the transformation takes place, the characteristics on which the item's classification are based, and the actions associated with each classification should be flexible and easily adaptable during system construction, but also, to some extent, during the actual system operation.

Based on the preceding discussion, it is debatable whether the traditional view of a measurement system as a centralized system with one main control loop is the most appropriate one. During framework development, we became convinced that the system should be viewed as a collection of communicating, active entities that cooperate to achieve the required system behavior. This improves the modularity of the system, decreases the dependencies between the various parts, and increases system flexibility. However, decomposing the system into active entities requires processes to be available to, or at least simulated by, the underlying operating system.

Another important aspect is the realtime behavior of the measurement system. In contrast to many realtime systems, a measurement system is not a periodic system. The realtime constraints in the system are, directly or indirectly, related to the triggering point where a product to be measured enters the system. Although when running at maximum performance this becomes a periodic behavior, the start is not determined by the clock, but by a physical event. In the ideal situation, the software engineer would specify the realtime constraints on the different activities in the system. Based on that specification, the system would schedule the activities such that the realtime constraints are met, or, if it is not possible to schedule all activities, it would respond to the software engineer with a message. However, in the current situation, the software engineer implements the tasks that have to be performed and performs a test run of the system. Often, the system does not meet all deadlines at first and the software engineer has to adjust the system to fulfill the requirements by, for example, changing the priorities of the different processes.

Finally, the requirements for modern measurement systems often result in systems that are no longer confined to a single processor. Distribution plays an increasingly important role in measurement systems. However, the presence of distribution should not require the software engineer to change the basic architecture of the system. The system should simply be extended with behavior for dealing with communication over address spaces.

11.1.1 Nonfunctional Requirements

Based on the previous discussion, we have distilled a number of requirements for measurement systems.

Intuitive. As with any software system, the designed framework should be based on concepts that have a direct correspondence to entities in the application domain. The way these concepts are used and combined should be logically consistent with the view of a domain expert.

Reusable. The framework should provide reusable components for the construction of measurement systems. This requires a delicate balance between generality and specialty. It also means that the components and decomposition dimensions have to be chosen such that relatively general components from different dimensions can be composed to form specific components that can be used in real systems with minimal extensions.

Flexible. Although flexibility would be considered a positive aspect of any system, the requirements for the flexibility of measurement systems are higher than average. As described, the actual composition of the system from its components, the analysis process, and the reaction by the system based on the analysis results need to be easily adaptable, both during application development and during system operation.

Realtime constraints. Although most traditional system construction approaches deal with realtime constraints by running tests on the system and measuring the system responses, we already discussed the advantages of expressing realtime constraints directly as part of the system. The difficulty with both realtime and concurrency is the platform dependence of the implementation of these techniques.

The version of the framework presented in this chapter does not deal with the issues of concurrency and distribution. The reason for this is that our project was most concerned with achieving a stable application architecture, and issues such as concurrency and distribution can be superimposed on top of the architecture. However, concurrency and distribution are relevant for measurement systems. As mentioned earlier in this section, considering the increasing complexity of measurement systems, it may easily become necessary to decompose a system into communicating, active components that are distributed among various processors. We intend to address these issues in a future version of the framework.

11.2 Measurement System Framework Design

When modeling a measurement system using object-oriented principles, we model the real world using objects that represent real-world entities. Both the sensors and the actuators clearly exist in the real world and are correspondingly modeled as objects. The measurement item, however, is a more complex question. The measurement item obviously exists in the real world, but it has to be instantiated every time a physical item enters the measurement system. However, when it is instantiated, it is empty and contains no data whatsoever concerning its physical counterpart. This information has to be obtained from the sensors that measure the relevant variables of the physical entity. This is where an important design decision concerning the boundaries between the sensor objects and the measurement item has to be made. Only in the simplest systems can the values measured by the sensor with an immediate corresponding hardware sensor be used directly by the measurement item. Very often the data have to be transformed—for example, condensed, cleaned of faults, or converted into other domains. The question is whether this is the task of the measurement item or of the sensor measuring the data. The answer, as for all difficult questions, is that it depends. Sometimes the data from one or more physical sensors need to be transformed before they represent the data that can be used by the measurement item, whereas in other cases the data form a logical part of the measurement and need to be transformed in the process intuitively associated with the measurement item. An example of the first is the use of redundancy. The designer of the system may make use of more than a single sensor to increase the reliability of a particular variable of the physical item. The measured values need to be compared and an average or most-votes result will be used as the value measured by the abstract sensor. An example of the second type is the repeated measurement of a variable in time. The sensor may measure the value of a variable multiple times for a measurement item; for example, the thickness of an item may be measured at several points to provide sufficient coverage of that aspect of the item.

11.2.1 The Measurement Process

Figure 11.1 shows the architecture of a simple measurement system. It consists of five entities that communicate with each other to achieve the required functionality.

- The trigger triggers the abstract factory when a physical item enters the system.
- The abstract factory creates a representation of the physical object in the software, that is, the measurement item.
- The measurement item requests the sensor to measure the physical object.
- The sensor sends back the result to the measurement item that stores the results.

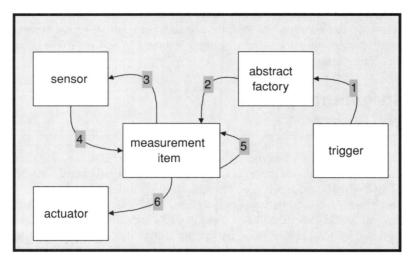

Figure 11.1   Architecture of a simple measurement system.

■ After collecting the required data, the measurement item compares the measured values with the ideal values.

■ The measurement item sends a message to the actuator requesting the actuation
appropriate for the measured data.

11.2.2 Sensor

The sensor is the software representation of a hardware device that measures one particular variable of the item in question. The sensor is responsible for maintaining an
accurate model of the hardware sensor. To achieve this, the sensor communicates with
the hardware sensor. The way the sensor updates itself with the data in the physical
sensor can vary, depending on the sensor type and the application. In the framework,
the updating of the sensor has been modeled as a separate strategy. The update strategy is discussed in the next section.

Another aspect of the sensor is that the data read from the hardware sensor has to be
converted into a value that has some meaning in the context of the software system.
This conversion process can be very different, depending on the application and the
way the sensor is used. Therefore, the conversion has also been abstracted as a calculation strategy. The details of the calculation strategy are described later in this chapter.

Figure 11.2 presents the class hierarchy of the sensor classes. The abstract superclass
Sensor has two subclasses, AbstractSensor and ConcreteSensor. A concrete sensor has
a one-to-one relationship to a hardware sensor; that is, for every hardware sensor a
concrete sensor exists. The abstract sensor is an instance of the Composite design pattern [Gamma 1995] and represents an abstraction of one or more sensors. For instance,
two concrete sensors, both of which measure the same aspect of an item, could be contained in an abstract sensor that calculates the average of the two and uses that as its
value. The concrete sensor has a subclass trigger that is used for triggering the abstract
factory when a physical item enters the measurement system.

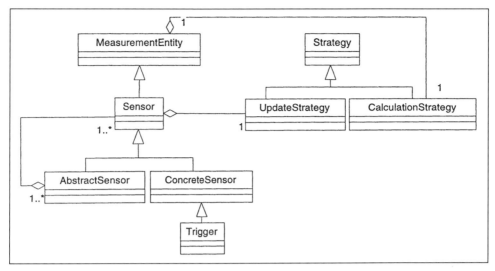

Figure 11.2   Class relations for Sensor.

The sensor has several methods, such as those for reading and setting the update and calculation strategies. However, the main method used by the measurement item is the getValue method:

```
getValue
    "returns the stored measured value."

    (self updateStrategy) clientUpdate.
    ^self measuredValue
```

This method first calls the update strategy, which, depending on the strategy type, might update the value stored in the sensor. Second, the object returns the measured value.

11.2.3 Update Strategy

The correct way of updating the sensor depends on the application and the type of sensor. Recognizing this caused us to abstract the updating behavior using the Strategy design pattern. So far, three strategies for updating have been defined:

Client update. This update strategy is used when the amount of computation on a sensor should be minimized. The sensor never updates itself, until it is called by a client. Upon receipt of the request, the sensor first updates itself and subsequently returns the (very recently) updated value.

Periodic update. The periodic update strategy requires a time interval as an input. At the beginning of each time interval, the sensor will update itself with fresh data from the physical sensor.

On-change update. This update strategy can be used when the physical sensor notifies the software system, either through an interrupt or otherwise, that its value has changed. Every time the sensor is notified, it will update itself.

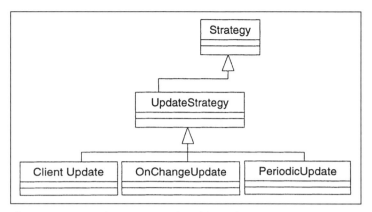

Figure 11.3   UpdateStrategy class hierarchy.

Figure 11.3 shows the different update strategies. In the current definition of the framework, these update strategies are mutually exclusive; in other words, only a single strategy can be active at any point in time. However, the update strategy of a sensor can be changed at runtime. Nevertheless, one could imagine that in certain applications two strategies should be combined—for example, the periodic and client-based update strategies.

11.2.4 Calculation Strategy

The calculation strategy is used for collecting and converting data from one representation into another. It is used by more than just sensors. Measurement items and other entities also make use of the calculation strategy, which is why the aggregation relation is placed at the level of the MeasurementEntity class. As shown in Figure 11.4, a concrete calculation strategy class hierarchy has been defined for concrete sensors. For the abstract sensor, no calculation strategies have been predefined, but these strategies are rather easy to define.

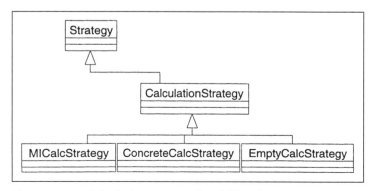

Figure 11.4   CalculationStrategy class hierarchy.

11.2.5 Measurement Item

The measurement item is the object that contains the data collected from the sensors concerning the physical measurement item. As shown in Figure 11.5, the measurement item inherits from the class MeasurementEntity, causing it to contain a calculation strategy. The calculation strategy was discussed in the preceding section. The measurement item has its own calculation strategy, EmptyCalcStrategy, which just forwards the calculation process to the measurement item itself. Other parts of the measurement item are a collection of measurement values, a collection of actuators, an actuation strategy, and a reference to the item factory that instantiated the measurement item.

A measurement item is invoked via its start method by the item factory after it has instantiated the item. The start method contains the top-level behavior for the measurement item with respect to its primary task—that is, to collect data on the physical item it represents and to actuate the actuators appropriately, based on the measured data and the comparison to the set data.

```
start

    (self calculationStrategy) performCalculation.
    (self actuationStrategy) actuate.
    ^self
```

The calculation phase of the measurement item is concerned with collecting the data and converting it to a value form that matches the requirements within the system. The only action performed by the measurement item is to invoke each measurement value that it contains with a request to collect the data from the sensor to which the measurement value is connected and to process this data. The actuation phase is concerned with generating the necessary effects on the actuators, based on the values collected during the calculation phase. The actuation strategy uses the set of actuator references stored by the measurement item to activate the various actuators. After the measurement item has sent the required actions to the actuators, it is removed from the system.

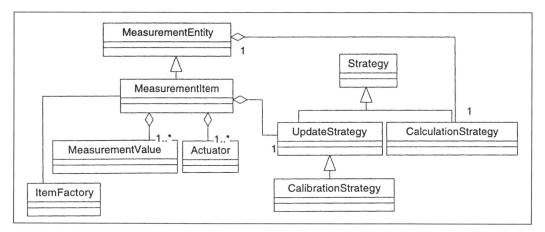

Figure 11.5   Relations for class MeasurementItem.

11.2.6 Measurement Value

The MeasurementValue class represents one aspect of the physical measurement item that is used by the system. A measurement value has zero, one, or more dimensions and a domain. Examples of a measurement value are the presence of a part of the item (zero-dimensional, boolean domain), the temperature of an item (zero-dimensional, real domain), the width of an item measured through a sequence of samples (one-dimensional, real domain), and a camera image (two-dimensional, 0–255 [gray-scale] domain). Each measurement value contains a set value representing the correct value, a measured value representing the value measured at the current physical item, and a compare method describing how to interpret differences between the measured and set values.

Multidimensional measurement values (one-dimensional and higher) are modeled using the Composite pattern [Gamma 1995]. The class organization is shown in Figure 11.6. The measurement value inherits from MeasurementEntity, which contains the behavior common for all entities in the measurement system. MeasurementValue has two subclasses: AtomicMV and ComposedMV. The first represents measurement values directly obtained from a sensor. These values generally are zero-dimensional, although exceptions exist. The latter represents the (multi-)dimensional measurement values (one-dimensional and higher), which are composed of measurement value instances.

As shown in Figure 11.6, one can, using the composed measurement value, construct multidimensional measurement values that can contain several values from the same sensor, but measured as different time points, as data values from various sensors that have to be composed in an integrated value, or as multidimensional data from one sensor, such as a camera.

11.2.7 Calibration Strategy

In measurement systems, *calibration* is the process of collecting the ideal values for the measurement item. This means that, as opposed to normal behavior, the values mea-

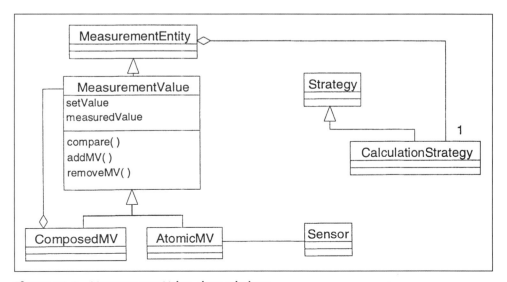

Figure 11.6   MeasurementValue class relations.

sured during this process are to be considered the correct values, rather than using the set values stored in the measurement item. Calibration influences the actuation strategy of the measurement item rather than the calculation strategy. Therefore, the normal actuation strategy of the measurement item is replaced with a calibration strategy that performs the actions required during calibration.

In order to fully understand the calibration process, it is important to see that the item factory and the measurement item both play a role. The item factory contains an instance of class MeasurementItem that is used as a prototype for generating measurement items during normal system operation. When the user of the system decides to calibrate, the first step is to notify the item factory that the next measurement item is to be used for calibration. When the trigger notifies the item factory, the item factory instantiates a measurement item, but replaces the normal actuation strategy with a calibration strategy instance. The measurement item performs its measurements and calculations and then activates its actuation strategy. The calibration strategy used in this framework looks like the following code sample. It first requests its context: the measurement item to calibrate itself. This causes the measured values to be stored as set values in the measurement item. The next step is to call the item factory with the measurement item as an argument. This causes the item factory to replace its current prototype item with the measurement item passed as an argument. Now, all following trigger events will result, in that the item factory instantiates a copy of the measurement item now stored as the prototype item; in other words, the prototype measurement item contains the new set values.

```
actuate
    "performs the required actuations for calibration after the
measurement is finished"

    context calibrate.
    (context factory) calibrate: context.
    ^self
```

11.2.8 Item Factory

The item factory incorporates both the Abstract Factory and the Prototype design patterns [Gamma 1995] and it is responsible for instantiating instances of class MeasurementItem whenever it receives a trigger event, to configure these instances and to activate each instance by providing it with a separate process or invoking its start method.

Figure 11.7 shows the class structure of ItemFactory. It contains an instance of MeasurementItem denoted as prototype item and a state variable, inCalibration, indicating whether the system is in calibration mode or in normal operation. The calibrate method is used to put the item factory in calibration mode, whereas the calibrate(anItem) method is used to replace the current prototype item with the passed argument.

The trigger method is the main method of the item factory, since it is responsible for instantiating new measurement items. The code of the method is shown as follows. First, a new copy of the prototype item is created. Second, it is determined whether the system is in calibration, causing a calibration strategy to be used as the actuation strategy, or whether the system is in normal operation, in which case the normal actuation strategy is used. Subsequently, the necessary references are bound and the measurement item is activated by invoking its start method.

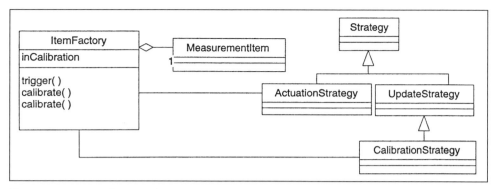

Figure 11.7   ItemFactory class.

```
trigger
     "called by the trigger to indicate that a measurement item has
entered the system"

     | mi as|
     mi := prototypeItem copy.
     (inCalibration)
          ifTrue: [ as := CalibrationStrategy new.
inCalibration := false]
          ifFalse: [as := ActuationStrategy new].
     as context: mi.
     mi actuationStrategy: as.
     mi factory: self.
     mi start.
     ^mi
```

11.2.9 Actuator

The actuator is used to perform actions in the real world based on the measurements taken by the measurement system on the measurement item at hand. Examples of actions performed by actuators are removing a dirty beer can from a conveyer belt or printing a code on the physical measurement item. So far, only the superclass Actuator has been defined. More concrete actuator classes are often so application-specific that they need to be defined for concrete applications.

The basic behavior of an actuator is to perform actions in the real world through an interface. These actions can vary widely—for example, removing an item from a conveyor belt or printing a code on the item that later is used for classifying the item. The actuator is invoked by the actuation strategy stored in the measurement item during the actuation phase. After instantiation, the measurement item first enters the calculation phase, during which it collects data from sensors that is stored in the measurement values. Subsequently, the measurement item enters the actuation phase, thereby invoking the actuation strategy to determine the appropriate actions. The actuation strategy will invoke the relevant actuators, causing the intended actions in the real world. The context of class Actuator is shown in Figure 11.8.

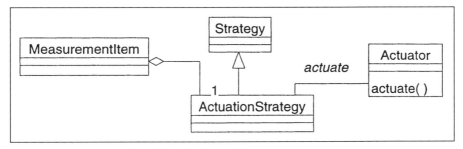

Figure 11.8   Context of class Actuator.

11.2.10 Realtime Aspects

Although time is not mentioned in the description of the classes in the framework, it does play an important role in the framework and in measurement systems in general. In a measurement system, an entity enters the system—for example, on a conveyor belt— and is detected by a trigger sensor, causing the actions described earlier. However, all subsequent actions need to be performed at certain time points and not arbitrarily. A sensor needs to read the data at the time when the measurement item passes the sensor, just as the actuator has to perform its action at the right point in time. Although failure of realtime constraints is not catastrophic, the correct operation of the system depends on it. Untimely behavior may stop the production process, and the system can therefore be viewed as relatively hard realtime. As opposed to most (hard) realtime systems, a measurement system is not a periodic system. Although there is repeated behavior in the system, this behavior is not triggered by a clock but by a trigger sensor. Since the amount of time between two items may vary, so may the computation requested from the system.

In the framework design, all time points are considered relative to the time at which the trigger detected an item entering the system. The trigger sensor sends a trigger event to the item factory with a time stamp in milliseconds as an argument. This time stamp is passed on to the measurement item object that is created in response to the event. The measurement item contains a calculation strategy and an actuation strategy, both of which need to be executed in a time-aware manner, for reasons previously described. Both the calculation and actuation strategies use the time stamp to time their reading and actuation actions. Since the strategies are highly application-dependent, it is no problem that these strategies hard-code the necessary delays between their actions.

One aspect not taken care of by this approach, and consequently left out of the framework, is the situation where the time points at which actions need to take place are dependent on some external factor. For example, if the conveyor belt has a variable speed, the time points for reading and actuating will depend on the speed of the conveyor belt.

11.3 Simulating Framework Applications

Any framework requires evaluation of its design after it has been defined. This is a necessary activity to validate the generality of the design and the degree of reusability that can be achieved from it. For the domain of measurement systems, constructing real applications only for testing the framework is not feasible due to the large cost involved, which is primarily the result of the expensive equipment in a measurement system. Therefore, before constructing actual systems using the framework, the developer should evaluate it carefully. Based on this, it was decided to develop some framework applications in a simulated context. Rather than running the framework application in a real measurement system, it would initially run in a simulated environment.

The notion of a simulated environment requires that entities be available that act as placeholders for the actual hardware that is part of the measurement system being simulated. In the case of measurement systems, these entities are primarily the physical sensors and actuators, since these are the entities that are connected to the Sensor and Actuator classes in the framework. A simulated framework application can be visually represented as shown in Figure 11.9. Three main parts are identifiable: the framework, the simulated environment, and, in between, the application code. The framework was described in *Section 11.2*. The application code refers to the code necessary to adapt the contents of the framework for the application at hand and to functionality that is so specific to the application that it is unlikely that it can be reused in other contexts. The simulated environment is discussed in the following subsections.

11.3.1 Physical Sensors

Instances of the Sensor class in the framework are supposed to be connected to a physical (hardware) sensor that provides measurement data. In a simulated environment, the physical sensor has to be simulated by a PhysicalSensor class. So far, as shown in Figure 11.10, only a few classes have been defined, but this can easily be extended since the interactions between the framework sensor and the physical sensor have explicitly been defined.

The PhysicalSensor class contains a sensor process, a dependent sensor, and a cycle. The process is used to represent the independent behavior of some hardware sensors to generate different data over time. The dependent sensor refers to the framework (software) sensor that is associated with the hardware sensor. As described earlier, the hardware sensor may notify the software sensor that its value has changed and, in order to do that, the hardware sensor needs a reference to it. The cycle instance variable indicates the speed of the simulation process inside the hardware sensor. Since this process is iterative, the cycle indicates the amount of time to wait before starting the subsequent iteration.

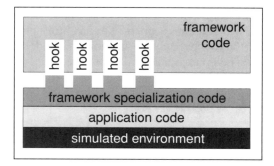

Figure 11.9   Simulated framework application.

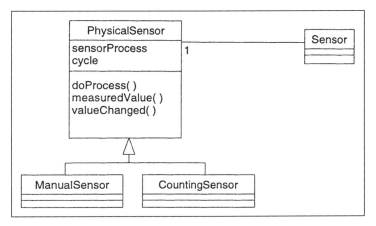

Figure 11.10   Subclasses of PhysicalSensor.

The manual sensor, a subclass of the hardware sensor, implements a simple testing sensor that allows the user of the simulation environment to test parts of the application by incrementing the value stored in the manual sensor, potentially causing triggers and other computation to occur inside the application. The counting sensor automatically counts and can be used to test the iterative behavior of the application. The counting sensor contains its own process, whereas the manual sensor is purely reactive and manipulated through the user interface.

11.3.2 Physical Actuator

Similar to the physical sensor, a physical actuator is connected to a framework (software) actuator, but the connection is only one-directional—from the actuator to the physical actuator—since no communication is required in the opposite direction. The software actuator can actuate the physical actuator through a reference to it.

As shown in Figure 11.11, only a few classes have been defined for the PhysicalActuator class. Each PhysicalActuator instance is accessed through the actuate method, defined as an abstract method at the PhysicalActuator superclass. Two concrete subclasses have been defined: ValveActuator and SlideBarActuator. The ValveActuator class simulates a valve and can be in two states (open and closed) and two active states (opening and closing). Each actuation causes the valve to change state from closed to open or the opposite. The SlideBarActuator class simulates extender behavior of some kind; that is, on each actuation the extender goes from base position to full extended position and back to the base position.

11.3.3 Example

For the simulation, a class was defined that could contain a configuration of a measurement system (see Figure 11.12). This configuration consists of the configurable parts of the measurement system (the sensors and the actuators) and the simulated

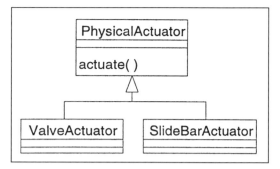

Figure 11.11   Subclasses of PhysicalActuator.

context of the measurement systems (the hardware sensors and the hardware actuators). The user can add, delete, and edit each of the entities. The link button is used to link a hardware sensor and a software sensor or an actuator to a hardware actuator. When all settings are made, the start button is pressed to instantiate the system, leading to the situation shown in Figure 11.13, where the four entities and an instance of the Trigger class are presented.

For adding and editing entities in the measurement system, a window as shown in Figure 11.14 is used. This example is used for adding and editing sensors. Each sensor has a class (selected from the set of subclasses of class Sensor) and two strategies, an update strategy and a calculation strategy. Each strategy can be selected from the available alternatives.

In Figure 11.14, the results of an instantiation of the preceding example are shown. In this example, the counting sensor has a separate process that counts from 0 to 50. For every increment, the sensor is notified. Since the sensor has an OnChangeUpdate strategy, the sensor will update its own value representation by reading the value of the counting sensor. When the sensor updates itself, the trigger is notified. Depending on the update strategy of the trigger, the trigger either reacts to the notification or reads

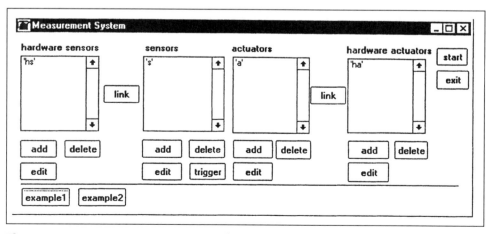

Figure 11.12   Measurement system configuration tool.

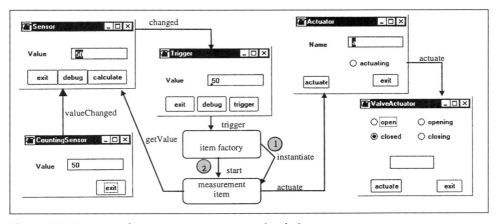

Figure 11.13   Example measurement system simulation.

the sensor in a periodic manner. The trigger's reaction consists of reading the value of the sensor, deciding whether the value justifies a trigger and, if it does, triggering the item factory. The item factory, in response, creates a copy of the prototype measurement item that it contains and starts the measurement item. The measurement item reads the sensors to which it is connected via its measurement value instances, performs a transformation of the acquired data, and, depending on its actuation strategy, may actuate one or more of the actuators to which it has stored references. Each actuator will, in reaction, actuate the hardware actuator to which it is connected—in this case, the valve actuator. The valve actuator will change state from closed to open or vice versa for each actuation. On each actuation, the actuator enters the active state—that is, opening or closing—and goes through an iterative process, opening or closing the slider bar in 10 steps.

11.4 Example: Beer Can System

In this section, we develop a simple example measurement system that illustrates the use of the measurement system framework.

The beer can system is placed at the entrance of a beer can filling factory and its goal is to remove from the input stream beer cans that are not clean, that is, cans that contain dirt of some kind. Clean cans should just pass the system without any further action. To achieve this, the measurement system consists of a triggering sensor, a camera, and an actuator that can remove cans from the conveyer belt. When a can enters the measurement system, the system receives a trigger event from the trigger in the hardware. After some amount of time, the camera will read a sample input, from which only a single picture line is returned. This sampling is repeated a few times and, subsequently, the measured values are compared to the ideal values and a decision about removing or not

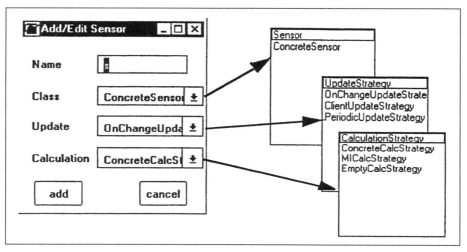

Figure 11.14 Sensor add and edit window.

removing the can is made. If the can should be removed, the actuator is invoked at a time point fixed relative to the time the trigger event took place, and the can is removed from the belt. Figure 11.15 presents the system graphically.

The camera reads a square area consisting of 256×256 pixels and 256 gray tones per pixel. The reason that the camera returns only a single picture line involves an implementation issue: Dealing with five line samples is much less computationally intensive than dealing with a complete matrix.

Since we intend to simulate this application, we also have to design the context of the measurement application. The context consists of the two sensors and the actuator. Since the trigger sensor and the camera are related to the same real-world process, these need to interact in order to generate realistic input for the measurement application. Thus, when the trigger generates an event, not only the application, but also the camera, is to be notified. We assume that the conveyor belt has a constant speed and that the beer cans pass through the system with a minimal interval, but not necessarily a constant interval. For the simulation, we assume that the minimal interval between two beer cans is 1.5 seconds. During the first second, the beer can passes the system and the subsequent 0.5 second cover the empty space until the next can. In order to be able to follow the simulation, the system runs at one tenth of the actual time; in other words, the 1.5 seconds between the cans in the simulation equals 15 seconds in realtime.

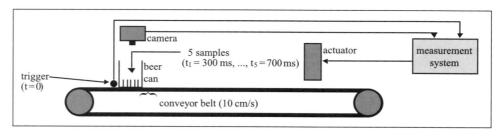

Figure 11.15 Example beer can measurement system.

To simulate the software of this measurement system, the first step is to define classes that represent the hardware entities of the measurement system—that is, the trigger, the camera, and the actuator for removing cans from the conveyor belt. Based on these classes, the necessary extensions to the framework that are needed to construct the application can be defined. In the following section, the hardware classes are defined. The application classes and the configuration of the beer can system are described in *Section 11.4.2.*

11.4.1 Physical Entity Classes

A number of hardware simulating classes are required to construct a realistic simulation of the beer can system. These are the physical trigger, the physical camera, and the physical actuator. For illustrative purposes, we also defined a clock class that allowed us to relate the occurrence of events to certain time points. In the following sections, the hardware simulating classes are described.

HWBCTrigger

The first class is the physical beer can trigger, HWBCTrigger (see Figure 11.17). In reality, the trigger might be a light sensor circuit where the light beam is broken by a beer can entering the system. Here, the physical trigger class has two modes, manual and automatic. In the manual mode, the user of the simulation can cause a trigger by pressing the trigger button. The trigger will pass the trigger event on to the software trigger, the hardware camera (discussed in the next section), and the clock. In the automatic mode, the trigger starts a process that creates a trigger event every 1.5 simulation seconds (that is, every 15 seconds in realtime).

HWBCCamera

The physical camera simulation class, HWBCCamera, is based on a real camera used by EC-Gruppen. The physical camera reads an area, but the processor in the physical camera takes only a single image line from the read area. The image line covers the relevant part of the conveyor belt over the width. Since the camera reads an image line every 100 milliseconds (ms) simulation time, a beer can will be read 10 times since it takes 1 second to pass the camera. Both the camera user interface and the image line principle are shown in Figure 11.16.

The physical camera can read and store data in many different ways, but the only aspect relevant for this system is whether an image line is a good line or a bad line. The good line indicates an image line that is read from a clean beer can, whereas a bad line is an image line read from a dirty beer can. When receiving a trigger event (either from the trigger button or from an external source), the camera starts a process that will generate 10 image lines, 100 ms apart. The reading radio button indicates when the camera is active. In reality, the camera would run constantly, but there is no reason to simulate that behavior since the beer can will pass in 1 second. The camera can run in three modes: only good, only bad, and random. In the only good mode, only good image lines are generated, in the only bad mode only bad image lines are generated, and in the

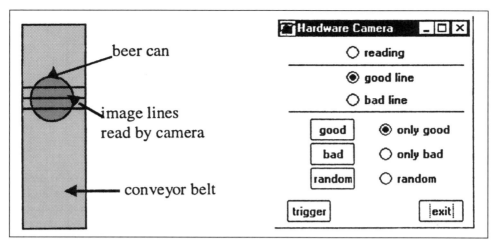

Figure 11.16 Image lines read by the camera.

random mode both types of lines are generated using a random number generator. In reality the percentage of dirty beer cans is very small, typically less than 1 percent or 1 pro mille, but the probability in the case of the simulated camera is larger—for example, 15 percent—to avoid having to wait for several hours before detecting a dirty can.

HWBCActuator

The physical actuator class, HWBCActuator, simulates a physical device for removing dirty beer cans from the conveyor belt. The device uses a mechanical leg that kicks the beer can from the belt into a container. The user interface of the actuator shows when the actuator is passive or active and the slide bar illustrates the mechanical leg.

11.4.2 Beer Can System

When designing the beer can software system that uses the hardware simulating classes described in the preceding section, we were very pleased to find that the extensions to the framework required to obtain system functionality were very limited and were located exactly where we intended them during framework design—that is, the strategies. As we will show later, only two new strategy classes had to be defined: the calculation strategy and the actuation strategy for the measurement item. In addition, we had to write a configuration specification to describe the required objects and their relationships. The configuration specification is shown as follows:

```
configurationBeerCanSystem
    | mi mv clock |
    hwTrigger := HWBCTrigger new.
    hwCamera := HWBCCamera new.
    hwTrigger hwCamera: hwCamera.
    swTrigger := Trigger new.
```

```
hwTrigger dependentSensor: swTrigger.
itemFactory := ItemFactory new.
swTrigger itemFactory: itemFactory.
swCamera := ConcreteSensor new.
swCamera calculationStrategy:
      (ConcreteCalcStrategy new context: swCamera).
swCamera updateStrategy:
      (OnChangeUpdateStrategy new context: swCamera).
swCamera hardwareSensor: hwCamera.
hwCamera dependentSensor: swCamera.
mi := itemFactory prototypeItem.
mi calculationStrategy: (BCMICalcStrategy new context: mi).
5 timesRepeat: [
      mv := (MeasurementValue new sensor: swCamera).
      mv calculationStrategy: (MICalcStrategy new context: mv).
      mi addMeasurementValue: mv.
].
itemFactory prototypeItem: mi.
itemFactory actuationStrategy: BCActuationStrategy new.
hwbcActuator := BCHWActuator new.
swActuator := Actuator new.
swActuator hardwareActuator: hwbcActuator.
mi addActuator: swActuator.
clock := BCClock new.
hwTrigger clock: clock.
hwTrigger open. hwCamera open. swTrigger open. itemFactory open.
swCamera open. hwbcActuator open. swActuator open. clock open.
```

Although the configuration consists of several lines, it is rather short if one bears in mind that it describes the complete beer can system, including both the hardware simulation part and the software system. The running simulation system consists of several windows and several concurrent processes. Figure 11.17 shows an annotated snapshot of the complete system.

BCMICalcStrategy

The beer can measurement item calculation strategy (BCMICalcStrategy) contains one method, performCalculation, that describes how and when the measurement item should read the sensor. The measurement item contains five measurement values, all of which are connected to the camera sensor. The idea is to read the camera sensor at five different points in time, in other words, at 300, 400, . . ., 700 ms after the trigger event. The results from these read operations are stored in the measurement values and will subsequently be used by the actuation strategy described in the next section. The code of the performCalculation method is shown here:

```
performCalculation
      | st mvs |
      st := context startTime.
      mvs := context measurementValues.
      "MV - 1"
```

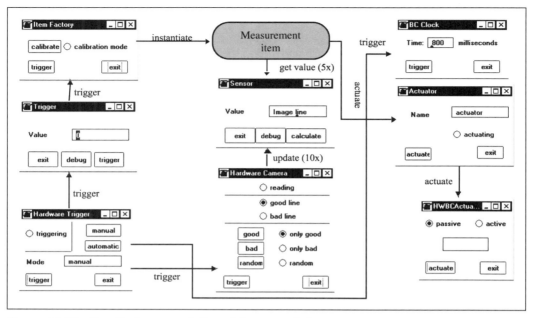

Figure 11.17   Graphical representation of the example beer can measurement system.

```
(Delay untilMilliseconds: st+3000) wait.
(mvs at: 1) performCalculation.
"MV - 2"
(Delay untilMilliseconds: st+4000) wait.
(mvs at: 2) performCalculation.
"MV - 3"
(Delay untilMilliseconds: st+5000) wait.
(mvs at: 3) performCalculation.
"MV - 4"
(Delay untilMilliseconds: st+6000) wait.
(mvs at: 4) performCalculation.
"MV - 5"
(Delay untilMilliseconds: st+7000) wait.
(mvs at: 5) performCalculation.
^self
```

BCActuationStrategy

The beer can actuation strategy class, BCActuationStrategy, also contains a single method, actuate. The actuation strategy is responsible for determining the appropriate actions by the measurement system, that is, whether or not to remove the beer can from the conveyor belt. The actuation strategy implemented in this system is that, at most, one of the read image lines may differ from the ideal image line. If more than one image line is different, the beer can will be removed. The time of actuation should be exactly 1 second after the trigger event, as shown in the following actuate method code:

```
actuate
    | act mvs st counter|
    act := (context actuators) at: 1.
    st := context startTime.
    mvs := context measurementValues.
    "count bad lines"
    counter := 0.
    1 to: 5 do: [ :n | | mv | mv := mvs at: n.
        ((mv measuredValue value at:1) = (mv idealValue at: 1))
            ifFalse: [ counter := counter + 1]
    ].
    (counter > 1) ifTrue: [ act actuate: st + 10000].
    ^self
```

11.5 Evaluation

Constructing an object-oriented framework from a number of example applications is a challenging activity that is easy to underestimate in its complexity and required time. One important problem is that every issue that comes up during the design process has to be evaluated with respect to generality, on the one hand, and real-world applicability, on the other hand. In this section, we perform an evaluation from two perspectives: first, an evaluation of the lessons learned during the design of this first version of the framework as presented in this chapter, and, second, an evaluation of the conventional object-oriented paradigm in itself. The latter evaluation, although perhaps unorthodox, is highly relevant for our research, since we use the object-oriented paradigm for modeling our applications and reusable components. If the object-oriented paradigm in itself lacks particular features or the expressiveness necessary for dealing with certain aspects of the domain, this should result in an adaptation of it.

11.5.1 Lessons Learned

The framework described in this chapter is the result of cooperation between the University of Karlskrona/Ronneby and EC-Gruppen, an industrial company producing, among other things, embedded systems. From this cooperation and the framework design in itself, we gained experience about a number of issues that we believe are relevant for similar projects.

Research Philosophy

Especially in a research project that is as concrete as the development of an object-oriented framework, the active involvement of the industrial partner(s) is of crucial importance. The traditional view of scientific development is that knowledge is developed at universities and then distributed to industry, which constitutes knowledge transfer. The modern view of this process, which we have experienced as much more accurate, is that knowledge develops in the process of meeting and discussing the topics. Knowledge is developed on both the industrial and the academic sides using input from each other.

In our project, the most intense situations were the design meetings, where both the academic and the industrial partners were involved. Academics constantly challenged the old way of doing things, whereas the industry people attacked the abstract and generic ideas provided by the academics and demanded to see concrete applications of them. All of us felt that the applications developed through these meetings. However, repeating our experiences requires that a few preconditions be fulfilled. First, the group should be small, maximally 5 to 10 people. In larger groups, creativity and discussions do not flow as freely. Second, the people in the group have to trust each other and must dare to say anything that comes to mind without feeling inhibited. Explicit attention should be directed to encouraging this, especially in multicultural groups (academia and industry). Finally, the group must find the right balance between developing a result in time and giving the team the opportunity to reflect. Although all members should have the goal of the project clearly in mind, we believe that explicit time pressure reduces the quality of the solution and does not pay off in the long run.

Project Size

Although project size has been identified as an issue by other authors as well, it was definitely valid for this project. Designing a framework is a very complex and time-consuming process that is easily underestimated. The amount of domain knowledge that is required to design a useful framework is much greater than that needed for normal application development. Also, a solid understanding of the design space of applications in the domain is very important. When entering the domain of interest as a novice, considerable amounts of time should be directed to studying the domain before a useful design can be made.

The abstract design of the measurement system framework consists of about 25 classes. Although this is not very large, a concrete instantiation of the framework will include several concrete classes inherited from the framework classes, increasing the size of the measurement system. The framework was designed as part of a government-sponsored project with a duration of one year which included approximately six people, about evenly divided between industry and academia. However, no one involved was working full-time with the framework design. Although the company has developed prototype instantiations of the framework, at the time of writing the development of their first product based on the framework had not yet started.

Boundary

Designing a framework for a domain may seem like a well-defined task, but in practice we found that drawing the boundary for the framework was extremely difficult. In our early discussions, we constantly extended the framework, since we all agreed that the framework would be even better if it included yet another feature. We soon realized that the size of the framework would be unmanageable for our project; however, prioritizing features is a difficult process. To give just one example, measurement systems are also used in the production of fluid and gas products. In those systems, the notion of a measurement item is not as clearly present as in the measurement systems discussed in this chapter. Initially, we decided without much discussion that this type of system should also be included, since it would make the framework even better. However, we soon found that, from a design perspective as well as from a time perspective, the framework should be focused to incorporate item-based measurement systems only. The design was complicated by including continuous production measurement, and the required time and effort exceeded our budget.

Hands On

When designing the framework, we found it to be very important to experiment with the identified concepts and to prototype the framework. We used Smalltalk-80 [Goldberg-Robson 1989] for this purpose, since it allowed us to rapidly create applications from the framework that also had some graphics associated. In addition, Smalltalk provides processes and contains a notion of time, resulting in a more realistic simulated prototype. In any case, prototyping the framework during design provides immediate feedback on the usefulness and flexibility of the design.

11.5.2 Evaluating the Object-Oriented Paradigm

The goal of the project was to create a reusable architecture and associated assets that could be used to construct measurement systems for less cost than when building them from scratch. The underlying paradigm used for the framework is the object-oriented approach. Although the object-oriented paradigm has several advantages over more traditional paradigms, the developer also has to critically evaluate the paradigm that is used. Such evaluations reveal the weaknesses of a paradigm and allow the developer to deal with them by circumventing them during application development and, whenever possible, to solve the weaknesses by extensions to the paradigm. Although the latter approach is traditionally considered to be infeasible, our experience with the layered object model, our research language, has shown that using an extensible language model with an extensible compiler that generates C++ code is quite feasible and provides considerable extended expressiveness as compared to a rather small implementation effort.

During the design of the measurement system framework, we identified a number of problems. These problems are related to the use of strategies, the calling direction between two objects, and the binding of the acquaintances of an object. Each of the problems is discussed in the following sections.

Strategies

In [Gamma 1995] the Strategy design pattern is introduced as a solution to the problem in which an application domain contains many similar classes that differ only in the algorithm used by the class. The Strategy design pattern separates the algorithm from the class by modeling the algorithm as an independent class. The class that requires the algorithm creates an instance of an algorithm class, stores it as a part object, and accesses the algorithm by calling its part object.

In the measurement system framework, we made extensive use of the Strategy pattern. For example, the Sensor class contains an update strategy that determines when the sensor updates itself, that is, when the hardware sensor indicates that something has changed, when a client calls the sensor, or as a periodic process. In addition to update strategies, we used calculation strategies that describe how to collect data and how to transform it, and actuation strategies that describe how to interpret the accumulated data and how to actuate via the actuators.

The problem that we experienced with the use of strategies is that, although a strategy increases the flexibility of a class, it also considerably complicates the interactions within the object and between the strategy object and the containing object. The way the Strategy pattern is presented in [Gamma 1995] is such that the object simply calls the strategy object, which, in response, just does its thing and returns. However, the strategies that were used in the measurement systems framework were much more interaction-oriented, in that the strategy had to call its context object to obtain data, reference to acquaintances, change state, and invoke methods. This created the need for a much more complex interface between the strategy object and the context object and, furthermore, since much internal interaction within the context object takes place via the strategy object, the understandability of the context object is decreased because the functionality of many of the methods is no longer so obvious.

When analyzing this problem, we identified that the Strategy design pattern implements one or more methods of the context object in such a way that these methods can easily be replaced by other implementations. However, since the Strategy pattern is implemented as a part object, it is not at the same level as the methods of the context object. This creates the complex interaction patterns within the context object. A solution to this problem would be an object model that allows the replacement of individual methods in an object or that manages to better integrate the strategy implementation into the object.

One could argue that the Strategy pattern was a bad choice for our cases and that, for example, subclasses would have been more appropriate. We disagree with this for several reasons. First, the reason for using the Strategy pattern (factoring out behavior) and our goal (being able to change aspects of the class behavior) are a perfect match and there is no reason to suspect difficulty. Second, we wanted to replace some strategies at runtime, and this is not supported by other approaches such as subclassing.

Calling Direction

The traditional object communication semantics are that a sender object sends a message to a known receiver object. This is a very clear and simple approach to communication between computational entities such as objects. However, this simple message transmission may represent many different relations between objects. As we identified in [Bosch 1996], many types of relations can exist between two objects or classes and all these relations are implemented using message passing.

In the design of the measurement system framework, we ran into a problem related to message passing in a number of places. The problem was that, in the situation where two objects had some relation, it was not clear which of the two objects would call the other object. This was particularly evident in two locations in the framework. The first was between the hardware sensor and the sensor objects. In some applications, the hardware sensor will actively invoke the sensor with newly collected data, whereas, in other applications, the sensor will call the hardware sensor and retrieve the most current data from the hardware sensor. Both approaches are equally valid, but which is used depends on the particular application. Keeping the flexibility to implement the required updating approach required that both objects be designed to contain update strategies such that each application could configure the update approach it required. In light of the problems described in the previous section, this use of strategies is less than ideal.

The second location at which the calling direction problem appeared was between the measurement item and the sensor. Depending on the application, either the measurement item invokes the sensor to collect that data or the sensor pushes the data toward the measurement item. Since we were unwilling to further complicate the interaction patterns between the entities in the framework, we decided to hard-code the first approach in the framework; in other words, the measurement item always collects the data from the various sensors rather than the other way around. However, ideally, we would have preferred to have flexibility in that respect also.

As a potential solution, it should be possible to define some type of relation between two objects that abstracts the calling direction between the two objects such that neither of the objects needs to be concerned with this. This issue is also related to the problem discussed in the next section.

Acquaintance Handling

Virtually all objects use other objects in the course of their operation. These other objects are referred to as *acquaintances* of the object. These acquaintances are bound to the object either through the use of global object names (and classes) or through the use of references, for which the updating has to be programmed explicitly. Although this is an accepted way of dealing with acquaintance selection and binding, we found it to be rather troublesome in our design of the framework and, especially, during experimentation with it.

The problem is that all application specifications based on the framework lead to rather large configuration specifications where all objects need to be explicitly bound to other relevant objects—not seldom, in both directions. This problem appeared in numerous places in the framework. One example is the strategies: For every strategy instantiated in an application, two bindings have to be explicitly specified (one binding from the context object to the strategy object and one binding in the other direction). Thus, despite the fact that the strategy object is located inside the context object, these objects still need to be configured with references to each other. Other examples are that the trigger has to be configured with a reference to the item factory, despite the fact that only a single item factory exists within the system, and that the prototype measurement item has to be bound to each sensor and actuator (and despite the fact that each sensor and actuator is of a particular type and could be identified very easily). As a result, in the specification of an application, up to two thirds of the code may function to bind objects to their acquaintances. The acquaintance handling increases complexity, reduces reusability, and requires a considerable amount of resources from the programmer.

We study this problem in more detail in [Bosch 1998], where we also propose a solution in the context of the layered object model; however, we can at least conclude that it is important to differentiate between the specification of the requirements an object has on its acquaintance and the actual selection and binding process. Then, in more advanced systems, the selection and binding process can be automated, relieving the software engineer from the configuration task.

11.6 Related Work

The domain of object-oriented frameworks has been studied by many authors; see, for example, [Johnson-Foote 1988; Mattsson 1996; Opdyke-Johnson 1990; Pree 1994]. Although some discussion remains, most authors agree that a framework consists of a set of classes that embodies an abstract design for an application or subsystem domain. Several frameworks have been designed for various domains ranging from operation systems [Yokote 1992] to user interfaces [Weinand- Gamma 1994]. In this chapter, we have used the advances made in object-oriented frameworks as input. For example, design patterns [Gamma 1995] are becoming increasingly popular as a means to design and describe frameworks [Beck-Johnson 1994]. We have used several design patterns throughout the chapter to model and explain parts of the framework.

To the best of our knowledge, no other object-oriented frameworks specifically for measurement systems have been defined. [Schmid 1995] reports on a framework for manufacturing that deals with much higher-level aspects than individual sensors and actuators. [Lea 1995] describes a framework for avionics that contains elements as sensors and actuators that are also present in our framework. However, the processing of data from the sensors and the activation of actuators are clearly different in the two frameworks because of a difference in application-domain requirements.

11.7 Summary

The advantages of measurement systems are generally improved performance/cost ratio and more consistent and accurate quality control, which obviate the need to be able to reuse existing measurement system software. As a solution to the lack of reusability, we have introduced and discussed a design for an architecture and a framework for the domain of measurement systems. The version of the framework presented here focuses primarily on the main elements of a measurement system such as its architecture; more concrete classes for such items as types of concrete sensors and actuators are lacking. However, adding these classes is relatively simple since the interface of the classes and the interactions to the other classes have been defined. Aspects such as realtime behavior, concurrency, and distribution have not been the primary focus in this presentation of the framework, although we acknowledge the importance of these aspects.

Several examples of framework instantiations have been presented in this chapter, and an extended evaluation of the lessons we learned during the design of the framework was also presented. In addition, we analyzed the expressiveness of the object-oriented paradigm and identified three situations in which the traditional object-oriented paradigm lacks expressiveness—dealing with strategies, the calling direction between objects, and the selection and binding of acquaintances. In our future research on extended object-oriented language models, we intend to address these issues.

11.8 References

[Beck-Johnson 1994] Beck, K., and R.E. Johnson. Patterns generate architecture. *Proceedings ECOOP 1994*, M. Tokoro and P. Pareschi, editors, LNCS 821 Springer-Verlag, Bologna, Italy, July 1994.

[Bosch 1996] Bosch, J. Relations as object model components. *Journal of Programming Languages* 4:39–61.

[Bosch 1998] Bosch, J. Object acquaintance selection and binding. Submitted for publication in *Theory and Practice of Object Systems,* 1998.

[Gamma 1995] Gamma, E., R. Helm, R. Johnson, and J. Vlissides. *Design Patterns: Elements of Reusable Object-Oriented Software.* Reading, MA: Addison-Wesley, 1994.

[Goldberg-Robson 1989] Goldberg, A., and D. Robson. *Smalltalk-80: The Language and Its Implementation.* Reading, MA: Addison-Wesley, 1989.

[Johnson-Foote 1988] Johnson, R.E., and B. Foote. Designing reusable classes. *Journal of Object-Oriented Programming* 1(2), June 1988.

[Lea 1995] Lea, D. *Design Patterns for Avionics Control Systems.* DSSA Adage Project ADAGE-OSW 94-01, 1995.

[Mattsson 1996] Mattsson, M. Object-oriented frameworks: A survey of methodological issues. LU-CS-TR:96-167, licentiate thesis, Lund University, 1996.

[Opdyke-Johnson 1990] Opdyke, W.F., and R.E. Johnson. Refactoring: An aid in designing object-oriented application frameworks. *Proceedings of Symposium on Object-Oriented Programming Emphasizing Practical Applications,* 1990.

[Pree 1994] Pree, W. Meta-patterns: A means for capturing the essential of reusable object-oriented design. *Proceedings ECOOP 1994,* M. Tokoro and P. Pareschi, editors, LNCS 821 Springer-Verlag, Bologna, Italy, July 1994.

[Schmid 1995] Schmid, H.A. Creating the architecture of a manufacturing framework by design pattern. OOPSLA 1995, pp. 370–384, Austin, Texas, October 1995.

[Weinand-Gamma 1994] Weinand, A., and E. Gamma. ET++: A portable, homogeneous class library and application framework. *Proceedings of the UBILAB 1994 Conference,* Zürich, Switzerland, September 1994.

[Yokote 1992] Yokote, Y. The Apertos Reflective Operating System: The concept and its implementation. *Proceedings OOPSLA 1992,* Vancouver, British Columbia, October 1992.

Distributed Systems Frameworks

Part Three describes several communication software and distributed systems frameworks. Developers of communication software and distributed systems face many challenges. Communication software and distributed systems contain both inherent complexities, such as fault detection and recovery, and accidental complexities, such as the continuous rediscovery and reinvention of key concepts and components. In addition, distributed systems are usually large scale and require a huge infrastructure. Therefore application framework technology is a perfect approach for building communication software and distributed systems. Part Three contains Chapters 12 through 17 and Sidebars 2 and 3.

Chapter 12, "Compound Active Documents," discusses CORBA/OpenDoc, COM/ OLE/ActiveX, and Java/JavaBeans, which concretely illustrate emerging principles of component and document design, such as the events-properties-methods model. They support components with visual, interactive listening membranes that transform blackbox computers into glass-box systems whose "picture windows" allow clients to both see and modify what is inside. Frameworks are viewed as extensible collaborating collections of components with goal-directed behavior.

Chapter 13, "Supervision and Control Systems Framework Architecture," describes a framework architecture to support the development of supervision and control systems based on CORBA. The architecture is centered around services and domains that help satisfy typical requirements of these systems, such as realtime and fault tolerance. A development method supported by prototype tools and based on the formal language TRIO is also presented to guide designers in the construction of their applications.

Chapter 14, "EPEE: A Framework for Supercomputing," proposes a framework in which the parallel codes can be encapsulated in object-oriented software components that can be reused, combined, and customized with confidence by library designers to offer application programmers easy-to-use programming models. This chapter illustrates an approach with \Paladinpunct, an object-oriented linear algebra library designed along these lines: \Paladin can be used at various levels of abstraction, ranging from a complete hiding of distribution issues down to the fine tuning of parallelism.

Sidebar 2, *Frameworks in the Healthcare Domain*, indicates that the message-oriented framework supports the development and exchange of messages among the server or repository side of applications. It may use object request brokering technologies (such as CORBA and ActiveX) for the exchange of messages. The service-oriented framework supports the development of healthcare-specific services that benefit fully from object request brokering architectures and the established distributed computing services and facilities. The visual integration framework focuses on desktop automation. These frameworks continue to evolve as the market changes and the technology matures.

Chapter 15, "The Bast Framework for Reliable Distributed Computing," describes Bast, an open object-oriented framework for building reliable distributed applications and middleware. Specialized environments, such as group communication toolkits (such as Isis or Totem) or transactional monitors (Encina or Tuxedo, for example), are hardly extensible or customizable for specific needs, because their underlying protocols are hidden and implemented in an ad hoc manner. In contrast, Bast provides customizable distributed protocols as basic components for reliable distributed computing.

Chapter 16, "Object-Oriented Realtime System Framework," attempts to exploit the key issues in the design and application of an object-oriented realtime system framework (OORTSF) for the development of realtime applications in embedded systems. First, the class hierarchy, a scenario for object collaboration in OORTSF, and an attempt to document OORTSF using some design patterns are described. Then, an example on the adaptation of this framework to implement a flight path control realtime system is illustrated.

Chapter 17, "JAWS: A Framework for High-Performance Web Servers," illustrates how to use frameworks and patterns for communication software to develop a high-performance web server called JAWS. JAWS is an object-oriented framework that supports the configuration of various web server strategies, such as a Thread Pool concurrency model with asynchronous I/O and LRU caching versus a Thread-per-Request concurrency model with synchronous I/O and LFU caching. Because JAWS is a framework, these strategies can be customized systematically and measured independently and collaboratively to determine the best strategy profiles. Using these profiles, JAWS can adapt its behavior statically and dynamically to deploy the most effective strategies for a given software/hardware platform and client workload. JAWS's adaptive software features make it a powerful application framework for constructing high-performance web servers.

Sidebar 3, *The Five-Module Framework for Internet Application Frameworks*, presents the five-module architecture of a framework for Internet application development. The five-module architecture was developed as part of an Internet development framework, the Distributed Interactive Web-site Builder (DIWB). The DIWB is built on top of two powerful Internet frameworks, WebObjects and OpenStep. The five-module architecture is designed to separate the tasks of application development, present a component-based software development, and facilitate software evolution. The five-module architecture separates the application into five modules: presentation, UI components, business logic, data management, and system infrastructure. This sidebar presents the functionality of each module, the interface between modules, and some evaluation scenarios of the framework. The architecture has been implemented, exercised, and deployed on the Web.

Compound Active Documents

The concepts *object, component, framework, document,* and *compound active document* have context-dependent meanings but may, as a first approximation, be defined as follows:

Object. Container with identity and interface operations that share a persistent state.

Component. Umbrella concept for variable-granularity, reusable, possibly off-the-shelf entities.

Framework. Having collaborating components with goal-directed extensible behavior through an API.

Document. Component with visible interactive interfaces for browsing and authoring.

Compound active document. Document with autonomous parts programmable through scripting.

Component is an open-ended umbrella concept that includes OpenDoc, COM, and JavaBeans components as well as off-the-shelf pluggable component-based software. *Frameworks,* the primary focus of this chapter, are collections of collaborating components with domain-specific extensible client interfaces. *Documents* are specialized components whose visible interfaces support browsing and authoring, while *compound active documents* consist of parts with autonomous functionality supported by multiple threads and scripting.

OpenDoc extends the file/folder desktop paradigm of the 1980s to provide a powerful and simple compound document model on top of CORBA's interoperable distributed objects. ActiveX provides a document model for World Wide Web (WWW) documents on top of Microsoft's COM/OLE. JavaBeans provides a Java-based application environment for managing components and building platforms out of beans (classes that conform to certain interface conventions) supplied in Java archive repositories (JARs). Comparison of OpenDoc, ActiveX, and JavaBeans document models yields principles for the design and implementation of frameworks of collaborative components with visible, interactive interfaces.

OpenDoc, COM/OLE, and Java have very different component models. OpenDoc components have identity, a state, and visual interfaces; COM/OLE components consist of collections of interfaces that provide time-independent services and treat identity and state as properties of special state-sensitive interfaces for containers, monikers and data transfer; while Java components have a core interface and security model extended by modular class libraries and tools.

OpenDoc specifies a language-independent infrastructure and document model from the ground up through an industry-wide effort coordinated by OMG. Its conceptual and architectural elegance provides a baseline for understanding document architectures, though it has been canceled as a product. ActiveX specializes Microsoft's component architecture COM/OLE to a Web-based document model. Java, with extensions specified in the class libraries java.lang, java.util, and java.awt, provides not only a language but also an environment for component-based technology, while JavaBeans extends the Java environment to provide a toolkit for component and document composition.

CORBA has played a central role in formulating concepts and architectures of interoperability. COM's interoperability at the binary (machine-language) level and Java's interoperability within a single well-designed language are less ambitious than CORBA's multilanguage approach. Interoperability is much simpler in an integrated language, environment, and component model such as Java, since accidental syntactic differences due to language are minimal and questions of semantic interoperability can be addressed directly. JavaBeans focuses on constructing composite beans from Java components, and leaves grafting of top-level application beans (applets) into Web or CORBA systems to higher-level software.

OpenDoc, ActiveX, and JavaBeans differ not only in their substance but also in their descriptive focus. This is reflected in our discussion, which focuses on structure and implementation for OpenDoc, controls for ActiveX, and interfaces and event models for JavaBeans.

12.1 CORBA Component-Based Software Architecture

CORBA's interoperability architecture aims to extend component reusability at the object level across multiple languages and distributed components. It offers four layers of progressively higher-level services.

12.1.1 CORBA's Layered Service Architecture

CORBA's layered service architecture is discussed in this section. The CORBA view emphasizes interactive services at four different levels: object, system, application, and end user. These levels are defined as follows:

Object services. Object-level interoperation among multiple languages, interfaces, and platforms.

System services. System-level components that provide distributed object services.

Application services. Services used to create applications organized as frameworks.

End-user services. Domain-specific services provided to end users.

The traditional 'onion' of system layers (see Figure 12.1a) includes an inner hardware layer, an operating system layer, a programming language layer, and an environment layer. The CORBA view focuses on interactive services at the object, system, application, and end-user levels. The difference in viewpoint between traditional layers of transformation and layers of interaction is significant from the viewpoint of interactive modeling, discussed in later sections. The four levels of interactive service in Figure 12.1b are associated with objects, components, frameworks, and user interfaces.

12.1.2 Primitive Architectural Elements

CORBA primitive architectural elements are objects, components, frameworks, and user interfaces that are defined as follows:

Objects. Interoperable object specification in an interface definition language (IDL).

Components (classes). System service requirements—CORBA common object services.

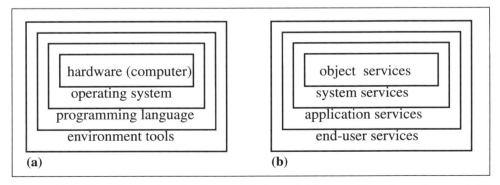

Figure 12.1 Two views of application architecture: (*a*) layers of transformation, and (*b*) layers of interaction.

Frameworks. Specified by API interfaces for developers—CORBA common facilities.

User interfaces. End-user human-computer interface requirements.

Since CORBA's object services and IDL have been widely described elsewhere [Orfali 1996; Wegner 1996] and our primary concern is application services provided by frameworks, the following section briefly examines CORBA's object and system services as a prelude to a more detailed examination of application services.

12.1.3 CORBA Object Services

CORBA's object services are realized by an object request broker (ORB) that handles communication among application objects and provides system and library services. Standard interfaces are specified in an IDL and stored in an interface repository. Interfaces of application objects are mapped to IDL by a language mapping that maps interfaces in specific object-oriented languages into language-independent IDL interfaces.

The ORB accepts requests from client objects through an IDL stub or a dynamic invocation for the services of server objects, transmits them for execution to the server, and returns the result to the client. It also accepts calls to system objects from both client and server objects and object-specific calls through an object adapter, as shown in Figure 12.2.

CORBA provides mediation services (half-bridges) from clients to the ORB and from the ORB to servers. Clients may invoke a service through a static stub or through a dynamic invocation created from the IDL specification at runtime. The ORB validates client requests against the IDL interface and dispatches them to the server, where arguments are unpacked (unmarshaled), methods are executed, and results are returned. Server-side software includes object adapters that bind object interfaces and manage object references, and a server skeleton that uses the output of object adapters to map operators to the methods that implement them.

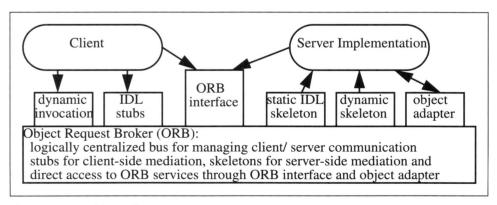

Figure 12.2   Object adapter.

12.2 CORBA System and Application Services

CORBA's system services (common object services) are described in [Orfali 1996], which lists 16 representative operating-system services implemented as classes of a class library.

12.2.1 CORBA System Services

CORBA's application services (common facilities) are classified into vertical (domain-dependent) and horizontal (domain-independent) services implemented by frameworks. *Vertical services* support frameworks for applications such as health and finance and are developed by service providers such as hospitals and banks rather than by computer companies. Horizontal services, expressed as frameworks of collaborating components, include interface, data, task, and system management services.

Naming. For managing, querying, and navigating through object name spaces.

Events. For registering the interest of users in events—push and pull invocation.

Life cycle. For creating, copying, moving, and deleting compound objects.

Trader. Repository of services available to users, analogous to yellow pages.

Transactions. For specifying and managing atomic transactions.

Concurrency control. For acquiring and releasing locks to control coordination of shared data.

Persistence. For managing components that persist beyond the lifetime of the creator in a database.

Query. For finding data that satisfies a query specification.

Collection. For allowing queries to return collections of data that satisfy the query.

Relationships. For keeping track of dynamic relationships among components.

Externalization. For writing the content of components into a stream.

Properties. A repository of properties dynamically associated with objects at runtime.

Time. For synchronizing time in a distributed system.

Security. For enforcing security and authentication of components.

Change management. For version control services.

Licensing. For enforcing licensing restrictions.

12.2.2 CORBA Domain-Independent (Horizontal) Application Services

User interface services are the visible part of an iceberg whose behavior is managed and implemented by hidden information, task, and system management services. Domain-independent services have hooks for domain-specific features that specialize services to a particular domain. OpenDoc specializes these services to documents with four subsystems that loosely correspond to the first three services listed.

Interface management. Interfaces with a common look and feel and hooks for domain-specific services.

Information management. Documents storage and data interchange for compound documents.

Task management. Manages workflows, long transactions, agents, scripting, rules, and task automation.

System management. Manages instrumenting, configuring, installing, operating, and repairing components.

12.2.3 OpenDoc Specialization of Application Services

CORBA interface services correspond to OpenDoc's layout, information management to storage and data transfer facilities, and task management to scripting.

Layout. Manages document presentation and layout within containers.

Storage. Accommodates arbitrary nesting for documents of varying type and size.

Data transfer. Allows for cut and paste, drag and drop, and integrity of linked documents.

Scripting. Supports dynamic execution of programs within active documents.

12.3 OpenDoc: A CORBA Framework for Compound Active Documents

OpenDoc is a CORBA-based document framework that evolved from HyperCard's browsing, authoring, and scripting facilities. Document technology was pioneered by Apple Computer in the early 1980s, was present in a mature form in Hypercard in the late 1980s, and has further evolved in the second and third generation systems described here. Our goal is to describe component-based document architectures of the mid-1990s and to identify underlying architectural models.

12.3.1 Document Structure

Documents have active parts whose interface behavior is specified by parts editors. They are dynamically created as sessions that persist and evolve over their life cycle.

OpenDoc documents are built up from active parts that know how to draw and print themselves and otherwise control their own destiny [OpenDoc 1996]. Interface behavior is controlled by part editors, implemented by subclasses that specialize general-purpose editing facilities to the particular part. Part editors define how the part is initialized, drawn, and moved (externalized) and specify events in which the part is interested. Operations for part handling common to many parts are realized by super-classes of a class hierarchy whose part-specific operations are specified in subclasses.

Each part autonomously controls the layout of its subparts, its interaction with other subparts, its animation and mobility, and its lifetime. Parts editors may be dynamically modified or entirely replaced so that the binding of part editors to parts is looser than that of operations to objects. Parts effectively have multiple editing interfaces that may evolve or be replaced over the lifetime of the part. Loose binding between an object and its interfaces scales up better to large persistent components than does tight bind-ing of operations in traditional objects.

Documents are dynamically created as sessions within a document shell environ-ment. Sessions of a shell are analogous to instances of classes, but scaling up instance creation to large components requires new technology to handle dependence on sup-port tools. Each session supports a name service for binding and accessing names, a storage service for managing persistent documents, an event service for registering and handling interesting events, a drawing service, and a user interface service that handles document presentation. Documents are heavy components that preserve object-based notions of interfaces and instances but have greater interface-accessing and instance-creation overhead than traditional objects.

12.3.2 Layout

OpenDoc's layout determines the visual rules of engagement that realize the user inter-face model; storage facilities implement static document structure and data transfer facil-ities express component mobility, while scripting supports user-specified functionality.

OpenDoc's layout facilities specify visual appearance through the use of frames to represent the visible space (real estate) occupied by a part, facets to control the visible behavior of parts, and canvases to describe the drawing environment in which draw-ing and rendering tools actually render the document part. Frames may have any shape (though they are usually rectangular) and may contain nested frames with autonomous behavior. A given part may appear in many frames with different repre-sentations and parts editors. Document parts can be directly selected independent of their level of nesting, and multiple parts of the document can be active at the same time provided there are no shared resource conflicts. Views in all frames are automatically updated when a part's state is changed.

Facets control the geometric relation of a frame to its containing document. Static canvases are used to render parts that do not change, while dynamic canvases are needed to represent video displays or animated objects. Documents can be recon-structed by reading in the frames, using facets to determine containment relations and asking facets to draw themselves on canvases.

12.3.3 Storage

OpenDoc's layout functionality is supported by a flexible storage system called Bento (after the Japanese compartmentalized food boxes). Bento manages storage for docu-ments by a four-part hierarchy:

Storage system: containers → documents → parts → drafts → storage units.

- A storage system has multiple flexible containers.

- Each container contains a compound active document.

- Each document consists of multiple parts, each having one or more drafts.

- Each draft resides in a flexible storage unit.

Storage units, the primitive low-level units for storing document parts, have a complex structure to model the complexity and versatility of document parts, with about 50 methods for managing the properties and contents of documents. Storage units have properties with values that can be arbitrarily large and include references to other storage units. Property value combinations, called *focuses,* provide a context for method invocation by pattern matching and permit access to values through a stream interface.

Drafts capture development history and facilitate version control. Documents consist of heterogeneous collections of versions of document parts that are stored in a container. The four-level hierarchy of containers, documents, drafts, and storage units supports very flexible parts at the lowest level; history and version control at the next level; composite documents with varied components at the third level; and a general notion of file-structured containers at the top level.

12.3.4 Data Transfer

The data transfer facilities of OpenDoc include drag-and-drop and cut-and-paste, and support automatic updating of links to transferred data. The receiver can decide whether to embed the data as a separate part or to incorporate it within a destination part (this corresponds to the difference between Cons and Append in LISP). If transfers involve a large amount of data, the source can issue a promise that the destination can call in when it is ready to receive the data. Data transfer, which entails the creation of a temporary storage unit, involves a complex sequence of actions.

Though assignment between fixed-size registers of computer memory is simple, scaled-up assignment with variable-size data containing links and other contextual information is complex and shows that scaling up requires qualitative changes in design. Memory structure likewise scales up from fixed-size memory registers to flexible multilevel containers. Part structure scales up from objects whose operations are tightly bound to a state to parts loosely associated with multiple parts editors, while the class-instance relation scales up so instances that must fend for themselves after they are created are replaced by sessions whose evolution over time is managed by system services.

12.3.5 Scaling up from Languages to Components

To scale up from languages to components, there are four concepts, as defined here:

Assignment. Data transfer of components (parts) with links, editors, and visible properties.

Memory register. Container with flexible parts, multiple drafts, and visual properties.

Tightly bound object operations. Loosely bound multiple interfaces that evolve over time.

Class instances. Document sessions with name, storage, and event services.

12.3.6 Scripting

User-defined actions on document parts are specified by script facilities that trigger *events* handled by the event model of Open Scripting Architecture (OSA). Scripts that execute on occurrence of an event are registered as events in an event registry.

Scripts provide a mechanism for adding functionality to a document after it has been created. Dialog boxes when documents are opened can enforce security and perform such other tasks as automatically adapting user interfaces to the skill level, language, and goals of the user. Roaming agents that gather information and represent the interests of nonlocal components can be created as active scriptable documents. Scripts can record and subsequently duplicate sequences of goal-directed user actions to learn patterns of frequent higher-level user behavior.

OpenDoc's attempt to extend Hypercard's neat interface and scripting functionality to distributed interoperable components taught us much about document design, though this project has been terminated. Though the preceding description is terse, it allows comparison of OpenDoc with COM/OLE/ActiveX and Java/JavaBeans.

12.4 Microsoft's Compound Document Architecture: COM/OLE/ActiveX

The component architecture of COM/OLE focuses on interoperability among nondistributed components conforming to interface and interaction constraints imposed by Microsoft's component object model. ActiveX specializes OLE to HTML-based WWW document technology.

COM supports interoperability of interfaces through function tables at the binary (machine language) level. It does not directly support higher-level IDLs for interoperation between C++, Smalltalk, and Java. Binary interoperability is universal, just as Turing machines are a universal computation mechanism, but it requires extra work to support language-sensitive interfaces.

COM's object model differs from that of traditional objects. It defines an object as a collection of interfaces rather than as a collection of operations sharing a common state. All objects have an interface called *Iunknown* that supports multiple interfaces through a query interface function. *QueryInterface* queries the set of interfaces to find a specific interface.

COM interfaces specify a component's plugs and sockets but do not directly support identity, so that clients are not guaranteed access to the same object on successive occasions of access [Orfali 1996]. This model expresses state-independent services, but not objects such as bank accounts whose services depend on their state. COM expresses objects by special-purpose interfaces such as the *dataobject* interface for data transfer and by monikers that provide a powerful naming facility for associating names with storage structures.

Though CORBA and COM differ in their component models, the functionality of each is supported by the other. Tight binding between object identifiers with a state, supported directly in CORBA, is realized in COM by monikers, while loose binding to an interface, the normal accessing mode in COM, is a special case of state-dependent access, and is realized in CORBA/OpenDoc by part editors and other state-independent object services. However, CORBA provides interoperability among distributed objects, whereas COM/OLE in its 1997 incarnation does not support distributed objects.

OLE is an acronym for *Object Linking and Embedding*. The distinction between data transfer by copying and linking to a shared copy is central to its design. OLE supports containers that contain compound components with visual interfaces that can be animated by scripts. It captures OpenDoc's document abstraction by a component abstraction that expresses interface behavior and resides in a container that supplies a persistent identity. Both containers and their contents are specified as collections of interfaces that may be accessed through multiple views, corresponding to OpenDoc's accessing of a document part through different part editors. Data transfer through cut-and-paste and drag-and-drop with updating of links is supported. Transferred data can be referenced by a link or can be directly embedded.

COM/OLE specifies primarily logical rather than visual properties of components and relies on languages like VisualBasic or Visual C++ to provide visual functionality. ActiveX extends the functionality of languages like VisualBasic so that the user can create and customize visual interfaces for controlling interaction. ActiveX is a cross-platform, language-independent technology that facilitates the creation, customization, and management of visual ActiveX controls, either by adding them to a visual programming language or by enhancing web browsers such as Netscape Navigator or Internet Explorer with a collection of customizable primitive controls for common tasks. ActiveX supports creation of controls by customization of generic standard controls or by specification of new controls from scratch.

Controls (called *widgets* in some systems) are visible interface elements such as buttons and dialog boxes that control the behavior of components. They are a visual analog of language control structures that control interactive behavior by user actions rather than controlling algorithmic instruction sequencing. Controls may be activated by user events, such as depressing a mouse, or by system events, such as storing a value of a property. Microsoft's primary goal for ActiveX is to enhance Internet Explorer, which aims to supplant Netscape Navigator as the browser and document manager of choice for web documents.

ActiveX controls control objects on web pages and support interaction among components by listening for the occurrence of events to realize collaborative behavior. They provide document control functionality comparable to that of OpenDoc parts editors and the Java abstract windowing toolkit (AWT), but as an add-on are not as well integrated into the underlying document model as are comparable features of OpenDoc and Java. However, factoring out interface control as an independent part of document models allows powerful interface control technology to be developed. ActiveX provides a growing library of components for layout, animation, virtual reality, and other forms of enrichment of HTML documents.

ActiveX controls can be implemented in a variety of scripting languages, including VBScript for VisualBasic and JScript, which is an open implementation of Javascript. Scripts are directly embedded in HTML code and are compiled when the document is read by Internet Explorer. The idea of visual controls whose functionality can be enhanced by scripting, which was already highly developed in the 1980s in Hypercard's buttons, fields, and dialog boxes, is central to compound active document technology.

ActiveX integrates stand-alone applications such as Excel into web documents by enhancing the functionality of Internet Explorer to handle directly the document format of specific applications. Spreadsheets and charts created in Excel can be directly opened through Internet Explorer or any other suitably enhanced browser. Instead of converting documents to HTML and viewing them with an HTML browser, the document browser is modified to accept documents in a variety of native formats.

The COM/OLE/ActiveX model is open in the sense that it can be extended to new document styles and scripting languages, but is proprietary in that it is designed to work with Microsoft-supported software such as Internet Explorer. Microsoft's strategy appears to be designed to make Internet Explorer the browser of choice for web documents by supporting major competing systems within the COM/OLE component paradigm, while making it hard to run Microsoft systems on CORBA or Java platforms.

12.5 Java Interfaces, Applets, and Beans

Java has been specifically designed to correct deficiencies of earlier object-oriented languages and support secure, modular component-based technology. It has a clean component model that is extended to visual document interfaces through the class library java.awt and is integrated with a well-designed component management system, JavaBeans, to provide a comprehensive compound active document technology.

12.5.1 Extending Interfaces and Implementing Classes

Java's interface model provides a foundation for its component technology by explicitly distinguishing between state-independent interfaces and state-dependent objects and classes [Arnold 1996]. Java interfaces may be viewed as an extreme form of abstract classes for which all operations have a deferred implementation:

Classes. Specify both object interface behavior and its implementation.

Class inheritance. Ambiguously mixes behavior and implementation inheritance.

Abstract classes. Specify object interface behavior; may implement some methods.

Partial implementation. Implementation that must be completed before instances can be created.

Java interfaces. Support pure behavior specification without any implementation.

Interactive composition. Behavior that is better modeled by interfaces than by classes.

The clean distinction between interfaces that specify services and implementations that track evolution over time allows concerns of these two aspects of modeling to be separated. Inheritance is better addressed at the interface level independently of issues of implementation. In particular, multiple inheritance of interfaces avoids problems that arise in multiple inheritance of classes. Java separates behavior extension by inheritance and behavior implementation by classes, as shown in Figure 12.3. Extended interfaces can be further extended, while extension of classes may create problems because of the conflicting open/closed role of classes as hooks for extension and templates for implementation.

Java permits class extension for compatibility with other object-oriented languages, but forbids it for multiple inheritance. Though Java permits extension of classes, it should be avoided in clean programs so that extension (inheritance) is restricted to interfaces and is conceptually independent of class implementation. This accords with the European view that the semantics of inheritance should be defined by specification, as opposed to the U.S. (Smalltalk) view that inheritance should be defined by implementation

Interfaces are transducers (filters) whose composition realizes composite transducers. Interface composition is an object-based analog of instruction composition, and the role of interfaces as a primitive for interaction is an analog of instructions as a primitive for algorithms. When interfaces are attached to components with state they lose their purity, and interaction among operations of an interface and among multiple interfaces makes their behavior difficult to specify. Extending pure interfaces is weaker in the behavior it can describe than extending classes because it cannot model sharing of state at the subclass level: Such behavior can be realized because Java allows extending classes as well as extending interfaces, but should be used only in cases where sharing at the subclass level is a necessary part of the behavior. Interfaces attached to components with state provide persistent services over time whose behavior is described by interaction histories rather than by transformations [Wegner 1997]. Methods of an interface are listening mechanisms triggered by events. Event models that provide a foundation for the semantics of interfaces are discussed in the next section in exploring the component model of JavaBeans.

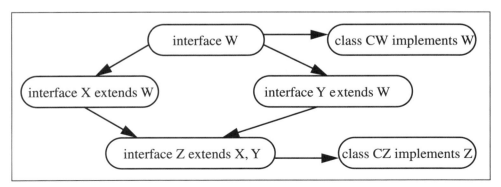

Figure 12.3   Separation of interface inheritance and class implementation.

12.5.2 Applets and JavaBeans

Java supports a flexible client-server model with lightweight servers that dynamically request functionality for specific tasks. Lightweight server technology is exemplified by Hot Java, whose applets can be moved from the server to the client to enhance client functionality dynamically by delegating and distributing server tasks to clients (see Figure 12.4). The greater flexibility of Hot Java than of traditional browsers such as Netscape Navigator is due to late (lazy) binding of protocols and modes of viewing on a call-by-need basis. Interactive client-server computing encourages demand-driven computing by clients that use mobile services on a call-by-need basis, whereas traditional client-server computing supports supply-driven computing by monolithic server resources.

Applets have environment-independent functionality that supports late (lazy) interactive binding of clients. They are mobile processes whose functionality can be harnessed by browsers independently of the environment in which they execute. Java gains great flexibility by its separation of interfaces and implementation, which yields not only cleaner interface inheritance but also process mobility through environment-independent interfaces and interactive binding of interface functionality.

Applets provide stand-alone functionality for documents (web pages), but can neither be used by builder tools in constructing composite components nor interact with their containing document. JavaBeans facilitates the construction of composite beans from collections of component beans, providing a systematic Java-based realization of the compound active document paradigm.

Java beans are reusable software components that provide both runtime functionality and design hooks for creating composite structures that can be manipulated in a builder tool [JavaBeans 1996]. JavaBeans is a construction environment that requires a builder and some beans (usually supplied in a Java archive resource (JAR) file) used as primitive components in constructing composite beans. Builders are tailored to alternative visual target environments and may provide general Web support like ActiveX, domain-specific layout or server applications, or document editing. The builder uses application beans from the JAR, system beans such as buttons, and introspection and customization provided by the JavaBeans system to build applications. Completed applications—for example, applets—may be tested in system-supplied testbeds.

JavaBeans + java.awt + builder + JAR → new beans (applets) constructed by the JavaBeans construction kit using Java's abstract window toolkit, domain-specific beans in JAR, and a builder that understands the target domain.

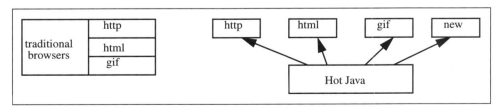

Figure 12.4 Eager versus lazy binding of protocols.

JavaBeans realizes interoperability among components by adaptors interposed between client and server beans. JavaBeans adaptors mediate only semantic needs and can therefore be much simpler than CORBA adaptors, whose main task is to mediate between different languages and interface presentation styles. Some forms of adaptation, such as that between buttons and their clients, can be realized by automatically generated adaptors.

12.6 The Event Model of Component Interaction

Event models allow actions of event listeners to be triggered by the occurrence of events at an event source. They provide a new control structure for component communication that extends the flexibility of procedure call and message passing. Procedure calls can be viewed as specialized events whose only function is to call a server to request a service and supply data parameters so the service can be provided.

Events cause actions as side effects, may be oblivious to the actions that they cause, and may cause multiple events in multiple components. Events decouple control from statement execution to a greater extent than procedure calling. Exceptions in traditional programming languages are a restricted form of events that cause the normal flow of control to be modified when exceptional actions are required. They are implemented by exception handlers that handle (catch) exceptions when they are raised (thrown). Event models elevate the exception mechanism to be the primary control structure and generalize it so that occurrence of an event can cause multiple components to be notified of its occurrence.

Event models are especially useful in modeling external input, since the effect of mouse clicks or other user-initiated inputs can be modeled by events occurring at the user interface that cause the system to perform desired actions. Thus, onmousedown was the most common event of the Hypercard event model, which also allowed events such as onopencard, caused by inner system actions. Since event models provide a uniform control structure to handle both external and internal events, all component and document models offer an event model for both user-interface control and control of certain inner operations.

Since JavaBeans has a nicely described event model, we use the JavaBeans model as the basis for discussion. It requires event listeners to register themselves in a registry for the event and causes event sources to notify all registered listeners whenever the event occurs. The data structure transmitted to listeners when they are notified of an event is an instance an event state class. Event-handling interfaces are defined in event listener interfaces that are specified by subclasses of an eventlisteners class.

Visual interfaces catch user events and cause actions by components listening for those events. They handle visual interaction through *listening membranes* activated by mouse clicks that transform blackbox computers to glass-box containers with windows that provide access to selected inner structure in browsing, authoring, and scripting modes. Input through a given interface is sequential, though input to a system with multiple input ports involves distributed multiple input streams that cannot, in general, be expressed as a sequential (serializable) input stream [Wegner 1996].

Components with visual interfaces, such as beans, are abstractly modeled by events, properties, and methods, which extend notions of control, variable, and operation to express the semantics of visual interaction. Components associated with user interfaces have interactively generated sequential streams of input events controlled by multiple internal threads that generally execute one at a time, as in monitors. Events trigger listening actions, properties have visual and/or internal attributes, and methods are callable both interactively and by system calls. Beans may have a visible GUI representation or be invisible and known just by their ability to call methods, fire events, and manage a persistent state.

Extensions from algorithms to visual, interactive components include:

Control. Execute unique next instruction → notify listeners of nonunique next event.

Variable. Hidden internal representation → visible attribute with interactive interface.

Operation. Procedure call → message event caused by interaction or inner system condition.

Properties (named attributes) extend variables so their values can uniformly represent both visual and inner attributes. Property attributes can be visual (such as being red or rectangular) and occupy real estate on the screen. Properties can be set either interactively by the user or algorithmically by the program. Setting the value of a property can be used to control actions through the event mechanism, so that interactive setting of visual attributes can trigger interactive events. Visual-input-sensitive interfaces are porous two-way listening membranes that expose what is inside and can be programmed to receive interactive mouse clicks on any part of their visual real estate at any time.

Methods can be invoked either by traditional system calls or through user- or system-generated events. Invocation of methods by events changes the execution paradigm, allowing nonsequential nondeterministic execution controlled by user interaction as well as program properties.

Traditional programs have restricted input events handled by read statements, do not allow properties (variables) to be set directly by the user, and do not allow methods to be interactively invoked by the user. Visual interfaces require notions of control, variables, and operations to be extended. Visibility and interaction play distinct roles in the new paradigm: Visibility by itself facilitates conceptual understanding through browsing, while visual interaction extends computational problem-solving power [Wegner 1996].

Visual (browsing) interfaces. Visual interfaces that support browsing enrich understanding and provide system programmers with alternative ways of presenting data. Netscape Navigator and Internet Explorer illustrate the power of noninteractive visual browsing interfaces.

Interactive (authoring and scripting) interfaces. Interaction at the level of authoring includes the use of existing operations for modifying interface objects, while scripting involves the creation of new properties and operators. Interactive interfaces have multiple listening points (one for each mouse position) that allow the user to select among alternative choices and thereby to quickly find objects in spaces with an exponential number of possibilities. The role of interaction in document systems is very different from that of visualization: Interaction is not only more convenient but actually is more expressive than algorithms as a problem-solving method.

The AWT/JavaBeans event model records the occurrence of events in event objects that are responsible for notifying registered listeners that the event has occurred. Event types are specified by subclasses of the event object class. Condition events notify the associated event object, which, in turn, notifies listeners. Mouse clicks and other input events are transformed through special hardware and software into messages to associated event objects. Visual interfaces such as buttons have implicit events activated by user-initiated mouseclicks on the visible real estate.

Introspection is the process of automatically figuring out the events, properties, and methods of beans. An introspection class provides a uniform method of introspecting by the use of syntactic patterns to automatically discover the events, properties, and methods of classes.

JavaBeans builds on the Java language, class libraries that specify the event and introspection models, and special-purpose interface hardware and software to provide a kit for constructing composite beans and applets from components. We would like to specify the abstract structure of beans by extending specification techniques of traditional programming languages. The event-property-method model of components is a first step in systematically specifying JavaBeans and, more generally, in describing design structure for compound active documents.

Beans may, as a first approximation, be viewed as collections of collaborating bean components with a beanlike interface. Thus, beans are frameworks for compound active documents, document interfaces are GUIs of frameworks, and bean and framework specification are related. Specification techniques for beans and frameworks are further examined later in the context of structured object-oriented programming.

JavaBeans has a language-dependent document model built on a sound language that supports pure interfaces and a lightweight client-server discipline exemplified by Hot Java. Its underlying model provides a simple foundation for dynamic document architectures. To achieve compatibility with CORBA components, JavaBeans supports IDL wrappers for Java components that provide bridges from the JavaBeans API to other component model architectures, allowing JavaBeans to operate in ActiveX, OpenDoc, or document environments yet to be designed.

Java and JavaBeans provide a language, system, and application framework that conforms to the layered CORBA services of Figure 12.1b but is better designed and better integrated than earlier systems. It may well become a standard that supersedes earlier designs and makes language interoperability with earlier languages unnecessary except for legacy code. The canceling of OpenDoc by Apple may well be a prelude to the wholesale canceling of CORBA by OMG in favor of a Java/JavaBeans component model.

12.7 Modes of Interaction

The semantics of software components is specified by their mode of interaction, while that of algorithms is specified by their mode of execution [Wegner 1997]. Modes of interaction provide an outside-in view of components that complements the inside-out view of algorithms. The analysis of systems by their mode of interaction is an interactive analog of the analysis of algorithms by their mode of execution. The expressiveness of components is measured by their ability to perceive and interact with the external world, while that of algorithms is measured by their ability to transform inputs noninteractively into outputs.

The irreducibility of components to algorithms can be proved very simply by showing that interactive systems cannot be modeled by Turing machines with finite initial input tapes [Wegner 1996]. Greater expressiveness follows from the fact that Turing machines with infinite tapes are known to be more expressive than regular Turing machines. The formal proof is corroborated by informal evidence. The following points constitute an assertion from Fred Brooks that there is no silver bullet for simply specifying systems:

- The assertion that everyone is talking about object-oriented programming but no one knows what it is

- The failure of the Japanese fifth-generation project to realize the goals of computing by logic

- The inability of pattern theory to develop formal pattern specifications

The design space of interactive systems, which includes software engineering (SE), artificial intelligence (AI), and virtual reality (VR) systems, is much richer in its variety of behaviors than the design space of algorithms. In the programming language world, types and classes specify values by their modes of interaction, whereas in the software engineering world, interfaces specify systems by their modes of interaction. Modes of interaction provide a qualitative framework for analysis, since quantitative complexity analysis is not applicable to systems.

To illustrate the power of qualitative analysis of interactive behavior, we briefly review modes of behavior for SE, AI, and VR. SE focuses on reactive systems that provide services by reacting to the requests of clients. AI focuses on proactive agents that act on their environment to realize external goals. VR focuses on real-time, multimodal, cognitively realistic interaction.

Reactive systems that passively supply services have simpler environment models than proactive agents that try to understand and change the world. If interactive expressiveness is defined by external modeling power, then AI and VR systems are more expressive than reactive SE systems. The reactive services provided by components to clients can be very complex, but clients are modeled as components that make syntactically simple requests specified by operations with parameters. Component interfaces provide both an abstraction of the external world to proactive agents looking outward and an abstraction of the inner worlds of reactive components to clients looking inward.

Modes of interaction provide a unifying descriptive framework for SE. Software architecture deals with alternative modes of interaction such as pipes, client-server, and blackboard models. Interoperability examines interaction among heterogeneous components that differ in platform and interface definition. Object-oriented design models, such as object modeling technique (OMT) [Rumbaugh 1991], specify interaction among objects differently from computation within objects. Design patterns and frameworks determine modes of interaction that can be classified and reused but cannot be proved correct, formally specified, or formally composed.

Modes of interaction also provide a unifying descriptive framework for AI. Learning, planning, and acting have characteristic modes of interaction. Proactive agents actively learn about the external world, build complex internal models of the world, and perform actions to change it. Agents use incremental data to update their model of the world as a basis for action. Planning systems combine updating their world model with the execution of policies that maximize their expected reward over finite or infinite time horizons, while learning systems explore the world and build models for later action.

VR aims to create machines that can simulate the real world in interacting realistically with humans. VR achieves its realism by integration of spatial, stereo, and temporal perspectives: Footprints in space are combined with footprints in time to create cognitively realistic virtual worlds. Though VR simulates environments rather than human behavior, it requires a detailed cognitive model to provide cognitively acceptable inputs and respond to human actions. Simulating each of the five senses involves entirely different modes of communication and perception that integrate mathematical techniques of pattern description with cognitive properties of perception. The cognitive reconstruction of three-dimensional images from stereo and temporal projections requires interaction patterns to match cognitive expectations if motion sickness is to be avoided. Making spatiotemporal inputs consistent with human cognitive limitations provides an extra dimension of difficulty over and above that of creating adequate interaction patterns.

Modes of interaction can be modeled mathematically as projections of the world on the input sensors of an agent. Stimuli S from an external world W are projections $S = P(W)$ onto input sensors such that the inverse cannot be completely known (W cannot be reconstructed from S). Projection mappings P provide a mathematical tool for analyzing modes of interaction. Incompleteness of S in specifying the world W is related to Godel incompleteness.

An agent's knowledge of the world is expressed by Plato's cave metaphor, which compares humans to cave dwellers who can observe only shadows on the walls of their cave (retina), not the true external world. S is the shadow cast by W on the wall of the agent's cave. However, S can include stereo inputs from multiple sensors (eyes and/or ears) and temporal inputs at successive points in time, and can indeed be a stereo-spatiotemporal interaction pattern more complex than a two-dimensional image on the wall of a cave.

12.8 Specifying Frameworks by Constraints on Component Behavior

Whereas algorithms are specified by the composition of primitive functionality to define composite functionality, interaction is more naturally specified by constraints on all possible behavior than by how it is built up from primitives. Composition from primitives is necessary to create components and systems, but once components have been created their interactive effect is better described by types and interfaces that constrain interaction than by how it has been constructed, for two distinct reasons:

Abstraction. Interactive behavior directly describes the effect on the user.

Noncompositionality. Composite behavior cannot be specified by the composition of primitive behavior.

Driving is initially learned by understanding controls such as the accelerator and the steering wheel, but rules of the road are better specified by constraints on keeping to the road and not hitting obstructions. Behavior for frameworks is more naturally specified by constraints on a space of all possible interactions than by the composition of primitive behaviors.

Constraint-based specification is a *sculpture paradigm* that removes unwanted behavior until only the desired behavior is left, just as the sculptor chips away unwanted material until the desired form emerges. Constraint specifications are realized by progressively constraining the superset of all possible behavior to a desired form, just as a sculpture is realized by progressively removing material from a block of marble. Behavior specification by constraints that eliminate possible behaviors rather than by composition of behavior is a new specification paradigm that uses the counterintuitive principle "less is more" for system specification.

Frameworks realize collaborative richness by sacrificing the freedom of components that collaborate, just as marriage partners give up some freedom to realize collaborative richness. Constraints are a more powerful behavior-specification technique than composition because they make no assumption about the behavior being constrained, allowing the behavior of nonalgorithmic noncompositional collaborative components to be described.

The abstract modeling of composition by behavior constraints, developed in [Wegner 1996], is illustrated in Figure 12.5, where the component C1 gives up behavioral freedom when constrained to collaborate exclusively with C2. Components that in isolation are interactive open systems, free to interact with any client, become noninteractive closed systems when constrained to interact exclusively with each other. Composition may cause open interactive systems to become closed and noninteractive: An open server that provides services to any client becomes closed if its services are entirely preempted by (dedicated to) a particular client. However, dedicated (closed) composition that entirely preempts the services of a component is a special case of open composition that yields a new open system that can be constrained by further composition.

The sacrifice of freedom for discipline to realize collaborative behavior is a feature of both software components and people who lose their freedom when they become cogs

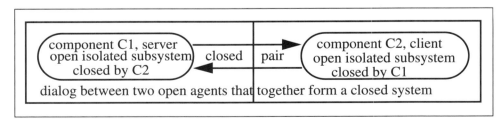

Figure 12.5 Component composition as a constraint on behavior.

(algorithms) in corporations. The advantages of application frameworks over class libraries are realized by sacrificing behavioral freedom of isolated objects and classes for collaborative discipline to serve users. Frameworks support the inversion of control from client-side calls to server-side callbacks through strong inner control constraints on components to realize useful interaction with clients.

Viewing composition as a constraint on interactive behavior provides a systematic basis for the mathematical modeling and algorithm composition duality. Each interactive composition step constrains behavior to a subset of its free behavior. Constraints are more widely applicable than composition because they can be applied to constrain noncompositional as well as compositional behaviors.

Goal-directed behavior may be created by bottom-up composition of smaller units or by top-down constraints on already existing components. The creation of frameworks from collections of objects, classes, and components clearly falls into the second category. Michelangelo could not have created his statue of David by gluing together small bits of marble.

12.9 Summary

To provide a framework for component-based technology, we combine the bottom-up analysis of three specific systems with top-down conceptual models of interaction. CORBA/OpenDoc, COM/OLE/ActiveX, and Java/JavaBeans concretely illustrate emerging principles of component and document design, such as the events-properties-methods model. They support components with visual, interactive listening membranes that transform blackbox computers into glass-box systems whose "picture windows" allow clients to both see and modify what is inside. Frameworks are viewed as extensible collaborating collections of components with goal-directed behavior.

12.10 References

[Arnold 1996] Arnold, K., and J. Gosling. *The Java Programming Language.* Reading, MA: Addison-Wesley, 1996

[JavaBeans 1996] *Java Beans 1.0 Specification.* Javasoft, December 1996.

[OpenDoc 1996] Apple Computer Inc. *OpenDoc Programmers Guide.* Reading, MA: Addison-Wesley, 1996.

[Orfali 1996] Orfali, R., D. Harkey, and J. Edwards. *The Essential Distributed Objects Survival Guide.* New York: John Wiley & Sons, 1996.

[Rumbaugh 1991] Rumbaugh, J., M. Blaha, W. Premerlani, F. Eddy, and W. Lorensen. *Object-Oriented Modeling and Design.* Englewood Cliffs, NJ: Prentice Hall, 1991.

[Wegner 1996] Wegner, P. Interactive software technology. In *Handbook of Computer Science and Engineering,* CRC Press, December 1996.

CHAPTER 13

Supervision and Control Systems Framework Architecture

Supervision and control (S&C) systems are typical computer applications that traditionally impose high reliability and realtime requirements—think, for example, of plant-monitoring systems, traffic control systems, and patient-monitoring systems—whose failures may result in high damage and even in loss of human lives. For this reason, to date they have been implemented as closed systems based on proprietary hardware and software, which has resulted in low cost-effectiveness. As a consequence, they are usually not portable and cannot easily be extended or integrated into more complex systems.

Recent technological advances, however, offer new chances for the development of more complex S&C applications at lower costs and with shorter times to market. In particular, powerful communication media such as the field bus [IEC 1993], local area networks (LANs) and wide area networks (WANs), and abstract, object-oriented (OO) software standards such as CORBA [Mowbray 1995] facilitate communications between heterogeneous distributed objects and improve the following qualities of distributed applications:

- High integration among different functions
- Openness
- Heterogeneity
- Interoperability
- Reduced development time and cost

In particular, the high-level abstract interface provided by CORBA allows connecting components running on different platforms (for example, a relational and an OO database), thus reducing development time and cost by exploiting a typical benefit of OO approaches.

S&C applications can certainly share these benefits. For instance, in the field of energy management systems there are several independent applications, such as diagnostic systems to monitor the state of the plant components, alarm-managing systems to react online and in realtime to plant malfunctions, and maintenance systems to reconfigure the plant in the event of new operating conditions. All such applications have their own sensors, hardware processors, databases, and specialized software, and the information they share could be managed more effectively in an integrated environment. For instance, alarms could be recorded by the alarm-managing subsystems and accessed through a global database by the diagnostic subsystem. This, in turn, could benefit from accessing remote information through a WAN to compare the performance of similar components located at different sites.

To fully achieve such a goal, however, two crucial issues must be addressed:

CORBA does not presently address a few issues that are critical for S&C systems, such as reliability and realtime. This creates a *semantic hole* that hampers rigorous design and verification.

A big gap must still be filled by design to move from system requirements to a complete implementation in terms of the CORBA architecture. This job could be highly fostered if the designer were provided with a rich environment supporting reuse of predefined objects and design paths that are typical of most S&C applications.

This chapter reports on our ongoing research, conducted within the OpenDREAMS Esprit project, aimed at exploiting CORBA and OO frameworks to build new-generation S&C applications with the extra qualities mentioned here. OO frameworks are a powerful generalization of traditional code libraries and can be seen as almost ready-to-use pieces of applications that just need to be tailored to specific needs and integrated into a complete system. Thus, to reach our goals we define both a collection of CORBA-compliant frameworks to support S&C-specific needs and a *development method* that guides the designer from requirements specification to design and verification.

In the past few years, much work has been done on OO frameworks. Among these frameworks, it is worth citing the Taligent Application Environment [Taligent 1994], which includes more than 100 specific frameworks comprising more than 2000 C++ classes, grouped into three main framework families. The SEMATECH CIM framework [SEMATECH 1996] is based on an object-oriented model of semiconductor manufacturing. It is specifically targeted at manufacturing information management and control for both the planning and operational phases of semiconductor wafer fabrication. G++ [Menga 1991] offers frameworks to handle concurrency and realtime, CORBA-style distribution, persistency, and MMI generation. Finally, the Manufacturing Virtual Enterprise (MVE) architecture was originally defined by the National Industrial Information Infrastructure Protocols (NIIIP) Consortium (led by IBM) as a mechanism to provide a manufacturing collaboration environment [NIIIP 1997]. MVE is built on top of CORBA and CORBAServices; it consists of a number of vertical market facilities.

None of these frameworks, however, specifically address the problems of S&C systems, though the G++ environment has been used to develop several industrial applications in the field of process control.

This chapter is organized as follows: *Section 13.1* presents a general view of the OpenDREAMS architecture and methodology. *Section 13.2* describes OpenDREAMS services, that is, the enrichments of the basic CORBA to fill the semantic holes previously mentioned. *Section 13.3* describes OpenDREAMS domains, specialized frameworks designed to fill the methodological gap previously mentioned. *Section 13.4* outlines the design method used in OpenDREAMS to guide application designers. The method is illustrated by means of a running example derived from a real industrial application developed during the project. Finally, *Section 13.5* summarizes the state of our research and illustrates the main lines for its further development.

The presentation is tutorial and skips technical details. Documentation is available in the referred bibliography, while all OpenDREAMS reports are available by anonymous ftp at the Web site ftp-lse.epfl.ch, directory pub/opendreams.

13.1 The OpenDREAMS Architecture and Methodology

According to the OMG reference architecture (OMA) the runtime structure of a CORBA-based S&C system can be described as a collection of objects communicating through the Object Request Broker (ORB; see Figure 13.1). The CORBAServices are system-level objects that extend the ORB, providing well-defined services packaged as components with interfaces defined in Interface Definition Language (IDL). They provide semantic additions that ensure properties needed by specific applications. For instance, S&C applications must satisfy realtime and fault-tolerance requirements, while banking applications have strong security requirements.

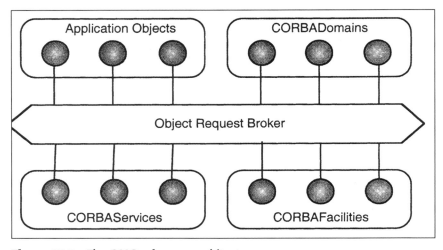

Figure 13.1 The OMG reference architecture.

The CORBAFacilities are interfaces and/or objects providing general-purpose capabilities applicable to most application domains [OMG 1995a, 1995b, 1995c]. The CORBADomains are objects specific to industrial vertical markets. These high-level components provide functionalities of direct interest to developers in particular application domains (for example, finance, healthcare, manufacturing, telecom, transportation, and S&C). At present, no CORBADomains have been adopted by the OMG. Finally, the Application Objects are the ultimate consumers of the CORBA infrastructure, being the components of specific end-user applications.

In a general sense, CORBAServices, CORBAFacilities, and CORBADomains are all OO frameworks supporting the construction of the whole CORBA application. Services, however, are lower-level and are implemented through traditional libraries. Facilities and domains, instead, are true, high-level frameworks, as they include real *application fragments* provided with their own policies and threads of control.

The OpenDREAMS project aims to build a CORBA-based *architecture* to support S&C applications and a complete *methodology*—provided with appropriate development tools—to guide their construction. Figure 13.2 shows a first description of our approach from a developmental viewpoint.

Services provide the first layer augmenting ORB's semantics to cope with special S&C requirements. Some services are already defined as CORBAServices by the OMG (but a few extensions have been defined in the OpenDREAMS project); others were defined in the OpenDREAMS project and are currently—or will be shortly—proposed for possible standardization to the OMG.

CORBADomains for S&C applications are the core of our project: An S&C application is built on top of S&C domains and facilities by including and using their features; furthermore, it may directly use some CORBAServices. For instance, a typical S&C application could consist of C++ code calling CORBA stubs standing for suitable services, domains, or facilities. In the OpenDREAMS project we did not design any CORBAFacilities. Facilities are in fact general-purpose frameworks that can be used to build several special-purpose domains. Thus, we expect that they will soon be available as commercial products.

Finally, the TRIO-based methodology drives the application developer from the initial phase of requirements specification down to the CORBA-based architectural design and to the implementation and verification phases.

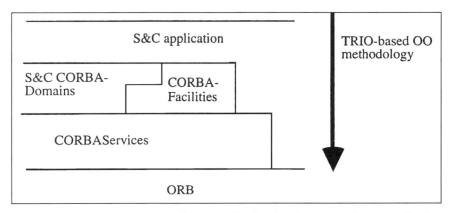

Figure 13.2   OpenDREAMS architecture for the development of S&C applications.

13.2 The CORBA/OpenDREAMS Services

CORBAServices are a collection of IDL interfaces providing the system-level functionalities that extend the ORB. During the OpenDREAMS project we defined and/or extended several services specifically tailored for S&C applications; here we list the main ones:

Replication service (not defined by OMG). In most S&C systems, several application objects have the highest availability and fault-tolerance requirements (for example, alarms in a nuclear power plant). To this purpose the OpenDREAMS platform offers a replication service that relieves the developer from most of the burden of explicitly defining *replicas* of critical objects: The developer need only provide a high-level specification of the desired *fault-tolerance requirements* of critical objects, and the service will automatically select the appropriate *replication policies* (number and hosts of instances, copying algorithms, and so on). The main difference between the OpenDREAMS replication service and other available solutions, such as Orbix+ISIS [IONA 1996] and Electra [Maffeis 1995], is that the former is built on top of the ORB while the latter are integrated into the ORB. As a consequence, the OpenDREAMS replication service is much more ORB-independent and can be easily ported from one ORB to another.

Transaction service. S&C applications have specific needs in terms of transaction management [OpenDREAMS 1996]. In particular, there is a strong requirement for an adaptable transaction model that permits (1) splitting a transaction into a hierarchy of subtransactions, each executing a specific task, and (2) defining *commit spheres* (parts of the hierarchy that can commit their updates before transaction end) and *abort spheres* (parts of the hierarchy that can abort without impacting the rest of the transaction). This results in an extension of the OMG-defined transaction service, providing primitives that allow an application to perform transactional updates of CORBA objects, either persistent or not. These primitives allow multiple distributed objects to cooperate to provide atomicity.

Persistency service. This service provides mechanisms for retaining and managing the persistent state of CORBA objects. It provides facilities to access, retrieve, and update objects from and to a relational or object-oriented database in a transparent way.

Query service. This service permits the querying of application objects, which are generally grouped into collections. It allows querying, in a uniform way, transient and/or persistent objects stored in several relational, object-oriented, or proprietary databases.

Event service. This service provides an event-based messaging environment. The OMG is currently specifying an event-based notification facility that will incorporate event classification according to, for instance, priority.

Realtime extensions. Most S&C operations must be completed within sometimes hard time constraints. Thus, we provided mechanisms both to specify time requirements for critical operations and to implement policies that guarantee such requirements (for example, priorities).

13.3 S&C CORBA/OpenDREAMS Domain

In the OpenDREAMS project, the S&C CORBADomain is a framework dedicated to the supervision and control area, defined as an OMA-compliant object-oriented framework. The definition and standardization of such a framework, modeling the objects of the S&C domain and the functions associated with them, will play a key role in the design and development of new-generation S&C systems. Of course, this framework is supported by the underlying ORB infrastructure, the services and the facilities.

The S&C domain provides a common environment for the integration of applications and the sharing of information in the S&C application field. Moreover, it could also be subsequently specialized and/or extended by industrial subdomains—for example, to define modules specific to electric power management activities. Such a further specialization is expected to be a smooth and gradual process, to be performed by the relevant industrial actors in a stepwise fashion; this aspect, however, is not pursued further in this chapter. When developing an application, framework classes may be used either as factories for ready-to-use objects—that is, in collaboration or composition relationships—or as abstract classes to be customized and/or specialized—for instance, through inheritance relationships.

Our S&C domain is structured into a collection of collaborating modules, each one describing a set of classes and their relationships, dedicated to an S&C-needed functionality. The framework modules can be subdivided into three functional groups: *utility modules, activity modules,* and *specialized utility modules.*

13.3.1 Utility Modules

These modules offer objects supporting all the basic mechanisms of the S&C activity. In the OpenDREAMS project we are developing the following utility modules:

Base process values management module. Provides objects the ability to manage and access the variables that represent physical values in the supervised process. This module also manages more complex data values—for example, the position of a process object, such as an airplane. The data values are normally augmented with validity and time-stamp attributes, and must be loggable through history functions for storing and retrieval purposes. In existing S&C systems, process variables are typically exposed through a proprietary *realtime database* (which is really a supervisory control and data acquisition [SCADA] component acting as a process variables repository). For example, suppose that a realtime database exposes a Float variable representing a temperature; an external module can subscribe to this value to render it on the MMI or to use it for further calculations. It must be possible to log the Float variable by creating a FloatLog and associating with it a LogController object, whose role is to monitor the Float variable and automatically feed the log.

Events management module. Offers ways to classify S&C-related events and to define their features. S&C events must be time-stamped, be loggable and retrievable, and support identification of their emitter. They should also support advanced notification policies and event filtering based on various criteria, such as an event's class, name, or emitting object. Information associated with an event should be extensible, and events should be partitionable into families. This module is based on the CORBA/OpenDREAMS event service. As an example, one might want to monitor all the actions of a given operator, and thus might define a specific OperatorEventDispatcher object to which the operator's events will be sent; this object will dispatch the events to any interested observer that demonstrates interest by subscribing to it. During the subscription, the observer can define the events of interest (such as the operator acknowledging alarms). One might also want to log selected events, and thus might create an EventLog and its associated EventLogController, and hook it to an EventDispatcher. By configuring the EventLogController, the user can select the events to be loggable.

History management module. Provides a means to log and retrieve recordable framework objects, such as process objects or supervision objects (alarms, events, operator actions, and so on). Logs are sequential records of an object's values as it evolves over time. Logs must offer functions to store time-stamped object values and to retrieve them, either by browsing a log or by requesting the value at a given time. This module maintains a list of available logs and permits starting and stopping the logging of a specific variable. This module should be easily extensible, and should accommodate new log classes for additional recordable objects that are unspecified in the current version of the framework. For example, a user might want to examine the history of a variable representing the temperature in some physical process; this will be done by browsing through a LogManager object to retrieve the Log object for that variable, then using the Log services to examine the temperature values as they evolve over time.

Alarm management module. Supplies objects to deal with abnormal conditions. Alarms are characterized by a description that includes a degree of severity. This module provides special alarm-related functionalities, such as different alarm acknowledgment policies, alarm filtering, and alarm logging and retrieving. This module also provides the structured classes needed to handle and manage alarms, such as alarm groups, alarm events, and so on, and manages lists of active and potential alarms. For example, a user might define an alarm group for power failures, and decide to acknowledge all the alarms included in the group at once, or else mask some of them.

Operators management module. Offers ways to manage groups of human operators and track their activity. Operators may belong to multiple groups, structured into subgroups. This module keeps records of all the operators and groups, and provides means to browse through them. It permits defining operator events to provide information about actions triggered by operators; operator events are time-stamped, carry the status of the operation, and must be loggable and retrievable.

Access control management module. Provides ways to define access control and authentication policies to framework objects, supporting the definition of a global strategy to control operators' actions, including definition of allowed operations for groups of operators, access rights enforcement, and notification of operator events to track their activity. It is based on specifications of the OMG's Security Service (defining interfaces for authentication and authorization of operations on objects).

13.3.2 Activity Modules

These framework modules offer objects for performing essential activities during the typical S&C process life cycle. To find the pertinent objects, we started from the general process model depicted by Lawson, which is abstract enough to fit with almost any S&C system. According to this model, supervision and control can be seen as a single loop, during which data from the process under supervision is first captured by sensors, then processed and combined to produce an observed picture of the situation. Anomalies are found by comparing the desired situation with the observed one; finally, remedy actions are planned and executed. Figure 13.3 shows an iteration of the loop and the objects produced at each step.

Among the different S&C activities we focused on during OpenDREAMS, we selected those intended to manage situation objects and anomalies, because these are the ones that exhibit the most generic behavior and that are also essential for the S&C process. Therefore, we are developing the following two activity modules:

Situation processing module. Aims to build *situation objects* by fusion and/or composition of elementary pieces of information. Situation objects include two main parts: the *static* part of the object, describing its structural characteristics (that is, how that object may be built, to which part of the process under supervision it is related, and so on); and the *dynamic* part, including the list of values relevant for that object. Note that depending on the supervision process, the number of used values may vary (the current value may suffice in some cases). The instantaneous values of variables are always paired with a validity factor and a time stamp. As a situation object may reflect the behavior of several variables, special attention is paid to how validity values and time stamps are managed. Note that as some situation objects may result from a quite complex and time-consuming process, the replication service is used to ensure high availability. As an example, a quite complex situation object might be an airport runway in an S&C application concerning airport ground traffic management. The dynamic part of this object must accommodate a huge amount of information, such as the vehicles on the runway, their respective positions and speed, and so on.

Anomalies detection module. Aims to detect anomalies by comparing the situation objects with some description of the nominal situation. Note that the identifica-

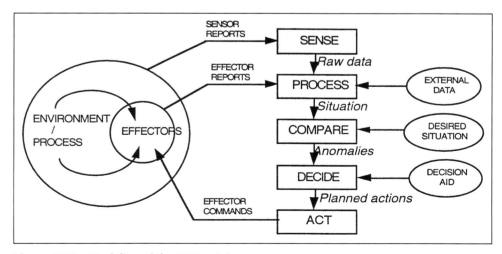

Figure 13.3   Modeling of the S&C activity.

tion of an anomaly is a process that may vary in complexity, depending on the system: In some cases, one anomaly may be related to a simple variable with the indication of a threshold; in other cases, when an anomaly is related to various conditions applying to several variables, a more complex description is needed. In addition, this module should be able to control the raising, enabling, and disabling of alarms (by using the alarm management module functionalities). For instance, in the case of an airport ground traffic management application, identifying a potential violation of the security limits among vehicles accessing the same runway, based on their position and speed, would require a complex modeling of the anomaly detection activity.

13.3.3 Specialized Utility Modules

This category includes modules that are further specialized to deal with more specific application domains, such as traffic control or energy management systems. For brevity, this chapter does not cover them.

13.4 The TRIO-Based Development Method

TRIO is a development methodology for S&C applications based on a formal specification language [Morzenti 1994]. It has been used for several years in industrial applications [Gargantini 1996; Basso 1995] and is now fairly well established. It is also supported by a few tools, though still at a prototype level [Felder 1994; Mandrioli 1995].

The TRIO language includes a basic temporal logic language for specifying in detail, an object-oriented extension that supports writing reusable modular specifications of complex systems, and a further extension that includes predefined higher-level application-oriented notions, such as events, states, processes, and pre- and postconditions. Within the OpenDREAMS project the TRIO methodology has been tailored to the development of CORBA-based applications, with most attention focused on the architectural design phase.

We next describe the TRIO/OpenDREAMS methodology as a *sequence of phases*. According to [Parnas 1986], however, this does not mean that they are to be executed exactly in the order they are described. Rather, a spiral software development model [Boehm 1988] appears to be more realistic: Only the final project documentation will be arranged *as if* the whole development process were executed in a rigid sequential manner.

13.4.1 Application Requirements Specification

This activity is now fairly well established. It is based on the following principles:

- It must produce a precise, complete, unambiguous document.
- It may involve several people having different roles. For instance, specification

documents often evolve from a first informal version delivered by users to a final version delivered by specialists on requirements specification.

■ To satisfy different and often contrasting goals (such as rigor and understandability by different types of readers) it is useful for specification documents to use (whenever needed) not only a mathematical formalism but also informal explanations. Graphical notations are very useful for this purpose.

■ Most qualities that are generally valuable for software products are important as well for specification documents. In particular, they must be easily maintainable and reusable; complex aspects must be explained and understood by exploiting incremental refinement (first the essential aspects, then adding details) and modularization.

The TRIO language helps to achieve these goals through some distinguishing features—in particular, the following:

■ The use of a mathematical notation to achieve maximum precision and rigor.

■ The use of an object-oriented approach to achieve good modularization, reusability, and maintainability of specification documents. In particular, genericity and inheritance allow writing specifications that can be easily tailored to specialized goals starting from generic documents. For instance, we can specify generic requirements for a whole category of power plants; then we can derive with little effort specialized requirements for a particular instance of such plants by choosing suitable parameters (such as the number and capacity of reservoirs and the generated power).

■ The use of a simple and natural graphical interface, supported by an interactive editor.

This chapter focuses on the object-oriented features of the TRIO language. For a more complete description of the mathematical aspects of the language and of their exploitation in the specification and analysis of critical requirements, the interested reader may refer to [Basso 1995; Ghezzi 1990].

Figure 13.4 provides a high-level—and highly simplified—description of a system for the diagnosis and monitoring of a steam condenser in a thermoelectric power system, which is used throughout this section as a running example to illustrate the various phases of the development method.

The boxes in Figure 13.4 represent the main objects that constitute the whole application.

PRECON. A diagnostic system designed to improve the efficiency and availability of the plant. It continuously monitors the performance of the condenser to detect faults and to support the operators by suggesting remedy actions. To achieve its goal, PRECON interacts with other parts of the S&C system (namely the following list entries).

Data acquisition and preprocessing (ACQ). Performs acquisition of data from the field for all S&C functionalities and stores them into the plant database (see "global plant database [GPDB]").

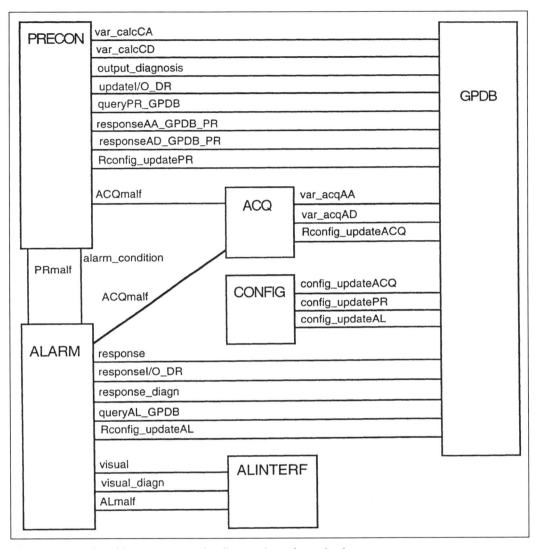

Figure 13.4 The object structure of a diagnostic and monitoring system.

Alarm management (ALARM). Traces the state of the alarms issued by all modules and manages operators' interactions, namely alarm visualization and alarm acknowledgment, through the ALINTERF module.

Configuration management (CONFIG). Allows the operator to configure parameters of each module of the S&C system. Through it the system can be easily adapted to the peculiar needs of single plants.

Global plant database (GPDB). A virtual database consisting of a set of distributed and even heterogeneous databases; it contains static and dynamic data coming from all the other components of the S&C system.

The lines connecting different boxes represent items such as *variables, predicates,* and *functions* that are shared by several objects. For instance, alarm_condition represents an event that is signaled by the alarm manager to PRECON.

Once the overall system structure has been specified through figures such as Figure 13.4, system requirements are specified in a structured textual notation, which can include formal and informal parts (our editor provides automatic translation from graphical notation to a textual *stub* to be filled by the specifier). For instance, in the example system there are requirements for object functionalities (the acquisition and preprocessing subsystem must make analogic and digital variables available every five minutes), and for fault tolerance (the alarm management subsystem should always be available).

13.4.2 Application Requirements Validation

In our approach, the critical activity of requirements validation exploits the use of a formal approach: Suitable tools in fact help in *prototyping specifications* (that is, deriving sample behaviors to check their adequacy with respect to user needs), checking desired properties, and so on. The same tools can also be exploited to support the verification of implementation correctness against the stated requirements [Felder 1994; Mandrioli 1995]. Verification and validation, however, are not within the scope of this chapter; therefore, these issues are not considered further here.

13.4.3 Deriving Architectural Design from Requirements Specification

This phase is the core of the whole application design. Two distinguishing features favor a smooth transition from requirements to design:

Both specifications and design are based on object-oriented approaches, which provides a natural guideline. In fact, in an S&C system it is quite likely that both specification and architectural design will refer to objects or classes such as sensors, alarms, historical repositories, and so on. Therefore, the designer's main goal will be to derive application objects for the S&C system runtime architecture from a similar (but not identical) object structure already provided in the specification document.

The use of generalized ready-to-integrate building blocks helps bridge the gap between the bare CORBA interface and application functions. In a bottom-up path they go from services to general frameworks devoted to a wide application field such as S&C to even more specialized frameworks.

Next we describe the architectural design phase by splitting it into more detailed subphases, as illustrated by the example diagnostic application.

Mapping Specification Objects into CORBA Application Objects

In practice, the transition from specification to design is seldom as sharp as described in idealized process models. This is even more true in object-oriented approaches, where it is often quite natural to identify *specification objects* with *design objects*. Thus, at least as a first step, we can consider Figure 13.4 as a starting point for an architectural design of a CORBA-based application in which the denoted objects are a first description of CORBA application objects.

A less trivial step identifies *object operations* (*methods*), driven by items connecting different specification objects. Often, however, several such items can be grouped into a single operation. For example, ALARM is connected to GPDB by the following items: queryAL_GPDB, response, response_diagn, and responseI/O_DR. These items represent a request of an operation that the ALARM object sends to the GPDB object (queryAL_GPDB) and the associated reply. Therefore, all these items are merged into a single operation that we call *query_by_alarm*.

At this point we have to identify the objects that will compose the application: The specification is restructured by splitting and composing the different specification objects until each of them can be viewed as a single application object. Here frameworks (CORBADomains and CORBAFacilities) come into play, as they constitute a major guide for the restructuring activity. In other words, the designer should restructure the specification objects trying to map some of them into the already existing objects belonging to one or more framework. For instance, using the anomalies detection module, the situation processing module, and the alarm management module, one can design part of PRECON and ALARM, as shown in Figure 13.5 (where the oval includes the used frameworks).

Specifying Client-Server Relationships

The next step concerns the identification of the client-server relationships among the application objects that do not belong to a framework. This is accomplished simply by adding an arrowhead to the lines that connect boxes and represent operations: The arrows go from the server *exporting* the operation to the client *importing* it.

Adding the Services

As stated in *Section 13.1*, a CORBA service is a set of IDL interfaces that can be inherited by application objects to achieve semantic properties necessary to guarantee application requirements. For example, the application object PRECON must repeatedly perform the following sequence of activities:

- Writing on the GPDB the set of computed variables by calling the operation put_var_calc

- Writing on the GPDB the diagnosis of the current situation by calling the operation output_diagnosis

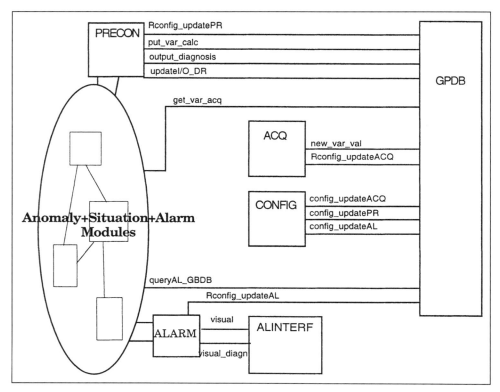

Figure 13.5 The use of frameworks.

- Writing on the GPDB the input output data relation associated with the current situation detected by calling the operation I/O_update

These three actions should be done *atomically* to ensure data integrity in GPDB. Therefore, they should be executed within a single transaction; hence, PRECON must use the *transaction service*. PRECON will also need the query service to access the GPDB. Similarly, ALARM will use the replication service and the query service. Furthermore, most operations will exploit *realtime extensions* since in most cases they must satisfy time requirements.

The result of the analysis of which services are used by which object is described by a new enrichment of the graphical notation:

- A box with rounded corners indicates a persistent object.

- A box in bold indicates a replicated object.

- The symbol *Qn* indicates a query request, where *n* identifies the query.

- The symbol *Tn* indicates that the operation is part of a transaction, where *n* identifies the transaction.

- A bold line denotes an operation that needs realtime extensions (for simplicity, here we do not distinguish between hard and soft realtime).

Figure 13.6 summarizes the result of these design steps and presents a complete object architecture that specifies all relationships among application objects, frameworks, and services.

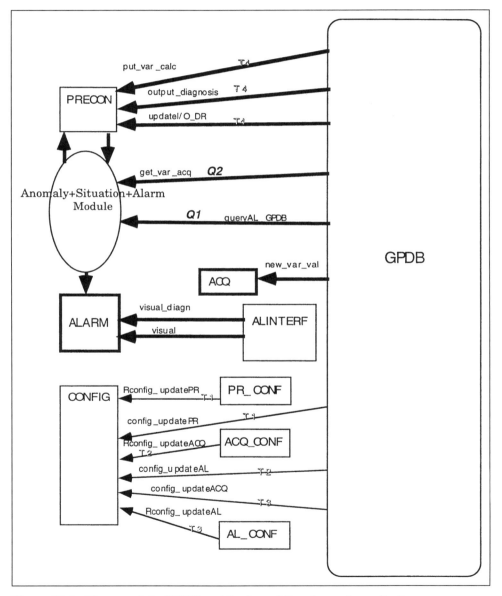

Figure 13.6   The complete CORBA architecture of the diagnosis application.

Generating IDL Interfaces

The next step consists of deriving the IDL interfaces for the objects identified during the previous step, using all the information contained in the class definition. Moreover, the use of a service implies that the IDL interface *inherits* from the corresponding IDL interface of the service. For example, an object that uses the replication service inherits from mGroupAdmin::GroupAccessor, while an object that will be replicated inherits from the interface mGroupAdmin::Groupable. With reference to Figure 13.6, Figure 13.7 displays the IDL interfaces of modules ALARM and ALINTERF.

Note that, in principle, one can *automatically* generate a complete stub structure from the graphical definition of the architecture. Such a translation is scheduled as a future development of the present prototype of the editing tool.

Implementing the Code

The architectural design is now complete. In the final step, actual code is obtained by filling the stubs generated by the previous phase. This requires essentially two types of coding:

- Coding the implementation of application objects, using abstract operations provided by IDL interfaces.

- Filling those parts of frameworks that are left parametric with respect to the application.

Thanks to the use of frameworks, the gap between application requirements and the implementation is easily bridged, and the design effort is focused on the few typical elements of the application (in our case, the diagnostic algorithms). More standard activities, such as managing alarms, querying databases, and so on, are simply imported through the OO mechanisms.

Verifying the Correctness of the Design

As previously stated, this chapter does not focus on the verification phase(s) of the software life cycle. We merely note that the joint use of formal methods (based on the TRIO language) and of CORBA services and frameworks offers the potentiality of achieving the typical benefits of formal verification at a reasonable price in terms of human effort. (By *formal verification* we mean not only traditional formal correctness proofs, but any verification method that is supported by some formalisms—for example, the semiautomatic derivation of test cases from formal requirement specifications.) In fact, we can formally specify not only application requirements, but even the semantics of critical services and frameworks (for example, time performance requirements). Then, we can devote a major effort to validating them *once and forever* against their formal semantics. The availability of highly reliable frameworks guaranteeing well-specified requirements greatly facilitates the verification of application requirements since the frameworks and services used in the application can be viewed as blackboxes whose properties have already been verified.

```
module_Alarm{
    typedef unsigned long AlarmID_type;
    interface Alarm:mGroupAdmin::Groupable{
    // Since this module is replicated it must inherit
    // from mGroupAdmin::Groupable
    oneway void alarm_condition
                    (    in AlarmID_type AlarmID,
                         in _main::func_type func,
                         in _main::level_type level);
    };
};


module_AlInterf{
    enum ii {InAlarm, BecomesInAlarm};
    typedef ii interface_type;
    typedef string description_type;
    typedef unsigned long varID_type;
    typedef struct{
        interface_type interf;
        varID_type varID;
        _Main::timetag_type timetag;
        _Main::level_type level;
        _Main::AnalogLevel_type AnalogLevel;
        float th;
        description_type description;
    }DisplayData_type;
    // DisplayData_type records the alarms
    interface AlInterf:_Persistence_Object::VarString{
    // AlInterf uses persistent objects;
    // it must inherit the ODL def
        oneway void visual (
                    in DisplayData_type DisplayData,
                    in _Main::func_type func);
        oneway void visual diagn(
                    in sequence <VarString> diagnostics,
                    in _Main::func_type func);
    // The actual structure will be defined at
    // implementation time
    };
};
```

Figure 13.7 IDL interfaces of CORBA application objects.

13.5 State of the Art and Future Development

We have described the essential features of ongoing research aimed at building a framework architecture and a development methodology for the construction of S&C

applications rooted in CORBA. The present state of our research consists of the following results:

- A precise definition of CORBAServices and CORBADomains and a partial implementation thereof
- A preliminary design methodology based on the formal language TRIO, presently mainly focused on the architectural design
- Two sample applications: a diagnostic system for power plants (from which this chapter's example has been extracted) and an airport ground traffic control system
- A few prototype tools supporting the development methodology

Future developments will consolidate and extend the present state: We will complete the implementation of services and domains (we plan to submit them to the OMG for possible standardization); we will complete the development methods and enhance the supporting tools. In particular, we expect major benefits from exploiting the formal approach based on TRIO, as pointed out in *Section 13.4*. Ultimately, our research should provide improvements both in S&C systems reliability and in development costs.

13.6 Summary

This chapter presents a framework architecture to support the development of supervision and control systems based on CORBA. The architecture is centered around services and domains that help to satisfy typical requirements of these systems, such as realtime and fault-tolerance. The chapter also presents a development method, supported by prototype tools and based on the formal language TRIO, to guide designers in the construction of their applications.

13.7 References

[Basso 1995] Basso, M., E. Ciapessoni, E. Crivelli, D. Mandrioli, A. Morzenti, E. Ratto, and P. San Pietro. Experimenting a logic-based approach to the specification and design of the control system of a pondage power plant. *ICSE-17 Workshop on Industrial Application of Formal Methods,* Seattle, WA, April 1995.

[Boehm 1988] Boehm, B.W. A spiral model of software development and enhancement. *IEEE Computer*, 21(5), May 1988: 61–72.

[Felder 1994] Felder, M., and A. Morzenti. Validating real-time systems by history-checking TRIO specifications. *ACM Transactions on Software Engineering and Methodologies*, 3(4), October 1994.

[Gargantini 1996] Gargantini, A., L. Liberati, A. Morzenti, and C. Zacchetti. Specifying, validating, and testing a traffic management system in the TRIO environment. *Proceedings of COMPASS, 11th Annual Conference on Computer Assurance*, Gaitersburg, MA, June 1996.

[Ghezzi 1990] Ghezzi, C., D. Mandrioli, and A. Morzenti. TRIO, a logic language for executable specifications of real-time systems. *Journal of Systems and Software,* 12(2), May 1990.

[IEC 1993] International Electrotechnical Commission. Field bus standard for use in industrial control system physical layer specification and service definition. Standard IEC—IS—1158-2. IEC, 1993.

[IONA 1996] IONA. *Orbix+ISIS Programmer's Guide.* ISIS Distributed Systems, IONA Technologies, 1996.

[Maffeis 1995] Maffeis, S. Adding group communication and fault-tolerance to CORBA. *Proceedings of the 1995 USENIX Conference on Object-Oriented Technologies,* Monterey, CA, June 1995.

[Mandrioli 1995] Mandrioli, D., S. Morasca, and A. Morzenti. Generating test cases for real-time systems from logic specifications. *ACM Transactions on Computer Systems,* 13(4), November 1995: 365–398.

[Menga 1991] Menga, G., P. Picchiottino, P. Gallo, and G. Lo Russo. Framework for object-oriented design and prototyping of manufacturing systems. *Journal of Object-Oriented Programming,* 1991.

[Morzenti 1994] Morzenti, A., and P. San Pietro. Object-oriented logic specifications of time critical systems. *ACM Transactions on Software Engineering and Methodologies,* 3(1), January 1994: 56–98.

[Mowbray 1995] Mowbray, T., and R. Zahavi. 1995. *The Essential CORBA: Systems Integration Using Distributed Objects.* New York: John Wiley & Sons, 1995.

[NIIIP 1997] NIIIP. National Industrial Information Infrastructure Protocols. www.niiip.org, 1997.

[OMG 1995a] Object Management Group. *CORBA: Architecture and Specification.* Framingham, MA: OMG, August 1995.

[OMG 1995b] Object Management Group. *CORBAServices.* Framingham, MA: OMG, April 1995.

[OMG 1995c] Object Management Group. *CORBAFacilities.* Framingham, MA: OMG, August 1995.

[OpenDREAMS 1996] OpenDREAMS. *Consolidated OpenDREAMS Architecture Description.* Deliv. WP1/T1.2-AAR-REP/R12b-V1. OpenDREAMS, September 1996.

[Parnas 1986] Parnas, D.L., and P.C. Clements. A rational design process: How and why to fake it. *IEEE Transactions on Software Engineering,* 12(2), February 1986: 251–257.

[SEMATECH 1996] SEMATECH. *Computer-Integrated Manufacturing Application Framework Specification 1.3.* Document 9306111697F-ENG. Austin, TX: SEMATECH, 1996.

[Taligent 1994] Taligent. *Developer's Guide to the Taligent Application Environment.* Vol. 1, *Preliminary.* Cupertino, CA: Taligent, Inc., 1994.

CHAPTER 14

EPEE: A Framework
for Supercomputing

A fair amount of the research in the field of supercomputing aims to ease the programming of distributed memory parallel computers (DMPCs). Indeed, while scientific programmers long for the computational power provided by modern DMPCs, they are generally reluctant to cope with the manual porting of their applications onto such machines because the tedious tasks of parallelization, distribution, process handling, and communication management are not among the most attractive features of DMPCs [Pancake 1990].

One of the main directions investigated to date lies in the design of semiautomatic parallelizing compilers. However, building compilers that generate efficient code for a language like High Performance Fortran (HPF) [HPF 1993] turns out to be more difficult than expected. Although many optimization techniques are known (message vectorization, loop restriction, and so on), their automatic application requires a comprehensive analysis of the program being compiled. It is also unlikely that this kind of semiautomatic parallelizing compiler could deal efficiently with application programs involving data redistribution or irregular computation patterns. Moreover, the semi-automatic parallelization approach offers no way to exploit the many hand-coded parallel algorithms that have been developed since parallelism became a mainstream research activity.

Propositions based on AI techniques have been made to deal with these problems [Fahringer 1992]. Based on the observation that only a limited number of basic operations are needed in the time-consuming inner loops of numeric programs, it is proposed in PARAMAT [Kessler 1994] to automatically identify these basic operations and substitute sequential expressions by equivalent optimized parallel counterparts.

Although this approach is interesting for parallelizing preexisting code, it is not the most straightforward way to develop new programs. Actually, once the basic operations have been identified and stored in a library, it should be possible to reuse them directly as building blocks for new application programs. The point is that such true reusability for a library requires an appropriate design and implementation emphasizing modularity. Too often in the parallel community, the provided libraries have failed in this goal because of the limitations of the programming language and the abstractions they rely on. One typical example is the classical libraries built for FORTRAN programs. Indeed, while dynamically redistributable data structures are eagerly awaited by end users, these libraries are not versatile enough to deal with the complex problems bound to the management of this functionality. We claim that object-oriented techniques are helpful to bring in such versatility and, to a greater extent, to facilitate the programming of DMPCs.

This chapter shows that by fostering the construction of reusable and extensible libraries of parallel software components, existing sequential object-oriented languages enable the efficient use of DMPCs at various levels of abstraction, ranging from a total hiding of distribution issues down to the fine-tuning of parallelism. *Section 14.1* outlines the design of an Eiffel Parallel Execution Environment (EPEE) that evolved from a small class library [Jézéquel 1993] toward a complete framework for encapsulating data sharing, message passing, synchronization, parallelism, and data distribution into reusable software components. *Section 14.2* illustrates how EPEE can be used to build application-specific frameworks, using as a case study the design of Paladin, an object-oriented library dedicated to linear algebra computation on DMPCs. The section illustrates how EPEE's components can be combined with sequential ones to provide useful parallel abstractions, enters some of the details of the implementation of distributed matrixes in Paladin, and discusses performance-related issues. *Section 14.3* shows how versatile applications can be built using Paladin with a range of abstraction levels such that, at the highest level, distribution and parallelism remain completely hidden from the application programmer. *Section 14.4* briefly discusses related work.

Note that EPEE is based on Eiffel [Meyer 1992] because this language most elegantly features all the concepts needed (strong encapsulation, static type checking, multiple inheritance, dynamic binding, and genericity). However, any other statically typed object-oriented language could have been used instead (for example, Java, Modula-3, Ada 95, or C++) at the price of a few contortions.

14.1 The EPEE Framework

The EPEE framework parallel programming model, framework architecture, basic communication and data sharing components, distributed management components, parallel operators, and the operator design pattern are discussed in detail in the following sections.

14.1.1 The EPEE Parallel Programming Model

The kind of parallelism we consider is inspired by Valiant's block synchronous parallel (BSP) model [Valiant 1990]. A computation that fits the BSP model can be seen as a succession of parallel phases separated by synchronizations and sequential phases.

In EPEE [Jézéquel 1993], Valiant's model is implemented based on the single program multiple data (SPMD) programming model. Data can be either distributed across the processors, or virtually shared if a distributed shared memory (DSM) is available on the target architecture. (A DSM implements the abstraction of a shared memory on top of a distributed memory [Li 1986]. It handles such issues as page faults, page caching, cache consistency, and so on.)

The performance increase comes from splitting the data into partitions that can be processed in parallel. EPEE provides a design framework in which data representations are totally encapsulated in regular Eiffel classes [Hamelin 1994], without any extension of the language or any modification of its semantics. Whether the data is distributed or virtually shared, the user still views the program as a sequential one, and the parallelism is derived from the data representation: Each processor runs a subset of the original execution flow. This subset is based on the owner write rule (that is, a processor may write only its own data partition), as introduced in [Callahan 1988] and described formally in [André 1990].

Our method for encapsulating parallelism within a class can be compared with the encapsulation of tricky pointer manipulations within a linked list class that provides the user with the abstraction of a list without any visible pointer handling. In contrast to concurrent object-oriented languages such as POOL-T [America 1987] or ABCL/1 [Yonezawa 1986], which were designed to tackle problems with explicit parallelism, our goal is to hide the parallelism, and optionally the data distribution, from the application programmer.

14.1.2 Structure of the EPEE Framework

The EPEE framework can be used at three main levels: the *application level,* the *applicative framework level,* and the *core framework level* (see Figure 14.1).

At the application level, the programmer programs to interfaces that are abstract datatypes (ADTs). The program behaves the same way regardless of whether it is running on a parallel computer; only performance improvements might show up if it is not. For a user of an ADT library designed with EPEE, it must be possible to handle distributed objects just like local (that is, nondistributed) ones, while having the possibility, but not the obligation, of fiddling about with data distribution directives.

The problem for the designer of a new ADT library is thus to extend the EPEE framework by implementing the set of relevant distributed objects, ensuring their portability and efficiency, and preserving a "sequential-like" interface for the sake of the user, from whom distribution and parallelization issues must be masked. The fundamental idea is to build a hierarchy of abstraction levels. Application programs are written in such a way

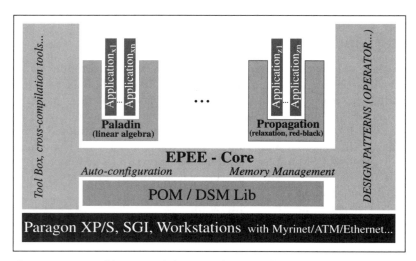

Figure 14.1 Architecture of the EPEE framework.

that they operate on abstract data structures, whose concrete (replicated, shared, or distributed) implementation is defined independently from the programs that use them.

The distribution of an object is usually achieved in two steps. The first step aims to provide the user with transparency. It consists of handling the actual representation of the object on the processors of a DMPC in such a way that the resulting object can be used in a SPMD program just like its local counterpart in a sequential program. In the case of distributed objects, one has to implement a mechanism ensuring a transparent remote access to nonlocal data. In the case of shared objects, this transparent access is automatically ensured by the DSM.

The second step mainly addresses performance issues. It consists of applying some design patterns to implement the methods that operate on the distributed or shared objects. The following sections essentially discuss distributed objects, but the underlying object-oriented techniques can be applied to shared objects in the same way.

EPEE facilitates the task of the ADT library designer by providing a number of design patterns supported by a collection of predefined parallel software components. These components constitute a kind of toolbox that remains fully extensible, since it can be augmented as and when new parallel components are developed to fit the needs of particular distributed applications. The following sections describe some of the components that the EPEE's toolbox provides to date.

14.1.3 Basic Communication and Data-Sharing Components

EPEE contains a set of basic communication facilities required for handling the distribution of ADT libraries. The class Parallel Observable Machine (POM) is a *façade* [Gamma 1995] hiding the complexities and platform dependencies of the EPEE communication subsystems. It includes functions that offer an abstract view of the parallel machine (number of nodes and identity of local node), as well as functions for sending and receiving messages in point-to-point or broadcast mode and for polling reception queues. The model optionally includes a complementary *observation node*, whose role is to collect and handle trace information related to the behavior of a distributed application [Guidec 1995]. POM is available for IP, Myrinet or ATM networks of Unix workstations, Silicon Graphic SGI, and Paragon XP/S.

Several Eiffel classes have been developed on top of POM. For example, the class Transmissible defines an interface for objects that need to be efficiently exchanged by the processors of a DMPC:

```
deferred class TRANSMISSIBLE
      -- An Eiffel deferred class is like a Java Interface
feature
    send (destination: INTEGER)
       -- Send object to 'destination'
    bcast
       -- Broadcast object to all nodes
    recv_bcast_from (source: INTEGER)
       -- Receive object from 'source' in broadcast mode
    recv_from (source: INTEGER)
       -- Receive object from 'source' in point-to-point mode
end -- TRANSMISSIBLE
```

Hence, an object A derived from Transmissible can be sent by processor source to processor target using the simple expression A.send(target); processor target receives the value of object A using the expression A.recv_from(source). Transmissible implementations use the basic communication facilities offered by POM.

To handle parallel computers where it is possible to actually *share* data among a number of processors, using either a physically shared memory or a DSM, EPEE includes a subsystem called *DSM-Lib*. It provides an interface for the minimal set of common operations for several kinds of shared memory implementations. To date, DSM-Lib is implemented for two platforms: the DSM running on the Paragon XP/S, and on Unix workstations (Solaris, Linux, and SGI) using standard interprocess communications. In both cases, the interface and the functionalities of DSM-Lib are the same. Sharing objects among processors sets a number of problems related to memory management and interactions with the Eiffel built-in garbage collector. We will not enter into the gory details of its implementation, because from a user's point of view, shared objects are created through an *abstract factory* and are transparently integrated within the Eiffel runtime system. As a consequence of this mechanism, any object that is allocated in shared memory becomes visible from any process of the parallel application, and can be used just as local ones, notwithstanding synchronization issues.

14.1.4 Distribution Management Components

In a programming model such as HPF, one can specify the partitioning of an object and the mapping of the resulting partitions on the processors of the target DMPC through compiler directives. We chose to reify these abstractions—that is, we provided the programmer with a set of classes for handling data distribution issues.

For instance, mechanisms for distributing bi-indexable objects (such as arrays, grids, matrixes, and tables) based on a blockwise partitioning are encapsulated in a class Distribution_2D. This class contains all the routines needed to perform global to local and local to global index conversions, to identify the owner of a block, to run iterations over local or non-null elements, and so on. The way in which Distribution_2D was developed is a typical example of code reuse based on the mechanism of multiple (actually, repeated) inheritance: It inherits twice from a more simple class Distribution_1D (see Figure 14.2). Note that a class dedicated to the distribution of three-dimensional objects could be built just as easily by combining the features of Distribution_1D and those of Distribution_2D.

The parameterization of the creation method (*class constructor* in C++ terminology) of class Distribution_2D is inspired by the syntax used in the HPF directive *distribute*, and it has roughly the same expressiveness. An application programmer willing to get involved in data distribution management may describe a distribution pattern by specifying the size of the index domain considered, the size of the basic building blocks in this domain, and how these blocks must be mapped on a set of processors. The definition of the mapping function is left abstract in the class Distribution_2D and encapsulated in a small hierarchy of classes dedicated to the mapping of two-dimensional structures on a set of processors (somewhat as in the Strategy pattern).

```
deferred class MAPPING_2D
feature
    map_block (bi, bj, bimax, bjmax, nproc: INTEGER):INTEGER is
-- Maps block(bi, bj) on a processor whose identifier
-- must be in the range [0, nproc]
      require
            bi_valid:   (bi >= 0) and (bi <= bimax)
            bj_valid:   (bj >= 0) and (bj <= bjmax)
      deferred
      ensure
            (Result >= 0) and (Result < nproc)
      end -- map_block
end -- class MAPPING_2D
```

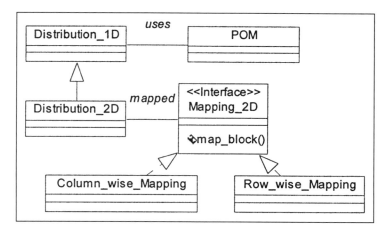

Figure 14.2   Distribution facilities in the EPEE toolbox.

Note that Eiffel lets us *specify* the semantics of this function thanks to *preconditions* (boolean assertions following the keyword require that must be respected upon entering the function) and *postconditions* (specifying what the function is supposed to do: The assertion following the keyword ensure must be respected when the function exits). Since assertions are inherited in Eiffel, the EPEE framework makes sure that any subclass of Mapping_2D respects the specifications expressed in the pre- and postconditions of the method map_block.

EPEE includes two effective classes that permit either row-wise or columnwise mapping of the blocks of a distributed object on a set of processors. In the class Row_Wise_Mapping, for example, the method map_block is implemented as follows:

```
expanded class ROW_WISE_MAPPING
-- expanded class instances are value objects instead of
-- references (e.g., in C/C++ (int) instead of (int*).
-- Since this class hold no data, its instances won't
-- take any space in memory.
inherit MAPPING_2D
feature
    map_block (bi, bj, bimax, bjmax, nproc: INTEGER): INTEGER is
        do
            Result := (bi * (bjmax + 1) + bj) \\ nproc
        end -- map_block
end -- class ROW_WISE_MAPPING
```

The implementation of Column_Wise_Mapping is, of course, similar to that of Row_Wise_Mapping. A user could easily propose alternative mapping policies (random mapping, diagonal mapping, and so on): The only thing a user must do is design a new class that inherits from Mapping_2D and that encapsulates an original implementation of the method map_block.

Figure 14.3 shows the creation of an instance of Distribution_2D. The instance of class Distribution_2D created in this example permits management of the distribution of a 10×10 index domain partitioned into 5×2 blocks mapped columnwise on a set of 4 processors.

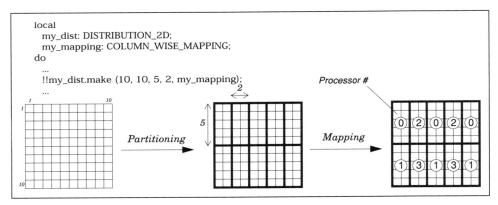

Figure 14.3 Example of a distribution allowed by class Distribution_2D.

Each distributed object must be associated at creation time with an instance of a subclass of Distribution, which plays the role of a distribution template for this object. This distribution template can be specified either explicitly—in which case a new instance of Distribution is created for the object—or implicitly by passing either a reference to an already existing distributed object or a reference to an existing distribution template as a parameter. Several distributed objects can thus share a common distribution pattern by referring to the same distribution template. It is most important to note that an instance of a class such as Distribution_2D does not actually store any data. It simply provides the mechanisms that are needed to handle the distribution of a bi-indexable object.

14.1.5 Parallel Operators

The basic communication and distribution components presented in the preceding sections can serve as basic building components to develop sophisticated parallel operators. The notion of *operator* relates to Booch's agent [Booch 1994]. It serves to encapsulate operations in a pure object-oriented model: An operator is an object created to execute a specific operation on behalf of another object. Classes describing such operators can be perceived as *algorithmic abstractions,* just as classes describing data structures are commonly perceived as data abstractions.

Consider the class Dist_Reductor, which is a quite simple implementation of a generic parallel reduction operator:

```
expanded class DIST_REDUCTOR [T]
-- T is a generic parameter, as in Ada (C++ template param.)
feature
   reduce (v: T; action: BINOP[T]): T is
      local proc: INTEGER;  tmp: T;  POM: POM;
      do
      Result := v -- Initialize return value to local value
      POM.bcast (Result) -- Broadcast local value
      -- Now receive values from other processors
      from proc := 0 until (proc = POM.nb_nodes) loop
          if (proc /= POM.node_id) then -- not me
             POM.recv_bcast_from (proc, tmp)
                  -- Invoke action on available values
             Result := action.op (Result, tmp)
          end -- if
          proc := proc + 1
      end -- loop
      end -- reduce
   . . .
end -- DIST_REDUCTOR
```

The role of an instance of Dist_Reductor is to perform an SPMD reduction. The class Dist_Reductor encapsulates a single function, reduce, which admits two parameters. The first is a variable v whose value must be the contribution of the local processor to the distributed reduction; the second is a variable action that must be a binary operator—that is, an operator featuring the binary operation that must be used to perform the actual reduction.

Note that although the code encapsulated in Dist_Reductor is intentionally very simple (each processor first broadcasts its contribution to the reduction; afterward, it starts collecting the values sent by all the other processors implied in the computation—the actual reduction is obtained by invoking the function op on agent action, with the intermediate result of the reduction and the last received value tmp as parameters), more sophisticated versions of the function reduce allowing for peculiarities of a given DMPC could be encapsulated in descendants of this class.

This distributed reductor is an example of a class encapsulating a general-purpose parallel mechanism. Several other parallel abstractions are available in the EPEE's toolbox, such as abstractions of general-purpose communication patterns (such as rotation and shift) and abstractions of generic computation schemes (such as apply and reduce), which are provided for both a parallel and a sequential execution environment. These operators constitute basic building blocks that can be combined in an algebraic fashion to build customized application-oriented operators.

Indeed, a minimal set of building blocks can be shown to provide a basis for expressing arbitrary operations on enumerations of collections in an architecture-independent way. The theory behind these operators has its roots in the algebra of monoids but is better known as the Bird-Meertens calculus [Skillicorn 1990]. To benefit from these abstractions, an application must be designed along the lines of the Operator design pattern [Pacherie 1998] outlined in the following section.

14.1.6 The Operator Design Pattern

The operator design pattern is discussed in the following sections.

Intent

The Operator pattern provides a generic design approach to express operations as autonomous agents working on data enumerations in an architecture-independent way. It builds on the Iterator pattern [Gamma 1995] and improves the reusability and extensibility of applications designed and implemented with it, most notably their ability to run efficiently on a DMPC.

Problem

We start with the design of data collection processing using the Iterator pattern. Consider the application of an operation over the items of a collection, for instance the scalar product of a vector. Using the Iterator design pattern and the encapsulation principle, one may think about encapsulating such an operation into the abstract Vector class. Following this idea, an implementation of the scalar product of a vector using an iterator can go as follows:

```
class VECTOR[E]
feature -- Vector Scalar product example implementation
   items : WRT_ITERATOR[E] is deferred end
     -- Factory method returning an iterator on the vector items
   scal (coef : E) is
```

```
            -- Scale this vector by coef
            local iterator : WRT_ITERATOR[E]
            do
            iterator := items
            from iterator.start until iterator.exhausted loop
                iterator.set_item(iterator.item*coef)
                iterator.next
            end -- loop
        end -- scal
    -- ...
end -- VECTOR
```

On second thought, this approach might not always be the best one. We can identify at least two issues related to the use of the encapsulation principle in this case.

The first issue concerns the reusability of the processing method. According to the encapsulation principle, the only way to reuse the scalar product operator would be to inherit from the class where this operation is defined. By encapsulating this operation within the Vector class, we have introduced a strong coupling between the collection and the operation abstraction, whereas this was not necessary. As an unexpected consequence, we have designed a (conceptually) general-purpose operation as an operation tightly bound to vectors.

The second issue relates to the extensibility of a whole library designed with this interpretation of the encapsulation principle. Indeed, each attempt to include a new operation brings alterations to the code of the collection classes. Besides, the collection classes are usually organized into a hierarchy of subclasses that collaborate with each other. Thus, even minor changes must be made very carefully to avoid any alteration in the behavior of the whole system.

Solution

A collection class should not encapsulate the operations modifying the state of the items stored in its structure. The only operations a collection abstraction (such as a class container) may provide are related to the management of the data structure used to hold these items (accessing, adding and removing items, sorting, and so on). In the design pattern we present, the data modification process is modeled with a dedicated abstraction that performs the related operation on an enumeration of the elements stored in the container.

In the previous code example, it is obvious that the scalar product does not use any information on the structure of the vector collection. Its only requirement is concerned with the ability of processed items to be multiplied by a constant factor. Thus, the scalar product operator requirement is just related to the type of processed items: here they must feature the multiplication (infix operator *).

Therefore, an operator is an autonomous abstraction, parameterized by a function argument. It is responsible for the application of that function over the items of an enumeration and for aggregating each result in a convenient fashion (for example, as a single item or another enumeration). In other words, an operator is itself a function taking an enumeration of items and a function working on these items (which we call the *regular operation*). In the Operator pattern, we reify this abstraction into the operator class.

Applicability

The Operator design pattern can be applied to implement the regular operation over data collections. The Operator pattern is relevant if the processing does not need any knowledge about the source of the enumeration it processes. In a general context, one can think about data collection processing as either a mutating process (that is, processing that changes the storage structure of the collection, such as for sorting) or as a nonmutating process (that is, processing that relies only on an enumeration of the processed collection). As soon as the goal is nonmutating collection processing, it is possible to use the Operator pattern.

Structure

The structure of the Operator pattern extends the Iterator pattern with an abstract Operator class that is a client of the iterator. Figure 14.4 presents the static structure of the pattern, outlining three class hierarchies. The basic pattern structure is made of only the operator, the iterator, and the collection abstract classes. This figure also includes two examples of concrete operators: the scalar product and the dot product.

Figure 14.5 presents the static diagram for collections. Note that the iterator hierarchy appears in both diagrams because iterators are the link between processing classes (operators) and collection classes.

In the original structure of the pattern, the operator is completely independent from the collection. However, there are cases where the client of the collection processing is the collection itself. In such a situation, the convenient trade-off between the pattern design guidelines and its practical application is to use a *factory method* [Gamma 1995] for the creation of the operator in the application collection class. The benefit of using such a pattern comes from the ability we have to redefine the concrete operator in subclasses of the abstract collection class. Indeed, we use this pattern to be able to redefine factory methods instantiating the parallel participants (distributed collection and parallel operator) in this pattern when it is applied to parallel computations.

Collaborations

The pattern structure is made of three participants: the *operator,* the *iterator,* and the *collection.* Each participant is responsible for a part of the pattern behavior. These responsibilities are stressed in the following collaborations:

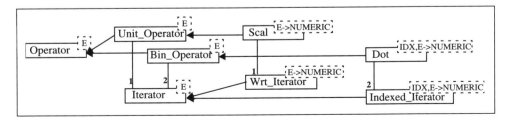

Figure 14.4   Operator static diagram.

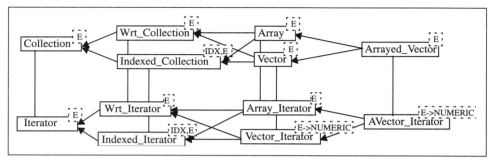

Figure 14.5   Collection static diagram.

Operator. The operator is created and executed by the client. To perform its work, the operator collaborates with an iterator supplied by the client. The constrained genericity of the operator ensures that its regular operation is meaningful for each processed item. Besides, the type of attachable iterators ensures that the enumeration (ordered, indexed, and so on) is suitable for the operator specifications.

Iterator. An iterator is responsible for building the sequence of items (for example, a collection traversal). There are special cases of iterators that are aware of indexes associated with yielded items; they include them in their interfaces. Besides, iterators might also implement specific traversal policies to yield their items (forward, backward, and so on) along with required properties (ordered items, filtered items, and so on).

Collection. A collection is responsible for gathering a set of data. The Collection abstraction includes the Aggregate abstraction but is not restricted to it. For example, a collection can be a handle to an IO medium such as a file, a socket, and so on. At the highest level of abstraction, a collection has, at least, an iterator factory method that is able to yield the collection items. Using inheritance and specialization, new collection classes are defined to include more features, such as indexes or ordering, and subsequently to define the corresponding iterators.

Implementation

The behavior of an operator can be split into three parts:

Preprocessing. This is the preparation of the computation, that is, the internal initialization needed by the concrete implementation of the computations that an operator must achieve. This preprocessing phase corresponds to the before_run method and is invoked each time this operator is run.

Enumeration processing. This phase is the application of the regular operation over the items of an enumeration. This phase corresponds to the do_all method of the operator class.

Postprocessing. At the time all the items are processed, a final computation might be required according to the global knowledge of the results computed by the regular operation over the collection. This computation is performed by the after_run method and is invoked as soon as the collection processing is finished.

```
deferred class UNIT_OPERATOR [ITEM]
inherit
   OPERATOR
feature
   make (iter : like items) is
       -- This method can be used as a constructor
       require iter_exists: iter /= Void
       do
       items := clone(iter) -- to avoid iterator sharing
       end
feature {UNIT_OPERATOR}
   item_action (item : E) is deferred end -- Unary operation
feature {NONE} - Means that the features below are protected
   do_all is
       -- Apply item_action over each item provided
       do
       from items.start until items.exhausted loop
          item_action(items.item)
          items.next
       end -- loop
       end -- do_all
   items : ITERATOR[E]
end -- UNIT_OPERATOR
```

It can be noted that the preprocessing and postprocessing phases might be defined by the application programmer according to the specific service to be implemented with the operator. On the contrary, the collection-processing phase is independent from any operator implementation, and the only thing the programmer has to define is the item_action method. Using this approach, we can implement the *operator* version of the scal method previously discussed.

```
class  SCAL [E -> NUMERIC] -- Generic parameter E
inherit                    -- must conform to NUMERIC
   UNIT_OPERATOR [E]
       rename make as make_from_operator
       redefine items end
creation make - Declare "make" as the constructor of the class
feature
   make (coef : E; iter : like items) is
       do
          make_from_operator(iter)
          coef := c
       end -- make
feature
   item_action (e : E) is -- Scal regular operation
       do
          iterator.set_item(iterator.item * coef)
       end -- item_action
feature {SCAL}
   items : WRT_ITERATOR [E]
end -- SCAL
```

Because the number of arguments required by a regular operation cannot be fixed at this level of abstraction, the Operator class has a deferred do_all method that should perform the enumeration processing. This do_all method is implemented to take a single argument in the class Unit_Operator that is inherited by Scal. But the Operator may be subclassed for operators handling more than one argument. The internal mechanisms of multiple operators are roughly the same as for the unit operator, except that they deal with two or more enumerations at once.

Consequences

The Operator design pattern allows the separation of the responsibilities between collections and operations and the relaxing of the interdependencies between those abstractions. It leads to three class hierarchies: The *collections* provide the *enumerations* that are processed by the *operators*. On one side, we model abstractions for collections; on the other side, we model processing over data as autonomous agents. Operators do not directly rely on collections but on enumerations. The connection between operators and collections is made by the enumeration abstraction, itself reified as the Iterator class in the pattern. The key point is that an enumeration is not restricted to an aggregate traversal in all possible situations. This design has several consequences:

Methodology. Collection processing is seen as the collaboration between a set of collections and a set of operators through enumerations. Processing these collections relies on applying several operators in turn.

Specialization. Improvement in the operator implementations can be made independently from collections; also, improvement in the internal collection representations can be made safely without drawbacks on operators.

Reusability. It is possible to provide concrete general-purpose operators focusing only on the semantics of the modeled operation. Most of the time, the regular operation implicates some requirements regarding the processed items and their enumerations. So far as these requirements can be expressed by typing (using constrained genericity and iterator redefinition), we are able to build concrete operators for a wide range of applications.

Extensibility. The set of available operators can be extended without any change to either the collection hierarchy or the existing operators.

This chapter's main interest in the Operator pattern is regarding its suitability for data parallel programs. Indeed, the following section shows how to build parallel operators from basic ones.

Parallel Operator

A parallel operator has the responsibility of ensuring that the parallel execution has the same effect as the sequential one. A parallel operator uses the synchronization methods implemented by a memory model concrete class (either shared or distributed) and the preprocessing and postprocessing methods (before_run and after_run) to recombine local contributions to build a global and shared result:

```
deferred class PARALLEL_OPERATOR
inherit
   OPERATOR
      redefine run end -- run is overridden
feature
   run is
      do
      memory.pre_sync
      before_run
      do_all
      after_run
      memory.post_sync
   end -- run
   attach_memory (m : MEMORY_MODEL) is
      -- Store the memory model used
      do
         memory := m
      end -- attach_memory
feature {PARALLEL_OPERATOR}
   memory : MEMORY_MODEL
end -- PARALLEL_OPERATOR
```

To build a concrete parallel operator, a library designer reuses the sequential one and combines it to the abstract parallel operator using multiple inheritance. Examples of the use of a parallel operator to parallelize the scalar product and the dot product are presented in *Section 14.2.3*.

14.2 Using EPEE to Build a Parallel Linear Algebra Library

This section illustrates how to use the EPEE framework to develop Paladin, an object-oriented library dedicated to linear algebra computations on DMPCs.

14.2.1 Design Principle of Paladin

The design principle of Paladin (abstracting and providing data representations) is discussed in this section.

Abstracting the Data Representation

Paladin is built around the specifications of the basic entities of linear algebra: matrixes and vectors. A fundamental design principle for this library is that the abstract specification of an entity is kept isolated from any assumption regarding the actual data representation (for example, dense, sparse, replicated, distributed, and shared). For example, the simplified abstract specification of a matrix entity is encapsulated in a deferred class Matrix, which contains many algorithms for performing matrix-based

computations but which provides no details about the way matrix objects are represented in memory:

```
deferred class MATRIX
feature -- Attributes
   nrow : INTEGER       -- Number of rows
   ncolumn : INTEGER    -- Number of columns
feature -- Scalar Accessors
   item (i, j: INTEGER): DOUBLE is
      -- Return current value of item(i, j)
      require
        valid_i:  (i > 0) and (i <= nrow)
        valid_j:  (j > 0) and (j <= ncolumn)
      deferred
      end -- item
   put (v: DOUBLE; i, j: INTEGER) is
      -- Put value v into item(i, j)
      require
        valid_i:  (i > 0) and (i <= nrow)
        valid_j:  (j > 0) and (j <= ncolumn)
      deferred
      ensure item (i, j) = v
      end -- put
feature -- Vectorial and submatrix Accessors
   row (i: INTEGER): VECTOR is
      -- Return a "window" on the ith row
   ...
feature -- Operators
   trace:  DOUBLE is do ... end
   add (B: MATRIX) is do ... end
   -- an infix variant to allow expressions such as R := A + B
   infix "+" (B: MATRIX) : MATRIX is do ... end
   mult (A, B: MATRIX) is do ... end
   LU is do ... end
   ...
end -- class MATRIX
```

The resulting class can be thought of as a partial implementation of the abstract
datatype of a matrix entity [Abelson 1985; Cardelli 1985]. Methods can be classified in
two categories, *accessors* and *operators*. The accessors are the methods that permit
accessing a matrix in read or write mode. They can be either scalar (such as put and
item), vectorial (returning a Vector which is actually a window on the matrix content)
or even two-dimensional (returning a submatrix). The implementation of accessors
depends on the format chosen to represent a matrix object in memory. Consequently, in
class Matrix, the accessors put and item are left deferred—that is, they are declared but
not defined (a deferred method in Eiffel is equivalent to a pure virtual function in
C++). Their signature is specified (number of arguments and types of these arguments), as well as the formal properties (pre- and postconditions) that have to be
respected by subclasses implementing these deferred methods.

Providing Various Data Representations

To get concrete matrix classes, we rely on the mechanism of multiple inheritance in order to combine the abstract Matrix class with some EPEE components that can take care of the actual data representation. For example, the class Local_Matrix implements nondistributed matrixes by combining the abstract class Matrix with the implementation facilities offered by a two-dimensional array (Array2). The names of the methods inherited from both ancestor classes are matched correctly through *renaming*, an Eiffel language mechanism that addresses this kind of problem.

```
class LOCAL_MATRIX
inherit
   MATRIX
   ARRAY2 [DOUBLE]
      rename height as nrow, width as ncolumn end
creation make -- declare 'make' as this class constructor,
   -- and that's all!
end -- class LOCAL_MATRIX
```

Since matrixes and vectors in Paladin admit several alternative representation layouts (for example, sparse matrixes are Arrays of sparse vectors), they must be considered as *polymorphic* entities—objects that assume different forms and whose form can change dynamically. The problem of choosing the most appropriate representation format for a matrix is even more crucial in the context of distributed computation, since matrixes can be partitioned and distributed on multiprocessor machines. Each distribution pattern for a matrix (distribution by rows, by columns, by blocks, and so on) can then be perceived as a particular implementation of this matrix. When designing an application program that deals with matrixes, the choice of the best representation layout for a given matrix is a crucial issue. Paladin makes it possible for the application programmer to change the representation format of a matrix at any time during a computation. For example, after a few computation steps an application program may need to convert a sparse matrix into a dense one, because the sparsity of the matrix has decreased during the first part of the computation. Likewise, it may sometimes be necessary to change the distribution pattern of a distributed matrix at runtime to adapt its distribution to the requirements of the computation. Paladin thus provides a facility to redistribute matrixes dynamically, as well as a facility to transform dynamically the internal representation format of a matrix (this is detailed in *Section 14.3.2*).

14.2.2 Implementation of Distributed Matrixes in Paladin

In Paladin, distributed matrixes are implemented using two abstraction levels: The first level focuses on distribution issues (using the relevant EPEE components), and the second level deals with the internal representation of a distributed matrix on each processor.

Dealing with Distribution Issues

The accessors declared in class Matrix must be implemented in accordance with the programming model introduced in *Section 14.1.1*. This is achieved in a new class Dist_Matrix that inherits from the abstract specification encapsulated in class Matrix and uses a distribution template (an instance of Distribution_2D) to deal with distribution issues. The accessor put is defined so as to conform to the owner write rule: The assignment of a matrix element is conditioned by a locality test using the distribution template of the matrix.

```
put (v:  DOUBLE; i, j:  INTEGER) is
   -- SPMD model: all processors run through this code
 do
   if dist.item_is_local(i, j) then
    local_put (v, i, j)
   end -- if
 end -- put
```

Likewise, the accessor item is defined so that remote accesses are properly dealt with: The processor that owns item (i, j) broadcasts its value so that all the other processors can receive it. The invocation M.item(i, j)thus returns the same value on all the processors implied in the computation:

```
item (i, j: INTEGER): DOUBLE is
 do
   if dist.item_is_local(i, j) then -- This procedure owns the item
     Result := local_item (i, j)
     POM.broadcast (Result)
   else -- Just wait for it
     Result:=POM.receive_from(dist.owner_of_item(i, j))
   end -- if
 end -- item
```

Managing the Internal Representation of a Distributed Matrix

The implementation of the methods put and item shown in the preceding section deals with the distribution of data, but not with the actual *access* to local data. This problem is tackled at a second level, in the body of the local accessors local_put and local_item, whose implementation is closely dependent on the format chosen to represent a part of the distributed matrix on each processor. Since there may be numerous ways to store a distributed matrix in memory (for example, the distributed matrix may still be dense or sparse), both methods local_put and local_item are left deferred in class Dist_Matrix. They must be defined in classes that are subclassed from Dist_Matrix and that encapsulate all the details relative to the internal representation of distributed matrixes. The class Dblock_Matrix is one of the many descendants of Dist_Matrix. It inherits from Dist_Matrix as well as from Array2[Local_Matrix], and therefore implements a dense matrix distributed by blocks as a two-dimensional table of local matrixes. Each entry in this table refers to a building block of the distributed matrix stored in memory as an instance of Local_Matrix (see Figure 14.6). A void entry in the table means that the local processor does not own the corresponding block matrix. In Dblock_Matrix, the local accessors local_put and local_item are defined so as to allow for indirection due to the table.

A Layered Class Hierarchy

The class hierarchy that results from our approach is clearly organized as a layering of abstraction levels. At the highest level, the class Matrix encapsulates the abstract specification of a matrix entity. The class Dist_Matrix corresponds to an intermediate level, where the problem of the distribution of a matrix is solved, while the problem of the actual storage of the matrix in memory is deferred. At the lowest level, classes such as Dblock_Matrix provide fully operational specifications for distributed matrixes. Besides Dblock_Matrix, the class hierarchy of Paladin includes classes such as Dcol_Matrix and Drow_Matrix that encapsulate alternative implementations for row-wise and columnwise distributed dense or sparse matrixes. In these classes, distributed matrixes are implemented as tables of local vectors, which in turn can be dense or sparse, and are made compatible with Fortran arrays to benefit from the very aggressively optimized basic linear algebra subroutines (BLASs) [Lawson 1989] available on many platforms. Some of the operators inherited from Matrix can then be redefined in Local_Matrix so that BLASs are automatically invoked whenever possible—that is, when the BLAS kernel is available on the target machine and when all the operands of an operation have a Fortran-compatible representation.

Other kinds of distribution patterns or other kinds of representation formats could be proposed. One could, for example, think of exotic distribution patterns based on a decomposition in heterogeneous blocks or on a random mapping policy. One could also decide to provide an implementation ad hoc for triangular or symmetric distributed matrixes. With the object-oriented approach, the extensibility of a class hierarchy such as that of Paladin has virtually no limit. It is always possible to incorporate new classes seamlessly into a preexisting class hierarchy.

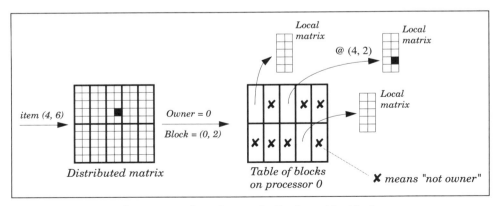

Figure 14.6 Internal representation of a matrix distributed by blocks.

14.2.3 Parallelization Techniques

The techniques presented in preceding sections permit the transparent distribution of an object: From the viewpoint of an application programmer, there is no fundamental difference between the services offered by a shared or a distributed object and those offered by a local (that is, nondistributed) one. It is just possible to handle larger objects due to the fact that the total memory offered by a DMPC usually amounts to several times that of a monoprocessor machine.

However, the flow of control of all methods is still sequential, so that little improvement in performance can be expected. To get better performance, it is necessary to redefine those operators of the distributed object that can be considered critical (that is, computation-intensive ones). The method consists of combining relevant operators with the abstract parallel operator. As outlined in *Section 14.1.6*, the purpose of a parallel operator is to make each of its local fragments collaborate with all the others to synchronize on individual contributions of a given operator, and then build the global result.

It must be noted that we do not propose new optimization techniques: Most of them actually result from research efforts that aim to transform sequential imperative languages such as Fortran and C into parallel languages (discarding useless remote reads, restricting iteration domains, optimizing index transformations, vectorizing data, and so on). The originality of our approach lies in the way these optimizations are incorporated in a parallel library: We propose to encapsulate them into reusable components (the parallel agents) that library designers may customize to implement their own optimized operators.

For example, the EPEE distribution management components (such as the class Distribution_2D introduced in *Section 14.1.4*) can be used at one and the same time for restricting iteration domains (because they provide methods to iterate over local elements only) and for optimizing index transformations (most of the index-related computations can be performed once, the results being stored in private tables). The following code example illustrates this idea, showing the parallelization of the scalar product operator as introduced in *Section 14.1.6*. The parallelization of this operator is straightforward because its computation does not require any postprocessing to gather partial results. Implementing the parallel scal operator leads to double inheritance between the Parallel_Operator class and the Scal operator. We just have to make sure that calling the run method of Parallel_Scal invokes the parallel run method of Parallel_Operator.

```
class PARALLEL_SCAL [E -> NUMERIC]
inherit
   SCAL [E]
      rename make as make_scal
      undefine run -- Undefine sequential run to use the
      end          -- definition from the parallel operator
   PARALLEL_OPERATOR [E]
creation make
feature
   make (iter : ITERATOR[E]; c : E; m : MEMORY_MODEL) is
     do
```

```
        make_scal(iter,c)
        attach_memory(m)
     end -- make
  end -- PARALLEL_SCAL
```

In the example of the parallel dot operator (implementing the dot product of two vectors), the postprocessing phase consists of gathering the partial dot products into a summation, using the Dist_Reductor parallel operator introduced in *Section 14.1.5*.

After this computation, performed into the method after_run, each processor holds the same value for the dot product. The EPEE toolbox also helps in the parallelization of more complex operators. Consider, for example, the method mult, which computes the product of two matrixes. It was implemented quite simply in class Matrix, based on three nested loops and the accessors put and item. However, this default implementation is purely sequential, and therefore is quite inefficient if at least one of the matrixes is distributed. We encapsulated in class Dblock_Matrix another method, mult_dblock, that also computes the matrix product, but only if the matrixes considered are distributed by blocks.

Instead of relying on the basic scalar accessors put and item, the algorithm of mult_dblock is directly expressed in terms of block matrix operations. The iteration domain is reduced thanks to locality tests, so each processor performs only local calculations. Communications, when they cannot be avoided, are naturally vectorized due to the fact that the data is exchanged as block matrixes instead of scalar elements.

Actually, vectorizing data access is not profitable to communications only. Restructuring the algorithms encapsulated in class Matrix and its descendants so that they perform block matrix operations in their inner loops globally enhances the performance of Paladin, because it contributes to reduce memory swapping and cache defaults on most modern processors. Providing a distributed object with multilevel accessors therefore has an interesting consequence: It permits enhancing the performance of operators thanks to better exploitation of the memory architecture and a reduction of the cost of data exchanges between the processors of a DMPC.

At this stage, it must be understood that this approach does *not* lead to an explosion of the number of methods in the library. For each operation considered, only a few distribution combinations can lead to an optimized parallel solver (for example, the matrix multiplication discussed previously). If the object distributions do not fit one of these distribution combinations, one can either use the default inherited algorithm or *redistribute* one or several of the objects so that an efficient solver can be selected (see *Section 14.3.2*).

14.2.4 Performance Issues

Since Eiffel is a modern object-oriented language, its superiority over more traditional languages such as C or Fortran is not debatable as far as software engineering is concerned. However, there always remains the suspicion among scientific programmers that the use of a high-level language necessarily implies low performance: Modularity, late (that is, dynamic) binding, and automatic garbage collection are features reputed to be costly, and thus unacceptable for scientific computation.

But these features are not as costly as they seem. In EPEE, for example, garbage collection facilities are exploited quite efficiently: On each processor of the DMPC, the garbage collection can be disabled during computations and incrementally enabled while the local processor is idle, waiting for a message to be received. Hence, the garbage collector behaves as a coroutine and allows the effective overlapping of memory management processing over communications.

As for the cost of modularity and dynamic binding, implementations of object-oriented languages have progressed considerably in the last few years. State-of-the-art compilers are now able to infer many dynamic types at compile time, allowing the general dynamic dispatching mechanism to be replaced with simple procedure calls, or even code inlining, opening the way for classical optimizations such as loop merging, common subexpression elimination, and so on.

Accordingly, experiments with Paladin demonstrate that with current compilation technologies efficiency is no longer a major issue; see [Guidec 1995] for detailed performance results.

14.3 Writing Applications with Paladin

Writing applications with Paladin has several advantages: it ensures dynamic interoperability and dynamic redistribution, and controls all parallel and distribution issues.

14.3.1 Interoperability

One of the major advantages of the Paladin class organization is that it ensures the dynamic interoperability of all kinds of matrixes and vectors, whatever their current data representation. A feature declared in class Matrix is inherited by all the descendants of this class, and sometimes is redefined to benefit from the available parallelism. Even if the dynamic type of a Matrix object is not known at compile time, the dynamic binding of methods to objects ensures that the relevant versions of parameterless methods (such as the method trace) are called.

The problem is more complex for operators that admit several operands because the relevant method must be selected based on the current data representation of all the objects involved in the computation. Such a mechanism of *multiple dispatching* is provided by some object-oriented languages (such as CLOS [Gabriel 1991] and Cecil [Chambers 1992]), but not by statically typed languages (such as Eiffel, Modula-3, Ada 95, or C++) whose *function overloading* is just a compile-time mechanism that does not take into account the dynamic types of the arguments. Multiple dispatching has been implemented in Paladin by performing explicit tests on the dynamic types of operands. While somewhat tedious to implement, it ensures that all internal representations can be combined transparently and dynamically.

For example, the user may write an expression such as R := A * B where matrix R distribution is left unspecified (R is just declared as of type Matrix), A is distributed by rows, and B is distributed by columns. If both objects referred by A and B would happen to be distributed by blocks at this point of the execution, then the method mult_dblock (introduced in *Section 14.2.3*) would be automatically called.

14.3.2 Dynamic Redistribution

It may sometimes be necessary to adapt the representation of a matrix or a vector to the requirements of the computation. A row-wise distributed matrix, for example, may have to be transformed dynamically in a columnwise distributed matrix, assuming that this new representation is likely to lead to better performance in some parts of an application program.

An algorithm that permits redistribution of a matrix can be obtained using the communication facilities provided by class Pom and the distribution facilities provided by class Distribution_2D. Blocks of matrixes are simply transferred from the source to the destination, the garbage collector taking care of blocks no longer available locally.

The gory details of the redistribute method do not show through the interface of class Dblock_Matrix. From the viewpoint of the application programmer, an instance of Dblock_Matrix can thus be redistributed quite simply. Consider the following small SPMD application program:

```
local
   A, B: DBLOCK_MATRIX [DOUBLE]
do
   -- !!A.make() ask for the creation of a new object A
   -- using the feature make as a constructor
   !!A.make (100, 100, 5, 2, ROW_WISE_MAPPING)
   !!B.make (100, 100, 7, 3, COLUMN_WISE_MAPPING)
     ...(1)...
   B.redistribute (A.dist)
     ...(2)...
end
```

Imagine that in this application the requirements of the computation mandate that matrixes A and B be distributed differently in the first part of the concurrent execution. On the other hand, the second part of the computation requires that A and B have the same distribution. Then the redistribution facility encapsulated in class Dblock_Matrix can be used to achieve the redistribution. Other classes of Paladin (such as Dist_Matrix, Dcol_Matrix, and Drow_Matrix) also encapsulate a version of redistribute whose implementation fits the characteristics of their distribution patterns.

14.3.3 Hiding All Parallel and Distribution Issues

Our approach for developing libraries of distributed objects permits hiding a lot of the tedious management of parallelism and distribution. However, the application programmer still remains responsible for deciding which representation format is the most appropriate for a given object. Hence, when transforming a sequential program into an SPMD one, the programmer must decide which object shall be distributed and how it shall be distributed. This may not always be an easy choice. Finding a "good" distribution may be quite difficult for complex application programs, and paradoxically requires a good understanding of the concurrent behavior of operations.

However, for most linear algebra operations, not so many different data distributions permit an efficient use of the underlying DMPC. The idea is thus to encapsulate this knowledge together with the operator, and to allow the operator to dynamically redistribute the matrix it is working on according to its particular needs in terms of distribution patterns. To achieve this goal, we need the concept of a *polymorphic matrix*, that is, a matrix capable of dynamically changing its internal representation without letting the user notice it. This is obtained by introducing a distinction between the data structure that contains the matrix data and the matrix itself. A polymorphic matrix is just a client of the class Matrix defined previously, and can thus change its representation dynamically.

```
class POLY_MATRIX
feature {NONE} -- Private handle on a matrix container
   container : MATRIX
feature -- Public Accessors
   item (i, j: INTEGER): DOUBLE is
     -- delegates to the container
     do
       Result := container.item (i, j)
     end
   put (v: like item; i, j: INTEGER) is
     -- delegates to the container
     do
       container.put (v, i, j)
     end
   ...
feature -- Operators
   ...
end -- POLY_MATRIX
```

A Poly_Matrix has the same interface as the class Matrix, but privately uses a Matrix for its implementation. Its basic accessors put and item are defined so as to access the data stored in the container, which can be of any subtype of Matrix. Likewise, each operator of Poly_Matrix is defined so as to call the corresponding operator in the container, after a possible change of its internal representation (polymorph self) and of that of its arguments (polymorph others). The following code snippet shows the implementation of the method add, whose argument is polymorphed so as to get the same distribution as that of the current matrix. The addition can then be performed most efficiently.

```
class POLY_MATRIX
   ...
feature -- Internal representation conversion
 redistribute_like (source : POLY_MATRIX) is
  local
     old_data : like container
  do
    if not container.conforms_to(source.container) then
```

```
      old_data := container -- save container
      -- get source type and share its distribution
      -- template
      container := clone(source.container)
      container.convert(old_data) -- transfer the data
    end -- if
  end -- redistribute_like
feature -- operators
  add (m : POLY_MATRIX) is
    -- make sure both matrices have the same
    -- distribution before calling actual add
  do
    m.redistribute_like(Current)
    container.add(m.container)
  end -- add
end -- class POLY_MATRIX
```

The application programmer using Poly_Matrix no longer has to care about distribution patterns; polymorphic matrixes are redistributed transparently as and when needed. Note that the performance overhead of the extra indirection in operator calls remains negligible with respect to the algorithmic complexity of the operations on the large matrixes considered in Paladin. However, redistributing a matrix—or changing its type—can be a costly operation. This could lead to concurrent executions in which most of the activity would consist of redistributing matrixes or vectors.

Hence, the concept of the polymorphic matrix built on top of Paladin does not put an end to all optimization problems. Rather, it provides an interesting framework for investigating global optimizations for distributed programs, concurrently allowing for the optimization of individual operations and for the optimization of their sequencing.

14.4 Related Work

The main approaches to handling massively parallel computations are discussed in the introduction. This section mainly concentrates on works based on object-oriented parallel and distributed approaches.

Most object-oriented languages enable interfacing a class hierarchy with facilities provided by precompiled modules or libraries: The notion of code reuse is not limited to the reuse of classes. The encapsulation mechanism also makes it possible to provide external code with an object-oriented interface. Precompiled external modules and libraries can thus be reused in an object-oriented context, even if they were not originally designed in an object-oriented way (this is actually the way Lapack.h++ [Vermeulen 1993] and ScaLAPACK++ [Dongarra 1993] were initially designed). Paladin has been designed the other way round: Start with an analysis of the domain to get a layered class hierarchy with each level dealing with one kind of problem (from bottom to top: communications, distribution, local memory representation, operators, and polymorphism). But Paladin is not an industrial-strength product, and in that sense it does not compete with comprehensive packages such as ScaLAPACK++ [Dongarra

1992] or similar commercial products. While being an operational Eiffel library running on various DMPCs, Paladin is basically a research demonstrator whose purpose is to investigate how an object-oriented framework can help in mastering the complexity of distributed programming.

A lot of work has recently been carried out in the context of High Performance C++, both in the United States with the HPC++ program itself [Gannon 1997], and also in Japan with MPC++ [Ishikawa 1996] and in Europe with the Europa working group on Parallel C++. These projects encompass work at three levels: runtime system, language extensions, and class libraries. Regarding the latter aspect, the general idea is to *parallelize* the C++ Standard Template Library, building on the well-designed iterators available there. Here, with the Operator design pattern, we go one step further in the uncoupling of the distributed collections and the operations running on them by reifying the abstractions defined in the Bird-Meertens formalism [Skillicorn 1990].

14.5 Summary

This chapter outlines a framework in which the parallel codes can be encapsulated in object-oriented software components that can be reused, combined, and customized with confidence by library designers to offer application programmers easy-to-use programming models. It illustrates our approach with the description of the design of Paladin, an object-oriented linear algebra library designed within the EPEE framework. Paladin can be used at various levels of abstraction, ranging down from the fine-tuning of parallelism up to a total hiding of all distribution issues.

At the lowest level, the ADT library designer has total control over parallelism management. The EPEE reusable software components (dealing with communication, data distribution, and operation parallelization issues) can be used to build higher-level abstractions (such as HPF-like distributed matrixes in Paladin), thus fostering a semi-transparent use of the underlying DMPC (the library user still has to specify the data distribution). For large computations, this chapter shows that the overhead due to the higher level of object-oriented languages remains small. By interfacing the internals of Paladin with the BLAS kernel, it is demonstrated that the object-oriented approach makes it possible to benefit from preexisting highly optimized machine code libraries and gives the best performance without sacrificing the conceptual high level of the user's point of view.

At the highest level—that is, when designing an application program that deals with matrixes—the choice of the best representation layout for a given matrix is a crucial issue. Paladin makes it possible to change the representation format of a matrix at any time during a computation. On this topic, the object-oriented approach has an unquestionable superiority over HPF compilers that can only bind methods to objects statically, thus producing very inefficient code if the dynamic redistribution pattern is not trivial. Redistribution in Paladin can be either controlled by the user or encapsulated with the methods needing special distributions to perform an operation efficiently. In the latter case, the user no longer has to care about parallelism or distribution patterns: All the matrixes are redistributed transparently as and when needed. Although this does not solve all optimization problems, it provides an interesting framework for investigating the interactions between local and global optimizations for distributed programs.

Since Paladin has been completed, other applicative frameworks have been developed in the context of EPEE:

N-body simulations. A framework for simulating N-body problems (such as galactic mechanics). Performance on various parallel computers and discussions on the design of this application can be found in [Jézéquel 1996].

Propagation problems. Many physical problems have no easy analytical solutions, but can still be discretized and then simulated on computers. This is especially true of propagation problems, where one needs to time-track the value of a physical variable (such as temperature) on various points of a three-dimensional space. We identified a number of relevant abstractions that help in the design of flexible solutions to propagation problems and implemented them in an applicative framework [Jézéquel 1996]. Another application of these mechanisms, applied to the field of telephone radio-wave propagations, can be found in [Guidec 1997].

Rain forest simulation. An applicative framework to let biologists simulate the dynamics of rain forests. This is an ongoing project for which the sequential design and implementation of the application is completed; we are still working on an efficient parallel version.

14.6 References

[Abelson 1985] Abelson, H., G.J. Sussman, and J. Sussman. *Structure and Interpretation of Computer Programs*. New York: MIT Press/McGraw-Hill, 1985.

[America 1987] America, P. Pool-T: A parallel object-oriented programming. In *Object-Oriented Concurrent Programming*, A. Yonezawa, editor. Cambridge, MA: MIT Press, 1987: 199–220.

[André 1990] André, F., J.-L. Pazat, and H. Thomas. Pandore: A system to manage data distribution. *ACM International Conference on Supercomputing*, June 11–15, 1990. New York: ACM Press, 1990.

[Booch 1994] Booch, G. *Object-Oriented Analysis and Design with Applications,* 2d ed. Redwood City, CA: Benjamin-Cummings, 1994.

[Callahan 1988] Callahan, D., and K. Kennedy. Compiling programs for distributed-memory multiprocessors. *Journal of Supercomputing*, 2, 1998: 151–169.

[Cardelli 1985] Cardelli, L., and P. Wegner. On understanding types, data abstraction, and polymorphism. *ACM Computing Surveys*, 17(4), 1985: 211–221.

[Chambers 1992] Chambers, C. Object-oriented multi-methods in Cecil. *Proceedings of the 1992 European Conference on Object-Oriented Programming (ECOOP 1992)*. O. Lehrmann Madsen, editor, LNCS 615, Springer-Verlag, Utrecht, Netherlands, June/July1992.

[Dongarra 1992] Dongarra, J., R. van de Geijn, and D. Walker. A look at scalable dense linear algebra libraries. *Scalable High-Performance Computing Conference*. Los Alamitos, CA: IEEE Computer Society Press, April 1992.

[Dongarra 1993] Dongarra, J., R. Pozo, and D.W. Walker. ScaLAPACK++: A design overview of object-oriented extensions for high-performance linear algebra. *Proceedings of SUPERCOMPUTING 1993*, Portland, Oregon, November 1993.

[Fahringer 1992] Fahringer, T., R. Blasko, and H.P. Zima. Automatic performance prediction to support parallelization of Fortran programs for massively parallel systems. *Proceedings of the 6th ACM International Conference on Supercomputing*, pp. 347–356, Washington, DC, July 1992. New York: ACM Press, 1992.

[Gabriel 1991] Gabriel, R., et al. CLOS: Integrating object-oriented and functional programming. *Communications of the ACM*, 34(9), 1991.

[Gamma 1995] Gamma, E., R. Helm, R. Johnson, and J. Vlissides. *Design Patterns: Elements of Reusable Object-Oriented Software*. Reading, MA: Addison-Wesley, 1995.

[Gannon 1997] Gannon, D., and E. Johnson. HPC++: Experiments with the standard template library. *ACM Editors, JSC 1997*. New York: ACM Press, 1997.

[Guidec 1995] Guidec, F. Un cadre conceptuel pour la programmation par objets des architectures parallèles distribuées: application à l'algèbre linéaire. Ph.D. thesis, IFSIC/University of Rennes, June 1995.

[Guidec 1997] Guidec, F., P. Calegari, and P. Kuonen. Parallel irregular software for wave propagation simulation. *HPCN Europe*, Vienna, Austria, April 1997. Lecture Notes in Computer Science series. Springer-Verlag, 1997.

[Hamelin 1994] Hamelin, F., J.-M. Jézéquel, and T. Priol. A Multi-paradigm object oriented parallel environment. *International Parallel Processing Symposium (IPPS 1994) Proceedings*, pp. 182–186, H.J. Siegel, editor. Los Alamitos, CA: IEEE Computer Society Press, April 1994.

[HPF 1993] HPF-Forum. *High Performance Fortran Language Specification*. Technical Report Version 1.0. Rice University, Houston, Texas, May 1993.

[Ishikawa 1996] Ishikawa, Y., et al. The MPC++ approach. *Reflexion 1996*.

[Jézéquel 1993] Jézéquel, J.-M. EPEE: an Eiffel environment to program distributed memory parallel computers. *Journal of Object Oriented Programming*, 6(2), May 1993: 48–54.

[Jézéquel 1996] Jézéquel, J.-M., and J.-L. Pacherie. Parallel Operators. Proceedings of the 1996 European Conference on Object-Oriented Programming (*ECOOP 1996*), pp. 384–405, P. Cointe, editor. Lecture Notes in Computer Science 1098. Springer-Verlag, Linz, Austria, July 1996.

[Kessler 1994] Kessler, C.W. Symbolic array data flow analysis and pattern recognition in dense matrix computations. *Proceedings of the Working Conference on Programming Environments for Massively Parallel Distributed Systems*. IFIP WG 10.3, April 1994.

[Lawson 1989] Lawson, C., R. Hanson, D. Kincaid, and F. Krogh. Basic linear algebra subprograms for Fortran. *ACM Transactions on Math. Software*, 14, 1989: 308–325.

[Li 1986] Li, K. Shared virtual memory on loosely coupled multiprocessors. Ph.D. thesis, Yale University, New September 1986.

[Meyer 1992] Meyer, B. *Eiffel: The Language*. Englewood Cliffs, NJ: Prentice-Hall, 1992.

[Pacherie 1998] Pacherie, J.-L. Operator design pattern for data parallel computation. *Technology of Object-Oriented Languages and Systems, TOOLS 23*, E. Raimund,

S. Madhu, and B. Meyer, editors. Los Alamitos, CA: IEEE Computer Society Press, 1998.

[Pancake 1990] Pancake, C., and D. Bergmark. Do parallel languages respond to the needs of scientific programmers? *IEEE Computer,* December 1990: 13–23.

[Skillicorn 1990] Skillicorn, B.D. Architecture-independent parallel computation. *IEEE Computer,* 23(12), December 1990: 28–33.

[Valiant 1990] Valiant, G.L. A bridging model for parallel computation. *Communications of the ACM*, 33(8), August 1990.

[Vermeulen 1993] Vermeulen, A. Eigenvalues in Rogue Wave Software's Lapack.h++. *Proceedings of the Object-Oriented Numerics Conference (OON-SKI 1993)*, 1993.

[Yonezawa 1986] Yonezawa, A., J.-P. Briot, and E. Shibayama. Object-oriented concurrent programming in ABCL/1. *Proceedings of the OOPSLA 1986 Conference on Object-Oriented Programming Systems, Languages, and Applications,* September 1986. New York: ACM Press, 1986.

SIDEBAR 2
FRAMEWORKS IN THE HEALTHCARE DOMAIN

SB2.1 Business Case

The healthcare market is undergoing a lot of change. The move to managed care is driving a need for cost reduction. Mergers among healthcare facilities have forced previously independent healthcare systems to work together. Physicians and healthcare professionals are asking to have multimedia medical data available at various workstations to assist in medical decision making. All of these changes require better means of exchanging and integrating information from a heterogeneous collection of sources. Existing medical information exchange protocols provide connectivity, but not interoperability. Connectivity guarantees that information from one system can be sent to another system without loss. Interoperability assumes connectivity, and is the ability of components to exchange structured information so that they can work together in a predictable, coordinated fashion to accomplish a common purpose [alSafadi 1998]. Thus, the evolving healthcare frameworks are aiming toward an interoperable software infrastructure that delivers plug&play capability and address the growth needs of healthcare enterprises.

To achieve the desired interoperability, three major frameworks have emerged, each focusing on a specific tier of the software architecture. First, the *message-oriented framework* focuses on the backend tier. Second, the *service-oriented* framework focuses on the middle tier. Third, the *visual integration framework* focuses on the front tier. These frameworks, depicted in Figure SB2.1, are promoted by a variety of industry groups and standards-developing organizations. The following sections briefly expose these frameworks and their orientation.

SB2.2 Message-Oriented Frameworks

These frameworks focus on supporting healthcare systems that work together by exchanging messages. These frameworks support either the development or the exchange of messages. A prominent healthcare messaging scheme is the Health Level 7 standard [HL7-1], which focuses on data exchange among hospital information systems. Version 3.0 [HL7-2] uses object-oriented message development framework. The framework is comprised of four models [Jacobson 1995]: the *use case model,* the *reference information model,* the *interaction model,* and the *message model.* This framework aims to define precise messages by removing optional fields and clarifying ambiguous semantics. Furthermore, the HL7 Special Interest Group on Object Brokering Technology (SIGOBT) [HL7-3] has defined a framework for representing HL7 messages and their fields as CORBA Interface Definition Language (IDL) and Microsoft's ActiveX representation.

The Andover Working Group [AWG] is implementing Version 3.0 of HL7 by providing real-world scenarios presented by its members [HL7-1]. The profiles of the messages generated by AWG using the HL7 framework are registered with the HL7 Conformance Special Interest Group. Systems conformant to these profiles will have reduced integration costs and timeframes. Furthermore, the AWG has implemented the HL7 SIGOBT specification as the Enterprise Communicator (EC). The EC provides three main features: It routes messages among applications, it enforces the adherence to conformance profiles by validating

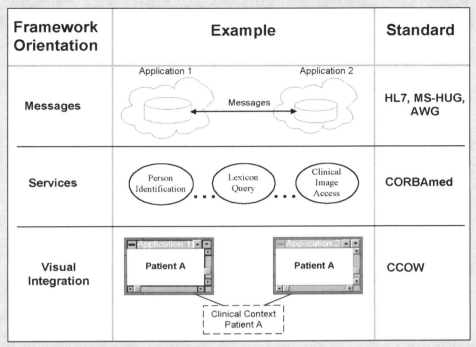

Framework Orientation	Example	Standard
Messages	Application 1 Application 2 / Messages	HL7, MS-HUG, AWG
Services	Person Identification … Lexicon Query … Clinical Image Access	CORBAmed
Visual Integration	Application 1 — Patient A Application 2 — Patient A / Clinical Context Patient A	CCOW

Figure SB2.1   Orientation of healthcare frameworks.

exchanged messages, and it provides a centralized configuration management for interoperating applications. Another contributor to the message-oriented framework is Microsoft's Healthcare User's Group (MS-HUG) [ActiveX], which encourages interaction among its members in the direction and application of Microsoft's ActiveX technology. MS-HUG has been very active in HL7 SIGOBT, providing technical and marketing support for the ActiveX efforts. ActiveX does not define any particular information content. It provides the ability to define objects, then concentrates on support for object sharing and interaction.

SB2.3 Service-Oriented Framework

CORBAmed is the healthcare domain task force of the Object Management Group [OMG]. The CORBAmed framework is based on the Object Management Architecture (OMA) and depends on CORBA services and facilities. This group standardizes interface specifications for distributed healthcare services using IDL. Example services are the Person Identification Service, the Lexicon Query Service, or the Clinical Image Access Service. The challenge for this group is to complement the interface definition (syntax) with the information model supporting the interface (semantics). This requires strong collaboration with other organizations, such as HL7.

Continues

SIDEBAR 2
FRAMEWORKS IN THE HEALTHCARE DOMAIN *(Continued)*

SB2.4 Visual Integration Framework

The Clinical Context Object Work Group [CCOWG] publishes standards for the visual integration of healthcare applications at the point of use (a personal computer or workstation). Visual integration is via information which is presented and/or entered at the client side, and all such applications must run in windows on the same desktop. This information is the clinical context that the users establish and modify as they interact with healthcare applications. Examples of a clinical context include the identity of a patient, a moment in time, or a particular patient encounter that the user wants to review via the applications. The underlying framework specified by CCOWG is technology neutral, permitting implementation environments based on Microsoft COM, CORBA, or Java. The initial deliverables and prototyping are based on COM.

SB2.5 Summary

The message-oriented framework supports the development and exchange of messages on the server or repository side of applications. It may use object request brokering technologies (such as CORBA and ActiveX) for the exchange of messages. The service-oriented framework supports the development of healthcare-specific services that benefit fully from object request brokering architectures and the established distributed computing services and facilities. The visual integration framework focuses on desktop automation. These frameworks continue to evolve as the market changes and the technology matures.

SB2.6 References

[ActiveX] ActiveX for Healthcare. www.mshug.org/activex/index.html.

[alSafadi 1998] alSafadi, Y., and Mankovich, N.J. PACS/Information systems interoperability using an enterprise communication framework. *IEEE Transactions on Information Technology in Biomedicine,* 2(2), July1998: 271–276.

[AWG] Andover Working Group. www.hp.com/mpg/newawgmain.html.

[CCOWG] Clinical Context Object Working Group. www.mcis.duke.edu/standards/CCOW/.

[HL7-1] HL7 ECF V.1.0, *Information Model, A/D/T.* Hewlett-Packard Publication M2125A, 2d ed. Hewlett-Packard, 1997.

[HL7-2] HL7 Quality Assurance/Data Modeling Committee. HL7 V.3.0, *Message Development Framework,* V.3.1. *www.mcis.duke.edu/standards/HL7/committees/,* January 1998.

[HL7-3] HL7 Special Interest Group on Object Brokering Technologies. www.mcis.duke.edu/standards/HL7/committees/SIGOBT/obt.html.

[Jacobson 1995] Jacobson, I., M. Christerson, P. Jonsson, and G. Övergaard. *Object-Oriented Software Engineering: A Use Case-Driven Approach.* Reading, MA: Addison-Wesley, 1995.

[OMG] CORBAmed Domain Task Force of the Object Management Group. www.omg.org/corbamed.

CHAPTER 15

The Bast Framework for Reliable Distributed Computing

Over the past 20 years, distributed systems have become commonplace in many computing domains: process controls for manufacturing plants and power stations, public switched telephone networks, air traffic control systems, and so on. In such systems, various physical components are driven by interconnected computers that cooperatively run so-called distributed applications. More recently, the infatuation with the Internet has brought distributed systems within reach of almost anyone who owns a personal computer (PC). Distribution is definitively emerging as one of the major trends in computing of this decade. Compared to a stand-alone computer, a distributed system bears a major difference: *partial failures*. As pointed out by L. Lamport, a distributed system can stop you from working *"when a machine you've never even heard of crashes"* [Mullender 1989]. When such a situation occurs, it is no longer possible to ignore that some computing resources are remote, and *transparency* is lost.

15.1 Chapter Overview

After an introduction about the importance of reliability (*Section 15.2*) and a brief introduction to the Bast framework (*Section 15.3*), *Section 15.4* provides an overview of distributed programming environments and discusses their limitations. In doing so, it presents

This chapter contains material that has appeared in Benoît Garbinato's Ph.D. thesis [Garbinato 1998a], as well as in papers presented at ECOOP 1996 [Garbinato 1996a], COOTS 1997 [Garbinato 1997b], and ICDCS 1998 [Garbinato 1998b].

the problems addressed by the Bast framework, arguing that existing platforms are *libraries* rather than frameworks. *Section 15.5* gives an overview of Bast from Peter's point of view—it describes what application programmers have to know to start building reliable distributed applications with Bast. *Section 15.6* gives an example of how Peter could use Bast to actively replicate a server object in some distributed application, in order to make it fault tolerant. *Section 15.7* presents Tori's point of view of Bast—what protocol programmers must know of its internals, mainly based on two design patterns, in order to be able to extend Bast. Then, *Sections 15.8* and *15.9* illustrate the various extensibility features of Bast through concrete examples. *Section 15.10* discusses some design and implementation issues, and presents performance measures. Finally, *Section 15.11* summarizes what the Bast framework offers, with some concluding remarks.

15.2 The Need for Reliability

In mission-critical applications, failures might result in the potential loss of lives, as in air traffic control systems; or in financial hardship, as in stock exchange applications. As an aspect of reliability, *fault tolerance* plays a central role because it consists of ensuring that a given service will not fail in a unexpected way. Intuitively, a distributed service is said to be fault tolerant if its clients can continue using it when failures occur, as if nothing happened. One way to achieve fault tolerance is by replicating the underlying servers without the clients knowing—that is, by ensuring replication transparency.

The starting point of the Bast framework lies in the observation that transparency and reliability are often desirable and closely related in distributed systems, but are difficult to achieve. From this perspective, software designers need a continuum of abstractions, so they can build distributed systems that tolerate various failure scenarios. This continuum should allow them to choose the transparency level that is most adequate to express solutions to their problems. Schematically, it should consist of an open collection of layered abstractions, each one hiding details irrelevant to its upper layer. In this context, we believe that the framework approach, based on the notions of callback and inheritance, is particularly well adapted.

15.2.1 Approaches to Reliability

Two approaches are most often adopted by computer scientists when reliability is a concern, each approach acting as background for a particular research and development effort. One such effort deals with the development of reliable distributed systems; we refer to it as the *engineering approach*. The other tries to come up with robust reliability protocols, so it is more of an *algorithmic approach*.

Engineering Approach

This approach considers distributed computing from a pragmatic viewpoint and tries to answer the question of what are the fundamental engineering abstractions for building reliable distributed systems. It was discussed in detail by the Delta-4 research project, together with a rich, specialized glossary [Laprie 1991; Powell 1991]. To be effective, those techniques must rely on well-understood problem/solution pairs, resulting from more theoretical and algorithmic research. This is precisely the approach described here.

Algorithmic Approach

Distributed algorithms are the cornerstone of any reliable distributed service. As far as fault tolerance is concerned, they can be regarded as providing a solid basis for the engineering techniques just mentioned. Here, research efforts try to answer the question of what are the fundamental algorithmic abstractions for solving classical reliability problems. This viewpoint is adopted by the theoretical distributed systems community, which often uses the terms *distributed algorithm* and *protocol* as synonyms.

15.2.2 Differentiating Design Skills

Although the two approaches described in the preceding section are complementary, they are often artificially opposed. On one side, theoretical considerations imply rather formal concepts, while on the other, practical software engineering requires flexible and modular off-the-shelf components. We think the framework approach can help in smoothly integrating the two viewpoints.

To simplify our discussion however, we often characterize programmers by dividing them into groups based on their skills and giving them nicknames; Figure 15.1 illustrates this distinction. Peter is our emblematic *application programmer*, who knows very little about distribution-related problems and their solutions. However, he is skilled in building distributed applications, through the use of specialized programming abstractions provided by some middleware layer. Tori, on the other hand, is our emblematic *system* or *middleware programmer*, who implements such specialized abstractions. She does so by applying distributed algorithms, in which she is skilled. We sometimes call her a *protocol programmer,* as well.

Figure 15.1   Divergent viewpoints of reliability?

Real-life programmers are somewhere in between these two emblematic viewpoints. Furthermore, they are most likely to shift as their skills evolve. As a consequence, an adequate framework should allow them to choose the abstraction level that their designs require and let them be able to change such a choice whenever they want.

Abstractions for Peter

The object model enables programmers to express client-server relationships naturally, which is probably why it is now widely used to build distributed applications. Furthermore, because object-oriented techniques promote modular and flexible design, objects help to manage these viewpoints in an orthogonal and incremental way. As a consequence, this is more and more frequently the distributed programming paradigm chosen by Peter in his engineering approach. The CORBA [OMG 1997] and Java [Gosling 1995] trends testify to this point. Distributed objects allow Peter to implement distributed application components in a clean and natural way.

As far as reliability issues are concerned, two models have emerged over the years: the *transaction model*, which originated from the database community in the 1970s, and the *group communication model*, which originated from the distributed systems community in the 1980s. They have been combined with object concepts in several existing environments. Both models enable the expression of some kind of failure atomicity on a set of actions—that is, guaranteeing that all actions or none will be performed with respect to failures. The difference is that transactions are primarily used for accessing several heterogeneous servers, whereas group communication generally serves the purpose of managing homogeneous copies of a replicated server.

Abstractions for Tori

Although the problems addressed by transactions and groups partially overlap, most dedicated programming environments make it very difficult to blend transactions and group communication. Furthermore, such environments provide very scarce facilities for customization and extension, which is far from being satisfactory for Tori. For example, she cannot plug in new state-of-the-art distributed algorithms. Those restrictions can be partly explained by the fact that groups and transactions are abstractions too coarse-grained to offer enough flexibility. Another reason has to do with the limited impact of object concepts on fault-tolerance techniques. Many of the existing environments are implemented as monolithic toolkits, which makes it difficult for Tori to extend them.

However, the Bast framework, as well as other recent developments [Hüni 1995; Van Renesse 1995], testifies that this is changing. In particular, object-orientation is a promising approach for factorizing fundamental abstractions on top of which transactions and groups can be built. Nevertheless, objects alone are too general, and more specialized abstractions are needed. Interestingly, both the transaction and the group models imply some underlying protocols, either explicitly or implicitly. As the following section shows, this observation is at the heart of the Bast framework.

15.3 The Bast Framework

In ancient Egypt, *Bast*, also known as *Bastet*, was a cat goddess worshipped in the delta city of Bubastis. Because cats are said to benefit from several lives, they are in some sense tolerant of a fair number of crashes. So, we thought the protectress of cats would be an appropriate namesake for our reliable distributed framework.

15.3.1 Design Origins

The Bast framework originated from the firm conviction that current fault-tolerance tools and techniques do not take advantage of research in object-oriented design in a satisfactory manner. As a consequence, customizations and extensions are made possible only for application programmers, not for middleware programmers. Yet design problems and solutions are often very similar for both kinds of programmers. Furthermore, reusing well-tested code is a key issue when it comes to building reliable distributed software.

More specifically, distributed protocols should be fundamental programming abstractions and should be manipulated as first-class components. Consequently, adequate means to express relationships between them are also crucial. It is incidentally surprising that protocols remain so well hidden in existing distributed environments, considering that distributed systems have to deal with increasingly complex interactions between remote entities. This is probably because such environments are primarily aimed at application programmers with, a priori, limited skills in distributed algorithms. Their goal is to preserve programmers from this complexity, so they can concentrate on applications. Furthermore, exposing protocols in a coherent and reusable way implies additional design and maintenance efforts. Not doing so, however, drastically restricts the adaptability of existing fault-tolerance platforms, and, in some sense, their applicability as well.

15.3.2 Decomposing and Recomposing Reliability

One fundamental feature of Bast is that it offers transparency as a choice, not as a constraint. To promote adequate flexibility, it allows each programmer to choose the abstraction level that is best suited. Being based on callback operations that can be redefined through inheritance, Bast is an object-oriented framework aimed at reliable distributed software and middleware. In comparison to similar environments, Bast goes one step further toward modular and flexible protocol composition. It provides an open and extensible architecture, based on various design levels. Standard fault-tolerance techniques are *decomposed* and then *recomposed* in terms of protocols and distributed algorithms. This decomposition process is based on solid foundations, resulting from recent advances by the theoretical distributed systems community. It leads to a hierarchy of specialized programming abstractions, which we believe to be generic and adequate to solve reliability problems. We support these claims by showing how this conceptual framework helps both application and protocol programmers.

With Bast, reliable distributed applications can be built by programmers who are not familiar with fault-tolerance techniques, whereas skilled protocol programmers can customize and create distributed protocols from existing ones. Protocol composition is a key concept in Bast, because it enables the reuse of robust implementations of basic protocols. We illustrate this point by presenting how both group communications and transactions can be built on top of foundational protocols that are manipulated via *objects* and *patterns*. This makes it possible for Bast to support a wide range of fault-tolerant distributed applications.

15.4 Reliable Distributed Programming

Reliable distributed software is challenging to build, because one potentially has to deal with many complex issues—safety and liveness, reliability of communication, detection of incorrect behaviors, replication of critical components, ordering of messages, group membership, management of atomic transactions, and so on. Each of these issues actually corresponds to a distributed problem that must be solved, and both Peter and Tori face a real jungle of such problems, as shown in Figure 15.2.

All those problems are related to each other, but they are managed at different abstraction levels. For example, applying a given replication policy (active, passive, and so on) to some distributed application component is usually a problem for Peter. On the contrary, the safety and liveness of distributed algorithms are concerns for Tori. She might then address the problem of ensuring such properties via failure detection and reliable communication. So, depending on the programming environment and on Tori's programming skills, she might use off-the-shelf software components, through callback redefinition, or build them from scratch, through protocol composition.

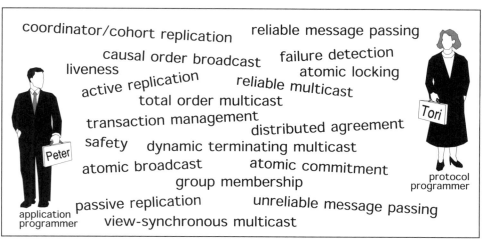

Figure 15.2   Facing a distributed problems jungle.

15.4.1 Problem/Solution Pairs

Over the last 10 years, theoretical research has laid the basis of *asynchronous distributed systems* augmented with *unreliable failure detectors* [Chandra 1992, 1996; Guerraoui 1997b], by identifying several distributed problems, pictured in Figure 15.2. Interestingly, the name of each of these problems can also designate an abstraction that solves the problem. The term *group membership,* for instance, not only refers to the problem of maintaining a consistent view of the group among its members; it also names distributed programming abstractions that help to solve the group membership problem. Such abstractions can then be used to support various replication policies, which are yet other abstractions that enable Peter to ensure the reliability of distributed applications. In other words, depending on the abstraction level, each item in Figure 15.2 can be understood either as a problem to solve or as an abstraction used to solve other problems. For this reason, such items are sometimes called *problem/solution pairs.*

In a reliability context, the intrinsic robustness of programming abstractions is a key feature. There are two issues to consider here: the nature of conceptual abstractions specific to this context, and the reuse of well-tested solutions through an adequate structuring approach. This second point is particularly important, considering that relationships between problem/solution pairs can be quite complex. Managing this complexity to reuse existing solutions is not easily done, because many different dimensions have to be considered. Is the underlying system synchronous or asynchronous? What types of failures do we consider? Do crashed network nodes recover? So, flexibility is yet another important issue, if we want programming abstractions that easily adapt to various system models or to new requirements.

15.4.2 Distributed Programming Environments

Several distributed programming environments provide specialized abstractions to achieve reliability, while others address the problem of representing distributed protocols. We say that the former are *reliability based* and that the latter are *protocol based*. Both kinds of platforms relate to Bast, although they do so in different manners. Reliability-based platforms can be further characterized as *transaction based* or *group based.*

Transaction-Based Platforms

The *transaction paradigm* [Lynch 1994] has proven to be very useful for distributed databaselike applications. However, the atomicity, consistency, isolation, and durability (ACID) properties of the original transaction model are too strong for several applications. For example, the *isolation* property is too strong for cooperative work applications, whereas the *atomicity* property is too strong for applications dealing with replicated data. This is partly due to the fact that underlying agreement protocols are designed and implemented in an ad hoc manner and cannot be modified. The rigidity of the original transaction model has lead many authors to explore the design of more flexible transactional models, such as nested transactions, but the underlying agreement protocol still cannot be modified.

In designing Bast, we adopted an alternative approach—providing the basic abstractions required in implementing various transaction models, rather than supporting one specific model. These abstractions implement support for reliable total order communications (enabling the building of distributed locking), atomic commitment, and so on.

Group-Based Platforms

Groupware toolkits such as Isis [Birman 1993] and GARF [Garbinato 1995] offer reliable communication primitives with various consistency levels, such as causal order multicast and total order multicast. These environments are based on the *group paradigm* as a fundamental abstraction for reliable distributed programming. The group concept is very helpful for handling replication: A replicated entity (a process in Isis or an object in GARF) is implemented as a group of replicas. It constitutes a convenient way of addressing replicated logical entities without having to explicitly designate each replica. When a failure occurs, members of a group are notified through a *group membership* protocol and consequently can act—for example, to elect a new primary in a primary backup replication scheme. However, the strong coupling between the group concept and consistency leads to the inability to support a reliable multicast that involves different replicated entities, that is, several groups. This limitation makes group-oriented environments unable to seamlessly integrate transaction models. Here again, underlying agreement protocols are hidden and, not being accessible, they cannot be customized.

A major characteristic of the Bast framework is that it enables the decoupling of the group notion from consistency issues: Groups are viewed merely as *logical addressing capabilities*, while reliable multicast communications are supported by adequate protocol classes based on a distributed agreement pattern. As a consequence, Bast naturally supports reliable multicasts involving different groups of replicas.

Protocol-Based Platforms

Pioneers in the domain modular operating systems, such as x-Kernel [Hutchinson 1988] and Choices [Campbell 1993], have shown that flexibility can be significantly increased by decomposing network support into elemental components supporting well-defined interfaces. Not surprisingly, several object-based operating systems have evolved toward platforms providing protocol-based abstractions. The limitations of such platforms have mainly to do with a lack of generic abstractions for dealing with fault-tolerance issues. Network protocols often constitute the implicit application domain of protocol-based platforms, and few explicitly address fault-tolerance issues.

For example, Avoca [O'Malley 1990] and Morpheus [Abbott 1993] are used to support a dynamic network architecture for RPC communication, built on top of TCP/IP and Ethernet. Similarly, in Conduits+ [Hüni 1995], information chunks and conduits make up a framework for network software and are used to implement TCP/IP protocols as well as a signaling system for ATM. As for platforms addressing fault tolerance, their abstractions are usually deeply influenced by some underlying model and thus are not generic. The Horus system [Van Renesse 1995], for instance, is exclusively based on group membership and virtual synchronous communication. As a consequence, Horus cannot do better than Isis when it comes to integrating groups and transactions. Likewise, the Consul communication substrate [Mishra 1993], a fault-tolerant extension of Avoca, bases its reliability support exclusively on group communication.

15.5 Bast Overview

The Bast framework is designed to help programmers build reliable distributed systems, and is based on protocols as basic structuring components. It aims to provide an extensible set of powerful abstractions that support the design and implementation of reliable distributed systems. Figure 15.3 presents an overview of Bast's architecture, based on a fully object-oriented design and implementation. In Bast, various abstraction levels are provided, depending on whether Peter or Tori is the user. At the highest level, all the complexity is hidden from Peter in ready-to-use components. Such components can be seen as an evolution of the GARF environment, which aimed to support reliable distributed programming in a fairly automated way [Garbinato 1995]. In GARF, however, reliability issues were dealt with by Isis, used as a blackbox toolkit, so reliable distributed protocols were not accessible. With the Bast framework, on the contrary, protocols are made directly available to Tori, who can customize and/or create protocols from existing ones. This section presents only what Peter needs to know to be able to use Bast. Extensibility features are left out here and are presented in *Section 15.7*, which considers Tori's point of view.

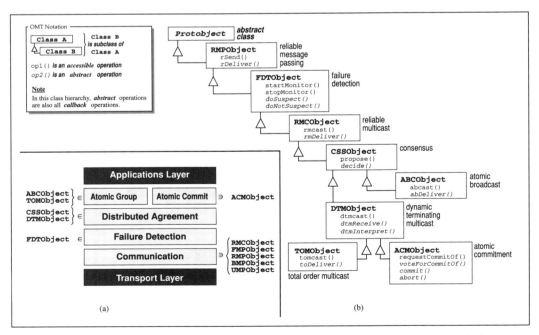

Figure 15.3 Overview of the Bast framework: (*a*) layered service architecture, and (*b*) some protocol classes.

15.5.1 System Model

In the Bast framework, we consider a distributed system to be composed of objects that have the means to remotely designate each other and to participate in various protocols. Distinct distributed objects reside, a priori, on different nodes, and faulty nodes are supposed to fail independently by crashing. We make no assumptions on the synchrony of the system, but instead use the notion of failure detectors (failure detectors enable hiding the synchrony of distributed systems and are abstractly defined through reliability properties [Chandra 1996]). We define *distributed protocol* π as a set of coordinated interactions between distributed objects, which aims to solve *problem* π. This implies a very broad view of what distributed protocols are, since it all depends on the specification of problem π. According to this definition, even a trivial unreliable communication between two remote objects is a distributed protocol. We believe, however, that the generality of this definition helps to make things simpler.

15.5.2 Ready-to-Use Components

Building fault-tolerant applications is normally a hard task, which requires highly skilled protocol programmers, because reliable distributed protocols can be very complex to understand and to implement. To make this task accessible to Peter, we need ready-to-use components that support adequate distributed protocols. For example, the atomic commitment protocol is essential to any application involving transactions, while the atomic broadcast protocol is the cornerstone of applications based on active replication. In this context, we believe that *protocol classes* are powerful tools that allow Peter to put complex protocols to work, but remain easy to understand and to use.

The *protocol class* concept can be defined as follows: A protocol class πObject implements the behavior of distributed objects that are capable of executing protocol π—that is, of solving distributed problem π. Instances of protocol classes are designated as *protocol objects*. We use πObject to refer to any protocol class, and a πObject to designate some distributed object of class πObject.

Figure 15.3b presents some ready-to-use protocol classes provided in Bast. This class diagram uses the standard Object Modeling Technique (OTM) notation [Rumbaugh 1991]; abstract operations are all callback operations. The root of this class hierarchy is the abstract superclass Protobject. Each πObject class provides a set of operations that interface protocol π: These operations act as entry points for applications using protocol π. For example, class RMPObject, which implements reliable point-to-point communications, provides operation rSend( ) and callback rDeliver( ), which enable reliably sending and receiving messages, respectively.

15.5.3 The Protocol Class Hierarchy

Bast's protocol class library is structured into layered services, each composed of one or more classes that implement related protocols; this is shown in Figure 15.3a. Peter is responsible for the application (top layer). At the bottom, the communication service relies on the transport layer; it is responsible for low-level communications between different network nodes and relies on operating system services (not shown in Figure

15.3a). Anything in between the application and the transport layers is part of Bast. Our model is not strictly *vertically* layered (although Figure 15.3a might suggest it), so Peter can use any existing Bast's service. An overview of the classes pictured in Figure 15.3 follows. *Section 15.10* discusses the implementation of these classes.

Basic Classes

Peter first has to learn about two classes: Protobject, which is the root of the protocol class hierarchy, and ProtobjectRef, which enables designating remote protocol objects. Those two classes provide no support for remote communications or any other protocol: Protobject is an abstract class, while ProtobjectRef serves only as an addressing facility.

Communication Service

This communication service provides the following protocol classes: UMPObject, BMPObject, RMPObject, FMPObject, and RMCObject. The first four implement *point-to-point* communication and differ in their delivery guarantees. They provide unreliable, best-effort, reliable and first-in, first-out (FIFO) point-to-point communication, respectively, through operations xSend() and xDeliver(), where $x \in$ {u, b, r, f}. Class RMCObject supports reliable *multicast* communication through operations rmcast() and rmDeliver().

Failure Detection Service

Protocol objects of class FDTObject are capable of monitoring one another through operations startMonitor() and stopMonitor(). Each instance manages a private set containing remote references of objects it suspects to be faulty, and is notified whenever this set has to be updated, through operations doSuspect() and doNotSuspect().

Distributed Agreement Service

The need to have distributed objects agree on some common value is central to many problems in fault-tolerant distributed computing. So, robust consensus-related protocols are the cornerstone of most fault-tolerant systems. In Bast, protocol classes CSSObject and DTMObject both provide operations that are capable of solving the distributed agreement problem even when some faulty nodes are involved. With class CSSObject, several nonconcerted objects can join the same consensus execution, by proposing any object as initial value through operation propose(). For this reason, we say that consensus is a *symmetrical* protocol. When agreement is reached, the decision value is delivered to each participant by the protocol through operation decide().

As for class DTMObject, it is at the heart of Bast's distributed agreement pattern, the *Dynamic Terminating Multicast* (DTM) [Guerraoui 1995b]. With this class, an initiator first multicasts an object to all participants through operation dtmcast(); each participant computes and returns a reply through operation dtmReceive(). Distributed agreement is then reached on a *collection* containing a subset of those replies. Finally, this collection is interpreted by each nonfaulty participant through operation dtmInterpret( ). *Section 15.8* presents in detail how a general atomic commitment and a total order multicast can be built by subclassing DTMObject and redefining its callback operations. Note that Peter is normally not supposed to use DTM directly, although nothing prevents him from doing so.

Atomic Group Service

When Peter wants to ensure fault-tolerant total ordering of messages on a group of protocol objects (groups are only logical addressing capabilities here—that is, no group membership is assumed necessary) he has the choice between two protocol classes, ABCObject and TOMObject, through operations $x$cast( ) and xDeliver( ), where $x \in$ {abc, tom}, respectively. The difference can be expressed as follows: As a member of two distinct groups, a TOMObject ensures total ordering of messages sent to either groups, whereas an ABCObject ensures total ordering only of messages that are sent within each group. For example, if messages m1 and m2 are multicast in two distinct yet overlapping groups, they might be seen in a different order by two objects of class ABCObject, but this is not possible for two objects of class TOMObject. Class ABCObject is adequate for ensuring consistency of a replicated object, whereas TOMObject makes it easy to perform distributed locking on replicated servers, even when some are faulty. As *Section 15.6.2* shows, class ABCObject is adequate for ensuring consistency of a replicated object.

Atomic Commit Service

Instances of class ACMObject are capable of solving various atomic commitment problems, depending on the desired semantics. For that purpose, an additional class hierarchy is provided, whose root is class AbstractTransaction. Currently, Bast offers two kinds of ready-to-use transaction classes, NonBlockingTransaction and ReplicatedTransaction. The atomic commitment protocol starts with someone asking all participants to commit some transaction through operation requestCommitOf( ). As a result, everyone computes and returns their votes to the protocol through operation voteOnCommitOf( ). Finally, the same decision to commit or to abort is delivered to each participant through operations commit( ) or abort( ).

15.6 Using Bast

In Bast, distributed protocols are said to be *generic*. In this context, genericity implies that the type of arguments passed to any protocol operation is not restricted; for example, operation rSend( ) can be used to send any object across the network. (More precisely, we should say any object that is *not* a protocol object; sending protocol objects across the network requires updating all their distributed references before subsequent uses. Migrating protocol objects is yet another distributed problem, but this chapter does not deal with this issue.) Genericity also means that callback operations, such as rDeliver( ), are supposed to be redefined by each application in order to meet its needs; callbacks are said to be *triggered by the protocol*.

Protocol classes are organized into a single inheritance hierarchy: Each protocol class implements only one protocol, but instances of some πObject class can execute any protocol inherited from πObject's superclasses (see Figure 15.3b). So, protocol objects are capable of running several executions of identical and/or distinct protocols concurrently.

15.6.1 Achieving Active Replication

To illustrate how protocol classes can help Peter build fault-tolerant distributed software, consider an application in which objects are running on a network of four workstations, and suppose he wants some critical distributed object S to be available even when some workstations crash. One way to achieve this consists of *actively replicating* object S on all four workstations; in this case, we say that S is a *replicated object*, and it is manipulated as a group of replica objects $g_s = \{S_1, S_2, S_3, S_4\}$. Whenever a workstation crashes, users working on the remaining three can go on with their work, because their local replica S_i is still available. Now the *liveness* of S is ensured, but Peter still has to make sure that all four replicas keep a consistent state throughout their execution; that is, he is now concerned with the *safety* of S. To ensure consistency, he can use total order multicast communications on group g_s: By making sure all update messages are received by the four replicas in the same order, he knows their states will remain identical. What Peter really needs here is a protocol class that solves the *atomic broadcast* problem; informally, the atomic broadcast requires that all correct replicas deliver the same update messages in the same order [Chandra 1996]. (The term *broadcast*, rather than *multicast*, is used here because the target group g_s is implicit for all update messages. *Multicast* suggests that each message could be sent to a different set of distributed objects, which is not the case in this example.)

15.6.2 Using Class ABCObject

The Bast framework provides a protocol class that solves the atomic broadcast— ABCObject, which defines operations abcast( ) and callback abDeliver( ). By subclassing ABCObject and by making replicas of S instances of that new class, Peter can actively replicate S very easily: The callback operation abDeliver( ) of such a subclass is implemented in order to update the local replica S_i in a deterministic way. More precisely, Peter has to implement each public operation of his subclass in such a way that it only calls abcast( ). He then has to implement the "real" code as private methods that are called by abDeliver( ).

Figure 15.4 depicts what happens after some user action on workstation 1 generates an update for replicated object S. Instead of directly applying the update to local replica S_1, the application builds an update message m and invokes operation abcast( ) on S_1, passing it m. The responsibility for propagating the update is now delegated to S_1. Operation abcast( ) starts an execution of the atomic broadcast protocol involving replicas S_1, S_2, S_3, and S_4. Eventually, the protocol triggers operation abDeliver( ) on each replica, including S_1. This operation has been implemented by Peter in ABCObject's subclass and performs the actual update, using message m. Because class ABCObject solves the atomic broadcast problem, Peter has the guarantee that any con-

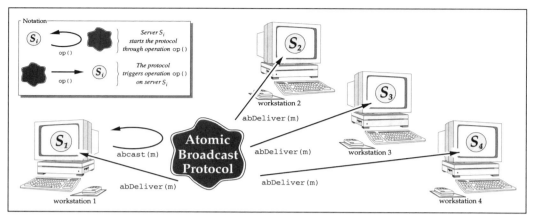

Figure 15.4   Active replication with class ABCObject.

current message will be identically ordered with respect to *m* on all replicas. Note that operations abcast( ) and abDeliver( ) can also be used to atomically transfer the most recent state to a replica that is recovering after a crash [Guerraoui 1997a].

15.7 In-Depth View of Bast

Sections 15.8 and 15.9 present another of Bast's key features—its extensibility. This feature concerns Tori, who has adequate skills in building fault-tolerant distributed protocols. However, before those sections present how new protocol classes are actually added to Bast, this section first discusses some aspects about the way we model protocol relationships. In particular, this section introduces the Strategy design pattern and shows how it is used recursively.

15.7.1 Protocol Dependencies

Fault-tolerant distributed protocols are challenging to build, because they involve many other underlying protocols. This can result in complex dependency relationships, as illustrated by Figure 15.5a. The DTM pattern implemented in Bast, for instance, is built on top of consensus, failure detections, and reliable communications. Consensus is itself based on failure detections and on reliable communications, both point-to-point and multicast; in turn, Bast's reliable multicast relies on reliable point-to-point communications. Figure 15.5b shows the corresponding protocol classes and their inheritance relationships, following the OMT notation.

In Bast, managing protocol dependencies is possible not only during the design and implementation phases (between protocol classes), but also at runtime (between protocol objects). This is partly due to the fact that protocol objects can execute more than one protocol at the same time. In this context, trying to compose protocols comes down to answering the questions of how protocol layers are assembled and how they cooperate.

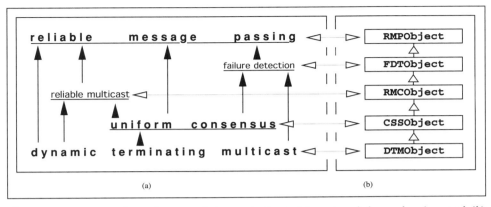

Figure 15.5 Protocols and protocol classes in Bast: (*a*) protocol dependencies, and (*b*) protocol class hierarchy.

Figure 15.6a presents an instance of class ABCObject during its execution. As previously seen, class ABCObject defines two entry operations to the atomic broadcast protocol, abcast() and abDeliver(). Besides those operations, the protocol object anABCObject is also capable of concurrently executing any protocol inherited by its class, such as consensus and reliable multicast communication (see Figure 15.3b). This is what makes the atomic broadcast easy to build.

15.7.2 Protocol Layer Interactions

Figure 15.6a shows anABCObject simultaneously running five different protocols on behalf of the application layer, while performing low-level calls to the transport layer for this job. Figure 15.6b focuses on the protocol stack dedicated to some atomic broadcast execution. Besides the atomic broadcast algorithm, this stack is made up of four other algorithms: consensus, reliable multicast, failure detection, and reliable message passing. As we shall see, each of these algorithms is an object (in the old days, they would have been separate modules manipulated by higher levels), so one can customize class ABCObject by changing them.

In Bast, protocol dependencies are modeled in a way similar to that of the *Open Systems Interconnection* (OSI) stack model [Rose 1990]. In our first attempt to structure protocol interactions, we adopted a strictly vertically layered approach. However, we were forced to face the fact that it does not always make sense in terms of protocol dependencies, as suggested by Figure 15.6b. In the end, only the *encapsulation* benefit of the layered approach was retained, while its strictly vertical nature was discarded. Our conclusion here concurs with the work done by [Hüni 1995] on a framework for network protocols. Coming back to anABCObject, each time the application layer invokes one of its operations, a new protocol stack is created. So, each protocol execution is supported by an independent protocol stack, as suggested in Figure 15.6a. Furthermore, each layer of that stack is in charge of only one protocol supported by class ABCObject. Focusing on the protocol object anABCObject, *protocol composition* here means to assemble various layers, each one running a protocol algorithm necessary to

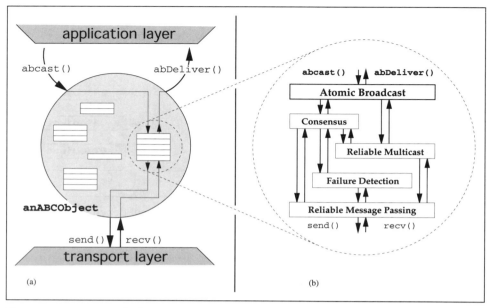

Figure 15.6 Protocol objects and the layered model: (*a*) an instance of ABCObject in execution, and (*b*) interacting protocol layers.

the execution of the atomic broadcast protocol. This is where protocol composition actually occurs, as the following section shows.

15.7.3 Algorithms as Objects

In order to separate protocol layers from their implementations, distributed algorithms are manipulated as separate objects. Consequently, each πObject protocol class is independent of the algorithm supporting protocol π, which makes protocol composition fully flexible. Distributed algorithm objects of class πAlgo are privately used by the corresponding πObject protocol objects and hold the actual implementation of distributed algorithm π. An algorithm object always executes *within* a protocol object: As a result, Peter deals only with protocol objects and knows nothing about algorithm objects, but Tori does.

Applying the Strategy Design Pattern

According to [Gamma 1995], the intent of the Strategy pattern is to "define a family of algorithms, encapsulate each one, and make them interchangeable." Making each πObject protocol class independent of the algorithm supporting protocol π is precisely what we provide for composing reliable distributed protocols in a flexible manner. In other words, the Strategy pattern is a key element in Bast, as far as flexible protocol composition is concerned. This design pattern is usually implemented by objectifying the algorithm [Gamma 1993], that is, by encapsulating it into a so-called *strategy* object; the latter is then used by a so-called *context* object.

In the Bast framework, strategy objects represent protocol algorithms, and they are instances of subclasses of class ProtoAlgo. A ProtoAlgo subclass that implements an algorithm for solving problem π is referred to as class πAlgo. In the Strategy pattern terminology, a protocol algorithm, an instance of some πAlgo class, is the *strategy*; a protocol object, an instance of some πObject class, is the *context*. A strategy and its context are strongly coupled, and the application layer only manipulates instances of πObject classes.

Figure 15.7a sketches the way protocol objects and algorithm objects interact. On the left side, protocol object aπObject offers the services it inherits from its superclasses, as well as the new services that are specific to protocol π. The actual algorithm implementing protocol π is not part of aπObject's code; instead, aπObject uses services provided by strategy aπAlgo seen on the right side of Figure 15.7a. Whenever an operation related to protocol π is invoked on aπObject, the execution of the protocol is delegated to strategy aπAlgo. In turn, the services required by the strategy to run protocol π are based on the inherited services of context aπObject. Such required services identify entry-point operations to underlying protocols needed to solve problem π. Figure 15.7b presents the relationship between classes πObject and πAlgo, using a class diagram based on the OMT notation.

Strategy–Context Interactions

The way in which aπObject and aπAlgo cooperate can also be seen as some kind of *symbiosis*: Two dissimilar objects participate in a mutually beneficial relationship. Instances of class πAlgo each represent a distinct execution of protocol π's algorithm. So, another way to look at algorithm objects can be expressed as follows: At runtime, each algorithm object represents a layer in one of the protocol stacks currently in execution within aπObject (see Figure 15.7c).

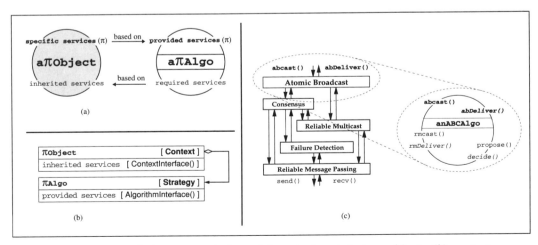

Figure 15.7 Strategy design pattern in Bast: (*a*) context and strategy objects, (*b*) context and strategy classes, and (*c*) strategy as protocol layer.

15.7.4 An Example: Reliable Multicast

In Bast, class RMCObject provides primitives rmcast( ) and rmDeliver( ), which enable the sending and receiving of a message m to a set of protocol objects referenced in $Dst(m)$, in a way that enforces reliable multicast properties [Chandra 1996]. The distributed algorithm on which protocol class RMCObject relies is supported by class RMCAlgo. The latter implements a Chandra-Toueg algorithm also presented in [Chandra 1996]. Figure 15.8 illustrates what happens respectively on the *initiator side* of the multicast and on some *target side*. The local interactions between instances of RMCObject and RMCAlgo are described for each side:

> **The protocol starts with operation rmcast() being invoked on some initiator object aRMCObject$_i$, passing it a message m and a destination set $Dst(m)$.** In this operation, the context aRMCObject$_i$ first creates a strategy aRMCAlgo$_i$ and then invokes operation rmcast( ) on it with the arguments it has just received. The strategy aRMCAlgo$_i$ builds message $\tilde{m}$, containing both m and $Dst(m)$. It then issues a reliable point-to-point communication with each protocol object referenced in $Dst(m)$. In order to do this, the strategy aRMCAlgo$_i$ relies on inherited service rSend( ) of the context aRMCObject$_i$.

> **When message $\tilde{m}$ reaches aRMCObject$_t$, one of the targets, callback rDeliver(), is triggered by the protocol.** Operation rDeliver( )—note that this is not operation *rm*Deliver( ) that is being called—detects that $\tilde{m}$ is a multicast message and for-

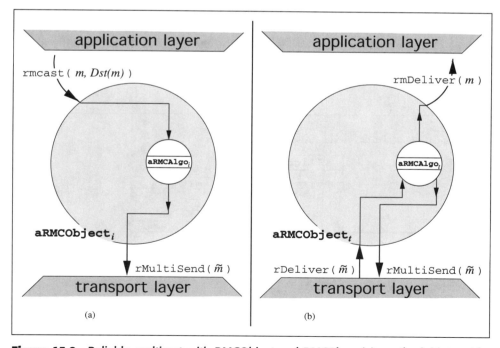

Figure 15.8   Reliable multicast with RMCObject and RMCAlgo: (*a*) on the initiator side, and (*b*) on some target side, first time.

wards it to aRMCAlgo$_t$, the strategy in charge of that particular execution of the reliable multicast protocol. If aRMCAlgo$_t$ does not already exist, aRMCObject$_t$ first creates it. When aRMCAlgo$_t$ receives $\bar{m}$ for the first time, it reissues a reliable point-to-point communication with each protocol object referenced in $Dst(m)$ (extracted from $\bar{m}$), and then invokes rmDeliver( ) on its context aRMCObject$_t$, passing it message m (also extracted from $\bar{m}$). This retransmission scheme ensures the Agreement property of the reliable multicast primitive, which requires that either all correct objects in $Dst(m)$ or none receive message m.

15.7.5 Natural Concurrency Management

Protocol algorithm classes define a completely separate inheritance hierarchy from that of the protocol objects (with ProtoAlgo as root). Each instance of some πAlgo class represents one execution of protocol π implemented by that class, and holds a reference to the context object for which it is running. Any call to the services required by the strategy will be issued to its context object. There might be more than one instance of the same ProtoAlgo's subclass used simultaneously by aπObject. At runtime, the latter maintains a table of all strategies that are currently in execution for it. Each message is tagged to enable aπObject to identify in which execution of what protocol that message is involved, and to dispatch it to the right strategy. As a consequence, concurrent protocol executions are managed in a straightforward manner.

15.7.6 Recursive Use of Strategies

As previously pointed out, Tori can focus strictly on protocol π and on its associated πObject and πAlgo classes. In particular, all protocols needed to support protocol π are hidden in inherited operations. The latter might also be implemented by applying the Strategy pattern, but this is transparently managed by superclasses of πObject. In this sense, Bast uses the Strategy pattern in a powerful *recursive* manner.

The recursive use of the Strategy pattern is illustrated in Figure 15.9. Figure 15.9 schematically presents a possible implementation of protocol class CSSObject, which enables the solution of the consensus problem by providing operations propose( ) and decide( ). In Figure 15.9, the gray oval is context class CSSObject, while the inner white circles are various πAlgo strategy classes. Arrows show the connections between provided services (top) and required services (bottom) of each strategy class. Operations provided by class CSSObject are grouped on the application-layer side (top). Each strategy class pictured in Figure 15.9 is managed by the corresponding context class in the protocol class hierarchy presented in Figure 15.3b.

15.7.7 Drawbacks and Limitations

One drawback of the Strategy pattern is the overhead due to local interactions between strategies and contexts. In distributed systems, however, this overhead is small compared to communication delays, especially when failures and/or complex protocols are involved (including marshaling). More specifically, the time for a local Smalltalk

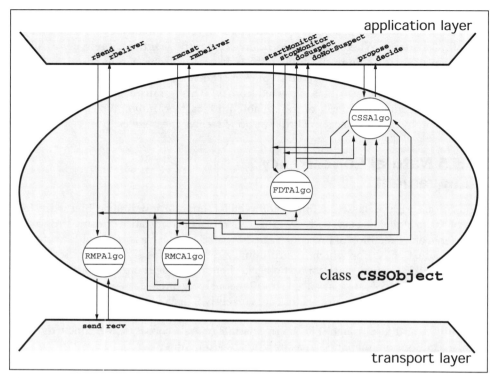

Figure 15.9 Recursive use of the Strategy pattern.

invocation is normally under 100 µs, whereas a reliable multicast communication usually takes more than 100 ms when 3 or more protocol objects are involved (on a 10-Mbit Ethernet connecting Sun SPARCstation 20 workstations)—without even considering failures or marshaling time. The gain in flexibility clearly overtakes the local overhead caused by the use of the Strategy pattern (see *Section 15.10*).

There is also a minor compatibility constraint among different protocol algorithms in order to make them interchangeable: Some new algorithm class $\pi Algo_n$ can replace defaultπAlgo *if and only if* $\pi Algo_n$ requires a subset of the services featured by the hosting protocol class. A detailed discussion on the use of the Strategy design pattern in Bast can be found in [Garbinato 1997b].

15.8 Protocol Composition and Tuning

Protocol programmers such as Tori have basically three ways of extending Bast: by *composing* protocol classes to build a brand-new one, by *tuning* some protocol class through changes made to its distributed algorithms, and by *customizing* a protocol class that implements a *distributed pattern*.

Protocol composition has to be used when the new protocol cannot be built by tuning existing distributed algorithms or by applying some distributed pattern, but it can be seen rather as an assembling of protocols already available in Bast. Then, protocol tuning is best suited when Tori wants to adapt some existing algorithm to a particular context—for example, to achieve better performance. In that case, she extends Bast not with a new protocol class, but rather with a new distributed algorithm class. As for distributed pattern customization, refer to *Section 15.9*.

15.8.1 Flexible Protocol Composition

The Strategy and Context separation offers full flexibility in protocol composition and makes it possible to change any protocol algorithm of any protocol class very easily. Protocol dependencies are expressed only at the specification level, through subclass relationships, whereas the implementations can vary. One could, for example, optimize the reliable multicast algorithm on which class ABCObject relies, while leaving it unchanged in other classes. Protocol algorithms could even be dynamically edited and/or chosen, according to criteria computed at runtime; this feature is analogous to the dynamic interpositioning of objects.

Another advantage is that Tori can focus strictly on protocol π and on the interaction between class Object and class πAlgo: She does not need to know how other protocols are implemented. Because aπObject must be able to execute all lower-level protocols on which protocol π is based, Tori is also forced to clearly *specify* what underlying protocols are required to implement the corresponding protocol π. She can then choose which protocol class to subclass in order to implement πObject.

Following is a five-step methodology that guides Tori in extending Bast. To illustrate this point, the method she would follow to build the DTMObject protocol class is presented. Figure 15.10 summarizes the methodology.

1. Establish what services the new protocol class DTMObject provides—that is, what operations are given to programmers wanting to use DTMObject. Those operations are dtmcast( ), dtmReceive( ), and dtmInterpret( ).

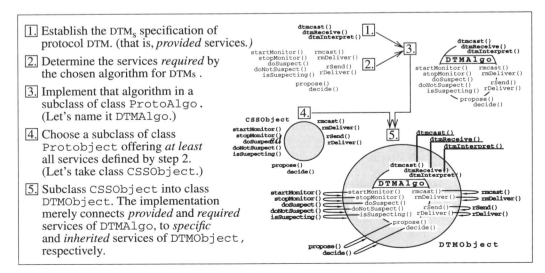

Figure 15.10 Extending Bast with protocol class DTMObject.

2. Choose an algorithm implementing DTM, and determine what services it requires by decomposing it in a way that enables the reuse of as many existing protocols as possible. Those services are consensus, failure detections, and reliable point-to-point and multicast communications (see [Guerraoui 1995a] for algorithmic details).

3. Implement the chosen algorithm in some DTMAlgo class; all calls to the required services are issued to an instance variable representing the context object—that is, an instance of class DTMObject.

4. Choose the protocol class that will be derived to obtain the new class DTMObject. The choice of class CSSObject is directly inferred from step 2, since the chosen superclass has to provide *at least* all the services required by protocol DTM.

5. Implement class DTMObject by connecting services provided by class DTMAlgo to the new DTM-specific services of class DTMObject, and by connecting services required by class DTMAlgo to the corresponding inherited services of class DTMObject.

15.8.2 Tuning Distributed Algorithms

Class CSSObject is at the heart of the DTM distributed pattern and, hence, at the heart of all agreement protocols that are built out of class DTMObject. This illustrates the fact that Bast considers consensus a fundamental building block in the design of agreement protocols [Guerraoui 1995a].

The actual consensus algorithm used by class CSSObject is encapsulated by class CSSAlgo (following the Strategy design pattern). The consensus algorithm we have considered in our current implementation is that of Chandra and Toueg [Chandra 1996]. In a crash-stop model, this algorithm was proved not to block as long as there is a majority of correct participant objects. Now, because class CSSObject is one of Bast's foundations, one might want to tune it to improve performance.

Schiper has introduced the notion of *latency degree,* in order to measure and compare the efficiency of distributed algorithms in consensus solution [Schiper 1997]. This measure considers only executions where no process crashes or is suspected (the most frequent runs in practice). For example, the solution currently implemented in Bast has a latency degree of 4, which means that it requires at least four communication steps to reach a decision. Schiper also proposes a new algorithm that is more efficient than that of Chandra and Toueg, since it requires only two communication steps, and he shows that a trivial optimization of Chandra and Toueg's solution leads to an algorithm with a latency degree of 3. This new algorithm is called the *early consensus.* While both algorithms produce roughly the same number of messages in the best case—that is, $O(n2)$ in a point-to-point network and $O(n)$ in a broadcast network—early consensus tends to generate more messages when failure suspicions occur. This is only an intuitive result, however, and further investigation is needed to gain better insight on when to choose one algorithm or the other. So, whatever the reason, Tori might be willing to alter the implementation of class CSSObject and base it on early consensus. She could even decide to trade fault tolerance for efficiency, and consider a blocking version of consensus, which requires even fewer messages to reach a decision. Indeed, it is sometimes reasonable to assume that the probability of having a crash during the execution of consensus is small enough to be neglected.

In Bast, changing consensus solution is achieved by merely creating a different algorithm object when one is needed. Note that when such a change is applied directly on class CSSObject, it implicitly impacts on the performance of class DTMObject, and hence on classes ABCObject, TOMObject, and ACMObject. Interestingly, the resulting algorithm for class ACMObject comes down to be the famous two-phase commit, which is indeed blocking [Bernstein 1987]. Then, the resulting algorithm for class TOMObject comes down to be roughly the old Isis total order algorithm [Birman 1993]. This is not surprising, since the aim of Bast is not to propose new agreement algorithms, but rather to design a framework for expressing these algorithms in a modular way.

15.9 Applying the DTM Agreement Pattern

This section illustrates distributed pattern customization in Bast by showing how Tori can apply the *DTM agreement pattern* to produce a nonblocking atomic commitment and a fault-tolerant total order multicast. Since both protocols are based on consensus, the DTM pattern is perfectly suited here. Such a method for extending Bast is adequate when the new protocol can be seen as an instance of another more general protocol (the distributed pattern). This feature is what makes Bast a framework in the sense that [Campbell 1993] defines it; therefore, this section discusses *protocol customization*.

15.9.1 The Distributed Agreement Pattern

The DTM distributed pattern enables an initiator object to reliably multicast a message m to $Dst(m)$, a destination set of remote participant objects, and to reach agreement on $Reply(m)$, a set of replies $reply_k$ returned by each $participant_k$ in response to m. This is why we say it is a *distributed agreement* pattern.

In order to customize the DTM distributed pattern, Tori has to subclass the protocol class DTMObject. Instances of such subclasses can play the role of both the *initiator* and the *participant*. Figure 15.11 objects and operations are involved while the protocol is executing: Fat arrows represent operation invocations on objects, bulleted arrows ($\bullet\!\rightarrow$) represent objects resulting from invocations, and circled numbers show the order in which invocations occur. The initiator object is on node A, while $participant_i$ and $participant_j$ are on node B and node C respectively; different nodes imply different address spaces. Since the interaction of the protocol with each participant is exactly the same, arrows are numbered for $participant_i$ only.

Protocol Overview

The DTM pattern's protocol starts by the invocation of dtmcast( ) of an initiator object, passing it a message m, a set of remote participants objects $Dst(m)$, and a *validity condition* (explained shortly); this invocation results in a reliable multicast to the set of participants. When message m reaches some $participant_k$, the latter is invoked by the

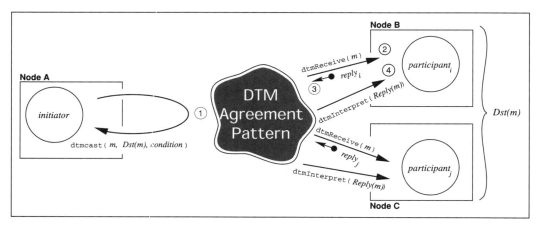

Figure 15.11 The DTM distributed pattern.

protocol through the dtmReceive() operation, taking m as argument. In turn, *participant$_k$* computes and returns its *reply$_k$*. Eventually, each nonfaulty participant is invoked through the dtmInterpret() operation with the *Reply(m)* set, on which consensus has been reached, as argument. So, as long as dtmInterpret() implements a deterministic algorithm, all participants will take the same decision. Operations dtmReceive() and dtmInterpret() are invoked through callbacks by DTM.

Why DTM Is a Pattern

Like any protocol class in Bast, DTMObject is generic in the sense that the message m sent by the initiator, the set of participants *Dst(m)*, the response *reply$_k$* computed by each *participant$_k$*, and the interpretation of *Reply(m)*—the set of replies on which agreement is reached—are not defined a priori. More specifically, m and *reply$_k$* can be any object, while the interpretation of *Reply(m)* is performed by a callback operation.

However, DTM is said to be a distributed *pattern* because it has something more: By customizing its generic dimensions, one can produce new protocols, not only use it in some specific application. (Note, however, that in earlier work [Garbinato 1996a, 1996b, 1997a, 1997b] we refer to DTM as a *generic protocol*. Our point of view, as well as our terminology, has since evolved.) In other words, DTM is primarily intended to serve Tori, not Peter. A distributed pattern, such as DTM, can also be described as a *template protocol* —that is, as some kind of *meta* or *abstract* distributed protocol that acts as a template for application-level protocols aimed at Peter.

Validity Condition

One very important generic dimension that makes DTM a distributed pattern is its *validity condition*, which enables constraining *Reply(m)*: When this constraint cannot be satisfied, the protocol blocks. The reliability property of the DTM pattern lies in the fact that its protocol will not *necessarily* block if one or more participants fail—the protocol is based on (possibly unreliable) failure detectors to decide whether an object is faulty.

It depends on the chosen *validity condition*. The *Reply(m)* set received by all nonfaulty participants might simply lack the replies of faulty participants. It is necessary to be able to express such a condition, since participants might fail and the *Reply(m)* set might have a content that does not permit making any satisfactory decision—for example, *Reply(m)* could be trivially empty. An example of validity condition is the *majority condition*, which can be expressed as $|Reply(m)| > |Dst(m)|/2$; that is, it requires a majority of nonfaulty participants for the protocol not to block.

Operation dtmcast() of class DTMObject takes such a validity condition as its third parameter. The latter can be any object, as long as it understands operation test(), which takes three sets of protocol object references as parameters. The validity condition is tested while the DTM pattern is collecting participants' replies, and is at the heart of reliability issues. When invoked by the protocol, operation test() receives three sets as arguments: *Dst(m)*, *Reply(m)*, and *Suspect(m)*, a subset of *Dst(m)* that contains objects of *Dst(m)* that are *suspected* to be faulty. Set *Suspect(m)* is necessary for instances of the DTM pattern where failures have to be considered in the agreement process— that is, when the condition on *Reply(m)* is expressed in terms of failures.

15.9.2 Atomic Commitment with DTM

The *atomic commitment problem* requires that participants in a transaction agree on *commit* or *abort* at the end of the transaction. If participants can fail and Tori still wants all correct participants to agree, the problem is known as the *nonblocking* atomic commitment (NB-AC) [Bernstein 1987]. In this case, the agreement should be to commit if and only if all participants vote yes and if no participant fails. It has been proved that this problem cannot be solved in asynchronous systems with unreliable failure detectors [Guerraoui 1995a]. This leads to the specification of a weaker problem: the nonblocking *weak* atomic commitment (NB-WAC), which requires merely that no participant is *ever suspected*. Because the DTM pattern makes no assumption on the properties of the failure detector it uses, both the NB-AC and the NB-WAC problems can be seen as instances of DTM, depending on the failure detector considered.

Class ACMObject

To solve the atomic commitment problem using the DTM distributed pattern, Tori subclasses DTMObject into ACMObject. This class defines new operations requestCommitOf(), voteForCommitOf(), commit(), and abort(); apart from the first one, all are triggered by callbacks. Class ACMObject also implements inherited operations dtmReceive() and dtmInterpret().

Operation requestCommitOf() initiates the protocol for a given transaction passed as an argument (an instance of some AbstractTransaction's subclass). The protocol terminates when either commit() or abort() is triggered; these two operations are also passed by the transaction that must be committed or aborted. Figure 15.12 shows an overview of the atomic commitment protocol based on DTM: On the far left is a *transaction manager* that is willing to commit an atomic sequence of operations performed by the two *data managers* on the far right. As in Figure 15.11, arrows represent invocations on objects, while numbers in circles show the order in which invocations occur;

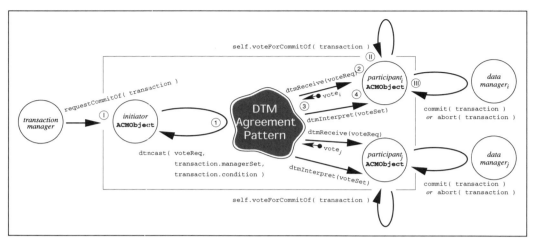

Figure 15.12   Atomic commitment with DTM: overview.

Arabic numerals indicate DTMObject-level operations and Roman numerals indicate ABCObject-level operations.

We next sketch how objects interact while the atomic commitment protocol is executing. Figure 15.13 presents the implementation of the main operations involved. The pseudocode used there is very simple: Statements are separated by semicolons; variables are untyped and declared as in ∥ voteReq ∥; the assignment symbol is ←; and the value returned by an operation is preceded by the symbol ↑.

Initiator Side

When the transaction manager wants to commit an atomic sequence of operations that occurs during a given transaction, it invokes operation requestCommitOf() on its ACMObject, passing it the corresponding transaction object. Transaction objects are instances of AbstractTransaction's subclasses and hold all relevant information for starting atomic commitment protocols.

Operation requestCommitOf() first creates a VoteRequest message, and stores it in a local variable voteReq (see Figure 15.13a). Class VoteRequest defines the instance variable transaction, which holds the actual transaction object. Then, operation requestCommitOf() starts the atomic commitment protocol by invoking the inherited operation dtmcast(). The generic set $Dst(m)$ and the generic validity condition, passed to dtmcast() as second and third arguments, respectively, are transaction's instance variables.

Participant Side

When the message voteReq reaches a participant ACMObject, callback operation dtmReceive() first extracts the transaction object (see Figure 15.13b). It then passes the transaction to the operation voteForCommitOf() defined by class ACMObject, which is expected to compute a vote concerning the commitment of the transaction (either yes or no); the vote is returned to DTM.

```
requestCommitOf( transaction )  ①              dtmReceive( voteReq )

   || voteReq ||                                   || transaction vote ||
   voteReq ← VoteRequest.new( transaction );       transaction ← voteReq.transaction;
   self.dtmcast( voteReq,                           vote ← self.voteForCommitOf ( transaction );  ⑪
                 transaction.managerSet,            ↑ vote;
                 transaction.condition );                                                      (b)
                                                                                              (d)
                                          (a)    dtmInterpret( voteSet )
                                          (c)
   test( managerSet, voteSet, suspectSet )           || transaction ||
                                                     transaction ← voteSet.anyVote.transaction;
   || predicate ||                                   if | voteSet | = | transaction.managerSet |  then
   predicate ← true ;                                  foreach  vote ∈ voteSet  do
   foreach participantₖ ∈ managerSet  do                 if  vote = no  then
     if voteₖ ∉ voteSet ∧ participantₖ ∉ suspectSet then    ↑ self.abort( anyVote.transaction );  ⎫
         predicate ← false ;                             else                                     ⎬ ⑪⑪⑪
     ↑ predicate;                                          ↑ self.abort( anyVote.transaction );  ⎭
                                                        ↑ self.commit( anyVote.transaction );
```

Figure 15.13   Atomic commitment with DTM: details: (*a*) operation requestCommitOf(), (*b*) callback operation dtmReceive(), (*c*) operation test(), and (*d*) operation dtmInterpret().

The DTM distributed pattern then collects the votes of all nonfaulty participants and put them into voteSet, a set implementing generic set *Reply(m)*. During this collecting phase, the validity condition may be tested several times. As soon as voteSet satisfies operation test() (see Figure 15.13c), the DTM pattern starts an agreement protocol by invoking inherited operation propose(), with voteSet as argument. Eventually, callback decide() is triggered on each nonfaulty participant. DTMObject's implementation of operation decide() merely calls dtmInterpret() and passes it the value on which agreement has been reached, namely voteSet. Operation dtmInterpret() then computes the final decision, which is *commit* only if all votes in voteSet are yes and if no participant ACMObject was suspected. In order to do this, dtmInterpret() first extracts the transaction object from any vote found in voteSet (see Figure 15.13d). It then compares the size of voteSet with the size of transaction.managerSet: If both have the same size, it means that no participant was suspected by DTM. It then goes through each vote to see if they all are yes. Operation dtmInterpret() ends up by invoking either commit() or abort()and passing it the transaction; these operations are consequently expected to act on the corresponding data manager.

Validity Condition

The semantics supported by object transaction directly depends on its validity condition, held in the variable transaction.condition. For example, an instance of ReplicatedTransaction holds a majority condition, whereas a NonBlockingTransaction holds the condition implemented by operation test() of Figure 15.13c. This operation is implemented in terms of participant failures as the following predicate: $\forall$ *participant$_k$* $\in$ *Dst(m)*: *reply$_k$* $\notin$ *Reply(m)* $\Rightarrow$ *participant$_k$* $\in$ *Suspect(m)*. Interestingly, the same condition is suitable for both NB-AC and NB-WAC problems, because it all depends on the actual failure detector the DTM pattern uses.

15.9.3 Total Order Multicast with DTM

The *reliable total order multicast* problem can be specified by two primitives, TO-multicast(m, $Dst(m)$) and TO-deliver(m), and by a set of conditions on those primitives. Those conditions express that consistency and liveness must be preserved despite object failures, and that if more than one object are in the intersection of several different $Dst(m)$ sets, they must all perform the corresponding TO-deliver( ) in the same order. Note that we are not talking of some broadcast primitive here: The TO-multicast(m, $Dst(m)$) primitive requires that the destination set $Dst(m)$ be explicitly specified, and this set can be different for each invocation. (In a broadcast primitive, the destination set is implicit: It is the whole system. See *Section 15.7*.) This is why the order condition is expressed in terms of several $Dst(m)$ sets. A formal definition of the total order multicast problem can be found in [Guerraoui 1997b].

To our knowledge, the algorithm presented here is the first *genuine multicast* protocol capable of ensuring total order in a distributed system with unreliable failure detectors. We use the term *genuine multicast* to indicate that the algorithm is not trivially based on a broadcast protocol (which would not be scalable). This algorithm has been described and proved elsewhere [Guerraoui 1997b] without using the DTM distributed pattern. Since it is quite a complex protocol, we first present it independently of DTM. Note that such a total order multicast protocol makes it straightforward to solve the distributed locking of several replicated servers, even when some replicas fail.

Overview of the Protocol

The basic idea of the algorithm presented here is to have each object in $Dst(m)$ propose a time stamp for message m, and to reach an agreement on the maximum of those time stamps; the latter is then used as a sequence number for message m, and messages are delivered according to their sequence numbers. Time stamps are based on Lamport's logical clocks [Lamport 1978]. So, when object o receives message m, it sends its current logical clock value as a proposed time stamp to all other objects in $Dst(m)$. It then stores m in a queue of *pending messages*—that is, all the messages in this queue do not have their sequence numbers computed yet. When agreement is reached on m's sequence number, object o moves m from the queue of pending messages to a queue of *delivery messages*—that is, all the messages in this queue do have their associated sequence numbers but have not yet been delivered. Finally, object o performs TO-deliver(m) for each message m in the delivery queue whose sequence number is smaller than the proposed time stamps of all messages in the pending queue.

Three additional conditions have to be fulfilled for the protocol to work: (C_1) *causal order* delivery must be ensured for all messages exchanged in the algorithm; (C_2) each logical object o in $Dst(m)$ has to be replicated, and its replication rate must be such that there is always a majority of correct replicas of o in the system; and (C_3) the sequence number has to be the maximum of the time stamps that have been proposed by a *qualified majority* of replica objects in $Dst(m)$.

Condition C_2 leads $Dst(m)$ to contain groups of objects (replicas) rather than individual objects, each group gathering the replicas of one logical object. The notion of *group* is used here merely as a naming facility—no group membership protocol (as in Isis [Birman 1993]) is necessary for the algorithm to be correct. In this context, *object o ∈ Dst(m)* is interpreted as *object o ∈ group g ∧ group g ∈ Dst(m)*. The qualified majority of *Dst(m)* is a set of objects that contains a majority of replicas of *every group* in *Dst(m)*. So, condition C_3 can be expressed as the following predicate: $\forall\, g \in Dst(m)$: $|tsSet_g|$ > $1/2 \times |g|$, where $tsSet_g$ is the set of time stamps proposed by replica objects in group *g* when *m*'s sequence number is computed. It is beyond the scope of this chapter to explain why these additional conditions are necessary; details can be found in [Guerraoui 1997b].

Class TOMObject

To implement the total order multicast protocol presented here using the DTM distributed pattern, Tori subclasses DTMObject into class TOMObject. This class defines new operations tomcast( ) and toDeliver( ), which implement the total order multicast primitives TO-multicast( ) and TO-deliver( ) respectively. Class TOMObject also implements inherited callbacks dtmReceive( ) and dtmInterpret( ).

From the clients' point of view, instances of class TOMObject represent some multicast service that allows them to initiate multicasts of totally ordered messages on *explicit* sets of replicated objects; this is precisely why the solution of the distributed locking problem is straightforward with class TOMObject. On the server side, each replica has an associated TOMObject that acts as an intermediary and participates in the protocol for it—that is, TOMObject instances are in charge of computing sequence numbers for messages and reordering them accordingly. Figure 15.14 presents an overview of the total order multicast based on the DTM pattern, following the same conventions as Figure 15.12. In Figure 15.14, *participant*$_{A_i}$ and *participant*$_{B_j}$ are two instances of class TOMObject managing replicas *i* and *j* of *server A* and *server B* respectively. When operation toDeliver( ) is triggered on a participant TOMObject, the message passed as argument is forwarded to the corresponding server replica, with the guarantee that total order is satisfied.

We next sketch how objects interact while the total order multicast protocol is executing. Figure 15.15 presents the main implementation operations involved; the pseudocode is the same as in Figure 15.13.

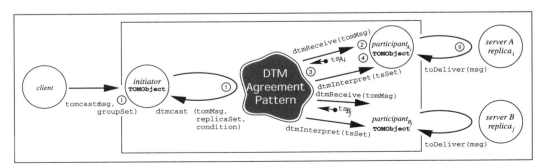

Figure 15.14   Total order multicast with DTMoverview.

```
tomcast ( msg, groupSet )  ①              dtmReceive ( tomMsg )
   || tomMsg replicaSet condition ||           || ts ||
   tomMsg ← TOMMessage.new( msg );            ts ← self.lamportClock.update( tomMsg );
   replicaSet ← ⋃ group                        tomMsg.ts ← ts;
             group ∈ groupSet                   self.pendingQueue.add( tomMsg );
   condition ← TOMCondition.new();             ↑ ts
   condition.groupSet ← groupSet;                                              (b)
   self.dtmcast( tomMsg,                                                       (d)
               replicaSet,                  dtmInterpret ( tsSet )
               condition );         (a)        || tomMsg ||
                                               tomMsg ← self.getMsgRelatedTo( tsSet );
                                   (c)         tomMsg.ts ← self.maxTimeStamp( tsSet );
test ( replicatSet, tsSet, suspectSet )      self.pendingQueue.remove( toMmsg );
   || predicate ||                            self.deliveryQueue.add( tomMsg );
   predicate ← true ;                         foreach m_d ∈ self.deliveryQueue do
   foreach group ∈ self.groupSet do              if ∀m_p ∈ self.pendingQueue : m_p.ts > m_d.ts  then
      if | self.select( tsSet, group ) | ≤ Ω × | group |  then    self.toDeliver( m_d.msg );  ⑩
         predicate ← false ;                       self.deliveryQueue.remove( m_d );
      ↑ predicate;
```

Figure 15.15   Total order multicast with DTMdetails: (*a*) operation tomcast( ), (*b*) callback operation dtmReceive( ), (*c*) operation test( ), and (*d*) operation dtmInterpret( ).

Initiator Side

When some client object wants to issue a total order multicast to a set of replicated server objects, it first has to build a set of groups, each containing the replicas' distributed references (instances of ProtobjectRef) to a logical server. Such groups of replicas might, for example, be provided by some separate naming service. The client then invokes operation tomcast( ) on the initiator TOMObject, representing the multicast service. Two arguments are passed to operation tomcast( ): msg, which can be any object, and to groupSet, the set of groups it just built.

Operation tomcast( ) is implemented as follows (see Figure 15.15a): An internal message tomMsg, an instance of class TOMMessage, is created, and its variable toMsg.msg is initialized with the original message msg; all groups of replicas are merged into replicaSet, a single set of protocol object references; a validity condition is created as an instance of class TOMCondition; and, finally, dtmcast( ) is invoked, with tomMsg, replicaSet, and condition as arguments.

Participant Side

Class TOMessage also defines the variable toMsg.ts, which is used by each participant TOMObject to hold the proposed time stamp when toMsg is stored in the pending queue, and toMsg's sequence number when it is stored in the delivery queue. The pending queue and the delivery queue are held in TOMObject's instance variables pendingQueue and deliveryQueue, respectively. So, when the message toMsg reaches some participant TOMObject, operation dtmReceive( ) updates its Lamport clock, sets toMsg.ts to the updated logical time, and stores toMsg in the pendingQueue (see Figure 15.15b). It then returns toMsg.ts to the DTM pattern. The variable toMsg.ts contains an instance of class TimeStamp, which implements generic $reply_k$ as Lamport's logical time.

The DTM distributed pattern then collects time stamps and puts them into tsSet, a set implementing the generic set $Reply(m)$. During this collecting phase, the validity condition may be tested several times. As soon as tsSet satisfies operation test() (see Figure 15.15c), the DTM pattern starts an agreement protocol by invoking inherited operation propose(), with tsSet as argument. Eventually, callback decide() is triggered on each nonfaulty participant. DTMObject's implementation of operation decide() merely calls dtmInterpret() and passes it the decision on which agreement has been reached, namely tsSet. Operation dtmInterpret() then computes toMsg's sequence number, moves toMsg from the pendingQueue to the deliveryQueue, and performs toDeliver() for all original messages toMsg.msg that have been made *deliverable* by the newly computed sequence number (see Figure 15.15d). Operation dtmInterpret() relies on private operations getMsgRelatedTo() and maxTimeStamp(), defined by class TOMObject. These two operations enable getting the message associated with tsSet and computing the maximum time stamp in tsSet, respectively.

Validity Condition

Class TOMCondition implements the validity condition of the total order multicast protocol—its test() operation evaluates the condition C_3 presented earlier, based on the notion of qualified majority. In this condition, $Dst(m)$ contains groups of objects rather than individual objects. So, TOMCondition's implementation of test() simply ignores the first argument passed to it by DTM—the first argument of test() is a set containing references to protocol objects, not references to groups (see Figure 15.15c). The instance variable groupSet is used instead, which holds the set of groups that was passed to operation tomcast() by the client. Private operation select(), defined by class TOM-Condition, extracts from tsSet the proposed time stamps of a particular group and puts them in a new set.

15.10 Implementation Issues

Our first prototype of the Bast framework was implemented using VisualWorks 2.x, the commercial Smalltalk [Goldberg 1983] platform by ParcPlace-Digitalk Inc. The development took place on a network of Sun SPARCstation 20s and UltraSPARC 1s, running the Solaris 2.x operating system. It was recently ported to Java, using Sun's Java Development Kit (JDK) on the same hardware and OS environment.

Because Smalltalk and Java are semantic twins, Bast's design is virtually the same in both languages. The only differences have to do with dynamic type checking in Smalltalk versus static type checking in Java, and with their respective standard libraries. None of those differences are relevant here. The following section discusses the overall architecture of Bast independently of the language, together with some key issues in design and implementation. Performance results of the Smalltalk implementation are also presented; preliminary tests tend to suggest that performance results of the Java version would be very similar.

15.10.1 Implementation Overview

As already discussed in *Section 15.5*, protocol classes are what Peter is given to build reliable distributed applications. Tori has to deal with an additional kind of classes: protocol algorithm classes, which are all subclasses of abstract class ProtoAlgo. This section presents an overview of how Bast's basic services have been implemented in Smalltalk, except for the atomic group and atomic commit services, which have already been extensively discussed in the previous sections.

Communication Classes

All point-to-point communications provided by classes UMPObject, BMPObject, RMPObject, and FMPObject are performed by the *private* class TransportLayer, which represents the transport layer on each network node. In our implementation, a node is a *virtual machine* (VM), in either Smalltalk or Java. Communications between VMs are implemented by class TransportLayer through a low-level layer written in C: the *Message Passing Layer* (MPL), which is not shown in Figure 15.3a. (VisualWorks and JDK both enable dynamic linking of C functions with Smalltalk and Java code, respectively.) MPL is based on UDP sockets and extends them with the delivery guarantees mentioned earlier in this chapter.

All algorithms for point-to-point communications are implemented within MPL: Class TransportLayer is responsible only for marshaling and unmarshaling messages and for dispatching them. As a consequence, none of the point-to-point communication objects uses private algorithm objects. However, MPL offers no support for reliable *multicast* communications. Class RMCObject is therefore based on algorithm class RMCAlgo, which implements a straightforward reliable multicast algorithm based on systematic retransmissions; details about this algorithm can be found in [Chandra 1996; Garbinato 1997b].

Failure Detection Classes

As previously mentioned, we assume that FDTObject instances on the same network node do not fail *independently*, which in our implementation means that we only consider failures of VMs. The monitoring of remote VMs is performed for class TransportLayer by MPL. Class TransportLayer merely dispatches suspicions and nonsuspicions to local protocol objects. MPL's failure detection scheme is implemented using timeouts and is assumed to behave as a failure detector of type $\lozenge S$. (Such failure detectors are said to be unreliable because they can make false suspicions; they have been proven to be sufficient to solve consensus in asynchronous systems [Chandra 1996].) As for protocol classes supporting point-to-point communications, class FDTObject does not rely on an algorithm class: The failure detection protocol is wired in the underlying transport layer.

Distributed Agreement Classes

Protocol class CSSObject relies on algorithm class CSSAlgo, which implements the $\lozenge S$-based consensus by Chandra and Toueg [Chandra 1996], while DTMObject is based on class DTMAlgo, implementing the DTM algorithm of Guerraoui and Schiper [Guerraoui 1995b]. Both algorithms require protocol objects to perform reliable point-to-point and multicast communications, so CSSObject and DTMObject are subclasses of RMPObject and RMCObject. Because objects participating in these protocols also have to monitor each other, classes CSSObject and DTMObject are subclasses of FDTObject, as well. Finally, class DTMObject is a subclass of CSSObject, which factors the actual agreement protocol.

15.10.2 Transport Layer Dependency

Depending on the semantics of the underlying transport layer, protocol classes can be more or less complex. Figure 15.16 illustrates this point for class CSSObject: Since the transport layer in Figure 15.16a is *unreliable*, reliable communications have to be ensured at the protocol class level, involving several different πAlgo classes. In Figure 15.16b, on the contrary, the transport layer supports reliable point-to-point communicationand failure detection as well as reliable multicast, so no algorithm object is needed for these protocols. (Our actual transport layer provides reliable point-to-point communication and failure detection, but no reliable multicast. It is a tradeoff between Figures 15.16a and 15.16b.) Having reliable communication algorithms wired in the transport layer reduces the complexity of class CSSObject and possibly increases performance. Furthermore, as long as the reliable transport layer still offers unreliable communications, no flexibility is lost: It is always possible for Tori to bypass wired-in reliable communications and reimplement them in adequate algorithm classes. This is also true for failure detection.

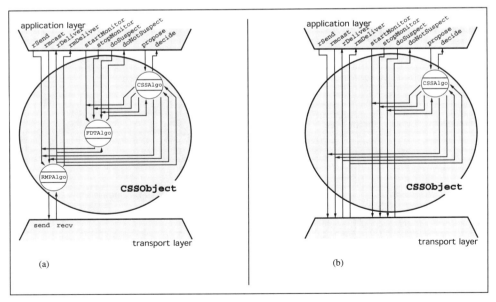

Figure 15.16 Dependency on the transport layer: (*a*) class CSSObject based on an unreliable transport layer, and (*b*) class CSSObject based on a reliable transport layer.

15.10.3 Design Alternatives

This section discusses some design alternatives that we considered when implementing our first prototype of Bast. Some of those alternatives have been part of an even earlier implementation but were later left out, while others are inspired by other existing frameworks.

Inheritance Alone

As presented in *Section 15.6,* inheritance is an appropriate mechanism to build fault-tolerant distributed applications from ready-to-use components: By subclassing appropriate protocol classes and by implementing their callback operations according to the desired semantics, Peter has the ability to tailor protocols to his needs. However, we pretend that inheritance alone is not sufficient as far as protocol composition goes, because it does not offer Tori enough flexibility. For example, inheritance does not allow her to easily implement a new algorithm for some existing protocol and to use it in whatever protocol class she wants.

This situation is illustrated in Figure 15.17: Given the pictured class hierarchy, suppose Tori wants to change the reliable multicast algorithm on which both the causal and the atomic broadcast protocols are based (classes CBCObject and ABCObject, respectively), while leaving it unchanged in all other classes (CSSObject and DTMObject in our case). With inheritance alone as a code reuse mechanism, she has to implement the new reliable multicast algorithm in both CBCObject and ABCObject classes; this not what Tori expects from Bast as a framework promoting flexible protocol composition and optimal code reuse. Furthermore, inheritance is not appropriate when it comes to choosing among several protocol algorithms *at runtime*. It is these limitations that led us to objectify distributed algorithms by recursively applying the Strategy design pattern, as presented in *Section 15.9.*

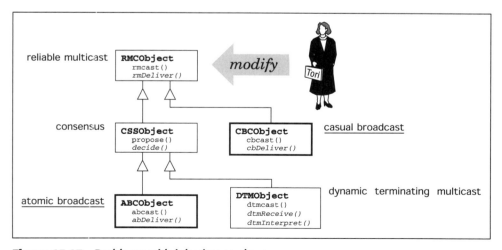

Figure 15.17   Problems with inheritance alone.

Mixin Classes

Assembling the various protocol layers through multiple inheritance is very appealing. Note, however, that neither Smalltalk nor Java offers multiple inheritance. Smalltalk reflective facilities have been proven to make it possible to add multiple inheritance [Ingalls 1982], while no such study has yet been published for Java. With multiple inheritance, each πObject class would implement only protocol π, while accessing all required underlying protocols through unimplemented operations. The latter would then be provided by other protocol classes through multiple inheritance. With such a design, protocol classes are all *abstract* and we usually refer to them as *mixin classes* or simply *mixins*.

There are several drawbacks with this approach, however. First, protocol classes are not mere ready-to-use components: Before actually creating a protocol object, one first has to build a new class deriving from all the necessary protocol classes. Peter can no longer ignore protocol dependencies. Then, because protocol layers are assembled through subclassing, it is very difficult to compose protocols at runtime. While fairly complex yet possible in Smalltalk, such runtime protocol composition is impossible in Java (classes can be created only at compile time in this language). Finally, concurrent protocol executions within the same protocol object still have to be managed, whereas this problem is handled naturally when each protocol execution is materialized as a separate algorithm object.

Toolbox Approach

Another possible approach to the reuse of protocol implementations is to provide programmers with a toolbox containing reusable components and associate them with design patterns. Both ACE [Schmidt 1994] and Conduits+ [Hüni 1995] frameworks are such toolboxes. The ACE framework provides collaborating C++ objects, plus some design patterns, that help to produce reusable communication infrastructures. In Conduits+, conduits and information chunks are assembled thanks to various patterns, in order to create protocol layers.

However, there are no such things as protocol objects in either of these frameworks. One of Bast's major aims is to provide programmers with the unifying notion of the protocol object, which is the cornerstone of the protocol-oriented approach. This enables the support of a continuum of abstraction levels, with no arbitrary boundaries. With a toolbox approach, on the contrary, elemental components (the tools) define abstraction boundaries in a fairly rigid manner. Consequently, the Bast framework is not based on a toolbox design. Furthermore, ACE does not promote protocol composition, whereas Conduits+ does it in a slightly different way than Bast, as the following section discusses.

Blackbox Reusability

In a *blackbox* framework, reusability is mainly achieved by assembling instances, whereas in a *whitebox* framework, it is mainly achieved through inheritance. A blackbox framework is known to be easier to use, but harder to design.

In Conduits+, the use of design patterns is motivated by the fact that traditional layered architectures do not enable code reuse across layers. Protocols can then be composed at a lower level than in Bast, through the assembling of conduits and information chunks, which are elementary blocks used to build protocol layers. In other words, the Conduits+ framework does not enable the manipulation of distributed algorithms as objects, but it further decomposes them: Conduits and information chunks are finer-grain objects than Bast's strategies. Indeed, strategies represent protocol layers, while conduits and information chunks are internal components of protocol layers. So, Conduits+ goes one step further in the process of objectifying distributed algorithms. This approach makes it easy for Conduits+ to be a pure blackbox framework, while Bast combines features of both blackbox and whitebox frameworks.

15.10.4 Performance

As mentioned earlier, Bast was primarily built as an *open* environment for teaching and prototyping reliable distributed algorithms. In particular, all optimizations that would compromise its extensibility and genericity were left out—allowing *any* object to be sent across the network has a cost. As a consequence, Bast's first implementation was slow. However, now that the first design and implementation of Bast is fully operational, we are currently conducting in-depth performance analysis in order to seek ways of optimizing it.

The rest of this section presents some of our first performance results and conclusions, as far as potential optimizations go. Preliminary tests indicate that Bast offers roughly the same performance on Smalltalk and on Java. (Compared to Bast built on JDK 1.0, the VisualWorks 2.x version was about 1.5 times faster. With JDK 1.1, performance is now the same.) Tests also tend to prove that both versions could be optimized in a very similar way. The following section discusses the performance only of the Smalltalk version.

Test Scenario

Our test scenario aims to test Bast's performance in the context of one-to-many communication protocols: such protocols are essential for replication management. Three protocols are tested:

- A *sequence of reliable point-to-point sends*, through operation rSend( ) and callback rDeliver( ) of class RMPObject

- A *reliable multicast*, through operation rmcast( ) and callback rmDeliver( ) of class RMCObject

- An *atomic broadcast*, through operation abcast( ) and callback abDeliver( ) of class ABCObject

In this scenario, we consider a logical ring composed of three protocol objects located on three different network nodes, with each protocol object o_i knowing its preceding object *pred*(o_i). Each object o_i sends its messages to all protocol objects in the ring (including itself), using some one-to-many communications operations (depending on the protocol being tested). Messages are said to be *empty*—that is, they hold a reference to the nil object—and they are sent in bursts of five: When protocol object o_i sends messages to all, it does so five times in a row. To implement fair access to the transport layer, each o_i waits until it *x*Delivers five messages from *pred*(o_i) before sending another burst of five messages to all, with $x \in$ {r, rm, abc}. At each network node, time is started when o_i *x*Delivers its first message and stopped when it has done so for 150 messages. By dividing 150 messages by the time o_i takes to deliver them all, we get the throughput of each protocol for our scenario.

Testing took place on a 10-Mbit Ethernet interconnecting 13 Sun SPARCstations during a normal workday. All workstations were running XWindows as well as several interactive applications (Netscape, emacs, and so on), so network and CPU loads were medium to high. Network nodes hosting protocol objects were three Sun UltraSPARC 1s, all equipped with 64 Mbytes of RAM and running Solaris 2.5. Each test was performed at least 20 times to get meaningful results.

Results with Smalltalk

Table 15.1 presents performance results of the Smalltalk implementation. The first column indicates which protocol is being tested, while the second column gives its throughput; performance worsens quickly as protocol complexity increases. The third column shows the number of low-level messages that go through the transport layer (MPL) in order to deliver 150 high-level messages. The fourth column shows how the average size of MPL messages evolves. Although high-level messages merely contain the nil object, lower-level messages contain additional information related to the various underlying protocols. This information gets bigger as protocols become more complex.

Not surprisingly, 300 MPL messages are processed by RMPObject objects performing reliable point-to-point communication: 150 are sent and 150 are received. Reliable multicast objects of class RMCObject process roughly four times more MPL messages to do their job: Each MPL message received for the first time triggers three more reliable point-to-point communications (because of the systematic retransmission scheme described earlier). For ABCObject objects performing atomic broadcasts, the number of MPL messages is more difficult to interpret: It includes many messages involved in underlying reliable multicast and consensus executions.

The fifth column gives the percentage of the overall time spent on marshaling and unmarshaling MPL messages: These results strongly suggest that marshaling is where optimization efforts should concentrate. The last column shows how many algorithm objects are created. Class RMPObject directly relies on the transport layer, so its instances create no algorithm objects. Instances of RMCObject create only RMCAlgo objects, whereas instances of ABCObject also create consensus algorithms. Out of 344 algorithm objects created, 53 are instances of class CSSAlgo, which indicates that so many consensus executions are necessary to abDeliver( ) 150 messages. Each consensus decides upon the ordering of about three atomically broadcast messages.

Table 15.1 Smalltalk Performance to xDeliver 150 msgs, $x \in \{r, rm, abc\}$

PROTOCOL CLASS	THROUGHPUT [MSGS/SEC]	NUMBER OF MPL-MSGS	MPL-MSG SIZE [BYTES]	MARSHALING [TIMEPERCENTAGE]	ALGORITHMS CREATED
RMPObject	15.1	300	700	54	—
RMCObject	4.4	1173	1334	88	150
ABCObject	1.4	3406	1873	79	344

Results with Java

Table 15.2 presents results of the performance tests with the Java version. Clearly, the Java implementation is two to three times faster than the Smalltalk one. Note that it creates one-third fewer algorithm objects, out of which 33 solve consensus. So, about four to five atomically broadcast messages are handled by each consensus execution. This partly explains why Java tests lead to better results for class ABCObject. We can also observe that marshaling is roughly 16 to 23 percent faster in Java than in Smalltalk.

Considering that no optimization has yet been performed, these results are quite encouraging—especially if we think that Sun's Java VM is purely interpreted. On the contrary, Visualworks Smalltalk relies on the Deutsch-Schiffman implementation technique, which dynamically translates compiled methods into machine code and maps contexts onto the processor stack [Deutsch 1984]. As soon as this approach, known as *just-in-time compilation,* becomes widely applied to Java VMs, we can expect even better results.

The MPL C Library Alone

Protocol class RMPObject was also compared with the MPL library, used alone in a C program implementing the scenario previously described (same network configuration, message size, burst size, and so on). Such performance results are interesting because class RMPObject directly relies on MPL. With this C program, we get a throughput of 306 messages/s. So, MPL alone is then about 20 times faster than class RMPObject in Smalltalk, and 8 times faster than it is in Java. This can be partly explained by the bad performance of the marshaling process, but further testing will be necessary to refine this analysis.

15.10.5 Possible Optimizations

As previously suggested, optimization should probably start at the marshaling level, in order to make it work faster and produce smaller messages. For instance, each empty high-level message sent through operation rSend( ) produces a 700-byte MPL message. This is far too large, even considering that an MPL message contains several other pieces of information, such as a unique message ID and the distributed reference of its sender object. This result is not surprising: Bast's marshaling is based on the VisualWorks *Binary Object Storage Service* (BOSS), which aims to make it easy to save *any* object onto stable storage (the Java implementation uses a similar service). Although BOSS semantics suits Bast's needs for marshaling (particularly in terms of genericity and modularity), it was designed with very different performance goals in mind.

Still, before even touching BOSS internal code, a very simple optimization principle can help us to cut down the marshaling overhead: reducing the number of low-level messages going through the transport layer. For test purposes, this optimization principle was applied in two straightforward ways: by avoiding systematic retransmission at the reliable multicast level and retransmitting messages only if their initial sender is suspected to be faulty, and by avoiding unmarshaling messages whenever an unused *ack* or *no ack* is received by the transport layer. With those two simple optimizations,

Table 15.2 Java Performance to xDeliver 150 Messages, $x \in \{r, rm, abc\}$

PROTOCOL CLASS	THROUGHPUT [MSGS/SEC]	NUMBER OF MPL-MSGS	MPL-MSG SIZE [BYTES]	MARSHALING [TIMEPERCENTAGE]	ALGORITHMS CREATED
RMPObject	38.6	300	710	80	—
RMCObject	8.5	1081	1020	87	150
ABCObject	3.5	2003	1316	79	227

class RMCObject raises its throughput from 4 to 12 messages, while class ABCObject doubles its throughput.

15.11 Summary

This chapter introduces Bast, an object-oriented framework for fault-tolerant distributed computing, based on protocol objects and patterns. Bast provides various ready-to-use protocols, such as the atomic broadcast and the atomic commitment, to support the development of reliable distributed applications. It also offers the Strategy and DTM design patterns, powerful tools for extending its protocol class library.

This chapter describes the way Bast was designed and points out issues in reusing and composing distributed protocols. In particular, it describes in detail how Bast's design patterns can be applied in order to create new protocols from existing ones. Further protocols, such as group membership or view synchronous communication, can then be easily developed, by using lower-level protocols provided by Bast.

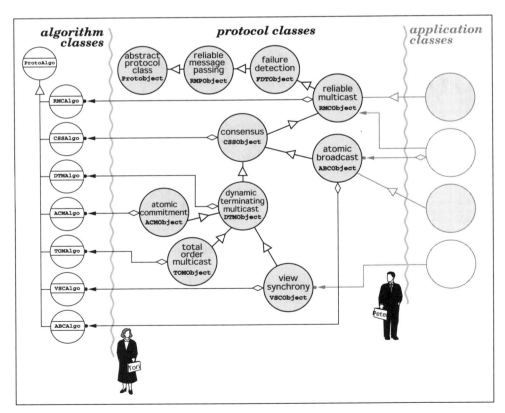

Figure 15.18   Viewpoint integration in Bast.

15.11.1 Viewpoint Integration

In the introduction to the chapter discusses two viewpoints of reliability that are often opposed (see Figure 15.1). From this perspective, one can see the Bast framework as a concrete means to integrate these viewpoints. Figure 15.18 illustrates this idea by presenting a synoptic view of Bast in which classes are grouped into three categories.

On the left are classes that implement the various distributed algorithms on which protocol classes, in the middle, are based. Roughly speaking, this is Tori's playground: She can tune and compose protocols by applying the Strategy design pattern, as well as system-level protocol patterns. On the right, Peter builds application classes by using protocol classes as off-the-shelf components, either through inheritance, aggregation, or referencing. In doing so, he applies application-level protocol patterns.

15.11.2 Current Status

Bast was first written in Smalltalk and then ported to Java. It has been used both for teaching reliable distributed algorithms and systems, and for prototyping new fault-tolerant distributed protocols. In order to make Bast useful for practical application development, we are currently working on performance testing and code optimization. More information about Bast can be found on the Web, at http://lsewww.epfl.ch/bast. Our first implementation is free to the public and is also available there.

15.12 References

[Abbott 1993] Abbott, M.B., and L.L. Peterson. A language-based approach to protocol implementation. *IEEE/ACM Transactions on Networking*, 1(1), 1993: 4–19.

[Bernstein 1987] Bernstein, P.A., V. Hadzilacos, and N. Goodman. *Concurrency Control and Recovery in Distributed Database Systems*. Reading, MA: Addison-Welsey, 1987.

[Birman 1993] Birman, K., and R. Van Renesse. *Reliable Distributed Computing with the Isis Toolkit*. Los Alamitos, CA: IEEE Computer Society Press, 1993.

[Campbell 1993] Campbell, R., N. Islam, D. Ralia, and P. Madany. Designing and implementing choices: An object-oriented system in C++. *Communications of the ACM*, Special Issue on Concurrent Object-Oriented Programming, 36(9), 1993: 117–126.

[Chandra 1992] Chandra, T.D., V. Hadzilacos, and S. Toueg. *The Weakest Failure Detector for Solving Consensus*. Technical Report 92-1293. Computer Science Department, Cornell University, Ithaca, NY, 1992. A preliminary version appears in *11th ACM Symposium on Principles of Distributed Computing*. New York: ACM Press, 1992.

[Chandra 1996] Chandra, T.D., and S. Toueg. Unreliable failure detectors for reliable distributed systems. *Journal of the ACM*, 34(1), 1996: 225–267.

[Deutsch 1984] Deutsch, P., and A.M. Schiffman. Efficient implementation of the Smalltalk-80 system. *Conference Record of the Eleventh Annual ACM Symposium on Principles of Programming Languages (PLoP 1984)*. New York: ACM Press, 1984: 297–302.

[Gamma 1993] Gamma, E., R. Helm, R. Johnson, and J. Vlissides. Design patterns: Abstraction and reuse of object-oriented design. *Proceedings of the 1993 European Conference on Object-Oriented Programming Proceedings (ECOOP 1993).* Lecture Notes in Computer Science 707. Springer-Verlag, 1993.

[Gamma 1995] Gamma, E., R. Helm, R. Johnson, and J. Vlissides. *Design Patterns: Elements of Reusable Object-Oriented Software.* Reading, MA: Addison-Wesley, 1995.

[Garbinato 1995] Garbinato, B., R. Guerraoui, and K.R. Mazouni. Implementation of the GARF replicated object platform. *Distributed Systems Engineering Journal,* 2, 1995: 14–27.

[Garbinato 1996a] Garbinato, B., P. Felber, and R. Guerraoui. Protocol classes for designing reliable distributed environments. *Proceedings of the 1996 European Conference on Object-Oriented Programming Proceedings (ECOOP 1996).* Lecture Notes in Computer Science 1098. Springer Verlag, 1996: 316–343.

[Garbinato 1996b] Garbinato, B., P. Felber, and R. Guerraoui. Modeling protocols as objects for structuring reliable distributed systems. *Proceedings of the Communication Networks and Distributed Systems Modeling and Simulation Conference (CNDS 1997),* pp. 165–171, 1996.

[Garbinato 1997a] Garbinato, B., P. Felber, and R. Guerraoui. Right abstractions on adequate frameworks for building adaptable distributed applications. In *Special Issues in Object-Oriented Programming,* Max Mühlhäuser, editor. dpunkt-Verlag, 1997: 24–28.

[Garbinato 1997b] Garbinato, B., and R. Guerraoui. Using the Strategy design Pattern to compose reliable distributed protocols. *Proceedings of the 3rd USENIX Conference on Object-Oriented Technologies and Systems (COOTS 1997),* pp. 221–232, Portland, Oregon, June 1997.

[Garbinato 1998a] B. Garbinato. Protocol objects and patterns for structuring reliable distributed systems. Ph.D. thesis, Swiss Federal Institute of Technology (EPFL), Lausanne, 1998.

[Garbinato 1998b] Garbinato, B., and R. Guerraoui. Flexible protocol composition in Bast. *Proceedings of the 18th International Conference on Distributed Computing Systems (ICDCS-18).* Los Alamitos, CA: IEEE Computer Society Press, 1998: 22–29.

[Goldberg 1983] Goldberg, A.J., and A.D. Robson. *SMALLTALK-80: The Language and Its Implementation.* Reading, MA: Addison-Wesley, 1983.

[Gosling 1995] Gosling, J., and H. McGilton. *The Java Language Environment: A White Paper.* Technical report. Palo Alto, CA, Sun Microsystems, 1995.

[Guerraoui 1995a] Guerraoui, R. Revisiting the relationship between non-blocking atomic commitment and consensus. *Distributed Algorithms—9th International Workshop on Distributed Algorithms (WDAG 1995),* J.-M. Hélary and M. Raynal, editors. Lecture Notes in Computer Science 972. Springer-Verlag, 1995: 87–100.

[Guerraoui 1995b] Guerraoui, R., and A. Schiper. Transaction model vs. virtual synchrony model: Bridging the gap. *Theory and Practice in Distributed Systems.* Lecture Notes in Computer Science 938. Springer Verlag, 1995: 121–132.

[Guerraoui 1997a] Guerraoui, R., and A. Schiper. Software based replication for fault-tolerance. *IEEE Computer,* 30(4), 1997: 68–74.

[Guerraoui 1997b] Guerraoui, R., and A. Schiper. Total order multicast to multiple groups. *Proceedings of the 17th International Conference on Distributed Computing Systems (ICDCS-17).* Los Alamitos, CA: IEEE Computer Society Press, 1997: 578–585.

[Hüni 1995] Hüni, H., R. Johnson, and R. Engel. A framework for network protocol software. *Proceedings of the OOPSLA 1995 Conference on Object-Oriented Programming Systems, Languages, and Applications.* New York: ACM Press, 1995.

[Hutchinson 1988] Hutchinson, N.C., and L.L. Peterson. Design of the x-kernel. *Proceedings of the SIGCOMM 1988 Symposium,* pp. 65–75, 1988.

[Ingalls 1982] Ingalls, D.H.H., and A.H. Borning. Multiple inheritance in Smalltalk-80. *Proceedings of the National Conference on Artificial Intelligence,* pp. 234–237, 1982.

[Lamport 1978] Lamport, L. Time, clocks, and the ordering of events in a distributed system. *Communications of the ACM,* 21(7), 1978: 558–565.

[Laprie 1991] Laprie, J.-C. Dependability concepts. In *Delta-4: A Generic Architecture for Dependable Distributed Computing,* D. Powell, editor. Springer-Verlag, 1991: 43–69.

[Lynch 1994] Lynch, N., M. Merrit, W. Weihl, and A. Fekete. *Atomic Transactions.* San Mateo, CA: Morgan Kaufmann, 1994.

[Mishra 1993] Mishra, S., L.L. Peterson, and R.D. Schlichting. Consul: A communication substrate for fault-tolerant distributed programs. *Distributed Systems Engineering Journal,* 1(2), 1993: 87–103.

[Mullender 1989] Mullender, S., ed. *Distributed Systems.* Frontier Series. Reading, MA: Addison-Wesley, 1989.

[O'Malley 1990] O'Malley, S.W. *Avoca: An Environment for Programming with Protocols.* Technical Report TR 90-31. Department of Computer of Science, University of Arizona, Tucson, 1990.

[OMG 1997] Object Management Group. *The Common Object Request Broker: Architecture and Specification,* Revision 2.1. Framingham, MA: OMG, 1997.

[Powell 1991] Powell, D., ed. *Delta-4: A Generic Architecture for Dependable Distributed Computing,* Vol. 1. Springer-Verlag, 1991.

[Rose 1990] Rose, M.T. *The Open Book: A Practical Perspective on OSI.* Englewood Cliffs, NJ: Prentice-Hall, 1990.

[Rumbaugh 1991] Rumbaugh, J., M. Blaha, W. Premerlani, F. Eddy, and W. Lorenson. *Object-Oriented Modeling and Design.* Englewood Cliffs, NJ: Prentice-Hall, 1991.

[Schiper 1997] Schiper, A. Early consensus in an asynchronous system with a weak failure detector. *Distributed Computing,* 10(3), 1997: 149–157.

[Schmidt 1994] Schmidt, D.C. ASX: An object-oriented framework for developing distributed applications. *Proceedings of the 6th USENIX C++ Technical Conference.* USENIX Association, 1994.

[Van Renesse 1995] van Renesse, R., K. Birman, R. Friedman, M. Hayden, and D. Karr. A framework for protocol composition in Horus. *Proceedings of the ACM Symposium on Principles of Distributed Computing (PODC 1995).* New York: ACM Press, 1995.

CHAPTER 16

Object-Oriented Realtime System Framework

Realtime systems belong to a category of application systems that need special design and implementation techniques. In addition to the domain knowledge, a realtime system designer should know about different scheduling algorithms for different domain-specific applications, techniques to support low-overhead context switching, and mechanisms to provide proper intertask communication and resource sharing. All these realtime system design techniques necessary in the implementation of a realtime system kernel form a prohibitive overhead for realtime application designers.

Object-oriented technologies, pledging reusability, now come to relieve the burden of realtime software system construction. Recently, we have successfully designed an object-oriented realtime system framework (OORTSF) in an attempt to provide a framework-oriented development tool for embedded realtime applications. This chapter describes the design issues of OORTSF, defines a five-step process for the development of realtime systems using this framework, and presents an example of the implementation of a realtime application system using OORTSF. It also presents a classification of some high-level reuse technologies to clarify the reusability of OORTSF in realtime system design.

A brief introduction to the Object Modeling Technique (OMT) [Rumbaugh 1991] notation used in this chapter is as follows: A *class* is represented by a rectangular box, and an *object instance* is represented by a rounded box. A class or object box is partitioned into three compartments: The class or object name is placed in the top compartment, attributes are placed in the middle compartment, and member functions and methods are placed in the lower compartment. Two specialized associations are used in this chapter: *generalization* (also known as *inheritance* or *is-a*) relationships and *aggre-*

gation (also known as *containment* or *has*) relationships. The generalization relationship between a superclass and its subclasses is represented by a triangle, a line that connects the superclass to the apex of the triangle, and lines that connect the subclasses to the base of the triangle. The aggregation relationship relates an assembly class (or object) to one component class (or object); aggregation is represented by a line with a diamond at the end denoting the assembly part of the relationship and lines at the other end denoting the component parts.

16.1 High-Level Reuse Techniques

Using terms similar to those that have been used in parallel processing, software reuse can be classified as low-level or fine-grain reuse, which reuses only a small amount of code segments at the programming level, and high-level or coarse-grain reuse, which reuses design concepts and/or a large amount of code. Promoting the level of reuse is important in increasing the scale of software reuse.

Promising technologies in high-level reuse, such as design patterns [Coad 1992; Gamma 1995; Pree 1994], frameworks [Gibbs 1994; Myers 1995], and software architectures [Garlan 1995; Krunchten 1995; Perry 1992; Shaw 1996], have been discussed elsewhere. A classification of these high-level reuse technologies using OMT notation is shown in Figure 16.1. The object-oriented reuse technologies are still evolving, even in the definition of the technology itself [Johnson 1997]. With the advance of object-oriented reuse technologies, the relations and interactions among different reuse technologies will also change. However, we try to organize these concepts of reuse technologies through the following definitions:

Design patterns. Provide general solutions to common design problems using sets of communicating classes and objects. The description of a design pattern often provides a metaphorical abstraction to help users capture the concept easily and

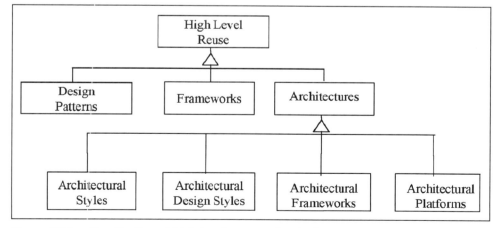

Figure 16.1 Classification of high-level reuse technologies.

use the pattern effectively. Typical examples of design patterns are the structural pattern *Façade* which intends to provide a unified interface to a set of interactions in a subsystem, and *Observer*, which defines a one-to-many dependence relationship to reflect the changes of an object state with different forms of view [Gamma 1995]. Design patterns have been used as a tool to document larger reusable software entities, especially the framework [Johnson 1992].

Frameworks. Provide a set of collaborating classes and runtime objects to facilitate the creation of software in some domain-specific applications [Gibbs 1994; Myers 1995]. The set of abstract and concrete classes in a framework can be easily adapted to meet the requirements of a specific application. In this way, the design and code of the framework can be reused.

Software Architectures. Crafting software is also called *architecting* software. An operational software has some sort of architectures inside. Reusable entities in software architectural technologies can be further divided into four different categories: architectural style, architectural design style, architectural framework, and architectural platform. The differences among them and examples for each category are described as follows:

- A software *architectural style* shows a well-established common form of global software organization. For example, seven styles of architectures have been introduced by Shaw and Garlan [Shaw 1996]: *pipes and filters, object-oriented organizations, implicit invocations, layered systems, repositories, interpreters,* and *process control.*

- An *architectural design style* shows a design methodology to foster the software architecture. Shaw [Shaw 1995] categorized the design styles as *functional decomposition, dataflow, object-oriented, state machine, event-oriented, process control, data structure,* and *decision table.*

- An *architectural framework* is a more detailed and complete framework using one or more architecture design styles for the development of some domain-specific application. A software architecture artifact designed with some styles can be reused as an architecture framework, only if it provides enough documentation and builds enough flexibility inside to encompass a certain application domain. An architectural framework for telecommunication infrastructure systems has been introduced in [van der Linden 1995].

- An *architectural platform* provides a flexible infrastructure to fit a wide range of applications. Architectural platforms are designed to provide a hardware-platform- and operating-system-independent environment for the interoperation of application software. They can be served as an infrastructure to promote object-level collaboration and reuse. The Common Object Request Broker (CORBA) Architecture and Specification of the Object Management Group (OMG) [Adler 1995] is an example of this.

Users of a framework do not need to have a thorough understanding of the design details of the framework. However, design patterns can be used as a description language to document a framework [Johnson 1992]. This will help a framework user to gain a quick understanding of the mechanisms used in the framework, especially when the user already has general domain knowledge about the design patterns used in the document.

Frameworks provide solutions for some domain-specific applications. However, they might not provide a total solution to the framework users. Sometimes, a software architectural view will help users to take a hierarchical view of the application system under development by placing the framework in a proper compartment inside the architecture and developing only the necessary domain objects to complete the system design. For example, realtime system designers can have a layered architectural view of the system under development by using our OORTSF framework as a base layer, and attaching the developed domain-specific objects to the underlying OORTSF. This kind of layered view will be very constructive in using frameworks to develop applications. This chapter later presents an example of the framework-oriented development of an application using OORTSF to verify this viewpoint.

16.2 Class Hierarchy in OORTSF

Realtime systems must be suitably constrained to meet critical timing requirements. One way to constrain a realtime system with predicted timing behaviors is to implement it as a system of periodic tasks. For periodic tasks, three realtime task-scheduling methods have been proven to be theoretically sound and practically useful: the *cyclic scheduler* (CYS), the *rate monotonic scheduler* (RMS), and the *earliest deadline first* (EDF) *scheduler*. Therefore, in our framework, these three scheduling methods are all supported such that users can choose the most appropriate one according to their needs.

The object-oriented paradigm pledges power in modeling real-world objects and reusability. Working with an object-oriented realtime system framework will help realtime application system developers integrate domain-specific objects into this framework more naturally. For this purpose, a reusable OORTSF was developed, in which the object-oriented abstract class concept is applied to extract common behavior of the framework component objects. This OORTSF provides necessary kernel objects, such as a scheduler object, some task-table objects, and supporting objects, for the development of realtime applications.

First, we define an abstract class CSchedulerBase, shown in Figure 16.2, to capture the basic behaviors of a scheduler such that inheritance can be used to specialize this abstract base class into three popular schedulers differentiated by their scheduling methods: CCYScheduler, CRMScheduler, and CEDFScheduler. In the figure, variable names that begin with C indicate class definitions.

Since a realtime application often requires intertask coordination, typical intertask coordination mechanisms such as mutual exclusion and synchronization must be supported. *Mutual exclusion* deals with the interlock among shared resources, which ensures an orderly execution of cooperating tasks to achieve consistency in shared data access. *Synchronization* mechanisms provide an execution sequence control between tasks. In general, semaphore is a simple and efficient mechanism that can be used to solve the mutual-exclusion and synchronization issues [Silberchatz 1994]. Therefore, in Figure 16.2 we define a semaphore class CSemaphore for this purpose, where member functions signal( ) and wait( ) are atomic functions to access the semaphore value Sem-

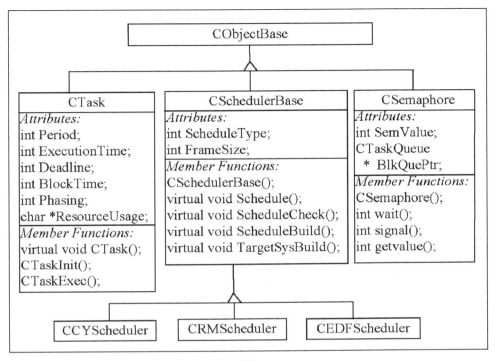

Figure 16.2 Major class hierarchy in OORTSF.

Value. A task queue—CTaskQueue in Figure 16.3—pointed to by a BlkQuePtr, is used to keep track of the tasks blocked by the wait( )function call in CSemaphore. Some tasks in CTaskQueue, if unblocked by the signal( ) function calls from some other tasks, will be moved to the CReadyQueue, shown in Figure 16.3. These tasks in CReadyQueue should be arranged according to the priority sequence prespecified by the scheduling algorithms.

System management is supported by classes derived from two base classes, CList-Base and CItemBase. As shown in Figure 16.3, CListBase is the base class of various task-table classes, message communication classes, and resource-sharing classes; CItemBase is the base class for the classes that handle system resources and messages. In contrast to the primitive CSemaphore, a higher-level message-queue class CMessageQueue is provided here for intertask communication, together with a resource-table class CResourceTable as an abstraction to encapsulate the resources shared among tasks. In the implementation of CMessageQueue and CResourceTable, CSemaphore is used as the underlying mechanism. Three TaskTable classes derived from CListBase, CCyclicTaskTable, CPeriodicTaskTable, and CSporadicTaskTable, are provided to store the information of application tasks for schedulability check and runtime scheduling. The classes CTaskQueue and CReadyQueue are related to CSemaphore and to the functions wait( ) and signal( ), respectively, as previously discussed.

Other system-supporting classes in OORTSF, such as CTimeBase, CFaultManager, and CExceptionHandler, shown at the bottom of Figure 16.3, are explained as follows.

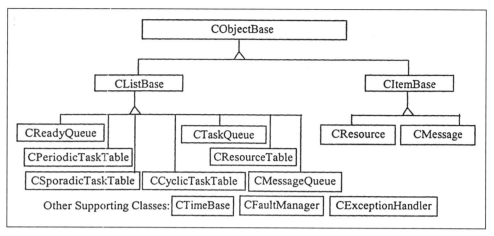

Figure 16.3   Supporting class hierarchy in OORTSF.

TimeBase. A time-related base class. A system time is provided by an object instantiation of this class. The system time resolution can be adjusted by refining the behavior of this class. The size of the execution time frame is also determined in this class for interrupting a system at periodic intervals.

FaultManager. A fault manager class (CFaultManager) is designed to collect information on system faults, such as type of fault, occurrence count, and time of occurrence.

ExceptionHandler. Any exception condition, such as a system power failure or machine error, will cause a system exception. During exception handling, the CExceptionHandler class is used to perform the system status saving and to invoke the fault manager for further handling and fault reporting.

16.3 Scenario of Object Collaboration in OORTSF

Assume that we have three application programs to be scheduled and included in a realtime embedded system. A scenario for developing such a system using OORTSF is depicted as follows. First, the three application task objects have to be attached to the framework via three instantiated CTask class objects. Each application task must be encapsulated in an instantiated object of CTask class or its derivation. The scheduling-related task parameters needed by the scheduler are defined as attributes of this class and should be provided by the system user. Therefore, framework users need an Adapter pattern [Gamma 1995] to adapt the application task to the task abstractions of OORTSF and to convert the application class interfaces to the task interfaces required by OORTSF. Then, the users need only specialize the virtual functions CTaskInit() and CTaskExec() to provide the application object initialization and functionality.

A task-table object, instantiated from one of the C*TaskTable classes in Figure 16.3 (for example, CCyclicTaskTable), is used to collect the application task objects. The collection operation is done via the TaskRegister( ) function in the task-table object (not shown in Figure 16.3). A scheduler object is an instance of one of the three algorithm-specific scheduler classes, CCYScheduler, CRMScheduler, and CEDFScheduler. All three of these classes are derived from CSchedulerBase. For a specific application, the application developer can choose a related scheduling method, which works like the Roles Played pattern [Coad 1992]; however, only one role will apply to a specific application. The structure of the CSchedulerBase class hierarchy is also similar to a Strategy pattern [Gamma 1995]. In a Strategy pattern, Strategy (Compositor) is used to define a common interface for the supporting algorithms; therefore, our CSchedulerBase is a Strategy. Similarly, a ConcreteStrategy represents the implementation of a specific algorithm derived from the Strategy interface; therefore, the three specific scheduler classes are ConcreteStrategies. To reduce memory size at runtime, only one selected scheduler code will be instantiated and be included in the final target code image.

Then, the OORTSF framework can be continued as follows: Start the schedulability check phase, and perform the application execution or code generation phase. In the schedulability check phase, all application tasks should have been registered into a corresponding task-table object via the TaskRegister( ) function before they can be analyzed by the ScheduleCheck( ) function in the scheduler object. If the application tasks pass through the schedulability check successfully, the tasks will be scheduled for normal system operations in the second phase. After the success of the schedulability check, the user has an option to generate a compact target system containing only the execution codes of application tasks and the framework kernel. This job is done via the TargetSys-Build( ) function in the scheduler object. Another way of entering the second phase is to use the Schedule( ) function in the scheduler object to start the application directly.

For the preceding operations, we have devised an interactive and user-friendly GUI for entering task parameters, generating schedulability check reports, and building application tasks [Kuan 1995]. When a typical realtime embedded system is built using OORTSF, the following basic set of collaborating objects are instantiated, as shown in Figure 16.4. A TimeBase object is used to count the system ticks and activate the Scheduler object. A Scheduler object is used to select one of the application tasks from the

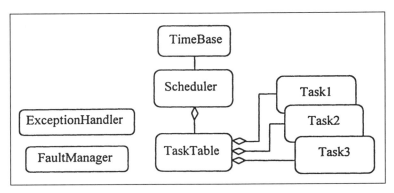

Figure 16.4 Typical collaborating objects in OORTSF.

TaskTable for execution under the control of a selected scheduling algorithm. As to the ExceptionHandler and FaultManager objects, they are supporting objects for exception handling during execution and system fault reporting and management, respectively.

16.4 Framework-Oriented Development of Application Systems

When using the OORTSF framework to develop realtime applications, the concept of layered software architecture [Krunchten 1995; Shaw 1996] is helpful. We can view OORTSF as a base layer that abstracts computation resources to the task level and provides an interface for the application task objects to reuse the realtime schedulability analysis and the scheduler design. Free from the implementation details of a realtime kernel and necessary scheduling algorithms, an OORTSF user can fully concentrate on domain-specific knowledge when developing a realtime application system.

From the description in *Section 16.3*, a five-step process is proposed for the framework-oriented development of realtime applications using OORTSF. The steps areas follows:

1. Identify and define the domain task objects.

2. Generate the realtime requirements for each of the domain task objects.

3. Use OORTSF to perform the schedulability check.

4. Use OORTSF to perform the target system generation.

5. Verify and validate the generated target system.

In the first step, users first have to identify and define the task objects needed in their domain applications. In the second step, the developers perform some analysis to figure out the realtime requirements of the application tasks under development. Each application task has its own realtime requirements (which include execution period and deadline, for example) attached to the abstracted OORTSF framework tasks via the instantiation of a CTask object using the parameters in the constructor of CTask. In the schedulability check phase, all application tasks first have to be registered to the corresponding task-table objects via the TaskRegister( ) function. Then, the schedulability check operation is performed by OORTSF. If a design passes through the schedulability check, the OORTSF framework will invoke the target system generation process to produce a compact target code by discarding unnecessary supporting codes. This code generation process controls the final target code generation to select the most proper source code file and object library. It also ensures that the scheduler code instantiated into the target code will contain only one best scheduler selected by the application designer. This is important in controlling the memory size of the final target image to fit in the often scarce memory resources in a realtime embedded system. In the final step, the target code is ready for the final step of system verification and validation.

An airborne vehicle flight-path control realtime application has been successfully implemented as a pilot project showing the reusability of OORTSF. This system consists of seven application domain objects: two external sensor data collection objects, GyroscopeSensorData and AccelerometerSensor Data; a velocity computation object,

VelocityCompute; a vehicle position computation object, PositionReconing; a vehicle direction and attitude computation object, DirectionAttitudeCompute, which takes the gyro sensor data to derive the flight direction and attitude of the vehicle; a vehicle flight-path control object, LaneAdjust; and a vehicle empennage control object, ActuatorData, which controls the empennage via actuator control interfaces. The task objects of this system are shown in Figure 16.5.

In this application, since the realtime requirements of the application tasks are assigned with an execution rate of 25 Hz, and all tasks are executed at 40-ms intervals, we first try to use a *cyclic executive* (via the CCYScheduler object) to schedule the application tasks. Using cyclic scheduling, the task execution sequence has to be predetermined, and accesses to the shared resources have to be sequential and, thus, automatically guaranteed [Klein 1994]. Though cyclic scheduling can suffer from the frame overrun situation, if we have enough CPU duty cycle reservation, the possibility of frame overrun will be very low. After performing ScheduleCheck( ) on the execution time required for each of the application tasks, we find that the total duty cycle utilization is under 50 percent. Therefore, we conclude that the schedulability of the application task set can be met accordingly. Since the cyclic scheduler has been chosen, the application tasks can then be integrated with the cyclic-scheduler-related framework codes to come up with a compact target system ready for realtime execution. The code generation of this target application can be further tuned according to the system-level verification and validation results.

Since an OORTSF user is supported with the reuses of both the high-level design concepts and the low-level scheduler code as well as various supporting mechanisms (for example, intertask synchronization and mutual exclusion), OORTSF is really a framework "that reuses both design and code" [Johnson 1997]. Using OORTSF and following the five-step design process, realtime system application developers need only focus on the application domain analysis, then hook the applications into the task abstraction of OORTSF and choose a proper scheduler provided by OORTSF. The small flight-path control example provides some sample realtime design tradeoff discussions that might also be helpful to other framework users.

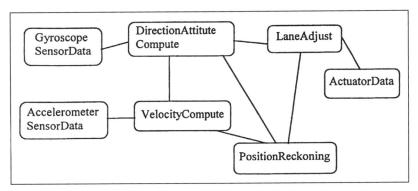

Figure 16.5 Task objects in an airborne vehicle flight-path control system.

Besides, different modeling views produce different abstractions. For example, the realtime object-oriented modeling (ROOM) method [Selic 1994] is another approach to realtime system modeling. In ROOM, application objects are modeled as Actors that have one or more communication Ports; behavior of an Actor is specified as a state transition diagram (ROOMchart) in which changes in behavior are caused by state transitions triggered by messages. The sending and receiving of messages between Ports provides a mechanism for Actor interaction. In OORTSF, Task and Scheduler abstractions can be explicitly specified. The behavior is associated with the application tasks. Using OORTSF abstractions, theoretically sound scheduling algorithms [Klein 1994] can be more intuitively integrated into a framework and applied to the application design and development.

16.5 Extending OORTSF

OORTSF is a realtime software framework designed with embedded systems as our target application domain. In OORTSF, we build schedulability check facilities for three well-established scheduling algorithms: cyclic executive, rate monotonic scheduling, and earliest deadline first. By adapting the OORTSF framework to an ORB of CORBA architecture, we have two ways of integrating OORTSF into a CORBA architecture: as an ORB client mode of operation, or as an ORB server mode of operation.

The first integration method is to use the OORTSF framework as an ORB client and integrate other ORB server tasks in a remote site as the application tasks required by the OORTSF framework. The timing overhead of the ORB services can be calculated and accumulated into the realtime scheduling task parameters of the OORTSF CTask objects, and then the schedulability check in the OORTSF framework can be done. After this schedulability verification, the OORTSF-developed application system can be executed in a CORBA-compliant environment. The second integration method is to let the OORTSF framework, which controls the scheduling of application tasks according to their realtime requirements, be adapted with an object adapter and act as an ORB server in response to the remote clients that need the service of this OORTSF framework.

In this way, the OORTSF framework can be extended to work in a distributed and heterogeneous CORBA-compliant execution environment. This is an example of integrating a framework into an architecture platform. We believe that this kind of interaction in high-level reuse technologies will extend the degree of software reuse.

In adapting cataloged design patterns [Gamma 1995] for realtime system design, we have found that realtime system design needs some patterns in its own right. For instance, the Proxy pattern defers the instantiation of objects until it is necessary. Yet, in a realtime situation we might prefer to instantiate the objects statically to reduce the time overhead required in instantiating objects during runtime. Hence, we believe that a dedicated set of design patterns has to be devised to help OORTSF framework users design their application objects and have these objects cooperate with the OORTSF framework efficiently. A set of realtime application system design patterns that can cooperate with the OORTSF framework to form a pattern language for realtime system development would be helpful for framework-oriented system developers.

16.6 Summary

This chapter presents the design of OORTSF for the development of embedded real-time application systems. Since OORTSF users can reuse both the high-level design concepts and the low-level code generated to construct the underlying realtime mechanisms, they have to focus only on the application domain analysis instead of on the implementation of scheduling methods and other supporting mechanisms.

In describing the instantiation of OORTSF collaborating objects, we tried to use some well-established design patterns. This chapter presents these discussions on documenting the framework, which will be helpful to framework users in capturing the design concepts and reusability of OORTSF. Furthermore, this chapter exploits the implementation of a real-time airborne vehicle flight-path control system as an example for the framework-oriented application system development using OORTSF. A categorization of three high-level reuse techniques—design patterns, frameworks, and software architectures—is provided to enlighten the relationships among these high-level reuse techniques and to establish a hierarchical view in the use of OORTSF as a framework-oriented application system development tool.

Last, this chapter discusses the extension of our OORTSF framework to operate in a distributed architecture platform such as CORBA, and finds that realtime system design needs design patterns in its own right. Our future work will propose a set of realtime application system design patterns that can cooperate with OORTSF to form a pattern language for the framework-oriented development of realtime application systems.

16.7 References

[Adler 1995] Adler, R.M. Emerging standards for component software. *IEEE Computer*, 28(3), March 1995: 68–77.

[Coad 1992] Coad, P. Object-oriented patterns. *Communications of the ACM*, 35(9), September 1992: 152–159.

[Gamma 1995] Gamma, E., R. Helm, R. Johnson, and J. Vlissides. *Design Patterns: Elements of Reusable Object-Oriented Software*. Reading, MA: Addison-Wesley, 1995.

[Garlan 1995] Garlan, D. Research directions in software architecture. *ACM Computing Surveys*, 27(2), June 1995: 257–261.

[Gibbs 1994] Gibbs, S.J., and D.C. Tsichritzis. *Multimedia Programming: Objects, Environments and Frameworks*. Reading, MA: Addison-Wesley, 1994.

[Johnson 1992] Johnson, R.E. Documenting frameworks using patterns. *Proceedings of the OOPSLA 1992 Conference on Object-Oriented Programming Systems, Languages, and Applications*, Vancouver, BC, October 1992. New York: ACM Press, 1992: 63–76.

[Johnson 1997] Johnson, R.E. Frameworks = (components + patterns). *Communications of the ACM*, Theme Issue on Object-Oriented Application Frameworks, M.E. Fayad and D. Schmidt, editors, 40(10), October 1997: 39–42.

[Klein 1994] Klein, M.H., J.P. Lehoczky, and R. Rajkumar. Rate-monotonic analysis for real-time industrial computing. *IEEE Computer*, 27(1), January 1994: 24–33.

[Krunchten 1995] Krunchten, P.B. The 4+1 view model of architecture. *IEEE Software*, 12(6), November 1995: 42–50.

[Kuan 1995] Kuan, T.Y., W.B. See, and S.J. Chen. An object-oriented real-time framework and development environment. Position paper for the OOPSLA 1995 Workshop 18, Austin, TX, 16 October 1995.

[Myers 1995] Myers, W. Taligent's CommonPoint: The promise of objects. *IEEE Computer*, 28(3), March 1995: 78–83.

[Perry 1992] Perry, D.E., and A. L. Wolf. Foundations for the study of software architecture. *ACM SIGSOFT Software Engineering Notes*, 17(4), October 1992: 40–52.

[Pree 1994] Pree, W. *Design Patterns for Object-Oriented Software Development*. Reading, MA: Addison-Wesley, 1994.

[Rumbaugh 1991] Rumbaugh, J., M. Blaha, W. Premerlani, F. Eddy, and W. Lorensen. *Object-Oriented Modeling and Design*. Englewood Cliffs, NJ: Prentice-Hall, 1991.

[Selic 1994] Selic, B., G. Gullekson, and P. Ward. *Real-Time Object-Oriented Modeling*. New York: John Wiley & Sons, 1994.

[Shaw 1995] Shaw, M. Comparing architectural design styles. *IEEE Software*, 12(6), November 1995: 27–41.

[Shaw 1996] Shaw, M., and D. Garlan. *Software Architecture: Perspectives on an Emerging Discipline*. Englewood Cliffs, NJ: Prentice Hall, 1996.

[Silberchatz 1994] Silberchatz, A., and P.B. Galvin. *Operating System Concepts,* 4th ed. Reading, MA: Addison-Wesley, 1994.

[van der Linden 1995] van der Linden and Jurgen K. Muller. Creating architectures with building blocks. *IEEE Software*, 12(6), November 1995: 51–60.

CHAPTER 17

JAWS: A Framework for High-Performance Web Servers

During the past several years, the volume of traffic on the World Wide Web has grown dramatically. Traffic increases are due largely to the proliferation of inexpensive and ubiquitous web browsers such as NCSA Mosaic, Netscape Navigator, and Internet Explorer. Likewise, web protocols and browsers are increasingly applied to specialized computationally expensive tasks, such as image-processing servers used by Siemens [Hu 1997] and Kodak [Pyarali 1996] and database search engines such as AltaVista and Lexis-Nexis.

To keep pace with increasing demand, it is essential to develop high-performance web servers. However, developers face a remarkably rich set of design strategies when configuring and optimizing web servers. For instance, developers must select from among a wide range of concurrency models (such as Thread-per-Request versus Thread Pool), dispatching models (such as synchronous versus asynchronous dispatching), file-caching models (such as LRU versus LFU), and protocol processing models (such as HTTP/1.0 versus HTTP/1.1). No single configuration is optimal for all hardware/software platforms and client workloads [Hu 1997, 1998].

The existence of all these alternative strategies ensures that web servers can be tailored to their users' needs. However, navigating through many design and optimization strategies is tedious and errorprone. Without guidance on which design and optimization strategies to apply, developers face the Herculean task of engineering web servers from the ground up, resulting in ad hoc solutions. Such systems are often hard to maintain, customize, and tune since much of the engineering effort is spent just trying to get the system operational.

We frequently refer to the terms *object-oriented (OO) class library*, *framework*, *pattern*, and *component* in this chapter. These terms refer to tools that are used to build reusable software systems. An *OO class library* is a collection of software object implementations that provide reusable functionality to users calling object methods. A *framework* is a reusable, semicomplete application that can be specialized to produce custom applications [Johnson 1997]. A *pattern* represents a recurring solution to a software development problem within a particular context [Gamma 1995]. A *component* refers to a *reifiable* (or abstractable) object with a well-defined interface. Both OO class libraries and frameworks are collections of components that are reified by instantiation and specialization. A pattern component is reified through codification.

This chapter illustrates how to produce flexible and efficient web servers using *OO application frameworks* and *design patterns*. Patterns and frameworks can be applied synergistically to improve the efficiency and flexibility of web servers. Patterns capture abstract designs and software architectures of high-performance and adaptive web servers in a systematic and comprehensible format. Frameworks capture the concrete designs, algorithms, and implementations of web servers in a particular programming language, such as C++ or Java. In contrast, OO class libraries provide the raw materials necessary to build applications, but provide little guidance as to how to put the pieces together.

This chapter focuses on the patterns and framework components used to develop a high-performance web server called *JAWS* [Hu 1997, 1998]. JAWS is both a web server and a framework from which other types of servers can be built. The JAWS framework itself was developed using the ACE framework [Schmidt 1994b, 1997b]. The ACE framework reifies key patterns [Gamma 1995] in the domain of communication software. The framework and patterns in JAWS and ACE are representative of solutions that have been applied successfully to communication systems ranging from telecommunication system management [Schmidt 1996a] to enterprise medical imaging [Pyarali 1996] and realtime avionics [Harrison 1997b].

The remainder of this chapter is organized as follows: *Section 17.1* presents an overview of patterns and frameworks and motivates the need for the style of communication software framework provided by JAWS; *Section 17.2* illustrates how patterns and components can be applied to develop high-performance web servers; *Section 17.3* compares the performance of JAWS with other high-performance web servers over high-speed ATM networks; and *Section 17.4* presents concluding remarks.

17.1 Applying Patterns and Frameworks to Web Servers

There is increasing demand for high-performance web servers that can provide services and content to the growing number of Internet and intranet users. Developers of web servers strive to build fast, scalable, and configurable systems. This task can be difficult, however, if care is not taken to avoid common traps and pitfalls, which include tedious and errorprone low-level programming details, lack of portability, and the wide range of design alternatives. This section presents a road map to these hazards. We then describe how patterns and frameworks can be applied to avoid these hazards by allowing developers to leverage both design and code reuse.

17.1.1 Common Pitfalls of Developing Web Server Software

Developers of web servers confront recurring challenges that are largely independent of their specific application requirements. For instance, like other communication software, web servers must perform various tasks related to connection establishment, service initialization, event demultiplexing, event handler dispatching, interprocess communication, memory management and file caching, static and dynamic component configuration, concurrency, synchronization, and persistence. In most web servers, these tasks are implemented in an ad hoc manner using low-level native operating system (OS) application programming interfaces (APIs), such as Win32 or POSIX, which are written in C.

Unfortunately, native OS APIs are not an effective way to develop web servers or other types of communication middleware and applications [Schmidt 1997c]. The following are common pitfalls associated with the use of native OS APIs:

Excessive low-level details. Building web servers with native OS APIs requires developers to have intimate knowledge of low-level OS details. Developers must carefully track which error codes are returned by each system call and handle these OS-specific problems in the server. Such details divert attention from the broader, more strategic issues, such as semantics and program structure. For example, UNIX developers who use the wait system call must distinguish between return errors due to no child processes being present and errors from signal interrupts. In the latter case, the wait must be reissued.

Continuous rediscovery and reinvention of incompatible higher-level programming abstractions. A common remedy for the excessive level of detail with OS APIs is to define higher-level programming abstractions. For instance, many web servers create a file cache to avoid accessing the filesystem for each client request. However, these types of abstractions are often rediscovered and reinvented independently by each developer or project. This ad hoc software process hampers productivity and creates incompatible components that are not readily reusable within and across projects in large software organizations.

High potential for errors. Programming to low-level OS APIs is tedious and error-prone due to their lack of type safety. For example, most web servers are programmed with the Socket API [McKusick 1996]. However, endpoints of communication in the Socket API are represented as untyped handles. This increases the potential for subtle programming mistakes and runtime errors.

Lack of portability. Low-level OS APIs are notoriously nonportable, even across releases of the same OS. For instance, implementations of the Socket API on Win32 platforms (WinSock) are subtly different than on UNIX platforms. Moreover, even WinSock implementations on different versions of Windows NT possess incompatible timing-related bugs that cause sporadic failures when performing non-blocking connections.

Steep learning curve. Due to the excessive level of detail, the effort required to master OS-level APIs can be very high. For instance, it is hard to learn how to program with POSIX asynchronous I/O [POS 1995] correctly. It is even harder to learn how to write a *portable* application using asynchronous I/O mechanisms since they differ widely across OS platforms.

Inability to handle increasing complexity. OS APIs define basic interfaces to mechanisms such as process and thread management, interprocess communication, filesystems, and memory management. However, these basic interfaces do not scale up gracefully as applications grow in size and complexity. For instance, a typical UNIX process allows a backlog of only ~7 pending connections [Stevens 1997]. This number is inadequate for heavily accessed web servers that must handle large numbers of simultaneous clients.

17.1.2 Overcoming Web Server Pitfalls with Patterns and Frameworks

Software reuse is a widely touted method of reducing development effort. Reuse leverages the domain knowledge and prior effort of experienced developers. When applied effectively, reuse can avoid recreating and revalidating common solutions to recurring application requirements and software design challenges.

Java's java.lang.net and RogueWave Net.h++ are two common examples of applying reusable OO class libraries to communication software. Although class libraries effectively support component reuse in the small, their scope is overly constrained. In particular, class libraries do not capture the canonical control flow and collaboration among families of related software components. Thus, developers who apply class-library-based reuse often reinvent and reimplement the overall software architecture for each new application.

A more powerful way to overcome the pitfalls described here is to identify the *patterns* that underlie proven web servers and reify these patterns in *object-oriented application frameworks*. Patterns and frameworks help alleviate the continual rediscovery and reinvention of key web server concepts and components by capturing solutions to common software development problems [Gamma 1995].

The Benefits of Patterns for Web Servers

Patterns document the structure and participants in common web server micro-architectures. For instance, the Reactor [Schmidt 1995a] and Active Object patterns [Lavender 1996] are used widely as web server dispatching and concurrency strategies, respectively. These patterns are generalizations of object structures that have proven useful in building flexible and efficient web servers.

Traditionally, the patterns used to develop web servers have either been locked in the heads of the expert developers or buried deep within the source code. Allowing this valuable information to reside only in these locations is risky and expensive, however.

For instance, the insights of experienced web server designers will be lost over time if they are not documented. Likewise, substantial effort may be necessary to reverse-engineer patterns from existing source code. Therefore, capturing and documenting web server patterns explicitly is essential to preserve design information for developers who enhance and maintain existing software. Moreover, knowledge of domain-specific patterns helps guide the design decisions of developers who are building new servers in other domains, such as medical imaging or telecommunications.

The Benefits of Frameworks for Web servers

Knowledge of patterns helps to reduce development effort and maintenance costs. However, reuse of patterns alone is not sufficient to create flexible and efficient web server software. While patterns enable reuse of abstract design and architecture knowledge, abstractions documented as patterns do not yield reusable code directly [Schmidt 1995b]. Therefore, it is essential to augment the study of patterns with the creation and use of application frameworks. Frameworks help developers avoid costly reinvention of standard web server components by implementing common design patterns and factoring out common implementation roles.

17.1.3 Relationship between Frameworks, Patterns, and Other Reuse Techniques

Frameworks provide reusable software components for applications by integrating sets of classes and defining standard ways that instances of these classes collaborate [Johnson 1997]. In general, the components are not self-contained since they usually depend upon functionality provided by other components within the framework. However, the collection of these components forms a partial implementation, that is, an application skeleton. This skeleton can be customized by inheriting and instantiating from reusable components in the framework.

The scope of reuse in a web server framework can be significantly larger than using traditional function libraries or OO class libraries of components. In particular, the JAWS framework described in *Section 17.2* is tailored for a wide range of web server tasks. These tasks include service initialization, error handling, flow control, event processing, file caching, concurrency control, and prototype pipelining. It is important to recognize that these also can be reused in many other types of communication software.

In general, frameworks and patterns enhance reuse techniques based on class libraries of components in the following ways:

> **Frameworks define semicomplete applications that embody domain-specific object structures and functionality [Fayad-Schmidt 1997].** Class libraries provide a relatively small granularity of reuse. For instance, the classes in Figure 17.1 are typically low-level, relatively independent, and general-purpose components such as strings, complex numbers, arrays, and bit sets.

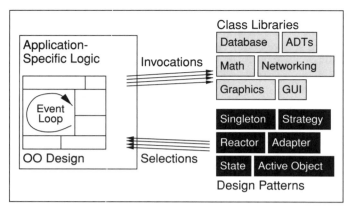

Figure 17.1   Class library component architecture.

In contrast, components in a framework collaborate to provide a customizable architectural skeleton for a family of related applications. Complete applications can be composed by inheriting from and/or instantiating framework components. As shown in Figure 17.2, frameworks reduce the amount of application-specific code since much of the domain-specific processing is factored into generic framework components.

Frameworks are active and exhibit inversion of control at runtime. Class library components generally behave *passively*. In particular, class library components often perform their processing by borrowing the thread(s) of control from application objects that are self-directed. Because application objects are self-directed, application developers are largely responsible for deciding how to combine the

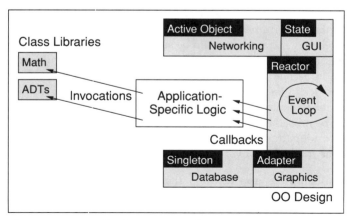

Figure 17.2   Application framework component architecture.

components and classes to form a complete system. For instance, the code to manage an event loop and determine the flow of control among reusable and application-specific components is generally rewritten for each new application.

The typical structure and dynamics of applications built with class libraries and components is illustrated in Figure 17.1. This figure also illustrates how design patterns can help guide the design, implementation, and use of class library components. Note that while class libraries provide tools to solve particular tasks (for example, establishing a network connection), they do not offer explicit guidance to system designers. In particular, software developers are solely responsible for identifying and applying patterns in designing their applications.

In contrast to class libraries, components in a framework are more *active*. In particular, they manage the canonical flow of control within an application via event dispatching patterns such as Reactor [Schmidt 1995a] and Observer [Gamma 1995]. The callback-driven runtime architecture of a framework is shown in Figure 17.2.

Figure 17.2 illustrates a key characteristic of a framework: its *inversion of control* at runtime. This design enables the canonical application processing steps to be customized by event-handler objects that are invoked via the framework's reactive dispatching mechanism [Schmidt 1995a]. When events occur, the framework's dispatcher reacts by invoking hook methods on preregistered handler objects, which perform application-specific processing on the events.

Inversion of control allows the framework, rather than each application, to determine which set of application-specific methods to invoke in response to external events (such as HTTP connections and data arriving on sockets). As a result, the framework reifies an integrated set of patterns, which are preapplied into collaborating components. This design paradigm reduces the burden for software developers.

In practice, frameworks, class libraries, and components are complementary technologies. Frameworks often utilize class libraries and components internally to simplify development of the framework. For instance, portions of the JAWS framework use the string and vector containers provided by the C++ Standard Template Library [Stepanoy 1994] to manage connection maps and other search structures. In addition, application-specific callbacks invoked by framework event handlers frequently use class library components to perform basic tasks such as time and date processing, file management, and numerical analysis.

To illustrate how OO patterns and frameworks have been applied successfully to develop flexible and efficient communication software, the remainder of this chapter examines the structure, use, and performance of the JAWS framework.

17.2 The JAWS Adaptive Web Server

The benefits of applying frameworks and patterns to communication software are best illustrated by example. This section describes the structure and functionality of JAWS. JAWS is a high-performance and adaptive web server that implements HTTP. In addition, it is a platform-independent application framework from which other types of communication servers can be built.

17.2.1 Overview of the JAWS Framework

Figure 17.3 illustrates the major structural components and design patterns that comprise the JAWS Adaptive Web Server (JAWS) framework. JAWS is designed to allow various web server strategies to be customized in response to environmental factors. These factors include *static* factors, such as support for kernel-level threading and/or asynchronous I/O in the OS, and the number of available CPUs, as well as *dynamic* factors, such as Web traffic patterns and workload characteristics.

JAWS is structured as a *framework of frameworks*. The overall JAWS framework contains the following components and frameworks: *Event Dispatcher*, *Concurrency Strategy*, *I/O Strategy*, *Protocol Pipeline*, *Protocol Handlers*, and *Cached Virtual Filesystem*. Each framework is structured as a set of collaborating objects implemented using components in ACE [Schmidt 1994a]. The collaborations among JAWS components and frameworks are guided by a family of patterns, which are listed along the borders in Figure 17.3. An outline of the key frameworks, components, and patterns in JAWS follows. *Section 17.2.2* presents a more detailed description of how these patterns have been applied to JAWS's design.

> **Event Dispatcher.** This component is responsible for coordinating JAWS's Concurrency Strategy with its I/O Strategy. The passive establishment of connections with web clients follows the *Acceptor* pattern [Schmidt 1997a]. New incoming requests are serviced by a concurrency strategy. As events are processed, they are dispatched to the Protocol Handler, which is parameterized by an I/O strategy.

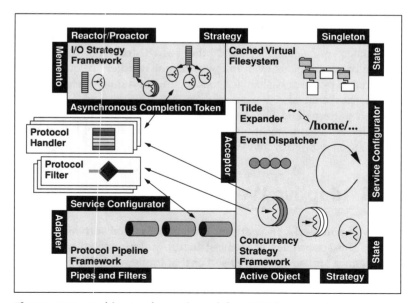

Figure 17.3   Architectural overview of the JAWS framework.

The ability to dynamically bind to a particular concurrency strategy and I/O strategy from a range of alternatives follows the *Strategy* pattern [Gamma 1995].

Concurrency Strategy. This framework implements concurrency mechanisms (such as Single Threaded, Thread-per-Request, or Thread Pool) that can be selected adaptively at runtime using the *State* pattern [Gamma 1995] or predetermined at initialization time. The *Service Configurator* pattern [Jain 1997b] is used to configure a particular concurrency strategy into a web server at runtime. When concurrency involves multiple threads, the strategy creates protocol handlers that follow the *Active Object* pattern [Lavender 1996].

I/O Strategy. This framework implements various I/O mechanisms, such as asynchronous, synchronous, and reactive I/O. Multiple I/O mechanisms can be used simultaneously. Asynchronous I/O is implemented via the *Proactor* [Harrison 1997a] and *Asynchronous Completion Token* patterns [Pyarali 1997]. Reactive I/O is accomplished through the *Reactor* pattern [Schmidt 1995a]. The framework utilizes the *Memento* pattern [Gamma 1995] to capture and externalize the state of a request so that it can be restored at a later time.

Protocol Handler. This framework allows system developers to apply the JAWS framework to a variety of web system applications. A protocol handler is parameterized by a concurrency strategy and an I/O strategy. These strategies remain opaque to the protocol handler by following the Adapter pattern [Gamma 1995]. In JAWS, this component implements the parsing and handling of HTTP/1.0 request methods. The abstraction allows for other protocols, such as HTTP/1.1 and DICOM, to be incorporated easily into JAWS. To add a new protocol, developers simply write a new Protocol Handler implementation, which is then configured into the JAWS framework.

Protocol Pipeline. This framework allows filter operations to be incorporated easily with the data being processed by the Protocol Handler. This integration is achieved by employing the Adapter pattern. Pipelines follow the *Pipes and Filters* pattern [Buschmann 1996] for input processing. Pipeline components can be linked dynamically at runtime using the Service Configurator pattern.

Cached Virtual Filesystem. This component improves web server performance by reducing the overhead of filesystem accesses. Various caching strategies, such as LRU, LFU, Hinted, and Structured, can be selected via the Strategy pattern [Gamma 1995]. This allows different caching strategies to be profiled for effectiveness and enables optimal strategies to be configured statically or dynamically. The cache for each web server is instantiated using the *Singleton* pattern [Gamma 1995].

Tilde Expander. This component is another cache component that uses a perfect hashtable [Schmidt 1990] that maps abbreviated user login names (for example, ~schmidt) to user home directories (for example, /home/cs/faculty/schmidt). When personal Web pages are stored in user home directories, and user directories do not reside in one common root, this component substantially reduces the disk I/O overhead required to access a system user information file, such as /etc/passwd. By virtue of the Service Configurator pattern, the Tilde Expander can be unlinked and relinked dynamically into the server—for example, when a new user is added to the system.

17.2.2 Overview of the Design Patterns in JAWS

The JAWS architecture diagram in Figure 17.3 illustrates *how* JAWS is structured, but not *why* it is structured using these particular components. To understand why JAWS contains frameworks and components such as Concurrency Strategy, I/O Strategy, Protocol Handler, and Event Dispatcher requires deeper knowledge of the design patterns underlying the domain of communication software in general and web servers in particular. Figure 17.4 illustrates the *strategic* and *tactical* patterns related to JAWS. These patterns are summarized in the following section.

Strategic Patterns

The following patterns are *strategic* to the overall software architecture of web servers. Their use widely impacts the level of interactions of a large number of components in the system. These patterns are also used to guide the architecture of many other types of communication software.

Acceptor. This pattern decouples passive connection establishment from the service performed once the connection is established [Schmidt 1997a]. JAWS uses the Acceptor pattern to adaptively change its concurrency and I/O strategies independently from its connection management strategy. Figure 17.5 illustrates the structure of the Acceptor pattern in the context of JAWS. The Acceptor is a factory [Gamma 1995]. It creates, accepts, and activates a new Protocol Handler whenever an Event Dispatcher notifies it that a connection has arrived from a client.

Reactor. This pattern decouples the synchronous event demultiplexing and event-handler notification dispatching logic of server applications from the services performed in response to events [Schmidt 1995a]. JAWS uses the Reactor pattern to process multiple synchronous events from multiple sources of events, *without* polling all event sources or blocking indefinitely on any single source of events. Figure 17.6 illustrates the structure of the Reactor pattern in the context of JAWS.

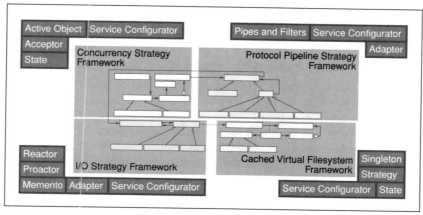

Figure 17.4   Design patterns used in the JAWS framework.

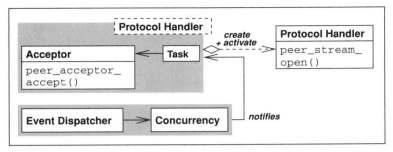

Figure 17.5 Structure of the Acceptor pattern in JAWS.

JAWS *Reactive IO Handler* objects register themselves with the *Initiation Dispatcher* for events (that is, input and output through connections established by HTTP requests). The Initiation Dispatcher invokes the handle_input notification hook method of these Reactive IO Handler objects when their associated events occur. The Reactor pattern is used by the Single-Threaded web server concurrency model presented in *Section 17.2.2*.

Proactor. This pattern decouples the asynchronous event demultiplexing and event-handler completion dispatching logic of server applications from the services performed in response to events [Harrison 1997a]. JAWS uses the Proactor pattern to perform server-specific processing, such as parsing the headers of a request, while processing other I/O events asynchronously. Figure 17.7 illustrates the structure of the Proactor pattern in the context of JAWS. JAWS *Proactive IO Handler* objects register themselves with the Completion Dispatcher for events (that is, receipt and delivery of files through connections established by HTTP requests).

The primary difference between the Reactor and Proactor patterns is that the Proactive IO Handler defines *completion* hooks, whereas the Reactive IO Handler defines *initiation* hooks. Therefore, when asynchronously invoked operations such as recv_file or send_file complete, the Completion Dispatcher invokes the appro-

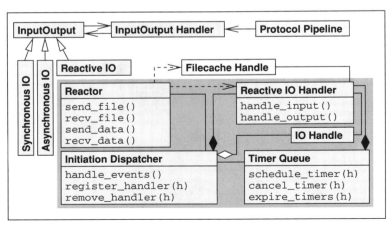

Figure 17.6 Structure of the Reactor pattern in JAWS.

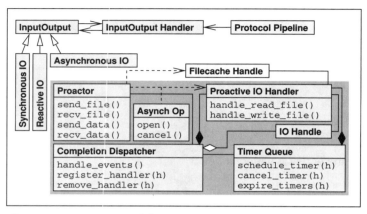

Figure 17.7 Structure of the Proactor pattern in JAWS.

priate completion hook method of these Proactive IO Handler objects. The Proactor pattern is used by the asynchronous variant of the Thread Pool in *Section 17.2.2*.

Active Object. This pattern decouples method invocation from method execution, allowing methods to run concurrently [Lavender 1996]. JAWS uses the Active Object pattern to execute client requests concurrently in separate threads of control. Figure 17.8 illustrates the structure of the Active Object pattern in the context of JAWS.

The Protocol Handler issues requests to the Scheduler, which transforms the request method (such as an HTTP request) into *Method Objects* that are stored on an *Activation Queue*. The Scheduler, which runs in a separate thread from the client, dequeues these Method Objects and transforms them back into method

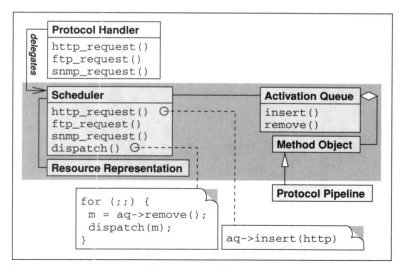

Figure 17.8 Structure of the Active Object pattern in JAWS.

calls to perform the specified protocol. The Active Object pattern is used in the Thread-per-Request, Thread Pool, and Thread-per-Session concurrency models described in *Section 17.2.2.*

Service Configurator. This pattern decouples the implementation of individual components in a system from the *time* when they are configured into the system. JAWS uses the Service Configurator pattern to optimize, control, and reconfigure the behavior of web server strategies dynamically at installation time or during runtime [Jain 1997a]. Figure 17.9 illustrates the structure of the Service Configurator pattern in the context of the *Protocol Pipeline, Filter,* and *Cache Strategy* components.

The figure depicts how the Service Configurator can dynamically manage *dynamically linked libraries* (DLLs). This allows the framework to configure different implementations of server strategies dynamically at runtime. The *Filter Repository* and *Cache Strategy Repository* inherit functionality from the *Service Repository.* Likewise, the strategy implementations (such as *Parse Request* and *LRU Strategy*) borrow interfaces from the *Service* component of the pattern so that they can be managed dynamically by the repository.

Tactical Patterns

Web servers also utilize many *tactical* patterns, which are more ubiquitous and domain-independent than the strategic patterns just described. The following tactical patterns are used in JAWS:

Strategy. This pattern defines a family of algorithms, encapsulates each one, and makes them interchangeable [Gamma 1995]. JAWS uses this pattern to selectively

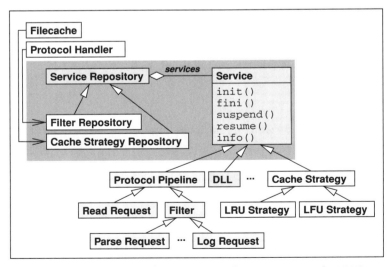

Figure 17.9   Structure of the Service Configurator pattern in JAWS.

configure different cache replacement strategies without affecting the core software architecture of the web server.

Adapter. This pattern transforms a nonconforming interface into one that can be used by a client [Gamma 1995]. JAWS uses this pattern in its I/O Strategy framework to uniformly encapsulate the operations of synchronous, asynchronous, and reactive I/O operations.

State. This pattern defines a composite object whose behavior depends on its state [Gamma 1995]. The Event Dispatcher component in JAWS uses the State pattern to seamlessly support various concurrency strategies and both synchronous and asynchronous I/O.

Singleton. This pattern ensures that a class has only one instance and provides a global point of access to it [Gamma 1995]. JAWS uses a Singleton to ensure that only one copy of its Cached Virtual Filesystem exists in a web server process.

In contrast to the strategic patterns described earlier, tactical patterns have a relatively localized impact on a software design. For instance, Singleton is a tactical pattern that is used to consolidate certain globally accessible resources in JAWS. Although this pattern is domain independent and thus widely applicable, the problem it addresses does not impact JAWS's software architecture as pervasively as strategic patterns such as Active Object and Reactor. A thorough understanding of tactical patterns is essential, however, to implement highly flexible software that is resilient to changes in application requirements and platform characteristics.

The remainder of this section discusses the structure of JAWS's frameworks for concurrency, I/O, protocol pipelining, and file caching. For each framework, we describe the key design challenges and outline the range of alternative solution strategies. Then, we explain how each JAWS framework is structured to support the configuration of alternative strategy profiles.

17.2.3 Concurrency Strategies

Concurrency strategies impact the design and performance of a web system significantly. Concurrency design challenges, alternative solution strategies, and JAWS concurrency strategy framework are discussed in the following sections.

Design Challenges

Empirical studies [Hu 1998] of existing web servers, including Roxen, Apache, PHTTPD, Zeus, Netscape, and the Java web server, indicate that a large portion of non-I/O-related web server overhead arises from the web server's concurrency strategy. Key overheads include synchronization, thread and process creation, and context switching. Therefore, choosing an efficient concurrency strategy is crucial to achieving high performance.

Alternative Solution Strategies

Selecting the right concurrency strategy is nontrivial. The factors influencing the decision are both static and dynamic. *Static* factors can be determined a priori. These factors include hardware configuration (such as number of processors, amount of memory, and speed of network connection), OS platform (such as availability of threads and asynchronous I/O), and web server use case (such as database interfacing, image server, or HTML server). *Dynamic* factors are those detectable and measurable conditions that occur during the execution of the system. These factors include machine load, number of simultaneous requests, dynamic memory use, and server workload.

Existing web servers use a wide range of concurrency strategies, reflecting the numerous factors involved. These strategies include single-threaded concurrency (such as Roxen), process-based concurrency (such as Apache and Zeus), and multithreaded concurrency (such as Netscape Enterprise, PHTTPD, and JAWS). Each strategy offers benefits and drawbacks, which must be analyzed and evaluated in the context of both static and dynamic factors. These tradeoffs are summarized in the following sections.

Thread-per-Request

This model handles each request from a client in a separate thread of control. Thus, as each request arrives, a new thread is created to process the request. This design allows each thread to use well-understood synchronous I/O mechanisms to read and write the requested file. Figure 17.10 illustrates this model in the context of the JAWS framework. An Acceptor thread iterates waiting for a connection, creating a Protocol Handler, and spawning a new thread so that the handler can continue processing the connection.

The advantage of Thread-per-Request is its simplicity and its ability to exploit parallelism on multiprocessor platforms. Its chief drawback is lack of scalability—the number of running threads may grow without bound, exhausting available memory and CPU resources. Therefore, Thread-per-Request is adequate for lightly loaded servers with low latency. However, it may be unsuitable for servers that are accessed frequently to perform time-consuming tasks.

Thread-per-Session

A *session* is a series of requests that one client makes to a server. In Thread-per-Session, all of these requests are submitted through a connection between each client and a separate thread in the web server process. Therefore, this model amortizes both thread creation and connection establishment costs across multiple requests.

Thread-per-Session is less resource intensive than Thread-per-Request since it does not spawn a separate thread for each request. However, it is still vulnerable to

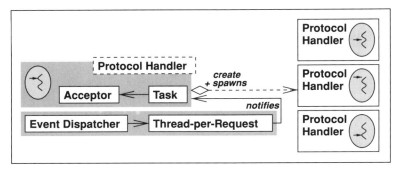

Figure 17.10   Thread-per-Request strategy in JAWS.

unbounded resource consumption as the number of clients grows. Also, the use of Thread-per-Session requires both the client and the server to support the concept of reusing an established connection with multiple requests. For example, if both the web client and the web server are HTTP/1.1 compliant, Thread-per-Session can be used between them. However, if either the client or the server supports only HTTP/1.0, then Thread-per-Session degrades to Thread-per-Request [Berners-Lee 1996; Fielding 1997].

Thread Pool

In this model, a group of threads is prespawned during web server initialization. Each thread from the pool retrieves a task from a job queue. While the thread is processing the job, it is removed from the pool. Upon finishing the task, the thread is returned to the pool. As illustrated in Figure 17.11, the job being retrieved is completion of the Acceptor. When it completes, the thread creates a Protocol Handler and lends its thread of control so the handler can process the connection.

Thread Pool generally has lower overhead than Thread-per-Request since the cost of thread creation is amortized through prespawning. Moreover, the number of resources the pool can consume is bounded since the pool size is fixed. However, if the pool is too small, it can become depleted. This causes new incoming requests to be dropped or to incur high latency. Furthermore, if the pool is too large, resource consumption may be as large as using Thread-per-Request.

Single-Threaded

In this model, all connections and requests are handled by the same thread of control. Simple implementations of Single-Threaded servers process requests iteratively. This is usually inadequate for high-volume production servers since subsequent requests are queued until they reach the head of the queue, creating unacceptable delays.

More sophisticated Single-Threaded implementations attempt to process multiple requests concurrently using asynchronous or reactive I/O (described in *Section 17.2.4*). Single-threaded concurrency strategies can perform better than multithreaded solutions on uniprocessor machines that support asynchronous I/O [Hu 1997]. Since JAWS's I/O framework is orthogonal to its concurrency framework, we consider the Single-Threaded concurrency strategy as a special case of the Thread Pool where the pool size is 1.

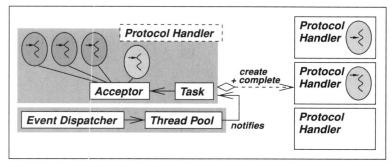

Figure 17.11   Thread Pool strategy in JAWS.

Experiments in [Hu 1997, 1998] demonstrate that the choice of concurrency and event-dispatching strategies significantly affect the performance of web servers that experience varying load conditions. In particular, no single server strategy provides optimal performance for all cases. Thus, a web server framework should provide at least two degrees of freedom:

Static adaptivity. The framework should allow web server developers to select a concurrency strategy that best meets the static requirements of the system. For example, a multiprocessor machine may be more suited to the Thread Pool strategy than a uniprocessor machine.

Dynamic adaptivity. The framework should allow its concurrency strategy to adapt dynamically to current server conditions to achieve optimal performance in the presence of dynamic server load conditions. For instance, to accommodate unanticipated load usage, it may be necessary to increase the number of available threads in the thread pool dynamically.

JAWS Concurrency Strategy Framework

As previously discussed, no single concurrency strategy performs optimally under all conditions. However, not all platforms can make effective use of all available concurrency strategies. To address these issues, the JAWS Concurrency Strategy framework supports both static and dynamic adaptivity with respect to its concurrency and event-dispatching strategies.

Figure 17.12 illustrates the OO design of JAWS's Concurrency Strategy framework. The Event Dispatcher and Concurrency objects interact according to the State pattern. As illustrated, the server can be changed to either Thread-per-Connection or Thread Pool between successive calls to server → dispatch(), allowing different concurrency mechanisms to take effect. The *Thread-per-Connection* strategy is an abstraction over

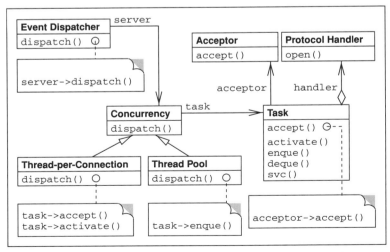

Figure 17.12   Structure of the Concurrency Strategy framework.

both the Thread-per-Request and Thread-per-Session strategies previously discussed. Each concurrency mechanism uses a *Task*. Depending on the choice of concurrency, a Task may represent a single Active Object or a collection of Active Objects. The behavior of the Concurrency object follows the Acceptor pattern. This architecture enables the server developer to integrate alternate concurrency strategies. With the aid of a strategy profile, the server can choose different strategies dynamically at runtime to achieve optimal performance.

17.2.4 I/O Strategies

I/O strategy is an important component of JAWS. I/O design challenges, alternative solution strategies, and JAWS I/O strategy framework are discussed in the following sections.

Design Challenges

Another key challenge for web server developers is to devise efficient data retrieval and delivery strategies, collectively referred to as *I/O*. The issues surrounding efficient I/O can be quite challenging. Often, a system developer must resolve how to arrange multiple I/O operations to utilize concurrency available from the hardware/software platform. For instance, a high-performance web server should simultaneously transfer files to and from the network, while concurrently parsing newly obtained incoming requests from other clients.

Certain types of I/O operations have different requirements than others. For example, a web transaction involving monetary fund transfer may need to run *synchronously*, that is, to complete before the user can continue. Conversely, web accesses to static information, such as CGI-based search engine queries, may run *asynchronously* since they can be canceled at any point. Resolving these various requirements yields different strategies for performing I/O.

Alternative Solution Strategies

As previously indicated, various factors influence which I/O strategy to choose. Web servers can be designed to use several different I/O strategies, including *synchronous*, *reactive*, and *asynchronous* I/O. The relative benefits of using these strategies are discussed in the following sections.

The Synchronous I/O Strategy

Synchronous I/O describes the model of I/O interaction between a web server process and the kernel. In this model, the kernel does not return the thread of control to the server until the requested I/O operation either completes, completes partially, or fails. [Hu 1997] shows that synchronous I/O usually performs well for small file transfers on Windows NT over high-speed ATM networks.

Synchronous I/O is well known to UNIX server programmers and is arguably the easiest strategy to use. However, there are disadvantages to this model. First, if combined with a Single-Threaded concurrency strategy, it is not possible to perform multiple synchronous I/O operations simultaneously. Second, when using multiple threads (or processes), it is still possible for an I/O request to block indefinitely. Thus, finite resources (such as socket handles or file descriptors) may become exhausted, making the server unresponsive.

The Reactive I/O Strategy

Early versions of UNIX provided synchronous I/O exclusively. System V UNIX introduced nonblocking I/O to avoid indefinite blocking. However, nonblocking I/O requires the web server to poll the kernel to discover if any input is available [McKusick 1996]. Reactive I/O alleviates the blocking problems of synchronous I/O without resorting to polling. In this model, a web server uses an OS event demultiplexing system call (such as select in UNIX or WaitForMultipleObjects in Win32) to determine which socket handles can perform I/O. When the call returns, the server can perform I/O on the returned handles; that is, the server *reacts* to multiple events occurring on separate handles.

Reactive I/O is widely used by event-driven applications (such as X Windows) and has been codified as the Reactor design pattern [Schmidt 1995a]. Unless reactive I/O is carefully encapsulated, however, the technique is errorprone due to the complexity of managing multiple I/O handles. Moreover, reactive I/O may not make effective use of multiple CPUs.

The Asynchronous I/O Strategy

Asynchronous I/O simplifies the demultiplexing of multiple events in one or more threads of control without blocking a web server. When a web server initiates an I/O operation, the kernel runs the operation asynchronously to completion while the server processes other requests. For instance, the TransmitFile operation in Windows NT can transfer an entire file from the server to the client asynchronously [Davis 1996].

The advantage of asynchronous I/O is that the web server need not block on I/O requests since they complete asynchronously. This allows the server to scale efficiently for operations with high I/O latency, such as large file transfers. The disadvantage of asynchronous I/O is that it is not available on many OS platforms (for example, UNIX). In addition, writing asynchronous programs can be more complicated than writing synchronous programs [Harrison 1997a; Pyarali 1997; Schmidt 1996b].

JAWS I/O Strategy Framework

Empirical studies in [Hu 1997] systematically subjected different server strategies to various load conditions. The results reveal that each I/O strategy behaves differently under different load conditions. Furthermore, no single I/O strategy performs optimally under all load conditions. The JAWS I/O Strategy framework addresses this issue by allowing the I/O strategy to adapt dynamically to runtime server conditions. Furthermore, if a new OS provides a custom I/O mechanism (such as asynchronous scatter/gather I/O) that can potentially provide better performance, the JAWS I/O Strategy framework can be easily adapted to use it.

Figure 17.13 illustrates the structure of the I/O Strategy framework provided by JAWS. *Perform Request* is a Filter that derives from Protocol Pipeline, which is explained

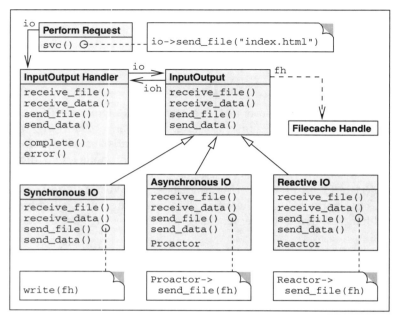

Figure 17.13   Structure of the I/O Strategy Framework.

in *Section 17.2.5*. In this example, Perform Request issues an I/O request to its *InputOutput Handler*. The InputOutput Handler delegates I/O requests made to it to the *InputOutput* object.

The JAWS framework provides *Synchronous IO, Asynchronous IO,* and *Reactive IO* component implementations derived from InputOutput. Each I/O strategy issues requests using the appropriate mechanism. For instance, the Synchronous IO component utilizes the traditional blocking read and write system calls; Asynchronous IO performs requests according to the Proactor pattern [Harrison 1997a]; and Reactive IO utilizes the Reactor pattern [Schmidt 1995a].

An InputOutput component is created with respect to the stream associated by the Acceptor from the Task component described in *Section 17.2.3*. File operations are performed with respect to a *Filecache Handle* component, described in *Section 17.2.6*. For example, a send_file operation sends the file represented by a Filecache Handle to the stream returned by the Acceptor.

17.2.5 Protocol Pipeline Strategies

Protocol pipeline design challenges, alternative solution strategies, and JAWS protocol pipeline framework are discussed in the following sections.

Design Challenges

Early web servers, such as the National Center for Supercomputer Applications's (NCSA) original httpd, performed very little file processing. They simply retrieved the requested file and transferred its contents to the requester. However, modern web servers perform data processing other than file retrieval. For instance, the HTTP/1.0 protocol can be used to determine various file characteristics, such as the file type (such as text, image, audio, or video), the file encoding and compression types, the file size, and its date of last modification. This information is returned to requesters via an HTTP header.

With the introduction of common gateway interface (CGI), web servers are able to perform an even wider variety of tasks. These include search engines, map generation, interfacing with database systems, and secure commercial and financial transactions. However, a limitation of CGI is that the server must spawn a new *process* to extend server functionality. It is typical for each request requiring CGI to spawn its own process to handle it, causing the server to behave as a *Process-per-Request* server, which can inhibit performance [Hu 1998]. The challenge for a high-performance web server framework is to allow developers to extend server functionality without resorting to CGI processes.

Alternative Solution Strategies

Most web servers conceptually process or transform a stream of data in several stages. For example, the stages of processing an HTTP/1.0 request can be organized as a sequence of tasks. These tasks involve reading in the request, parsing the request, parsing the request header information, performing the request, and logging the request. This sequence forms a *pipeline* of tasks that manipulates an incoming request, as shown in Figure 17.14.

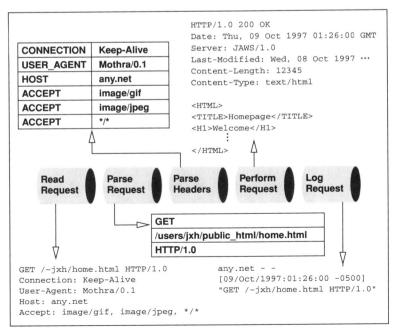

Figure 17.14 The pipeline of tasks to perform for HTTP requests.

The tasks performed to process HTTP/1.0 requests have a fixed structure. Thus, Figure 17.14 illustrates a *static pipeline* configuration. Static configurations are useful for server requests that perform a fixed number of processing operations in a fixed order. If these operations are relatively few and are known a priori, they can be prefabricated and used directly during the execution of the server. Examples of static processing operations include marshaling and demarshaling data, data demultiplexing through custom web protocol layers, and compiling applet code. Incorporating static pipelines into the server makes it possible to extend server functionality without resorting to spawning external processes. The Apache web server provides this type of extensibility by allowing *modules*, which encapsulate static processing, to be dynamically linked to the web server.

However, situations may arise that require a pipeline of operations to be configured *dynamically*. These occur when web server extensions involve arbitrary processing pipeline configurations, so the number is essentially unlimited. This can happen if there is a large number of intermediary pipeline components that can be arranged into arbitrary sequences. If the operations on the data are known only during the execution of the program, dynamic construction of the pipeline from components provides an economical solution. There are many examples of when dynamic pipelines may be useful, including the following:

Advanced search engines. Search engines may construct data filters dynamically depending on the provided query string. For instance, a query such as (performance AND (NOT symphonic)), requesting Web pages containing the word performance but not the word symphonic, could be implemented as a pipeline of a positive match component coupled with a negative match component.

Image servers. Image servers may construct filters dynamically depending on the operations requested by the user. As an example, a user may request that the image be cropped, scaled, rotated, and dithered.

Adaptive Web content. Web content can be dynamically delivered dependent on characteristics of the end user. For example, a personal digital assistant (PDA) should receive Web content overviews and smaller images, whereas a workstation could receive full multimedia enriched pages. Likewise, parents may choose to block certain types of content on their home computers.

Existing solutions that allow server developers to enhance web server functionality dynamically are either too application specific or too generic. For example, Netscape's NetDynamics focuses entirely on integrating web servers with existing database applications. Conversely, Java-based web servers (such as Sun's Java Server and W3C's Jigsaw) allow arbitrary server extensibility since Java applications are capable of dynamically executing Java byte code. However, the problem of *how* to provide a dynamically configurable pipeline of operations must still be resolved by server developers. Similarly, *servlets* extend web servers by providing services in a process executing independently of the main server. However, each servlet must be implemented as its own stand-alone application. Thus, developers must custom engineer their own solutions without the benefits of an application framework based on design patterns.

Structuring a server to process data in logical stages is known as the *Pipes and Filters* pattern [Buschmann 1996]. While the pattern helps developers recognize how to organize the components of a processing pipeline, it does not provide a framework for doing so. Without a framework, the task of adapting a custom server to efficiently adopt new protocol features may be too costly and difficult, and may result in high-maintenance code.

JAWS Protocol Pipeline Strategy Framework

The preceding discussion motivates the need for developers to extend server functionality without resorting to external processes. In addition, we describe how the Pipes and Filters pattern can be applied to create static and dynamic information processing pipelines. JAWS's Protocol Pipeline framework is designed to simplify the effort required to program these pipelines. This is accomplished by providing *task skeletons* of pipeline components. When the developer completes the pipeline component logic, the component can then be composed with other components to create a pipeline. The completed components are stored in a repository so they are accessible while the server is running. This enables the server framework to dynamically create pipelines as necessary at runtime while the web server executes.

Figure 17.15 provides an illustration of the structure of the framework. The figure depicts a Protocol Handler that utilizes the Protocol Pipeline to process incoming requests. A Filter component derives from Protocol Pipeline, and serves as a task skeleton for the pipeline component.

Pipeline implementors derive from Filter to create pipeline components. The svc method of each pipeline component first calls into the parent svc, which retrieves the

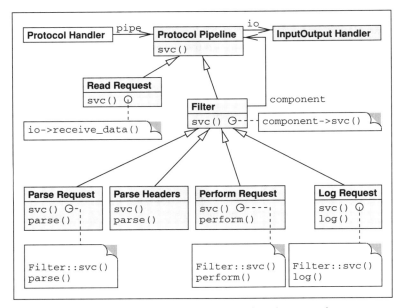

Figure 17.15   Structure of the Protocol Pipeline framework.

data to be processed and then performs its component-specific logic upon the data. The parent invokes the svc method of the preceding component. Thus, the composition of the components causes a chain of calls pulling data through the pipeline. The chain ends at the component responsible for retrieving the raw input, which derives directly from the Protocol Pipeline abstraction.

17.2.6 File-Caching Strategies

File caching design challenges, alternative solution strategies, and JWAS cached virtual filesystem framework are discussed in the following sections.

Design Challenges

The results in [Hu 1998] show that accessing the filesystem is a significant source of web server overhead. Most distributed applications can benefit from caching, and web servers are no exception. Therefore, it is not surprising that research on web server performance focuses on file caching to achieve better performance [Mogul 1996; Williams 1996].

A *cache* is a storage medium that provides more efficient retrieval than the medium on which the desired information is normally located. In the case of a web server, the cache resides in the server's main memory. Since memory is a limited resource, files reside in the cache only temporarily. Thus, the issues surrounding optimal cache performance are driven by *quantity* (how much information should be stored in the cache) and *duration* (how long information should stay in the cache).

Alternative Solution Strategies

Quantity and duration are strongly influenced by the size allocated to the cache. If memory is scarce, it may by undesirable to cache a few large files since caching many smaller files will give better average performance. If more memory is available, caching larger files may be feasible. Resolving these factors gives rise to a number of different file-caching strategies:

Least recently used (LRU) caching. This cache-replacement strategy assumes that most requests for cached files have *temporal* locality, that is, a requested file soon will be requested again. Thus, when the act of inserting a new file into the cache requires the removal of another file, the file that was *least recently used* is removed. This strategy is relevant to web systems that serve content with temporal properties, such as daily news reports and stock quotes.

Least frequently used (LFU) caching. This cache-replacement strategy assumes that files that have been requested frequently are more likely to be requested again, which is another form of temporal locality. Thus, cache files that have been *least frequently used* are the first to be replaced in the cache. This strategy is relevant to web systems with relatively static content, such as Lexis-Nexis and other databases of historical facts.

Hinted caching. This form of caching is proposed in [Mogul 1996]. The hinted caching strategy stems from analysis of Web page retrieval patterns that seem to indicate that Web pages have *spatial* locality; that is, a user browsing a Web page is likely to browse the links within the page. Hinted caching is related to *prefetching*, though [Mogul 1996] suggests that the HTTP protocol be altered to allow statistical information about the links (or *hints*) to be sent back to the requester. This modification allows the client to decide which pages to prefetch. The same statistical information can be used to allow the server to determine which pages to *precache*.

Structured caching. This refers to caches that have knowledge of the data being cached. For HTML pages, structured caching refers to storing the cached files to support hierarchical browsing of a single Web page. Thus, the cache takes advantage of the structure present in a Web page to determine the most relevant portions to be transmitted to the client (for example, a top-level view of the page). This can potentially speed up Web access for clients with limited bandwidth and main memory, such as PDAs. Structured caching is related to the use of B-tree structures in databases, which minimize the number of disk accesses required to retrieve data for a query.

JAWS Cached Virtual Filesystem Framework

The solutions just described present several strategies for implementing a web server file cache. However, employing a fixed caching strategy does not always provide optimal performance [Markatos 1996]. The JAWS Cached Virtual Filesystem framework addresses this issue in two ways. For one, it allows the cache-replacement algorithms and cache strategy to be integrated easily into the framework. Furthermore, by utilizing strategy profiles, these algorithms and strategies can be dynamically selected to optimize performance in the presence of changing server load conditions.

Figure 17.16 illustrates the components in JAWS that collaborate to define its Cached Virtual Filesystem framework. The InputOutput object instantiates a Filecache Handle, through which file interactions, such as reading and writing, are conducted. The Filecache Handle references a Filecache Object, which is managed by the Filecache component. The Filecache Object maintains information that is shared across all handles that reference it, such as the base address of the memory-mapped file. The Filecache component is the heart of the Cached Virtual Filesystem framework. It manages Filecache Objects through hashing and follows the State pattern as it chooses a Cache Strategy to fulfill the file request. The Cache Strategy component utilizes the Strategy pattern to allow different cache-replacement algorithms, such as LRU and LFU, to be interchangeable.

17.2.7 The JAWS Framework Revisited

Section 17.1 motivates the need for frameworks and patterns to build high-performance web servers. We use JAWS as an example of how frameworks and patterns can enable programmers to avoid common pitfalls of developing web server software. Together, patterns and frameworks support the reuse of integrated components and design abstractions [Johnson 1997].

Section 17.2 describes how the JAWS framework is designed and the strategies it provides. To articulate the organization of JAWS's design, we outline the strategic and tac-

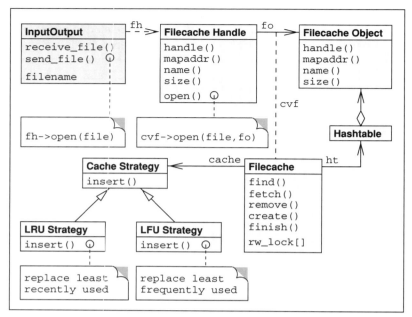

Figure 17.16 Structure of the Cached Virtual Filesystem.

tical design patterns that have the largest impact on the JAWS framework. The Acceptor, Reactor, Proactor, Active Object, and Service Configurator patterns are among the most significant strategic patterns. The Strategy, Adapter, State, and Singleton patterns are influential tactical patterns used in JAWS.

The patterns described in this chapter were chosen to provide the scaffolding of the JAWS architecture. These patterns capture the necessary collaborating entities, which take the form of smaller components. From this, the major components of the framework (such as the Concurrency Strategy, IO Strategy, Protocol Pipeline, and Cached Virtual Filesystem frameworks) are constructed and integrated into a skeleton application. Developers can use this skeleton to construct specialized web server software systems by customizing certain subcomponents of the framework (such as Filters and Cache Strategies).

Figure 17.17 shows how all the patterns and components of the JAWS framework are integrated. The JAWS framework promotes the construction of high-performance web servers in the following ways. First, it provides several preconfigured concurrency and I/O dispatching models, a file cache offering standard cache-replacement strategies, and a framework to implement protocol pipelines. Second, the patterns used in the JAWS framework help to decouple web server strategies from implementation details and configuration time. This decoupling enables new strategies to be integrated easily into JAWS. Finally, JAWS is designed to allow the server to alter its behavior statically and dynamically. For instance, with an appropriate strategy profile (empirical benchmarking data of various server configurations under various server conditions), JAWS can accommodate different conditions that may occur during the runtime execution of a web server. By applying these extensible strategies and compo-

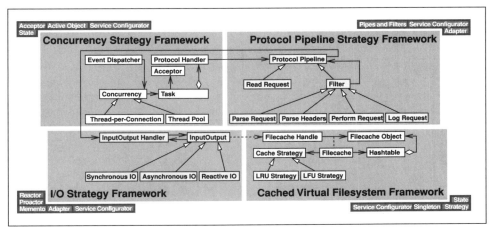

Figure 17.17   The JAWS web server framework.

nents with dynamic adaptation, JAWS simplifies the development and configuration of high-performance web servers.

17.3 Web Server Benchmarking Testbed and Empirical Results

Section 17.2 describes the patterns and framework components that enable JAWS to adapt statically and dynamically to its environment. Although this flexibility is beneficial, the success of a web server ultimately depends on how well it meets the performance demands of the Internet, as well as corporate intranets. Satisfying these demands requires a thorough understanding of the key factors that affect web server performance.

This section describes performance results obtained while systematically applying different load conditions on alternative configurations of JAWS. The results illustrate how no single configuration performs optimally for all load conditions. This demonstrates the need for flexible frameworks like JAWS that can be reconfigured to achieve optimal performance under changing load conditions.

17.3.1 Hardware Testbed

Our hardware testbed is shown in Figure 17.18. The testbed consists of two Micron Millennia PRO2 plus workstations. Each PRO2 has 128 Mbytes of RAM and is equipped with 2 Pentium Pro processors. The client machine has a clock speed of 200 MHz, while the server machine runs at 180 MHz. In addition, each PRO2 has an ENI-155P-MF-S ATM card made by Efficient Networks, Inc., and is driven by Orca 3.01 driver software. The two workstations are connected via an ATM network running through a FORE Systems ASX-200BX, with a maximum bandwidth of 622 Mbps. However, due to limitations of the LAN emulation mode, the peak bandwidth of our testbed is approximately 120 Mbps.

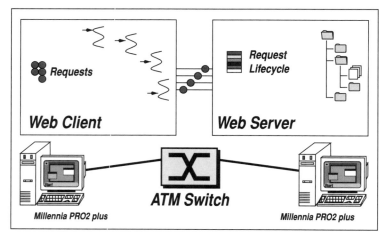

Figure 17.18 Benchmarking testbed overview.

17.3.2 Software Request Generator

We used the WebSTONE v2.0 benchmarking software [Trent 1995] to collect client- and server-side metrics. These metrics include *average server throughput* and *average client latency*. WebSTONE is a standard benchmarking utility, capable of generating load requests that simulate typical web server file access patterns. Our experiments used WebSTONE to generate loads and gather statistics for particular file sizes in order to determine the impacts of different concurrency and event-dispatching strategies.

The file access pattern used in the tests is shown in Table 17.1. This table represents actual load conditions on popular servers, based on a study of file access patterns conducted by the Standard Performance Evaluation Corporation (SPEC) [Carlton 1996].

17.3.3 Experimental Results

The results presented in this chapter compare the performance of several different adaptations of the JAWS web server. We discuss the effect of different event-dispatching and I/O models on throughput and latency. For this experiment, three adaptations of JAWS were used:

Table 17.1 File Access Patterns

DOCUMENT SIZE	FREQUENCY
500 byte	35%
5 Kbyte	50%
50 Kbyte	14%
5 Mbyte	1%

Synchronous Thread-per-Request. In this adaptation, JAWS was configured to spawn a new thread to handle each incoming request and to use synchronous I/O.

Synchronous Thread Pool. JAWS was configured to prespawn a thread pool to handle the incoming requests and to use synchronous I/O.

Asynchronous Thread Pool. For this configuration, JAWS was configured to prespawn a thread pool to handle incoming requests, while using Transmit-File for asynchronous I/O. TransmitFile is a custom Win32 function that sends file data over a network connection, either synchronously or asynchronously [Davis 1996].

Throughput is defined as the average number of bits received per second by the client. A high-resolution timer for throughput measurement is started before the client benchmarking software sends the HTTP request. The high-resolution timer stops just after the connection is closed by the client. The number of bits received includes the HTML headers sent by the server.

Latency is defined as the average amount of delay in milliseconds seen by the client from the time it sends the request to the time it completely receives the file. It measures how long an end user must wait after sending an HTTP GET request to a web server and before the content begins to arrive at the client. The timer for latency measurement is started just before the client benchmarking software sends the HTTP request and stops just after the client finishes receiving the requested file from the server.

The five graphs shown for each of throughput and latency represent different file sizes used in each experiment, 500 bytes through 5 Mbytes by factors of 10. These file sizes represent the spectrum of file sizes benchmarked in our experiments, to determine empirically the impact file size has on performance.

Throughput Comparisons

Figures 17.19 through 17.23 demonstrate the variance of throughput as the size of the requested file and the server hit rate are increased systematically. As expected, the throughput for each connection generally degrades as the connections per second increase. This stems from the growing number of simultaneous connections being maintained, which decreases the throughput per connection.

As shown in Figure 17.21, the throughput of Thread-per-Request degrades rapidly for smaller files as the connection load increases. In contrast, the throughput of the synchronous Thread Pool implementation degrades more gracefully. The reason for this difference is that Thread-per-Request incurs higher thread creation overhead since a new thread is spawned for each GET request. In contrast, thread creation overhead in the Thread Pool strategy is amortized by prespawning threads when the server begins execution.

The results in Figures 17.19 through 17.23 illustrate that TransmitFile performs extremely poorly for small files (<50 Kbyte). Our experiments indicate that the performance of TransmitFile depends directly upon the number of simultaneous requests. We believe that during heavy server loads (that is, high hit rates), TransmitFile is forced to wait while the kernel services incoming requests. This creates a high number of simultaneous connections, degrading overall server performance.

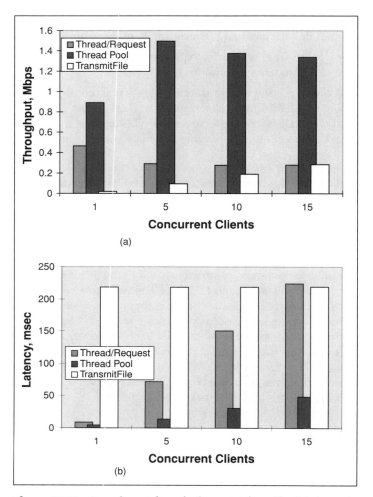

Figure 17.19 Experimental results from 500-byte file: (*a*) through-put, and (*b*) latency.

As the size of the file grows, however, TransmitFile rapidly outperforms the synchronous dispatching models. For instance, at heavy loads with the 5-Mbyte file (shown in Figure 17.23), it outperforms the next closest model by nearly 40 percent. TransmitFile is optimized to take advantage of Windows NT kernel features, thereby reducing the number of data copies and context switches.

Latency Comparisons

Figures 17.19 through 17.23 demonstrate the variance of latency performance as the size of the requested file and the server hit rate increase. As expected, as the connections per second increases, the latency generally increases, as well. This reflects the additional load placed on the server, which reduces its ability to service new client requests.

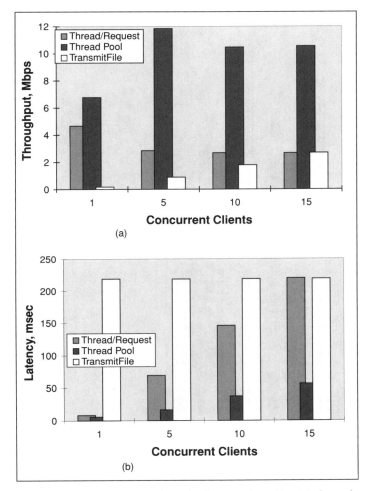

Figure 17.20   Experimental results from 5-Kbyte file: (*a*) throughput, and (*b*) latency.

As before, TransmitFile performs extremely poorly for small files. However, as the file size grows, its latency rapidly improves relative to synchronous dispatching during light loads.

Summary of Benchmark Results

As illustrated by the results in this section, there is significant variance in throughput and latency depending on the concurrency and event-dispatching mechanisms. For small files, the synchronous Thread Pool strategy provides better overall performance. Under moderate loads, the synchronous event-dispatching model provides slightly better latency than the asynchronous model. Under heavy loads and with large file transfers, however, the asynchronous model using TransmitFile provides better qual-

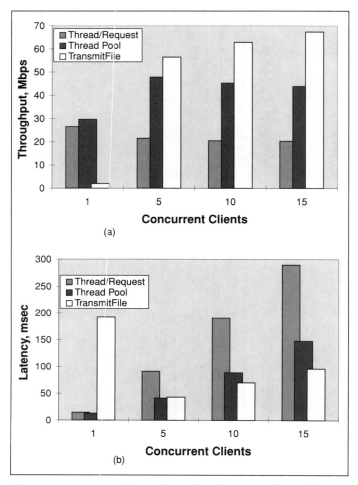

Figure 17.21 Experimental results from 50-Kbyte file: (*a*) throughput, and (*b*) latency.

ity of service. Thus, under Windows NT, an optimal web server should adapt itself to either event dispatching and file I/O model, depending on the server's workload and distribution of file requests.

17.3.4 A Summary of Techniques for Optimizing Web Servers

From our research, we have found that it is possible to improve server performance with a superior server design (a similar observation was made in [Nielsen 1997]). Thus, while it is undeniable that a hard-coded server (that is, one that uses fixed concurrency, I/O, and caching strategies) can provide excellent performance, a flexible server framework, such as JAWS, does not necessarily correlate with poor performance. This section

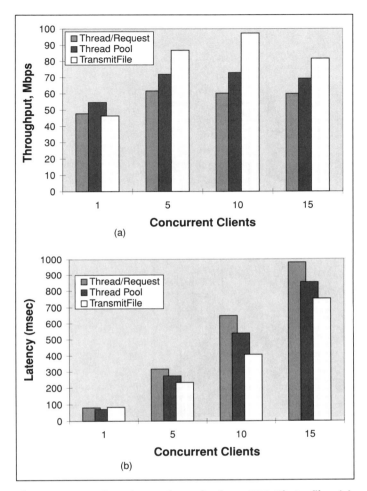

Figure 17.22 Experimental results from 500-Kbyte file: (*a*) throughput, and (*b*) latency.

summarizes the most significant determinants of web server performance. These observations are based on our studies [Hu 1997, 1998] of existing web server designs and implementation strategies, as well as our experience tuning JAWS. These studies reveal the primary targets for optimizations to develop high-performance web servers.

Lightweight Concurrency

Process-based concurrency mechanisms can yield poor performance, as seen in [Hu 1998]. In multiprocessor systems, a process-based concurrency mechanism might perform well, especially when the number of processes is equal to the number of processors. In this case, each processor can run a web server process, and context-switching overhead is minimized.

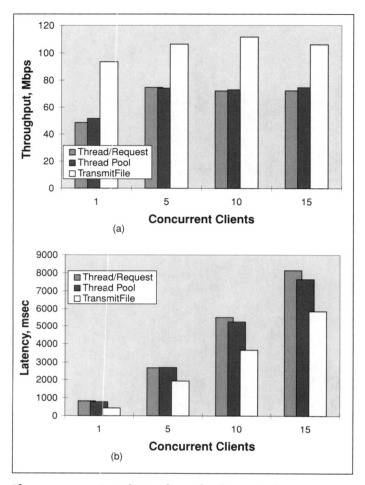

Figure 17.23 Experimental results from 5-Mbyte file: (*a*) throughput, and (*b*) latency.

In general, processes should be *preforked* to avoid the overhead of dynamic process creation. However, it is preferable to use lightweight concurrency mechanisms (such as using POSIX threads) to minimize context-switching overhead. As with processes, dynamic thread creation overhead can be avoided by *prespawning* threads into a pool at server start-up.

Specialized OS Features

OS vendors often will provide custom programming interfaces that provide higher performance. For example, Windows NT 4.0 provides the TransmitFile function, which uses the Windows NT virtual memory cache manager to retrieve the file data. Transmit-File allows data to be prepended and appended before and after the file data, respectively. This is particularly well suited for web servers since they typically send HTTP header data with the requested file. Hence, all the data to the client can be sent in a single system call, which minimizes mode-switching overhead.

Specialized OS APIs must be benchmarked carefully against standard APIs to understand the conditions for which the special interface will give better performance. In the case of TransmitFile, for instance, our empirical data indicate that the asynchronous form of TransmitFile is the most efficient mechanism for transferring large files over sockets on Windows NT, as shown in *Section 17.3.3*.

Request Lifecycle System Call Overhead

The *request lifecycle* in a web server is defined as the sequence of instructions that must be executed by the server after it receives an HTTP request from the client and before it sends out the requested file. The time taken to execute the request lifecycle directly impacts the latency observed by clients. Therefore, it is important to minimize system call overhead and other processing in this path. The following describes various places in web servers where such overhead can be reduced.

Minimizing synchronization. When dealing with concurrency, synchronization is often needed to serialize access to shared resources (such as the Cached Virtual Filesystem). However, the use synchronization penalizes performance. Thus, it is important to minimize the number of locks acquired and released during the request lifecycle. In [Hu 1998], it is shown that servers with a lower number of lock operations per request perform much better than servers that perform a high number of lock operations.

In some cases, acquiring and releasing locks can also result in *preemption*. Thus, if a thread reads in an HTTP request and then attempts to acquire a lock, it might be preempted, and may wait for a relatively long time before it is dispatched again. This increases the latency incurred by a web client.

Caching files. If the web server does not perform file caching, at least two sources of overhead are incurred. First, there is overhead from the open system call. Second, there is accumulated overhead from iterative use of the read and write system calls to access the filesystem, unless the file is small enough to be retrieved or saved in a single call. Caching can be effectively performed using memory-mapped files, available in most forms of UNIX and on Windows NT.

Using gather-write. On UNIX systems, the writev system call allows multiple buffers to be written to a device in a single system call. This gather-write function is useful for web servers since the typical server response contains a number of header lines in addition to the requested file. By using gather-write, header lines need not be concatenated into a single buffer before being sent, avoiding unnecessary data copying.

Precomputing HTTP responses. Typical HTTP requests result in the server sending back the HTTP header, which contains the HTTP success code and the MIME type of the file requested (for example, text/plain). Since such responses are part of the expected case, they can be precomputed. When a file enters the cache, the corresponding HTTP response can also be stored along with the file. When an HTTP request arrives, the header is thus directly available in the cache.

Logging Overhead

Most web servers support features that allow administrators to log the number of hits on various pages they serve. Logging is often done to estimate the load on the server at various times during the day. It is also commonly performed for commercial reasons; for example, Web sites might base their advertising rates on page hit frequencies. However, logging HTTP requests produces significant overhead for the following reasons:

Filesystem access. A heavily loaded web server makes a significant number of I/O calls, which stresses the filesystem and underlying hardware. Writing data to log files increases this stress and thus contributes to lower performance. Keeping log files and the HTTP files on separate filesystems and, if possible, on separate physical devices can limit this overhead.

Synchronization overhead. A typical web server has multiple active threads or processes serving requests. If these threads or processes log requests to a common shared log file, access to this log file must be synchronized; that is, at most one thread or process can write to the shared log file at any time. This synchronization introduces additional overhead and is thus detrimental to performance. This overhead can be reduced by keeping multiple independent log files. If memory buffers are used, these should be stored in *thread-specific storage* to eliminate locking contention.

Reverse hostname lookups. The IP address of the client is available to a web server locally. However, the hostname is typically more useful information in the log file. Thus, the IP address of the client needs to be converted into the corresponding hostname. This is typically done using *reverse DNS lookups*. Since these lookups often involve network I/O, they are very costly. Therefore, they should be avoided or completed asynchronously using threads or asynchronous I/O.

Ident lookups. The Ident protocol [Johnson 1993] allows a web server to obtain the user name for a given HTTP connection. This typically involves setting up a new TCP/IP connection to the user's machine and thus involves a round-trip delay. Also, the Ident lookup must be performed while the HTTP connection is active and therefore cannot be performed lazily. To achieve high performance, such lookups must thus be avoided whenever possible.

In some applications, logging is essential for maintaining accounting information, providing security, or marketing analysis. However, excessive logging is detrimental to performance. If performance is essential, then web server developers should seek to minimize the amount of information that is being logged.

Transport Layer Optimizations

The following transport layer options should be configured to improve web server performance over high-speed networks:

Listen backlog. Most TCP implementations buffer incoming HTTP connections on a kernel-resident *listen queue* so that servers can dequeue and service them using accept. If the TCP listen queue exceeds the backlog parameter to the listen call, new connections are refused by TCP. Thus, if the volume of incoming connections is expected to be high, the capacity of the kernel queue should be increased by giving a higher backlog parameter. This may require modifications to the OS kernel.

Socket send buffers. Associated with every socket is a send buffer, which holds data sent by the server while it is being transmitted across the network. For high performance, it should be set to the highest permissible limit (that is, large buffers). On Solaris 2.5, this limit is 64 Kbyte.

Nagle's algorithm (RFC 896). Some TCP/IP implementations implement Nagle's algorithm to avoid congestion. This can often result in data getting delayed by the network layer before it is actually sent over the network. Several latency-critical applications (such as X Windows) disable this algorithm (for example, Solaris supports the TCP_NO_DELAY socket option). Disabling this algorithm can improve latency by forcing the network layer to send packets out as soon as possible.

17.4 Summary

As computing power and network bandwidth have increased dramatically over the past decade, so has the complexity involved in developing communication software. In particular, the design and implementation of high-performance web server software is expensive and errorprone. Much of the cost and effort stems from the continual rediscovery and reinvention of fundamental design patterns and framework components. Moreover, the growing heterogeneity of hardware architectures and diversity of OS and network platforms make it hard to build correct, portable, and efficient web servers from scratch.

Building a high-performance web server requires an understanding of the performance impact of each subsystem in the server—for example, concurrency and event dispatching, server request processing, filesystem access, and data transfer. Efficiently implementing and integrating these subsystems requires developers to meet various design challenges and navigate through alternative solutions. Understanding the tradeoffs among these alternatives is essential to providing optimal performance. However, the effort required to develop ad hoc designs is often not cost-effective as requirements (inevitably) change. For example, the performance may prove to be inadequate, additional functionality may be required, or the software may need to be ported to a different architecture.

Object-oriented application frameworks and design patterns help to reduce the cost and improve the quality of software by leveraging proven software designs and implementations to produce reusable components that can be customized to meet new application requirements. The JAWS framework described in this chapter demonstrates how the development of high-performance web servers can be simplified and unified. The key to the success of JAWS is its ability to capture common communication software design patterns and consolidate these patterns into flexible framework components that efficiently encapsulate and enhance low-level OS mechanisms for concurrency, event demultiplexing, dynamic configuration, and file caching. The benchmarking results presented in *Section 17.3* demonstrate the effectiveness of using frameworks to develop high-performance applications and illustrate that flexible software is not antithetical to performance. The source code and documentation for JAWS are available at www.cs.wustl.edu/~schmidt/ACE.html.

17.5 References

[Berners-Lee 1996] Berners-Lee, T., R.T. Fielding, and H. Frystyk. Hypertext Transfer Protocol HTTP/1.0. Informational RFC 1945. Network Working Group, www.w3.org, May 1996.

[Buschmann 1996] Buschmann, F., R. Meunier, H. Rohnert, P. Sommerlad, and M. Stal. *Pattern-Oriented Software Architecture: A System of Patterns.* New York: John Wiley & Sons, 1996.

[Carlton 1996] Carlton, A. An explanation of the SPECweb96 benchmark. White paper. Standard Performance Evaluation Corporation, www.specbench.org, 1996.

[Davis 1996] Davis, R. *Win32 Network Programming.* Reading, MA: Addison-Wesley, 1996.

[Fayad-Schmidt 1997] Fayad, M.E., and D. Schmidt. Object-Oriented Application Frameworks, *Communications of the ACM,* 40(10), October 1997.

[Fielding 1997] Fielding, R., J. Gettys, J. Mogul, H. Frystyk, and T. Berners-Lee. Hypertext Transfer Protocol HTTP/1.1. Standards Track RFC 2068. Network Working Group, *www.w3.org,* January 1997.

[Gamma 1995] Gamma, E., R. Helm, R. Johnson, and J. Vlissides. *Design Patterns: Elements of Reusable Object-Oriented Software.* Reading, MA: Addison-Wesley, 1995.

[Harrison 1997a] Harrison, T., I. Pyarali, D.C. Schmidt, and T. Jordan. Proactor: An object behavioral pattern for dispatching asynchronous event handlers. *Proceedings of the 4th Pattern Languages of Programming Conference,* Monticello, Illinois, September 1997.

[Harrison 1997b] Harrison, T.H., D.L. Levine, and D.C. Schmidt. The design and performance of a real-time CORBA event service. *Proceedings of the OOPSLA 1997 Conference on Object-Oriented Programming Systems, Languages, and Applications,* Atlanta, GA, October 1997. New York: ACM Press, 1997.

[Hu 1997] Hu, J., I. Pyarali, and D.C. Schmidt. Measuring the impact of event dispatching and concurrency models on web server performance over high-speed networks. *Proceedings of the 2nd Global Internet Conference,* November 1997. Los Alamitos, CA: IEEE Computer Society Press, 1997.

[Hu 1998] Hu, J., S. Mungee, and D.C. Schmidt. Principles for developing and measuring high-performance web servers over ATM. *Proceedings of the INFOCOM 1998 Conference,* April 1998. Los Alamitos, CA: IEEE Computer Society Press, 1998.

[Jain 1997a] Jain, P., and D.C. Schmidt. Service Configurator: A pattern for dynamic configuration and reconfiguration of communication services. *The 3rd Pattern Languages of Programming Conference.* Technical report WUCS-97-07. Washington University, St. Louis, MO, February 1997.

[Jain 1997b] Jain, P., and D.C. Schmidt. Service Configurator: A pattern for dynamic configuration of services. *Proceedings of the 3rd USENIX Conference on Object-Oriented Technologies and Systems (COOTS 1997),* Portland, Oregon, June 1997.

[Johnson 1993] Johns, M.S. Identification Protocol. Network Information Center RFC 1413. Network Working Group, *www.w3.org,* February 1993.

[Johnson 1997] Johnson, R. Frameworks = patterns + components. *Communications of the ACM, Special Issue on Object-Oriented Application Frameworks, M.E. Fayad and D. Schmidt, editors,* 40(10), October 1997.

[Lavender 1996] Lavender, R.G., and D.C. Schmidt. Active Object: an object behavioral pattern for concurrent programming. In *Pattern Languages of Program Design,* J.O. Coplien, J. Vlissides, and N. Kerth, editors. Reading, MA: Addison-Wesley, 1996.

[Markatos 1996] Markatos, E.P. Main memory caching of web documents. *Proceedings of the Fifth International World Wide Web Conference,* Paris, France, May 1996.

[McKusick 1996] McKusick, M.K., K. Bostic, M.J. Karels, and J.S. Quarterman. *The Design and Implementation of the 4.4BSD Operating System.* Reading, MA: Addison-Wesley, 1996.

[Mogul 1996] Mogul, J.C. Hinted caching in the web. *Proceedings of the Seventh SIGOPS European Workshop: Systems Support for Worldwide Applications,* 1996.

[Nielsen 1997] Nielsen, H.F., J. Gettys, A. Baird-Smith, E. Prud'hommeaux, H.W. Lie, and C. Lilley. Network performance effects of HTTP/1.1, CSS1, and PNG. *Proceedings of the ACM SIGCOMM 1997 Conference.* New York: ACM Press, 1997.

[POS 1995] *Information Technology Portable Operating System Interface (POSIX).* Part 1, *System Application: Program Interface (API) [C Language],* 1995.

[Pyarali 1996] Pyarali, I., T.H. Harrison, and D.C. Schmidt. Design and performance of an object-oriented framework for high-performance electronic medical imaging, *USENIX Computing Systems,* 9, November/December 1996.

[Pyarali 1997]Pyarali, I., T.H. Harrison, and D.C. Schmidt. Asynchronous Completion Token: An object behavioral pattern for efficient asynchronous event handling. In *Pattern Languages of Program Design,* R. Martin, F. Buschmann, and D. Riehle, editors. Reading, MA: Addison-Wesley, 1997.

[Schmidt 1990] Schmidt, D.C. GPERF: A perfect hash function generator. *Proceedings of the 2nd USENIX C++ Technical Conference,* San Francisco, CA, April 1990. USENIX Association, 1990: 87–102.

[Schmidt 1994a] Schmidt, D.C. ACE: An object-oriented framework for developing distributed applications. *Proceedings of the 6th USENIX C++ Technical Conference,* Cambridge, MA, April 1994. USENIX Association, 1994.

[Schmidt 1994b] Schmidt, D.C., and T. Suda. An object-oriented framework for dynamically configuring extensible distributed communication systems. *IEE/BCS Distributed Systems Engineering Journal,* Special Issue on Configurable Distributed Systems, 2, December 1994: 280–293.

[Schmidt 1995a] Schmidt, D.C. Reactor: An object behavioral pattern for concurrent event demultiplexing and event handler dispatching. In *Pattern Languages of Program Design,* J.O. Coplien and D.C. Schmidt, editors. Reading, MA: Addison-Wesley, 1995: 529–545.

[Schmidt 1995b] Schmidt, D.C. Experience using design patterns to develop reusable object-oriented communication software. *Communications of the ACM,* Special Issue on Object-Oriented Experiences, M.E. Fayad and W.T. Tsai, editors, 38(10) October 1995.

[Schmidt 1996a] Schmidt, D.C. A family of design patterns for application-level gateways. *The Theory and Practice of Object Systems,* Special Issue on Patterns and Pattern Languages, 2(1), 1996.

[Schmidt 1996b] Schmidt, D.C., and C.D. Cranor. Half-sync/half-async: An architectural pattern for efficient and well-structured concurrent I/O. In *Pattern Languages of Program Design,* J.O. Coplien, J. Vlissides, and N. Kerth, editors. Reading, MA: Addison-Wesley, 1996.

[Schmidt 1997a] Schmidt, D.C. Acceptor and Connector: Design patterns for initializing communication services. In *Pattern Languages of Program Design,* R. Martin, F. Buschmann, and D. Riehle, editors. Reading, MA: Addison-Wesley, 1997.

[Schmidt 1997b] Schmidt, D.C. Applying design patterns and frameworks to develop object-oriented communication software. In *Handbook of Programming Languages,* P. Salus, editor. New York: Macmillan Computer Publishing, 1997.

[Schmidt 1997c] Schmidt, D.C., and C. Cleeland. Applying patterns to develop extensible and maintainable ORB middleware. *Communications of the ACM,* December 1997.

[Stevens 1997] Stevens, W.R. *UNIX Network Programming,* 2d ed. Englewood Cliffs, NJ: Prentice Hall, 1997.

[Stepanoy 1994] Stepanoy, A., and M. Lee. *The Standard Template Library.* Technical Report HPL-94-34. Palo Alto, CA: Hewlett-Packard Laboratories, April 1994.

[Trent 1995] Trent, G., and M. Sake. WebSTONE: The first generation in HTTP server benchmarking. White paper. Silicon Graphics, www.sgi.com, February 1995.

[Williams 1996] Williams, S., M. Abrams, C.R. Standridge, G. Abdulla, and E.A. Fox. Removal policies in network caches for World Wide Web documents. *Proceedings of the SIGCOMM 1996 Conference,* Stanford, CA, August 1996. New York: ACM Press, 1996: 293–305.

Most current web application development uses a three-layer approach [Lhotka 1997]. The three layers are the presentation layer, the business logic layer, and the system layer. The presentation layer is responsible for presenting the content with a user-friendly interface. This is typically accomplished with application development software such as Visual-Basic or Visual C++. The business logic layer implements most of the business logic and provides services to the user interface (UI) components in the presentation layer. The system layer provides the network, operating system, and persistent storage for data. The three-layer architecture has proven useful in Internet applications. However, it has the following limitations:

A system implemented using this architecture has a close connection between the presentation and the business logic. Usually a static binding between the presentation and the business logic exists because the presentation calls the functions contained in the business logic layer. If there is a change in the presentation or in the business logic, then the parts of the application that reference them must also change.

The business logic and system layers are tightly coupled. Therefore, changing the platform, operating system, or database management system may cause many changes in the business logic and sometimes even in the presentation layer.

In the presentation layer, layout information, navigation information, and UI components are sometimes mixed together. These are different types of data that are handled by different experts (domain experts, media experts, and programmers). The architecture should reflect these differences.

To address these limitations, we proposed a five-module architecture: presentation, UI components, business logic, data management, and system infrastructure (see Figure SB3.1). The five-module architecture explicitly separates the data model from the data source. In this manner, it is possible to change the underlying database management system with minimum effort. In addition, the five-module architecture uses a broker [Buschmann 1996] interface between the modules. This interface technology allows developers to add, delete, and modify components with minimum effort. By definition, the layered approach only allows a layer to communicate with the layers directly above and below it. Decomposition of the presentation and system layers requires that the business logic communicate with the presentation, UI components, and data management. This violates the layered principle, thus requiring that the architecture be composed of modules and not layers.

Presentation. This module prepares the content data for display on the web browser. It also provides the runtime binding between the UI components and the business logic. This presentation module functions independently of the content of the page. Therefore, it is possible to change the business logic or UI components without changing the presentation module.

Continues

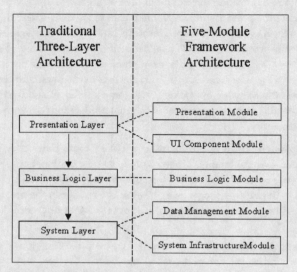

Figure SB3.1   The traditional three-layer architecture and the five-module framework architecture.

UI components. This module provides UI components for display by the presentation
  module. It is possible to add UI components without changing the presentation. The
  UI components convey information to the user through the presentation layer and
  also accept user input through the presentation layer. Typical UI components are
  text, images, text fields, radio buttons, video, hyperlinks, scroll bars, and tables.

Business logic. This module provides the services that the user can request from the
  application by interaction with the UI components in the presentation module.

Data management. The module provides persistent data storage and management for
  the application independent of the underlying database. This module provides an
  abstract interface to the database and a database adapter that allows the system to
  use databases from various vendors. The data management layer can store and
  retrieve *code and data*. All portions of the architecture that use the services of the
  data management are stored within the data management, along with the data that
  they generate.

System infrastructure. This module provides configuration and maintenance of the
  underlying hardware, operating system, and network.

  In an application built using the five-module architecture, the presentation module
loads the specification for a page from the database through the data management module. The presentation module creates the HTML for the layout of the page from the speci-

fications. Then the business logic object associated with each UI component is invoked to allow initialization of the UI component. Then the UI component creates the HTML for its display in the browser. Then the page is assembled and transmitted to the user. When the user generates a response to the page, the response passes to the business logic objects associated with the UI components. Then the response passes to the business logic object associated with the entire page. Then the data management layer saves the response and any data generated by the logic objects to the database with a reference to the page and the user who generated the response.

The architecture allows the developers to build many applications by binding standard code (the business logic) to standard components. Then if the developer needs custom behavior he or she adds new business logic objects and UI components to the data management layer and binds those to the page or UI components within the page. This allows the capabilities of the system to change without changes to the underlying application or architecture. The five-module architecture has been implemented in Distributed Interactive Web-Site (DIWB) builder [Ebner 1997; Shao 1998] on top of two Internet frameworks, WebObjects and OpenStep [McCormick 1996].

References

[Buschmann 1996] Buschmann, F., R. Meunier, H. Rohnert, P. Sommerlad, and M. Stal. *Pattern-Oriented Software Architecture: A System of Patterns.* New York: John Wiley & Sons, 1996.

[Ebner 1997] Ebner, E., W. Shao, and W.T. Tsai. *The Distributed Interactive Web-Site Builder: A Five-Module Framework For Internet Application Development,* at http://war.cs.umn.edu/DIWBFramework.pdf, 1997.

[Lhotka 1997] Lhotka, R., *Business Objects.* Chicago: Wrox Press, 1997.

[McCormick 1996] McCormick, K., and K. Toshach. *Enterprise Objects Framework Developers Guide.* Redwood City, CA: NeXT Computer, 1996.

[Shao 1998] Shao, W., W.T. Tsai, S. Raydurgam, and R. Lai. An agent architecture for supporting individualized services for Internet applications. Submitted for publication in *Proceedings of IEEE International Conference on Tools with Artificial Intelligence,* 1998.

PART

Four

Network and Telecommunication Frameworks

Part Four introduces network management and telecommunication frameworks, such as FIONA and MultiTEL. In today's global economy, communication networks are a key success factor for businesses, organization, and institutes. Planning cost-effective networks that meet the quantitative and qualitative needs is hard, because of the increasingly stringent requirements as well as the proliferation of network technologies and services. Although there are numerous commercial tools for network planning and design available, they are always nonextensible and built for a restricted set of network architectures and problems. We believe that application framework technology is a perfect approach for developing and maintaining stable communication network systems. Part Four contains Chapters 18 through 22 and Sidebar 4.

Chapter 18, "A Framework for Network Management Agents," discusses the design of an object-oriented framework dedicated to the implementation of the network management interfaces in telecommunication networks. The framework is part of the control system architecture of the Alcatel 1641SX SDH Cross-Connect. Although the framework was designed for network management applications, many design principles are of general interest. The framework provides, on the one hand, a complete operation environment for an agent in a telecommunication network. It supports the processing of management requests and allows spontaneous notifications to be issued to the management system. On the other hand, the framework provides sophisticated support for the efficient implementation of the network management interface for a concrete application. It provides tools to generate substantial parts of the code from a formal interface specification.

Chapter 19, "Telecommunication Network Planning Framework," proposes a flexible, object-oriented software framework for the development of integrated network planning and design tools. The framework implements several reusable components that are essential to network planning and design, such as a generic network model, graphical user interfaces, and algorithm and controller components. It also provides standard interactions between these components, thereby allowing an application programmer to integrate new applications into a framework application easily.

Chapter 20, "FIONA: A Framework for Integrating Distributed C^{3}I Applications," allows distributed C^{3}I application components to share a common presentation facility. FIONA component skeletons and patterns provide a standard internal component structure, hide the details of the underlying CORBA middleware, and make it possible to plug and play components at runtime. Some examples of the patterns implemented in FIONA are Publish/Subscribe, Object Serialization, Command, and Composite.

Chapter 21, "MultiTEL: Multimedia Telecommunication Services Framework," presents a compositional framework (MultiTEL) that encapsulates an architecture of multimedia telecommunication services (MTSs) as a collection of computational components controlled by connectors that abstract coordination patterns. The compositional model enforces framework deployment by the specialization of standard components, common interaction patterns, and service architecture. We propose visual composition as a way of building telecommunication services from plug-compatible components and connectors, which can be verifiable with formal methods. MultiTEL also defines a distributed platform that supports dynamic composition of components and connectors, by using Java/RMI technology and the Web.

Chapter 22, "Event Filter Framework and Applications," describes the main components of the event-filtering framework. The chapter covers how the objected-oriented event-filtering framework is designed and implemented. An email event-filtering application has been developed on top of the event-filtering framework. It has been shown that the event-filtering framework is reusable and extensible for developing event management applications with minimal development effort and cost. It also discusses the guidelines for how to extend this framework to adapt different domain-specific applications.

Sidebar 4, *Layla: Network Management Interfaces Framework*, defines a network management interface (NMI) as the middle layer of a network management system, situated between the high-level control processes and the low-level components of the system. Developing NMIs is a challenging task involving multiple software layers, specification languages, and tools. In order to ease the job of NMI developers, this sidebar introduces Layla, a prototype application framework supporting Open Systems Interconnection (OSI) NMIs and using OSI's Common Management Information Service (CMIS).

CHAPTER 18

A Framework for Network Management Agents

This chapter discusses the design of an object-oriented framework dedicated to the implementation of the network management interfaces in telecommunication networks. The framework has been developed for the control system architecture of the Alcatel 1641SX Digital Cross-Connect. This software evolved over several years using object-oriented methods [Booch 1994] and an iterative development process [Booch 1995; McConnell 1996]. The current release has been in operation for about two years now. Meanwhile, it has also been incorporated into other Alcatel products. Although the framework was designed for network management applications, many design principles are of general interest.

In order to manage the high degree of complexity of telecommunication networks and to enable interoperability in multivendor networks, ITU-T developed the Telecommunication Management Network (TMN) as a unique architecture with standardized protocols and interfaces for the communication between network management systems and network elements. The network elements work as local agents for the network manager. Communication between a management system and network elements can work only if shared management knowledge exists, which is defined by a management information model. The information model is an abstraction of the physical and logical resources provided by network elements.

These resources are modeled as *managed objects* (MOs) and stored in the network element's *management information base* (MIB). The manager operates on the network element exclusively via management operations on the MOs. The network element is responsible for transforming these operations, such as modification of the transmission signal structure, into effects on the represented physical resources. MOs are also modified internally by the network element itself to reflect state changes of its physical resources, such as defects of the hardware or errors in a received transmission signal. Such changes are forwarded to the management system using event reports. Figure 18.1 illustrates the manager-agent relationship between a network management system and a controlled network element. More information on network management can be found in [Black 1992] and [Stallings 1993].

The MOs of an information model are specified in a formal, object-oriented language according to the *Guidelines for the Definition of Managed Objects* (GDMO). A *managed object class* (MOC) is defined by its attributes, operations, actions, and the notification types it can emit. The formal specification is restricted mainly to syntactical aspects, whereas the semantic aspects, the behavior of attribute-oriented operations, and actions are specified as plaintext. GDMO makes use of several object-oriented concepts, including multiple inheritance.

Management operations between management system and network elements are exchanged in the form of standardized OSI CMIS/CMIP messages. The manager may retrieve information from MOs via get requests and may modify MOs using set and action requests. The manager may also create or delete MOs in the MIB. The MOs report state changes to the manager by sending event reports.

The software architecture of the 1641SX defines several functional layers (see Figure 18.1). The access layer provides the interfaces to the network management system and to local operator terminals. The MIB layer contains the management information base with all managed objects. It provides the management services to the network management system and the local terminal. The MIB layer is placed on top of a hardware abstraction layer, called the virtual hardware management (VHM). This layer offers a logical interface to all hardware resources that is independent from any specific information model. It transforms logical requests from the MIB layer to

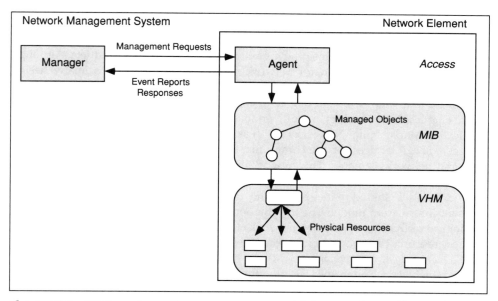

Figure 18.1   TMNoverview with manager-agent model (1641 SX internal layers shown in italic).

board-specific requests on the hardware. It is also responsible for detecting defects within transmission signals and of hardware components. Corresponding alarms are reported to the MIB.

The amount of work at different layers might vary vastly. Also, requests within one layer vary in complexity and processing speed. Some requests might even be handled locally within one layer. To guarantee instant response times, layers must not be blocked while an adjacent layer is busy. Therefore, layers must be decoupled as far as possible. To achieve this goal, requests are processed asynchronously and layers communicate with each other using a message-based protocol. Each layer processes requests locally first. Responses are returned as soon as the information has been validated and the internal data has been updated. A systemwide flow control concept avoids communication overloads and ensures that requests to adjacent layers are forwarded whenever the layer is ready to accept them.

While this section showed how the MIB layer fits into the overall system architecture, the rest of this chapter discusses in more detail the approach we have taken with MIB development.

18.1 MIB Framework

Although the basic structure and behavior of information models have been standardized, there are still different models available. Mostly for historical reasons, these models differ mainly in how the functionality of a transmission system is mapped to managed objects. However, while the resulting structure varies among different information models, the basic patterns of request and alarm processing are the same in all models. Therefore, it makes sense to extract the common parts into a generic framework.

Before we decided to build our own framework, we looked for a commercial solution. However, it became apparent quickly that the frameworks offered on the market were very limited in comparison to what we had in mind. They mostly provided support in decoding the incoming network protocol information into data structures and generated a thin layer centered around accessing attributes of managed objects. Additional behavior must be coded manually, which has to be redone for all similar information models. Also, those frameworks were implemented using structured methods and provided only limited support for extending underlying services such as modifying request processing strategies. Even those solutions that offered C++ interfaces weren't really designed with object-oriented methods in mind. Therefore, we decided to develop a more flexible, fully object-oriented framework that provides a generic network management agent for use with any information model that follows the ITU-T standards.

When we looked more deeply into the subject, we noticed that a framework alone would not be sufficient to support our ambitious reuse goals among different information models. While a framework allows the effective sharing of those parts of an MIB implementation that remain the same for all information models, it cannot support slightly different structure or behavior of individual managed objects. To avoid hand-coding several hundred managed objects per information model, we decided to use a mixture of different technologies.

Our overall design architecture for the MIB implementation is threefold: First, we separated common behavior into a framework. Second, we looked for structures and behavior that followed similar patterns. For those parts, we decided to use code generators to expand generic code templates into individual C++ source files. Finally, specific behavior can be added by overriding methods of the generated classes. The following sections describe the operation of the framework, our approach to managed object implementation and code generation, and how those fit together.

18.1.1 Operation of the Framework

Because MOs must be implemented for each information model, we concentrated our efforts on making this task as simple as possible, even if the framework would become more complex. However, we believe the resulting framework is still simple and easy to understand.

The MIB framework represents a generic agent that is able to process management operations on the MIB. To illustrate the interworking of the major parts of the framework, we will use a set-request that replaces the value of some attributes of an MO as an example. This scenario is outlined as a unified modeling language (UML) collaboration diagram in Figure 18.2. Event handling follows similar design principles and is not discussed here.

The Q-Interface Controller contains a communication protocol stack that runs as a separate process. It converts requests and event reports between the standardized external representation and the internal format that is used throughout the MIB layer.

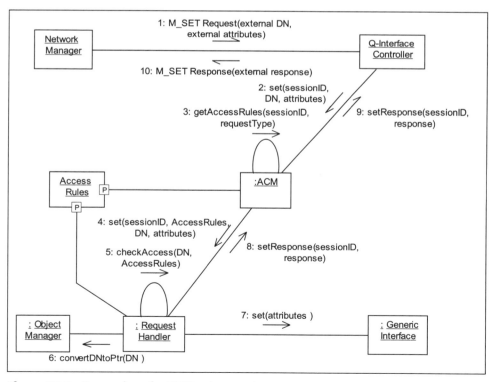

Figure 18.2   Processing of a CMIS set request.

The latter uses C++ data types and is much more efficient than the external representation. The encoded request is sent together with all arguments to the AccessControl-Manager (ACM) class of the MIB process. The ACM is able to control multiple concurrent communication sessions with different clients simultaneously. It receives client requests and dispatches responses and event reports to them. Apart from network managers, which communicate via the Q-Stack, local terminals may access the system directly using the internal message format.

Furthermore, the ACM is responsible for user authentication and security management. For each request, it retrieves the relevant set of access rules objects, depending on the user and the current request type. Because access violations are checked at the individual MO level, these objects are passed along with the request to the request handler.

All managed objects are organized in a tree structure—the *containment tree*—with the named entity (NE) at the root. Each MO has a *distinguished name* (DN) that unambiguously describes its position within the tree. All MOs are under the authority of the ObjectManager class. It translates the DN to an object pointer and dynamically loads the object in memory in case it hasn't been loaded yet.

Some requests involve more than one MO. The RequestHandler uses iterator classes provided by the ObjectManager to traverse the naming tree. It then applies a filter that is part of the request parameters to find the set of target MOs. These MOs are checked against the access rules objects that were supplied by the ACM. Any access violations are reported to the caller and the MO is skipped.

The RequestHandler forwards the request to the target MO via the GenericInterface class. All MOs derive from this abstract class. It offers an interface for all CMIS request types. Create and delete requests are delegated to the ObjectManager. A Builder pattern similar to the one described in [Gamma 1995] is used to decouple the ObjectManager from actual creation of MOs. For get, set, and, action requests, the GenericInterface checks all request parameters against available attributes and the allowed operations. It then decomposes the request into single attribute-oriented operations and dispatches the operations in cooperation with the MO implementation classes to the appropriate attribute or action. Finally, the results of the called methods are collected in a response and returned to the RequestHandler, which forwards it to the caller via the ACM. MOs must override several operations of the GenericInterface class to react to a request in an MO-specific way.

Most of the framework services are designed using a few fundamental patterns; for example, to decouple the framework from the application, abstract classes are used that define the protocol of a service. Application classes must derive from these classes to implement the required functionality.

To ensure that all changes happen completely or don't take place at all, a transaction concept has been introduced. Special objects have been defined to simplify the use of transactions. To open a transaction, it is sufficient to create a local transaction object on the stack. The constructor of the object calls the global TransactionManager to open the transaction. If the transaction has not been committed when the object is destructed, a rollback is triggered automatically. This simplifies the use of transactions considerably. If something goes wrong within a member function, a simple return statement triggers the rollback of the transaction, which undoes all changes.

The ObjectManager uses the TransactionManager to include all accessed MOs in the current transaction during the logical name–to–object pointer translation. This is completely transparent for other MOs and increases the overall quality by removing a common source of errors.

Object persistency is closely coupled with transactions. When a transaction is committed, the current state of a modified object is written to disk. In case of a rollback, the previous object state is simply reloaded from persistent storage.

18.1.2 MOC Implementation— Generic Part

Because MOs need all the previously described services, the following class hierarchy can be constructed (see Figure 18.3). The TransactionControl class is the abstract base class for all transaction-related services. It offers the member functions that are called

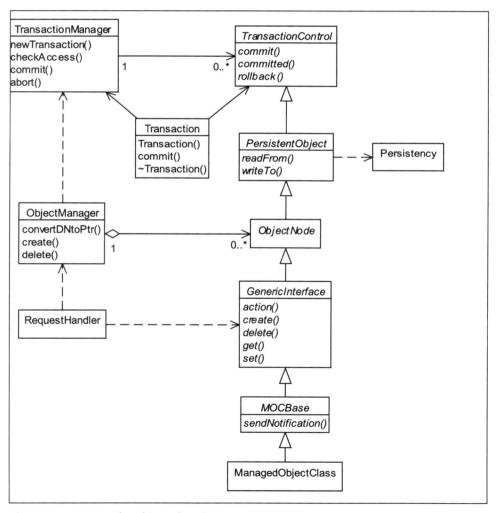

Figure 18.3   Base class hierarchy of an MO.

during a two-phase commit or rollback of a transaction. PersistentObject derives directly from TransactionControl to implement the persistency mechanism. PersistentObject overrides the commit and rollback functions to call the persistency read and write functions in case of write transactions.

The ObjectManager controls all MOs via the abstract ObjectNode class interface. Because the effects of object creation and deletion must be made persistent, the ObjectNode class is derived from PersistentObject. This also ensures that object creation and deletion are performed under transaction control.

The GenericInterface class, which has already been discussed, derives from Object-Node. Finally, MOCBase offers information model–independent services to all managed object classes. One of these services is handling of notifications. The MO passes the parameters of the notification to be sent to the corresponding MOCBase method. The notifications are stored until the end of the current transaction. Upon successful termination of the transaction, the notifications are forwarded as event reports to management users. If more than one notification is stored within MOCBase, they are combined if possible.

The class diagram shows that most services are loosely coupled. Complex services are build on top of simpler services and all services are clearly separated from the application. It follows the software architecture that is outlined in [Kruchten 1995] and has a strict layering [Shaw 1996]. Simple structures are the ultimate goal of any good software architecture. Common mechanisms are used wherever possible, which lend themselves to the use of design patterns. The use of abstract classes in the framework leads to dependency inversion as it is discussed in [Martin 1995]. All framework classes are decoupled from application classes.

Some services that we haven't covered yet are common mechanisms for error handling and fault logging, tracing, interprocess communication, and event report handling. They follow similar principles. Some of these packages are actually part of a basic framework, as they are used in other functional layers as well.

18.1.3 MOC Implementation— Specific Part

Each MOC of the information model is represented in the MIB by (at least) one implementation class. The inheritance structure of the information model is preserved. Each MO is represented by one object. The behavior of managed objects must be compliant with the definition in the information model. The general concepts, the behavior common to all attribute-oriented operations, and the behavior of operations that affect the MO as a whole can be found in the X.700 series of ITU-T standards, which are also described in [Black 1992].

The framework handles all attributes as generic data types. The methods of the MO implementation classes do not handle the complex attribute representation, but use the internal data types representing the attributes syntax. This simplifies the MOC implementation significantly. However, the conversion between attribute representation and internal data types must be performed by the specific MOC.

With the framework in place, MOs must provide only a couple of services. They must implement persistency and conversion functions for all attributes and they must satisfy the requirements of the generic interface by offering operations to manipulate attributes with requests. MOs must handle alarms and issue notifications if values of certain key attributes change. Finally, they must handle any specific behavior that is associated with state changes and they must inform the virtual hardware management layer to update hardware-related information.

While this doesn't seem much, these services must be provided for all the hundreds of MOCs of an information model. Even if the complete framework can be reused for different implementations of the MIB, the effort to implement all required MOs is still significant. Additionally, many of the required services are conceptually straightforward to implement but cannot be put in the framework because they have to be implemented for many different data types. Storing attributes to disk is such an example. It would be nice if the implementation of these services could be automated. However, most of the required features proved different enough that the C++ template mechanism could not be used.

18.1.4 Code Generation

Since information models are defined in GDMO, a formal language, the MOC implementation can be automatically generated to a large extent. This includes the basic structure of all MOCs with their attributes, attribute-oriented access functions, conversion routines, and persistency support. Moreover, all functions that are required for interworking with the GenericInterface class are generated. This reduces the amount of hand-written code significantly.

Unfortunately, within the GDMO description important parts of an information model—mainly the behavior of the MOCs—is described in plaintext. To likewise be able to generate parts of the MOC code related to the behavior description, we enhanced the GDMO with additional language elements to the *Extended GDMO* (XDMO). For example, in XDMO it is possible to mark all attributes for which attribute value change notifications must be emitted. Pairs of attributes can be labeled as relationship attributes where an update of one causes a consistent update of its peer. Finally, attributes can be specified as hardware-related. Modifications of such attributes lead to corresponding requests to the virtual hardware management layer.

The MOC implementation classes generated from XDMO are called *MO data classes*. The data classes are generated using our tool chain. First, a GDMO parser reads the specifications of the information model in the extended GDMO syntax (XDMO) and generates an intermediate representation. The so-called IMGenerator takes the intermediate representation as well as code templates as input and produces the C++ header and implementation files. The template-based approach allows not only the generation of C++ code but also the generation of textual representations of the information model, such as HTML documents.

Since XDMO cannot reflect the complete behavior of an MOC as specified in an information model, the functionality of the data classes has to be extended in the *behavior classes* by redefining data class methods. Figure 18.4 shows a sample inheritance lattice of data and behavior classes. The basic goal of this structure was to decouple data and behavior classes as far as possible. This allows data classes to be compiled without any behavior class. Code generation is also used for several behavior classes that are quite similar, such as different types of equipment of the Cross-Connect, which have the same attributes but only slightly different behavior.

The split into data and behavior classes has several advantages. An MIB with basic functionality can be generated from the information model specification and tested without the need for hand-crafted code. Based on that, MIB functionality can be

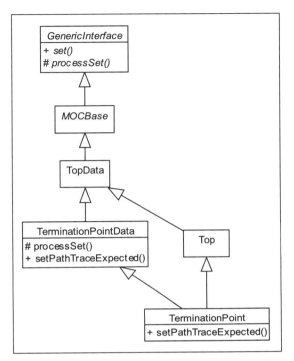

Figure 18.4 Sample inheritance hierarchy of a managed object class.

extended by incrementally adding behavior classes. The implementation of the basic functionality can be optimized by replacing the data class implementation with an improved version. This approach and the use of code generation for the data classes significantly reduce effort to upgrade or change the information model. The data classes allow the evolution from reduced functionality to full functionality. The decoupling reduces test and maintenance effort.

18.1.5 Interworking of Generic and MOC-Specific Part

To explain the interworking of the framework and generated and hand-written code in more detail, we show how an attribute of a managed object is changed. This example uses a termination point managed object, which represents the end point of a transmission path. A path is identified by its path trace, which is inserted at the source site and supervised at the receiving sink site. The expected path trace identifier can be set as an attribute of the termination point MO.

Figure 18.5 shows the collaboration diagram, while Figure 18.4 represents the corresponding class diagram. Note that GenericInterface, TerminationPointData, and TerminationPoint are drawn as separate objects, although they are subobjects of one TerminationPoint object. We did this to show the interaction between different base classes.

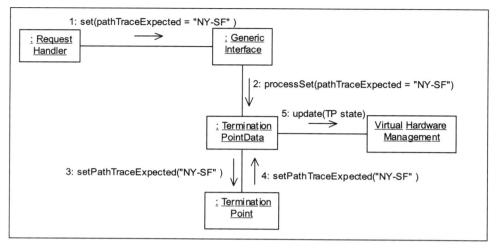

Figure 18.5 Internal processing of a set request.

The scenario starts with a set operation performed by the RequestHandler on the GenericInterface part of the object. The GenericInterface uses the Strategy pattern described in [Gamma 1995] to perform all steps of the set operation. It calls the process-Set() operation, which is overridden in the data class, to dispatch the generic set operation to the attribute-specific operation. This function is generated from the GDMO specification. It converts the generic attribute data type to the concrete path trace attribute and calls the set operation for it. The set operation is overridden in the Termination-Point class to perform additional checks on the path trace parameter. In many cases, the generated default implementation of the base class is sufficient and the operation doesn't need to be overridden in the behavior class.

Then the set operation of the base class is invoked. This generated operation triggers the update of the termination point characteristics on the hardware and saves the new expected path trace value to disk. Hardware access for this attribute is generated because the attribute has been marked accordingly in the XDMO description. If an error occurs during execution of the scenario, it is reported back to the GenericInterface, which transforms the result into a standardized error message. Otherwise, GenericInterface returns a successful response to the framework RequestHandler. In both cases, the result is returned to the network manager, according to the scenario shown in Figure 18.2.

This example shows how the framework and the generated code work hand in hand and that both can be easily extended by overriding operations in derived classes. Overall, our strategy to combine a framework with massive code generation led to very positive results. First, because of code generation we had a working MIB very early in the development life cycle. This allowed developers to test with the generated MOCs. It saved us from writing many stubs and supported an evolutionary programming style whereby the generated data classes were replaced with the behavior classes as they became available. Second, code generation can be seen as using a more abstract, problem-oriented language. It saved effort and guaranteed consistency in the implementation of services. Third, we can present massive reuse figures, as shown in Table 8.1.

Table 18.1   Reuse Figures

SYSTEM PART	LINES OF CODE	NUMBER OF CLASSES	PERCENT OF LOC
Framework	564,000	670	52.8
Generated code	425,000	845	39.7
Handwritten code	80,000	260	7.5
Total	**1,069,000**	**1775**	**100.0**

As can be deduced from the table, code generation improved the reuse potential significantly. The framework code is handwritten but contains the large Q-Protocol stack software (about 280 kLOC) that was bought from a third-party vendor. If this part would be subtracted from the preceding numbers, the generated code would be 53.9 percent, and therefore would contribute even more to the overall success. Code generation could only be used because formal specifications for all managed objects were available. Also, to make full use of code generation, some effort must be spent to set up the XDMO definitions and to write master code for generated behavior classes. However, this effort is far less than that required for writing all implementation code manually.

18.2 Summary

Our experience with the approach taken is very positive so far. The framework has proven to be very stable and flexible over time. We are currently implementing the fourth MIB project based on the described approach. Although we had to enhance the framework for each project, all changes had relatively local effects. Additionally, all modifications were upwardly compatible so that we could reintroduce them into existing projects.

The MIB framework, together with the generated code, gave developers clear guidelines, which even allowed us to outsource one MIB implementation to a contractor. Our focus on a clean software architecture paid off when we introduced new features into the system. While the first version did support only simple password verification, later iterations of the framework supported the full-blown security management scheme described previously. This major change in policy affected only the ACM and RequestHandler components. An even more striking example is the evolution of the request processing strategy. We started with a version that offered only limited concurrency. However, this scheme proved to be too inefficient and not flexible enough. We now create a RequestHandler object for each session. Request processing uses a cooperative scheduling approach to guarantee fairness between user requests and to avoid the problem that large requests can lock up the machine. While this caused heavy changes in the request-handling part of the framework, the rest of the system was not affected. In particular, we didn't have to change any MOC. This shows the advantages of a well-layered architecture with loose coupling among components. Interestingly enough, we discovered and used many patterns even before the pattern movement became popular. If books on patterns had been available at that time, we would have saved design and documentation effort. Therefore, we believe it is essential to communicate patterns and stop reinventing the wheel.

The use of code generation reduced the amount of hand-written code significantly. We believe that these impressive results show the potential of a software architecture–centric approach that uses object technology together with a modern iterative and incremental software development process. Introducing functional layers and the use of systemwide concepts leads to systems that are better structured and that support a clear separation of concerns. The combination of a sophisticated framework and code generation allowed us to produce better software with less effort and better quality and consistency. Our experience showed that similar concepts should be applicable to other domains as well. For example, for a new generation of operator terminals, most of the graphical representation is directly generated from attribute specifications.

18.3 References

[Black 1992] Black, U. *Network Management Standards*. New York: McGraw-Hill, 1992.

[Booch 1994] Booch, G. *Object-Oriented Analysis and Design with Applications*. Redwood City, CA: Benjamin Cummings, 1994.

[Booch 1995] Booch, G. *Object Solutions: Managing the Object-Oriented Project*. Menlo Park, CA: Addison-Wesley, 1995.

[Gamma 1995] Gamma, E., R. Helm, R. Johnson, and J. Vlissides. *Design Patterns: Elements of Reusable Object-Oriented Software*. Reading, MA: Addison-Wesley, 1995.

[Kruchten 1995] Kruchten, P. The 4+1 view model of architecture. *IEEE Software*, November 1995, pp. 42–50.

[Martin 1995] Martin, R. *Designing Object-Oriented C++ Applications Using the Booch Method*. Englewood Cliffs, NJ: Prentice Hall, 1995.

[McConnell 1996] McConnell, S. *Rapid Development: Taming Wild Software Schedules*. Redmond, WA: Microsoft Press, 1996.

[Shaw 1996] Shaw, M., and D. Garlan. *Software Architecture: Perspectives on an Emerging Discipline*. Upper Saddle River, NJ: Prentice Hall, 1996.

[Stallings 1993] Stallings, W. (editor). *Network Management*. Los Alamitos, CA: IEEE Computer Society Press, 1993.

CHAPTER 19

Telecommunication Network Planning Framework

With the upcoming worldwide liberalization of the telecommunication market on the one hand and the increasing demand for a variety of communication services on the other hand, the planning, the design, and the management of telecommunication networks have become a vital issue for telecommunication companies, service providers, and software companies. Telecommunication networks must be designed considering both installation costs and required capacity, services must be developed and evaluated, the performance of new protocols have to be tested, and so on. Although numerous commercial tools exist for these tasks, they all have one major disadvantage. To the application programmer, they present themselves as a blackbox. While they offer a certain range of solutions to problems such as backbone design and clocking analysis, they cannot be adapted to integrate new optimization algorithms or special analysis methods. Consequently, they are only useful to a certain degree, but more often than not fail to provide the desired techniques. However, for a telecom operator such as Swisscom, it is important to be able to test new products and study aspects of existing ones whenever the need arises. Hence, we have decided to build an open, object-oriented system for the development of planning, design, and optimization applications.

Clearly, one possibility for building such a system would be to create a set of class libraries or a toolkit containing various planning, design, and optimization methods. New applications could be built by reusing classes and methods contained in the toolkit. However, this approach limits code reuse to classes and methods. The interaction between classes must be designed for each application from scratch, thus making the integration of applications in a standard environment very difficult. This, however, is crucial in a problem domain, where individual applications share a large number of standard features. For example, most applications dealing with networks require the possibility of querying, displaying, and modifying the network configuration data. Using only a toolkit, the application programmer would have to rewrite the basic editing features of the application every time. Frameworks are an elegant and increasingly popular way of solving these problems [Booch 1994; Taligent 1995].

Unlike a toolkit or libraries, a framework not only provides the user with standard components, but also implements the interaction between these components. That is, a framework defines a standard default application frame and requires users to add components to the application rather than to write applications completely by themselves. Consequently, it is possible to integrate new applications into the same system by reusing the default application components, such as an editor or a controller component.

Usually, the kind of interactions and relationships defined by a framework originate in the area of graphical user interfaces and the interface between the user and the application in general. However, we also apply framework concepts to the organization of algorithms. The motivation for organizing the interaction between algorithms in a framework structure comes from the domain of *compositional modeling* [Falkenhainer 1991]. In compositional modeling, a problem structure is decomposed into semi-independent problem fragments that can then be automatically composed according to various assumptions and conditions. This technique has been successfully applied to domains such as software agents [Brazier 1996] and reactive physical systems [Nadjm 1997]. There are two main advantages of compositional modeling. First, the model fragments may be reused in other applications, while it might not be possible to reuse a single large model. Second, the model composition process is hidden from the application, thereby allowing for new model fragments to be added to the system and made immediately available to each application that uses the composed model. Clearly, these advantages can also be of benefit in the domain of network planning and design. In particular, in the analysis and simulation of network protocols and services there are algorithms that can be decomposed according to the protocol layers and then reused in the sense of compositional modeling.

In this chapter, we present the framework NETPLAN [Messmer 1997]. NETPLAN is a framework of frameworks, integrating both the traditional framework concepts dealing with graphical user interfaces as well as a basic compositional modeling framework for algorithms. NETPLAN is based on object-oriented technology extensively using the paradigm of design patterns [Buschmann 1996; Gamma 1995]. So far, our experience indicates that NETPLAN facilitates the development of new, tailored network applications and, in particular, allows the integration of these new applications, resulting in a high degree of acceptance by the application users.

The remainder of this chapter is organized in the following manner. *Section 19.1.1* gives an overview of the framework and *Section 19.1.2* considers some implementation issues. In *Section 19.1.3*, a simple HTTP delay application is introduced for tutorial purposes. Next, in *Sections 19.1.4* through *19.1.7*, the various features of the framework are explained with respect to this practical example application. Finally, *Section 19.2* summarizes the implementation of the example application based on the framework and *Section 19.3* draws some conclusions.

19.1 The Framework NETPLAN

Throughout this chapter, we use the object modeling technique (OMT) notation whenever possible to describe the various relationships between classes and objects of the framework. In Figure 19.1, the most important elements of the OMT notation are listed.

19.1.1 Framework Overview

In order to understand the kind of facilities that are required by an application in the domain of network planning and design, the basic components of such an application are outlined in Figure 19.2.

At the core of any application is an *application controller.* This controller is responsible for creating and maintaining all the objects and modules that make up the application. In particular, the controller creates and controls an object representing a network and all data items related to the network. Furthermore, it controls all graphical user interfaces that are required by the application, such as views of the network topology and the network data and panels for the display of specific results. Naturally, interface events issued by the user must also be handled by the controller. Finally, the controller is also responsible for calling algorithms that perform the actual tasks of the specific

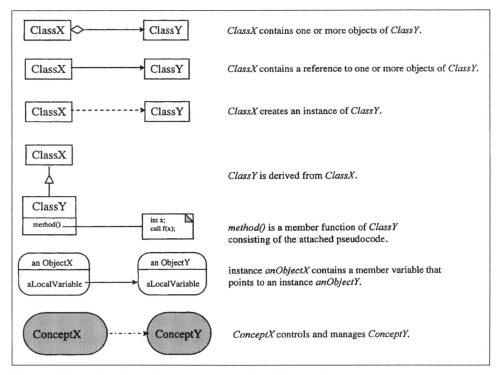

Figure 19.1   OMT class interaction and relationship notation.

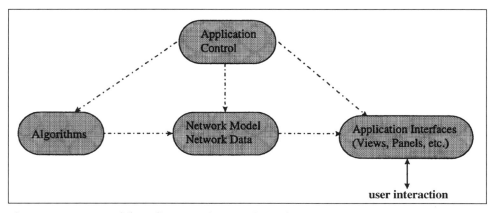

Figure 19.2   Control flow diagram of a generic application.

application. Based on a library or a toolkit, all of these objects and interactions can be implemented using a classical programming technique. However, no code and functionality reuse between different applications will be possible.

On the other hand, when the application structure in Figure 19.2 is realized on the basis of the NETPLAN framework, interactions between the different components are already handled and can therefore be reused in the current and in future applications. In Figure 19.3, the general structure of the NETPLAN framework and the position of the application components from Figure 19.2 are displayed. The framework components are shown in light gray, while the user application components are given in dark gray. The overall structure of the framework was influenced by the proposed segmentation of a framework into subframeworks in [Taligent 1995]. The NETPLAN framework is made of a *global framework* and three subframeworks: the *application* framework, the *interface* framework, and the *algorithm* framework. A vital part of the global framework is that the generic network model interacts with the subframeworks in a predefined manner. Furthermore, each framework provides certain standard objects that form the body of the default application along with standard control paths that allow the objects of the different frameworks to interact with each other. In the following paragraphs, we briefly explain the features and the importance of each framework and its relationships with the other frameworks.

The global framework contains the three subframeworks, the general network model, and a network data component. It provides standard interactions between these frameworks and the generic network model and also organizes the handling of the network data component. This component contains both standard network configuration data that is provided by the framework and also application-specific network information. Notice that, while in the general application diagram in Figure 19.2 the network component includes both the network topology and the configuration information, this is not the case in NETPLAN. The topology of a network model is handled completely by the predefined component, network model, of the global framework. The application-specific network aspects, however, such as new protocols or hardware technologies are handled by the network data component. This component can be accessed and manipulated by the application through standard interfaces defined by

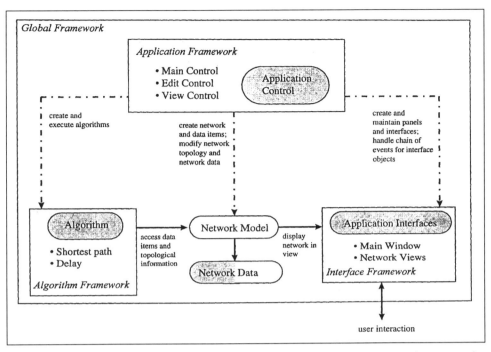

Figure 19.3 Organization of the NETPLAN framework and interaction between the different subframeworks.

the global framework. All other application components are not embedded directly into the global framework, but instead, they are to be linked with and embedded into the subframeworks.

At the core of the global framework is the application subframework. It consists of a main controller object that coordinates all activities in an application and several default controller objects such as an edit and a view controller. Among the actions performed by objects in the application framework are the creation of interface and algorithm objects, and creation and maintenance of the network model (indicated by dashed lines in Figure 19.3). Note that the application control object from the general application in Figure 19.2 must be embedded into the application framework, ensuring that the interaction with the network model, interfaces, and algorithms are already handled.

The interface framework consists of a set of objects and classes defining the standard user interface of any network application built with the framework and the views that are used in order to visualize the network topology. Additionally, user interaction events, such as mouseclicks in views and menu item selections, are handled in a standard fashion and can be directly relayed to controller objects in the application framework—in other words, the interface object in the general application given in Figure 19.2 must be embedded into the interface framework. Hence, user actions such as choosing a node in a network view are collected by framework components and sent to the application controller for processing.

The network model is a graph that represents the network topology in terms of nodes and links. Network components in the context of telecommunication, such as routers, bridges, and ISDN terminals, are not directly mapped onto some network object, but instead they are modeled by using a generic node in the network graph. A special data item describing the properties and parameters required for a router, bridge, or ISDN terminal is attached to this generic node. As previously mentioned, the data items are part of the network data component that is managed by the global framework. The network model offers a standard interface to register and retrieve data items in and from a network object. This allows an application to register new data items that are immediately recognized by the edit and view controller. NETPLAN provides three different types of data attributes: user-defined, database-dependent, and computed items. As problem domains exist for which the computations in the data items are fairly complex, it is sensible to collect some of the computational rules in algorithmic form. Hence, the data items in network objects must, under certain circumstances, access objects of the algorithm framework.

The algorithm framework is organized according to the compositional modeling paradigm. That is, algorithms are organized in so-called families of algorithms, where each family is responsible for a specific problem. The algorithms represent different approaches to a problem that can be used under different conditions (network topology, presence of protocols, and so on) and requirements (precision, available time, preferences, and so on). Depending on the conditions and requirements for a given problem, the algorithms are then automatically selected, hierarchically composed, and applied to solve the given problem.

Each application component described in Figure 19.2 can be embedded in a subframework or directly mapped onto a general framework component such as the generic network model. Before we explain these subframeworks in more detail, we elaborate briefly on issues related to the general implementation principles, the development environment, and the platform.

19.1.2 Implementation and Platform Considerations

The realization and implementation of the framework architecture, as described in the previous section, requires various mechanisms that are currently best provided by object-oriented languages such as C++ and Smalltalk. In particular, the reuse of framework components and the interaction between these components can be realized by the object-oriented paradigms *virtual inheritance* and *polymorphism*.

The design and implementation of NETPLAN are heavily influenced by the concept of design patterns as described in patterns [Buschmann 1996; Gamma 1995]. Design patterns represent a method to describe recurring and well-known patterns in software solutions and to provide a common language for software engineers and designers by giving names to these patterns. Based on design patterns, it becomes easier to explain the design and implementation concepts of NETPLAN.

In order to illustrate the basic principle of how framework components or *classes* can be inherited and the relationship between different components can be reused, we give a simple example in Figure 19.4 based on the design pattern Abstract Factory [Gamma 1995]. This pattern is used mainly in the formulation of the relationship

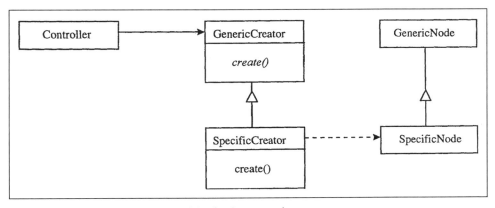

Figure 19.4 Factory pattern used in the framework.

between the edit controller and the network model. That is, whenever a new network node is to be created, the edit controller uses a factory or creator object to do so. For this purpose, the controller class keeps a reference to an object of class GenericCreator, which contains a virtual member function, create(). In its default implementation, create() returns a node object of class GenericNode. Hence, the controller receives a GenericNode object and adds this to the network model. This behavior can now be changed by subclassing both the GenericCreator and the GenericNode class into classes SpecificCreator and SpecificNode, respectively, such that the overloaded function create() in SpecificCreator creates and returns an instance of class SpecificNode. For the controller to know about the new network object classes, an instance of SpecificCreator must be registered with it. The registration process causes, among other things, the controller to inform the edit controller to add a new network object type to the selection box in the network editor panel (see Figure 19.9 later in this chapter). As a consequence, if the user or an application selects the new object type for creation, the controller automatically calls the derived method create() of SpecificCreator and, hence, a node of class SpecificNode is added to the network model. This, of course, is possible only because create() is a virtual function of GenericCreator. Clearly, based on this scheme, it is possible to reuse framework classes and the interactions and communication paths between these classes very efficiently.

Concerning the implementation, one of the requirements that the framework has met is that it be portable over a variety of platforms. Hence, the development of the graphical user interface framework was based on a commercial toolkit, namely, the ILOG Views toolkit from the French company ILOG [ILOG 1996]. ILOG Views is a portable, object-oriented library for implementing graphical user interfaces. Based on ILOG Views it was possible to develop the framework under Unix and Motif and then port it to Windows 95 without any adjustment or development overhead. An example of an interface written with ILOG Views is given in Figure 19.9.

In the following, we briefly outline an application and its requirements in the context of the framework. Based on this sample application, it is possible to explain the details of each framework component on a practical basis.

19.1.3 A Sample Application: Delay Behavior of TCP/IP over ISDN

In order to better understand the requirements of a network application in the context of the framework, consider the following example.

Let us suppose that for network testing purposes one needs to know how much time it would take to load and view the home page of a particular WWW site. That is, the user would like to know the response time of an HTTP request in a particular network.

HTTP applications (server and client) use TCP/IP for communication between the client and the server. The network connecting the HTTP client to the HTTP server is assumed to be an ISDN network. The datalink layer is assumed to be a variant of PPP. The protocol stack of the example application, as outlined in Figure 19.5, shows how the various protocol blocks interact with each other.

Clearly, such an application requires the possibility of creating and modifying a network containing communication nodes that are connected via ISDN links. Furthermore, it requires information about the various network components and the protocols. The calculation of TCP round-trip delay, for example, depends on several parameters related to the TCP protocol such as the size of the sliding window mechanism, maximum size of a data segment, and the acknowledgment strategy. It is clear that the calculation of the TCP delay between two sites on a communication network is not trivial and that it involves, for example, querying the network in order to find a valid ISDN route and access static and computed parameters from different network objects. Finally, the results of the computation must be displayed to the user for further analysis.

Based on this sample application and the general outline of the framework given in *Section 19.1.1*, we now study each framework component in detail.

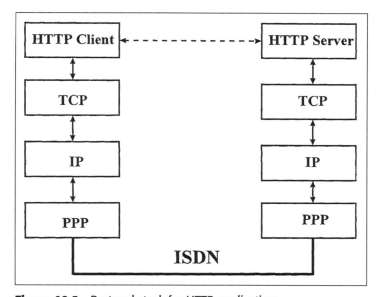

Figure 19.5 Protocol stack for HTTP application.

19.1.4 The Network Model

From the overview of the framework given in Figure 19.3, it is obvious that all of the subframeworks have a close relationship and interactions with the network model. For example, in the case of the HTTP application, it is clear that the network model must be able to accommodate nodes that represent servers and clients, links connecting these nodes directly or indirectly via intermediate communication nodes, and demands that represent requests for a home-page from a client to a particular server node. These and future requirements from other network applications demand a very general and flexible network model.

In Figure 19.6, the class and relationship diagram of the network model that is integrated into the framework and makes up the generic network model is displayed. Note that there is a class Network, which contains objects of class NetworkObjects. The task of Network is to provide a common interface to the other framework components and allow such basic operations as adding and deleting nodes and links and accessing links that are incident from and incident to a node. The objects on which these operations are performed are all instances of classes that are derived from the generic class NetworkObject. This class provides a standard interface to each network object to access data items that are of class DataObject. Objects of class DataObject are stored in network objects under specific access keys. Some of these keys are framework-defined and, for example, force the framework to store for each network object a data item that describes its technology type. Other keys can be defined by an application and can be used to store simulation or analysis data in specific network objects. Separating the information about an object from the actual network object allows for flexible handling of network configuration information at runtime. For example, given the fact that the basic topology of an existing network is to be used by a new application (such as the HTTP application described in this chapter), it is possible to add the data objects necessary for the new application at runtime to the network elements in the stored network. This would not be possible if configuration data items were to be encapsulated in the network object classes.

The information and data-handling features provided by the NetworkObject class are inherited by the subclasses of the NetworkObject class, namely, the GenericNode and the GenericLink class. The class GenericNode is an abstract class that is used mainly to implement some general properties of network nodes. Derived from this

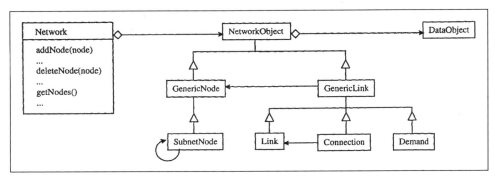

Figure 19.6 Inheritance and part-of relationships in the network model.

class is the class SubnetNode that supports the concept of subnetworks. That is, each instance of SubnetNode may again contain a set of SubnetNode objects. Hence, it is possible to model the concept of local area networks (LANs) being interconnected to form wide area networks (WANs), by using single instances of SubnetNode to represent complete LANs, whose components are then represented by SubnetNode objects within those LAN nodes. For the representation of link objects, three different classes are derived from class GenericLink: Link, Demand, and Connection. All of these classes keep references to a start and an end node. The class Connection is used to represent paths in a network; hence, it is capable of also holding references to Link objects. Note that there is no restriction on the number of links, demands or connections that can exist between two nodes. Furthermore, GenericLink objects may be either directed or undirected, depending on the requirements of the application (for example, ATM works with directed connections).

While this network model allows the representation of a large number of different network architectures and topologies, the framework also provides some standard access methods with the intention of providing easy access to network components and their data objects. The two most important access schemes are based on the design patterns Iterator and Visitor. In the case of the framework, a network iterator is a class that offers a standard interface for the traversal of the network structure, depending on the needs of the application.

For example, in the HTTP application it is necessary to traverse the network along an ISDN connection; that is, a path between two nodes has to be found and each link in this path has to be returned to the application for computation purposes. Similarly, the network visitor class offers a standard interface to visit a set of selected network objects by using a specific iterator. For each of the visited objects, an action or operation is then performed. For example, in the HTTP application, the maximum delay over all link components in a path must be determined. Hence, a visitor object that looks at each link in a path, reads the delays from the associated DataObject objects, and returns the maximum delay, can be used.

19.1.5 Controller Framework

Every application requires some form of control mechanism that organizes the interaction with the user, maintains the graphical user interface, and executes the actual application algorithms (see also Figure 19.2). In a toolkit environment, the control mechanism that is written by the application programmer needs to create all the components such as a network or the main interface. Hence, it must be rewritten for each new application. This is not the case in a framework environment. As indicated in the overview in Figure 19.3, the framework incorporates an application subframework, which contains certain control components such as a MainControl, an EditControl, and a ViewControl. Note that the general idea behind this architecture was influenced by the Model/View/Controller pattern described in [Gamma 1995]. These components are responsible for tasks that are normally provided by an application. For example, the MainControl object creates and maintains the network object, the main default window (see Figure 19.9), and the EditControl and the ViewControl objects. The Edit-Control object, on the other hand, manages all buttons and menu items in the default window that are involved in the process of editing, creating, and modifying a network, while the ViewControl displays or hides labels and legends and the splitting of the main network view.

Due to the fact that all of these controlling objects have some significant commonalities, the framework contains a class GenericController, from which all controlling classes are derived (see Figure 19.7). In particular, the MainController is the class from which a single object is instantiated that controls the network and the main interfaces. The ApplicationController class, on the other hand, is the superclass of the EditController and ViewController class that implement the behavior of the aforementioned EditControl and ViewControl objects. Among the member functions implemented by ApplicationController are access functions to the network object and the main interfaces created by the MainController object to which a reference is kept. Also, a standard event-handling scheme for keyboard and mouse events is integrated into the ApplicationController class. Furthermore, a special handshake scheme is implemented in the ApplicationController in order to prevent by default that user applications can be run concurrently. That is, ApplicationController contains a method startApplication that calls the function closeCurrentApplication of the MainController class. This function in turn calls the closeApplication method of the currently running application, asking it to close down and clean up. If the current application refuses to close down, the new application cannot be started. This handshake scheme is particularly useful when applications change the network graphical features (such as changing the color of links) or when special data objects are added to the network. Before other applications can be run in the default environment, the additions and settings initiated by the previous application must be undone. This process can be performed in the closeApplication that is called by the handshake procedure. Note that the handshake may be bypassed by application programmers, if concurrent activation of applications is desired.

It is important to note that any new application that is built with the framework must incorporate a controller object that is derived from ApplicationController. This guaran-

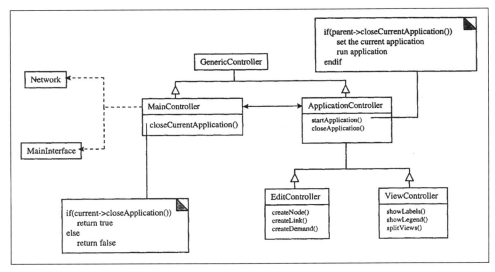

Figure 19.7 Inheritance and reference relationships in the controller framework.

tees that the application has access to all resources, the network and the main interfaces objects, the EditControl, and the ViewControl. Other components of an application such as an algorithm (*Section 19.1.7*) and a panel for querying parameters from the user and displaying algorithm results (*Section 19.1.6*) must be created in the new application controller class. Once a new application controller has been created it must be registered in the MainControl object as the current application. Thanks to this registration process, mouse and keyboard events can be sent from the MainControl object to the current application, where they may be handled in an application-specific fashion.

In the case of the HTTP application example, a controller class is required to instantiate an algorithm for delay computation, creates a new panel for the display of delay information, and handles possible user interaction such as mouseclicks in the application panel. An instance of this controller class must then be created and registered with the MainControl object in order to make it available in the framework.

We conclude that the concept of a global and different application controller provides a standard and easy interface for an application programmer to interact with the interface and the network components of the framework. The same control mechanisms provided by the global controller can be reused by several user applications without any modification to the global controller.

19.1.6 Interface Framework

From a user's point of view, a very important requirement of a network planning and design application is the availability of an easy-to-use graphical user interface (GUI). Clearly, this interface must provide both standard functionalities (such as allowing the modification of a network in a graphical environment where zooming, selecting, and printing are supported) as well as application-specific features (such as text and matrix panels providing additional information about an application). It is easy to see that creating and maintaining an interface that supports editing and viewing a network is no trivial matter. Hence, one of the main advantages of the framework is that it contains an interface subframework that offers a default interface for user operations on a network object. Furthermore, it provides a number of standard panels that can be subclassed and adapted to specific needs.

In Figure 19.8, the relationships among the most important classes in the interface framework are displayed. At the core of this subframework, there is a class CpcGeneric-Interface that implements general features and methods for the organization of buttons, menu items, text fields, scrolling fields, and more. In particular, it allows the construction and storage of interfaces outside of the framework by using a GUI editor. This makes it possible to change and modify interfaces at runtime. Note that this particular functionality is inherited from classes provided by the ILOG Views toolkit. Also, the GUI editor for these text-based descriptions is part of the ILOG Views package.

Besides creating interface objects and organizing them in windows or views, the class GenericInterface also implements callback functions for the graphical objects that are created by it. For example, each button described in the text file is first created and then registered with a standard callback function. The purpose of these callback functions is to link buttons or menu items in a panel to member functions in a controller object because all the intelligence of the application should be incorporated in the controller and not in the interface objects. However, before a method of a controller object can be

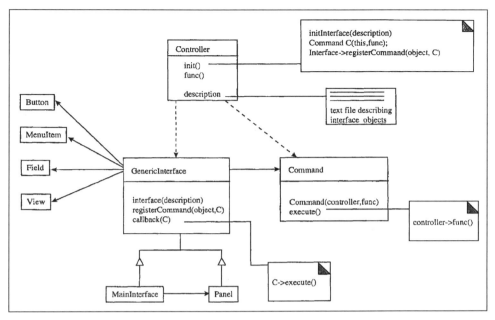

Figure 19.8   Inheritance and class relationships of interface framework.

executed by a callback function in a GenericInterface object, a link between the interface object and the controller method must be made. For this purpose, the framework contains a class Command, which is basically an implementation of the design pattern Command. Objects of this class are used to encapsulate a pointer to a controller class and a pointer to a method of this class. When attached to an interface object such as a button, the Command object is executed in the callback function and, in turn, the method of the controller gets called. In Figure 19.8, this control flow scheme is indicated in the Controller function init( ), in the function callback( ) of GenericInterface, and in the method execute( ) of the Command class. The main advantage of this scheme is that methods of an application controller can be easily connected to interface objects.

All of the functionalities of GenericInterface previously described are also available in the class MainInterface (that implements the default main window of any framework application) and in the class Panel (based on which application-specific panels may be built). In Figure 19.9, some of the most important features of MainInterface are summarized. For example, the main view, in which the network topology is displayed, may be split as well as stacked with additional views. Particularly the latter feature enables an application to add a panel to the main view. The user may then switch between network view and application panel. Other features include an overview window, a button area, and the main menu bar. The overview window indicates the current magnification and scroll position, providing the user with the necessary orientation in a large network. The button area is maintained by the EditController and provides standard buttons for editing a network such as addition, deletion, or modification buttons. Finally, the main menu bar is the place from which all framework-provided and user-defined applications are started.

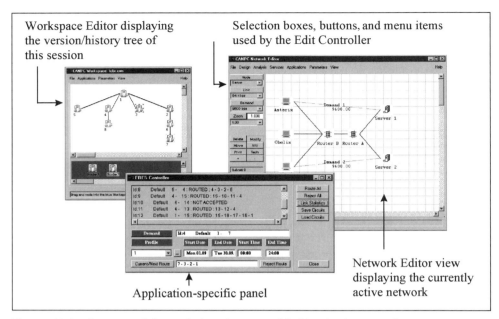

Workspace Editor displaying the version/history tree of this session

Selection boxes, buttons, and menu items used by the Edit Controller

Network Editor view displaying the currently active network

Application-specific panel

Figure 19.9 Features of the main interfaces provided by the framework.

The interface subframework plays an important role in helping the application programmer to write applications that are integrated within the framework and work in a well-defined and, to the user, well-known environment. For example, in the HTTP application a new panel must be created that allows the user to input application-specific parameters such as server think time and response size. Furthermore, the panel must also contain a scrolling text list in which the delay results for each communication request can be displayed. Finally, it will be necessary to add a new menu item to the main menu bar—a menu item that points to the new delay applications. All of these interface components can be subclassed from and integrated into the interface framework as described in this section.

Note also that because all of the interface classes defined by the framework are based on ILOG Views classes, applications written with the framework are fully portable from one operating system platform to the other.

19.1.7 Algorithm Framework

While the controller and the interface framework encapsulate design ideas that are easily understandable from the point of view of a programmer implementing some generic application, the need for an algorithm framework may not be evident immediately. In order to explain why an algorithm framework is necessary in a network planning and design framework, we consider one particular aspect of the HTTP example application from *Section 19.1.3* in more detail.

For the actual computation of an HTTP delay between two communication nodes, it is necessary to first compute the Transport Communication Protocol (TCP) delay. The

TCP delay, on the other hand, depends on the Internet Protocol (IP) delay. However, it is easy to see that the IP delay differs from one network technology to the other. That is, if the underlying network is an asynchronous transfer mode (ATM) network, then the IP delay is computed in a different manner compared to the case where the network is based on ISDN. Furthermore, in an ISDN network, the IP delay also depends on the type of service (primary or basic) that is used. In Figure 19.10, the dependencies of the different delay models are hierarchically displayed.

Clearly, in a classical programming approach the code fragments for the different IP delay calculations would be integrated into a single algorithm IP delay, which would be directly called by the TCP delay code. This procedure works fine as long as there is no need to add new IP delay models for new types of networks. In any of these cases, however, code maintenance and reuse become very difficult. Hence, we propose an algorithm framework, which aims at facilitating the reuse, addition, and composition of special algorithm fragments.

The aspect of composing algorithm fragments makes the algorithm framework interesting for application domains where algorithms depend on a large number of conditions and on circumstances such as the technology and the topology of a network. For example, in the call scheme displayed in Figure 19.10, the computation of the TCP delay actually requires that several decisions be made concerning the algorithm fragments. That is, the TCP delay is calculated dynamically from the various fragments. This approach to composing algorithms is similar to the compositional modeling approach introduced in [Falkenhainer 1991] for describing thermodynamic systems. In order for the algorithm fragments to be automatically composed, each fragment must specify the conditions and assumptions under which it can be applied. For

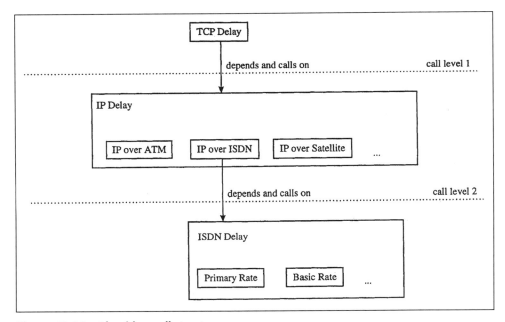

Figure 19.10   Algorithm call structure.

example, if a user or an application requires that the IP delay in a given network is computed, each algorithm fragment for IP delay computation must verify whether the network conditions and parameters for it to compute the delay correctly are provided. Hence, a fragment computing the IP over ATM delay must ensure that the underlying network is, in fact, an ATM network and all the necessary parameters describing an ATM network are available. Furthermore, in order to provide the user or the application with an interface to the algorithm fragments, these fragments must be encapsulated and collected in a container according to their meaning and output; that is, all IP delay fragments must be collected and organized in a container for IP delay computation. This container must implement a common interface to the algorithm fragments, thus allowing the automatic selection and the composition of the fragments that are valid under the current circumstances. Finally, it must support the addition of new fragments without the need to adjust existing applications.

In the algorithm framework, we propose so-called *algorithm families,* in which the algorithm fragments, or *algorithm models,* are collected. In Figure 19.11, the class diagram for the algorithm framework is displayed. For the algorithm families there is a class AlgorithmFamily, whose purpose it is to implement a common interface for the selection and execution of the algorithm models that are contained in it. For the algorithm models themselves, there is a generic class Algorithm, which offers a common interface for accessing the assumptions and the computations inherent in an algorithm model. It also implements a standard method for the retrieval of parameters from the current controller object. The actual implementation of an algorithm model is done in a subclass of the generic Algorithm class. For example, in Figure 19.11, there are two algorithm models—TCPDelay and IPoverISDN—indicated as subclasses of Algorithm. An instance of each of these classes exists in the application and these instances are kept within an object of class AlgorithmFamily. Hence, in the HTTP example application, there will be one AlgorithmFamily object encapsulating all TCP delay algorithms,

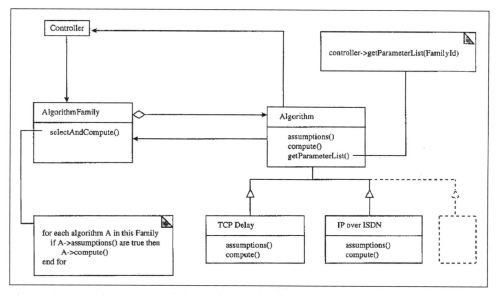

Figure 19.11 Inheritance and class relationship diagram of algorithm framework.

another one for all IP delay algorithms, and a further one for the ISDN delay models. At runtime, the actual selection of the right algorithm model in each AlgorithmFamily is performed in the method selectAndCompute( ) of AlgorithmFamily (see Figure 19.11). It is this method that is called from within an application controller. Its task is to call the assumptions of each of the algorithm models it contains and to finally compute the requested value with the algorithm model that suits the current situation. Clearly, new algorithm models may be added to an AlgorithmFamily object at any time, even at runtime, without the need to upgrade or inform the applications that use that particular AlgorithmFamily object. Furthermore, all details concerning the actual selection, computation, and composition process of a certain algorithm are hidden from the application programmer. Hence, complicated algorithms may be used in an application without the need to understand their implementation details and still it is guaranteed that the correct algorithm fragments are chosen according to the current circumstances.

In Figure 19.12, the object relationship diagram for some of the algorithm families used in the HTTP example is given. As already mentioned, for the computation of an HTTP

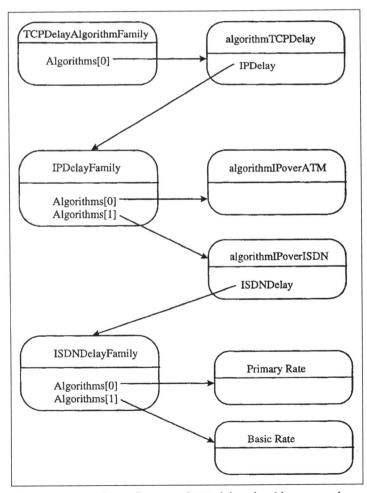

Figure 19.12 Object diagram of TCP delay algorithm example.

delay, the TCP delay is required. Hence, there is an AlgorithmFamily object named TCPDelayAlgorithmFamily, which holds an instance of an object of class algorithmTCPDelay. In this algorithm, the IPDelayFamily is called. This algorithm family, in turn, contains two algorithm models: an object of class algorithmIPoverATM and another object of class algorithmIPoverISDN. Again, IP over ISDN requires the ISDN delay and, thus, calls the family ISDNDelayFamily object, which will then select either the model Primary Rate or the model Basic Rate, depending on the service available in the underlying network.

We conclude that the algorithm framework provides a mechanism for the addition and the deletion of algorithms and for the automatic choice of the right algorithm to suit the requirements of a user application. The concept of an algorithm family aids the reuse of existing algorithms and the addition of new algorithm fragments (to accommodate the needs of future network technology) without any modifications to the user applications.

19.2 Example Application

In the previous sections, we have explained in detail the four subframeworks and the generic network model, as well as the relationships among these components. For a better understanding, the HTTP application was always used as a reference and the components and classes from the subframework that were to be subclassed were indicated. In this section, we briefly summarize the steps that are necessary in order to implement an application such as the HTTP example on the basis of the framework (see also Figure 19.12 and Table 19.1).

Table 19.1   Requirements and Implementations in HTTP Example

REQUIREMENT FOR . . .	IMPLEMENTATION
A controller mechanism that creates an application interface and organizes the communication between the user, the delay algorithm, the network, and the interface.	Subclass the ApplicationController class into an HTTPController. Create a new object of this class and link it to a menu in the default framework interface.
An application interface that queries the user for details and displays results.	Subclass ApplicationInterface into a class HTTPinterface and create an interface description for this class with the GUI builder program. Register the interface in the HTTPController object.
Special links representing ISDN links over which a TCP connection is set up.	Subclass DataObject into classes TCPDelay, IPDelay, and ISDNproperties, and attach objects of these classes to link objects. For the computed attributes, subclass ValueModel into corresponding DelayModels and register them in an object of ValueFamily
An algorithm for the computation of the HTTP delay.	subclass class Algorithm into HTTP-AlgorithmModel and register this algorithm model in a family HTTPAlgorithm.

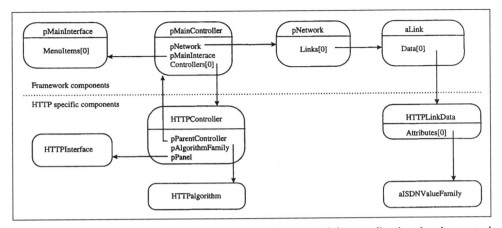

Figure 19.13 Object relationship diagram of the HTTP delay application implemented with the framework.

Figure 19.13 shows an object diagram describing the most important components and objects in the HTTP application and their relationship to the standard components provided by the framework. Notice that there are basically two places where application-specific objects are linked into framework components: in the MainControl object pMainController, which holds a reference to the pHTTPController object, and in the link object such as aLink, where an object aHTTPLinkData is attached, which contains, among other things, a reference to an ISDNValueFamily object. In the HTTPController there is also a reference to the HTTPInterface object. In Figure 19.14, a screen shot of the HTTP application displays both this HTTPInterface and the main interface of the framework. Furthermore, it also shows how the attributes that have been newly defined by the HTTP application are recognized by the EditControl object which lists them in the modification panel.

19.3 Summary

We have presented a framework of frameworks for the development of network planning, design, and optimization applications. This framework has already been used successfully for the development of four distinct applications by different groups, of which two were not directly involved in the development of the framework itself. From the experience gained in these four projects, the following main advantages are worth mentioning:

- The framework is well suited for the fast development of prototypes, which can then be used to further develop a productive version. Hence, the time lost on coding that is often experienced when using languages such as VisualBasic for prototyping does not occur when a framework like NETPLAN is applied.

- It is easy to integrate different applications within a master application. Hence, a user may analyze, optimize, or merely study the same network in conjunction with applications that were developed by different parties without having to switch applications and keep copies of the network in each of these applications.

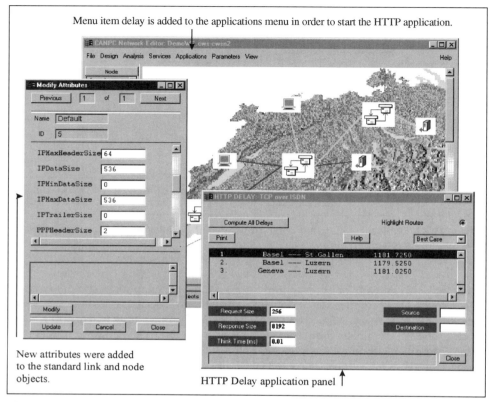

Figure 19.14 HTTP application panel and Modify panel displaying new attributes.

- The compositional modeling approach used in the algorithm and the data management subframeworks allows the realization of open and scalable systems.

- The facilities provided by the ILOG Views library make the framework truly portable. This is particularly important for applications that must run both in a backoffice environment such as a Unix system and also on the customer front, where Window-based platforms are more popular.

As with any system, there are still a number of features missing that may be required in other domains. In particular, we intend to move the framework from a single process philosophy to a distributed processing scheme by introducing CORBA [Siegel 1996] aspects in the following manner. The algorithm subframework and the network model will be encapsulated in a single server object, while the interface framework will be wrapped in a Web-based client object, which will gain access to the other subframeworks via an application framework server. Hence, a three-tier architecture will be formed whereby the interface framework client can run on any user machine that is connected via the inter/intranet to the application server component. This server component, in turn, will have access to the network model and the algorithm framework component. In this manner, it will be possible to have several people working with the same network model, provided that each user touches only on subareas of the network that are disjoint from the subareas of other users. We believe that a framework that provides basic functionalities and standard applications for such a distributed architecture and also offers all of the application development features described in this chapter would be of tremendous interest to the telecommunication and information technology industry.

19.4 References

[Booch 1994] Booch, G. Designing an application framework. *Dr. Dobb's Journal* 19(2), 1994.

[Brazier 1996] Brazier, F.M.T., B.M. Dunin Keplicz, N.R. Jennings, and J. Treur. DESIRE: Modeling multi-agent systems in a compositional formal framework. *International Journal of Cooperative Information Systems,* Special Issue on Formal Methods in Cooperative Information Systems: Multi-Agent Systems, M. Huhns and M. Singh, editors, 1997.

[Buschmann 1996] Buschmann, F., R. Meunier, H. Rohnert, P. Sommerlad, and M. Stal. *Pattern-Oriented Software Architecture: A System of Patterns.* New York: John Wiley & Sons, 1996.

[Falkenhainer 1991] Falkenhainer, B., and K. Forbus. Compositional modeling: Finding the right model for the job. *Artificial Intelligence* 51:95–143.

[Gamma 1995] Gamma, E., R. Helm, R. Johnson, and J. Vlissides. *Design Patterns: Elements of Reusable Object-Oriented Software.* Reading, MA: Addison-Wesley, 1995.

[ILOG 1996] ILOG S.A. *ILOG Views—Reference Manual Version 2.3.* France: ILOG S.A., 1996.

[Messmer 1997] Messmer, B. *NETPLAN: An Object Oriented Framework for Network Planning and Design.* Software documentation, Corporate Information Technology, Swisscom, 1997.

[Nadjm 1997] Nadjm-Tehrani, S. Reactive systems in physical environments: Compositional modeling and framework for verification. Dissertation No. 338, Ph.D. thesis, Department of Computer and Information Science, Linköping University, 1997.

[Siegel 1996] Siegel, J. *CORBA Fundamentals and Programming.* New York: John Wiley & Sons, 1996.

[Taligent 1995] Taligent, Inc. *The Power of Frameworks.* Reading, MA: Addison-Wesley (The Taligent Reference Library), 1995.

FIONA: A Framework for Integrating Distributed C³I Applications

FIONA has been developed by Origin as part of the EUCLID RTP6.1 R&D contract undertaken by the GRACE Consortium (Grouping for Research into Advanced C³I for Europe) led by Logica UK Limited. The focus of this project is to accelerate the application of advanced artificial intelligence (AI), human-computer interface (HCI), and distributed computing technologies to command, control, communications, and intelligence (C³I) systems. Such systems are increasingly important for battlefield, naval, and air operations; they also have civilian applications in areas such as air traffic control and emergency services.

The motivation behind the RTP6.1 research program is twofold. First, the situation on the battlefield is rapidly changing because of the following factors:

- Longer range and more sophisticated weapons

- The increased amount, diversity, and complexity of military intelligence information

- The change of focus from large-scale, east-west conflict scenarios, to smaller-scale, UN peacekeeping-type scenarios

- Decreased staffing

Second, the current operational C³I systems often possess the following problems:

- Poor user interfaces

- Expensive, monolithic, proprietary, noninteroperable, stovepipe systems

- Difficult to adapt, modify, and maintain
- Technology quickly becomes obsolete

The overall objective of the RTP6.1 project has therefore been to develop a modular, multiagent, open-standard-based, intelligent C³I architecture, which will be evaluated through the implementation of two technology demonstrators, one for the army domain, and one for the navy domain. The facilities and components created by the various parties in the project are integrated into one system in the GRACE demonstrator application; see Figure 20.1.

The main components of the GRACE demonstrator are the following:

Naval or army simulator. Scenarios are described using a particular script language. A scenario script describes the initial tactical situation and the following sequence of events.

Automated report analysis (ARA). This module receives reports from the simulator. The reports are identified and the information extracted and analyzed. The output of the ARA module is a *wide area picture* (WAP) database, which is a data model describing the current tactical situation.

Decision support, planning, and tasking (DSPT) facilities. These are facilities, or applications, providing support for things such as: situation and tactical threat analysis, terrain analysis, course of action construction, resource allocation, and engagement coordination planning. Important goals with these facilities are that they be modular and reusable, and that they provide services for each other.

The GRACE system architecture. This consists of two main parts: the CABLE multi-agent framework and the FIONA HCI-framework.

Test harness. This provides services that allow components in the system to be analyzed and evaluated.

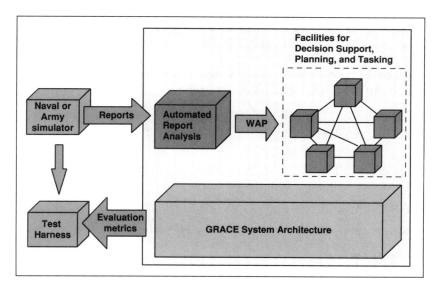

Figure 20.1 The GRACE C³I technology demonstrator.

The focus of this chapter is on the FIONA framework, which, together with the CABLE agent framework, forms the system architecture developed in the RTP6.1 project. First we will give a brief overview of the overall GRACE system architecture, then the FIONA framework will be described in more detail, and finally we will draw conclusions. The notation used in the chapter is the object management technology (OMT)–based notation developed by Gamma, et al. [Gamma 1995], with some additions here and there from the Unified Modeling Language (UML) [Booch 1996].

20.1 The GRACE System Architecture

The GRACE system architecture supports distributed components of the following types (as shown in Figure 20.2):

Agent. This is an autonomously operating component without a user-interface. It can cooperate intelligently with other agents, and it has deep knowledge of the application domain.

Applet. These are the user-interface components. They have (in general) little knowledge about the application domain. Each applet runs as a separate process with its own windows, menus, and dialogs.

Agent-applet. A combination of an agent and an applet that provides the link between the application-domain of the agents and the user-domain of the applets.

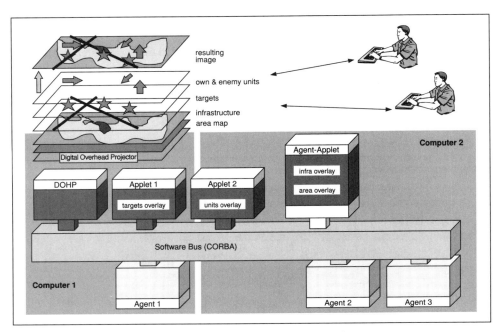

Figure 20.2 The main components in the GRACE system architecture.

Digital overhead projector (DOHP). This is a central, shared presentation facility used to display map and dynamic data in a fashion similar to that of an overhead projector. In order to place a graphical object on the DOHP, an applet first has to create a transparent overlay, which is used as a placeholder for the object. The resulting picture on the DOHP is the combination of all the overlays owned by different applets. Other functionalities provided by the DOHP include: turning the visibility of overlays on and off, changing the order of the overlays, panning and zooming, applet event callbacks, groupworking, and a publish-and-subscribe mechanism.

Agent components are constructed with the CABLE agent building environment, while applet components are constructed with the FIONA framework. The DOHP is a ready-to-use component provided by FIONA.

Figure 20.3 shows the common off-the-shelf (COTS) products used. CORBA was chosen as the distributed object middleware because it provides a high-level, object-oriented mechanism for communication between distributed objects; it is an open standard, and it is available on a large range of platforms. By using CORBA, it is furthermore easy to support runtime plug and play of distributed components, as the technical infrastructure to do this is provided by CORBA [OMG 1996]. ILOG Views is a cross-platform GUI builder and user interface toolkit providing a powerful set of classes for creating advanced graphical applications [ILOG 1995]. STL is part of the C++ standard and provides a library of collection and utility classes.

The programming language we chose to use was C++, as this was the most suitable language at the time for a number of theoretical and practical reasons: It is a powerful object-oriented language, it is available on all platforms, and it had the largest collection of available COTS products. There are, however, also a number of drawbacks: The language is very complex and thus very error prone, it does not support garbage collection, and it is a compiled language, which limits its flexibility at runtime. If we were to choose a programming language today we would very likely have opted for Java, as it is much easier and safer to use than C++ [Arnold 1996]; it provides garbage collection, built-in multithreading support, a very large collection of standard classes and frameworks, and a powerful component model; and its interpreted nature opens up a whole new set of possibilities for constructing and deploying applications.

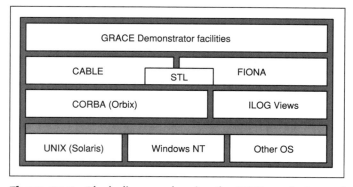

Figure 20.3 Block diagram showing the COTS products used in the GRACE system architecture.

20.2 The FIONA Framework

The FIONA framework is a pattern- and object-oriented framework for constructing user interface components (applets) that fit into the GRACE architecture. It has been designed to make it easy for developers to create new components by use of well-known design patterns and by providing an applet framework that encapsulates all the generic code that is needed for creating applets. Care has also been taken to encapsulate all the CORBA-related code in just a few classes. This makes the rest of the framework much cleaner, it makes it easy to switch to another CORBA implementation, and it makes the framework easy to use for developers with little or no CORBA experience. The main classes and modules in the framework are shown in Figure 20.4.

The patterns implemented in FIONA are:

Storable (or Object Serialization). This is used to make it possible to pass C++ objects by value via CORBA and to provide lightweight persistence support [OMG 1996]. This provides a much more flexible and generic method for communicating between distributed objects than that provided by the standard CORBA facilities, and it can greatly reduce the number of CORBA calls needed to pass data back and forth between components (see [Buschmann 1996; Coplien 1995; Mowbray 1997]).

Anonymous Publish-Subscribe. This is similar to the Observer pattern in [Gamma 1995], but it decouples the publisher (subject) and subscriber (observer) even more. It allows applets to subscribe to specific events, which can be published by

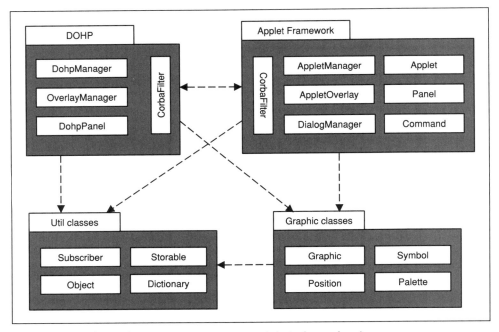

Figure 20.4   The main FIONA components and their dependencies.

other applets or by the DOHP. A *publishing agent* (or broker) is used for subscribing and publishing. The subscribers will receive a notification only for those events to which they have subscribed. All sorts of data can be passed in the notification call.

Composite. This is used for the Graphic classes. This allows a composite graphic to be treated in the same way as a single graphic object and thus helps to keep interfaces small and generic [Gamma 1995].

Extended Command pattern. This lets user actions be encapsulated as command-objects, which makes it possible to queue or log the actions and to support reversible operations. The Command pattern in FIONA also supports *dependencies* between commands and *multiple views* (buttons, menu items, and so on) attached to a command. Command dependencies mean that commands can be *enabled* and *disabled* depending on the state of other commands [Gamma 1995; Young 1992].

Template and Hooks pattern. This is used in many places where abstract classes provide generic functionality, which can be extended in Hook methods by subclasses [Gamma 1995].

Method pattern. This is used by the Panel class to let subclasses instantiate the overlay object [Gamma 1995].

These patterns, together with the applet-component skeleton provided by the Applet framework, make the FIONA framework flexible, extensible, and easy to use. The Publish-Subscribe pattern, for instance, provides a very generic communication mechanism between the participating objects. This makes it easy to plug and play publishers and subscribers in a blackbox fashion. Some of the patterns will be described in more detail later.

20.2.1 Combining CORBA with GUI Software

Both the DOHP and FIONA applets make use of CORBA in conjunction with graphical user interface (GUI) software. Using CORBA together with GUI software such as ILOG Views is not without problems, as both systems use a *main event loop* to process events. In the case of CORBA, these events will be CORBA messages (requests), and in the case of the GUI software, they will be user events.

A solution to this problem is to use two threads to run the main loops, but this creates a new problem since ILOG Views is not thread-safe and (for some technical reason that we won't go into here) requires that all calls to ILOG Views must be made from one single thread; in other words, it is not enough to use semaphores around the calls made to ILOG Views from different threads [ILOG 1995]. As the CORBA requests could also result in user interface calls, this meant that a solution had to be found that would allow the ILOG Views thread to handle the CORBA requests as well [ILOG 1995].

Orbix helps to solve this problem via its *filter* mechanism [Orbix 1995]. Orbix filters allow a programmer to specify that additional code is to be executed before or after the normal code of an operation. This makes it possible to perform security checks, provide logging, start up a thread per request, and so on. In our case, we used the filter

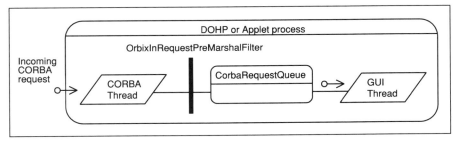

Figure 20.5 The mechanism used to ensure that all GUI calls are handled by a single thread.

mechanism to intercept incoming CORBA requests and put them into a request queue. The CORBA call is returned immediately after the request has been put in the queue; that is, the request is not handled further by the CORBA thread. The requests entered into the request queue are then removed from the queue by the GUI thread and processed further, as shown in Figure 20.5.

20.3 Design Patterns Used in FIONA

This section provides a more detailed description of the most important patterns used in FIONA. Other patterns were briefly described previously.

20.3.1 The Storable Pattern

The motivation for implementing this pattern in FIONA arose from the need to pass C++ objects *by value* via CORBA. The current CORBA standard (v2.0) only supports passing primitive types, structs (such as C structs), and references to remote objects between the communicating objects [OMG 1996]. This is cumbersome and inefficient when the information that must be communicated is contained in complex object structures, such as all the data needed to produce a map picture in an overlay on the DOHP; and, just as important, it interferes with the object-oriented way of programming, as illustrated in Exhibit 20.1.

Exhibit 20.1 Nongeneric Interface as a Result of Limitations in CORBA-IDL (v2.0)

```
typedef struct { .. } Point;
typedef struct { .. } Rect;
typedef sequence<Point> Points;

interface DOHP {
    oneway void AddPolyline( in string id, in Points pts, .. );
    oneway void AddPolygon( in string id, in Points pts, .. );
    oneway void AddEllipse( in string id, in Rect r, .. );
    <etc>..
};
```

This type of interface does not follow good object-oriented practices, as it requires the interface to be extended with every new type of graphic class that is added to the system, and composite graphical objects would have to be broken up and sent one by one. A good object-oriented solution to this problem would be to use the Composite pattern and define an abstract Graphic class, as shown in Exhibit 20.2.

This is a generic interface that would allow all types of graphic objects, including composites, to be passed. Adding new graphical classes to the system will have no impact on the interface. Regrettably, this type of interface is currently not (directly) possible in CORBA IDL.

One solution to this problem is the Storable pattern presented here. This is a pattern that makes it easy to add lightweight persistency support to a class. An intentional side effect is that this also makes it easy to pass (C++) objects *as strings* via CORBA. A similar pattern is the Serialize mechanism supported by Java [Arnold 1996]. The Serialize mechanism goes further, however, as it not only supports passing the data but also the code if this is not already present at the receiving end. This is possible in Java since it includes a runtime system that allows code to be dynamically loaded (interpreted). The Storable pattern presented here requires that the code for the objects that is passed by value via CORBA must be present on both the sending and the receiving side (see Figure 20.6).

The TutlStorableManager is an internal class that manages a dictionary containing class names of storable classes and their read functions. Objects are restored from their string representation by using the read functions in this dictionary. The abstract Tutl-Storable class defines the storable interface that must be implemented by all storable classes. There are four methods that must be implemented:

<classname>(istream). The stream constructor; it should reconstruct the object from its stringified representation.

Read. The (static) read function used to restore the object. This is the method that will be called by the TutlStorableManager.

Write. This method should save the state of the object to the stream.

ClassName. This method should return the name of the class.

The *finalized* methods: ToString, Save, Restore, and RestoreState, should not be overridden by subclasses. They are *template* methods (as in the Template and Hooks pattern), which should be used as provided. The TutlStorableType class is used to register

Exhibit 20.2   Wanted: A Generic, Object-Oriented Interface

```
class Graphic { .. };  // an abstract graphic class which supports the
                       //Composite pattern

interface DOHP {
    oneway void AddGraphic( in Graphic g, .. );
};
```

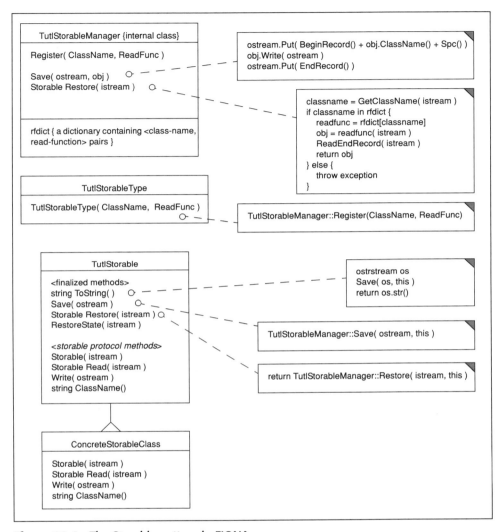

Figure 20.6 The Storable pattern in FIONA.

a new storable type with the TutlStorableManager. One instance of this class must be created for every new Storable class.

A limitation of the pattern, as presented here, is that it does not support object references; that is, saving a pointer to an object that has already been saved will cause a copy of the object to be written to the stream. The ability to save and restore pointers to objects can be provided by adding an instance-container to the TutlStorableManager class and changing the Save and Restore methods as shown in Exhibits 20.3 and 20.4.

Using the Storable pattern, we can now define the DOHP interface in a generic, object-oriented manner as shown in Exhibit 20.5.

Exhibit 20.3 Improved Save Method That Supports Restoring Object References

```
TutlStorableManager::Save( ostream os, Storable obj )
{
    // start saving with an empty instance container
    if os.AtBeginning() {
        instances.EraseAll()
    }

    if instances.Contains( obj ) {
        os.Put( BeginRecord() + "Ref " + instances.GetLocation(obj) +
Spc() + EndRecord() )
    } else {
        os.Put( BeginRecord() + obj.ClassName() + Spc() )
        obj.Write( os )
        os.Put( EndRecord() )
        instances.Add( obj )
    }
}
```

Exhibit 20.4 Improved Restore Method That Supports Restoring Object References

```
Storable
StorableManager::Restore( istream is )
{
    // start restoring with an empty instance container
    if is.AtBeginning() {
        instances.EraseAll()
    }

    ReadBeginRecord( is )
    w = GetWord( is )

    if IsRef( w ) {
        obj = instances.Get( GetInstanceCount( is ) )
        ReadEndRecord( is )
        return obj
    } else if w in rfdict {
        readfunc = rfdict[w]
        obj = readfunc( is )
        instances.Add( obj )
        ReadEndRecord( is )
        return obj
    } else {
        throw exception
    }
}
```

Exhibit 20.5   A Generic, Object-Oriented Interface Using the Storable Pattern

```
typedef string Graphic;

interface DOHP {
    oneway void AddGraphic( in Graphic g, .. );
};
```

20.3.2 The Anonymous Publish-Subscribe Pattern

The Publish-Subscribe pattern is a very commonly used pattern in object-oriented systems. The original idea comes from the Model/View/Controller framework in Smalltalk, and its intent is to define a one-to-many dependency between objects so that when one object changes state (publishes an event), all its dependants (subscribers) are notified and updated automatically. There are two main uses of this pattern in FIONA (as shown in Figure 20.7):

- To be used by the DOHP to signal user interface events to the applets. The difference with this and the normal overlay callbacks is that they will be received only by the *owner* of the overlay, while events coming via the Publish-Subscribe mechanism can be received by anybody.

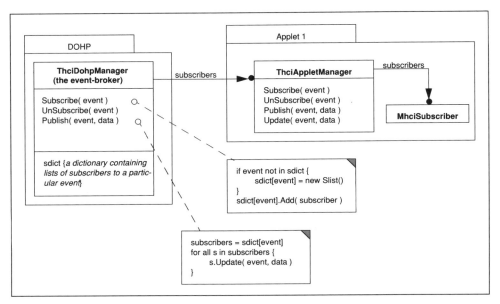

Figure 20.7   Implementation of the Anonymous Publish-Subscribe pattern in FIONA.

■ To facilitate anonymous peer-to-peer communication between the applets themselves.

The Anonymous Publish-Subscribe pattern implemented in FIONA differs in the following ways from the Observer pattern [Gamma 1995]:

Global event broker. Using an event broker the DOHP decouples the publishers and their subscribers. This makes the pattern very robust and easy to use since a subscriber does not have to find out which publisher it should subscribe to. This means that a subscriber will never miss an important notification because it happened to use the wrong publisher, as might be the case in the standard Observer pattern. The robustness resulting from the decoupling is especially useful in distributed systems where all sorts of errors can occur.

Events types. Subscribers can specify areas of interest by supplying an event argument. The addition of events to the mechanism eases the burden on the subscribers since they only receive Update notifications concerning events that are of interest to them.

The data are passed together with the event in the Update call. Passing the data along with the Update notification reduces the communication overhead (which is important in a distributed system) and ensures that the event and data are synchronized (something that might be difficult to ensure in a distributed system otherwise).

A two-level subscription mechanism. A two-level subscription mechanism is used to allow objects inside an applet process to act as subscribers and publishers. This fact is hidden from the DOHP (the event-broker), which sees the applet components only as a whole as a publisher and/or a subscriber.

The event and data that are published can be anything: It is up to the DOHP and individual applets to decide what they want to publish. Complex data can be transmitted as a string by using the Storable pattern, which is described later in this chapter.

20.3.3 The Command Pattern

The Command classes are designed according to the Command pattern in [Gamma 1995; Young 1992]. The intention of this pattern is to encapsulate the user actions (use cases) inside command objects, which makes it possible to queue or log the actions and to support undoable operations (the initial implementation in FIONA will *not* support undoable actions). In addition to the functionality described in [Gamma 1995], the design described here also supports dependencies between commands and multiple views attached to a command. Command dependencies mean that commands can be enabled and disabled depending on the state of other commands. The idea of command dependencies and multiple command views comes from [Young 1992].

A command object is coupled to one or more command-views, which are the graphical presentation of the command. When the state of the command changes, for instance, from enabled to disabled, then all the command-views will reflect this change. The Command pattern can therefore be seen as a special implementation of the Observer pattern. In addition to the advantages already mentioned, this pattern makes

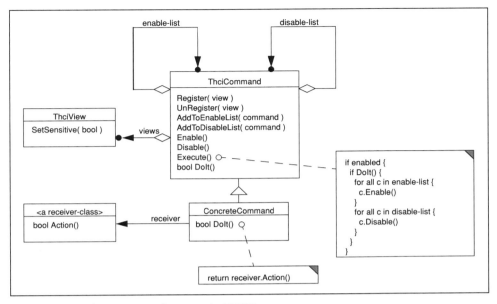

Figure 20.8   The Command pattern in FIONA.

it possible to create a library of common, generic commands that can be reused by all applet developers.

The receiver would typically be a panel (a subclass of MhciPanel), and the command views would be one or more graphic objects (normally buttons and menu items). Figure 20.8 illustrates the Command pattern in FIONA.

20.4 The Applet Framework

The applet framework defines a generic skeleton for an applet. This ensures that all applets have the same internal structure, and it greatly reduces the amount of code that needs to be added by the applet developer to create a specific applet. Besides providing a generic skeleton and thus relieving the burden on the applet developer, the applet framework also makes it much easier to ensure a consistent user interface, since a lot of prebuilt user interaction components can be provided by the framework.

Figure 20.9 shows the main components of the applet framework in FIONA. Most of the classes are internal classes, which are visible only inside the applet component, as only the ThciAppletManager and the ThciAppletOverlay classes are exposed via CORBA IDL interfaces. This high degree of encapsulation makes it easy to change the internals of an applet-component without affecting other parts of the system. The applet developer makes a concrete applet component by taking this applet skeleton and adding the concrete classes at the bottom of the figure.

There are two globally accessible objects in the applet framework: theApplet to access the ThciApplet instance and theDialogManager to access the ThciDialogManager instance. The services provided by these two classes are needed in many places

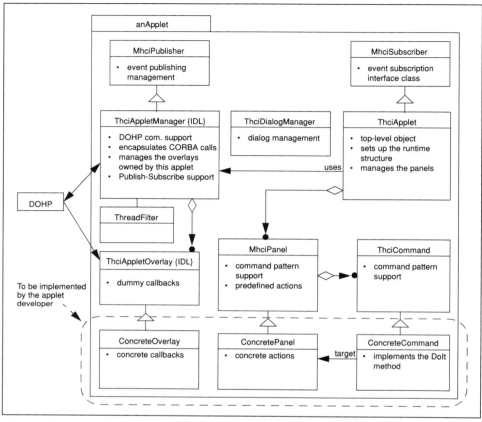

Figure 20.9   Overview of the applet framework.

inside the applet framework. Making them accessible via global references make them easy to use and prevents spreading references to these objects all over the framework. The following gives a brief description of the classes in the applet framework:

ThciApplet. This class parses the command-line arguments received via the main function, sets up the runtime structure of the applet, and manages the windows belonging to the applet.

ThciAppletManager {IDL}. The main responsibility of this class is to administer the DOHP connection and to encapsulate all the CORBA code related to communication from the applet to the DOHP. Other responsibilities are management of the applet overlay-proxies and internal Publish-Subscribe support.

ThciAppletOverlay {IDL}. This is an abstract, protocol class that implements the corresponding IDL interface. Its responsibility is to define the overlay callbacks that can be called by the DOHP. The implementation of the callbacks must be provided in subclasses.

MhciPanel. This is a mixin class that both specifies the protocol and at the same time implements the generic functionality required for the receiver part of the Command pattern.

ThciCommand. This class has already been described in the section describing the Command pattern.

ThciDialogManager. This is a concrete class (with only a single instance) that provides support for creating and displaying common dialogs.

The general approach used when making a new applet component is to use the ILOG Views GUI builder to lay out the user interface gadgets (buttons, menus, and so on) in an interactive fashion. Next, the generated user interface code is tied in with the applet framework via mix-in inheritance. The final part is to add the application-specific code.

20.5 Lessons Learned

The following list summarizes some of the important points highlighted in this chapter.

CORBA—good points. The decision to base the system architecture on CORBA has proven to be a good choice. CORBA IDL is a nice language for specifying component interfaces. During the design phase it helps the designer to focus on the interfaces instead of the details of the implementation, and during the implementation phase it makes it easy for the developers to work independently of each other, as they can develop a component without requiring the implementation of another component to be present.

CORBA—current problem areas. The current (v2.0) CORBA standard still misses some important features, such as the ability to pass objects by value, and a messaging service. A messaging service (providing guaranteed quality of service) is vital for the construction of robust distributed systems that are connected via fragile and/or low-bandwidth networks. Both of these issues will, however, be resolved in the new version of the CORBA standard.

Use of COTS products. The COTS products used (ILOG Views, STL, and Orbix) have proven to be very useful and have saved us lots of work. Their platform independence, for instance, made it possible to port the whole system architecture (totalling around 130,000 lines of code for FIONA and CABLE combined) from Solaris to Windows NT with little effort.

Version management of COTS products. One potential problem when using COTS tools is version management, as all parties involved must use the same versions. In a big project involving many different parties and many different COTS tools, this can become an issue.

Avoid COTS-centric architectures. Another potential problem with the use of COTS products is that the system architecture becomes COTS-centric, that is, too dependent on the particular COTS products that have been used. This makes the architecture less adaptable, less portable, and more difficult to maintain. Care should therefore be taken to avoid this pitfall by encapsulating the COTS tools so that the product-specific code is concentrated in a few areas.

Use of open standards. Using an open standard such as CORBA is, in our minds, also the best way to ensure that the system will be future-proof. Open standards tend to be more stable and tend to have a longer life than proprietary standards. Other important benefits are, of course, the ability to mix and match COTS tools and to make interoperable systems. The most powerful example of this is the Internet, which would not have been possible without open standards such as TCP/IP, HTML, HTTP, and SMTP.

Use of C++. C++ is a powerful object-oriented language. It is also a very complicated, error-prone language, which puts a large burden on the programmer, making it, in fact, not suited for the development of mission-critical systems. The arrival of Java, which has finally brought forward a widely supported language with all the necessary characteristics for the development of mission-critical systems, therefore spells the end of C++ [Java 1997].

20.6 Summary

Experience with the use of the FIONA framework within the GRACE consortium has been positive. By using the framework, it was easy to integrate components provided by different parties in the consortium. Such an integration using a traditional non-CORBA approach would have been a major undertaking, especially in a large, multination project. Using a pattern-oriented, CORBA-based framework such as FIONA has also improved the quality of the system, enabled reuse, made it possible to support runtime plug-and-play components, and made it easy for nonspecialists to develop components.

The most important possible future improvement would be to port FIONA to Java. This would make the framework simpler and less dependent on COTS products, as the Java toolkit has built-in support for object serialization, collection classes, and platform-independent GUI classes [Java 1997]. The powerful JavaBean client-side component model would furthermore make it possible to reduce the window clutter, as user interface components could share the same window space at runtime, and it would make it easy to provide web browser access to the system.

The combination of distributed components, middleware based on open standards, and object-oriented frameworks is clearly the way forward for building complex C^{3}I systems, or any other large mission-critical system.

20.7 References

[Arnold 1996] Arnold, K., and J. Gosling. *The Java Programming Language*. Reading, MA: Addison-Wesley, 1996.

[Booch 1996] Booch, G., J. Rumbaugh, and I. Jacobson. *The Unified Modeling Language for Object-Oriented Development*. Rational Software Corporation, 1996.

[Buschmann 1996] Buschmann, F., R. Muenier, H. Rohnert, P. Sommerlad, and M. Stal. *A System of Patterns: Pattern-Oriented Software Architecture*. New York: John Wiley & Sons, 1996.

[Coplien 1995] Coplien, J., and D. Schmidt. *Pattern Languages of Program Design.* Reading, MA: Addison-Wesley, 1995.

[Gamma 1995] Gamma, E., R. Helm, R. Johnson, and J. Vlissides. *Design Patterns: Elements of Reusable Object-Oriented Software.* Reading, MA: Addison-Wesley, 1995.

[ILOG 1995] ILOG. *ILOG Views User's Manual,* version 2.2. ILOG, 1995.

[Java 1997] Java. *Java Object Serialization Specification,* part of JDK 1.1 documentation. SUN Microsystems, Palo Alto, CA, 1997.

[Mowbray 1997] Mowbray, T.J., and R.C. Malveau. *CORBA Design Patterns.*, New York: John Wiley & Sons, 1997.

[OMG 1996] Object Management Group. *CORBA: Architecture and Specification.* OMG, 1996.

[Orbix 1995] Orbix. *Orbix 2 Programming Guide.* IONA Technologies Ltd., 1995.

[Young 1992] Young, D.A. *Object-Oriented Programming with C++ and OSF/Motif.* Englewood Cliffs, NJ: Prentice Hall, 1992.

MultiTEL: Multimedia Telecommunication Service Framework

Nowadays, we are facing an explosion of sophisticated multimedia telecommunication services (MTSs) developed by many independent service providers. The customer is able to choose from a number of similar services that differ in such things as pricing and quality of service. This kind of competitive market and the complexity of the application domain constitute important factors that contribute to the effective application of any reuse paradigm [Schmidt-Fayad 1997]. Besides this, multimedia services have many characteristics in common: (1) a logic service that involves the definition of the user interaction model, service accessibility, and the event scheduling of the service; (2) multimedia programming; and (3) realtime multipoint channels that meet broadband requirements, which provide appropriate conditions for developing an application framework. Examples of these services are video on demand (VoD), business meetings, conferences, remote education, chats, and computer-supported collaborative work (CSCW).

Work regarding multimedia applications shows that there have been considerable efforts made in developing specific multimedia programs for different application domains [Posnak 1997; Simon 1995], but little work has been done in defining a generic architecture that will integrate all aspects of MTSs. Besides this, other approaches that claim to be open offer only a very small and simple architecture, and so the effort of programming new services is large [Lazar 1995; Rajagopalan 1995]. Furthermore, the most important project concerning the definition of a distributed software architecture is the Telecommunication Intelligent Network Architecture (TINA) [TINA-C, 1995]. Although implementations of TINA complying with Common Object Request Broker Architecture (CORBA) specifications exist, providing a complete environment for the design and development of multimedia telecommunication services remains an open issue [Saridakis 1997].

Moreover, multimedia telecommunication services impose the challenge of building an open service infrastructure for supporting the distributed execution of these applications. The rapid adoption of Internet standards is producing an avalanche of new products and also the emergence of Web-based information networks called *intranets*. Therefore, providing wide access to Web-based collaborative platforms is the key. However, all the processing is tied to Web servers, which do not adequately support the coordination of distributed applications running in client machines. In addition, the Web cannot be used as a distributed processing platform like CORBA [OMG 1995], because it does not provide any kind of object localization service (object request broker, or ORB). There are many approaches [Chandy 1997; Ciancarini 1996; Hirano 1997] that try to overcome these deficiencies by using the mobility characteristics offered by Java applets [Sun 1998].

In order to integrate multimedia services on the Web, we have constructed a complete extensible compositional framework called MultiTEL (short for "multimedia telecommunication services") that tries to shorten the development time of multimedia services [Fuentes-Troya 1999].

Component-oriented frameworks are reusable designs of all or part of a software system described by a set of abstract components and by the way in which instances of these components collaborate. Therefore, frameworks define a reusable context for components, providing a template for implementing them. Our challenge, at first, was to define a new component-oriented model that separates interaction patterns from data processing. The goal of our compositional model is to help service designers in modifying a distributed application to obtain another one with the same patterns of communication and synchronization. Indeed, the service designer can reuse the difficult part (the concurrency management components), while freely modifying the internal processing part of the application components.

Frameworks are powerful, not just because they provide libraries of reusable components, but because they define a generic architecture that can be specialized to produce custom-built applications [Fayad-Schmidt 1997]. The architecture of MultiTEL follows our compositional model, defining standard components and common patterns of user interactions found in the literature. Then, we have identified the coordination patterns of the MTS domain and developed appropriate components, connectors, and a set of base services that show how common collaboration patterns can be tailored to obtain new services.

Furthermore, MultiTEL defines a distributed platform that supports the dynamic composition of MTS components and connectors by using Java/RMI technologies [Fuentes-Troya 1997]. In fact, MultiTEL implements a dynamic binding method that plugs components into connectors at runtime. This makes the system architecture more open since there is no need to know the references of components and connectors at compile time, facilitating the construction of customizable services. For instance, in a VoD service the framework can decide in runtime which connector will control movie reproduction according to the customer's profile. For subscribed customers, the connector will order the playing of the complete film, while for nonsubscribed ones it only plays a trailer for service advertising purposes.

Adequate documentation that supports the derivation process of a framework is the prerequisite to its success as a reusability paradigm. MultiTEL defines a set of tools designed to facilitate the extension of the framework. First of all, MultiTEL encourages the reuse of standard components, connectors, and MTS services by providing access to a shared distributed repository, accessed across the Internet. Additionally, visual environments are becoming very popular and there are several proposals that include a kind of visual composition [Mey de 1995]. We agree with the statement that interactive visualization of design patterns occurring in a framework contributes to the programming understanding of the underlying software architecture [Lange 1995; Meusel 1997]. Accordingly, MultiTEL defines a *visual builder* (VB) tool that guides the construction of new services by visual composition of existing components and connectors.

The specialization of the base classes and interfaces may be performed directly by the inheritance mechanism of Java or by using the *formal specification* (FS) tool. We can reason about components and connectors, and demonstrate properties of a certain composition pattern by using formal description techniques (FDTs). The architecture of the framework has been specified with the formal description technique LOTOS (Language of Temporal Ordering Specification) [ISO 1989], allowing validation of service architectures [Fuentes-Troya 1997]. The FS tool verifies the synchronization protocols encapsulated in connectors. After that, the framework's tools generate Java templates, including the interaction patterns of new connectors already validated. Finally, generic services with unbound parameters may be tailored to customer preferences and resources by the *application directory* (AD) tool. It also lists MultiTEL available applications the users can join.

The structure of this chapter is as follows. *Section 21.1* presents the model of components and connectors that is the base of the compositional framework. The basic components and connectors described in *Section 21.2* constitute the MTS architecture of the MultiTEL framework. We complete this section with a video on demand example, which is used to illustrate the new concepts proposed by MultiTEL throughout the rest of this chapter. The implementation of the compositional model in Java is presented in *Section 21.3*. It includes the definition of base classes that model components, connectors, and the service architecture. *Section 21.4* describes the middleware platform that supports the distributed execution of MultiTEL services. Finally, in *Section 21.5*, we show how to extend the framework's components to design new validated customizable services.

21.1 Component-Oriented Model

An ideal reuse technology provides components with standard interfaces that can be easily connected to make a new system. Software developers do not have to know the internal implementation of a component, and it is easy for them to learn how to use it [Johnson 1997]. However, components are not isolated entities; they usually interact with others to achieve their computation. Therefore, we should distinguish between how a component achieves its computation and how that computation is combined with others in the overall system [Nierstrasz 1996].

First, our challenge was the definition of a new composition model that separates computation from coordination. The compositional units of the model are the component that encapsulates computation and the connector that encapsulates a coordination protocol. Connections between components and connectors define the architecture of an application and are governed by a set of plug compatibility rules. In addition, this model defines a dynamic binding mechanism that plugs components into connectors at runtime. In consequence, the compositional model defines a new design pattern that will be the base technology for an application framework.

21.1.1 Components

Components are passive computational elements that encapsulate data and computation. They model real entities of the system such as databases, users, or multimedia devices. The interface of a component is a set of signatures as in CORBA Interface Definition Languages (IDLs), together with the list of events that this component may throw to the environment. When a component receives a message, it throws an event to a connector with the primitive *event* (see Figure 21.1). The processing that a component carries out upon message arrival is related to the manipulation of data or user interaction.

However, components do not know how the reception of a message and their computations influence the rest of the system. We have taken out the coordination protocol from components, which is placed in a connector. So, components should have an identity independent of the different interactions in which they could engage. Components do not encapsulate or understand protocols; they only obey the connectors' orders. A component may participate in more than one connector protocol, but never sends messages or events to other components.

21.1.2 Connectors

On the other hand, connectors are abstractions of coordination patterns. They implement communication protocols among two or more components and handle the events propagated by these or by other components with the primitive *catch* (see Figure 21.1). The specification of a connector includes the definition of a list of input events and a state transition diagram, which describes a coordination pattern. Connectors really know how message exchange affects the behavior of participant components. Each

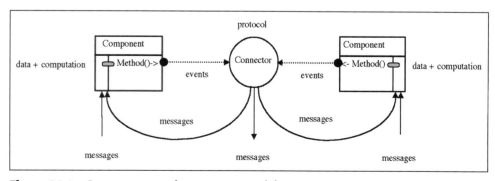

Figure 21.1   Components and connectors model.

component is plugged into one or more connectors that control its execution and ensure that it participates in the system according to the connector protocol. Therefore, communication between components is always performed through a mediator, that is, the connector element. The architectural pattern defined by this model is focused on the definition of connectors, which coordinate interactions among distributed components.

We may establish two kinds of connections between components and connectors. A connector is related to several components in a *control relationship*, if it can catch the events propagated by them. Connectors react to these events by sending messages to components, defining a *use relationship*. A component may participate in a use relationship with a connector, as long as it provides an interface compatible to the connector's output messages. Whereas components propagate events to unknown connectors, connectors have to specify the types of components to which they connect. Although connectors may specify target component types, components should not be aware of the use or control relationships in which they may engage.

21.1.3 Composition of Components and Connectors

In this section, we discuss the composition mechanisms of components and connectors. The compositional model defines composition inside the *application context* (AC) scope. The global AC is formed by the components and connectors that are bound for a particular distributed service. The role of the AC is to delimit the binding region in which components and connectors are searched during the object selection process. Since application execution is controlled by connectors, they also may create and delete other connectors and components modifying the AC context at runtime. They are spread over a distributed platform, so the references placed in the AC may be local or remote.

We subsequently will explain how to design a system architecture, that is, how to establish use and control relationships between the components and connectors of the system. The control relationship is defined by a *dynamic binding* mechanism that is able to find the appropriate connectors that have to handle a propagated event. Also, the model defines the use relationship by extending the method invocation defined by the object-oriented paradigm with three new types.

Composition Rules

The composition rules listed in this section define plug compatibility between components and connectors. Therefore, the design of a system architecture must be done according to these. This process will be supported by a visual tool that guides users in the design of new services, which will be explained in *Section 21.5*.

- A component can propagate events to different connectors in such a way that we could program specific connectors to handle different kinds of events.

- A connector can handle events from more than one component. Connectors specify protocols that must be understood by all the components involved.

- A connector may send messages both to components that propagate events to it and to other components that do not.

- Computations performed inside a component do not necessarily generate events. Only those actions that could be relevant to other components will be propagated as events.

- A component may define private components for modularization purposes, including as part of its interface the subcomponents' input messages and then delegating those messages to them.

- Also, in order to make a more modular design, a connector can delegate the handling of some events to private connectors.

When several components coordinate their behavior through a certain connector, a change in the coordination pattern can be simply achieved by replacing the connector, without modifying the code of the components involved. Likewise, modifying the internal structure of a component does not affect related connectors.

Dynamic Binding

The compositional model defines a binding method that plugs components into connectors at runtime. Binding is performed by matching the list of events of both components and connectors. A connector with a list of events α_1 is compatible with a component with a list of events α_2 if $(\alpha_1 \cap \alpha_2) \neq \emptyset$. This binding method is applied each time a component propagates an event. It looks up in the AC which connector is supposed to handle the propagated event according to the architecture of the application.

The decision about which connector may handle an event is taken outside of components and at runtime. This characteristic eases the design of open and dynamic systems, where the architecture of the system may be changing dynamically, adapting connections between components and connectors to the execution environment (customer profiles or system resources). Dynamic binding also enforces the construction of tailorable applications. The designer may define several connectors that might be candidates to catch the same event. Later the system will decide, for a certain customer, which is the connector that matches her or his profile. Therefore, users' profiles will determine which connectors will control the execution of a multimedia service.

Message Delivery

From the use relationship point of view, connectors send messages to components. Connectors control the execution of the application so they need to know some information about components' destination addresses. Communication in object-oriented paradigms is based on a direct dialog between a sender and a receiver object. However, this communication mechanism is insufficient for communication in open component-based systems. There are several approaches that extend this schema for distributed system programming [Bosch 1996]. We extend this concept with three types of message delivery.

Class-based invocation. Selection of a target object is based on the component's class name. This binding is very flexible in the sense that connectors do not know object references; they only have to know the class name of target components.

The class name of components is defined in an architectural context. A compositional architecture that models a family of applications defines types of components and connectors (base classes) and connections between them.

Name-based invocation. In this case a connector knows the name or reference associated with the target components, which will be assigned by a framework architecture. An architectural name defines the role that the component will play in a particular context, which may be redefined when reusing components in other contexts. This approach is similar to conventional object-oriented binding, but in this proposal component references are role names defined at architectural levels.

Address-based invocation. In distributed systems, processes reside in different machines. This binding is used when source and target components do not reside in the same context and the connector knows where the target component is expected to be. The format of the address will depend on the underlying middleware platform. In the implementation section we propose the use of uniform resource locators (URLs) as component addresses.

Nevertheless, the result of the selection process might be more than one component. Traditionally, an object always sends a message to a single object. However, it might be the intention to broadcast a message to a set of related components. For instance, the joining of a new participant in a videoconference service may be reported to the rest of them. This model defines mechanisms for broadcasting a message to all suitable components. By combining the class-based or the name-based invocation with the broadcast mechanism, we can express interaction patterns according to component types. For example, a connector can send a message to all the components that play the customer role in a videoconference.

21.2 The Compositional Architecture of MultiTEL

This work addresses the needs of interactive multimedia services basically derived from video on demand and videoconference generic services. Examples of them are subscribed VoD, remote education, chats, and conferences. However, the size of the set of possible multimedia services is open ended. We present an MTS architecture that is based on component orientation and distributed computing, which provides flexibility for designing and operating services over a wide variety of network and multimedia technologies. This vision implies a software architecture that offers reusable software components, eases service construction, and hides from the service designer the details of underlying technologies and the complexity of interaction patterns. This architecture will be the core of an application framework (MultiTEL) for the derivation of multimedia services.

In order to deal with this complexity, it is essential to divide the architecture into subsystems, where each subsystem has a well-defined scope and the relationships between them are also well-defined. Subsystems of the global architecture follow the base model of components and connectors, and communication between them is performed as usual through events and message passing.

Service subsystem. Defines a set of components and connectors for the specification, design, and implementation of telecommunication services.

Multimedia subsystem. Defines a set of components and connectors for the allocation and control of multimedia devices.

Network subsystem. Defines a set of components and connectors for the management and reservation of broadband multimedia channels.

Figure 21.2 shows the first level of abstraction of a multimedia service, which is composed by components modeling customers (participants), a multimedia component that represents the multimedia resources available in the system, and a network component that models internetworking issues.

The Service connector implements an interaction protocol among the participants, the network, and the multimedia devices. It accepts three kinds of events: service commands, multimedia device control, and network management. The protocol of this connector encapsulates the *service logic*, that is, the definition of user interaction models. Service logic is divided into several phases, each one controlled by one or more connectors. Following a hierarchical approach, we will discuss the composition of the service connector and the multimedia and network components in separate subsections.

21.2.1 Service Subsystem

We have designed a family of multimedia services rather than a single application. The building of MTS family products was based on a general understanding of service variations rather than on a precise service definition. The resulting MTS architecture aims to define a set of components and connectors that models one-party and multi-party interactive multimedia services. Examples of one-party services are multimedia mailing, video on demand, and multimedia database access; and examples of multi-party ones are conferences, seminars, and casual meetings.

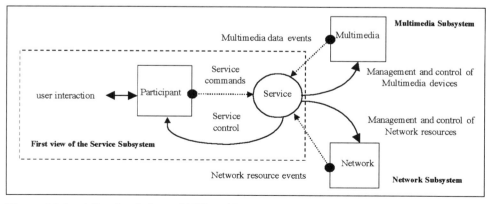

Figure 21.2   A first-level view of MTS architecture.

The design of standard components and connectors that take part in this architecture is based on proposals found in the literature [TINA-C, 1995]. This is a complex environment, so it is important to clarify who are the actors involved in the service provisioning process. Customers can join a service playing one of these three roles: organizer, manager, or participant.

Organizer. Customers of a service could be end users or operators who want to resell a service to their own customers. Service operators may tailor a generic service by giving values to component or connector parameters, and mapping network and multimedia resources to their local addresses. Designers may define generic services that will be configured by an organizer user. For instance, in video on demand the address of the video server will be bound by the purchaser of the service.

Manager. The manager is in charge of starting an organized service. In multiparty services, the manager controls the service scheduling. The manager includes a control panel for access control, service scheduling, or resource renegotiations.

Participant. Simple participants can receive video and audio from the service provider or from other participants. However, they may send multimedia data only when the service logic allows it.

The generic behavior of customer components is very simple and does not need to be changed for other services. A participant can connect, speak, introduce a service command (of access, scheduling, or service), or disconnect. Moreover, a participant component models a graphical user interface (GUI), so it encapsulates a control panel with a list of service commands. Control panels displayed by interactive components are generic areas that will be fulfilled by the connector that currently has the control. Each connector class defines a user interaction model corresponding to each service phase.

Sometimes access to a service is restricted for billing or security reasons and then participants must undergo an admission process. In fact, to be allowed to see a video or to attend a lecture, a participant should be previously subscribed to that service. Accepting new participants is a decision that may be taken according to an access protocol. The SCAccess connector processes the access parameters propagated from the participants inside events and asks the manager for an opinion. However, the decision is made by the SMAccess connector, which encapsulates the decision criteria associated with the manager. Figure 21.3 shows the access architecture of videoconference services where the SMAccess connector's protocol handles an access event by consulting the manager user, an *access constraints database* (ACDB) component that encapsulates the list of subscribed customers, and the network component, before sending a response to all participant components. In intranet environments the designer may define several access levels, each one defining the set of allowed actions. Accordingly, service provisioning begins with an access phase that controls users joining to services. The result of this phase will be acceptance or rejection.

Multimedia services might involve a large number of participants with a model of interpersonal communication that determines the utility of a service. For instance, in seminars only one participant is allowed to speak all the time, and the rest simply listen. However, in colloquial chats all participants are allowed to speak. So we have two examples of multimedia services that differ only in the interpersonal communi-

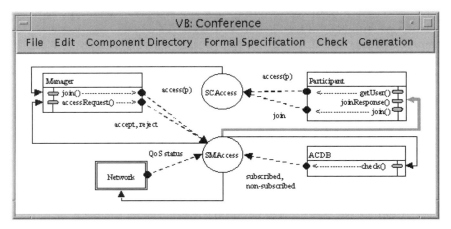

Figure 21.3   Access protocol for a videoconference service.

cation model. Besides this, there are several services that have to be scheduled in advance—for instance, conferences and collaborative work sessions. The component EventAgenda is designed to store data structures with temporal scheduling events.

The scheduling protocol modeled with the SSchedPP connector catches time set events and decides whose turn it is to speak. When timeout is reached, the connector inhibits the current participation. Also, the manager could make some personal decisions about the scheduling of a conference, for instance, censoring one of the participants, extending participation time, or shutting down the conference. The event scheduling protocol of the manager is implemented by the connector SschedMP, which controls the manager user actions and the time events (see Figure 21.4).

Each service has a set of commands that allows the controlling of service execution by service users. For instance, the video on demand service has commands to select a movie and in videoconference services, the turning on of a participant role may be another. In consequence, this part of the service logic may be personalized for each service extending the appropriate SPartProt connector. To sum up, a generic participant of videoconference services accepts three types of commands: access, scheduling, or service. We have defined at least one connector for handling each of these kinds of messages.

21.2.2 Multimedia Subsystem

Multimedia architecture is a collection of components and connectors that model multimedia devices and control data read/write operations. This compositional model helps to insulate application developers from management and volatility control in multimedia programming. Connectors characterize the dynamic relationships among the components that model multimedia devices.

A multimedia device gets its input data from *input ports* and sends its output data through *output ports*. Each port has an associated set of format components that represents the media format understood by it. Connections between device components are established based on format compatibility between input and output ports. The imple-

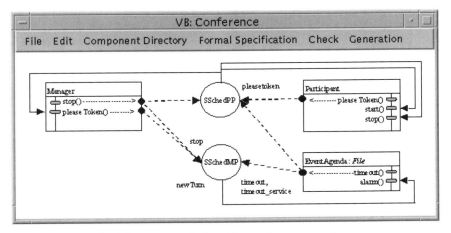

Figure 21.4 Scheduling protocol of a videoconference service.

mentation of the multimedia device component changes with the platform, but throws the same events. This architecture dynamically reconfigures its multimedia devices according to the kernel of the clients' environment. The allocation of devices is controlled by the AllocCont connector, according to local users' resources and quality-of-service requirements, which are negotiated for each participant. Therefore, we may include participants with heterogeneous multimedia devices in the same videoconference service.

A multimedia device (MultimediaDevice) is plugged into a ContCom connector that encapsulates its data control commands (Start, Pause, and so on). In order to control the movement of data, a user must also be plugged into this connector, which contains the state transition diagram of each type of multimedia device (file movie, camera, microphone, and so on). Another connector, SynProt, encapsulates the synchronization of frames that are delivered concurrently, by two or more MultimediaDevice components. The services that need to allocate several devices should use this connector for data controlling, instead of a ContCom connector. The MultimediaSAP component encapsulates all the multimedia resources of one service session (see Figure 21.5). It encapsulates a logical connection graph (LCG) that defines the possible connections among participants. There are some typical interaction models, such as the Star or Fully Connected patterns.

21.2.3 Network Subsystem

Network architecture makes the management and reservation of broadband streams transparent to the rest of the system. The ConnectC connector initiates connections between local multimedia devices and the network according to the logical connection graph encapsulated by the MultimediaSAP component. The VirtualConnection component encapsulates transport connections of a single participant. We define two components inheriting from it, which model unicast and multicast connections. A VirtualConnection component is plugged into the ConnectC connector, which controls

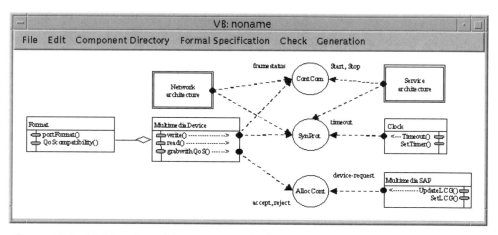

Figure 21.5 Multimedia architecture control relationships.

the establishment of connections between local devices and the rest of the participants and also handles disconnections initiated by the network. The architecture assigns an instance of a VirtualConnection component to each participant machine, which models the LCG of the service, but tailored for this participant. This component is responsible for the setup and the release of connections on traditional or asynchronous transfer mode (ATM) networks.

The NetworkSAP component abstracts the set of connections and network resources of a single service. The architecture includes a protocol of network resource reservation to guarantee delivery of data with a requested quality of service. The reservation protocol is applied to components that model links and switches. Finally, the computation about the amount of network resources spent by the members of a service is a task of the AccountC connector. The network architecture is shown in Figure 21.6.

A Video on Demand Service

We will illustrate the MTS architecture and every concept introduced by MultiTEL with a video on demand service. It provides digital video images to subscribed customers. The user interface is modeled with a nonconversational participant component, which defines three different menus: common (connect and disconnect commands), access, and service commands. It is a unicast service with an access and a service phase.

The access menu is used to read the user name, which is propagated as the access(params) event to the SCAccess base connector that is used for controlling this phase. Subscribed users have been stored in the base component ACDB, which is consulted by the SCAccess connector invoking the check( ) method. Afterwards, the service phase is controlled by a VoD-specific connector (Movie selector, Mselector), which displays a list of movies and accepts the user choice. The DoM (Directory of Movies) component encapsulates an index of movies organized by categories, therefore propagating only one event: listMovies( ). Typical methods to get, store, retrieve, and update items from the database are also implemented. The Mselector interface implements access to the appropriate DoM component. The protocol says that users may have 10 minutes for film selection; otherwise they will be disconnected. Future changes in film

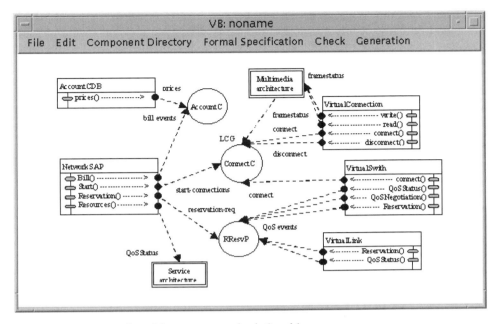

Figure 21.6   Network architecture control relationships.

selection policies will impact this connector only while the rest of the system remains unchanged (see Figure 21.7).

The next phase corresponds to movie reproduction, so it is controlled by ContCom connectors, which control the reproduction of the film, handling the Start, Fwd, Rew, Pause, and Stop events concurrently. The VoD architecture says that these events have to be handled by all instances of ContCom type stored in the current application context. Multimedia device reservation and the establishment of connections between devices is performed as explained in the preceding sections. In consequence, Figure 21.8 shows only those components and connectors that participate in video image transmis-

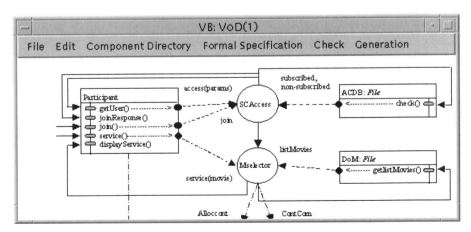

Figure 21.7   Access and movie selection phases of a VoD service.

sion. Each ContCom connector controls its local multimedia devices such as Window-Movie and FileMovie components, and the read/write operations on them. The UnicastConnection component of the server machine reads from the FileMovie component and writes on a stream. On the other hand, we have a component of the same type in the client machine that reads frames from an input stream and writes them in the WindowMovie device. The component that has the participant role is composed by Participant and ControlPanel components, but is considered as a single component.

21.3 MultiTEL: An MTS Framework in Java

In this section, we present the implementation details of the MultiTEL framework. MultiTEL encapsulates the compositional MTS architecture, but is implemented in the object-oriented language Java. Objects will run on a distributed platform that uses Java/RMI and Web services, which have become the most important way of coordinating distributed applications over the Internet. Moreover, they facilitate the development of interactive Web applications. As shown in Figure 21.9, MultiTEL implementation is structured in two different levels: an object-oriented implementation of the compositional model, and a middleware platform that provides common services for the distributed execution of applications. The first one is divided into two parts:

Application level (AL). This is the application level where service components and connectors are running in threads. Components and connectors of different services coexist and cooperate within this layer. Figure 21.9 shows two graphic user interfaces (GUIs) and a multimedia database (DB) coordinated by two connectors (CCs).

User-service part (USP). USPs are persistent representations of users in a specific service. Users join a multimedia service by running the corresponding USP applet from a browser. This class deals with the dynamic composition of components and connectors, using Java/RMI for communicating USPs among them and with the local kernel. It is also responsible for guaranteeing the fault-tolerance of the system

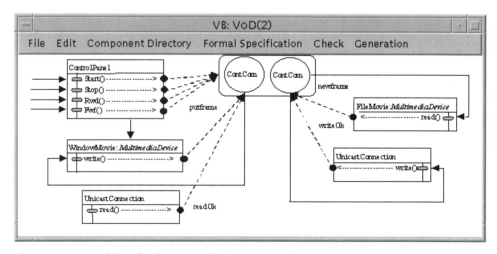

Figure 21.8   Multimedia data transfer in a VoD service.

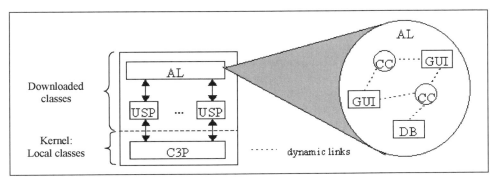

Figure 21.9 Java platform architecture.

by collecting incoming messages from other computers when the components or connectors have died and for restarting them from a previous stored state.

The second level of the framework is the middleware platform:

Common component-connector part (C³P). This is the kernel of the middleware platform, in charge of looking for the appropriate components and connectors, binding them to the application's generic references, and downloading them on execution. It also includes MultiTEL deployment tools for the derivation of new services.

In this section, we are going to focus on the first level of the framework, that is, the implementation of the component model. MultiTEL provides three base classes that encapsulate the functionality needed for building domain-specific applications. The framework provides a base class Component that is the root of the components hierarchy, a base class Connector that is the root of the connectors hierarchy, and last, the base class Dynamic Composition, which is the root of the service architecture hierarchy.

21.3.1 Component Base Classes

A use interface and the list of events it may propagate characterizes the Component class. The propagation of events is implemented by the event( ) method of this class (see Figure 21.10). This method is invoked by the descendent classes after the reception

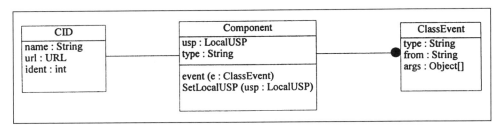

Figure 21.10 Component, Event, and Component ID (CID) classes.

of a message that is considered relevant to the environment. In this way, the throwing of events is transparent to the programmer and there is no need to redefine it.

Events are delegated to a binding class (USP class, described later), which implements the dynamic linking of components; therefore, components propagate events to unknown connectors. Likewise, it is important to point out that connector method invocations do not appear in the components' code. Since components do not contain references to other system entities, they should be reused in any service context, which has to provide appropriate connectors for event handling. In addition, each component has a unique global address defined by its CID class. This address will be used by connectors for sending response messages.

The Component class is the root of the component hierarchy; consequently, MTS components will be descendents of it. Programming a new component class only entails inheriting the corresponding base class and implementing a Java interface, which means defining a new MTS component type. Therefore, MTS component types are architectural types identified by an interface name. All components of the same type that implement the same interface might propagate events to the same connectors. This is very useful for building open customizable services because a service designer can define several connectors that handle the same events but with each one reacting differently to them. Components model real-world items, so they tend to be located next to the modeled entity. For example, the graphical user interface of a participant is implemented as a component that runs in the customer machine.

21.3.2 Connector Base Classes

The Connector class is identified by the list of events that it may catch and also by the list of components that it manages. We have already said that this special component encapsulates a synchronization protocol, so it implements a state transition diagram (STD). The Connector class handles the events with the catchEvent( ) method, shown in Figure 21.11, that trigger its state transition diagram. The implementation of connector protocols follows the State pattern [Gamma 1995], where each state is implemented as a class with a method by each input event. This pattern is used when an object has to exhibit state-dependent behavior; that is, depending on the state, the object reacts differently to the same requests. We have successfully integrated the design patterns into the compositional model, showing that both are good and complementary techniques for developing open systems.

Figure 21.11 shows the implementation of the SCAccess connector (SCAccess1 class) used by the VoD service for controlling the access phase. Its protocol (SCAccess1_Prot) expresses that in the Idle state (SCAccess1_Idle), it may handle the access event and change to the Check state (SCAccess1_Check), in which it may handle the subscribed and nonsubscribed events. If SCAccess's protocol final decision is of acceptance, immediately afterward it will send an alterContext message to the local USP, saying which are the appropriate connectors of the next phase that match the participant profile. Therefore, this connector customizes services by setting in the application context the components and connectors that fit the client's profile. Further, the components and connectors of the next phase are a parameter of SCAccess1 class, enforcing the devel-

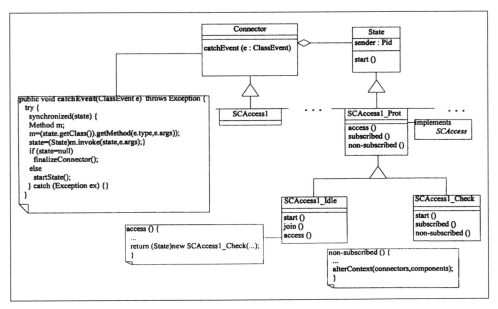

Figure 21.11 Connector classes. State design pattern.

opment of multimedia services by the composition of service phases. In fact, we reuse this connector in a seminar and in a remote classroom (TeleUni) service.

The catchEvent( ) implementation uses the Reflect packet of Java for event method invocation. The startState( ) method runs the initialization code of each state implemented in the start( ) method of the State class. This class also stores in the sender variable the CID of the object component that sent the last message to it. This is very useful for request-response communication, in which a connector sends a response message to the component that threw the last event.

The Connector class is the root of the connector hierarchy; thus, any MultiTEL connector extends the Connector class (such as SCAccess1) and also implements a Java interface (such as SCAccess) with the list of events that it is able to catch and also includes the list of managed component identifiers (MTS type).

In order to increase application efficiency, the user is encouraged to define small connectors. The platform tries to put connectors close to components that they manage. As a consequence, we distinguish between ephemeral connectors (needed only for a short time) and perpetual ones (needed during the whole service execution). MultiTEL implements the migration of frozen connectors to another machine. When somebody starts a service, a permanent home address is assigned to each connector. The permanent state of the connector is stored in this home address, so any object of the framework can resume the execution of a frozen connector. The kernel of the framework installed in this home machine is responsible for maintaining the consistency of this state. Moreover, connector migration also implies sending all the components related to it. One example is the scheduling connector used by the manager of a scheduled service. Since manager location may be changing during service provisioning, this connector should migrate to the current manager's machine.

The USP class that will be described in the next section manages the runtime linking of components and connectors. This binding class also provides remote references of the managed components.

21.3.3 Dynamic Composition Base Classes

We have already explained that MultiTEL implements a distributed platform for running MTSs. Since these service applications must be available for invocation from any customer machine, this platform publishes MultiTEL applications by using the Web services. In order to facilitate access to any service, we use the mobility characteristics offered by Java applets.

The USP class is an applet class that performs the setup and the runtime linking of an application. By loading USP applets, embedded in HTML documents, across the network we also retrieve all the required classes from the net. The advantage of this approach is that all the applications of this platform are always available for customers. Consequently, they do not need to have them installed in the local terminal. Also the maintenance of existing MTSs is performed directly on the server machines; therefore, service providers do not have to install new versions in client terminals.

The USP class contains information about the architecture of the application, that is, how components have to be plugged into connectors. We can consider it as a global configuration object that performs the runtime composition of components according to the service architecture. In this section we explain implementation details of the service architecture and the application context, and the role they play in the runtime linking of components. We also present how connectors send messages to remote components by using USP services.

Service Architecture Representation

Frameworks that encapsulate a reusable, tailorable software architecture are particularly important for developing open systems in which not only functionality but architecture is reused across a family of related applications [Demeyer 1997]. MultiTEL encapsulates the MTS architecture that has to be tailored to meet different multimedia service requirements. The architecture of a service defines the static or dynamic links that may be established during service execution. The SA is implemented as USP data structures that store information about how to plug components into connectors. The service designer has to set up the architecture of a system by supplying the control and use information as shown in Figure 21.12.

The application context concept defined by the compositional model is included in these data structures. The local AC is formed by SA entries that have bound the Reference field. Service architecture may define different component-connector connections, depending on the user's role (such as participant or manager); therefore, this information is

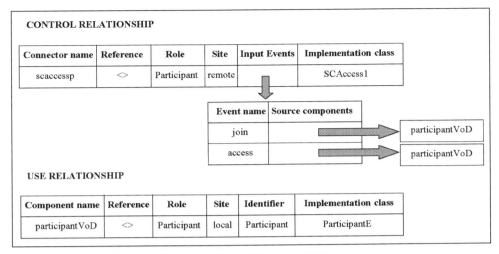

Figure 21.12   Implementation of service architecture (SA).

stored in the Role field. The Site field holds information concerning components and connector distribution. A local value indicates that the component or the connector is in the local AC, the remote value indicates that the USP has to search for the object throughout the global AC, and, finally, a URL value indicates the precise location of the object.

The control relationship defined by the compositional model specifies that a connector may handle an input event, Event name, if and only if it was propagated by the component, Source component. The control relationship of Figure 21.12 says that scaccessp is the object name of the SCAccess connector (defined by the MTS architecture), which will be in the global AC and is implemented by the SCAccess1 class. We want to point out that a designer may change the access protocol of a service only by changing the name of the implementation class. On the other hand, the use relationship shows information about a Participant descendent component (the identifier is Participant in Figure 21.12) with the name participantVoD, which is implemented by the ParticipantE class. Connectors will consult this structure to obtain component references.

A service designer has to program the architecture of a service by supplying components, connectors, and connections between them. This global configuration object represents the architecture of a service, and then by replacing it a designer may adapt the framework without changing the implementation of the other objects. USP provides one framework hot spot in which the programmer can tailor system configuration by specifying the connections that should be established during service execution. MultiTEL defines architectural patterns for the video on demand and videoconference generic services. Moreover, our approach considers the definition of incomplete services that may be organized by a customer who has to supply values to the Site, Role, and Implementation class parameters. Configuration of generic applications will be explained in the *Framework Deployment* section later in this chapter.

Dynamic Binding

The USP class also encapsulates the dynamic binding method applied to components and connectors. It implements the event() method that is invoked by local components for the propagation of an event. When a USP object receives a request to catch an event—event(e)—it looks up which connector is supposed to handle the propagated event in the current application context and in the service architecture. Finally, the USP calls the catchEvent() method of the target connector by a simple or Remote Method Invocation (RMI) call. The dynamic binding mechanism may be considered as a kind of ORB service of the middleware platform provided by MultiTEL. Figure 21.13 shows how the connector scaccessp catches the join event propagated by the participant participantVoD of a multicast distribution of movies service.

The architecture may specify dynamic connections where several connectors are candidates for catching an event. Service connectors are responsible for putting the appropriate connector in the application context, according to customer profiles. We can use this characteristic and the dynamic binding for building customizable services. For instance, we can add to the VoD architecture a new connection that links a ControlPanel component to a simple version of ContCom connector for service advertising purposes. Subscribed customers can watch complete movies while nonsubscribed ones can only see the trailers. A GUI component (ControlPanel) includes the control panel with Start, Fwd, Rew, Pause, and Stop buttons. The subscribed ContCom connector enables all buttons, whereas the nonsubscribed one enables the Stop button only.

Message Delivery

Since connectors have to decide which components will receive a message, they are supposed to have some information about component addresses. First of all, if a con-

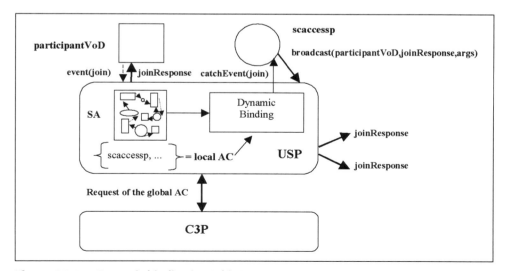

Figure 21.13 Dynamic binding in MultiTEL.

nector has the object reference of the target component, it simply calls the corresponding method. However, when components and connectors belong to different contexts, connectors may invoke one of the following versions of the USP's sendMessage( ) method:

```
sendMessage(name, "participantVoD", "getUser", args)
sendMessage(class, "FileMovie", movieURL, "read", args)
```

Sometimes, connectors only need to know the role that the target component plays in the service architecture, which is stored in the use relationship of SA structures. In this case the first version of this method is applied, providing a component name as its first argument. The USP object will look in the current AC for a component object that plays the role defined by the component name. In the example, the SCAccess connector sends the getUser message to a component that has the participantVoD identifier. In the second method, a connector provides the MTS type of the target component (class name) and also sets the address (URL) of where to look for components.

```
sendMessage(sender, "start", args)
```

Since components send their IDs (CIDs) inside events, connectors may store CIDs in the sender variable, so connectors can answer components' messages by specifying their CIDs. In a videoconference service, the manager sends the start message to the participant that previously asked to speak.

```
broadcast(name, "participantVC", "joinResponse", args)
broadcast(class, "ParticipantE", "stop", args)
```

Finally, the framework has built-in mechanisms for broadcasting messages to groups of components identified by a class or a component name. For instance, in videoconference services or in multicast VoD services the access connector of the manager (SMAccess) has to forward a joinResponse message to all the participants, informing them that a new user has been accepted in the conference (see Figure 21.13). However, the SSchedPP connector uses the broadcast by class for sending a stop message to all participants, including the manager, informing them that a participant timeout has occurred.

21.4 Middleware Platform

Each machine participating on MultiTEL has a kernel (C^3P) running on a Java virtual machine (JVM). The Java language solves heterogeneity of hardware and software, so we can say that MultiTEL fulfills the interoperability requirement. MultiTEL defines a distributed platform written in Java that runs on top of the Internet, which supports the distributed execution of multimedia services. The C^3P kernel stores information relevant to the service execution about local USPs, components, and connectors.

Regarding the distribution of the kernels' private information, we define an interkernel communication that provides efficient access to all the information stored in the platform. This approach can lead to scalability problems due to the amount of overhead for replication. We take a flexible approach to structuring the system to overcome these problems, following the Internet approach to scalability. The set of machines participating in MultiTEL is organized in hierarchical domains, where each machine inside a domain is responsible for its local components, connectors, and services. Besides this, there is one machine per domain that is defined as a gateway to other domains. Each gateway has a *routing table* that instructs it as to which other domains it has to forward the requests to. Thus, the distribution structure can be statically or dynamically configured, the same as in the Internet Protocol (IP).

Furthermore, C^3Ps manage communication with other domains and control local USPs. Their main objects are the *component directory* (CD) and the *application directory* (AD) described in the following sections.

21.4.1 Component Directory

MultiTEL offers a component and connector localization service to local users and sometimes to local USPs. The global AC is stored in the C^3P of the application's home machine. USPs ask for the global AC from their local C^3Ps, which they retrieve from the corresponding home machine. The USP base class is also considered part of this middleware platform because it performs operations related to object localization.

On the other hand, public components and connectors developed at a server machine are stored in a local repository. The component directory manages access to components and connectors that are distributed over the MultiTEL platform. We have already explained that components and connectors are distributed throughout the platform by domains, so the CD provides a search engine per domain.

In addition, service designers may retrieve public components and connector code with the purpose of reusing them in their own services. Thus, C^3P classes operate as HTTP servers that wait for component code requests. On the other hand, this object may download component or connector classes from other machines when local customers demand it.

An important task performed by the kernel is the storing of local *frozen* connectors, which will be bound from the last computed state. The component directory is the home of its local permanent connectors, so as long as a permanent connector remains in the active state—that is to say that it is running at a remote machine—the kernel queues all the connector's incoming requests. It also starts the migration of frozen connectors to another machine. After that, the connector remains locked in the active state.

21.4.2 Application Directory

The application directory holds and displays the list of local and remote services that are being offered by the MultiTEL platform. Services may be distributed throughout the platform by domains. When an application changes to a different state, the local kernel sends a reporting message. This information is propagated to the gateways of the platform and after that each machine will update the information that is being displayed at this moment by the local AD.

Generic services are installed in the AD with the *unbound* state. A generic service entry has a reference to the organization file that will guide its configuration. The output file of an organization service is also stored by the AD of the home machine. Regarding service execution, the AD holds the global context of each instance of service applications. It assigns a unique identification to service USPs to distinguish between several instances of the same service running at the same machine.

21.4.3 Remote Communications

The policy of the framework follows the Web principle of information distribution. A customer is able to run a service belonging to any MultiTEL machine. We cope with the difficulties of communication between the local objects of the kernel and the remote USP class by applying the RMI method of Java. RMI enables the programmer to create distributed Java-to-Java applications, in which the methods of remote Java objects can be invoked from another Java virtual machine, possibly on different hosts.

A Java program can make a call on a remote object, once it obtains its reference either by looking up the remote object in the bootstrap service provided by RMI or by receiving the reference as an argument or a return value. A client can call a remote object in a server, and that server can also be a client of other remote objects.

In this way, when a USP object arrives at a new machine it looks up the reference of the C^3P object. This is done in the init( ) method of the applet. Communication between components, connectors, and the USP is the usual message passing used by local objects. A USP has to collect component messages and connector events, so it is implemented as a remote object identified by a unique URL.

21.5 Framework Deployment

The framework architecture is structured in layers such that each one provides a set of common services. Nevertheless, the service designer only has to extend the MTS base classes following the compositional service development process proposed in this section. Our approach helps application developers to deal with the building of reliable, complete, and robust MTSs. The MultiTEL initial window is shown in Figure 21.14.

MultiTEL provides a set of tools that help the service designer in the development of new services following the framework methodology. These tools are the component directory, visual builder, formal specification, and application directory.

21.5.1 Using the Component Directory

The MultiTEL philosophy is the sharing of components, connectors, and services over the network. In this way, service designers may reuse public software developed by other companies that conforms to MultiTEL framework principles. The component directory tool helps application engineers in obtaining knowledge about components, connectors, and services that they may reuse in other contexts, by documenting how classes might be composed and derived to meet new service requirements.

This common service displays the list of components, connectors, and services by domains (see Figure 21.15). This application is a kind of search engine, very similar to

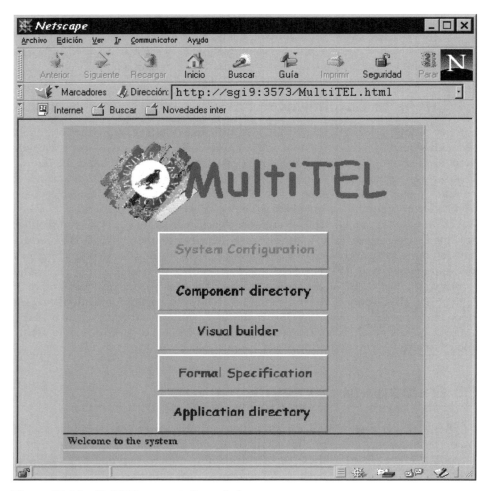

Figure 21.14   MultiTEL presentation window.

those available on the Web, but it searches components, connectors, and services instead of general information. One entry has the following structure:

```
CD Entry = { type, name, description, URL, interface, architectural role }
```

The user may select one or more fields to make a query (see Figure 21.15). A CD entry includes the type field identifying whether it is a component, a connector, or a service; the name; a brief description of the behavior; the URL; and important information related to framework specialization.

For each component, the CD lists the method signatures of the methods that are relevant to framework extension, that is, methods that propagate events (MTS type defined by a Java interface) and the generic role that the component may play in any service architecture. The connector interface lists the names of input events and the

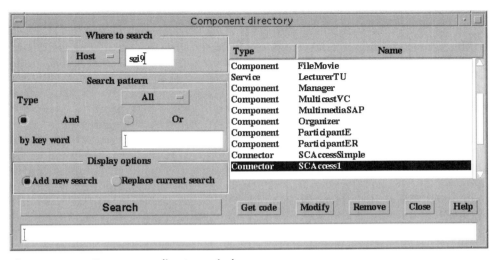

Figure 21.15   Component directory window.

messages that may be sent to components identified by their MTS types. In addition, the connector interface includes the internal protocol specified in a formal description technique and the generic role that may play its protocol in a service architecture. FDTs allow us to express connector reactive behavior and, also, allow connector protocol verification. Finally, each service entry lists the components and connectors that participate in the service architecture and, only for generic services, the list of service parameters as well.

Visual Builder

Our approach encourages the reuse of components in as many contexts as possible by defining event interfaces for connectors and message interfaces for components that can be part of the framework via component composition. This kind of framework extension is known as *blackbox*. We define a visual tool for the design of service architectures, adapting MTS components and connectors to target service requirements. This tool supports telecommunication services programming by visual component-connector composition. A new service can be created by the composition of basic or new components and connectors. Designers may extend MultiTEL by setting the application architecture (a MultiTEL hot spot) of new services. Components are drawn following our graphic notation as shown in the description of MTS architecture. The resulting graph of components and connectors is the architecture of the new application.

The visual builder displays the MTS service architecture corresponding to generic services such as videoconference and video on demand services. Designers have to tailor this MTS architecture, providing concrete components and connectors to each MTS role, adding and deleting connections, and extending components and connectors with new functionality. This tool has a link to the component directory to retrieve components that will be inserted in the service architecture by the designer. In this way, the framework encourages the sharing of components between MultiTEL platform developers, perceiving the distributed platform as a single component library.

This interactive environment is responsible for ensuring that framework entities are used correctly and are composed in a control or use relationship according to the rules of the compositional model (see *Section 21.2*). This visual environment checks the correctness of attempted connections by verifying whether each event that will be propagated has a connector to handle it, whether the messages that might be sent have a receiver, and, finally, whether all the defined events could be propagated.

The graphic notation has a textual representation (LDS) that serves as the back end to the visual builder composition environment. This textual notation provides an architectural description of a service and will be used to generate partial specifications at the basic code level [Fuentes-Troya 1999]. Those aspects not supported by the generator are filled in the implementation phase by the service engineer. This generative approach is considered as a good alternative to reduce the gap between framework design and implementation.

The Generate option will activate the building of the application context class, that is, the USP class of this service. The service architecture defined in the LDS is transformed by the generator into a private service inside a USP object. The programmer provides the list of components, connectors, and dynamic or static connections that may be established during service execution. The generator also will produce code for those new components or connectors defined inside the service. Figure 21.16 shows the access phase of the VoD service graphically and the corresponding USP code that defines its architecture that will be completed after the configuration phase explained in *Section 21.6*. Component and connector information added to the SA includes the role name and the class name.

Formal Specification

We have already shown how the visual builder helps service designers with the building of new services by composition. However, designing a service may imply the definition of new connectors, introducing new and unverified protocols into the system. This fact leads to the evolution of a nontested framework, which is not desired. Thus, we define a formal specification tool dedicated to the specification, simulation, and validation of multimedia services.

The visual builder checks the list of events propagated by a component with the list of events handled by a set of connectors, although this is not enough to guarantee the correctness of newly developed services. First, the verification of system/environment interactions is needed, to check if the resulting application fulfills service requirements. Also, the composition of connector protocols may be validated against nondesired conditions such as process deadlock or unreachable transitions.

MultiTEL components and connectors are specified with the FDT LOTOS [ISO 1989] in [Fuentes-Troya 1999, 1997b]. LOTOS is a formal abstract description language derived from process algebra, which enables a system to be described in a precise way, abstracting away realization details. Using formal specification tools, the user may introduce new components specified in LOTOS for simulation and validation purposes. The specification of components consists in defining methods and the propagation of events modeled in LOTOS as a synchronization gate. Connectors encapsulate

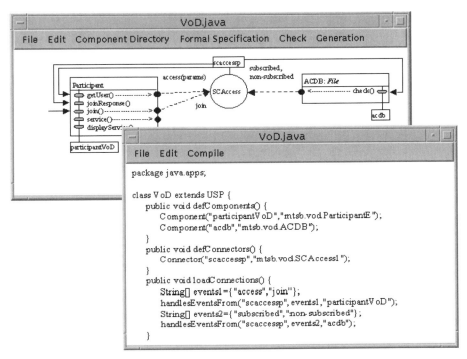

Figure 21.16 Visual programming of VoD service.

communication protocols and synchronize their behavior with its managed components by sharing the list of gates corresponding to the common events, and send messages to them also through a list of shared gates. The requirement analysis determines the interaction of the service with its environment, usually the service customer. This system/environment interaction is specified using scenarios. The simulation of this resulting prototype is another option of this tool, which is implemented with the LOLA (LOtos LAboratory) simulation tool. The validation of the system is also performed with LOLA by means of behavior matching against one scenario.

In conclusion, the specification and validation of new services guarantees the correct evolution of the framework. Another important advantage of this approach is the rapid prototyping of new services that allows the validation of system requirements. Users get immediate feedback on their actions and are informed when their actions cause nondesired situations. In general, the use of this formal environment provides a way for studying the critical parts of a system or also for the demonstration of interesting properties.

21.5.2 Using the Application Directory

The framework provides an application directory that shows the list of available services (see Figure 21.17). The AD lists for each multimedia service the application state and

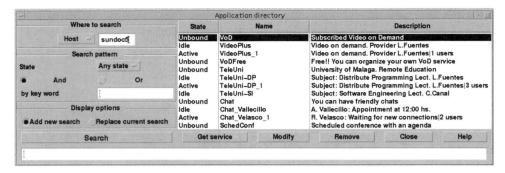

Figure 21.17 Application directory window.

name, a string describing the service offered by it, the URL of the USP, and a miscellany field. This last field lists relevant information that is specific to the service. Examples of this are the date and the time scheduled to initiate a videoconference service.

```
AD entry = { State, Name, Description, URL, Miscellany}
```

A service may be in unbound, idle, active, or frozen state. Unbound services are those that have to be configured before execution, idle services are ready to be executed in the future, an active service is currently running at one or several machines, and a service in the frozen state has been running in the past and should be resumed in the future. Obviously, only authorized users can initiate, resume, or join a service. The access connector of the application encapsulates the specific service criteria.

Service Configuration

MultiTEL customers might be end users or organizer users, as explained in *Section 21.3*. Organizers are potential operators that buy services for reselling to their customers. Service operators will adapt generic services to their resources and preferences. The configuration of a service means mapping logical names to physical names and giving values to parameters. For instance, in a video on demand the operator has to provide the URL of the FileMovie component and the file name of subscribed customers modeled by the ACDB component. Generic services are installed in the AD with the unbound state, and the organization service will start as somebody picks this entry.

A service configuration is described by the script language LCF. The organization connector interprets this input configuration file and asks a customer for parameter values. A service organization delivers an output file (.cfg) with all the parameters bound to a concrete value. The USP will load this file, which will be consulted by connectors for component-connector creation purposes. The following example corresponds to the configuration of a VoD service:

```
set parties unicast
set acdb, filemovie, dom "http://sgi9.lcc.uma.es/VoD"
```

```
set participantVoD local
set scaccessp remote
...
put text "Access Data Base" parname acdb::filename
value="acdb.jdb"
put text "Movie format" parname filemovie::format value="mpg"
        default "jpg" in "mpg", "jpg", "avi"
put text "Participant class" implementation participantVoD
value="ParticpantE" in "ParticipantE",
"GUIParticipant"
```

One-party services can be instantiated only one time, although multiparty ones accept many user connections. The application directory consults the set parties statement for service running control. Besides this, with the set statement, organizers map component and connector logical names to physical names. The local attribute indicates that the searching of components/connectors is limited only to the local application context (such as a participant of a VoD). However, remote components or connectors could be in local or in remote machines. Finally, components that model system resources (access database, filemovie, and so on) could be configured by the URL that identifies its physical name. This attribute will be stored by the USP object in the SA.

The purpose of the put statement is to set values to component-connector parameters. Later, the organizers will give values to them, according to their preferences. In the example, an access database will need the name of the subscribers file, the multimedia device FileMovie component will accept a format parameter, the organizer will set the implementation class of the participant component, and so on. This is a generic and open way of configuring services; that is, the set of service parameters is not predetermined.

21.6 Summary

Multimedia telecommunication services are often quite complex and hard to build. We have shown how a component-oriented framework defines a set of components and connectors that are relatively easy to build and maintain. The compositional model combines the composition and the separation of concerns issues, maximizing the reusability of the framework architecture. One of the main contributions of this work is to apply the component-oriented design to a large-scale system such as the MTS domain. The architecture of MultiTEL defines repositories of components and interaction patterns that model the most representative multimedia services of intranet areas. MultiTEL services run on a distributed platform over the Internet and the Web.

Multimedia services should be developed in steps with the aid of MultiTEL tools. The evolution of the framework led to an ideal state where the programming of new components is not required. This means that someone using the framework can concentrate on just components and connector links that need to be customized, and in this sense we can affirm that MultiTEL is a blackbox framework. However, the extension of the MTS architecture achieved by inheritance is also addressed in this proposal, so in this sense MultiTEL is a whitebox framework. In fact, we think that open and flexible frameworks may be extended by composition and inheritance, thus obtaining all their advantages.

Visual composition tools contribute to framework understanding, even for end users. Correctness issues are also addressed by the definition of a specific tool that performs the validation of critical protocols of the system. Owing to the high degree of reusability obtained using MultiTEL, we have been able to significantly shorten the development times of different VoD and videoconferences services, including lecturers, conferences, business meetings, and remote education. The MultiTEL environment is successfully running on Sun and Silicon Graphics workstations with Digital Media Library. Check the Web site for this book for code examples.

21.7 References

[Bosch 1996] Bosch, J. Language support for component communication in LayOM. *Proceedings of the ECOOP 1996 Workshop on Component-Oriented Programming (WCOP 1996).* Linz, Austria, July 1996. Also available at: www.pt.hk-r.se.se/~bosch.

[Chandy 1997] Chandy, K.M., and A. Rifkin. 1997. Systematic composition of objects in distributed Internet applications: Processes and sessions. *Proceedings of the 30th Hawaii International Conference on System Sciences.* Maui, Hawaii, January 1997.

[Ciancarini 1996] Ciancarini, P., et al. PageSpace: An architecture to coordinate distributed applications on the Web. *Proceedings of the Communication Fifth International WWW Conference (WWW 1996).* Paris, France, May 1996.

[Demeyer 1997] Demeyer, S., T.D. Meijler, O. Nierstrasz, and P. Steyaert. Design guidelines for tailorable frameworks. *Communications of the ACM,* Theme Issue on Object-Oriented Application Frameworks, M.E. Fayad and D. Schmidt, editors. 40(10):60–64, October 1997.

[Fayad-Schmidt 1997] Fayad, M., and D. Schmidt. Object-oriented application frameworks. *Communications of the ACM* 40(10):32–38, October 1997.

[Fuentes-Troya 1997] Fuentes, L., and J.M. Troya. Component oriented service architecture as a flexible service creation framework. *Proceedings of the Communication Networks and Distributed Systems Modeling* (CNDS 1997), pp. 68–73.

[Fuentes-Troya 1999] Fuentes, L., and J.M. Troya. Towards an open multimedia service framework. *ACM Computing Surveys, Symposium on Object-Oriented Application Frameworks,* M.E. Fayad, editor. September 1999.

[Gamma 1995] Gamma, E., R. Helm, R. Johnson, and J. Vlissides. *Design Patterns: Elements of Reusable Object-Oriented Software.* Reading, MA: Addison-Wesley, 1995.

[Hirano 1997] Hirano, S. HORB: Distributed execution of Java programs. *WorldWide Computing and Its Applications,* No. 1274 in LNCS, Springer Verlag, 1997, pp. 29–42.

[ISO 1989] ISO. Information Processing Systems—Open Systems Interconnection. *LOTOS—A Formal Description Technique Based on the Temporal Ordering of Observational Behavior.* IS-8807, 1989.

[Johnson 1997] Johnson, R.E. Frameworks = (components + patterns). *Communications of the ACM,* Theme Issue on Object-Oriented Application Frameworks, M.E. Fayad and D. Schmidt, editors. 40(10):39–42, October 1997.

[Lange 1995] Lange, D.B., and Y. Nakamura. Interactive visualization of design patterns can help in framework understanding. *Proceedings of the OOPSLA 1995*, pp. 342–357, Austin, Texas, 1995.

[Lazar 1995] Lazar, A., S. Bhonsle, and K. Lim. A binding architecture for multimedia networks. *Journal of Parallel and Distributed Systems* 30, November 1995.

[Meusel 1997] Meusel, M., K. Czarnecki, and W. Köpf. A model for structuring user documentation of object-oriented frameworks using patterns and hypertext. *Proceedings of the ECOOP '97*, June 1997.

[Mey de 1995] Mey de, V., 1995. Visual Composition of Software Applications. *Object-Oriented Software Composition*. Prentice Hall. Chapter 10, pp. 275–303, 1995.

[Nierstrasz 1996] Nierstrasz, O., Schneider J.G. and Lumpe, M., 1996. Formalizing Composable Software Systems—A Research Agenda. *Proceedings of the 1st IFIP Workshop on Formal Methods for Open Object-Based Distributed Systems (FMOODS 1996)*, France, March 1996.

[OMG 1995] Object Management Group. *Common Object Request Broker: Architecture and Specification*. OMG document, January 1995.

[Posnak 1997] Posnak, J., G. Lavender, and H.M. Vin. An adaptive framework for developing multimedia software components. *Communications of the ACM*, Theme Issue on Object-Oriented Application Frameworks, M.E. Fayad and D. Schmidt, editors. 40(10):43–47, October 1997.

[Rajagopalan 1995] Rajagopalan, B. Membership protocols for distributed conference control. *Computer Communications* 18(10):695–708, October 1995.

[Saridakis 1997] Saridakis, T., C. Bidan, and V. Issarny. A programming system for the development of TINA services. *Proceedings of the Open Distributed Processing and Distributed Platforms.* Chapman & Hall, 1997, pp. 3–14.

[Schmidt-Fayad 1997] Schmidt, D., and M. Fayad. Lessons learned: Building reusable OO frameworks for distributed software. *Communications of the ACM*, Theme Issue on Object-Oriented Application Frameworks, M.E. Fayad and D. Schmidt, editors. 40(10):85–87, October 1997.

[Simon 1995] Simon, R., et al. Multimedia MedNet. *Computer*, May 1995, pp. 65–73.

[Sun 1998] Sun Microsystems. *The Java Language Version 1.1.4.* 1998.

[TINA-C 1995]. TINA-C. *Overall Concepts and Principles of TINA.* TINA-C Deliverable, February 1995, www.tinac.com/95/file.list.html.

Event Filter Framework
and Applications

With the increasing development and growth of the Internet, huge volumes of events are on the network. It is necessary to manage such large volumes of events. There have been many event management applications, such as decision support in information systems, monitoring distributed systems and performance, fault network management, knowledge dissemination, and production control operations. Event filtering is used to support the event management applications through detecting specified events, reducing the volume of events, and efficiently delivering events to the corresponding users. This eliminates unnecessary network traffic and unnecessary processing by end-point management applications and enhances the performance of the network.

Event filtering has been used in several specific application domains such as Junkfilter [Sutter 1998], ASIST realtime command and control for spacecraft control system applications [GSFC 1998], and WebFilter [Boldt 1998]. Each application has its own specific domain requirements. In order to improve the reusability and extensibility of the event filtering in these domains, an object-oriented filtering framework is worthwhile to develop. It is very important not only to improve the existing event-filtering applications but also to develop new ones with the least amount of effort and cost.

This chapter is organized as follows: *Section 22.1* describes the components of the filtering framework. *Section 22.2* illustrates the design of the filtering framework. *Section 22.3* shows the implementation of the filtering framework. *Section 22.4* presents an example of event-filtering applications using the event-filtering framework. *Section 22.5* gives the experiences and lessons learned. *Section 22.6* is the conclusion and discusses the outlook for future work.

22.1 Event-Filtering Framework Components

Regardless of the event applications, event filtering involves event definition, filtering subscription, filter iterator, and action. Many existing event-filtering mechanisms are application dependent because they are modeled based only on their application domain requirements, so that they are impossible to reuse. We are going to build an event-filtering framework that consists of four core components of event filtering: the event definition constructor (EDC) component, the subscription component, the filter iterator component, and the action component. The different applications can be easily developed based on these components.

22.1.1 Event Definition Constructor Component

The first step in event filtering is the user specifying the event format. The EDC component is a set of related classes that provide basic interfaces to define events [Al-Shaer 1999]. An *event* is a significant occurrence in a system that is reported by a notification message. An event can be a primitive or a composite event. A *primitive event* is a basic event that does not depend on the occurrence of the other events. In contrast, a *composite event* is composed of multiple primitive events. The EDC component consists of several classes that construct event attributes, event operator, and event types.

22.1.2 Subscription Component

The subscription component serves the event management users by specifying their filtering criteria represented as filter programs. These programs define the target events to be detected and the associated actions. They consist of a set of predicates joined together using special operators called *filtering expression operators.* The second task of the subscription component is to build the filter for the target events by constructing the filter's internal representation. The subscription component includes the filter expression, the filter programming interface, and the filter builder. The filter builder is the key issue in designing the event-filtering framework. It utilizes the filter's internal representation to determine the structure and the operation of the filtering mechanism. The filter operations are specified by the algorithms and data structures used to classify and detect events. There are several filter internal representations. Some filter representations classify only primitive events such as boolean expression tree representation (BET) and directed acyclic graphs (DAGs). Other filter representations can detect composite events such as petri-nets (PNs) and deterministic finite automata (DFA).

22.1.3 Filter Iterator Component

The filter iterator component operates the filter internal representation called the *filter composer.* This component has several services such as inserting, deleting, and modifying filter programs in the internal representation. It also contains the event processor class, which inspects the incoming events from the observed system and determines if an event is detected or rejected. The developers can customize the filtering framework to adapt the different alternative filter internal representations. This makes the filtering framework adaptable to many alternative designs in event management applications [Al-Shaer 1997; Fayad-Cline 1996].

22.1.4 Action Component

When the filter iterator component detects a target event, it notifies the action component that performs the actions specified in the filter program and then operates on the filtered events either disseminating or dispatching them to the end users or consumers. It has two classes: event dispatcher and filter action.

22.2 Event-Filtering Framework Design

The object-oriented application framework is a reusable, semicomplete application that can be utilized to produce custom applications [Fayad-Schmidt 1997]. As previously discussed, this framework mainly consists of four components that include several design patterns such as the Adaptor pattern, the Builder pattern, the Interpreter pattern, the Interface pattern, and the Iterator pattern [Schmidt 1996]. In each component/design pattern, there is a set of classes and interfaces. The main classes of the

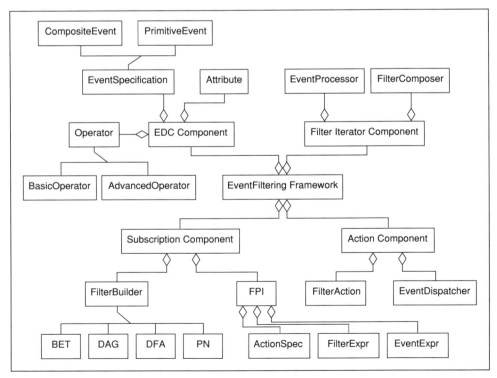

Figure 22.1 The event-filtering framework classes.

event-filtering framework are shown in Figure 22.1. The details of the component design are elaborated on the following pages. The class diagram for the EDC component is shown in Figure 22.2.

The class EventSpecification and class Attribute are abstract classes that contain only the definition of the operations. The clients will implement them, for example, as follows:

```
abstract class EventSpecification {
            abstract List PrimitiveEvent();
       abstract List CompositeEvent();
       }
       class myEventSpecification {
            myEventSpecification (List evtSpecs){
                   eventList = evtSpecs;
            }
```

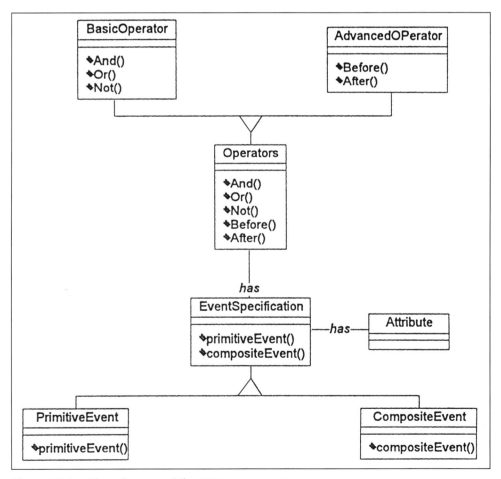

Figure 22.2 Class diagram of the EDC component.

```
            public List PrimitiveEvent() {
                    return eventList;
            }
            private List eventList;
    }
```

The operator class is used to implement all the boolean expressions including the basic operators *AND, OR,* and *NOR* and advanced operators *before* and *after.*

The subscription component is an important user interface component. The class diagram is shown in Figure 22.3. Users can specify their filtering criteria, the filter's internal representation, and associated actions.

The Interpreter pattern is the key part of this component. It is used for representing the sentences submitted by the users and then interpreting them. For example, in the email filtering application, a user submits his or her sentences as follows:

```
    Sender: johnson, hu edu, !ca
```

The interpreter represents "," as boolean operator "|," "hu edu" as "hu & edu," and ", !ca" as "| ! ca." And then interprets it as a boolean expression:

```
    Sender: johnson | hu & edu  | ! ca
```

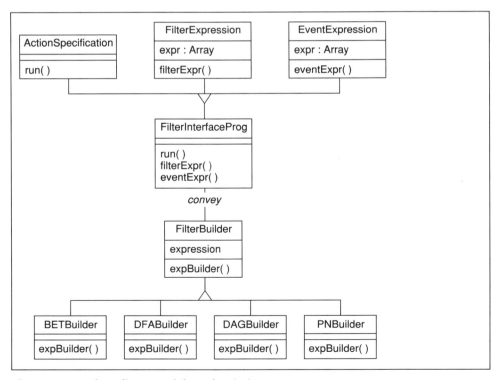

Figure 22.3   Class diagram of the subscription component.

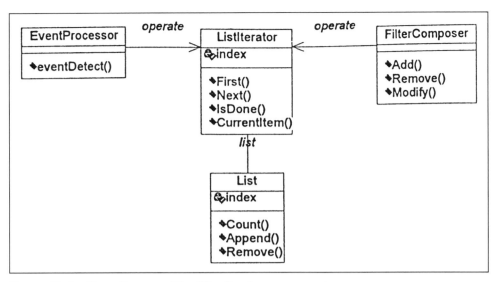

Figure 22.4 Class diagram of the filter iterator component.

After the users submit their filtering demands, the filter iterator begins to operate the filter internal representation constructed by the subscription component. This iterator can be designed using the Iterator pattern [Gamma 1995]. For the preceding example, the iterator maps a boolean function to all the variable elements of the expression and then evaluates it so that it can determine if an event or events are detected or rejected. In this component the users can also modify the filter programs through the filter composer, as shown in Figure 22.4.

When an interesting event is detected, the filter action component will instantaneously perform the action(s) specified in the filter program. Its class diagram is shown in Figure 22.5.

In addition, several utility classes are involved, including input/output (I/O) operations, network management, and multithreads.

The interaction diagram of these four components is shown in Figure 22.6. First of all, the users specify the event formats using the EDC component. Second, the users submit their filter demands and the associated actions by means of the subscription component. And then the filter iterator component is used to detect the specified event(s). The users can also use this component to modify their filter demands. If the specified event(s) is (are) detected, the action component is notified to perform the associated actions.

22.3 Implementation of the Event-Filtering Framework

The implementation of the event-filtering framework includes the preceding design pattern and other related classes, such as utility classes.

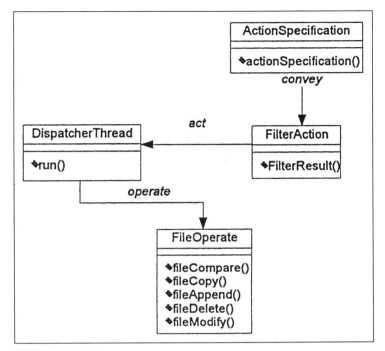

Figure 22.5 Class diagram of the action component.

An interface encapsulates a coherent set of services and attributes without explicitly binding this functionality to that of any particular object or code. For example, the java.lang.Runnable interface is simply as follows:

```
public interface Runnable {
        Public abstract void run();
}
```

The users implement it in concrete applications (see the Wiley Web site for examples at www.wiley.com/compbooks/fayad).

The Builder pattern separates the construction of a complex object from its representation, so that the same construction process can create different representations. Here it is used for constructing the internal representation of a filter whose construction process is the same. *Sections 22.1* and *22.3* show four kinds of filtering internal representations: BET, DAG, DFA, and PN. When a set of boolean expressions submits, the suitable filter internal representation can be built depending on the event specification and user selection. At first, an abstract class is defined as here:

```
abstract class filterRepresent {
        filterRepresent() { }
        abstract List filterRepresentation();
}
```

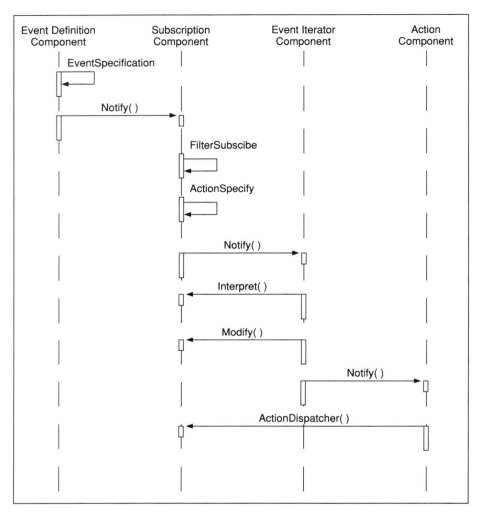

Figure 22.6   Interaction diagram of the event filter framework components.

If the user chooses DAG internal representation, as shown in Figure 22.7, then the concrete implementation of DAG is shown as follows:

```
class DAGBuilder {
        DAGBuilder(List expr, List cont) {
            Expression = expr;
            Context = cont;
        }
        public List FilterRepresent( ) {
            ...
        }
        public List add(Expression expr ) {
            ...
        }
```

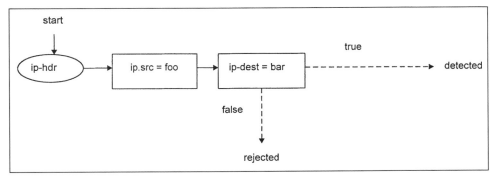

Figure 22.7   Directed acyclic graph representation.

```
public List remove(Expression expr) {
...
}
private List expression;
private List context;
}
```

The Adaptor pattern allows incompatible classes to work together by converting the interface of one class into an interface expected by the clients. The types of event attributes could be any data types such as boolean, integer, float, double, character, or string. Each data type's array adaptor is implemented based on Java Native Array, seen in Appendix A.

The iterator provides ways to access elements of an aggregate object sequentially without exposing the underlying structure of the object. It is used for mapping the predicate function to all the filter's internal representation elements, seen in Appendix A.

The Interpreter pattern defines a grammatical representation for a language and an interpreter to interpret the grammar. The terminal symbols in this language are boolean values, that is, the constants true and false. Nonterminal symbols represent expressions containing &, |, and !. The grammar for regular expressions is defined as follows:

BooleanExp :: = VariableExp | Constant | OrExp | AndExp | NotExp | '(' BooleanExp ')'

AndExp ::= BooleanExp '&' BooleanExp

OrExp ::= BooleanExp '|' BooleanExp

NotExp ::= '!' BooleanExp

Constant ::='true' | 'false'

VariableExp ::= 'A' | 'B' | ... | 'X' | 'Y' | 'Z'

The symbol BooleanExp is the start symbol, and Constant is the terminal symbol defining simple values. The grammar is represented by six classes, as shown in Figure 22.8.

Its implementation is shown subsequently. The function Evaluate evaluates a boolean expression in a context that assigns a true or false value to each variable. The function Replace produces a new boolean expression by replacing a variable with the

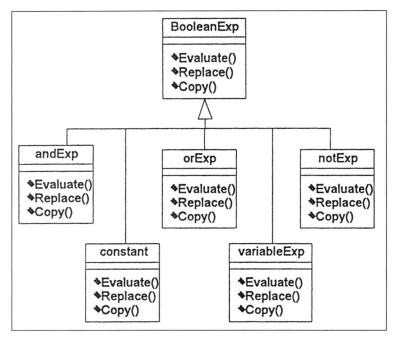

Figure 22.8 Class diagram of the Interpreter pattern.

expression. Here are the details booleanExp, variableExp, and andExp classes. Classes orExp and NotExp are similar to andExp. The Constant class represents the boolean constants.

```
abstract class booleanExp{
    public abstract boolean Evaluate(Context cnt);
    public abstract booleanExp Replace(String str, booleanExp
        blnExp);
    public abstract booleanExp Copy();
}

class Context {
    public boolean lookUp(String str){return true;}
    public void Assign(variableExp vblExp, boolean boolValue){}
}

class variableExp extends booleanExp {
    variableExp(String str) {
        string = str;
    }

public boolean Evaluate(Context cnt) {
    return cnt.lookUp(string);
}
```

```
        public booleanExp Copy() {
            return new variableExp(string);
        }
        public booleanExp Replace(String str, booleanExp exp) {
            if ( string.equals(str) )
                return exp.Copy();
            else
                return new variableExp(str);
        }

        private String string;
    }

class andExp extends booleanExp {
    andExp(booleanExp opd1, booleanExp opd2) {
        operand1 = opd1;
        operand2 = opd2;
    }

    public boolean Evaluate(Context cnt) {
        return (operand1.Evaluate(cnt) && operand2.Evaluate(cnt));
    }

    public booleanExp Copy() {
        return new andExp(operand1.Copy(), operand2.Copy());
    }
    public booleanExp Replace(String str, booleanExp exp) {
        return new andExp(operand1.Replace(str, exp),
operand2.Replace(str,          exp));
    }

    private booleanExp operand1;
    private booleanExp operand2;
}
```

The filter expression operators are realized in the unary predicate and binary predicate that are implemented combining with their relative function objects.

All the components are tested with serial small testing programs. After they pass the component tests, they are packed into different packages according to the functions of the components. As long as the users have the whole package, they can develop their own applications [Fayad 1998].

22.4 Event-Filtering Framework Applications

The event-filtering framework can be used to build event management applications for detecting and classifying events produced by event sources such as running programs or network elements and performing the associated actions. In this chapter, an email filtering application based on the event-filtering framework has been built. It also briefly gives the guidelines for building the Web filter and network management applications.

22.4.1 Email Filter Application

For the email application, the email event can be considered a primitive event and the event format can consider only the input stream both for the incoming mails and the existing mails. The event attributes are SENDER, SUBJECT, STATUS, specific words in the message content, or more. The associated actions could be ignore, delete, display, forward, or hide. For the existing mails, each message is separated as a file in order to save memory and to improve the performance of the application.

Two graphical user interfaces (GUIs) are implemented as shown in Figure 22.9 and Figure 22.10. At first, users select their filtering objects—either incoming mails or existing mails (see Figure 22.9). And then users specify their filtering demands and actions using the filter subscription user interface (see Figure 22.10). Users can specify sender name, sender domain, subject, or content key words, and their associated actions such as delete, ignore, display, classify, or search the specific messages in the incoming mails or existing messages. When new mail comes, the filter iterator component is used to determine if it is detected or rejected corresponding to the filtering demands. If detected, the iterator component notifies the action component to perform the associated actions. The implementation of the filter subscription user interface is a little bit complicated. It implements BorderLayout, choice box, CardLayout, GridLayout, Button, TextField, and Label.

When the subscription menu is selected under the FilterMonitor menu, the Subscribe filter demands window pops up. The default filter action is ignore (Figure 22.10). Users can input their filter demands for the ignore action. Users can also specify their

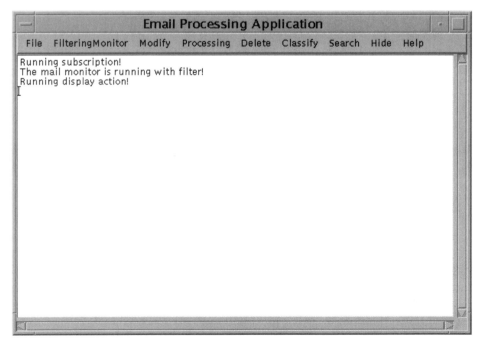

Figure 22.9 User interface of email filtering application.

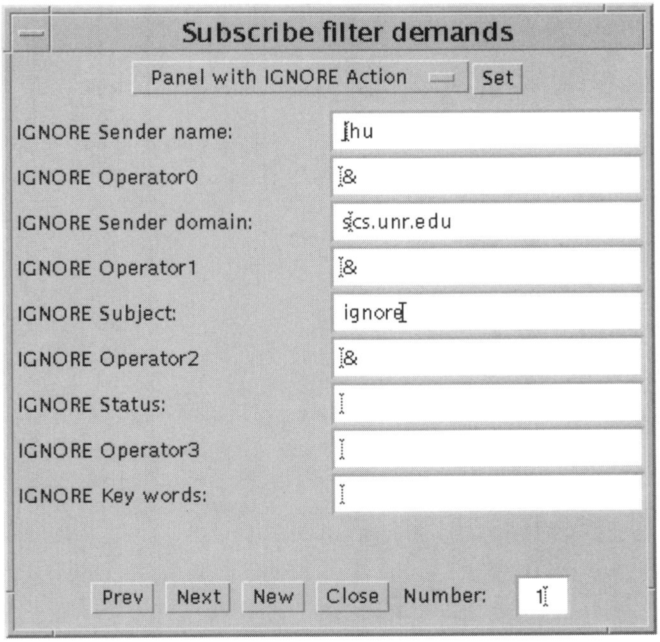

Figure 22.10   Filter subscription user interface for the ignore action.

filter demands corresponding to the other actions, such as delete, forward, and display, by clicking the choice button, as shown in Figures 22.11, 22.12, and 22.13.

In addition, users can modify their filter demands using the Modify filter demands interface, as shown in Figures 22.14 and 22.15. The modifying operations include deleting and inserting the filter demands in runtime.

When the new mail comes, a new window pops up with the sender name and subject, so that you can decide whether it needs reading or not, as shown in Figure 22.16.

Figure 22.17 shows the display action window when incoming mail meets the filter demands of the display action.

22.4.2 Web Filter Application

With the increasing growth of the Internet, there are various huge Web sites on the network. Users are not interested in all the Web sites nor in the complete contents of their specified sites. Furthermore, children also frequently visit the Web, and it is necessary to keep from them exposing them to unhealthy Web sites such as those featuring sex, crime, and adult themes. The Web filter application can be built on top of the filtering framework. It performs several functions such as filtering Web sites, extracting user-specified Web contents, and searching user-specified information.

For example, users can use the Web filter to specify the key words both in the domain name and their contents and associated actions such as submit, display, delete, and save. When parents are not home, they may wish to protect their children from exposure to undesirable Web sites; they can configure the Web filter so that only sites that are

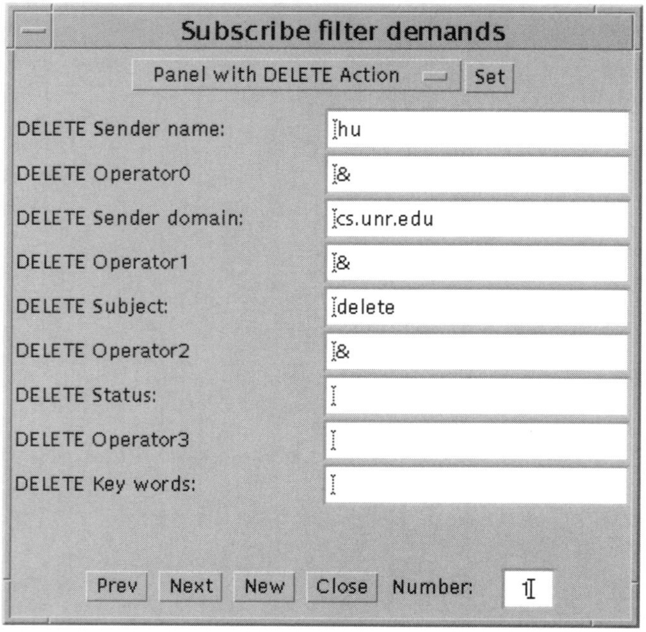

Subscribe filter demands

Panel with DELETE Action — | Set

DELETE Sender name:	hu
DELETE Operator0	&
DELETE Sender domain:	cs.unr.edu
DELETE Operator1	&
DELETE Subject:	delete
DELETE Operator2	&
DELETE Status:	
DELETE Operator3	
DELETE Key words:	

Prev | Next | New | Close | Number: | 1

Figure 22.11 Filter subscription user interface for the delete action.

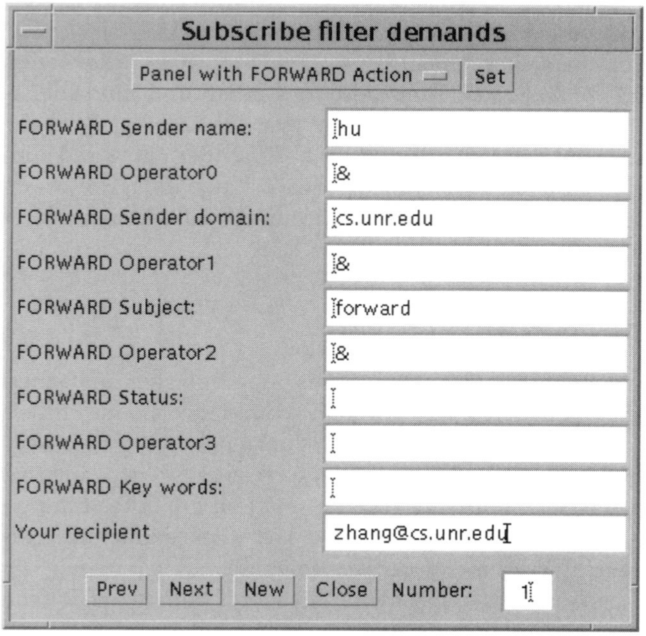

Subscribe filter demands

Panel with FORWARD Action — | Set

FORWARD Sender name:	hu
FORWARD Operator0	&
FORWARD Sender domain:	cs.unr.edu
FORWARD Operator1	&
FORWARD Subject:	forward
FORWARD Operator2	&
FORWARD Status:	
FORWARD Operator3	
FORWARD Key words:	
Your recipient	zhang@cs.unr.edu

Prev | Next | New | Close | Number: | 1

Figure 22.12 Filter subscription user interface for the forward action.

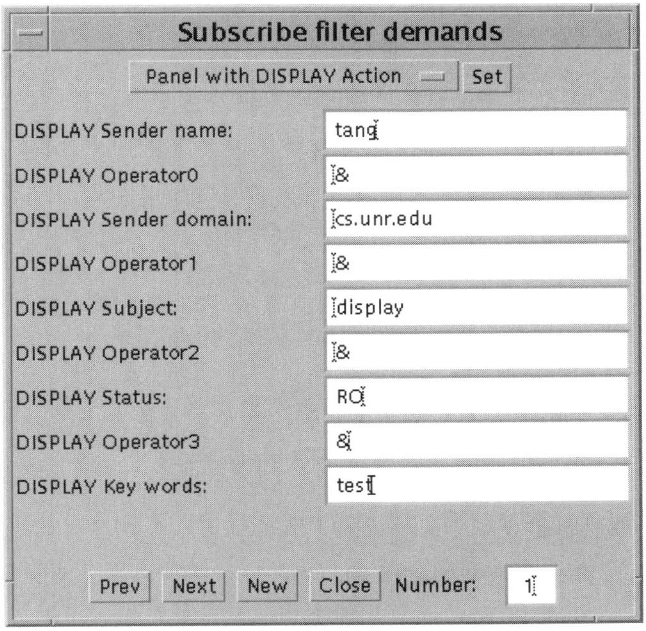

Figure 22.13   Filter subscription user interface for the display action.

suitable for children can go into their Web browsers. The Web filter not only makes use of the Web browsers more efficient, but also decreases the network traffic problem.

22.4.3 Network Management Application

The network management application can be easily built using the event-filtering framework. This application is used to monitor the status of specified hosts, gathering statistics about packets in the network, analyzing traffic patterns, and decreasing the traffic problems in the network.

Users can check whether the specified producers or consumers are available or alive; they can also determine the data transmission precision between local hosts and remote hosts by submitting the remote host address/host name. The producers can generate a huge volume of information, while the consumers may need only a portion of it. Users can use the event filter subscription component to specify their filter demands so that the end-user task is greatly decreased.

22.5 Experiences and Lessons Learned

Framework development is harder than application development. Application development focuses on a concrete problem, whereas framework development focuses on

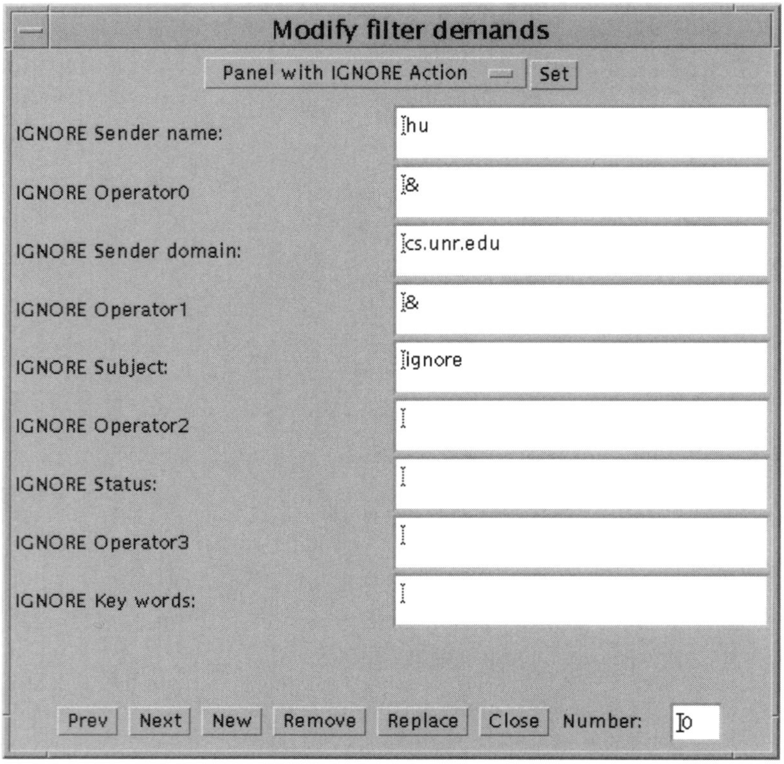

Figure 22.14   Filter modifying user interface for the ignore action.

the abstraction of the concrete applications. Designing abstractions from application examples is the most important step in framework development. Without abstraction, there are no abstract classes of frameworks.

Framework designers need to know many design patterns to develop frameworks. Knowing many design patterns is very helpful for generalizing abstract classes. On the other hand, design patterns cannot solve all the problems.

In order to reduce the production cycle of the framework, the framework test should start right after the framework design. The steps involved in the framework test should follow this rule: pattern by pattern, component by component, and framework by framework.

Reusing the existing frameworks and components is a very efficient way to develop new frameworks. For example, the Java AWT toolkit is a reusable component to develop GUIs, and the Java Generic Library [ObjectSpace 1998] is a great library on data structures. Both of these greatly reduce the effort and time required to develop this event-filtering framework.

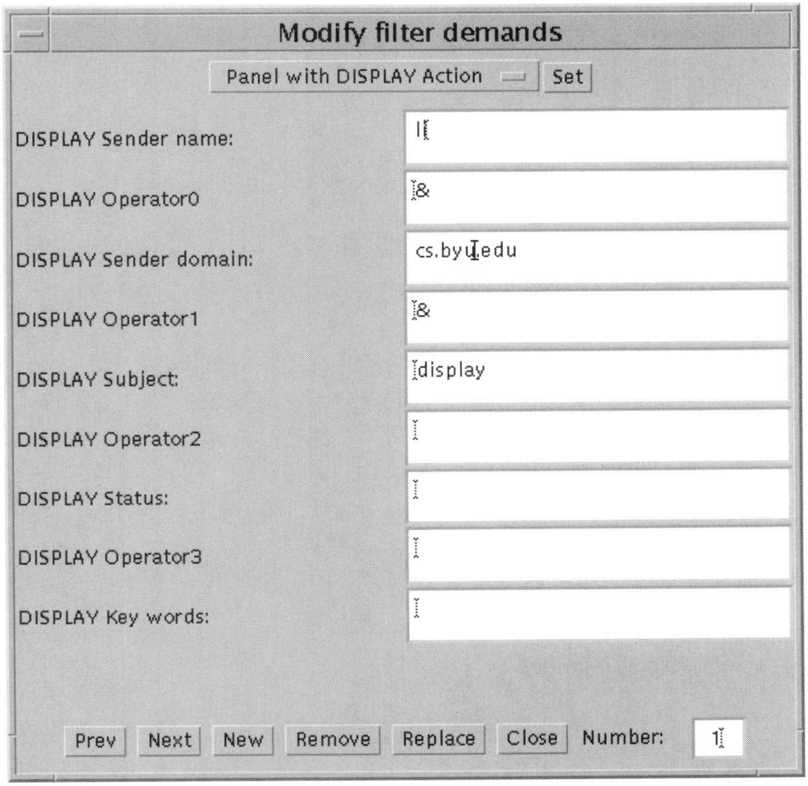

Modify filter demands

Panel with DISPLAY Action — | Set

DISPLAY Sender name: I

DISPLAY Operator0   &

DISPLAY Sender domain: cs.byu.edu

DISPLAY Operator1   &

DISPLAY Subject: display

DISPLAY Operator2   I

DISPLAY Status: I

DISPLAY Operator3   I

DISPLAY Key words: I

Prev | Next | New | Remove | Replace | Close | Number: 1

Figure 22.15   Filter modifying user interface for the display action.

In addition, choosing the object-oriented programming language is also an issue in developing frameworks. For example, Java is platform independent, which makes the developed framework more interoperable, and Java JDK is a powerful reusable toolkit. The heuristics involved in developing and applying the event-filtering framework are listed in the *Heuristics* sidebar.

— New mail com ·

You have new mail from:
Sender: hu
Subject: ignore

OK

Figure 22.16   New mail coming window.

Figure 22.17   New mail display window.

22.6 Summary

Event-filtering mechanisms are widely used by several key application domains, such as network and system management and distributed system toolkits. Each application has its own specific domain requirements. In order to reduce the development effort and costs of these event-filtering applications, it is necessary to build an event-filtering framework.

In this chapter, the event-filtering framework was developed. An email event-filtering application is built on top of this framework. The application tests have shown that the event-filtering framework is reusable, extensible, and reliable. In the same way, this framework can be used effectively to develop many event management applications, including security management, fault management, information and news dissemination, and quality and safety assurance in large-scale organizations. It can also be extended for other related frameworks.

The near future should introduce other related work, including the development of a more powerful filtering programming interface, efficient composition optimization techniques, parallel filtering in a cluster computing environment, and integrating an automated action mechanism in the event-filtering framework.

We will also build more event-filtering framework applications for network and system management, distributed system monitoring, World Wide Web monitoring, and news filtering, so that the reusability and extensibility of this event-filtering framework can be greatly improved.

HEURISTICS

Framework development is much harder than application development. Framework design is much more complex than application design, especially for the enterprise frameworks. It requires development teams with a wide range of skills to create robust, efficient, and reusable application frameworks. It needs expert analysts and designers who have mastered design patterns, software architectures, and protocols in order to alleviate the inherent and accidental complexities of complex software.

Design patterns are design reuse for framework development. Design patterns are the micro-architecture of frameworks.

Studying application examples and existing frameworks is an efficient way to develop new frameworks. Before developing a reusable component or implementing a design pattern, it is necessary to determine whether one exists or whether there is a related component available. If so, it can greatly reduce the effort and cost needed for development.

Generalization is the most important step in framework development. A framework consists of a set of abstract classes generalized from the concrete example abstraction.

The framework development group must be separate from the framework test group. If both groups are not separate, or if the framework developers also work for the framework test group, it will constrain the framework's reusability and extensibility.

Iteration is important in framework development. Reusable code requires many iterations. Only the framework has been tested to be workable in many examples; it is reusable.

The framework should be easy to separate. The components and frameworks within a framework should be easy to use independently, so that they can be reused and extended to the development of applications and new frameworks.

22.7 References

[Al-Shaer 1997] Al-Shaer, E. Event filtering framework: key criteria and design trade-offs. *Proceedings of the IEEE International Conference on Computer Software and Application,* pp. 84–89. Los Alamitos, CA: IEEE Computer Society Press, 1997.

[Al-Shaer 1999] Al-Shaer, E., M. Fayad, H. Abdel-Wahab, and K. Maly. Adaptive object-oriented framework for event management applications. *ACM Computing Surveys,* Theme Issue on Application Frameworks, M.E. Fayad, editor, September 1999.

[Boldt 1998] Boldt, A. *Filtering the Web using WebFilter,* http://math-www.unipaderborn.de/~axel/NoShit/, 1998.

[Fayad 1998] Fayad, M.E. *OO filter framework,* www.cs.unr.edu/~fayad/filter.framework, 1998.

[Fayad-Cline 1996] Fayad, M.E., and M.P. Cline. Aspects of software adaptability. *Communications of the ACM* 39(10):58–59, October 1996.

[Fayad-Schmidt 1997] Fayad, M.E., and D. Schmidt. Object-oriented application frameworks. *Communications of the ACM* 40(10):26–31, October 1997.

[Gamma 1995] Gamma, E., R. Helm, R., Johnson, and J. Vlissides., *Design Patterns: Elements of Reusable Software Architecture.* Reading, MA: Addison-Wesley, 1995.

[GFSC 1998] Goddard Electric Systems Integration Branch. Goddard Flight Space Center(GFSC), http://rs733.gsfc.nasa.gov, 1998.

[Hu-Fayad 1998] Hu, Jingkun, and Mohamed E. Fayad. Development of Object-Oriented Filtering Framework for Event Management Applications. Technical Report, TRCS-98-013, University of Nevada, Reno, June 1998.

[ObjectSpace 1998] ObjectSpace, Inc. Java Generic Library, www.objectspace.com, 1998.

[Schmidt 1996] Schmidt, D., M.E. Fayad, and R. Johnson. Software patterns. *Communications of the ACM* 39(10):36–39, October 1996.

[Sutter 1998] Sutter, G., and M. Hunt. Junk Mail Filtration with Procmail, www.pobox.com/~gsutter/junkfilter/, 1998.

SIDEBAR 4
LAYLA: NETWORK MANAGEMENT INTERFACES FRAMEWORK

Network management systems are used to control and monitor the components of distributed systems such as communication networks, where many different subsystems need to collaborate to offer a service. We define a network management interface (NMI) as the middle layer of a network management system, situated between the high-level control processes and the low-level components of the system. Developing NMIs is a challenging task involving multiple software layers, specification languages, and tools. In order to ease the job of NMI developers, we have developed Layla, a prototype application framework supporting Open Systems Interconnection (OSI) NMIs and using OSI's Common Management Information Service (CMIS).

Many software manufacturers offer packaged solutions for implementing NMIs, often called *application programming interfaces* (APIs). Network management APIs are a powerful development tool, since they take care of many low-level communication issues, yet they exhibit several shortcomings. We felt that these shortcomings would be best addressed by devising Layla as an application framework to mediate between the application and the API. The developer then simply has to deal with the object-oriented specification of the NMI and the Layla framework, and is shielded from the API, which typically provides a procedural interface. Also, generated code is hidden within the framework. Furthermore, Layla is designed to provide minimum but sufficient functionality for building NMIs, including high-level services.

At an early stage in the development of Layla, we decided to take an approach based on design patterns [Gamma 1995; Schmidt 1995]. The resulting framework architecture can be described as a heterogeneous system of design patterns. The system consists of previously published, general-purpose patterns, several new and domain-specific patterns taken from NMI standards (Manager-Agent, Remote Operation, and Managed Object patterns), as well as a couple of basic patterns relevant in Layla's API [Keller 1998] (online documentation of Layla is available at www.iro.umontreal.ca/labs/gelo/layla/). NMIs interact with one another using the Manager-Agent pattern, with each NMI either playing a manager or an agent role. The management protocol between managers and agents is described using the Remote Operation pattern. Agent NMIs use the Managed Object pattern to model their resources. All the patterns are implemented as a system of C++ classes that form the framework. The framework encapsulates to a large extent the underlying communication API, as has been shown with the adoption of two different, commercially available APIs.

Developing a Layla application, whether it is an agent, a manager, or both, is closely tied to the specification of the information to be exchanged. The development procedure consists of five steps. The first two steps consist in preparing the specification for use by the NMI and change little with the introduction of Layla. The remaining three steps deal with the development of the NMI itself and comprise the implementation of the managed objects, the agent application, and the manager application. The amount of work required for these latter steps is an order of magnitude lower, if Layla is used instead of a pure API. Remember that Layla supports OSI NMIs and uses CMIS.

Continues

SIDEBAR 4
LAYLA: NETWORK MANAGEMENT INTERFACES FRAMEWORK *(Continued)*

Using Layla, we have built, in cooperation with our industrial partner, several NMIs. Yet, a broader implementation base is needed to further validate the introduced concepts and the genericity of the framework. Layla's development demonstrates that pattern-based frameworks can be built for the demanding NMI domain. Experimentation with Layla makes us believe that pattern benefits such as flexibility, reusability, and documentation value of the framework and the resulting applications can indeed be reaped. And we concur with Schmidt [Schmidt 1995] that the "integration of design patterns together with frameworks" will be among the areas of increased attention in the years to come.

References

[Gamma 1995] Gamma, Erich, Richard Helm, Ralph Johnson, and John Vlissides. *Design Patterns: Elements of Reusable Object-Oriented Software.* Reading, MA: Addison-Wesley, 1994.

[Keller 1998] Keller, Rudolf K., Jean Tessier, and Gregor V. Bochmann. A pattern system for network management interfaces. *Communications of the ACM* 41(9):86–93.

[Schmidt 1995] Schmidt, Douglas C. Using design patterns to develop reusable object-oriented communication software. *Communications of the ACM,* Theme Issue on Object-Oriented Experiences, M.E. Fayad and W.T. Tsai, editors, 38(10):65–74, October 1995.

PART

Five

Environments

Part Five introduces environments frameworks, such as Beyond-Sniff (Chapter 23), Ecce (Chapter 24), Amulet (Chapter 25), Jadve (Chapter 26), Object Environments (Chapter 27), and OOPM (Chapter 28). Part Five contains Chapters 23 through 28.

Chapter 23, "Beyond-Sniff: A Framework-Based Component System," presents the framework-specific experience gained in developing Sniff and Beyond-Sniff from the architecture's perspective as well as the development process's perspective. It also shows that Beyond-Sniff consists of a layered system of frameworks. The smaller frameworks consist of a few classes, while the larger ones are component-collaboration frameworks comprising building blocks, application frameworks, and components.

Chapter 24, "Extensible Computational Chemistry Environment (Ecce)," introduces Ecce, which is a comprehensive, object-oriented environment for molecular modeling, analysis, and simulation. The key technical concepts include a seamless integration of software tools, accomplished through a standardized architecture for molecular modeling applications, and an extensible object-oriented chemistry data model to support the management of molecular and experimental data. Ecce is an integration of visualization tools, an object-oriented database management system, and a graphical user interface development tool. The principal contribution is providing an environment to chemists that enhances the productivity, software adaptability, system reliability, and maintainability of their computational results. Ecce serves as a development framework for the extended-functionality, chemistry-specific software that is required to meet the mission of the Department of Energy's Environmental Molecular Sciences Laboratory (EMSL).

Chapter 25, "The Amulet Prototype-Instance Framework," discusses the Amulet framework. Amulet is a new kind of object-oriented framework for user interface development that is based on a *prototype-instance* object system instead of the conventional class-instance object system. In a prototype-instance object system, there is no concept of a *class*, since every object can serve as a prototype for other objects and any instance can override any methods or data values. Amulet is also differentiated by high-level encapsulations of interactive behaviors and by the ubiquitous use of *constraints*, which are relationships that the programmer declares once and then are enforced by the system. The result is that programs written using the Amulet framework have a different style from those written with conventional frameworks. For instance, Amulet applications are typically constructed by combining instances of the built-in objects, rather than by subclassing the built-in classes or writing methods. Amulet is written in C++ and is portable across Windows NT and 95, Unix X/11, and the Macintosh.

Chapter 26, "Jadve: Graph-Based Data Visualization Framework," presents the design and implementation, as well as example applications of Jadve, a framework for graph-based data visualization applications written in Java. The main contributions of this work are these: (1) Compared with traditional graph editor frameworks, Jadve has built-in distributed processing and multiuser collaboration support, and (2) by utilizing Java's dynamic and portable features, applications can be easily constructed on top of Jadve and can run on virtually all platforms. Jadve provides a Java application programming interface (API) for programmers to build client-server applications that need to visualize information in terms of graphs, such as business work-flow or program dependencies. Through subclassing, the classes that implement a specific application inherit, customize, and enhance the Jadve graph representation, presentation, and layout services. Jadve employs a client-server architecture: The frontend client supports interactive editing, display, and browsing of graphs, whereas the backend server provides graph layout, storage, concurrency control, and collaboration management services. Three applications have been built on top of Jadve: a new version of Improvise, a process modeling environment; Chava, a graphical navigator for Java programs and document repositories; and Classifier Visualizer, a data classifier display and analysis module within a data mining environment.

Chapter 27, "Object Environments," describes a set of useful interfaces required by most objects and should come under the management of the targeted application. These interfaces include configuration, logging, timers, and application events (configure, shutdown, and so on) and can be impacted by the targeted application's operating system, event loop, or interprocesses communication mechanisms. The framework takes advantage of many design patterns to physically decouple the lower-level objects from the implementation mechanisms of the application. Implementation components are written and are available to the targeted application writer for insertion into the runtime environment.

Chapter 28, "Multimodeling Simulation Framework," discusses the Object-Oriented Physical Multimodeling (OOPM) framework. OOPM is an application framework for modeling and simulation under development at the University of Florida. OOPM extends object-oriented design with visualization and a definition of system modeling that reinforces the relation of model to program. OOPM is a natural mechanism for modeling large-scale systems and facilitates effective integration of disparate pieces of code into one simulation. The model author interacts with OOPM via a graphical user interface (GUI), which captures the model design, controls the model execution, and provides output visualization. The distributed model repository (DMR) facilitates collaborative and distributed model definitions and model reuse. The translator converts model definitions to simulation programs in C++, then compiles and links this simulation program, adding runtime support and creating an executable that runs under control of Scenario to provide output visualization using VRML (Virtual Reality Modeling Language). Heterogeneous multimodeling is the basis for geometry and dynamic behavior models, including finite state machine, the functional block model, the equation constraint model, and the rule-based and system dynamics models. Model authors may also create C++ code methods. Model types may be freely combined via multimodeling, which glues together models of the same or different types, produced during model refinement and reflecting various abstraction perspectives to adjust model fidelity during development and at runtime. Every model is built out of multimodel units (MMUs).

CHAPTER 23

Beyond-Sniff: A Framework-Based Component

The development of Sniff, a full-fledged C++ programming environment, started in 1990. Sniff [Bischofberger 1992] focuses on the individual developer and provides powerful browsing, exploration, and configuration management support for developing large projects [TakeFive 1996]. In late 1993, the Beyond-Sniff project was launched. Starting in 1995, Beyond-Sniff was applied on its own evolution. At the beginning of 1996, we finished the active development of Beyond-Sniff and sold the major parts to a programming environment vendor. Beyond-Sniff provides programming environment support as known from Sniff and complements it with pervasive collaboration and coordination support for team-based evolutionary development of large object-oriented software systems. The user's view of how Beyond-Sniff supports cooperative software engineering is described in [Bischofberger 1995a, 1995b].

From a technical perspective, each user works with a dynamically configurable set of independent but closely integrated tools such as class browsers, editors, or cross-referencers. All tools work on the same information model. It comprises all necessary development-related information, including source code, documentation, build information, and test data. The information model can be dynamically extended. Since all tools share the same model, it is physically separated from the tools and divided into logically cohesive partitions. Distinguished information model services manage these partitions.

In contrast to Sniff, Beyond-Sniff is not just one particular integrated development environment but serves different purposes for different clients: (1) It provides a defined set of tools to the software developers (Beyond-Sniff's end users). (2) It provides the technical infrastructure to support the building of new development tools to the tool makers (Beyond-Sniff ISVs). In order to meet the requirements of these two groups of clients, we designed and implemented Beyond-Sniff as a distributed component system. Based on our group's long experience in developing and applying frameworks—in particular, the application framework ET++ [Weinand 1994]—a framework-based approach to the design and implementation of this component system naturally evolved.

Beyond-Sniff's tools are closely integrated, meaning that all running tools are in synch and, in each context, any semantically useful service of any installed tool is accessible. Independently of its runtime distribution, Beyond-Sniff appears to the end user as one homogeneous tool. From our perspective, this kind of integration, combined with a high degree of flexibility in installing and replacing tools, is best achieved by implementing each tool as a separate component.

New tools sometimes require an extended information model, which can entail the introduction of new information model services. Similar to a tool, each information model service is a separate component. Thus, the Beyond-Sniff administrator can easily integrate newly required and evolved services into a running system. The information provided by these services is immediately accessible for all tools. Furthermore, the administrators can freely configure the distribution of tools and services at runtime according to changing performance requirements and changing conditions of the infrastructure in use.

For Beyond-Sniff ISVs, it is essential that they can quickly compose and adapt existing components and easily develop new ones. Object-oriented application frameworks for both tool as well as service components have the advantage of helping to meet the adaptation and development requirements. The tool component application framework implements a useful but empty tool component that already comprises all the integration, synchronization, and collaboration capabilities. The server component application framework does the same with respect to server components.

Frameworks not only have the ability to speed up component development and adaptation, but they are also well suited for abstracting and implementing component collaboration. In systems such as Beyond-Sniff, component collaboration is rather complex and follows recurring patterns. It is therefore ideally suited to be implemented as a framework. Of course, the resulting component-collaboration frameworks can be used inside or in combination with the tool and the service component application framework. Figure 23.1 depicts the resulting structure.

In addition to the requirements of the application domain, a software architecture is always shaped according to nonfunctional requirements as well. During the development of Beyond-Sniff, we learned that ease of evolution is one of the most important nonfunctional requirements of its design.

Although we were highly familiar with the application domain, we had to use an exploratory and evolutionary style of programming in order to develop appropriate technical solutions and to thoroughly elaborate the consequences of collaboration for software development tools. The more complex the system became, the more expense each evolutionary step required.

In order to decrease the burden of evolutionary changes, a software design has to exhibit several characteristics, such as an appropriate structural decomposition and a low degree of coupling between the structural units. The Beyond-Sniff component system provides sensible decomposition and decoupling at a coarse-grained level. In

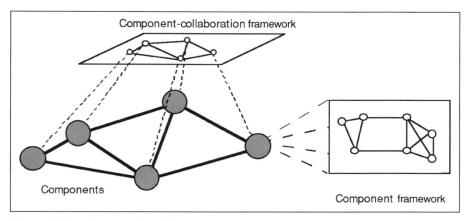

Figure 23.1 Framework architecture.

addition, we evolved Beyond-Sniff toward an architecture of horizontal layers. Each layer uses its subsequent layer only through its public blackbox interface. Due to the inversion of the control flow in frameworks, upcalls in the neighboring layer are allowed under certain circumstances. Layers can be individually adapted by using their inheritance interface.

Our experience indicates that Beyond-Sniff's components and layers are useful but suffer from inflexibility regarding minor evolutionary changes such as rearranged parameter lists, renamed parameters, and method name changes. That is even more serious considering the fact that these changes make up the majority of all changes. Therefore, we decided to introduce highly flexible coupling mechanisms that are used to make component as well as framework layer coupling as resistant as possible to such minor changes.

In this chapter, we present the framework-related experience we gained during the Beyond-Sniff project. We do so by focusing on Beyond-Sniff's architecture and on the experience we gained in evolving it.

The chapter is structured as follows: In *Section 23.1*, we give a short overview of Sniff and describe the most relevant aspects regarding the transition to Beyond-Sniff. *Section 23.2* focuses on Beyond-Sniff's architecture. We show which kinds of frameworks we developed for a seamlessly integrated component system. In *Section 23.3*, we describe detailed aspects of the Tool Integration framework as a particular example of a component-collaboration framework. In *Section 23.4*, we discuss the issue of high iteration costs during the development of complex software systems and present our approaches to keeping them as low as possible. The chapter finishes with a short case study (*Section 23.5*) and a compilation of our lessons learned in *Section 23.6*.

23.1 From Sniff to Beyond-Sniff

Sniff [Bischofberger 1992] is a single-user, one-process programming environment implemented on top of the ET++ application framework [TakeFive 1996]. Sniff can be configured to use different kinds of compilers, debuggers, and configuration management tools. In the core of Sniff, there is already a separation between services and tools. The project manager and the symbol table services manage shared information and guarantee its consistency. The tools, such as the class browser and project editor, serve to visualize and manipulate this information.

In developing Sniff it became clear that many aspects of tools could be generalized. They were implemented in the tool framework, an extension of the ET++ application framework. Examples for functionality in the tool framework are handling of shared menus, event forwarding between tools, and multidimensional information filtering.

Our experience in developing Sniff on top of ET++ [Weinand 1994] and the tool framework was very favorable. A considerable part of Sniff's user-friendliness is due to the culture and reusable solutions implemented in these frameworks. Sniff's architecture is optimized for structuring and handling large projects. Its browsing support is generally considered to be excellent. At the end of the Sniff project, we decided to move into a new area and develop Beyond-Sniff, an environment for cooperative software engineering. This decision led us to a number of new requirements and approaches:

Sniff's only support for cooperation is provided by the underlying configuration management system. Support of innovative synchronous and asynchronous cooperation requires coordinating agents. We therefore implemented sharable services that manage information and serve as coordinators.

Envisioned new tools made it necessary to handle larger amounts of information and to run expensive algorithms over them. For this reason we implemented a service scheme that made it possible to share the information and to parallelize the computing-intensive tasks.

Sniff's set of services and tools is fixed. Updates and additional tools can be distributed only with a new version of Sniff. This led us to the development of a plug-and-play component model for the Beyond-Sniff services and tools.

It must be cheap to implement new services and tools to be able to experiment with different solutions for cooperation support. It must be even cheaper than within Sniff, although in Beyond-Sniff the distribution aspects have to be handled as well. For this reason we decided from the beginning to develop frameworks that provide as much standardizable service and tool functionality as possible. It was our goal that these frameworks hide most of the complexity of the component model from the developer.

23.2 Beyond-Sniff's Architecture

This section provides four different views of Beyond-Sniff's architecture. The component view describes the overall component architecture and provides a glimpse of the kind of service and tool components that are available. The component structure view zooms into a service and a tool component to show their layered architecture. The framework structure view discusses the various frameworks according to the architectural layers by example of the tool framework. The framework reuse view shows which parts of which kinds of frameworks can be reused in a heterogeneous environment.

23.2.1 Component View

Beyond-Sniff consists of an open set of tools and services providing the support known from Sniff as well as functionality that is specific for cooperative software engineering. A screen dump of Beyond-Sniff looks similar to a screen dump of Sniff with the exception that there are a number of new and improved tools. Contrary to Sniff, the services and tools of Beyond-Sniff are based on a well defined, distributed, plug-and-play component model. The Beyond-Sniff component model defines a number of aspects of the way that components cooperate. The most important of them are the following:

- Communication
  - Request and notification encoding and distribution
- Component management
  - Service broker model for globally shared and project-specific services
  - User-level tool management model
- Tool integration
  - Declaration, distribution, and handling of the capabilities of the installed tools
  - Capability-based user interface handling
  - Capability-based request dispatching between tools

Components adhering to Beyond-Sniff's component model can be easily inserted into and removed from a running Beyond-Sniff installation. Furthermore, users of Beyond-Sniff do not have to be aware that they are working with separate tools and services, because the component model defines how tools can be seamlessly integrated.

In the rest of this section, we describe communication and component management aspects. Our tool integration approach is discussed in *Section 23.3*.

Figure 23.2 gives a high-level overview of the Beyond-Sniff components at runtime. The component model defines no restricting relationships between components and operating system processes. Each of the components depicted in Figure 23.2 could thus

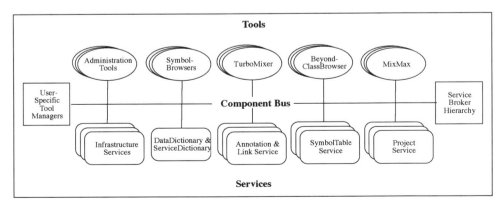

Figure 23.2 Component view of Beyond-Sniff.

be running in a process of its own or they could all be running in the same process. All other distributions are also possible.

Components communicate by means of self-describing requests. A request is an Any item. Anys are a universal semantic data representation mechanism (SDRM) that supports the definition of programming language–independent data types. Anys provide the management of the instances of these data types, including garbage collection and declarative data access. All instances are self-reflective; thus, they can be dynamically typechecked. Further information about Anys can be found in [Mätzel 1996].

Requests are exchanged using the component bus. This bus supports anonymous as well as peer-to-peer communication. Anonymous communication follows the publish/ subscribe principle. Requests in which a component is interested are described by request patterns, which are represented as Anys as well. Peer-to-peer communication requires a connection establishment prior to request exchange. A component requests a connection by describing the kind of service in which it is interested. The request is handled by a hierarchy of service brokers. The brokers at each hierarchical level have differently detailed responsibilities. For example, a Symbol Browser requests the symbol table of a particular project. The request travels from the general service broker, via the general SymbolTable Service Broker, to the project-specific SymbolTable Service Broker, which selects an appropriate SymbolTable Service and returns a reference to the requester.

Each component manages a request dispatcher that maps requests to the component's methods. Besides its specific functional interface, a component supports an introspection as well as a management interface. The latter serves, for example, to manipulate a component's request dispatcher dynamically.

23.2.2 Component Structure View

Figure 23.3 details the internal structure of services and tools. Both services and tools are implemented as layered systems of frameworks. Layers use each other mostly as blackboxes.

The Component Bus Access framework provides services and tools with access to the component bus. The tool-specific layers consist of the following:

- The Service Access frameworks provide a number of proxy objects that serve to use remote services transparently, as well as to execute some functionality locally and manage caches for efficiency reasons.

- The Tool Aspect frameworks provide several abstractions for functionality such as tool integration, browsing, and annotation and link handling. They comprise component-collaboration frameworks as well as extensions of ET++. These extensions integrate the component-collaboration frameworks into the application framework. They hide the fact that a lot of the tool functionality is based on the functionality provided by teams of services.

- The Tool Application framework, an ET++ extension, integrates the Tool Aspect frameworks into a homogeneous standard tool abstraction.

The service-specific layers consist of the following:

- The Data Management framework, which implements an object query language (OQL) queriable RAM database

- The Service framework, which abstracts functionality such as state management, data management, locking, and change propagation

Starting with these two-layered framework systems and the existing services and tools, it is a matter of days to implement a programming environment for a particular programming language. This environment automatically provides support for documentation, annotation and linking, configuration management, editing, and much more.

23.2.3 Framework Structure View

Figure 23.4 gives a more detailed view of the layers of the Tool Application framework. The Service Application framework is based on the same principles. The figure depicts the Tool Application framework, as well as the most important subframeworks. Compared to Figure 23.3, it provides further details about the Tool Aspect frameworks layer. This layer is of particular interest because it contains component frameworks that make use of various component-overlapping frameworks.

All gray frameworks depend on ET++. They are specific extensions of ET++ that implement user interface–related tool aspects in a generic way. The resulting Tool Application framework allows a developer to implement, for example, a new browser that corresponds to the standard browsing model with a few lines of code. The Tool Aspect frameworks consist of three kinds of parts:

- Proxies represent the components in component-collaboration frameworks.

- Building blocks provide higher-level, easy-to-use interfaces to the functionality of component-collaboration frameworks. They resemble facades that abstract the tool-relevant aspects of these frameworks. In addition, building blocks encapsulate the initialization of these frameworks. Whenever possible, a component-

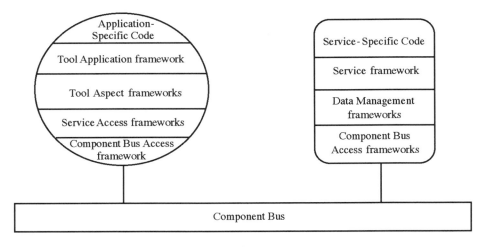

Figure 23.3 Component structure view of Beyond-Sniff.

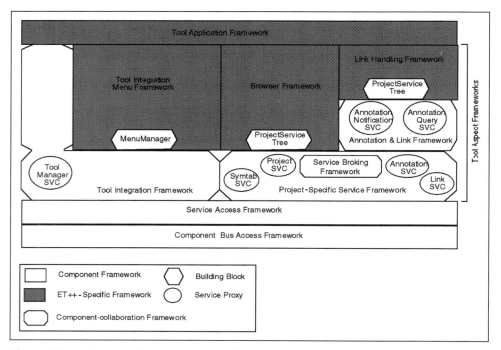

Figure 23.4 Framework structure view of tool components.

collaboration framework is used through a building block. This isolates the tools from various kinds of modifications of the framework.

■ ET++-specific frameworks implement the tool-specific parts of the component-collaboration frameworks and integrate the functionality closely into ET++.

The discussion of the Tool Integration framework in the next section is a scenario that provides examples for all three kinds of parts.

23.2.4 Framework Reuse View

While living in a closed world where the platform and framework developer can decide which languages and libraries are used in developing new services and tools, large parts of the design and code of a new service and tool can be reused. In a hetero-geneous world this is not always the case. For example, it can be a sensible decision to implement a new simple tool in Tcl/Tk. In this case the ET++-based frameworks cannot be reused, but at least the Service Access framework can be bound into Tcl and reused. Another example is the integration of an existing tool implemented in whatever language based on whatever GUI library, which are not C++ compatible. In this case only the design can be reused and the existing code has to be modified or wrapped in such a way that the tool participates at least in the Tool Integration framework and the Annotation and Link framework.

Table 23.1 shows which reusable parts of Beyond-Sniff depend on which infra-structure.

Table 23.1   Compatibility Restrictions

ARTIFACTS DEPEND ON	DEPENDING ARTIFACTS USED IN TOOLS
ET++	Tool Application framework, Tool Aspect frameworks, Component Bus Access framework
C++	Service Access framework, service proxies, building blocks, wrappers for component-overlapping frameworks
Component model	Reusable architecture concepts needed to participate in the component-overlapping frameworks

23.3 The Tool Integration Framework: A Component-Collaboration Framework

In this section we discuss, based on a specific example, how components cooperate, where the various parts such as building blocks and proxies reside, and how they are used to build component-collaboration frameworks.

All Beyond-Sniff tools obey the following scheme: Operations on the currently selected object are triggered via a command-issuing mechanism, which is usually a pull-down menu but could also be a button or a pop-up menu. For example, the icon representing a class is selected in the class hierarchy browser. The Class menu is pulled down and the Browse Class command is selected to show it in the class browser.

To achieve a seamless integration, all tools have to provide the same Class menu when a class is selected. This menu then depends on the installed tools and the class-related operations they provide. The same should be true for more direct interaction such as double-clicking.

The Tool Integration framework supports this kind of context-sensitive, homogeneous menu and direct interaction handling. It avoids any modifications of already existing tools if new tools are dynamically inserted or existing tools are replaced. It allows tools to share menus virtually as soon as they are able to display the same kinds of objects.

It does this by having a central, user-specific service, the ToolManager, which keeps track of which tools are installed, which ones are running for the corresponding user, and which operations they can perform on a given type of object. For all installed tools the ToolManager maintains *tool capabilities*. They describe how an instance of that tool can be activated and what operations it supports. The description of an operation consists of, among other things, what type of artifact it works on, from which menu it can be activated with which command, and whether it can be activated with a default action such as a double-click. All tools enroll themselves with the ToolManager at startup and remove themselves at exit.

Instead of using the ToolManager directly, a tool communicates via a Menu-Manager. The MenuManager is an example of a building block. It provides a more abstract and convenient interface to the ToolManager's functionality. There is no one-to-one correspondence between the interface of the MenuManager and the Tool-

Manager. The implementation of the MenuManager uses a local ToolManager proxy to access the ToolManager. Figure 23.5 gives an overview of how the different entities of the Tool Integration framework cooperate.

The Tool Integration Menu framework binds the Tool Integration framework into ET++, as depicted in Figure 23.4. It extends the ET++ menu-handling mechanism and is an integral part of the Tool Application framework. In ET++, the menu-handling control flow is implemented mainly in the class Manager. For each window of an ET++ application, there is exactly one Manager instance. Manager defines the following four methods that are relevant in the context of the Tool Integration framework. The factory method DoMakeMenuBar specifies which manager-specific menus have to be combined with the menu bar. DoMakeMenu is a factory method, which is called to initially create a menu. DoSetupMenu is called every time a menu gets exposed. DoMenuCommand is called as soon as a menu entry has been selected.

The Tool Integration Menu framework defines a new Manager subclass, which overwrites the described four methods. The implementations make use of a MenuManager. Let's consider the Class menu. Within DoMakeMenuBar, the MenuManager asks the ToolManager whether there is a Class menu category. If there is such a category, DoMakeMenu is used to create the Class menu. For that, the MenuManager retrieves from the ToolManager all tool capabilities that belong to the Class category. Each capa-

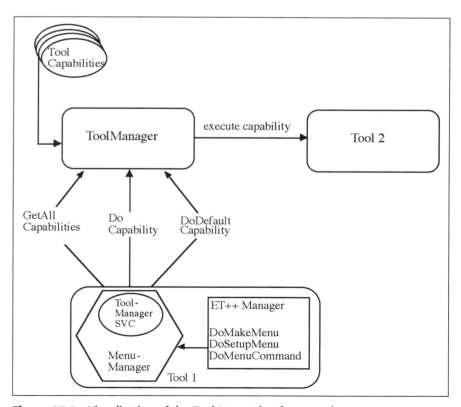

Figure 23.5 Visualization of the Tool Integration framework.

bility found is represented by a menu item. The menu item label is given by the capability itself. Each call of DoSetupMenuItem checks whether the constructed Class menu is still up-to-date. In addition, it enables and disables the menu's items depending on the actual selection. If a menu item of the Class menu is selected, the DoMenuCommand method is called. It provides the MenuManager with a description of the currently selected objects. The MenuManager passes this information to the ToolManager, which initiates the command execution associated with the originally provided tool capability by an appropriate tool. If there is no proper tool running, the ToolManager launches one.

23.4 Architectural Support for Iterative Development and Evolution

It is generally accepted that successful frameworks evolve in an iterative process. This process is tightly coupled with the development process of particular applications. During each iteration, common functionality is being extracted from the applications and shifted to the framework. The framework's class hierarchy is changed by means of refactoring, generalization, remodularization, and so forth.

The Beyond-Sniff frameworks were shaped by such an iterative process as well. The number of frameworks, their structure, responsibilities, and relationships have converged continuously toward the described architecture. This architecture was actively used for two years to develop some custom-made development environments. During this time, the major frameworks and architectural key abstractions remained stable.

This was, for obvious reasons, not the case during the first two years of the iterative evolutionary development process. We, rather, experienced that the cooperative, continuously ongoing evolution process can result in large expenses in developing large frameworks. In each step, the changing of particular parts of a system raised the issue of necessary adaptations of all the other parts depending on them. This was the case for the frameworks as well as for the framework-based applications.

After the first major redesign of Beyond-Sniff's architecture, we had to pay a high price in reorganizing our code base, educating all team members, and adapting our frameworks and applications.

One major problem was that it was not possible to cheaply provide evolution results to a subset of the application programmers because the cost we incurred in reorganizing our code base was too large. This resulted in overlarge evolutionary steps in the frameworks before they were tested in the context of the large applications. Furthermore, it was hard for the application programmers to adapt their applications to the changed frameworks because they had no tool support to quickly find out what was changed between two versions of the frameworks.

These two problems were eased very much by migrating to SNiFF+ version 2.0 [Take-Five 1996]. Its workspace-based cooperation support and its advanced history management and browsing support allowed us to reduce the administrative overhead to such a degree that it became possible to evolve our frameworks and applications in small steps.

Our experience is that tool support is crucial for an evolutionary development approach with more than two or three developers. Further information can be found in [Bischofberger 1995a].

It is quite obvious that reducing the costs of evolution with tools is only the second choice if it is possible to avoid them by designing evolution-friendlier architectures. For this reason, we started to concentrate on designing our frameworks and applications for ease of evolution. To achieve this goal, we used a few structural design approaches, which made our architecture more flexibly adaptable. The following three of these are discussed in the rest of this section:

- Blackbox frameworks of homogeneous abstractions (framework layers, components)

- Design patterns focusing on modularization and object coupling

- Flexible coupling between interacting objects/components

23.4.1 Components and Framework Layers

We designed our frameworks as layered systems, with layers representing abstractions of increasing specialization and functionality, as shown in *Section 23.2*. Each layer provides solutions for a particular problem domain and therefore has a well-defined and focused purpose. Its interfaces define a particular abstraction level. In Beyond-Sniff, the various levels of abstraction reach from a generic component model at the lowest layer to highly specialized, development-environment-specific tools and services at the top layer.

Higher layers naturally depend on the interfaces and semantics of lower layers. Accessing the functionality of layers only by a sound but narrow interface reduces the interlayer dependencies. We usually provide two different kinds of interfaces to a layer. First, the usage interface of the framework representing a particular layer is broad enough to be useful but highly focused. In addition, we provide an even more compact interface to a layer by means of building blocks. Building blocks provide single access points to layers covering instantiation and usage. Thus, by plugging building blocks together, framework layers are actually stacked. The internals of layers can be changed without affecting higher layers. For example, the ProjectServiceTree building block depicted in Figure 23.4 provides an interface to the Project-Specific Service framework, which itself provides a proper interface to a component-collaboration framework. Any change of the Project-Specific Service framework is hidden by the ProjectServiceTree.

The reduction of interlayer relationships has to be accompanied by a reduction of the dependencies within the layers. Well-focused problem solutions are encapsulated and provided with an appropriate usage interface. In Beyond-Sniff, this resulted in the described mixture of components, building blocks, and component-collaboration frameworks.

In our experience, layering is an approach that becomes very sensible once the application domain is, to a certain degree, understood. This means that this technique just starts to reduce evolution costs during later cycles. However, layering is not a comprehensive remedy regarding evolution issues because the inverted control flow of frameworks usually violates the layered structure.

Design Patterns

In order to cope with a number of expected changes, Beyond-Sniff intensively uses design patterns. In particular, these are the Facade, Adaptor, Mediator, Abstract Factory, Bridge, and Observer patterns [Gamma 1995]. Each of these patterns considers a particular aspect to be an anticipated subject of change and makes it therefore an explicit part of the suggested design.

Depending on the expected change and the amount of flexibility actually required, we used different, more or less flexible implementations of these patterns. Two examples for the application of design patterns are as follows:

> **The ProjectServiceTree building block is a facade for the Project-Specific Service framework.** It hides all intrinsics from the user. There is no particularly strong requirement for flexibility regarding change. Therefore, the ProjectServiceTree is implemented in a straightforward manner as, for example, recommended by [Gamma 1995]. However, it is used in a stronger sense than a facade, since if used, it is the only allowed interface to the framework. (See Figure 23.4.)

> **The Beyond-Sniff service brokers implement the Broker pattern but are involved only during connection establishment.** Furthermore, the Beyond-Sniff service brokers form a hierarchy that defines their collaboration structure. This hierarchy can be dynamically changed by means of managers. In order to request a service, the client specifies which kind of component it needs and sends this specification to the broker at the top of the hierarchy. The broker forwards the request along the hierarchy until a responsible broker is found. This broker then either creates an appropriate service instance or just replies with a service reference. The service broker reduces the coupling between the invoking client and the delivered product. It makes its clients independent of the strategy for how the type of service is chosen among different kinds of services that provide the same functionality. Furthermore, it hides how the service is created [Buschmann 1996]. (See Figure 23.2.)

Flexible Coupling

Layering and patterns work very well for expected changes. Evolutionary changes cannot ever be anticipated; however, we know that they always result in lots of minor evolutionary changes such as rearranged parameter lists, renamed parameters, method name changes, and so on. Thus, Beyond-Sniff uses flexible coupling mechanisms between components, as well as between frameworks and components, which are as resistant as possible to these changes.

Coupling exists as the result of dependencies. Dependencies are either static or dynamic. Beyond-Sniff reduces the static inter- and intralayer dependencies by the mechanisms previously explained. In addition, it reduces the dynamic relationships by providing flexibility along the various dimensions of collaboration. Among these dimensions, data representation, data model and interfaces, as well as connection management, are of special importance.

As already explained, the Beyond-Sniff service brokers provide a flexibly adaptable solution to the issues of connection management. Flexibility along the other dimensions is accomplished by reflective data representation using the Any SDRM (*Section 23.2*).

Anys are used to represent all project-specific and other relevant information. The self-describing nature of Anys allows a certain tolerance between the actual format of available data and the expected data format of the component. This means that data consumers are not affected by many kinds of modifications of the producer's data model. An example of such a modification is the delivery of instances of extended or (partially) renamed types.

Similar to the change-absorbing effect concerning data model changes, Anys are used to hide interface changes from depending parts. As mentioned in *Section 23.2*, the communication with components relies on the exchange of Anys. This makes a client independent from, for example, the actual sequence of the formal parameters on the server side. The server's request dispatcher is still able to perform its work correctly.

In general, flexible coupling between components and objects gains more importance the higher the embodied level of abstraction becomes and also with the increasing size of the system. [Mätzel 1997] describes in detail our current work on flexible coupling in the context of system evolution.

23.5 Case Study: Boar

Beyond-Sniff was used during the past two years to develop a number of specific programming environments such as the Gremlin, a GDMO development environment [Muss 1996]. GDMO stands for Guidelines to the Definition of Managed Objects and provides a language for the definition of managed objects within Telecommunications Management Networks (TMN). These developments were relatively straightforward because we were able to reuse the tool and component frameworks as is.

For this reason we discuss in this section the development of Boar, an adaptation of Beyond-Sniff to a particular commercial environment and its business requirements. Boar proved to be the most appropriate test case for the claims we made about the adaptability of Beyond-Sniff's framework architecture.

The requirements for Boar can be summarized as follows: It has to provide the highest possible performance for several dozens of developers working in parallel on projects of around 20 million lines of C++ code. Performance and sharing of resources are more important than absolute flexibility in selecting service distribution strategies. It has to be Common Object Request Broker Architecture (CORBA) compliant.

To meet these requirements, it was necessary to change Beyond-Sniff's service management and allocation strategies, as well as the collaboration patterns in the Project-Specific Service framework. We combined several fine-grained services to more coarse-grained services and optimized data management and sharing inside these larger services. In addition, we introduced load balancing. For Boar, it is sufficient to provide support for manual load balancing since Boar is supposed to be running in a tailored hardware environment. We wrote a graphical tool in order to manage load balancing based on a few project characteristics. In order to make the system CORBA compliant, we exchanged the component bus and adapted the Component Bus Access framework.

From a purely structural point of view, these changes are radical. However, the layering and component structure of the whole framework system proved to be good. The Service Broker abstraction described in *Section 23.2* and *Section 23.4* isolated clients from the changes in the service management and allocation strategies. The Project-ServiceTree described in *Section 23.4* isolated the tools from the modifications of the Project-Specific Service framework. The adaptations of the Component Bus Access framework were only slight and did not affect the Information Service framework because the interfaces between the Component Bus Access framework and the Service Access framework described in *Section 23.2* remained stable.

In developing Boar, the Beyond-Sniff architecture absorbed most of the changes at the intended locations (edges of the layers, component interfaces, and so on) and it allowed us to perform these changes without losing time in adapting all our applications.

23.6 Lessons Learned

Large-scale framework-based systems have to meet strict requirements of adaptability, evolution friendliness, and ease of use in order to make them economically evolvable. In the Beyond-Sniff project we learned that framework layers providing appropriate levels of abstraction and components providing blackbox abstraction are essential to fulfilling these requirements.

In Beyond-Sniff we developed component frameworks that make it easy to implement new services and tools. These frameworks provide a wide variety of abstractions, which range from completely generic to strongly domain-specific. The need for the generic frameworks, such as the Component Bus Access framework, is usually obvious from the beginning. Useful areas for domain-specific frameworks are, rather, found during the iterative evolution process which was the case, for example, with the Tool Integration framework. Our experience has also confirmed our expectation that the number of economically sensible component frameworks depends on the number of functionally similar components.

A further lesson we learned is that the usefulness of frameworks does not end at the boundary of components. On the contrary, we found that it was very efficient to abstract the generic interaction patterns between components in component-collaboration frameworks. Without these frameworks, it would have been impossible for relatively inexperienced developers to implement new services and tools that integrate seamlessly with the existing set of services and tools.

Considering an iterative development process and the evolution of software systems in general, the question of flexible coupling between components and between framework layers is of particular interest. Flexible coupling can be accomplished most effectively by making the various aspects of coupling explicit. The most promising approach lies in reflective architectures. They require intensive infrastructure support, which cannot always be provided. More moderate approaches are to apply coupling- and information hiding–related design patterns. Often-used patterns are the Facade, the Bridge, and the Strategy design patterns. Each one of these patterns objectifies certain aspects of coupling. For example, a facade can be considered an instantiated subsystem interface or module interface, resulting in the fact that a module can support multiple dynamically exchangeable interfaces. The application of coupling- and information hiding–related design patterns was very successful in the Beyond-Sniff project, as shown in the case study in *Section 23.5*. Nonetheless, we would place more emphasis on reflectivity today, based on the experience we gained this year in our new project [Bischofberger 1996a, 1996b].

Semantic data representation mechanisms (SDRMs) such as Anys can be used to achieve modification-tolerant data integration and communication. In Beyond-Sniff it proved economically very successful to represent all externally accessible information, including the requests exchanged between components, by means of an SDRM. This made it possible, for example, to flexibly exchange the dispatch requester and to install new backward-compatible service interfaces on the fly. The application of Anys to the connection establishment between components also proved important for flexible coupling. The application of an SDRM made it possible to define the interface of a component as a set of particular type instances, which is a prerequisite for a trading-based, highly dynamic connection establishment scheme.

Our experience in the Beyond-Sniff project clearly shows that sensible structuring and flexible coupling, together with tool support for cooperative software engineering, considerably speed up the iterative development process of frameworks and framework-based applications. The iterative development process naturally supports and accelerates the creation of framework layers as well as the usage of components and the aforementioned design pattern. We consider such heterogeneous frameworks consisting of components, building blocks, and component-overlapping frameworks, a natural solution for any kind of problem of an order of magnitude similar to that of Beyond-Sniff. Therefore, we expect this kind of framework architecture to gain more importance and visibility in the near future.

23.7 Summary

During the past seven years we developed Sniff and Beyond-Sniff. Sniff is a single-user, one-process programming environment that was implemented on top of the ET++ application framework. Beyond-Sniff is an environment for cooperative software engineering. It consists of a component bus and an open set of seamlessly integrated components (services and tools). In this chapter, we presented the framework-specific experience gained in developing Sniff and Beyond-Sniff from the architecture's perspective, as well as the development process's perspective. By discussing the architecture, we showed that Beyond-Sniff consists of a layered system of frameworks. The smaller frameworks consist of a few classes, while the larger ones are component-collaboration frameworks comprising building blocks, application frameworks, and components. Based on our experience, we argue that component-collaboration frameworks and layering come naturally for systems with a similar degree of distribution because they make it easier to handle the overall complexity. The iterative development of powerful distributed frameworks can be very expensive if the components are coupled too closely. Our experience shows that flexible coupling mechanisms, allowing for slippage between the components, and tool support can considerably reduce the costs of iterations.

23.8 References

[Bischofberger 1992] Bischofberger, Walter. Sniff—A pragmatic approach to a C++ programming environment. *Proceedings of USENIX C++ Conference 1992,* pp. 67–82. Portland, OR, August 1992. Berkeley: USENIX Association.

[Bischofberger 1995a] Bischofberger, Walter, Christian Kleinferchner, and Kai-Uwe Mätzel. Evolving a programming environment into a cooperative software engineering environment. *Proceedings of CONSEG 1995,* pp. 95–106. New Delhi, India, February 1995. New Delhi : Tata McGraw-Hill.

[Bischofberger 1995b] Bischofberger, Walter, Thomas Kofler, Kai-Uwe Mätzel, and Bruno Schäffer. Computer supported cooperative software engineering with Beyond-Sniff. *Proceedings of the 7th Conference on Software Engineering Environments,* pp. 135–143. Noorwijkerhout, Netherlands, April 1995. Los Alamitos, CA: IEEE Computer Society Press.

[Bischofberger 1996a] Bischofberger, Walter, Mike Guttman, and Dirk Riehle. Architecture support for global business objects: Requirements and solutions. *Joint Proceedings of the SIGSOFT 1996 Workshops,* pp. 143–146. ISAW-2, San Francisco, CA, October 1996. New York: ACM/SIGSOFT.

[Bischofberger 1996b] Bischofberger, Walter, and Dirk Riehle. Global business objects— Requirements and solutions. *Proceedings of the Ubilab Conference 1996,* pp. 79–98. Zürich, Switzerland, November 1996. *Computer Science Research at Ubilab, Research Projects 1995/96,* Kai-Uwe Mätzel and Hans-Peter Frei, editors. Konstanz: Universitätsverlag.

[Buschmann 1996] Buschmann, Frank, R. Meunier, H, Rohnert, O. Sommerlad, M. Stal. *Pattern-Oriented Software Architecture: A System of Patterns.* New York: John Wiley & Sons, 1996.

[Gamma 1995] Gamma, Erich, Richard Helm, Ralph Johnson, and John Vlissides. *Design Patterns: Elements of Reusable Object-Oriented Software.* Reading, MA: Addison-Wesley, 1995.

[Mätzel 1996] Mätzel, Kai-Uwe, and Walter Bischofberger. The Any framework—A pragmatic approach to flexibility. *Proceedings of COOTS 1996,* pp. 179–190. Toronto, ON, June 1996. Berkeley: USENIX Association.

[Mätzel 1997] Mätzel, Kai-Uwe, and Walter Bischofberger. Designing object systems for evolution. *Theory and Practice of Object Systems* 3(4). New York: John Wiley & Sons, 1997.

[Muus 1996] Muus, Wenka. *Konzeption und prototypische Realisierung einer GDMO-Entwicklungsumgebung auf Basis der generischen Entwicklungsumgebung Beyond-Sniff.* Master thesis (in German). Department of Computer Science, University of Hamburg.

[TakeFive 1996] TakeFive Inc., *SNiFF+ Manual,* www.takefive.com.

[Weinand 1994] Weinand, André, and Erich Gamma. ET++—A portable, homogeneous class library and application framework. *Proceedings of the Ubilab Conference 1994,* pp. 66–92. Zürich, Switzerland, September 1994. *Computer Science Research at UBILAB, Strategy and Projects,* Walter Bischofberger and Hans-Peter Frei, editors. Konstanz, Switzerland: Universitätsverlag Konstanz.

CHAPTER 24

Extensible Computational Chemistry Environment (Ecce)

24.1 What Is Ecce?

The Extensible Computational Chemistry Environment (Ecce) is an integrated problem-solving environment for computational chemistry. The Ecce software was developed at the Department of Energy's Pacific Northwest National Laboratory (PNNL) to support the Environmental Molecular Sciences Laboratory (EMSL). Ecce enables research scientists to easily use computational programs to perform complex molecular modeling and analysis tasks, accessing networked, high-performance computers from their desktop workstations. The mission of the EMSL is to provide the fundamental molecular science needed to develop the novel technologies used to clean up nuclear production sites. Ecce serves as a development framework for the extended functionality and chemistry-specific software that is required to meet the mission of the EMSL. Figure 24.1 illustrates the Ecce logo.

The Ecce environment, illustrated in Figure 24.2, is a problem-solving framework that uses an object-oriented database management system (OODBMS) to implement an extensible model for computational and experimental molecular science data. The OODBMS enables data tracking and complex data searches and the data model supports a common application programming interface (API) through which applications can access both the derived data and the metadata [Keller 1996]. The OODBMS also combines automated metadata management, derived data management, database management, modern intelligent graphical user interfaces (GUIs), scientific visualization and analysis tools, and access to a hierarchical mass storage (HMS) system. The

Figure 24.1 Ecce logo.

Ecce data model facilitates the integration of multiple software modules beneath a unifying graphical user interface that provides a common look and feel. The capabilities in Ecce will permit scientists to store, retrieve, and analyze the rapidly growing volumes of data produced by computational studies.

24.2 Design Objectives

The complex nature of the research at the EMSL facility demands that the software be flexible to meet an ever changing set of user requirements. Many challenges occur in

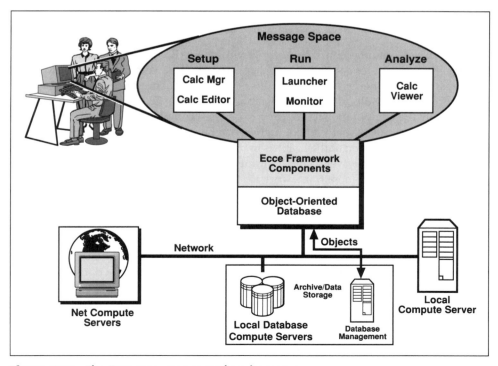

Figure 24.2 The Ecce resources control environment.

the design and development of such an extensible environment. It is sufficient here to summarize a few pertinent Ecce design objectives.

Design for extensibility (and thus longevity) in the following key areas:

- Different types of computational chemistry application areas (ab initio electronic structure, molecular dynamics, and so on).

- Different computational chemistry and data analysis codes (each chemist has a favorite code).

- Areas of chemistry besides computational (thermodynamics, spectroscopy, geochemical data, and so on).

- Dynamic network environment (resources and their availability are dynamic).

- Support for job management mechanisms or queuing systems.

- Provide a user-customizable chemistry desktop that gives users access to any Ecce tool. The desktop and Ecce tools will adhere to a common style that is built upon industry standards and will be designed to work in a heterogeneous desktop environment.

- All Ecce tools will be created utilizing the underlying chemistry and experiment data-centered model. This approach will facilitate the integration of Ecce tools, build reference data sets to facilitate data sharing, provide a common design basis for all tools, and build sophisticated tools for browsing and extracting data rather than recreating data sets. By enabling better integration of different applications, we can build sophisticated tools that integrate disparate steps of the scientific process.

- Support a variety of computational codes currently in use in EMSL and plan for the future integration of other such codes.

- Support any compute servers available in the EMSL networked environment as well as supporting systems at other sites accessible by collaborators.

24.3 Data-Centered Design

Many current software packages [Bowie 1995] consider scientific analysis as three separate and distinct data processing activities: preprocessing, solving, and postprocessing. We call this approach *process-centered software design*. This process-centered software design approach arose from the need for individual data analysis tools, each optimized for a particular purpose. Each software package typically has a unique proprietary method for handling data, with a host of input and output formats specific to that package. Furthermore, each of the separate software systems of a package usually communicates through file translation mechanisms.

Although process-centered software applications can process data effectively and efficiently, they pose a problem for users as they proliferate. The GUIs of such applications, if available at all, may differ in appearance, style, and behavior conventions. Scarce research hours must be spent writing translation utilities to integrate the individual applications. Similar translators may be written and maintained by many different users and are often shared among fellow scientists. The users of such systems are forced to concentrate too much of their effort on dealing with the nuances of the various software packages, thus disrupting the scientific discovery process.

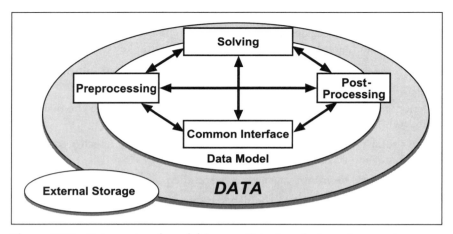

Figure 24.3 Data-centered model for an efficient analysis environment.

A preferred model for the scientific analysis is an object-oriented, data-centered model (illustrated in Figure 24.3). This approach emphasizes a single data model throughout all analysis activities. The data-centered model allows free interchange of information among all resources in the system. Users of such a system have control over all activities without directing extra effort to software specifics. Such a system does not have a preconceived analysis process built into the design. It should be discovery-flexible, allowing the user to proceed freely and creatively. The data-centered model, if designed correctly, will have a consistent user interface across all activities, methods, tools, and applications. That consistency should be limited only by the need to access some packages with predefined GUIs for an application. Thus, users will spend their time learning a single interactive approach instead of many.

The data-centered model simplifies program development as well. Much of the required data is defined in a data API layer. This model provides a single, common data representation and access library or API. Data translators can be written to and from a standard representation, reducing the required number of translators ($2n$ translators instead of $n[n-1]$ translators). Common behavior and functionality are immediately available to new applications. Developers can develop tools that communicate directly with other tools in the environment. Furthermore, the data-centered approach enables a development framework in which much of developed software can be reused, permitting functionality to be extended with minimal effort.

24.4 Why an Object-Oriented Framework?

Much has been said in the current literature about the use of object-oriented frameworks [Adair 1995; Appley 1996; Casais 1995; Taligent 1994]. An object-oriented framework captures a reusable software design that supports common capabilities within a specific problem domain. Architectures based on a framework developed with commercial technology directly supports our needs and enhances the transition into practical use.

An object-oriented framework for computational chemistry:

- Reduces a complex problem domain into manageable parts

- Encapsulates domain expertise applicable to many programs, making it feasible to efficiently create custom applications for specific problems

- Reduces development time by ensuring that developers do not have to design and implement the same thing over and over again

- Makes maintenance and extensions easier, thus improving the quality of the resulting application

- Enables the development of chemistry software tools that use the terminology of the problem domain, simplifying setup and expanding the potential user base

- Provides system-level services, such as file access, distributed computing, and job control

- Provides a sufficient usable lifetime for the software, thereby lowering costs

24.5 Problem Domain: Computational Chemistry

Within the chemistry community, computational chemistry tools have been used principally by specialists because of the large body of expertise required for their successful application [Hehre 1986]. The reasons for this are evident in a typical use scenario:

Research and preliminary calculations. Literature searching and preliminary calculations on analogous chemical systems are necessary to assess the performance of available physical models and approximations for the problem of interest. This context is also needed for the interpretation of results.

Choice of theoretical method/chemical model. As the processing and storage costs of computational chemistry methods scale anywhere from $O(N \log N)$ to $O(N!)$, where N is the number of basis functions, inappropriate choices can lead to meaningless or overly expensive results.

Code selection. Codes that can carry out the desired calculations are selected. No single application code supports all of the most important electronic structure models and methods. Different codes perform best on different architectures. In particular, the NWChem suite of distributed-data parallel computational chemistry codes, developed at PNNL, is specifically designed to perform well on massively parallel architectures [QCS 1995].

Compute server selection. An appropriate compute platform must be selected. For methods that may scale in cost from $O(N^2)$ to as rapidly as $O(N^7)$, this can mean a workstation or a large massively parallel processor (MPP) for calculations that differ only in the details of the model.

Prepare input. Input files with formats specific to each code must be generated. Run scripts that may be specific to a particular queue management system must also be generated.

Launch and monitor job. Run the calculation (transfer files, monitor batch queues, and so on) The practical details of running and monitoring 10 calculations at a time on as many different machines may consume half the workday of a computational chemist.

Analyze job. Results must be validated (did the wave function or geometry optimization calculation converge?) and extracted from output files.

The computational chemist therefore needs expert knowledge of:

- The chemical system in question
- The underlying theoretical models
- The capabilities and input options of one or more computational chemistry codes
- The use of a heterogeneous, distributed computing environment (workstations, vector machines, and MPPs)
- Extraordinary organizational skills (for managing the results of hundreds or even thousands of calculations a year)

Hardware, software, and theoretical advances are rapidly increasing the range of problems accessible to theoretical chemistry. It is important to make these tools useful to a broader range of molecular scientists. These new users are experts in the chemistry but require support with the theoretical models, codes, computing environments, and organization. In addition, it is important to store the growing body of these often-costly computational results in a sharable, searchable form [Feller 1996a, 1996b].

24.6 Ecce Architecture

The overall Ecce architecture consists of four API layers (illustrated in Figure 24.4). These layers are:

Core software components. This layer includes the low-level building blocks used to construct toolkits and applications for the EMSL Unix environment. They are generally purchased but sometimes acquired from the public domain or through collaborators.

Framework components. This layer includes software applications and toolkits developed or enhanced for EMSL. It represents the tools and conventions for providing an extensible environment for chemistry research. The purpose of this layer is to isolate, simplify, and standardize the construction of applications on top of the core components and to standardize a mechanism for applications to exchange messages and data.

Software applications/tools. EMSL applications fall into two main categories: user applications and administrative/developer tools. The latter are used by developers and system administrators to build user applications and to monitor the per-

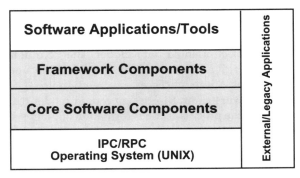

Figure 24.4   Ecce layers architecture.

formance or integrity of various hardware and software components of the EMSL architecture.

External/legacy applications. This layer represents software that is not intended for complete and comprehensive integration into the Ecce architecture. Comprehensive integration requires that all software adhere to a common protocol for communication and information exchange. Software must therefore be built to that protocol or modified to support it in order to be integrated comprehensively. Some software in the Ecce architecture will be commercial and not modifiable for EMSL, such as commercial graphing and plotting applications. Other software may continue to be developed using technology common to the field it represents, such as the batch-style computational codes.

24.7 Framework Components

In this section we focus exclusively on the Ecce framework components. The framework components we have developed fulfill our requirements for extensibility and provide a data-centered architecture for computational chemistry. Keep in mind, however, that these frameworks are applicable for domains other than computational chemistry. We describe four different types of frameworks developed for Ecce:

Chemistry Data Model framework. Ecce is based on an object-oriented data model whose abstract classes provide a framework that can be extended through inheritance.

Calculation Processing framework. As a software system for running legacy applications, we provide a framework for the semantic description of a legacy application's functional capabilities.

Calculation Setup framework. We employ a framework for handling the generation and parsing of application-specific input and output file formats.

Property Analysis framework. By using abstract data model classes, Ecce provides generic viewing capabilities for properties produced by applications.

24.8 Chemistry Data Model Framework

Central to the architecture of Ecce is an object-oriented data model. The Ecce data model is the common data interface between all Ecce applications, the OODBMS, and the scientific applications that Ecce manages. Although Ecce is currently tailored to computational chemistry applications, we were careful to design a data model that would be a framework capable of modeling the processes and information of other scientific domains. There are three important aspects to our data model: extensibility through inheritance, runtime determination of types, and extensibility through generic associations and classes.

Figure 24.5 depicts a simplified Ecce data model in Rumbaugh notation [Rumbaugh 1991]. Our data model consists of three main hierarchies: Experiment, Chemical System, and Property. The Experiment hierarchy manages information about the scientific process or experiments. We recognize that, at the abstract level, scientific experiments have some subject of study (Chemical Systems in our domain) and produce some results (Properties). We further classify experiments by whether they are computational and involve computer programs (Calculation) or physical and involve instruments or laboratory equipment (Lab Experiment). These terms reflect a paradigm shift now under way in scientific investigation. Originally, there were two scientific approaches: analytical theory and experimental observation. With the advances in computers over the last 20 years, simulation is becoming the third branch of science, bridging analytical theory and experimental observation. Therefore we define *experiment* in this chapter as either a set of observations of a natural property or simulations of that property.

The current Ecce software supports one classification of computational chemistry applications called Electronic Structure codes. By creating new, concrete classes of applications, through inheritance at the appropriate level of the Experiment hierarchy, the remainder of the Ecce framework is easily extended. Figure 24.5 shows four instances (dashed outlines) of extending the data model through inheritance in the Experiment, Calculation, and Chemical System hierarchies.

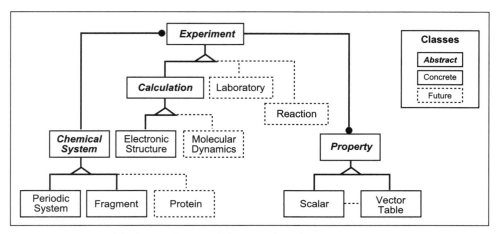

Figure 24.5 Simplified Ecce data model in Rumbaugh notation.

All Ecce user applications are written to communicate at the highest level of abstraction. However, many of the tools are appropriate only for specific subclasses of Experiments or Chemical Systems. In order to make the tools as generic as possible, Ecce implements a *runtime type information capability* that allows Ecce applications to customize their behavior for future extensions to the data model.

The final aspect to using our data model as a framework is the results or Property hierarchy. Our approach to handling future, unpredictable results from applications is to create a generic, structural Property model. Figure 24.5 indicates the range of results that Ecce currently is capable of storing, from zero-dimensional values (Scalar) to three-dimensional vectors of matrices or tables (Vector Table). In the computational chemistry domain, a Vector Table is used to track changes in Chemical System geometries such as those that a Molecular Dynamics Simulation might produce. We decided to make the Property model generic in this fashion because of the large number of results that can be produced by any Experiment. It is also the case that this part of the data model, if we needed to extend it by inheritance, would be the most volatile. Incorporating new properties does not require a change to the data model. Instead, Ecce users can register a new Property definition by using a configuration file. Registering a new property requires the following information: a description, a classification (for interface purposes), the units of the Property values, and the Property subclass to use as a representation.

24.8.1 Calculation Processing Framework

The largest, most complex framework is the one for setting up and running arbitrary computational chemistry codes. As mentioned previously, a major goal of Ecce is to improve the accessibility of these codes. Their accessibility to nonspecialists has been poor because of their variety and complexity, both in user interface and underlying theoretical basis. The initial focus of Ecce is on electronic structure codes; these are codes that construct a mathematical description of the quantum-mechanical electronic wave function of a molecular system. Any physical property of the system, including energetics, geometry, and spectral properties, may then be extracted from this model. These models vary enormously in computational cost and, hence, range of applicability.

The Calculation Processing framework encompasses the full cycle of setting up a calculation (discussed in the following section), launching the calculation anywhere on a heterogeneous global network of compute machines, and extracting arbitrary properties into Ecce for analysis.

Figure 24.6 shows a simplified view of the framework. The area inside the line represents the internals of Ecce. The elements outside the line are information and scripts used by Ecce, at runtime, to support a chemistry code. The following list briefly outlines each part of the framework:

Basic code information. This includes information such as the code name, version, where it is installed, and the name of an execution script that sets up the user's run environment on the compute server, as necessary for each code.

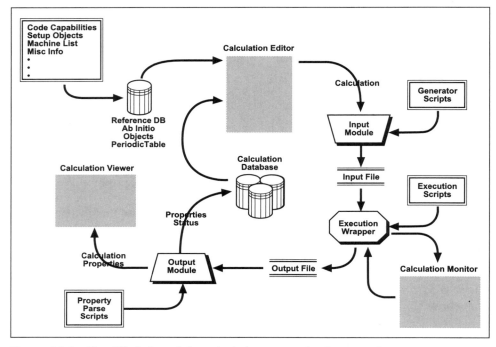

Figure 24.6   Simplified view of the calculation processing framework.

General capabilities of the code. This includes such information as the range of electronic models and target properties available from each code. It also includes detailed information about the capabilities, conventions, and limitations of the code. For example, for an electronic structure code this would include details of the primitive spatial functions (basis functions) available for the expansion of the molecular orbitals. This type of information is necessary to prevent users from setting up calculations that will fail or, worse, run to completion at great expense but with meaningless results.

Calculation setup objects. This portion of the Calculation Processing framework is described as the following Calculation Setup framework.

Scripts for generating input files. Once a user has specified the parameters for a calculation in the GUI, the input module (see Figure 24.6) invokes the input file generator script registered for the selected code. The script is passed a dictionary of the options and values chosen by the user and produces a correctly formatted input file.

Scripts for bring output properties into Ecce. Each calculation generates a set of properties of interest to the chemist. These properties are just part of the results typically dumped to an output file during the simulation with formats, units, and conventions specific to each code. Scripts, which must be registered with Ecce, then find and extract each property in the output. As each output property is detected, a script is invoked to reformat the data into a standard format that is automatically imported to the Ecce database and thus made available to all Ecce tools.

Scripts to import existing output files. There is an enormous accumulation of output from calculations run before Ecce was created, representing a storehouse of poorly accessible information. Loading these calculations in the Ecce database requires the property scripts previously described, plus additional scripts to parse setup information for each calculation.

24.8.2 Calculation Setup Framework

Each computational chemistry code may have hundreds of input options to specify the details of the model and the calculation. Options that are shared among some or all of the codes may still differ in terminology, default settings, or conventions for units. Consequently, it is challenging for expert users to use different codes, even for similar calculations; it is very difficult for chemists who are not specialists. To make computational chemistry useful to a wider audience and to support efficient use of computational resources, we have developed a framework that supports the creation of GUIs that are code-sensitive without embedding knowledge of specific codes into the applications. Figure 24.7 shows the general structure of the Calculation Setup framework.

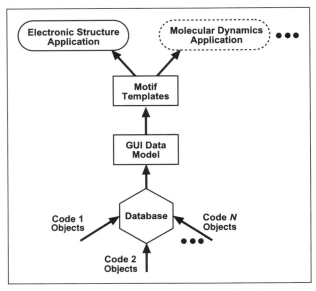

Figure 24.7   General structure of the calculation setup framework.

GUI Data Model

At the base of this framework is the GUI data model, which captures information about the available options for a calculation. Each concrete class in Figure 24.8 represents an instance of an object that can be realized in a GUI. The correspondence to standard GUI constructs is straightforward. The implementation of each GUI control is, however, independent of the model. For example, a GUIList may be realized as a list box, an option menu, or radio buttons. The choice is left to the GUI designer.

When a computational code is registered in Ecce, an expert user of a given code will provide information about the options supported by that code, specify validations to be performed on the input, and specify any dependencies that may exist between input objects.

On top of the basic GUI data model, we have created a set of GUI template classes. Each of these classes realizes the more abstract data model objects previously described as an actual GUI control. Each GUI template class is instanced with a unique identifier that corresponds to an input option. This information enables the object to access the base data model object to create the control, provide defaults, present options, and validate input.

Finally, at the application level, a set of GUI templates is pulled together to represent all the options available to the user. The application may also incorporate special chemistry knowledge. As is shown in Figure 24.7, applications can be built for different fields of chemistry using the same basic building blocks.

One important capability of the underlying GUI data model is that it supports a limited set of constraints between objects. For example, it may be specified that the default convergence tolerance for the electronic wave function calculation be tightened for target properties that are particularly sensitive. The supported codes incorporate these types of constraints, so the GUI must as well.

24.8.3 Property Analysis Framework

Once a simulation has been run and various properties have been stored in an Ecce database, users will examine these properties as part of their analysis. As mentioned

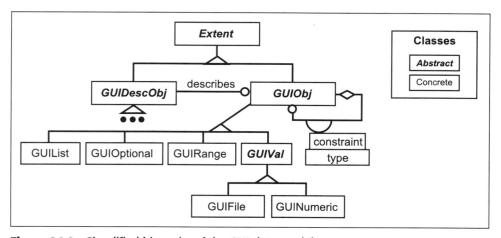

Figure 24.8 Simplified hierarchy of the GUI data model.

previously, a complete list of properties is not built into Ecce but controlled by a simple configuration file. Any calculation may produce any set of properties that can be calculated with a given computer code.

To support the viewing and analysis of whatever properties are produced, we have created a property viewer application and a framework for instancing and managing user interfaces for the properties. Since the property data model is structural, we can create default user interfaces for any property, according to its rank (scalar, vector, matrix, or tensor) and, for nonscalars, the type of each index. For example, the default display of a vector V(I,) when i ranges over the atoms of a molecule, is different from the default display when i ranges over a set of basis (spatial expansion) functions. The former case suggests a table and/or display of the values as labels on a three-dimensional image of the molecule; the latter case would be displayed as a three-dimensional density over the framework of the molecule. Default interfaces are useful, but often more specialized interfaces are desired; the framework is designed to first look for a specialized interface, then default to a generic interface.

To support all of this, an abstract class PropGUI was defined. This class includes all methods necessary for the property viewer application to instance and control the interfaces. It essentially serves as a property interface manager and includes support for tables, graphs, and three-dimensional visualization. A simplified class hierarchy is shown in Figure 24.9. In summary, this framework can be extended through subclassing or the definition of new properties.

24.9 Experiences

Ecce is currently being used within the EMSL environment at PNNL and by collaborators at other laboratories and educational institutions. Ecce supports two computational chemistry codes: Gaussian –9x and NWChem, the distributed-data parallel code developed at PNNL. A wide variety of electronic structure methods are supported by the GUI. Registration of further codes will be relatively easy, since only registration files and Perl scripts are required for input generation and output parsing. At recent count, Ecce includes over 569,000 lines of code, of which about half are newly written code. The balance of the code is software provided by automatic code generation and reused code. Such a project would not be practical without a coherent global design strategy.

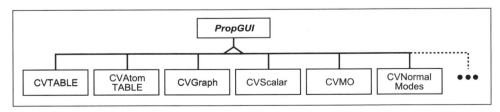

Figure 24.9 Simplified hierarchy of the properties.

Of course, difficulties always arise in developing a complex system. For instance, it was a significant shift for the software developers to think in terms of database and data-centered applications. We revised the chemistry data model often, as we became more familiar with the research chemistry domain. As new or not fully understood data emerged, we modified the design. We quickly learned that the structure had to be flexible because of the different needs of specific chemistry subdomains. This became evident in learning the terminology of the domain. Many of the experts use different terms for similar data types.

Internal structure problems occurred as well. Calculation data in the GUI data model were originally stored in a too-compact form and were not accessible enough. The data boundary between the GUI data model and the chemistry data model was also troublesome.

24.10 Future Work

Ecce contains a very large database of chemistry calculations. We plan to use this collection of information to develop advisors for novice users. We hope to provide the necessary advice on specific parts of the calculation process. For example, Ecce could suggest input parameters for a specific calculation and advise which compute server and code should be used to run a particular calculation efficiently. Advisor programs would help Ecce scientists to use the available compute resources optimally.

To keep up with the changing technologies, we will begin a porting effort to move Ecce to a Common Object Request Broker Architecture (CORBA)/Java–based environment that supports a three-tiered architecture and a larger variety of client platforms. This move will provide flexibility and platform independence for future development. The underlying architecture will remain, but will be split into three layers: one to support the user interface; a middle layer to communicate with compute resources, the database, and the hierarchical management system; and a third layer for the database client-server interactions.

Ecce is designed to accommodate the research activities at the EMSL. It is difficult to say where the next extension will be. However, with most of the basic structure complete, we now plan to extend the software to include other but similar problem domains. We will begin with data model extension to include molecular dynamics, groundwater simulations, and experimental data from nuclear magnetic resonance (NMR) instrumentation. Other parts of Ecce, including the GUI data model and calculation management, should require little or no modification.

24.11 Summary

Ecce began with a number of abstractions that have been encoded in frameworks. We have developed a distributed, heterogeneous computing environment for unifying the process of computational chemistry. This new environment has incorporated four different frameworks:

An object-oriented science data model. The Ecce chemistry data model manages information concerning the scientific process in terms of experiments (where a Calculation is one type of experiment). It incorporates the abstraction that an Experiment has a subject of study (a Chemical System) and produces results (Properties). Extension from this model is carried out both by inheritance to new concrete classes and by the definition of new Properties via registration files.

A framework for the semantic description of legacy code capabilities. The addition of an abstraction layer via the GUI data model has enabled the design of general GUIs that are then specialized for each supported code. The GUI data model is based on two parallel class hierarchies for the storage of code-independent and code-specific information. An extension to accommodate new computational chemistry codes and features requires only modifications to registration files.

A framework for handling the generation and parsing of application-specific input and output formats. A combination of registration files and code-specific Perl scripts is used for parsing and input formatting.

A framework for property analysis. A generic viewing capability is available for each output property based on its abstract data type.

We have developed a flexible environment for the user that enhances usability, productivity, software adaptability, system reliability, code extensibility, and maintainability. Ecce serves as a development framework for the extended functionality, chemistry-specific software that is required to meet the mission of the EMSL.

24.12 References

[Adair 1995] Adair, D. Building object-oriented frameworks. *AIXpert*, February and May 1995.

[Appley 1996] Appley, G., and M. Gallaher. A framework for manufacturing—Process simulation software. *Object Magazine*, May 1996.

[Bowie 1995] Bowie, J.E., and A.J. Olson (eds.). *Data Visualization in Molecular Science.* Reading, MA: Addison-Wesley, 1995.

[Casais 1995] Casais, E.(ed.). An experiment in framework development—Issues and results. *Architectures and Processes for Systematic Software Construction.* FZI-Publication 1/95, Forschungszentrum Informatik Karlsruhe, 1995.

[Feller 1996a] Feller, D. The role of databases in support of computational chemistry calculations. *Journal Computational Chemistry*, vol. 17(13):1571–1586.

[Feller 1996b] Feller, D.F., T.L. Keller, and D.R. Jones. The role of databases in support of computational chemistry. ACTC 1996 Conference, Park City, Utah, July 1996.

[Hehre 1986] Hehre, W.J., L. Radom, P. Schleyer, and J.A. Pople. *Ab Initio Molecular Orbital Theory.* New York: John Wiley & Sons, 1986.

[Keller 1996] Keller, T.L., and D.R. Jones. Metadata: The foundation of effective experiment management. *Proceedings of the IEEE First Metadata Conference*, Silver Spring, Maryland, April 1996.

[QCS 1995] Guest, M.F., E. Apra, D.E. Bernholdt, H.A. Fruechtl, R.J. Harrison, R.A. Kendall, R.A. Kutteh, X. Long, J.B. Nicholas, J.A. Nichols, H.L. Taylor, A.T. Wong, G.I. Fann, R.J. Littlefield, and J. Niepolcha. High performance computing: Issues, methods and applications. *Int. J. Quantum Chem: Quantum Chem. Symp.,* vol. 29, p. 475.

[Rumbaugh 1991] Rumbaugh, J., M. Blaha, W. Premerlani, F. Eddy, and W. Lorensen. *Object-Oriented Modeling and Design.* Englewood Cliffs, NJ: Prentice Hall, 1991.

[Taligent 1994] Taligent Inc. *Building Object-Oriented Frameworks.* Taligent white paper, 1994.

CHAPTER 25

The Amulet Prototype-Instance Framework

Creating user interface software has proven to be very difficult and expensive because it is often large and complex and challenging to implement, debug, and modify. Most of today's application frameworks for user interfaces still leave far too much of the application to the programmer. The Amulet user interface development framework tries to overcome this problem by supplying high-level support for the *insides* of application windows, which most other frameworks ignore. For example, whereas most frameworks do a good job of managing the creation of windows and the main menus, they leave the *contents* of the window to be programmed at the low-level window manager level, accepting events such as "mouse left-button down at 30,50" and using routines such as "draw-line." In contrast, Amulet supplies high-level support for the graphics and interactive behaviors of application-specific objects. The result is that many behaviors, such as creating, moving, selecting, and manipulating objects, cut/copy/paste, save and load, and undoing of operations, can often be incorporated into applications without writing any methods at all.

A key reason that Amulet provides a high level of support is that all of the user interface objects are available at runtime for inspection and manipulation through a standard protocol. This allows high-level, built-in utilities to be provided, which, in other toolkits and frameworks, must be reimplemented for each application. For example, the graphical selection handles widget can get the list of objects in a window, find out which ones are graphical, and move and resize a selected object, all using standard protocols, even if the objects are custom-created and application-specific.

The result is that creating applications in Amulet is quite different from other frameworks. In fact, much of Amulet programming is done without writing methods [Myers

1992], but instead by creating instances of built-in objects, setting their properties, and combining them into groups.

In addition to incorporating innovations into its own design, Amulet has an open architecture to enable user interface researchers and developers to easily investigate their own innovations. For example, Amulet is the first system that supports multiple constraint *solvers* operating at the same time, so that researchers might be able to investigate new kinds of constraint solvers. The undo model also supports new designs. The *widgets* (the Unix name for elements of the toolkit like scrollbars, buttons, and menus; sometimes called *controls* on the PC) are implemented in an open fashion using the Amulet intrinsics so that researchers can replace or modify the widgets. The goal is that researchers will only have to implement the parts that they are interested in, relying on the Amulet library for everything else. In addition, we aim for Amulet to be useful for students and general developers. Therefore, we have tried to make Amulet easy to learn and to have sufficient robustness, performance, and documentation to attract a wide audience.

Amulet, which stands for automatic manufacture of usable and learnable editors and toolkits [Myers 1997], is being developed as a research project at Carnegie Mellon University. It is implemented in C++ and runs on X/11, Windows 95, Windows NT, and the Macintosh. Applications created using Amulet can simply be recompiled to run on any of the machines.

25.1 Layered Design

The Amulet framework is divided into a number of layers (see Figure 25.1). These layers include an abstract interface to the window managers; novel models for objects,

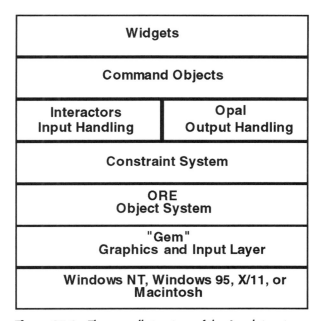

Figure 25.1   The overall structure of the Amulet system.

constraints, input, output, and commands; and a set of widgets. The following sections describe the overall design of each of these.

25.1.1 Gem: Abstract Interface to the Window Managers

Amulet provides a portable interface to various window managers called *Gem,* which stands for the Graphics and Events Manager. Gem uses C++ mechanisms to provide a simple graphics and input interface used by the rest of Amulet. Any code written using Gem will port to different windowing systems (Windows 95 or NT, Macintosh, or X/11) without change. Most other toolkits and frameworks only provide an interface at the Gem level or require that all graphics use the underlying low-level window manager drawing interface. However, typical Amulet users never see the Gem interface, since the higher-level parts of the Amulet framework provide access to the same capabilities in an easier-to-use way. We export the Gem interface mainly for advanced Amulet users. If the programmer wants to make something very efficient, calling Gem directly may be appropriate.

25.1.2 Object System

The *Ore* (object registering and encoding) layer of Amulet implements a *prototype-instance* object and constraint system [Lieberman 1986] on top of C++. In Amulet's prototype-instance object system, there is no concept of a class, since every object can serve as a prototype for other objects. An object comprises a set of *slots.* A slot has a name and can hold a value of any type; for example, the slot named Am_LEFT might hold the value 10. Slots are similar to member variables or instance variables in other object systems. A new object is created by making an *instance* of another object, which is called the *prototype.* Creating an instance is like making a copy of an object, except for the way that inheritance works. One of the innovations in Amulet is that if an object has parts, then the instance will also get instances of the parts (see Figure 25.2). We call this *structural inheritance.*

An instance starts off inheriting all of its slot values from the prototype, so that initially the instance and its prototype have all the same values. Then, the programmer will typically set some slots of the instance with new values. If a slot is *not* set in the instance, then its value will change if the prototype's value is later changed. The object system is *dynamic* in that slots in objects can be added and removed from objects at runtime, and the types in slots can also change.

For example, the following Amulet code creates a Node_Bitmap as an instance of the built-in Am_Bitmap object, and then sets the Am_IMAGE slot to the appropriate picture.

```
Am_Object Node_Bitmap = Am_Bitmap.Create()
                     .Set(Am_IMAGE, simple_rect_pic);
```

There is nothing special about the objects in the library (like the Am_Bitmap object used here). Any object can serve as a prototype from which to create other objects. For example, the following code creates an instance of the Node_Bitmap, changes the picture, and then puts it in a particular place. Other slots that are not set, such as the Am_VISIBLE slot, retain their default, inherited value.

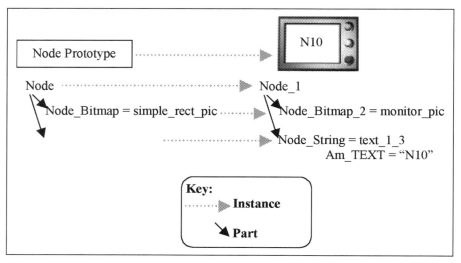

Figure 25.2   When an instance is made of the node prototype, an instance is also made of each of the parts.

```
Am_Object Node_Bitmap_2 = Node_Bitmap.Create()
                          .Set(Am_IMAGE, monitor_pic)
                          .Set(Am_LEFT, 10)
                          .Set(Am_TOP, 43);
```

An important feature of Amulet's object system is that there is no distinction between *methods* and *data*: Any instance can override an inherited method as easily as inherited data. In a conventional class-instance model such as Smalltalk or C++, instances can have different data, but only subclasses can have different methods. Thus, in cases where each instance needs a unique method, conventional systems must use a mechanism other than the regular method invocation or create a new subclass and a single instance of that subclass each time. For example, a button widget might use a regular C++ method for drawing, but would have to use a different mechanism for the callback procedure used when the user clicks on the button, since each instance of the button needs a different callback. In Amulet, the draw method and the callback use the same mechanism.

As an example, the following sets the DO method of the command in a button to be my_method (command objects are described subsequently). Then, my_method will be called whenever the user hits the button.

```
my_button.Get_Object(Am_COMMAND).Set(Am_DO_METHOD, my_method);
```

Amulet's object system also contains many other features that may be useful for programmers. An automatic memory management mechanism, which uses a reference counting scheme, manages Amulet's objects. A complete set of querying functions makes it easy to determine objects' properties at runtime. These are used by the debugging facilities described later, and they can also be useful for application programs. For example, a program can query the list of slots of an object and whether each slot is local or inherited. For each slot, the name of the slot (for example, LEFT), current value (for example, 10), and type of the current value (for example, Am_INT_TYPE) can be retrieved. Since there is no distinction between method and data slots, this one mechanism is used to discover all of the properties of an object.

Programming with a prototype-instance object system is a quite different style from that used in conventional object-oriented languages. Much of the code is devoted to listing the slots and default values for prototype objects, usually at initialization time, and then creating instances, possibly overriding some slots, as the program is running. This declarative style of programming seems to be intuitive and less error prone, and it makes it easier for more of the code to be created and analyzed by interactive design tools, such as interface builders.

There are many other advantages of the prototype-instance model. Having no distinction between classes and instances, or between methods and data, means that there are fewer concepts for the programmer to learn and that a consistent mechanism can be used everywhere. Another advantage of the prototype-instance object system is that it is very dynamic and flexible. All of the properties of objects can be set and queried at runtime, and interactive tools can easily read and set these properties. In fact, most of today's frameworks and toolkits implement some form of *attribute-value pairs* to hold the properties of the widgets, but Amulet's object system provides significantly more flexibility and capabilities.

Another advantage of our prototype-instance object systems over C++ is the ability to treat classes as first-class objects. In C++, one cannot store a class object in a variable so that different kinds of objects can be created at runtime. For example, C++ does not allow code like the following:

```
obj_to_create = Rectangle;        //NOT ALLOWED IN C++
...
new_object = new obj_to_create;   //NOT ALLOWED IN C++
```

Instead, the operand of the new operator must be a fixed class, leading to large case statements and other inflexible and error-prone constructs. In contrast, since we can create an instance of any object in a prototype-instance object system, we can store a reference to an object in a variable and later use the variable to create a new object:

```
Am_Object obj_to_create = Am_Rectangle; //Typical Amulet code
...
Am_Object new_object = obj_to_create.Create();
```

Amulet's predecessor, Garnet, also used a prototype-instance object system [Myers 1992]. Amulet's design is more complete and flexible, and we fixed a number of problems we experienced with Garnet. For example, we added the ability for a programmer to declare that certain slots are *not* inherited, so that each instance will start out with no value for that slot. For example, the Am_Drawonable slot of a Window object holds the machine-specific pointer to the underlying window manager window, and should not be inherited by instances of the window. Each instance of a Window must create and assign its own value for the Am_Drawonable slot. Finally, it is worth pointing out that Amulet is able to provide dynamic slot typing, a dynamic prototype-instance system, and constraints in C++ without using a preprocessor or a scripting language.

Although designed to support the creation of graphical objects, many Amulet users have discovered that the prototype-instance object system is useful for representing their internal application data whenever flexible and dynamically changing data types are desired.

The main disadvantage of the prototype-instance model over the conventional class-instance model is performance. When a slot is accessed, the system must perform a search through the object to see if the slot is there, and if not, it must search the prototypes up to the root. The same search is needed for both method and data slots. We have investigated various indexing and hashing schemes to help reduce this overhead, including hardwiring some common slots, but this increases complexity and sometimes does not improve performance. Dynamic typechecking also adds some overhead. The forward and backward pointers and space for the types add space overhead. The Self prototype-instance system [Unger 1987; Chambers 1989] uses extensive compiler techniques to try to remove some of this search, but we have not found this necessary to achieve adequate performance on modern platforms. One reason that Self needs this is that it uses the prototype-instance system for *everything*, right down to integer arithmetic, whereas Amulet uses the efficient underlying C and C++ mechanisms for basic computation and only uses the prototype-instance model for the user interface.

Another disadvantage of our dynamic prototype-instance model is the lack of compile-time checking. Instead, Amulet uses runtime typechecking. However, our experience over the past 10 years is that very few bugs are caused by type errors found at runtime, and the added flexibility far outweighs the problems.

25.1.3 Constraints

Amulet integrates *constraint solving* with the object system. This means that instead of containing a constant value like a number or a string, any slot of any object can contain an expression that computes the value. If the expression refers to slots of other objects, then when those objects are changed, the expression is automatically reevaluated. This kind of constraint resembles a spreadsheet formula, so it is called a *formula constraint* in Amulet. Constraint expressions can contain arbitrary C++ code. This works because the standard Get method that accesses values of slots can tell whether it is being invoked from inside of a formula, and if so, in addition to returning the value, it also sets up a dependency. Then, whenever a slot's value changes, Amulet knows which constraints depend on that value and can cause the constraints to recalculate.

Although many other research systems have provided constraints, we were the first to truly integrate them with the object system and make them general purpose. An important result of this is that constraints are used throughout the system in many different ways. For example, the built-in text object has constraints in its width and height slots that compute the dimensions based on the current string and font.

Amulet does not use a special preprocessor, so the syntax for specifying constraints is somewhat verbose. In C++, it is impossible to create new functions inside of other functions, so all formulas must be defined at the top level before they are used. For example:

```
// define a formula called right_of_tool_panel_formula which returns an
int
Am_Define_Formula(int, right_of_tool_panel_formula) {
  // 5 pixels away from the right of the tool_panel
  return (int)tool_panel.Get(Am_LEFT) +
           (int)tool_panel.Get(Am_WIDTH) + 5;
}
...
// now use the formula to compute the left of the scrolling_window
scrolling_window.Set(Am_LEFT, right_of_tool_panel_formula);
```

The macro Am_Define_Formula creates a formula named with the second argument (here, right_of_tool_panel_formula), which returns the type of its first argument (here int). The Am_Define_Formula macro defines a procedure to be executed by the formula, and the code following the macro is used as the procedure's body. The formula contains a pointer to the procedure to execute, the name of the constraint for debugging and tracing, and the list of slots used by this constraint.

Slots are accessed the same way whether they contain constraints or constant values, and the user's code does not know how the value was calculated. Furthermore, constraints can be used for computing any type of value, not just integers for layout. For example, the label shown in a button widget can contain a constraint to choose the label based on some property of an object. The following toggles the button's label based on the Am_VALUE slot of the object other_obj.

```
Am_Define_Formula(char*, compute_label_formula) {
    if (other_obj.Get(Am_VALUE) == true) return "Turn off value";
    else return "Turn on value";
}
my_button.Set(Am_LABEL, compute_label_formula);
```

The button widget does not care that the string was computed with a constraint. Whenever the value of a slot of an object changes, either because the programmer explicitly set the slot or because it contains a constraint that was automatically recalculated, the object will be redrawn if necessary, so here the button will be redrawn whenever other_obj's Am_VALUE slot changes.

Our constraint system was the first to allow the dynamic computation of the objects to which a constraint refers, so a constraint can not only compute the value to return, but also *which objects* and slots to reference. This allows such constraints as "the width is the maximum of all the components," which will be updated whenever components are added or removed as well as when one of the components' positions changes. Most other constraint systems cannot handle these kinds of constraints. These indirect constraints [Vander Zanden 1994] are also important for supporting object inheritance. When an instance of an object is created, Amulet also creates instances of any constraints in that object. These constraints refer to other objects indirectly. This is a form of *procedural abstraction,* since the constraints can be considered as relationships that can be reused in multiple places. In fact, Amulet supplies a library of predefined constraints, which can be used for many of the basic relationships found frequently in user interfaces.

An important research area in user interface software is creating new kinds of constraint *solvers* ([Borning 1981; Hudson 1996]). Therefore, Amulet contains an architecture that allows multiple solvers to coexist. Currently, in addition to the one-way formula solver already described, Amulet supports a multi-output, multiway solver and an *animation* constraint solver [Myers 1996b]. The animation constraint solver allows values of objects to change smoothly through time. Instead of jumping to a new value, the animation constraint forces the slot to take on a series of values interpolated between the old and new values. Animation constraints can work on any type of value, interpolating numbers, colors, or the point-list of a polygon. Special animation constraints are available for visibility, to cause an object to fade in and out, or grow and shrink (see Figure 25.3).

There is an important distinction between the style of programming supported by constraints and that of conventional approaches. In a conventional framework, every place where an object might be changed must also know about the other things that might be affected by that change. For example, suppose the nodes of Figure 25.2 had lines pointing to them. Then, every place that could move or change the size of the nodes would also have to know about adjusting the lines so they stay attached. In a conventional object-oriented framework, this might be programmed by having the move and grow methods of the nodes know about the attached lines. In a non-object-oriented system like VisualBasic, code would have to be added to every place where the position or size of a node was set to deal with the lines. In both styles, if a new kind of object also wants to be informed of the node's position, the node would have to be reprogrammed to know about these new objects as well.

In contrast, in a constraint system, the *lines themselves* know how they are attached to the node, so the information is localized at the appropriate place. If some new object wants to stay attached to the node, a constraint can be put into the new object itself, and the code for the node does not have to be changed. Thus, constraints tend to more successfully modularize an application's code because the information about which objects depend on values is maintained automatically by the system and does not need to be recoded into each manipulator of the value.

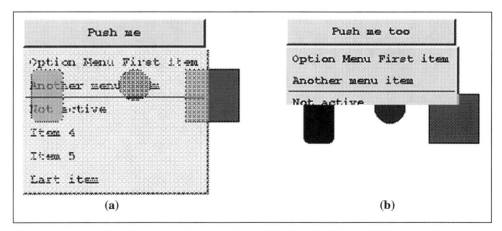

(a)   (b)

Figure 25.3 Animation constraints can be added to the Am_VISIBLE slot of a pop-up menu to make it *(a)* fade in using halftoning or *(b)* grow from the top.

25.1.4 Opal Output Model

The graphical object layer of Amulet is called *Opal*, the object programming aggregate layer. Opal hides the graphics part of Gem and provides a convenient interface to the programmer by using a retained object model, also called a *structured graphics model* or a *display list.* The programmer creates instances of the built-in graphical object prototypes, like rectangles, lines, text, circles, and polygons, and adds them to a group or window. Then Amulet automatically redraws the appropriate parts of the window if it becomes uncovered or if any properties of the objects change. This frees the programmer from having to deal with refresh. Objects can simply be created and deleted and their properties can be set. Furthermore, Opal automatically handles object creation and layout when the data can be displayed as lists or tables.

Opal makes heavy use of the object and constraint models of Amulet. Of course, all graphical objects are Amulet objects. The properties of objects that programmers do not care about can simply be ignored because they will inherit appropriate default values from prototypes. Groups use the ORE-level structural inheritance so that the parts of prototypes are created in instances (see Figure 25.2). This means that the programmer can simply create instances or copies of groups in the same way as primitive objects and in many cases will not even know if an object is a primitive or a group. For example, some of the widgets are implemented as a group of objects and others as a single object with a custom draw method. Due to this integration and uniform structure, simple programs are quite short and there are fewer concepts and features to learn. For example, *any kind* of object (even a group of objects) can be added as the label of a button or menu (not just strings or bitmaps as in Motif).

The retained object model allows Amulet to provide many facilities that must be programmed by each application in other frameworks and toolkits, including automatic refresh. Amulet uses a relatively efficient algorithm that calculates which objects will be affected when the object is erased, and redraws only the affected objects from back to front. Double buffering is provided by Amulet to eliminate flicker.

As an example, the following is the complete "hello world" program in Amulet, which displays a string and redraws the string if the window becomes covered and then uncovered. This program would be about two pages long in Motif.

```
#include <amulet.h>
void main (void) {
  Am_Initialize ();  //initialize Amulet
  Am_Screen
    .Add_Part ( Am_Window.Create () //add a window to the screen using
all of the default values
      .Add_Part ( Am_Text.Create ()  //create a text object and add it
to the window
        .Set ( Am_TEXT, "Hello World!"))); //set the string
  Am_Main_Event_Loop ();  //display the window and then handle all input
events
  Am_Cleanup (); //clean up Amulet
}
```

25.1.5 Interactors

Programming interactive behaviors has always been the hardest part of creating user interface software, especially since many frameworks only provide a stream of raw input events for each window, which the programmer must interpret and manage. To solve this problem, we introduced the Interactor model for handling input [Myers 1990a], whereby each Interactor object type implements a particular kind of interactive behavior, such as moving an object with the mouse or selecting one of a set of objects. To make a graphical object respond to input, the programmer simply attaches an instance of the appropriate type of Interactor to the graphics. The graphical object itself does not handle input events.

The Interactor design is one of the first to successfully separate the Controller from the View in the Model/View/Controller idea from Smalltalk [Krasner 1988]. The model contains the data, the view presents the data, and the controller manipulates the view. Most previous systems, including the original Smalltalk implementation, had the View and Controller tightly linked, in that the controller would have to be reimplemented whenever the view was changed, and vice versa. Indeed, many later systems such as Andrew [Palay 1988] and InterViews [Linton 1989] combined the view and controller and called both the View. In contrast, Amulet's Interactors are independent of graphics and can be reused in many different contexts.

Internally, each Interactor operates similarly. It waits for a particular starting event over a particular object or over any of a set of objects. For example, an Interactor to move the nodes of Figure 25.2 might wait for a left mouse button down over any of the nodes. When that event is seen, the Interactor starts running on the particular object clicked on, processing certain events. The moving Interactor processes mouse move events, while looking for a left button up event or an abort event (usually Control-G, Command-dot, or ESC). While the Interactor is running, the user is supplied feedback, either as a separate object (such as a dotted rectangle following the mouse) or by having the original object itself move. If the Interactor is aborted because the user hits the appropriate key or by a program calling the abort method, the original object is restored to its original state, the feedback object is hidden, and the Interactor goes back to waiting for a start event. If the Interactor completes normally (because the mouse button was released), then the feedback is hidden, the graphical object is updated appropriately, and a *command object* is allocated (see *Section 25.1.7*). Interactors are highly parameterized so that the programmer can specify the start, end, and abort events and the objects the Interactor operates over and uses for feedback, along with other aspects such as gridding and how many objects can be selected. As a result, Amulet's six types of Interactors are sufficient to cover all the behaviors found in today's interfaces. Evidence for this claim is that in *none* of the applications that have been created so far with Amulet did programmers ever need to go around the Interactors to get to the underlying window manager events.

The six types of Interactors in Amulet are *Choice Interactor*, which is used to choose one or more objects from a set; *One Shot Interactor*, which is used to cause something to happen immediately when an event occurs; *Move-Grow Interactor*, which is used to have a graphical object move or change size with the mouse; *New Points Interactor*, which is used to enter new points, such as when creating new objects; *Text Edit Interactor*, which supports editing the text string of a text object; and *Gesture Interactor*, which supports freehand gestures, such as drawing an X over an object to delete it or encircling a set of objects to select them.

The Interactors are implemented using Amulet objects, so parameters are simply slots the programmer can set or leave at their default values. Constraints can also be used to compute the parameters. For example, the Am_ACTIVE slot of an Interactor often contains a constraint depending on the global mode, and a constraint in a single Move-Grow Interactor might determine whether objects are moved or grown based on which mouse button was held down.

Normally, the Interactor operates on the object to which it is attached. An important feature of Amulet's Interactors is that they can also operate on a *set* of objects. For example, the Choice Interactor can select among the elements of a group, and the Move-Grow Interactor can be attached to a window to manipulate any object added as a part of the window. By default, Interactors make this choice based on the type of object they are attached to (group versus nongroup), but the programmer can explicitly specify which is desired.

As an example of the use of Interactors, the following code might be used to create new lines. Note that the constraint line_tool_is_selected is used to make this behavior be available only when the correct tool in the palette is selected.

```
all_objs.Add_Part (Am_New_Points_Interactor.Create("create_line")
            .Set(Am_AS_LINE, true)  //want to create a new line
            .Set(Am_FEEDBACK_OBJECT, lfeedback) //feedback while
dragging
            .Set(Am_CREATE_NEW_OBJECT_METHOD, create_new_line)
            .Set(Am_ACTIVE, line_tool_is_selected))
```

The following are some examples that show how Interactors can be used for moving and selecting objects. Note that in the simplest cases, an object can be made interactive with a single line of code:

```
//allow my_object to be moved while the left mouse button is held down
my_object.Add_Part(Am_Move_Grow_Interactor.Create());

//allow any part added to my_group to be grown using the right button
my_group.Add_Part(Am_Move_Grow_Interactor.Create()
                .Set(Am_GROWING, true)
                .Set(Am_START_EVENT, "right_down"));

//allow one or more parts of my_group to be selected with the left
button
my_group.Add_Part(Am_Choice_Interactor.Create()
                .Set(Am_HOW_SET, Am_CHOICE_LIST_TOGGLE));
```

A common design in other frameworks is for each graphical object to have a standard set of methods for the events that it handles. VisualBasic is an example of this design, where the programmer can write methods that are activated when the user clicks on or drags an object. There are a number of advantages to Amulet's design of having *explicit* objects (the Interactors) to represent the behaviors of the graphics. First, it provides significantly greater reuse for such common features as gridding, undo, and enabling and disabling operations, since these are provided in a single place, instead of being reimplemented with each graphical object. Second, being able to analyze, inspect, and manipulate the behavior objects makes debugging and tracing easier and enables external agents, tutors, and alternative interfaces like speech and gestures to control the interface without modifying the graphical objects or the existing behavior logic.

25.1.6 Widgets

Amulet supplies a large set of widgets, including pull-down menus, buttons, check boxes, radio buttons, text-input fields, and scroll bars. Each widget has a different drawing routine for the Motif, Microsoft Windows, and the Macintosh look and feel. By default, the widgets will appear appropriately to the native machine, but the programmer can switch to any look on any machine (for testing). Amulet reimplements all the widgets rather than using the built-in widgets from the various toolkits so that we can provide flexibility and control to programmers who want to investigate new widget behaviors. This is necessary, for example, to create a scroll bar with two handles or to support multiple people operating with a widget at the same time for a multiuser application. Widgets are completely integrated with the object, constraint, and command models, so properties of widgets can be computed by constraints, and the actions of widgets are represented by command objects (see next section), so they are easily undone. The various kinds of button and menu widgets can accept arbitrary Amulet objects including strings and bitmaps to display as the labels. This is easy in Amulet since there is a standard way for the buttons to query objects for their size and tell them where to draw.

Since widgets are objects, constraints are often used to compute their parameters—for example, to enable and disable the widgets based on the current global state and to lay out the widgets based on the window's current size. Amulet's widgets also have an extra parameter to disable them without graying out, which was added so the actual widgets can be used by interface-builder programs that need the widgets to be selected and moved when clicked on, instead of performing their normal functions.

In addition, Amulet supplies other widgets for the *insides* of application programs. For example, the selections-handles widget implements the familiar squares around the edges of graphical objects that show what is selected and allows the selected objects to be moved and resized. All other toolkits require programmers to reimplement selection handles and all their standard behaviors in every application, but in Amulet, programmers only need to add an instance of this widget to their window.

There are also built-in dialog boxes, such as message and error boxes, but mostly dialog boxes are just ordinary Amulet windows that are made visible and then made invisible (by simply setting the Am_VISIBLE slot of the window). Often, dialog boxes will be designed using Amulet's interface builder, called *Gilt*, which stands for "graphical interface layout tool." Gilt allows widgets to be laid out interactively using the mouse, and it can set their properties.

25.1.7 Command Objects

Often, the Interactors and widgets operate simply by setting the appropriate slots of objects and having the values computed by constraints. In other cases, extra actions are required. Rather than using a *callback procedure* (which is an application-specific procedure attached to a widget and called when the widget is clicked on by the user), Amulet allocates a *command object* and calls its DO method [Myers 1996a]. Amulet's command objects also provide slots and methods to handle undo, selective undo and repeat, enabling and disabling the command (graying it out), help, and balloon help messages. Thus, unlike in Apple's MacApp framework [Wilson 1990] (where the information about when a command is available is not programmed as a method of the command), the command objects in Amulet provide a single place for describing a behavior.

Furthermore, the command object architecture promotes reuse because commands for such high-level behaviors such as move-object, create-object, change-property, become-selected, cut, copy, paste, duplicate, quit, to-top and -bottom, group and ungroup, undo and redo, and drag-and-drop are supplied in a library and can often be used by applications *without change*. This is possible because the retained object model means that there is a standard way to access and manipulate even application-specific objects. As a simple example, the following creates a button that uses the built-in Quit command to exit the program when the button is pressed.

```
Am_Object my_button = Am_Button.Create ()
    .Add_Part(Am_COMMAND, Am_Quit_Command.Create()
        .Set (Am_LABEL, "Goodbye, world!"));
```

The commands in Amulet are *hierarchical*, so that a behavior may be composed of high-level and low-level commands [Myers 1996a]. For example, a scroll bar command might internally use a move-object command. This improves modularity and reuse because each command is limited to its own local actions.

All of the built-in operations in Amulet support undo. Thus, if a programmer uses the standard Interactors and command objects, all operations are automatically undoable without writing any extra code. If the programmer creates custom commands that perform application-specific actions, then a custom undo method will have to be written as well. However, we have found that the Amulet object and constraint models make writing undo methods very easy, since any needed data can be stored as slots in the command objects, and due to constraints, undoing operations is usually only a matter of resetting some slots. For example, the built-in command for moving objects simply saves the old position of the graphical object as the Am_OLD_VALUE slot of the command, so to undo the operation, the old position can simply be set into the slots of the graphical object. The graphical object itself does not need to have any methods or saved state to support undo.

Other buttons operate on the command selected in the list (in Figure 25.4, number 15), and will undo it, repeat it, or repeat it on new objects. Flash Object shows the object associated with the command. The Expand button will allow a command that operates on multiple objects to be separated into separate commands. The display of each command shows the action, the name of the objects affected, and the new value. The radio buttons on the right cause scrolling and selection commands to be queued, so that, for example, an accidental deselection of a set of objects can be undone.

Amulet's commands also support investigation of various undo mechanisms. Currently, Amulet supplies three different undo mechanisms from which the developer can choose: single undo like the Macintosh, multiple undo like Microsoft Word Version 6

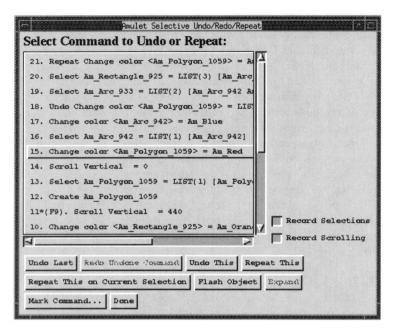

Figure 25.4 The experimental dialog box that allows users to access the regular undo and redo operations (the first two buttons below the scrolling list).

and Emacs, and a novel form of undo and repeat, where any previous command, including scrolling and selections, can be selectively undone, repeated on the *same* object, or repeated on a new selection [Myers 1996a]. Figure 25.4 shows the experimental dialog box that is supplied to support this new style and allow users to select a previously executed command. Researchers can also create their own undo mechanism and integrate it into the Amulet system.

Amulet also supports scripting by generalizing a sequence of recorded commands [Myers 1998]. The user can select some commands in Figure 25.4 for a script and then give it a name. Parameters of the commands can be automatically or explicitly generalized so the script will work in various contexts. Scripts can be edited and the user can also specify various ways they can be invoked.

25.2 Outline of Typical Applications

Due to Amulet's prototype-instance object system, Interactors, and constraints, writing applications for Amulet requires a quite different style from other object-oriented frameworks [Myers 1992]. The first step is usually to create a set of prototype objects that will be used by the application, such as, for example, the Node of Figure 25.2. Next, a main window is created and added to the screen, as shown in the code for the "Hello World" example. Next, the programmer will usually add the necessary widgets and subwindows to the window. Various slots for all these objects might be computed by constraints. Any dialog boxes or other secondary windows would also be created in the same way as the main windows, but their Am_VISIBLE slots will be set to false until they are needed. Finally, the Interactors and commands will be attached to objects. If necessary, custom DO and UNDO methods might be written for the command objects. However, unlike other frameworks, methods for drawing, saving, and printing are unnecessary due to the structured graphics model. Methods for the common interactive behaviors are also not necessary due to the Interactors and built-in command objects.

25.3 Debugging Tools

Debugging interactive applications requires additional mechanisms than those supplied with conventional development environments. This has been a neglected area in other frameworks. Amulet provides an interactive *Inspector* that displays the object's properties, traces the execution of Interactors, pauses, single-steps and traces animations, and displays the dependencies of constraints and the properties of slots (see Figure 25.5). From the Inspector, programmers can also set breakpoints or have messages printed whenever the value of a slot changes. Furthermore, extensive error checking (when debugging is enabled) and helpful messages make Amulet applications easy to develop and debug. We try to make sure that programmers using Amulet never see "Segmentation fault" or other common but unhelpful C++ error messages.

In Figure 25.5, the slots that are inherited are shown in gray and the local slots are shown in black. Notice that the high-level names of methods, constraints, and objects are shown. Values can be edited by the programmer to see how the changes will affect the object.

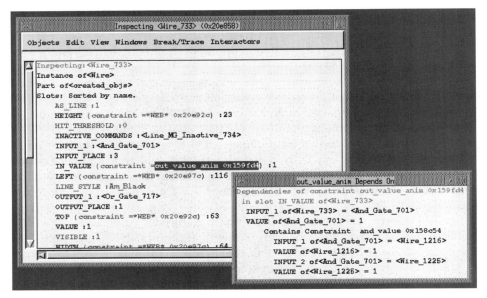

Figure 25.5 Inspecting a wire object and the constraint in its IN_VALUE slot.

25.4 Status and Future Work

The current version of Amulet (v3.0) has been released for Unix, Windows NT, Windows 95, and the Macintosh (to get Amulet, see www.cs.cmu.edu/~amulet). Amulet has been downloaded over 11,000 times in the past year (over 200 times a week), and many research and commercial applications have been built using it.

In the future, we will be investigating techniques to support sound output, visualizations, World Wide Web access and editing, and multiple people operating at the same time (also called *computer-supported cooperative work*—CSCW). An important focus will be on *interactive tools* that allow most of the user interface to be specified without conventional programming.

25.5 Related Work

Amulet builds on many years of work on user interface toolkits and frameworks (see [Myers 1995] for a survey). It is primarily influenced by our previous Garnet framework [Myers 1990b].

The first prototype-instance object system was probably ThingLab [Borning 1981], which did not use inheritance. Self [Ungar 1987] is the primary other language currently investigating the prototype-instance style. There are many differences between the Self and Amulet models. Self is its own language, so it does not have to integrate with an existing language. Self uses pure copy-down semantics, so after an instance is created, changes to the prototype are not reflected in the instances. Finally, Self does not support constraints. Other systems that have used the prototype-instance object model include Apple's NewtonScript and Sk8 languages, and General Magic's MagicCap. However, none of these supports structural inheritance or constraints.

There are many research systems that support constraints. The first system with constraints was probably SketchPad [Sutherland 1963]. Many systems have used constraints as part of an object system, but none is as general purpose or fully integrated as Amulet. The first integrated constraint and object system was ThingLab [Borning 1981], which supported multiway constraints. Rendezvous was designed to help create multiuser applications in Lisp. Like Amulet, Rendezvous [Hill 1994] allows multiple one-way constraints to be attached to a variable, but Rendezvous requires that variables be explicitly declared and uses a different implementation algorithm. SubArctic [Hudson 1996] supports an efficient implementation of a few simple layout constraints in Java, but does not have a general-purpose constraint solver.

Using command objects to support undo was introduced in Apple's MacApp [Wilson 1990] and has been used in many systems, including InterViews and Gina [Berlage 1994]. There is a long history of research into various new undo mechanisms, and Amulet is specifically designed to allow new mechanisms to be explored. The selective undo mechanism in Amulet is closest to the Gina mechanism [Berlage 1994], but adds the ability to repeat previous commands and to undo selections and scrolling.

25.6 Summary

We are very excited about the effectiveness of Amulet as a useful platform with which to perform user interface research. We hope it will also continue to be popular for user interface education and for the implementation of real systems. The innovations in Amulet and the integration of novel object, constraint, input, output, command, and undo models make it an attractive candidate for supporting both today's and tomorrow's user interfaces.

25.7 References

[Berlage 1994] Berlage, Thomas. A selective undo mechanism for graphical user interfaces based on command objects. *ACM Transactions on Computer Human Interaction.* 1994. 1(3). pp. 269-294.

[Borning 1981] Borning, Alan. The programming language aspects of Thinglab: a constraint-oriented simulation laboratory. *ACM Transactions on Programming Languages and Systems.* 1981. 3(4). pp. 353-387.

[Hill 1994] Hill, Ralph D., Tom Brinck, Steven L. Rohall, John F. Patterson, and Wayne Wilner. The rendezvous architecture and language for constructing multiuser applications. *ACM Transactions on Computer-Human Interaction.* 1994. 1(2). pp. 81-125.

[Hudson 1996] Hudson, Scott E., and Ian Smith. Ultra-lightweight constraints. *ACM SIGGRAPH Symposium on User Interface Software and Technology, Proceedings UIST'96.* Seattle, WA, November, 1996. pp. 147-155. www.cc.gatech.edu/gvu/ui/sub_arctic/.

[Krasner 1988] Krasner, Glenn E., and Stephen T. Pope. A description of the model-view-controller user interface paradigm in the Smalltalk-80 system. *Journal of Object Oriented Programming.* 1988. 1(3). pp. 26-49.

[Lieberman 1986] Lieberman, Henry. Using prototypical objects to implement shared behavior in object-oriented systems. *Sigplan Notices.* 1986. 21(11). pp. 214-223. *ACM Conference on Object-Oriented Programming; Systems Languages and Applications; OOPSLA'86,* Portland, Oregon, November 1986.

[Linton 1989] Linton, Mark A., John M. Vlissides and Paul R. Calder. Composing user interfaces with InterViews. *IEEE Computer.* February 1989. 22(2). pp. 8-22.

[Myers 1995] Myers, Brad A. User interface software tools. *ACM Transactions on Computer Human Interaction.* January 1995. 2(1). pp. 64-103.

[Myers 1998] Myers, Brad A. Scripting graphical applications by demonstration. *Human Factors in Computing Systems, Proceedings SIGCHI'98.* Los Angeles, CA, April 1998. pp. 534-541.

[Myers 1992] Myers, Brad A., Dario Giuse, and Brad Vander Zanden. Declarative programming in a prototype-instance system: object-oriented programming without writing methods. *Sigplan Notices.* 1992. 27(10). pp. 184-200. *ACM Conference on Object-Oriented Programming; Systems Languages and Applications; OOPSLA'92* Vancouver, British Columbia, Canada, October 1992.

[Myers 1990] Myers, Brad A., Dario A. Giuse, Roger B. Dannenberg, Brad Vander Zanden, David S. Kosbie, Edward Pervin, Andrew Mickish, and Philippe Marchal. Garnet: comprehensive support for graphical, highly-interactive user interfaces. *IEEE Computer.* November 1990. 23(11). pp. 71-85.

[Myers 1996a] Myers, Brad A. and David Kosbie. Reusable hierarchical command objects. *Proceedings CHI'96: Human Factors in Computing Systems,* Vancouver, BC, Canada, April 14-18, 1996a. pp. 260-267.

[Myers 1997] Myers, Brad A., Richard G. McDaniel, Robert C. Miller, Alan Ferrency, Andrew Faulring, Bruce D. Kyle, Andrew Mickish, Alex Klimovitski, and Patrick Doane. The Amulet environment: new models for effective user interface software development. *IEEE Transactions on Software Engineering.* June 1997. 23(6). pp. 347-365. June.

[Myers 1996b] Myers, Brad A., Robert C. Miller, Rich McDaniel, and Alan Ferrency. Easily adding animations to interfaces using constraints. *ACM SIGGRAPH Symposium on User Interface Software and Technology, Proceedings UIST'96.* Seattle, WA, November 1996. pp. 119-128. www.cs.cmu.edu/~amulet.

[Palay 1988] Palay, Andrew J., Wilfred J. Hansen, Michael Kazar, Mark Sherman, Maria Wadlow, Tom Neuendorffer, Zalman Stern, Miles Bader, and Thom Peters. The Andrew toolkit—an overview. *Proceedings Winter Usenix Technical Conference*, Dallas, Texas, February 1988. pp. 9-21.

[Sutherland 1963] Sutherland, Ivan E. SketchPad: a man-machine graphical communication system. *AFIPS Spring Joint Computer Conference*, 1963. pp. 329-346.

[Ungar 1987] Ungar, David and Randall B. Smith. Self: the power of simplicity. *SIGPLAN Notices.* 1987. 22 pp. 241-247. *ACM Conference on Object-Oriented Programming, Systems, Languages and Applications; OOPSLA'87*, Orlando, Florida, December 1987.

[Vander Zanden 1994] Vander Zanden, Brad, Brad A. Myers, Dario Giuse, and Pedro Szekely. Integrating pointer variables into one-way constraint models, *ACM Transactions on Computer Human Interaction.* 1994. 1(2). pp. 161-213.

[Wilson 1990] Wilson, David. *Programming with MacApp.* Reading, MA: Addison-Wesley, 1990.

Jadve: Graph-Based Data Visualization Framework

Data visualization is a very important and valuable tool to show the structure of technical information. Various data visualization technologies have been developed for different application domains. For example, computer mapping is now an integral part of Geographical Information Systems (GISs); numerical data displays (curves, bar charts, pie charts, and so on) are widely used in business and scientific computing; and directed attributed graphs (DAGs) representing the semantics of the underlying data are also used extensively in applications such as process (work-flow) modeling, program visualization and understanding, and data mining.

An interesting example of graph-based data visualization applications is *Improvise* [Barghouti 1995], a multimedia system for modeling, visualizing, and documenting software and business processes and work flow. It represents a process flow as a multi-layered directed graph and provides a graphical user interface (GUI) for displaying, editing, and browsing the graphs. Improvise uses nodes and edges that have different shapes and styles to represent different types of process entities. For example, a box (rectangle) with two horizontal lines in it represents a *manual task*, and an ellipse represents a *computer process*. It provides an object selection template that contains the different types (shapes and styles) of nodes and edges so that the user can insert a node or an edge to the graph by simply selecting an object from the template and clicking at a point (location) on the canvas. The user can also annotate each node and edge with multimedia information, such as video clips and executable attachments, by defining its attributes. In many simple graph-drawing environments, the user has to make a lot of effort to consider the size and placement of each node and edge in order to make a good presentation of the graph. Improvise completely eliminates such burdens by using *dot* [Koutsofios 1993], a graph layout generator, to compute the graph drawings, that is, the size and placement of each node and edge. Thus, the user only needs to place the nodes and edges on the canvas casually, and can issue a layout request to obtain high-quality graph drawings.

From Improvise and other advanced systems, we see that a graph-based data visualization application typically includes these basic modules (functions):

Graph representation. Allows the user to define graphs that represent application-specific information.

Graph presentation. Displays the graphs using a GUI, and allows the user to edit and browse the graphs.

Graph layout. Generates graph drawings automatically, using algorithms that consider graph characteristics (planarity, orientation, and so on) and aesthetic criteria (for example, maximization of the display of symmetries).

With the increasing importance of Web-based and, more generally, distributed computing, many applications also need to have these more advanced features: remote graph-drawing services and multiuser collaboration support. By *remote graph drawing,* we mean the ability for an application running on a client machine to request graph-drawing (layout) services from a server running on another machine anywhere on the network. By *collaboration,* we refer to the situation in which multiple users from different machines on the network share the same set of graphs for editing and viewing.

This chapter presents Jadve, a framework for graph-based data visualization applications. The motivation of building Jadve is not only to provide the standard (built-in) graph representation, presentation, (remote) layout services, and collaboration support, but also to facilitate rapid application development. Jadve thus provides an application programming interface (API) so that its standard services can be customized to accomplish the application-specific tasks. Jadve employs client-server architecture. The Jadve server provides collaboration support and employs dot to compute graph layout; the frontend client supports interactive graph editing and browsing, and can be launched from any node in the network and be connected to the server. This architecture has the advantage of saving computing resources since the computational-intensive graph layout process need not be on every client machine; in addition, graph representation can be stored by the server and shared by multiple clients.

The advent of Java [Arnold 1996] motivated us to exploit the features it provides, such as portability, GUI generation facilities, and distributed computing features. We implemented Jadve in Java, which allows the front ends of Jadve-based applications to be built as applets that can be executed over the WWW via any Java-enabled Web browser; this greatly facilitates the distribution of the application software and enhances its availability.

The rest of this chapter is organized as follows: *Section 26.1* discusses the design and implementation of Jadve. *Section 26.2* describes the Jadve API. *Section 26.3* presents three example applications developed on top of Jadve. *Section 26.4* compares Jadve with other related frameworks. *Section 26.5* contains a discussion of future work, and *Section 26.6* concludes the chapter with an evaluation and summary of topics covered in this chapter.

26.1 The Design and Implementation of Jadve

This section first discusses the overall design goals of Jadve and the advantages of using Java technologies for its implementation. It then discusses the design considerations of its main functionalities—namely, graph representation, presentation, layout, and collaboration support. This section describes the implementation of Jadve by presenting its main components.

26.1.1 Design Goals

From a framework technology point of view, we had three main requirements in building Jadve: extensibility, portability, and customizability. *Extensibility* allows for a natural evolution path, wherein new services can be incorporated into the framework. *Portability* is essential in the multiplatform world we live in. *Customizability* allows many different applications to be built on top of the framework, reusing its services and avoiding rewriting a lot of code.

The following sections consider how to accomplish these design goals and the required functionalities (services). Choosing the right language for implementation is the important first step because the strengths and weaknesses of the language affect the detail design of the system. We used Java because of the following features:

Object-oriented design. Adopting an object-oriented programming paradigm often results in a good component-based software architecture, which is essential for the extensibility of a system. Moreover, object-oriented design is natural for Jadve, which is graph based. A graph has a composite structure of graph objects, such as nodes, edges, and subgraphs. More important, there is a natural inheritance hierarchy among graph objects of different shapes and styles. For example, an edge with an arrowhead can be derived from a plain edge (a straight line with no arrow).

Distributed design. The Java Development Kit (JDK) includes a networking library to use sockets and TCP/IP protocols such as HTTP and FTP. These Java functions are essential for the multiuser collaboration support services.

Neutral and portable architecture. These Java features ensure that Jadve can run on any computing platform that supports the Java Virtual Machine. In other words, Jadve is portable.

Multithreaded design. This enables Jadve to perform more than one task for the user at the same time. For example, when the user requests a graph layout, a separate new thread (in the background) contacts the server and waits for the reply. In the meantime, the original thread continues to interact with the user.

Dynamic design. In Java, finding out runtime type (class) information is straightforward. Therefore, new classes can be easily added to a running program by supplying their full class names, which indicate the search paths for the classes, to the program. Using this Java feature, the Jadve API essentially facilitates the integration of application-specific functions (classes) into Jadve at runtime, thus enabling Jadve to be customized for specific applications.

26.1.2 Graph Representation, Presentation, and Layout

Graph representation deals with using graphs to capture the semantics of application data. The nodes and edges of the graph are therefore application data entities. Applications normally use different symbols to represent different types of application data. In Jadve, these symbols are just template nodes and edges, each of which has a different shape and drawing style.

For graph presentation, the Jadve front end displays the graphs and provides functions to edit (add, delete, copy, and paste) a node or edge and to browse (zoom and scroll) and analyze the graph, for example to find all reachable nodes from a given node. Some of these functions, such as the browse functions, are generic in the sense that they have the same well-defined behavior and consequences across all applications. On the other hand, other functions can have additional application-specific semantics. For example, an application may have different data-driven processing when a computer process is deleted than when a manual task is deleted. Therefore, these functions need to include two parts: the standard operations, and the application- and datatype-specific operations.

For graph layout, the Jadve front end simply provides a command for the user to request a layout. The layout procedure is generic to all graphs since it computes the drawing attributes—that is, the sizes and placements—of the nodes and edges by considering only their shapes, labels, and connection information.

We can see from the above discussion that graph objects—namely, graphs, nodes, edges, and their attributes—are the central elements in Jadve because its basic services are essentially operations on these objects. There are both general and application-specific graph representations and operations in Jadve. We can conceptually think of two types of graph objects: abstract objects and application objects. *Abstract* graph objects are the defining elements of a generic graph, that is, the subgraphs, the nodes, and the edges. The *application* objects are the results of overlaying application semantics on top of the abstract objects. It is important to realize that it is neither possible nor appropriate to design Jadve to include, as built-in, all possible application-specific graph objects (their representations and operations) since it is intended as an application framework on top of which a wide variety of systems can be developed. The challenge is to design Jadve in such a way that application objects and operations can be seamlessly integrated with its built-in generic graph representation, presentation, and layout services.

26.1.3 Multiuser Collaboration Support

Collaboration in data visualization is normally in the form of sharing (reviewing) the edit of a graph by others. There are many possible application-specific scenarios, such as the following examples:

- Before users can make changes to a graph, they are required to first obtain an exclusive lock on it so that no other user can make changes to the same graph at the same time. The lock is released once the user deposits the changed graph to the master repository.

- Before users make changes to a graph, they first check out (download) the latest version of the graph from the master repository. No lock is placed on the graph. When the user deposits the changed graph, if another user has already deposited changes to the same graph, they need to negotiate and merge their changes.

- Before users can deposit their changes, they need to present the changes to all other users and get their approval.

It is thus evident that Jadve should not be hard-coded to support a fixed collaborative work flow. Rather, it should provide the following general primitives and support mechanisms:

File management. Provides a repository for (shared) graph files; supports the lock/unlock and checkout/deposit operations.

User management. Defines a group as a set of users that collaboratively work on a collection of graph files (it is assumed that no files are shared between two groups); supports communications within a group (for example, broadcasts a message to all users, or sends a message from one user to another).

Application-specific concurrency control. Enforces a group-specific policy, which is a sequence of operations that must all succeed before a deposit can be made to the repository. For example, a policy with a single operation *no* indicates that no concurrency control is in place (that is, the Unix semantics is assumed); whereas a policy *lock;review* specifies that a lock must be obtained first, and a group review and approval process needs to take place.

Utilities. A function that compares two graphs and highlights the differences; a review-viewing facility that allows a user to display, in realtime, a changed graph remotely to other users in the group.

26.1.4 The Components of Jadve

This section presents the architectural components of Jadve, as shown in Figure 26.1 (generated using dot). The ellipses in the figure represent the modules (classes or methods), and the directed edges with their labels represent the data flowing between the modules. The two boxes, *front end* and *back end*, represent the main (container) modules of the Jadve client and server, respectively. The server and the client are two different programs that communicate through the networks.

Graph Object Definitions

We first discuss the implementation of graph objects, which is the foundation of all Jadve components.

Figure 26.2 shows the definitions of Jadve abstract objects. The solid edges in the figure represent the composite relations. The dotted edges represent the inheritance relations; for example, DotNode is extended from DotElement. Here DotGraph defines a graph as having a set of attributes, nodes, edges, and subgraphs. A graph element, a node or an edge, is defined by DotElement, which also has a set of attributes. Dot-

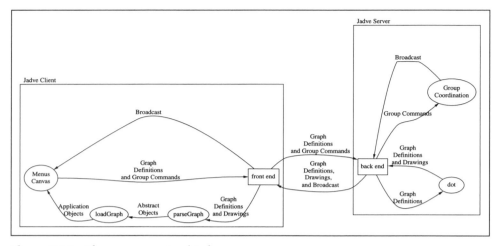

Figure 26.1 The components of Jadve.

Attribute defines an attribute as a (name, value) pair. Some details are not shown in the figure. For example, each DotElement has a pointer to its container, DotGraph, and each DotEdge has pointers to its two end nodes. Using these pointers, the composite structure of the entire graph can be traversed starting from any of its nodes or edges.

The abstract objects describe only the compositions of a graph. The application objects are the result of adding application representation and operation semantics to the abstract objects. As an application framework, Jadve facilitates the definitions of application objects using the class hierarchy shown in Figure 26.3. Again, the solid edges in the figure represent the composite relations, and the dotted edges represent

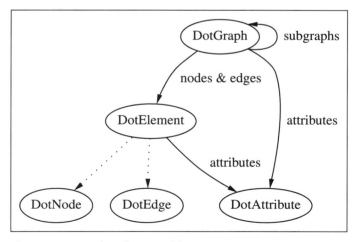

Figure 26.2 Jadve abstract objects.

the inheritance relations. JadveObject defines the most general aspects of an application object. The one-to-one correspondence between an application object and its abstract object is represented by the reference to its DotElement. JadveObject defines methods for drawing, locating (deciding whether the mouse position is within the object boundary), highlighting (painting the object in red), scaling (enlarging or shrinking the object when the view is zoomed in or out), translating (modifying the object position when the view is scrolled), and so on. The draw method is overridden by the subclasses, such as Box, which have detailed information about the shapes of the objects. Jadve also includes, as built-in, a number of subclasses of JadveObject, each with a commonly used shape and style. These include Box, Ellipse, Diamond, PlainEdge, DirectedEdge (an edge with an arrowhead), and so on. Application-specific graph objects are derived from JadveObject or one of its subclasses. For example, in Improvise, ManualTask is implemented by subclassing Box. It extends (overrides) the draw method of Box by adding two horizontal lines to divide the rectangle into three sections, and displaying the task name, description, and organization in the three sections, respectively.

Here we have separate definitions for abstract objects and application objects. There are alternative approaches for implementing the graph objects. For example, JadveObject and DotElement can be combined into a single class hierarchy (the combined class is still part of the DotGraph composition hierarchy). The motivation of our approach comes from the principle of separation of concern. DotGraph and DotElement deal with defining a graph, whereas JadveObject and its subclasses deal with the representation of application semantics. Customizing Jadve normally involves only extending the JadveObject classes.

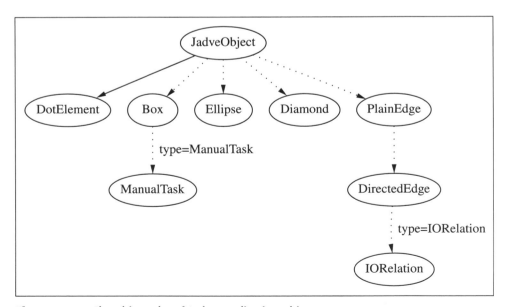

Figure 26.3 Class hierarchy of Jadve application objects.

The Jadve Client

The Jadve client handles most of the interactions with the end user. Its GUI is constructed using the standard Java Abstract Windowing Toolkit (AWT), with a template of application objects, pull-down menus for edit, display and analysis commands, and canvasses for displaying (drawing) graph objects.

As the front end to application users, the Jadve client provides the seamless integration of application-specific graph representations and operations with the generic Jadve services. Using Improvise as an example, when the user adds a manual task to a process flow graph, a ManualTask object is created and added to the list of graph objects (Jadve-Objects) displayed on the canvas (defined as JadveCanvas). In addition, its corresponding DotElement is created, with attributes (shape, box) and (type, ManualTask), and added as one of the nodes of the DotGraph associated with the JadveCanvas. When the user requests a layout, the writeGraph method of DotGraph writes out the graph definitions (in text form) according to the dot syntax. A layout request along with the graph definitions is then sent to the server. When the client gets back the graph drawings (also in text form and in the dot syntax), the Jadve parser, parseGraph, reads the drawing descriptions and constructs a new DotGraph accordingly. Each new Dot-Element is just the old one (before layout) with the new size and position attributes. To transform these new abstract objects to the corresponding application graph objects, the loadGraph method of JadveCanvas utilizes the dynamic feature of Java to first look for the type attribute of each DotElement object, then create a new object instance of type (if the type attribute is null, as in the vanilla Jadve environment, the shape attribute is used instead). For example, if a DotElement is of type ManualTask, then its corresponding new JadveObject is a ManualTask object. The last few steps of load-Graph are to erase the list of old graph objects, and display the new objects on Jadve-Canvas by invoking the draw method of each JadveObject. From this point on, the graph objects on the canvas carry the application representation and operation semantics. *Section 26.2* describes how application-specific object operations are supported.

The Jadve client also provides support for multiuser collaboration. Users in a group coordinate their operations by passing proper messages. Each client has a thread that sends and receives messages to and from other clients (by using the server as the relay; see next section, *The Jadve Server*). For example, when the concurrency control policy requires the review operation, a user, Joe, can let others review his edited graph by broadcasting a review message to the group. Upon receiving this message, each client creates a review view displaying Joe's changed graph for the corresponding group member. These review views are the slaves of Joe's workspace view, where he has made his changes. They have exactly the same display as Joe's view even when it zooms, scrolls, or highlights a graph object. Joe can therefore walk the reviewers through his specific changes.

The Jadve client has a tool called *diff*. It compares the graph on the canvas with another graph (not displayed) and highlights the deleted, inserted, and modified graph objects using different colors. This command can be used to show the differences between two versions of the same graph. For example, after failing to deposit his changes because user Diana has just updated the same graph, user Joe can use the diff command to compare his version with Diana's version. He can then try to merge all the changes and deposit again.

The Jadve Server

The main function of the Jadve backend concurrent server is to process client requests for graph layout and group communications. It listens to a socket for incoming messages and creates a Java thread to process each message. The header of each message between the server and the client specifies its message type. For a layout message, the server invokes the dot process to compute a graph layout. As shown in Figure 26.1, the server passes to dot the message body (the graph definitions), and sends the dot output (the graph definitions enriched with drawing information) back to the client.

The server supports multiuser collaboration according to the configuration file that defines the groups, and for each group, the users, graph files, and concurrency control policy. When a client sends a *register* message, the server first checks whether the user belongs to the group he or she intends to join. It then records the client's IP address and port number. Knowing the members of the group and the IP addresses and port numbers, the server can use sockets to relate group messages from one member to the others in the group. For example, during the review session, when user Joe, the member who has requested the review, zooms in the graph, the corresponding client sends a *group command* message to the server. The server then sends a *broadcast* message with the same message body, which is the command ZoomIn, to other clients. Upon receiving such a broadcasted command, each client executes it on its review view so that the group member sees exactly the same graph display as Joe.

The Jadve server also manages the master (centralized) repository of graph files and supports the lock/unlock and checkout/deposit operations. The lock/unlock operations are straightforward since the server is the only process that can access the files in the master repository. The server maintains a list where each entry contains a file and the user that holds the lock. For each checkout or (successful) deposit, the server also records the user ID and the time stamp. When user Joe attempts to deposit a graph, if the server discovers that Joe's checkout time stamp of the graph is smaller (earlier) than user Diana's deposit time stamp, it rejects Joe's deposit. The server sends a *reject* message, along with the "new" graph (updated by Diana) to Joe. The corresponding client then automatically invokes the diff command to show Joe the differences between the two versions. The server also deletes Joe's old checkout entry and creates a new one with the current time stamp, so that Joe can deposit after merging the two versions.

26.2 The Jadve API

The purpose of the Jadve API is to provide a means for developers to extend and customize Jadve. Using this API, an application-specific Jadve class is defined as the subclass of a built-in Jadve class. Application-specific behavior can then be implemented by adding new data members and methods to the built-in class and overriding its existing methods. This section gives only high-level descriptions of the essential Jadve classes, and is not intended to be a complete reference manual.

As described in *Section 26.1.4*, application-specific graph objects can be defined by subclassing JadveObject and implementing their own draw functions. Most applications require functions to analyze the structure of a graph. The reference from an application object JadveObject to the corresponding abstract object DotElement is an entry into the graph composition hierarchy. DotGraph provides traversing methods to visit every element of a graph.

JadveCanvas implements the canvas. Application objects displayed on the canvas can be accessed through two methods: getListOfObjects returns the list of all application objects, and getSelectedObject returns the selected (highlighted) object. To modify the behavior of Jadve built-in graph operations (delete, zoom, and so on), application-specific actions can be defined in the Jadve_eventHandle method, which is invoked whenever a Jadve built-in command is issued. Its default implementation is an empty function, thus allowing the standard operations to take place.

JadveMenu implements the pull-down menus. Menu commands that operate on graph objects are passed to the JadveCanvas attached to the menu bar. The addMenu and addMenuItem methods allow application-specific commands—that is, commands not provided as built-in by Jadve—to be added to the pull-down menus. For each application command—for example, Import—a corresponding class Import needs to be implemented as a subclass of JadveAppCommand. The actual command actions are specified in its execute method, which is invoked when the command is selected from the pull-down menus.

JadveObjectTemplate implements the object template window. Similar to Jadve-Canvas, it has the getListOfTemplates and getSelectedTemplate methods for accessing the template objects, each of which is a JadveObject. addTemplate and deleteTemplate can be used to add and delete a template object, respectively. JadveClient implements the frontend client. It contains a JadveObjectTemplate and a number of JadveMenus, each of which has an attached JadveCanvas.

JadveServer implements the backend server. Its addMessageType method enables the server to process messages other than layout requests and group commands. Similar to JadveMenu, for each new message type—for example, executeChava—a corresponding class executeChava needs to be implemented as a subclass of JadveAppMessage. The actual message-handling actions are specified in its execute method, which is invoked whenever the server gets such a message.

Finally, in a single-user environment, the only service that the Jadve server provides is the graph layout; therefore, it is desirable that the Jadve client have the option to invoke the dot process locally (thus eliminating the need to communicate with the server across the network). DotLayout is provided to support single-user applications. It has methods for parsing graph definitions and invoking dot to layout a graph. The doLayout method of JadveCanvas, which by default sends a layout message to the server, can be overridden to instead use the DotLayout methods.

26.3 Jadve Applications

This section briefly describes several examples to demonstrate how various data visualization applications can be constructed on top of Jadve. Note that the vanilla Jadve environment is different from these applications in that it contains no application-specific graph objects and operations. For example, its object template window contains only the built-in JadveObjects; that is, Box, Diamond, and so on.

26.3.1 Example 1: Improvise

The Java version of Improvise is the first comprehensive customization of Jadve. In fact, Jadve was extended to include new components (such as the object template window) once we realized that some Improvise functions need general support from the framework.

Improvise is a process (work-flow) modeling and analysis environment. Each type of Improvise work-flow object has its own special shape and drawing style. Therefore, a rich set of application objects, such as ManualTask, ComputerProcess, IORelation, and so on, is implemented. ImproviseObjectTemplate is extended from JadveObject-Template. It replaces the built-in JadveObjects with the entire set of Improvise application objects (see Figure 26.4).

Figure 26.5 shows the Improvise menu and canvas displaying a work-flow graph. The user has just added a ManualTask to the graph, by selecting it in the object template window and clicking an unoccupied position on the canvas. This new object is automatically highlighted (selected) so that any subsequent object command is operated on it. For example, the attribute command (in the object pull-down menu) can be used to specify its attributes—name, organization, and so on.

Improvise has a set of process analysis commands. For example, when the expand graph command is issued upon a node that represents a subgraph (a next-layer process graph), the entire subgraph takes the place of the node in the current graph. This command requires complex graph-traversing operations, and is not implemented in Jadve. To add this command, ImproviseMenu is implemented as a subclass of JadveMenu. It has the expand graph menu item added to the graph pull-down menu. An instance of expandgraph (a subclass of JadveAppCommand) is created when the ImproviseMenu is instantiated. The constructor of expandgraph has, as input parameter, a reference to the ImproviseMenu. From this reference, expandgraph methods, such as execute and expandInPlace, can access the JadveCanvas and, hence, the Improvise objects and work-flow graphs.

Improvise is multimedia enabled. That is, some of the Improvise objects can have associated multimedia (audio and/or video) data. Two new commands, playAudio and playVideo, are added to the object pull-down menu. These commands are disabled unless the highlighted object has the appropriate media files. The Jadve_event-Handle method of ImproviseCanvas (a subclass of JadveCanvas) specifies these Improvise-specific operations for the built-in highlight event (triggered when a graph

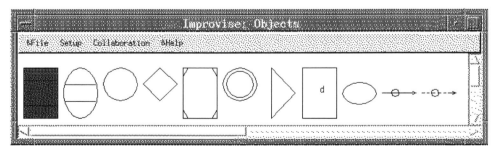

Figure 26.4 Improvise template objects.

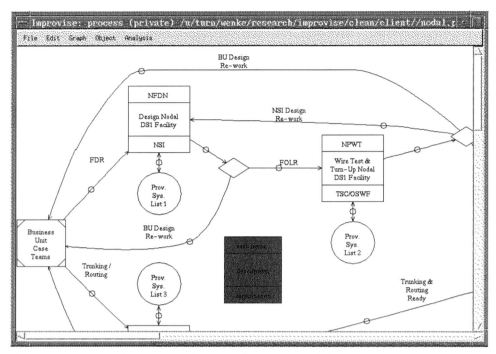

Figure 26.5   Improvise menu and canvas showing a work flow.

object is selected): If the audio attribute of the highlighted object is not null, enable the play audit command; if the video attribute is not null, enable the play video command. playAudio and playVideo are each implemented as a subclass of JadveAppCommand. Their execute methods implement the operations to play the media of the highlighted object. Improvise also fully utilizes the built-in multiuser collaboration services of Jadve to support shared editing and viewing of process graphs.

26.3.2 Example 2: Chava

Chava [Korn 1996] is a graphical navigator for analyzing the structures (such as class hierarchy or message-passing relations among classes) of Java programs. It was originally implemented using *lefty* [Koutsofios 1991] and *ciao* [Chen-Fowler 1995]. To use Chava, the user needs to first run a set of Chava scripts in the directory containing the Java programs. These scripts analyze the programs and build databases of Java program entities. A graphical front end can then display the program entities and their relations.

   The Jadve version of Chava is a simple customization. A new command runChava (a subclass of JadveAppCommand) is added to the JadveMenu and a new message type of executeChava (a subclass of JadveAppMessage) is added to the JadveServer. The runChava object on the client side is responsible for sending an executeChava message, which contains the directory path of the Java programs to be analyzed, to the server. The executeChava object on the server side runs the Chava scripts and sends the output (which is already in dot format) back to the client for display. Compared with its original implementation, the benefit of using Jadve is that Chava users can take advantage of the group collaboration features—for example, to review a Java program together.

26.3.3 Example 3: Classifier Visualizer

An important issue in knowledge discovery and data mining (KDD) is the presentation of the discovered knowledge [Fayyad 1996]. A human expert needs to understand and inspect (judge) the knowledge before it can be made useful (for example, put into a report). A large number of data-mining algorithms produce classifiers, which can classify a data item into one of the predefined categories (labels). There are many kinds of data classifiers, such as a decision tree, that can be represented as a DAG. We therefore wanted to apply Jadve to this application domain.

Figure 26.6 shows a decision tree in which the leaf nodes represent classes (decisions), the nonleaf nodes represent the attributes under test, and the edges represent the attribute values. The Attributes window in this figure shows the following decision information about the highlighted leaf node (with class label 0): for a data item, if its p-1 value is 3 and its p-18 value is 5, then it belongs to class 0 (with .938 probability).

The Classifier Visualizer is an example of utilizing only some of the components of Jadve. Here, the JadveCanvas is plugged into a host data-mining environment, *JAM*

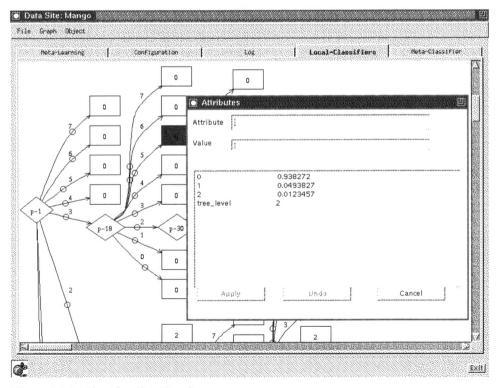

Figure 26.6 The Classifier Visualizer.

[Stolfo 1997]: Instead of using JadveMenu, the graph menu items were added to the menu bar of JAM. When a graph command, for example, Zoom In, is selected, the corresponding method, zoomIn, of JadveCanvas is invoked. The doLayout method is overridden to use methods in DotLayout, instead of communicating with a Jadve-Server. A load command is also added to transform data classifiers into graph descriptions and invoke doLayout to obtain the graph drawings.

26.4 Related Work

Related extensible graph editors include *EDGE* [Newbery 1988], *dotty* [Koutsofios 1994], and *HotDraw* [Johnson 1993]. These systems all treat pictures of graphs as structured objects, support a general set of menu-driven graph-viewing and -editing operations, and allow programmers to add application-specific functions. EDGE and dotty also provide on-demand graph layout services.

Dotty has two main components: lefty as the front end and dot as the back end. The *lefty* process runs a program written in the lefty (procedural) scripting language. This program includes functions to edit graph objects and to draw the objects according to their attributes (for example, color, shape, and style). It also has a graph layout function that communicates with the *dot* process running in the background. Customizing dotty involves directly (and freely) changing the lefty program (since the source code is always accessible to the user). For example, the leftdown function is called when a user presses the left mouse button. It by default calls insertnode to insert a new node in the position of the cursor. The user can rewrite the leftdown function to perform other operations, for example, to pop up a menu. It can be argued that dotty gives complete freedom to programmers to build applications since they can access and modify all functions. However, customizing dotty may have large overhead because one needs to understand the internals of the lefty program and to learn lefty, a nonstandard language. Jadve provides all of the functions supported by dotty. In addition, by providing a standard Java API, it hides the implementation details from the application programmers, and guarantees a degree of uniformity in terms of user-system interaction across different applications.

HotDraw is a framework for structured semantic drawing editors. It is written in Smalltalk, and is therefore object-oriented. The most important class in HotDraw is Figure, which is the superclass of all drawing elements in a HotDraw application. Each subclass of Figure redefines its drawing methods and attributes to represent application-specific information. Application programmers can further customize HotDraw by creating subclasses of (and making changes to) the important classes, such as Drawing (which represents the entire drawing), Tool, Handle, and Drawing-Editor. A major difference from Jadve is that HotDraw has built-in support for semantic operations. The elements of a semantic drawing can have constraints on their behavior. For example, an attribute of one element can be a function of the attributes of other elements. Constraints in HotDraw are implemented as objects. A Constraint object is created if a constraint is needed between two figures. It gets notification from the constraining figure and changes the constrained figure to satisfy the constraint. Jadve can, in principle, be extended to support constraints. The constraining Jadve-

Object can have a DotAttribute ("constraint", constraint_name) specifying the name of (a subclass of) JadveConstraint, and a list of ("constraining", element_id) specifying the list of constrained graph objects. As the triggering operation is performed on the constraining object, the Jadve_eventHandle method of JadveCanvas can invoke the execute method of the corresponding JadveConstraint object, which, in turn, traverses all constrained objects and makes proper changes. It should be noted that Jadve is not just an *editor*. Its client-server architecture and multiuser collaboration support, as well as the use of Java, are all aimed at providing a framework for building more advanced distributed applications.

26.5 Future Work

We plan to adopt a process-centered approach to support multiuser collaboration. The Jadve server can be integrated with a process engine (a work-flow management component) that supports project-specific process (work-flow step) definition. In such an architecture, the Jadve server is still responsible for supporting group communications. However, it needs to coordinate group activities according to the process states managed by the process engine. For example, when a Jadve client sends a review request to the server, the Jadve server passes this message to the process engine, which, in turn, enters the initial process state of a review session. Thereafter, as the session progresses, the process engine gets new process data from the clients (through the Jadve server), and moves through the next logical process steps. The Jadve, in turn, instructs the clients in the correct actions to take according to these steps. The advantages of using a process engine is separation of concern: Jadve can provide the generic support (group membership, message passing, concurrency control, and so on) that is required for all collaborative activities; the process engine is responsible for ensuring that the activities are carried out according to the defined (process) semantics.

It is our belief that different frameworks should complement each other in terms of the services they provide. Thus, an interesting extension to Jadve is to integrate it with other existing frameworks and provide data visualization services. The portable common tool environment (PCTE) [Long-Morris 1993] is a framework to facilitate the development of software development environments (SDEs). It has three main sets of services: user interfaces, communications, and object storage and management. PCTE provides Motif-compliant tools for GUI development, message passing and notification for CASE tool communications, and a standard objectbase for all artifacts of an SDE. Jadve can be added to the PCTE framework to provide visualization services, for example, to display and analyze the object hierarchy of its object base and the relations among the CASE tools.

26.6 Summary

There are two basic requirements for an application framework: First, it needs to provide a set of standard services valuable to the application domain; second, these services must be able to be extended and customized to accomplish application-specific tasks.

This chapter presents Jadve as a framework for graph-based data visualization applications. Jadve implements, as built-in, a set of graph representation, presentation, and layout services, as well as multiuser collaboration support. To facilitate application development, Jadve goes beyond simply providing an API. The central theme in its design and implementation is the seamless integration of application-specific graph objects and operations with the generic Jadve services. The separation of abstract objects from application objects is the most important design decision. Components (services) that operate on abstract objects can generally be protected from applications, whereas those that use application objects need to provide support for application-specific operations.

In addition to a component-based design, Java's object-oriented, architecture-neutral, and dynamic features are critical to ensuring the extensibility, portability, and customizability of Jadve. The three example applications demonstrate that Jadve can indeed be a framework to develop wide varieties of data visualization systems.

26.7 References

[Arnold 1996] Arnold, K., and J. Gosling. *The Java Programming Language.* Reading, MA: Addison-Wesley, 1996.

[Barghouti 1995] Barghouti, N.S., E. Koutsofios, and E. Cohen. Improvise: An interactive multimedia process visualization environment. *Proceedings of the 5th European Software Engineering Conference (ESEC 1995),* Barcelona, Spain, September 1995. Springer-Verlag, 1995.

[Chen-Fowler 1995] Chen, Y.-F., G.S. Fowler, E. Koutsofios, and R.S. Wallach. Ciao: A graphical navigator for software and document repositories. *International Conference on Software Maintenance,* Nice, France, October 1995.

[Fayyad 1996] Fayyad, U., G. Piatetsky-Shapiro, and P. Smyth. The KDD process for extracting useful knowledge from data. *Communications of the ACM,* 39(11), November 1996: 27–34.

[Johnson 1993] Johnson, R.E. Documenting frameworks using patterns. *Proceedings of the OOPSLA 1993 Conference on Object-Oriented Programming Systems, Languages, and Applications.* Washington, DC, September/October 1993: 63–76.

[Korn 1996] Korn, J., and E. Koutsofios. Chava: Ciao for Java. www.cs.princeton.edu/~jlk/chava, 1996.

[Koutsofios 1991] Koutsofios, E., and D. Dobkin. Lefty: A two-view editor for technical pictures. *Proceedings of the Graphics Interface 1991 Conference,* pp. 68–76, Calgary, Alberta, June 1991.

[Koutsofios 1993] Koutsofios, E., and S.C. North. *Drawing Graphs with Dot.* AT&T Bell Laboratories, October 1993.

[Koutsofios 1994] Koutsofios, E., and S.C. North. Applications of graph visualization. *Proceedings of the Graphics Interface 1994 Conference,* pp. 235–245, May 1994.

[Long-Morris 1993] Long, F., and E. Morris. An overview of PCTE: A basis for a portable common tool environment. Technical Report CMU/SEI-93-TR-1, ESC-TR-93-175. Software Engineering Institute, Carnegie-Mellon University, Pittsburgh, PA, March 1993.

[Newbery 1988] Newbery, F.J. EDGE: An extendible directed graph editor. Technical Report 8/88. Institute for Informatics, University of Karlsruhe, Karlsruhe, Germany, June 1988.

[Stolfo 1997] Stolfo, S., A. Prodromidis, S. Tselepis, W. Lee, D. Fan, and P. Chan. JAM: Java agents for meta-learning over distributed databases. *Proceedings of the 3rd International Conference on Knowledge Discovery and Data Mining*, Newport Beach, CA, August 1997.

CHAPTER 27

Object Environments

Frameworks are the instantiation of an architecture within a particular domain. These domains can be horizontal (graphical user interfaces [GUIs], databases, distributed systems, and so on) or vertical (healthcare, finance, and so on) in nature. They identify common abstractions (classes) within the domain and design the interaction between those abstractions. The application writer will either specialize the framework classes by inheriting from the abstract classes or by supplying parameters to concrete classes. In either case, much of the design is dictated to the user, leaving only use-specific extensions to be supplied.

While components (strings, lists, and so on) provide opportunities for low-level component reuse, and patterns (Observer, Strategy, and so on [Gamma 1995]) provide for conceptual design reuse, frameworks provide the opportunity for design and component reuse. A set of projects using a common framework will either all benefit from good design and components or will all suffer from a less-than-ideal design and/or faulty components. For this reason, organizations puzzle over whether to build frameworks from previously solved domains (I call them *street sweepers*) or to aid in completing future domains (I call them *snowplows*). It is true that advance frameworks built by snowplows could potentially benefit the projects that follow. However, since these are new domains, there are no guarantees that the first solution picked will be the proper solution. It is only after seeing what worked and what did not that the street sweepers can clearly pick from proven solutions. When it comes to building frameworks and locking into particular designs for a set of projects, I believe we should be street sweepers, using as many completed solutions as possible to determine the best design to be used by future systems. Although application teams routinely borrow architecture ideas from others, I find it extremely difficult to get them to reuse wholesale designs unless there is some evidence of its success. Frameworks tend to eliminate the artistic freedom of application developers. It is much easier for them to swallow if the art is something that they actually appreciate. The miniframeworks discussed here comprise a basic set of capabilities that have been implemented many times. These successful solutions (the unsuccessful ones were well hidden) were investigated and a merged set of solutions was created to provide a common framework for all future projects to develop from. This provides not only a proven framework to build from, but a level of consistency between projects for moving reusable (nonframework) code between them.

27.1 Framework for Building an Object Environment

During my travels through many object-oriented projects, one common theme always occurs—the need to create objects. Although this seems obvious at first, what has often been missed is a common environment to support similar functions performed by the objects. Whether doing GUIs, clients, servers, equipment control, product management, or analysis applications, there exists the generic horizontal domain of *Object*, which requires that certain capabilities be integrated under the control of the application without coupling all objects to the specifics of the application. The packages of abstractions include the following:

Compound status. Ability to pass and return not only status, but complex status information about a function or value.

Debug logging. Ability to log events significant to the programmer and have it under the runtime control of the user of the application.

Configuration. Ability to supply or obtain parameters at runtime from sources such as the command line, shell environment, or configuration file.

Callbacks. Ability to notify subscribers of events without inheriting from the publisher.

Alarms. Ability to publish operator information without being coupled to the distribution and processing mechanisms.

Timers. Ability to create timed callbacks to an object so that a single thread can be shared between two or more actions without blocking the thread.

Application. Ability to perform a coordinated start-up or shutdown between autonomous objects and manage the event loop.

From the object's perspective, these actually look like components. They are slightly higher in the food chain than strings or lists, but still just components. On the other hand, from the infrastructure's perspective, these create miniframeworks that are made up of abstract and concrete classes that get extended and configured by the application.

No matter what higher-level domain framework is being considered, the Object domain has continued to be a dependency. As street sweepers, we have collected many of the past solutions used for these categories and have provided a framework for applications to extend them while coupling the generic objects to nothing more than a foundation class library. This chapter addresses the needs of the generic and CORBA objects [OMG 1995]. There are many documented frameworks on the needs of GUI objects, and these are not repeated here.

27.2 Package Overview

The following sections present an overview for each package of object functionality. They are arranged in the order of coupling, where the earlier sections do not depend on the later sections and the later sections build on the earlier ones. The categories are made up of a varying degree of abstract classes. Most of the categories contain concrete implementations that need only to be selected by the application and configured for application-specific use. Others contain abstract classes that more classically fit the definition of a framework. Each section begins with a brief overview and then is followed up with details from the user's perspective (external view) and then the framework component developer's perspective (internal view). The diagrams provided are meant to capture essential details of each package and are not meant to be a complete design. The code provided is a gist of the details from the real implementation. The framework is implemented in C++, and the presentation assumes some knowledge of that language. However, most of the patterns and architecture can apply to other languages.

27.2.1 Compound Status

The compound status allows objects to pass and return information and status about that information in a consistent manner without relying on global data. This allows many of the object interfaces to keep from being *thread dumb*. The compound status is the only nonextensible class in the miniframework and is included for completeness.

Overview

There are two primary abstractions in the compound status. These are shown in Figure 27.1.

Status. A value-message compound status pair that encapsulates the type of status reported as well as carrying the textual data. This class can be passed, returned, or thrown anywhere status is required.

ReturnValue. A value-status compound pair that encapsulates not only the value, but the validity of the value. This is commonly used when there is an error in a pointer passed or returned during a function without throwing an exception.

Status User Perspective

The most common class to be used is the *Status* class. It contains the normal int status that is expected of a function, as well as an additional text message. The Status objects are usually passed by value so they may remain intact in the event of their clients run-

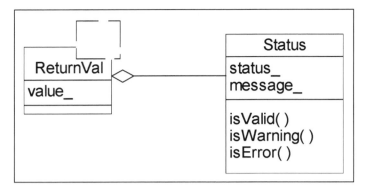

Figure 27.1   Status classes.

ning in separate threads. The following code demonstrates the usage of the Status class as a function return as well as a thrown object. The Status objects are as follows:

```
"Status Callee::method() throw() {
   Status status = 0;    //default to no error
      //detect an error
   status = Status(Status::eWarning,"warning explanation");
   return status;        //return status on stack
}
void MiddleMan::method() throw(Status) {
   Callee callee;
   Status status = callee.method();  //call a method we know
                                     //will only return a status
   if (status.isWarning())
      //try to fix some things
   else if (status.isError())
      throw status;                  //big error
}
void Caller::method() throw() {
   MiddleMan middleMan;
   try {
      middleMan.method();
   }
   catch (Status& status) { //throw by value,
                            //   catch by reference [Meyers 1996]
      cerr << status.message() << "(" << status.value << ")" << endl;
   }
}
```

The other, less common, class to be used is the *ReturnValue<T>* template class. It is used to return status about a returned value and is best used when trying to avoid exceptions. With the ReturnValue<T> class, one can return any value that would normally have been returned, as well as a status of that value.

```
ReturnValue<Element*> List::find(...) {
    //. . . detect and error
  return ReturnValue<Element*>(0,Status(Status::eError,"..text.."));
    //. . . no error located
  return 0;
}


void Caller() throw(Status) {
    //call a method that will either return the element or
    //status explaining error
  ReturnValue<Element*> element = list.find(...);
  if (element.status().isValid())
    (*element).method();      //everything is okay, use element
  else if (element.status().isError())
    throw element.status();  //woops, problem, throw supplied status
  ...
}
```

Status Component Perspective

The Status class basically has just two values, *status* and *message*. These values are augmented with some design rules as to whether the status is valid, a warning, or an error. The Status objects are copied by value so the message text needs to be efficiently copied from one instance to another. Once set, the message text is rarely augmented. Therefore, the copy-on-write [Meyers 1996] techniques employed by most string classes work well here.

```
class Status {
public:
   enum { eValid=0, eWarning=-1, eError=-2 };
   Status(int value=eValid, const String& message="");
      //valid is >=0, warnings are odd and errors are even
   int isValid() const    { return status_ >= 0; }
   int isWarning() const  { return status_ && (status % 2); }
   int isError() const    { return status_ && !(status % 2); }
   //more...
private:
   int status_;
   String message_;
};
```

The ReturnValue<T> class involves a single templated value and a wrapped status about that value. Simple conversion operators allow for the return value to be accessed easily.

```
template <class T>
class ReturnValue {
```

```
        ReturnVal(const T& value, const Status status=Status(0));
        const Status& status() const        { return status_; }
        operator const T&() const           { return value_; }
        const T& operator=(const T& value); { value_=value; return value_; }
        T& operator*()                      { return value_; }
        //more...
    private:
        T value_;
        Status status_;
    };
```

Status Summary

As stated, some classes in the framework are simply concrete building blocks for the remainder of the framework. The Status and ReturnValue<T> classes are concrete implementations that allow both compound status and compound status about a value to be conveniently returned as a group, eliminating the need to cache off status information in global or static variables.

27.2.2 Debug Logging

In almost every object's development, the need exists to output some kind of status or debug information to the programmer to provide a better understanding of how things are going under the hood. A programmer or an application administrator can use the output debug information in the event that an autopsy needs to be performed on a run of the application. These logs are meant to assist the software developer or maintainer. They are not meant to be read by the user.

In producing consistent, informative, coordinated debug information we need help from the object and the application. The object supplies the event and the low-level information to be output. The application determines where and what portions to write. The framework provides the base abstractions and some implementation components to complete this set of functionality without coupling the object to a specific application.

There are three primary abstractions within the debug log package. These are shown in Figure 27.2.

LogEntry. Captures information about an event, including source, level, and text. This class is meant to be concrete, but could be extended if needed.

Logger. Writes information to the designated target. This is an abstract class that will be implemented by a do-nothing logger (NoopLogger), a logger that will simply write data to a stream (StreamLogger), a logger that will write and manage the size of a log (FileLogger), and a log that will integrate messages from difference processes (CORBALogger).

DebugLog. Manages the logger(s) and the form of entries put in the logs. Individual projects will create derived classes (ProjectDebugLog) to configure the debug-logging framework.

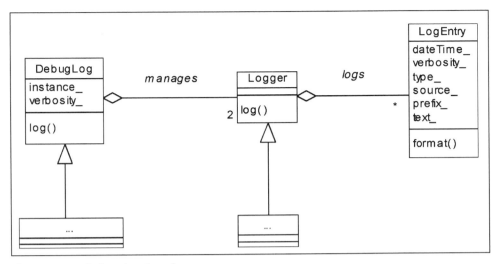

Figure 27.2 Debug logging classes.

Debug Log User Perspective

The users of the debug-logging capability will log their entry information to the DebugLog singleton class through a set of macros. These macros are used to do the following:

- Instantiate temporary instance of the logentry.
- Determine the source file (supplied by the preprocessor directive __FILE__) and line number (supplied by the preprocessor directive __LINE__).
- Tag the type of entry (entry, exit, error, warning, message, stub, and so on).
- Tag the level of entry (application or component).

This usage looks something like the following:

```
void SampleClass::method(int value) {
    AppEntry << METHOD(SampleClass, method)
             << "(value=" << value
             << ")" << Log;
    //do something
    AppExit << METHOD(SampleClass, method)
            << "- result=" << result
            << Log;
}
```

This will provide a log entry that looks something like the following:

```
JDate:Time, FileName:LineNo, Tag>text
```

```
001:080000, SampleClass.C:101,
   APENTR> SampleClass<0x12345678>::method(value=5)
001:080000, SampleClass.C:106,
   APEXIT> SampleClass<0x12345678>::method - result = good
```

The entries will be filtered out of the log if their designated verbosity is greater than the one set within the DebugLog class. This value is set at runtime with the aid of a derived class of DebugLog and the Configuration classes.

There are two levels of entries: application and components. *Application entries* are entries made by objects with a clear overall vision of the application's purpose. *Component entries* are entries made by objects that are much lower in nature and do not have real knowledge of the application's overall purpose. In general, application entries have a louder verbosity than component entries. This allows the end user to quiet the logs of noisy components and retain state information from the application.

There are several types of entries. Using the appropriate one for the job at hand allows for better entry filtering at runtime. The types have the tags *App* or *Cmp* added to them.

Entry. Entry to a function.

Exit. Exit from a function.

Path. Path within a function.

Status. Extra information added to Entry, Exit, and Path.

Stub. Entry into a stubbed method.

Message. Like a cout, it writes the text to standard out and also to the log.

Warning. Possible harm could be occurring.

Error. Harm being done, print to standard out as well as log.

State. Pretty print of object's state.

There are several canned text entries that allow for more consistent logging.

CTOR(ClassName). Expands to ClassName<0xthis>::ctor for constructors.

DTOR(ClassName). Expands to ClassName<0xthis>::dtor for destructors.

METHOD(ClassName, Method). Expands to ClassName<0xthis>::Method for methods.

SMETHOD(ClassName, Method). Expands to ClassName::Method for static methods.

The Log command terminates the entry and puts it in the log.

Debug Log Component Perspective

There are several ways to extend the debug-logging framework:

- Implement loggers
- Configure loggers
- Configure log entries

Implementing loggers is done by inheriting from the abstract Logger class and creating methods that take care of actually writing information to the log and participating in housekeeping.

```
class Logger {
public:
    virtual Status log(const LogEntry& entry)=0;
    virtual long size() const=0;
    virtual Logger& copyFrom(const Logger&,long amount)=0;
    //more..
};
```

The log( ) and size( ) methods are fairly self-explanatory. The copyFrom( ) method is used to create one log into another in the event of a crossover between logs.

To configure the logs, it simply takes a derived class of DebugLog to instantiate a logger (for logged entries) and filtered logger (for entries thrown away) when asked. There are default implementations of these methods in the base class. Normally the default implementations do not know where the logs should be written for a particular project or the naming convention to be used.

```
class DebugLog {
public:
    virtual Status open()
        logger_ = &newLogger(); //use helper methods to get both normal
        filteredLogger_ = &newFilteredLogger(); // and filtered loggers
        return 0;
    }
//more...
    //single properties added as well
protected:
    virtual Logger& newLogger() {          //default helper method impl
        return *new StreamLogger(*new ofstream("debuglog.dat"),1);
    }
    virtual Logger& newFilteredLogger() { //default helper method impl
        return *new NoopLogger;
    }
private:
    Logger *logger_;
    Logger *filteredLogger_;
};
class ProjectDebugLog : public DebugLog {
protected:
    //implement creating and configuring the logs by
    //    overriding helper methods
};
```

Configuring the log entries requires a compile-time override of the macros and templated configurations defined in the DebugLog class. One example of this is when we move a class between a development area and a submitted library area. The log entries for the object are configured to be louder in the development area than they are in the library area. Of note, the AppEntry shown in the "Debug Log User's Perspective" example expands to the following:

```
LogEntry(__FILE__, __LINE__, DebugLogConfig<LogLevel>::EntryTag(), \
    DebugLogConfig<LogLevel>::AppEntryVerbosity)
```

This accomplishes the following:

- Creates an instance of LogEntry with all required parameters. This instance is created as a temporary object and will be eliminated once we get past the Log statement. Project-specific extensions might create derived classes of the concrete LogEntry class to add anything they see necessary for log entries.
- Extracts the file (__FILE__) and line number (__LINE__) information from the preprocessor.
- Specifies the tag to be used in the log for the entry (DebugLogConfig<Log Level>::EntryTag()). This can be changed by the project.
- Specifies the verbosity to be used for the log entry (DebugLogConfig<Log Level>::AppEntryVerbosity). This can be changed by the project.
- Allows the LogLevel class name to be defined at compile time.

Debug Log Summary

As discussed, the debug-logging facility allows high-level as well as low-level objects to log tagged information without being concerned whether the information will ever make it to the logs. This is under runtime control. This, however, still does not allow the programmer total freedom to blindly add logging statements all through the code. Even if filtered, some extra processing will take place to determine at runtime what does and what does not get logged.

One thing not discussed is the issue of logging during static initializers and destructors. Since C++ does not assure the construction and destruction order of global objects when placed in multiple files, the debug-logging mechanism must be ready to log information before it has becomes fully configured and after it has been shut down. This is handled in the real implementation by creating a BufferedLogger that buffers all log entries until the debug log has been initialized. This buffering can be in memory or on disk. Shutdown is another matter. All we can do there is guess at when we think we are done and flush any remaining data. However, we always need to account for late-dying global objects logging their last bit of information unless we are willing to put shutdown code into each file that includes the DebugLog.

27.2.3 Callbacks

Callbacks involve sending messages to objects of an unknown type. Normal object-oriented programming would involve inheriting from the publisher and implementing a *Hook* [Pree 1995] abstract method. This approach can work when there is only one subscriber to handle the event and there are no further derivations of the publisher. Since objects commonly distribute their events to 0 to N subscribers, independent of their inheritance chain, there needs to be a linkage to the Hook through a Strategy pattern [Gamma 1995] rather than a Template method [Gamma 1995]. The strategy approach to callbacks involves the creation of an event handler that the publisher may post to. This is a simple concept; however, the strong typing of C++ requires that base classes be defined to glue the publisher and subscriber together and still maintain proper decoupling.

There are three primary abstractions within the *Callback* package. These are shown in Figure 27.3.

Callback. Defines a function object interface that the publisher will invoke and the subscriber will be notified by. This class is actually a series of callback classes all named Callback1<T1>, Callback2<T1,T2>, and Callback3<T1,T2,T3>, depending on the number of parameters being passed to the callback. This example uses Callback2<T1,T2> and passes it an EventType and void* (for call data).

CallbackAdapter. Defines a derived instance of a Callback that dispatches the event to the subscriber method. This class is actually a matching series of classes for the Callback classes in which the one taking two parameters is defined Callback2 Adapter<Class, Data, T1, T2>. The *Class* and *Data* templated parameters are used to determine the type of Subscriber to notify and the type of client data to pass back to them. The *T1* and *T2* parameters, just like Callback2<T1,T2>, are used to define the type of the parameters passed from the publisher.

Model. Encapsulates the *Subject* [Gamma 1995] functionality of managing and dispatching to multiple subscribers. The publisher usually contains the *Model* class rather than inheriting from it, since we normally know the primary object types that we are registering with.

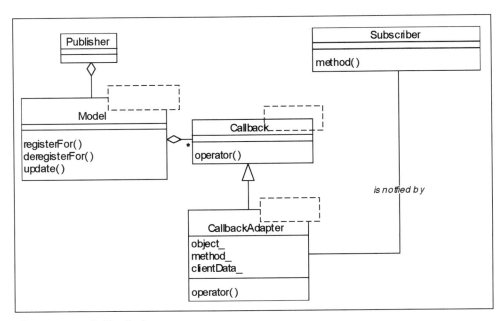

Figure 27.3 Callback classes.

Callback User Perspective

There are several types of users of the callback mechanisms. Some publishers have only a single subscriber and thus do not need the services of a Model class. Some publishers distribute well-known events such as *press* and *de-press* for a button. Other publishers distribute on-the-fly-events such as *request X completed* and *request Y timed out*. Each is touched upon here. First, consider the subscriber, since it rarely changes for each publisher type.

The subscriber classes are going to be notified by either a publisher or a model kind of class. The subscriber, rather than inherit from the publisher and implement a virtual method, will act more like a strategy and be pointed to. The publisher will invoke a method in Callback2<T1,T2>:

```
//publisher or model code
(*subscriber_)(event, eventData);
```

This, of course, is an abstract method (operator( )(T1,T2)) in the Callback2<T1,T2> class that gets implemented in the Callback2Adapter<Class,Data,T1,T2> class. The subscriber could have implemented the inheritance directly from the abstract callback class. However, this would have required an inheritance hierarchy of the subscriber (which may have multiple publishers), and would have either eliminated the client data or caused the publisher to start managing it in parallel with the callback registration. The normal route is to implement the interface through the *Adapter* [Gamma 1995] style interface. The subscriber creates the adapter with the following code:

```
class Subscriber {
public:
      //since the callback is contained by value in the class
      // it must be instantiated during the constructor
   Subscriber(Publisher& p) : cb_(this,&Subscriber::method,"hello") {
         //we register the callback adapter and not ourselves since
         //the callback adapter implements the inheritance from the
         //abstract callback class.
      p.registerFor(EventFilter(1), cb_);
   }
private:
         //the callback adapter will call this method when invoked
         //because we told it to in the constructor.
   void method(EventType event,
      void* callData, const char* clientData);
         //this actually declares the callback adapter, by value,
         //inside the class it is calling.
   Callback2Adapter<Subscriber,const char*, EventType, void*> cb_;
};
```

The publisher to single subscribers simply stores a pointer to that single subscriber within its class. Since there is only one object to be notified, there should not be enough re-entrance problems to warrant using the Model class. The publisher simply does the following:

```
class Publisher {
   typedef int EventType;
   Publisher(Callback<EventType, void*> *subscriber);
   //methods where something has happened
   {
       (*subscriber_)(event,callData);
          //a call to subscriber_->operator()(event,callData);
   }
private:
   Callback2<EventType, void*> *subscriber_;
};
```

The publisher of multiple events simply must add the Model class by either inheriting or delegating to a contained instance. Macros within the Model class definition make the delegation very easy and eliminate the need for a specific inheritance. The addition of the Model class takes care of cases where the publisher gets registration and deregistration requests while in the middle of an event dispatch to one of its subscribers.

```
class PublisherToN {
public:
   typeDef int EventType;
       //this macro declares a protected Model class with the name
       //subscribers_. It declares public method that directs all
       //function calls to the private instance for processing.
   DECLARE_MODEL2(EventType, void*, subscribers_)
   //methods where something has happened
   {
       subscribers_->changed(event, eventData);
   }
};
```

The publisher of well-known events simply adds some public static properties to its class that allows the subscribers to check to see which event they have been posted.

```
class PublisherWellKnown {
public:
   typedef int EventType;
   DECLARE_MODEL2(EventType, void*, subscribers_)
   static const EventType& pressEvent()   { return pressEvent_; }
   static const EventType& depressEvent() { return depressEvent_; }
   //some method where press event occurs
   {
       subscribers_->changed(pressEvent(), 0);
   }
private:
   static EventType pressEvent_;
   static EventType depressEvent_;
};
```

The publisher of on-the-fly events must maintain a system of keeping events unique and registering clients when they make a request. The outstanding client requests are held in the Model waiting for a reply. The client passes in their callback during the request and an on-the-fly event is created to track the transaction. This event is passed back to the client so clients may know why they are called later or if they need to cancel the request. The dispatch to the client will pass the call data along and automatically deregister the callback if there are no further needs to post that event.

```
class PublisherOnTheFly {
public:
    typedef int EventType;
    DECLARE_MODEL2(EventType, void*, clients_)
    typedef callback2<EventType, void*> Client;
    ReturnValue<EventType*> request(..., Client &client_) {
        //assuming the request is valid...
        EventType *event = &nextEvent();     //get the next event
        clients_.registerFor(client,*event);//register them for callback
            //now we need to remember, somehow the event to post
            //when the request completes
        return event;    //so they know what they will be called with
    }
protected:
    void dispatchCompletion(const EventType& event, void* callData) {
        clients_->changed(event, callData);//notify waiting client
        clients_->removeAllFor(event);     //we are done with that event
    }
private:
    static int nextID_;
    static EventType& nextEvent() {
        return *new EventType(nextID_++);
    }
};
```

Callback Component Perspective

The internal perspective of the callbacks is simple once one understands virtual functions, operator overloading, templates, and the adapter pattern. There is a specific callback class created for the number of parameters being passed by the publisher. The callback class is templated on the types of these parameters. The parameters are passed to a pure virtual function, implemented through the operator() overload.

```
template <class T1, class T2>
class Callback2 {
    virtual void operator()(T1 p1, T2 p2)=0;
};
```

The callback adapter class stores off any overhead for calling the client object. This is usually a pointer to the object, a pointer to the method to call, and a set of client data to pass back to the client so that it knows a context for which it has been called. The callback adapter classes implement the required inheritance from the callback class. A callback adapter class is created for the number of arguments a publisher will be passing. The callback adapter class will be templated not only on the type of data it will be passing through, but also on the type of object it is calling and the type of client data it will hold or return.

```
template <class Class, class Data, class T1, class T2>
class Callback2Adapter : public Callback2<T1, T2> {
public:
        //declare a type of method we will be calling
    typedef void (Class::*Method)(T1, T2, Data);
        //we need to know the object, method to call, and context
    Callback2Adapter(Class &object, Method method, Data clientData);
        //this is where we adapt from callback to client
    virtual void operator()(T1 p1, T2 p2) {
        (object_.*method)(p1, p2, clientData);
    }
private:
    Class &object_;
    Method method_;
    Data clientData_;
};
```

These classes are provided by the callback package. However, the real clients and subscribers may make their own inheritance from the callback classes.

Callback Summary

The brief overview of the callback mechanisms provides some insight of how to flexibly connect a publisher (of varying types) to a subscriber without the publisher knowing or having to manage much of the subscriber information. Much of the management is done in the Model and callback adapter classes.

One aspect not really discussed is filtering. Events are passed to clients if they match a criterion. Either the client or the Model must filter the events before passing them to the client. This is an additional piece of data that can be placed in the callback adapter so that it does not pass on events that are not for its client.

Clients will get callbacks from multiple sources. The events passed to the clients in these examples have been simplified into ints. This would not provide enough detail for a single client to distinguish replies from two publishers. The distinction can be done by the Model passing itself during the invocation or by the client adding ID information in the client data. However, one can also create a class out of the EventType and add domain information within the events that would be unique per publisher.

And, last, recursion and threads. What normally happens during a callback is that the client changes registration information about itself, someone you have already called, or someone you are about to call. The client may have also deleted you during the callback. The Model class handles such recursion and needs to allow for reentrances within its current thread.

27.2.4 Alarms

Whereas the debug logging is almost exclusively for software status reporting, the Alarms package creates a small framework for generating, describing, and distributing end-user information. Alarms are usually discovered by low-level objects and must be reported at a level where they cannot be coupled to the environment of the targeted applications. Alarms are usually generated with much less frequency than debug information and are of interest to a much broader audience.

There are three primary abstractions in the Alarm package. These are shown in Figure 27.4.

Alarm. Captures information about an event, including source, ID, text, and so on. This is meant to be a concrete class; however, it is open to extension.

AlarmMgr. A *Singleton* [Gamma 1995] base class interface for accepting alarms and managing alarm distribution. Anyone generating an alarm will add them to the alarm manager, who will distribute them to the appropriate subscribers. These subscribers can be storage mechanisms or displays and are notified through the Model framework from the Callback package. The Alarm package is a prime example usage of the Callback package.

CORBAAlarmMgr. An alarm manager that adds distributed processing extensions to the intraprocess capability. The Alarm is issued to distributed clients through the Object Management Group (OMG)'s Common Object Services Event Service. CORBAAlarmMgrs will be clients of other CORBAAlarmMgrs through the event service.

Alarm User Perspective

The generators of Alarms add their information to the framework by using the AlarmMgr as a factory for creating the Alarm object and adding it to the appropriate

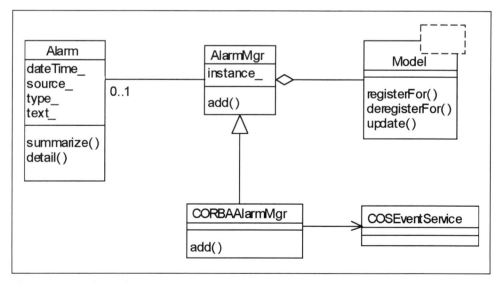

Figure 27.4   Alarm classes.

places without coupling the generator to the distribution techniques or subscribers. The generator code invokes one of several macros defined in the AlarmMgr class. These macros create an Alarm with an error (software or hardware error), alert (problem domain error), event (significant event occurrence), or progress (status of long-running process) by passing file, line, and alarm type to the AlarmMgr factory function. The AlarmMgr adds high-level process information to the Alarm, while project-specific derived classes of the AlarmMgr may add details of their own. The returned Alarm has additional information added to it through a streamed interface of type-tagged values. Particular tagged values consist of *AlarmID* (for registering alarms with user manuals), *AlarmSummary* (a short, one-line summary of the alarm), and *AlarmDetail* (a lengthy, multiline clarification of the alarm). At the completion of the line, the generator code logs the information to the AlarmMgr using the Log, a manipulator object (similar to the C++ iostream endl or flush manipulators). The AlarmMgr class distributes the alarms to the appropriate locations. These locations are extensions to the framework.

```
AlarmError << AlarmID("...")
           << AlarmSummary("error processing file")
           << AlarmDetail("...") << Log;
AlarmAlert << AlarmID("...")
           << AlarmSummary("calculation error") << Log;
```

Alarm Component Perspective

The Alarm framework can be extended in several ways:

- Alarm content
- Alarm subscribers
- Distributed alarm managers

Alarm content is impacted by having a derived class of the singleton AlarmMgr class implement the factory method. The content changes are limited to high-level process information since the low-level content is added by the generator and not the factory.

```
class ProjectAlarmMgr : public AlarmMgr {
public:
    Alarm& createAlarm(const string& file, int line, ...stuff...) {
        return ProjectAlarm(...all that data...)
    }
};
```

Intraprocess Alarm subscribers are added by registering for new Alarm events from the AlarmMgr. One example of an Alarm subscribers might log the entries into a database, and another might be a window on someone's display.

```
class AlarmLogger {
    AlarmLogger() : cb_(*this, &AlarmLogger::newAlarm, 0) {
```

```
AlarmMgr::instance().registerFor(&cb_,AlarmMgr::newAlarmEvent());
   }
   void newAlarm(AlarmEvent, Alarm* alarm, void*) {
      //called when new alarm added to AlarmMgr - now just log it
   }
private:
   Callback2Adapter<AlarmLogger, void*, AlarmEvent, Alarm*> cb_;
};
```

Extending the Alarm framework for distributed processing is straightforward. One could either add the distributed processing as an Alarm subscriber as with the Alarm-Logger or create a derived class of the AlarmMgr. The inherited approach seems to be the better approach since it keeps the distribution of alarms within the same (layered into inherited classes) object. The CORBAAlarmMgr derives from the AlarmMgr class and waits for anyone to either add an alarm or register for alarms. Added alarms are sent to the appropriate event channel. These same event channels are subscribed to when an object within the process is interested in hearing those alarms.

Alarm Summary

In implementing Alarms, developers need to provide a balance between rigid, registered text and flexible, descriptive text. Having alarm text come out of a standard file can help standardize a system output at the risk of having it not be able to describe this particular situation. The actual approach taken by the framework is to standardize the summary text and leave the detailed text up to the programmer to fill out. That way we get some uniformity and the ability to fully describe the impact at the same time.

27.2.5 Configuration

Class implementers are always looking for ways to defer sizes, ranges, values, and so on, to runtime parameters under the control of the administrator of the application. The Configuration package integrates several configuration sources together for the application so that low-level objects may be able to have values defined for them at runtime.

There are three primary abstractions in the Configuration package. These are shown in Figure 27.5.

ConfigurationElement. A data-value pair obtained from a configuration source.

ConfigurationSource. An abstract base class of data sources supporting find first/last/all types of queries. Configuration is one of the inheritors, implementing a *Composite* [Gamma 1995] of ConfigSources. Other ConfigSources are the command line, configuration file, and shell environment. Each of these sources are named in case the client wants a value from a particular source.

Configuration. A Singleton manager for the various configuration sources.

Configuration User Perspective

To use the configuration classes, the client programmer simply defines a set of named tags that will be located through a regular expression match. The client calls a global

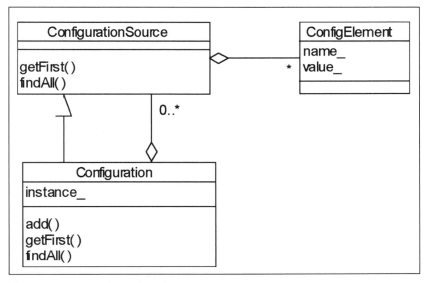

Figure 27.5 Configuration classes.

function, declared in the Configuration module, which resolves to the singleton and returns the values of the requested expression. The client passes in the expression, a default value in case it is not found, and the direction to search.

```
string user = Value("system.user","guest"); //direction def=forward
```

The named tags are usually hierarchical, so one might have a system.user as well as a system.host or request.user. The expression could attempt to locate the first *user. With regular expressions, the list of possibilities is endless and outside the scope of the configuration classes. The default value is the value returned to the caller in the event that there is no defined value for the tag. The direction will obviously impact which value is found first or the list order of values found in the event that there is more than one match. The return value is a string and must be converted to another form by the caller:

```
int age = atoi(Value("user.age","0"));
```

In the event that users would like to know not only the value of the entry that matched, but would also like to know the name of the entity, more robust services are defined in the Configuration class itself:

```
ConfigElement *element = Configuration::instance().findFirst(...);
if (element) {
    element->name();
}
```

If users would like a list of several elements, they may also return not just the first, but all matching elements:

```
List<ConfigElement*> elements = Configuration::instance().findAll(...);
```

If users need a particular source, such as the command line, they can access that source directly:

```
ConfigSource *cmdLine = Configuration::instance().source("CmdLine");
cout << "argc=" << ((CommandLine*)cmdLine)->argc();
```

Configuration Component Perspective

Internally, we can extend the Configuration framework by:

- Providing configuration sources
- Configuring the configuration

We create new configuration sources by implementing the abstract interfaces of the ConfigSource:

```
class ConfigFile : public ConfigSource {
public:
    virtual string name() const { return "ConfigFile"; }
    virtual string getFirst(...all that stuff...) {
        //try to locate a match to the expression -or- return the
        //default if we fail
    }
};
```

We configure the Configuration by either creating a derived class of the Configuration or just calling the add() method to add instantiated configurations.

Configuration Summary

Adding the Configuration package greatly reduces our reliance on programmer-selected defaults and puts real power in the hands of system administrators. Its simple user interface, flexibility, and extensibility (without coupling the client to the implementation) makes it quite popular.

27.2.6 Timers

Threaded applications are becoming increasingly common these days. However, this implementation technique can be very error prone and unnecessary in many situations. There are many times when a single thread can be shared between cooperating objects. The objects perform their actions upon request and activate timers to initiate a timed callback to regain control when necessary (such as a request timeout) without blocking the application.

There are two primary abstractions in the Timer package. These are shown in Figure 27.6.

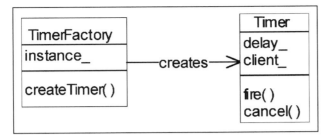

Figure 27.6   Timer classes.

Timer. The abstract base class of something that will fire after a set delay. This class is specialized by a concrete timer based on the specific event loop employed.

TimerFactory. A Singleton, Abstract Factory [Gamma 1995] for creating event-loop-specific timers. This class is specialized by a concrete timer factory based on the specific event loop employed.

Timer User Perspective

Using the timer abstractions makes the client code much more portable since it is the application classes that will decide the concrete implementation of the Timer and not the client. The client simply locates the TimerFactory through a Singleton reference and requests that a Timer be created with the passed-in parameters. One of those parameters will be the callback or callback adapter from the callback package. The other is the number of seconds to wait before being called back. The Timer returned is configured to run in the current environment and is activated by the start() method. The user's callback is called with the expired timer when it fires. The Timer can be reactivated by the user at that time. Cleanup is done by the user. The user must keep track of the Timer in the event that the cycle must be stopped.

```
class WakeUp {
public:
    WakeUp() : cb_(*this, &WakeUp::kick, 0) {
        //create a timer that will call us in 10 secs
        myTimer_ = TimerFactory::instance().createTimer(cb_,10);
        myTimer_->start();
    }
    void kick(Timer* timer, void*) {
        //do something now that we've been woken up
        myTimer_->set(10);
        myTimer_->start();
    }
    ~WakeUp() {
        //ok, now we have to stop this thing
        myTimer_->cancel();
        delete myTimer_;
```

```
    }
private:
    Callback1Adapter<WakeUp,void*,Timer*> cb_;
    Timer *myTimer_;
};
```

Timer Component Perspective

Extending the Timer framework is a simple matter of creating a tandem of a concrete timer and a concrete timer factory. The concrete timer knows how to communicate with the event loop implementation. The concrete factory will know which Timer to create. The application will install the proper timer factory at start-up.

```
class Timer {
public:
    Timer(int secs, Callback<Timer*> &client);
    virtual void start()=0;
    virtual void cancel()=0;
    virtual void fire() {
        (*client_)(this);
    }
    virtual void set(int secs) {
        secs_ = secs; // get ready, but wait for start()
    }
protected:
    int secs_;
    Callback1<Timer*> *client_;
};

class ConcreteTimer : public Timer {
public:
    virtual void start()  { /* start the countdown process */ }
    virtual void cancel() { /* kill the timer and just pause */ }
};

class TimerFactory {
    virtual Timer& createTimer(int secs, Callback1<Timer*> client)=0
    //more...singleton stuff
};

class ConcreteTimerFactory : public TimerFactory {
public:
    virtual Timer& createTimer(int secs, Callback1<Timer*> client) {
        return *new ConcreteTimer(secs, client);
    }
};
```

Timer Summary

It is up to the concrete implementations of the Timer and TimerFactory classes to determine how to regain control of the thread and fire the timer. This can be implemented with a separate thread within the concrete classes or by interfacing with other event loop mechanisms. The interface to timed events within the X Windows event loop is straightforward; however, the CORBA event loop does not seem to directly support timers. In any event, using an abstract Timer interface and a singleton TimerFactory interface, we shield the users of the timers from the specifics of how this is being accomplished.

27.2.7 Application Events

As objects become more independent, there becomes a need to develop a startup and shutdown protocol between them and the application. The application package defines properties related to startup and shutdown events as well as maintaining control of the event loop.

There are three primary abstractions in the Application package. These are shown in Figure 27.7.

Application. This is a singleton base class that defines the basic functionality of an application that does not rely on X Windows or CORBA. It has abstract methods of run( ) (start the event loop) and terminate( ) (end the event loop).

CORBAApplication. This is a derived application class that integrates CORBA concepts into the application responsibilities.

XApplication. This is a derived application class that integrates X Windows concepts into the application responsibilities.

The CORBAApplication and XApplication class interfaces also get integrated into a collective implementation. This, however, is done by the actual application.

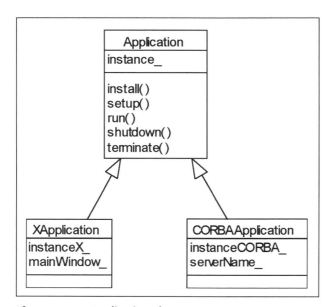

Figure 27.7 Application classes.

Application User Perspective

An object makes use of the Application package by registering for various events that will be published:

setupEvent. Configuration is known; it's okay to start interacting with other global objects.

runEvent. The application is totally set up and is about to go into the event loop.

shutdownEvent. Start shutting down objects under your control and prepare to terminate.

terminateEvent. Terminate without communicating with any global objects.

The following is an example of the registration process. The Sample class is an example of an independent object (such as a GUI editor window) that needs to do the following:

- Know when it can read the configuration (by registering for the setup event)
- Send out a request before the program enters the event loop (by registering for the run event)
- Have some time to close out dirty displays (by registering for the shutdown event)
- Get a last notification before the application terminates (by registering for the terminate event)

The registration to the application does not use the singleton instance( ) method. This is because many of the registrations will take place before we have an Application in place. The registrations are held in a static Model within the Application class rather than as an instance variable as in previous usages.

```
class Sample {
                        //create all the callback adapters
    Sample() : setup_(*this, &Sample::setup,0),
            run_(*this, &Sample::run, 0),
            shutdown_(*this, &Sample::shutdown, 0),
            terminate_(*this, &Sample::terminate, 0) {
        //now register the adapters for selected events
    Application::registerFor(
                        Application::setupEvent(),&setup_);
    Application::registerFor(
                        Application::runEvent(),&run_);
    Application::registerFor(
                        Application::shutdownEvent(),&shutdown_);
    Application::registerFor(
                        Application::terminateEvent(),&terminate_);
    }
    //read config and get
    void setup(Model*,EventType, void* ,void*); ready to go
    //last chance to do anything
    void run(Model*,EventType,void*,void*);
```

```
        //clean up our dirty objects and terminate
    void shutdown(Model*,EventType,void*,void*);
        //too late, get out now!!!
    void terminate(Model*,EventType,void*,void*);
  public:
    typedef Callback3Adapter<Sample,void*,Model*,EventType,void*>
                                            CallbackAdapter;

    CallbackAdapter setUp_;
    CallbackAdapter run_;
    CallbackAdapter shutdown_;
    CallbackAdapter terminate_;
  };
```

The main() writer simply puts together the following code. It demonstrates the usage of a global object and a couple of local objects. The global object will register with the Application class before we actually construct an Application object. That, again, is the reason for making the Model *static* in the Application class.

```
Sample object1;      //this is a global object, alive before main & app
main(int argc, char** argv) {
      //setup the application to run a CORBA event loop
    Application::install(new CORBAApplication("ServerName"));
      //create a few independent objects
    Sample object1;
    Sample object2;
      //tell everybody its time to read the config
    if (Application::instance().setup(argc,argv).isValid()) {
        //now go into the main loop
      Application::instance().run();
    }
  }
```

Application Component Perspective

To extend the Application framework, one must either derive from the Application class to implement a new main loop or tie together additional concepts with the XApplication and/or CORBAApplication classes. In either case, it will be the writer of main that instantiates the correct implementation.

Application Summary

One problem that was uncovered in early implementations of the Application classes was making them too knowledgeable. This is not a class that knows what a program does. It is an abstraction about what is available within the program, and it allows others to extend and implement that behavior. It is important to determine what will be configuration dependent. If the type of application to be instantiated comes from the configuration, then we have to initialize the configuration before constructing the application.

27.3 Summary

No matter what application domain we set out to design and implement, having a good handle on the object environment helps considerably. Early implementations of the environment, lacking a framework approach, resulted in follow-on projects having to modify source code to configure the classes for their areas. Newer miniframework designs have identified the firm areas (Template [Pree 1995]) of the components and placed them in base classes, while providing Hook [Pree 1995] definitions for either derived classes or strategy classes to implement. I don't really consider what has been presented so far as a full-fledged framework. However, it is definitely the basis of many other more robust frameworks and can be used to demonstrate some of the useful qualities of a framework on a small scale. Some of the areas discussed have been fully developed and used in several areas. Others are still in the theory state. It is hard to find sufficient time to address framework issues over specific project deadlines. Extensions to the environment are adding the dynamic loading of objects and beefing up thread safety. In developing the designs, I have found the referenced texts incredibly helpful.

27.4 References

[Gamma 1995] Gamma, E., R. Helm, R. Johnson, and J. Vlissides. *Design Patterns: Elements of Reusable Object-Oriented Software*. Reading, MA: Addison-Wesley, 1995.

[Meyers 1996] Meyers, S. *More Effective C++*. Reading, MA: Addison-Wesley, 1996.

[OMG 1995] Object Management Group. *The Common Object Request Broker: Architecture and Specification, Revision 2.0*. Framingham, MA: Object Management Group, 1995.

[Pree 1995] Pree, W. *Design Patterns for Object-Oriented Software Development*. Reading MA: Addison-Wesley, 1995.

CHAPTER 28

A Multimodeling
Simulation Framework

Object-oriented physical multimodeling (OOPM) is an application framework providing components and patterns [Johnson 1997] for modeling and simulation. For modeling, OOPM components take the form of multimodel units (MMUs), including a number of predefined MMUs for queuing, control, and geometry management. Patterns include class relations, containers, fuzzy types, multimodel topology, and heterogeneous multimodel hierarchy, all discussed here. OOPM handles details of translating models to programs. At simulation runtime, OOPM provides control of simulation program execution, event scheduling, and communication between the simulation program and output visualization. Two-dimensional output visualization support includes x-y plots, histograms, and moving sprites.

   OOPM embodies an approach to modeling and simulation that not only tightly couples a model author into the evolving modeling and simulation process through an intuitive human-computer interface (HCI), but also helps the model author do any or all of the following: (1) think clearly about, better understand, or elucidate a model; (2) participate in a collaborative modeling effort; (3) repeatedly refine a model as required to achieve adequate fidelity at minimal development cost; (4) build integrated models using existing proven small models as subsystems; (5) start from a conceptual model that is intuitively clear to domain experts, and unambiguously and automatically convert this to a simulation program; (6) create or change a simulation program without being a programmer; and (7) perform simulation model execution and present simulation results in a meaningful way that facilitates the other objectives mentioned here. In some cases modeling alone, without executing a simulation program, suffices to achieve the model author's objectives, which may be to learn about or better understand a phenomenon or system, or to communicate with colleagues. Usually, however, a model author wishes not only to model but also to construct and execute a simulation program to empirically validate the model based on observed behavior, to select or adjust various parameters and values and observe their effect, to measure performance, or to gauge model fidelity and assess its adequacy.

Figure 28.1 is a metamodel for modeling and simulation, highlighting distinctions among modeling, constructing simulation programs, and executing simulations. Model authors collaborate to develop a model, from which a simulation program is constructed, translated to executable form, and executed. The results are visualized or otherwise analyzed. Simulation programs developed directly without a platform-independent specification (model) are problematic: They are vulnerable to platform or language change, with low readability, low extensibility, low maintainability, and low reuse potential. Even when modeling is used, problems remain: expensive duplication of effort, low quality of reproduced external subsystems, limitations in expressivity of modeling frameworks, and limitations on the feasibility envelope imposed by the complexity of the development process. Currently the modeling and simulation (M&S) community suffers all these problems. The efficiency and productivity of model authors is low, evidence of this being that work usually cannot be reused or readily integrated into larger new systems [Dahmann 1998]. These problems propagate to every realm where modeling and simulation are used. When a model author sketches a whiteboard model with annotations and uses this to describe to programmers the design of a simulation program to be written, there are pitfalls. The programmers write a program, *but there is not necessarily a relation between the model described and the program produced*. More formal approaches such as requirements specifications and a traceability matrix reduce ambiguity but often introduce an unmanageably complex representation and a textual tabular format that is decidedly nonintuitive.

With OOPM, the model author uses visual metaphors in a framework for constructing the model, from which a simulation program is unambiguously and automatically built. Advantages include (1) built-in model validation; (2) partial automation of the development process; (3) extensibility and flexibility to accommodate unexpected change [Booch 1994]; (4) reduction in development time; and (5) the ability to model source systems of greater inherent complexity by integrating tried-and-true existing

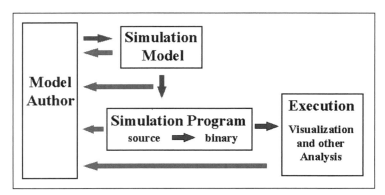

Figure 28.1   Metamodel for modeling and simulation.

models as subsystems, because "a complex system that works is invariably found to have evolved from a simpler system that worked. A complex system designed from scratch never works and cannot be patched up to make it work" [Booch 1994].

The extent of detail in a model reflects the abstraction perspective. Model refinement can produce greater fidelity, if required by the model author's abstraction perspective or by external criteria. *Multimodeling* is a recent development [Fishwick-Zeigler 1992, 1993, 1996] that provides multiple levels of abstraction to represent geometry and especially the dynamic behavior of a model. Multimodeling facilitates model development (as previously enumerated), integration and reuse of object-oriented distributed simulation models, and extensibility of the framework itself to accommodate future model types.

Figure 28.2 shows the elements of OOPM. The model author is interacting with the visual human-computer interface (HCI). The HCI has two graphical user interfaces (GUIs), each supporting a different purpose: *Modeler,* which is the model author interface (MAI), and *Scenario,* a simulation runtime visualization enabler. The model author interacts with Modeler to design the model. Modeler relies on the *distributed model repository* (DMR, discussed later) for model definitions. Scenario activates and initializes simulation execution (which we name *Engine*). Scenario maintains synchronous interaction with Engine, displaying Engine output in a form meaningful to the user, optionally allowing the user to interact with Engine, including modifying simulation parameters and changing the rate of simulation progress.

There are two kinds of distributed modeling and simulation: distributed model definitions with various model components defined on different hosts and distributed execution running simultaneously on a number of hosts. OOPM focuses on the first. The OOPM library consists of the DMR and the *mobile object store* (MOS). The MOS holds object data, and the DMR holds metadata. The DMR stores model definitions

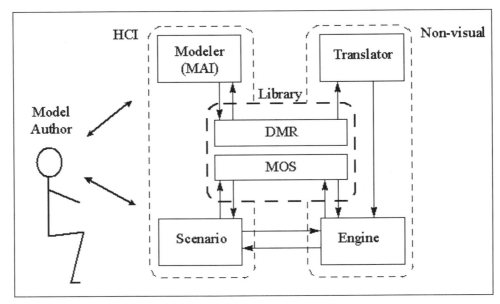

Figure 28.2 Elements of OOPM; principal interactions indicated by arrows.

defined and used by both Modeler and Translator. Models and model components are available for browsing and reuse. Class libraries, such as sets for modeling collections and popular geometries for spatial models, are available to the model author. Model definitions can be distributed over several locations.

The DMR hides location-dependent details. This facilitates collaboration and distributed modeling. Reuse of models, classes, and objects is thus mediated by the DMR. (Reuse examples appear later in this chapter.) The DMR supports the modeling application framework with more than just a class library: Classes are related in such a way that a class is not used in isolation but within a design encouraged and supported by the framework. The DMR stores not only a collection of classes available for reuse, but also relations among models, classes, and objects, and for geometry and behavior.

The language-neutral model definition by which Modeler and Translator communicate with the DMR uses the Distributed Multimodeling Language (DMML) developed by the authors and described elsewhere [Cubert 1998]. The MOS does for objects much of what the DMR does for models. The way the MOS works with Engine and Scenario is similar to the way the DMR works with Modeler and Translator. The MOS manages object persistence. The MOS is architecturally important; however, as our focus is on modeling and most MOS issues relate to simulation runtime, our MOS implementation is, to date, minimal. In Figure 28.1, Translator is the arrow between the simulation model and the simulation program: Translator gets from the DMR a language-neutral model definition produced by Modeler and maps it to a computer program for the simulation corresponding to the model, in a Translator Target Language (TTL). The TTL is presently C++; potentially, TTL can be any language. The C++ simulation program emitted by Translator is called Engine. Once compiled and linked with Engine runtime support, the Engine executable program is activated under control of Scenario.

To accompany explanations that follow, a landscape ecology model is used as the example throughout this chapter. The model is set in Florida's Everglades and is concerned with population models of apple snails within a two-dimensional spatial array. Apple snails live on sawgrass and are the staple food of the snail kite, a bird that is an endangered species. Reuse of the apple snail model in a snail kite model will assist in developing the snail kite model. The snail kite model may help scientists learn how to prevent extinction of the snail kite, within an even larger model, whose objective is to study ways of preserving the Everglades ecosystem.

The balance of this chapter is organized as follows : Discussion of some related work is followed by an explanation of the object orientation of OOPM. Then we discuss how and why OOPM employs multimodeling. A description of the visual elements of OOPM such as conceptual models and dynamic behavior models is followed by a description of the nonvisual elements of OOPM such as Translator and the DMR. Finally, we state our plans and conclusion.

28.1 An Overview

Research efforts, software engineering tools, and object-oriented commercial M&S products abound. OOPM differs from each of these that have been surveyed in one or more of the following ways: (1) Our primary focus is on the architecture and representation for distributed model reuse, (2) our model author interface is wholly graphical, and (3) multiple-level behavioral abstractions may be represented in any of several alternative ways, each with a formal basis in the literature and each with a community of advocates.

In the Discrete Event System Specifications (DEVS) system [Zeigler 1995, 1997], there are hierarchical behavior models based on proven formalism and a one-to-one relation between model specification formalism and simulator functionality. Behavior is modeled with one kind of dynamic model based on state machines. OOPM, in contrast, provides five kinds of dynamic multimodels that may be arbitrarily mixed and matched recursively (heterogeneous multimodeling). We are talking with the DEVS team to determine whether we can combine the modeling strength of OOPM with the strength of the DEVS formalisms and its support for a simulation runtime infrastructure.

Unified Modeling Language (UML) is an object-oriented analysis and design (OOA&D) technique that derives principally from two antecedents: the Booch method [Booch 1994] and the object modeling technique (OMT) proposed by Rumbaugh. A useful survey of these and other object-oriented analysis and design techniques as they apply to M&S is given by [Hill 1992; Hill-Vigor 1997]. Ways in which UML differs from the OOPM visual modeling environment include the following: (1) UML dynamics are through one type of dynamic model—state charts—whereas OOPM provides five kinds of dynamic multimodels that may be arbitrarily mixed and matched recursively (heterogeneous multimodeling), and (2) UML state charts are associated with a whole class, whereas an OOPM dynamic multimodel is associated with each method of a class.

OOPM is targeted at making distributed model reuse practical in a visual setting. JavaBeans, which provides reusable components in a visual builder tool, shares many of our objectives: It has a visual interface, components may be brought from anywhere, and components are self-identifying and self-configuring. The JavaBeans GUI Bean Box bean builder tool has three areas: a toolbox, a property sheet, and a design area where applications are built by associating events of one bean with methods of another. Differences from OOPM include the following: (1) There is no concept analogous to the DMR, (2) nor is there a concept analogous to DMML (the OOPM model specification language), and (3) the GUI is not a modeling framework and does not represent multimodel semantics.

28.2 Object-Oriented Approach to Modeling Geometry and Dynamics

Classes, objects, and relations that form the conceptual model in the OOPM digital world correspond to elements and relations in the source system. This is standard object-oriented methodology. This approach (1) facilitates object identification, which is capturing elements of meaning that must be represented in the model; (2) is intuitive to model authors; and (3) serves as documentation that makes a model more self-explanatory to anyone with application domain expertise. Most model authors find at least one of the OOPM dynamic behavior multimodel types to be intuitive and to be a natural way to express behavior of the source system.

During class and object identification, the model author is guided to explicitly recognize the nature of relations among classes. Among these relations are specialization, generalization, and aggregation [Booch 1994; Riel 1996], as depicted in Figure 28.3. *Specialization* is the relationship of derived class (subclass) to base class (superclass). An example from biological taxonomy is:

Conch and snail are kinds of gastropod mollusk.

Generalization is just the reverse:

Gastropod mollusks include whelk and periwinkle.

Specialization often happens when one needs to extend a class in one or several directions; generalization often happens after the fact, as common natures are recognized and factored out. Specialization and generalization are associated with inheritance, in which a derived class possesses characteristics of its base class; for example, mollusks have a foot, so Snail, a subclass of Mollusk, also has a foot. Coplien [Coplien 1992] recognizes inheritance as a solution domain concept that can be used for subtyping and for code reuse. Subtyping has corresponding meaning in the source system; code reuse does not. Coplien suggests public derivation for subtyping and private derivation for code reuse. Delegation (which implies aggregation) is sometimes better than inheritance for code reuse. In what Coplien calls "forwarding," a weak form of delegation, a selected subset of constituent class methods is made accessible via methods of the aggregate class. *Aggregation* comprises not one but numerous overlapping relations, including *containment, composition, usage,* and *association* [Booch 1994; Riel 1996, Zeigler 1997], among others. Some examples are:

A marsh ecosystem contains a matrix of patches; a patch consists of water and biomass.

A snail uses sawgrass for food.

A patch is associated with climate and hydrology.

Sometimes deciding which relation applies is problematic; relations should be examined in the context of the source system. Sometimes distinctions cannot be drawn

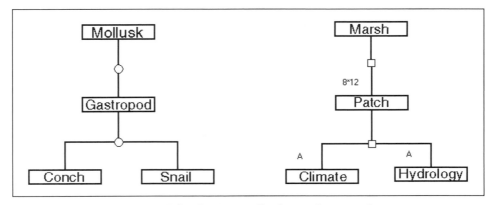

Figure 28.3   Relations: specialization/generalization and aggregation.

with certainty, but models can still be elucidated adequately without deciding the issue in one particular *right* way, as long as decisions are reasonable and consistent. Benefit arises from thinking about, discussing, and categorizing relations. A reasonable amount of effort spent here is worthwhile; the benefit is as much from the process as from the results. An example of drawing such distinctions is *containment by reference* versus *association by referential attribute* [Riel 1996]. Both are pointers, so there is no implementation issue; but the difference is regarding lifetimes: In the first case, the object contained by reference should live and die with the containing object; in the second case, the objects have independent lifetimes. Drawing this distinction may be important to the model author.

As the model author performs object identification through the OOPM MAI, a conceptual model is constructed. This visual representation is, like the whiteboard model mentioned previously, useful for communication with coworkers. Elucidating the classes, objects, and relations, the model author gains understanding as a result. The process may surface questions and ambiguities that must be addressed to achieve modeling or simulation objectives. When these matters are resolved, the completed model definition is unambiguously and automatically convertible to a simulation program in C++. The model author is thus tightly coupled into the modeling and simulation development loop.

OOPM permits attributes of each class to be primitive data types (integer, real, and string) or user-defined abstract data types (ADTs). ADTs are defined through classes in the model. Aggregation is represented by making constituent elements attributes of the aggregating class. The best representation depends on cardinality (the number of items of a constituent type, such as the 96 patches in the marsh of Figure 28.3), whether cardinality is known in advance and fixed or is inherently variable, and the nature of the relation, as previously discussed. *Cardinality* choices include (1) *many,* which causes a container to be created to hold contained objects of the aggregated class; (2) a numeric cardinality, such as *96,* which also causes a container to be created but additionally automatically populates the container with the designated number of contained anonymous objects; (3) *A,* indicating an association, meaning a referential attribute, which is a reference (pointer) to a named object whose lifetime is independent of the lifetime of the object of the aggregating class; and (4) *V,* indicating containment by value, which generates a value attribute within the aggregating class.

When the cardinality of a constituent class is 1, an ADT attribute will be created in the aggregating class, but a choice remains between the value and the referential. The *lifetime test* is one decision criterion: If the constituent object lifetime is independent of the lifetime of the aggregating object, then an association, represented by a reference or pointer, is best. It is also possible for the model author to choose a referential attribute when lifetimes coincide, but referential attributes require more management than do value attributes, so value attributes are chosen whenever possible.

A second criterion is the *name test.* If the object of the aggregated class needs to be a named object created in another part of the model by the model author, a referential attribute, represented by a reference or pointer, is in order, irrespective of lifetime. We find named objects the exception rather than the rule, because names are often irrelevant, named objects force more work onto the model author, and unnamed objects are just as accessible as named objects. OOPM's ability to create *anonymous objects* is quite useful—for example, 1000 individual models of free-roaming entities, such as snail kites (birds) in a marsh. The model author considers snail kite objects a fungible collection and has no need to provide each snail kite a name as long as it is somehow accessible. OOPM supports this accessibility through containers.

When cardinality is greater than 1, and especially when the number is uncertain, the attribute is a *container class* object, holding objects of the contained type. For example, SnailKiteS, a container class, may be instantiated as a value attribute of the marsh class and may hold 1000 snail kite objects. Alternatively, a SnailKiteS container may hold an arbitrary number of snail kites. Container classes represent an important aspect of aggregation. Provision is made for optional automatic population of containers with a specified number of contained objects; alternatively, model authors may populate containers and initialize their objects. Container classes can be specified directly by the model author but are usually generated automatically by the cardinality of the aggregation. Container behaviors include sending information to contained objects, executing methods of contained objects, and selecting a subset of contained objects based on a criterion. These features are similar to Zeigler [Zeigler-Moon 1997], and may be extended by the model author.

Another aspect of aggregation is how to relate an attribute of an aggregate class with the corresponding attribute in its constituent classes, when such correspondence exists. In contrast to delegation, the problem here is to invoke a method of *every* constituent class and transform the results into an overall result for the aggregate class. A container known to an object of the aggregate class obtains such information from all its contained objects, a set of objects of constituent classes. The approach is similar to ensemble methods [Zeigler-Moon 1997]. In a container, all contained objects can be dealt with in the same way using polymorphism. An example is the biomass of snails of several age classes (for example, eggs, juveniles, adults) in an ecosystem simulation. A snail's biomass is its weight. Total biomass is the sum of the weights of every age class of snail. Moving to a higher level of aggregation, a marsh in the Everglades has a biomass that is the sum of the biomasses of all populations in each of a number of patches, which are areas of the marsh. Here the relation is *summation*, and the common base class has this functionality. While summation is common, it is not universal, and a model author is free to specify appropriate functionality.

28.3 Model Refinement

Modeling is usually iterative and incremental in nature. As the process unfolds, a class hierarchy develops, taking on a tree-like appearance. Levels in this tree are usually related to the level of abstraction that one associates with thinking about and describing the model, with the most general classes near the root and the most specific classes at the leaves. Similarly, as dynamic behavior models are specified, using any one of several model types, it may be desirable to refine any one element of a model into another model in its own right. Each element of a model is termed a multimodel unit. Examples of MMUs in a finite state machine (FSM) are *state* and *transition*. The model within the MMU may be the same type or a different type as the type of the larger model containing the MMU. When one can mix and match model types arbitrarily in a hierarchy of any depth, this is a heterogeneous model hierarchy.

To support an arbitrary heterogeneous model hierarchy, our models must be *closed under coupling*. This suggests that the method of coupling one model component to another must be clearly defined. Two kinds of coupling exist: intralevel and interlevel. Intralevel coupling reflects model components coupled to one another in the same model. For example, one needs to specify rules of how petri-nets, compartmental models, and system dynamics graphs are formed. With a system dynamics graph, a rule of model building defines that any level has an input rate and an output rate.

A more interesting case arises in interlevel coupling, since we must ensure that we define rules for how model components from one model can be refined into models of different types. Can a finite state machine state be refined into a petri-net, or can a functional block model contain finite state machines inside blocks? What are the rules to guide this refinement? The rule for interlevel coupling is based on MMU decomposition. Each model is defined as a graph, and each graph component is defined as an MMU. This generalizes the semantics normally associated with most components to the extent that each component now maintains the power and flexibility of an object, with its own attributes and methods. For example, an FSM can be our candidate dynamic model. Since it is, by default, expressed as a graph, we take each state and transition and define each as an MMU. State names become MMU names and transitions become boolean methods within the MMU that they define. Also, the FSM itself is an MMU, so that a model becomes an MMU defined in terms of connected MMUs, which is an architecture that lends itself to recursively defined coupling. The semantics of model simulation uses the Simulate( ) method in each MMU comprising a model.

Multimodeling [Fishwick 1992, 1993, 1996] provides multiple levels of abstraction to represent geometry and dynamic behavior of a model. In OOPM, multimodeling permits a variety of dynamic model types, including FSM, functional block model (FBM), differential or algebraic equations (EQN), rule-based model (RBM), and system dynamics model (SDM). When these dynamic multimodel types are not appropriate, model authors may create code methods for dynamic behavior or as wrappers to encapsulate legacy code. Support for a variety of model types is an important intentional departure from the norm. Variety contributes breadth, which can accommodate diversity of background and preference in model authors. Breadth is also needed to accommodate variety in source systems and application domains. OOPM has the capability to seamlessly mix and match heterogeneous dynamic behavior model types at model definition time and also to hot-swap components at simulation runtime. Multimodeling facilitates (1) model development, selective refinement to achieved required fidelity or model extensibility, and accommodating unanticipated change; (2) integration and reuse of object-oriented distributed simulation models; and (3) extensibility of the framework itself to accommodate future model types.

Because model development resources are limited, we typically refine using a breadth-first approach, and this tree-like structure accordingly takes on an uneven shape, with some parts of the tree being of greater height and others being shorter, reflecting the underlying decision criterion to refine only as needed to achieve required model fidelity. Development is often iterative and incremental. We usually take a model to a simulation, run it, and use the results to determine where more modeling work is needed. Multimodeling can conserve development resources by providing an orderly framework within which refinement as needed may proceed. A shallow model can be run, and analysis can pinpoint model subtrees where additional fidelity is needed. This adaptive mechanism can focus and guide development. The evolving model is thus its own prototype. It needn't be discarded, as in throwaway prototyping, nor does it suffer the chaos that often accompanies the exploratory prototyping or exploratory programming approach.

The multimodel definition is recursive: Refinement proceeds as far as needed. The level of refinement may be bound at model definition time or at simulation runtime. When bound at model definition time, the simulation program will not change its components on the fly. When refinement is bound at simulation runtime, this permits hot-swapping of components. For example, refinement of such a multimodel changes on the fly in response to system constraints. A typical constraint is a realtime constraint on when the simulation must complete. Presently, OOPM does not provide the executive logic that decides when to change refinement depth, but, given such logic, OOPM has implemented a capability to reconfigure model refinement on the fly. Others are working on providing the executive logic for this kind of multimodeling in OOPM [Lee-Fishwick 1997].

28.4 Visual Elements of OOPM

Visual elements of OOPM include a conceptual modeler, use of Virtual Reality Modeling Language (VRML) for geometry models, several OOPM editors (one for each of five types of dynamic multimodels), and Scenario, which provides simulation runtime output visualization. Supported platforms for visual elements of OOPM include the Solaris dialect of Unix, Microsoft Windows NT4.0, and Windows 95.

28.4.1 Conceptual Models

The OOPM MAI is a graphical user interface. Modeler relies on the distributed model repository (discussed later) to store model definitions as they are constructed and as a source of components for reuse. The main part of the MAI is the conceptual modeler, discussed here. Additional parts of the MAI are a set of dynamic model editors, discussed in the "Dynamic Behavior" section. A model can be created from scratch or can be an integration reusing proven smaller models as subsystems obtained from the DMR. The conceptual model defines classes, objects, relations among classes, and relations among objects (aggregation and specialization or generalization). An example appears in Figure 28.4a. Small rectangles representing classes are arranged using their relations to form aggregation and specialization/generalization hierarchies. When a small class rectangle is double-clicked, it opens to reveal class detail, as in Figure 28.4b, including the name of the class, its attributes, its methods, and its named objects. Within each method, the model author may specify input parameters, output parameters, return type, and which dynamic model type the method is to be, or whether it is to be a code method or a constructor method.

Geometry

Our focus is to apply multimodeling to geometry, as we have done with behavior (see "Dynamic Behavior"). We do not seek to invent a solution for geometry. We prefer to

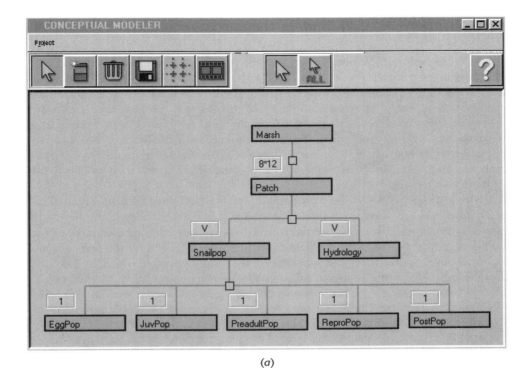

(a)

(b)

Figure 28.4 (a) OOPM conceptual model; (b) detail of one class.

reuse existing solutions. We seek to provide the framework to allow powerful capabilities of geometry representations such as VRML to be available to the OOPM model author. Geometry relates objects over a space. The OOPM Geometry class library has classes such as Matrix, which represents a two-dimensional grid, like the patches in a marsh, and provides two services: dereferencing and iteration. Dereferencing takes two coordinate values and returns the object at that coordinate. Iteration evokes a particular behavior of every object in a set. Matrix is a base class of marsh. This confers on marsh an ability to manage its geometry. Many source systems and their models fit this geometry metamodel.

Other geometry types under consideration for the Geometry class library are hierarchy trees, such as constructive solid geometry (CSG) and quad-tree. In the matrix geometry metamodel, source systems typically have free-roaming entities that interact and evolve over a field, with the field influenced and changed by the presence and activities of the entities, defining properties of the space over which the field is defined and through which entities move. Additionally, each spatial unit may contain objects that are fixed to reside in that unit; often a diffusion process is active over the field. This metamodel is descriptive of a wide variety of source systems, from polymer chemistry to ecosystems. An example of free-roaming entities is snail kites (birds) in a marsh. An example of a fixed object is the snail population in each patch of the marsh. Diffusion operates along gradients in snail population density between adjacent patches.

Early work with OOPM Scenario was done in the GUI toolkit (Tk) of Tcl/Tk. This has since been supplanted with VRML for several reasons: VRML is more immersive, VRML is better suited to Web-based operation than Tcl applets (Tclets), and VRML has better authoring tools. Each class in a model can have a VRML attribute. Figure 28.5a shows a VRML model of a marsh, with the size of the circle in each patch indicating abundance of snails in that patch. The affinity of snails for deeper water can be seen in the way the pattern of circles follows the deeper channels in the marsh. In a class that is an aggregation, such as a patch, the VRML model may include VRML models of some constituent classes. To illustrate this, consider a patch in a marsh, with a spatially fixed snail population in the patch, as in the first example; further, suppose the simulation runtime visualization is the relative abundance of three age classes of snails (eggs, juveniles, and reproductive adults) in each patch and over all the patches in the marsh. The three age classes are snail subclasses; each has a VRML model that is a texture-mapped shape representing the age class. The patch VRML model has the three snail subclass VRML models in close juxtaposition, with the size of each shape indicating relative abundance of that group. The marsh VRML model replicates the patch VRML model over the matrix. Figure 28.5b shows a variant in which the relative abundance of the three age classes of snails is shown for each patch of this marsh VRML model.

Dynamic Behavior

In OOPM classes, dynamic behavior is represented by *dynamic multimodels*, allowing the model author to specify a model (and thus its corresponding simulation program) without being a programmer. OOPM presently incorporates five kinds of dynamic multimodel, each presented here. The model author is free to use or avoid any particular multimodel type, either because of the diversity of backgrounds and preferences

(a)

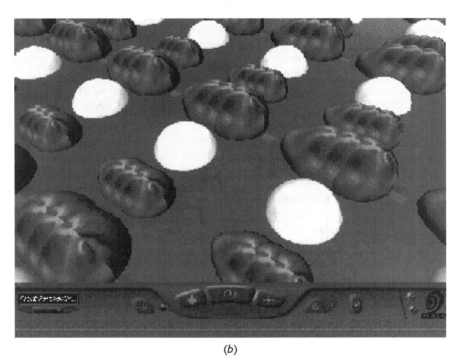

(b)

Figure 28.5 VRML marsh geometry: *(a)* snail abundance indicated by size of circles; *(b)* abundance of three age classes in each cell.

of the model authors, or because certain source systems and application domains lend themselves more naturally to one multimodel type than to another. The model author can mix and match various dynamic model types arbitrarily to define methods of the classes of the model. Each dynamic multimodel is created by an OOPM visual editor, involves drawing pictures like the whiteboard pictures mentioned in the chapter introduction, and has the rigor of the formalism that underlies the multimodel type.

Every OOPM dynamic model is (potentially) a multimodel, with a structure (subordinate elements), a topology (how those subordinate elements are connected), inputs, and outputs. In OOPM, every subordinate element of every dynamic model (for example, a state of a finite state machine) is an object of a derived class of a universal behavior base class, and so can in turn be another multimodel of any type, in principle, ad infinitum. This not only facilitates model refinement, it also supports heterogeneous multimodels and runtime multimodels (to be discussed later). Each method M_j of class C_i is a dynamic multimodel of some type. Within $C_i::M_j$ are subordinate elements. Each such element may be any method: (1) of C_i, (2) of any value attribute of C_i that is an abstract data type, (3) of any referential attribute of C_i that is an ADT, or (4) of any associated object. The first two groups are bound at class declaration time. The third and fourth groups permit dynamic binding, and so support *polymorphism*, in which an association to an object of some base class, such as Mollusk, can be satisfied by any object of any derived class of Mollusk, such as Snail, and a (virtual) method call will result in a call to a method of the appropriate derived class corresponding to the type of the associated object (snail), without the specific type of the associated object being known to the calling code. The use of polymorphism permits hot-swapping of one model for an equivalent model on the fly at runtime, thus supporting runtime multimodeling [Lee-Fishwick 1997].

The model author designates a method of a class as a finite state machine and then uses the OOPM FSM editor to construct the FSM. An FSM is a directed graph, consisting of states (the nodes) and transitions (the arcs). On each transition appears a predicate. Each state and each transition of the FSM may be another multimodel. At any time the FSM has a current state. Its dynamic behavior causes the FSM to change state from state$_i$ to state$_j$ when the predicate of transition$_{ij}$ is true. If several transitions have true predicates, ties are broken arbitrarily. An OOPM FSM is shown in Figure 28.6, representing snail population response to changing ambient temperature.

The model author designates a method as a *functional block model* and uses the OOPM FBM editor to construct the FBM. An FBM has blocks and traces. Blocks appear on the canvas as rectangles, like chips on a circuit board. Inputs and outputs of each block look like pins on a chip. The model author connects various output pins on one block to various input pins on another block. These *traces* form the FBM's topology. Inputs to the FBM, if any, are connected to block inputs. Outputs of the FBM, if any, are from output pins of various blocks. Cycles are permitted, and these propagate a value at one time step to the next time step. Several class libraries of prewritten blocks are available but not required, including *control applications* (Add, Subtract, Multiply, Divide, Integrate, Constant, PseudoRandom, and Accumulate), *queuing model* (Source, Sink, Fork, Join, and Facility), and *flowchart model* (Begin, End, Decision, Process, and Auxiliary). An OOPM FBM is shown in Figure 28.7 representing the life cycle of snails. In the forward direction, eggs grow to juveniles, then mature to adults. A cycle is explicitly indicated by the trace from reproductive adult to egg. The block at the bottom with many inputs records results for the experimental frame.

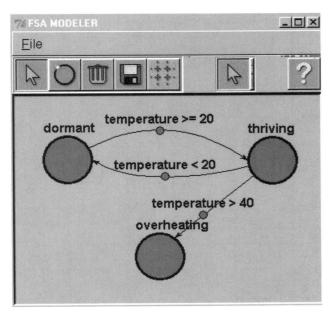

Figure 28.6 Dynamic multimodel: finite state machine (FSM) for snail population response to changing ambient temperature.

The model author designates a method of a class as an equations constraint model [Fishwick 1995] and then uses the OOPM EQN editor to construct the EQN. An EQN model consists of a system of any number of nth-order differential equations, as well as algebraic equations. The syntax is similar to that of C++, and math functions such as $\sin(x)$ may be used. Differential equations are represented using symbols such as x, x' for the first derivative, and x'' for the second derivative of x. Several state variables may appear. The output of the system may be any-order derivative of any variable. If a state variable used in the system of equations has the same name as an attribute of the class to which the EQN model belongs, then the attribute and the state variable denote the same entity. Either may then be used to update the other. In addition to variables and their derivatives, a set of equations may contain (additive and multiplicative) parameters and input signals. Parameters may be attributes of the class to which the model belongs, or they may be input parameters to the EQN method, or they may be multimodels.

The model author designates a method of a class as a system dynamics model [Fishwick 1995] and then uses the OOPM SDM editor to construct the SDM. System dynamic modeling is a functional modeling technique with a variable-based, rather than a function-based, approach. Elements of an SDM include levels, rates, sources, sinks, constants, and auxiliaries, as well as two kinds of arcs: flow arcs and cause-and-effect arcs. As with other models, elements may be multimodels. An OOPM SDM is shown in Figure 28.8, representing dynamic behavior of a reproductive adult snail population. Rates that affect population level include maturation, death, and senes-

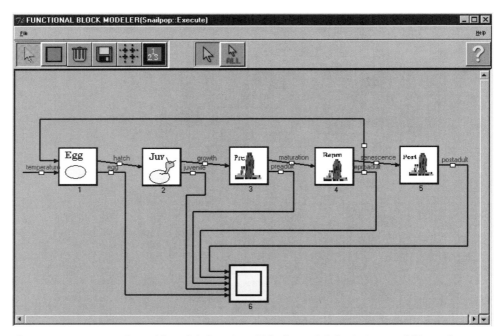

Figure 28.7 Dynamic multimodel: functional block model depicting snail life cycle.

cence (aging). The SDM is equivalent to an EQN model, but some model authors prefer the SDM form. Output of SDM editor is identical in to output of the EQN editor of an equivalent model. OOPM Translator does not know the difference between EQN and SDM. SDM is the first multimodel type developed in terms of another multimodel type. This approach is an example of reuse that may serve again in the future to further broaden the model author interface while minimizing development effort.

The model author designates a method of a class as a rule-based model (RBM) and then uses the OOPM RBM editor to construct the RBM. An RBM has a set of rules, each expressed as a conditional expression: if *premise,* then *consequence.* Each premise and each consequence can be another multimodel. The RBM editor has a premise pane and a consequence pane, each of which offers eligible items from lists, and for specifying relational and logical operators. An OOPM RBM is shown in Figure 28.9, representing the snail egg population response to changing ambient temperature. This RBM is a lower-level multimodel within the higher-level system dynamics multimodel described in the *System Dynamics Model* section.

Although models can be constructed without writing any programs, there may be times when no dynamic model type does what the model author wishes to do. Or the model author may have a piece of code for a specific algorithm, or some legacy code. For any of these reasons, OOPM permits a model author to write the body of a dynamic model in C++ code as a code method, and to integrate that with the rest of the model. The model author interface provides a simple text editing capability for code methods, but the model author is free to use his or her favorite editor instead (any text editor that works with ASCII files).

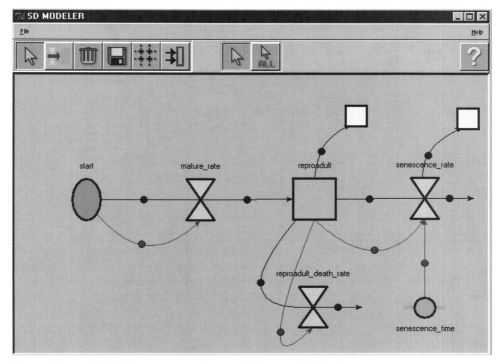

Figure 28.8   OOPM System dynamics model for snail behavior.

Scenario

Analysis of simulation execution has often in the past focused on massive amounts of tabular data. Output visualization is effective in facilitating analysis and understanding. Scenario does this; additionally, Scenario can initialize parameters and pass them to Engine. This is a Model/View/Controller architecture, where Scenario is the view and controller and Engine is the model. The new OOPM geometry representation is VRML. Each class may have a geometry attribute, which can be or include a VRML world. VRML authoring tools are external to OOPM; nonetheless, the ability of classes to bring with them their VRML representation is valuable for reuse and integration.

OOPM Scenario is a visualization enabler. Scenario activates and initializes simulation model execution by running the program we call Engine, at the request of the user. Scenario maintains synchronous bidirectional interaction with Engine. In the visualization role, Scenario displays Engine output in a form meaningful to the user. In the controlling role, Scenario allows the user to interact with Engine, modifying simulation parameters and changing the rate of simulation progress. Engine can be allowed to free-run, it can be made to single-step through one event at a time (the default), or it can be made to run at any pace in between. As a separate feature, simulation clock time scales can be stretched or compressed. Both can be combined to generate animations with which the model author can interact. Things that would happen too fast can be

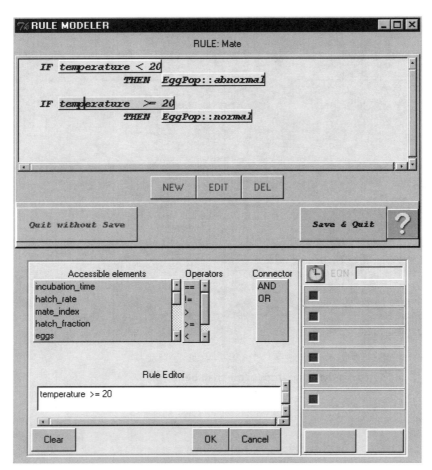

Figure 28.9   Dynamic multimodel: rule-based model for snail egg population response to changing ambient temperature.

slowed down. The rate of progress can be adjusted to focus on parts of the simulation execution that are of particular interest.

The first Scenario was Tcl/Tk-based. The new Scenario is VRML-based. Both use TCP/IP to communicate between Engine and Scenario. Tcl/Tk Scenario communication is between Engine and the Tcl/Tk interpreter. VRML Scenario communication is between Engine and a Java applet that resides on a Web page with a VRML browser plugin (CosmoPlayer 2.0) for the world being executed. The Java applet communicates with the VRML plugin using the external authoring interface (EAI). Activation of the Java applet and the VRML plugin are mediated by our DMX control panel, which is a coordinator for Web-based operation of OOPM. This is outside the scope of this chapter, but is described by the authors elsewhere [Cubert 1998]. Scenario detail is unique to each model. OOPM has visualization instruments for reuse, including dials and gauges, x-y plot graphs, and terrain maps. Nonetheless, some simulation output isn't necessarily amenable to graphical realtime treatment, and there is a necessary role for traditional analysis [Law-Kelton 1991]. OOPM can support this in two ways: Engine can send output for this purpose to standard output examined by Scenario or to a separate file. Further analysis can be handled by additional software provided by the model author—for example, MATLAB.

28.5 Nonvisual Elements of OOPM

In addition to the visual elements previously discussed, OOPM has nonvisual elements, including the distributed model repository, which holds model definitions; Translator, which maps model definitions to simulation programs written in C++; and Engine, the simulation program including its runtime support libraries. Translator converts a model definition obtained from DMR into a simulation program; Engine is that program. Supported platforms for nonvisual elements of OOPM include the supported platforms for the visual elements (Solaris dialect of Unix, Microsoft Windows NT4.0, and Windows 95), as well as MS-DOS and OS/2.

28.5.1 Translator

This element obtains a model definition from the DMR and uses it to construct a simulation program in Translator Target Language. The present TTL is C++. Translator output is a complete Engine program written in C++ including engine.h, a header file consisting primarily of class declarations, and engine.cpp, a source file containing a C++ translation of each dynamic model method and each code method, as well as code to invoke engine runtime support and to synchronize with and accept commands from Scenario.

28.5.2 Engine

Engine is the C++ simulation program generated by Translator. It is necessary to compile and link Engine source code to create the Engine executable. This is done automatically using the make utility program; alternatively, Engine can be compiled and linked using the interactive development environment (IDE) of a compiler such as Visual C++. At link time, runtime support is added from object libraries, the most important of which is ooSim [Cubert 1995]. Dynamic behavior multimodels are translated into C++ code, which relies on the underlying event scheduling of the ooSim dispatcher for propagating event chains. ooSim is event-scheduling simulation queuing model software, which is an object-oriented reimplementation and extension of the SimPack Toolkit [Fishwick-Zeigler 1992, 1995]; SimPack is, in turn, based on Simulation Modeling and Programming Language (SMPL) [MacDougall 1992]. In addition to event scheduling, ooSim provides other support, such as pseudorandom-number generation.

The Engine source file contains code to initiate one or more event chains. These event chains propagate independently, and the time step of each event chain is independent of the time step of every other event chain. The event scheduler propagates each event chain until that event chain terminates itself or until the simulation clock reaches the overall time limit specified for the simulation in the model definition. In general, an event chain propagates by rescheduling a specific event routine, which the model author identifies. This is accomplished by the auto_propagate feature, which is enabled by default. It is also possible for the model author to disable auto_propagate, in which case the model itself may generate any number of event chains following any logic. This is an advanced feature that is recommended only to those who are familiar with event scheduling in ooSim and wish to (or need to) have the additional flexibility that manual event scheduling provides. Manual event scheduling is *not* required to get OOPM models to run. As Engine runs, it executes one simulation event after another, driven by its underlying ooSim Future Event List (FEL). As an event executes, it may generate output on standard output. All such output is presented to Scenario (see the *Scenario* section). After executing each simulation event, Engine checks with Scenario for instructions and new parameter values. The relation between Engine and Scenario is inherently interactive and bidirectional. Scenario can inject events into the FEL of a running Engine. This feature supports distributed execution.

Distributed Model Repository (DMR)

In the original development of OOPM, model definition persistence was accomplished via textual format, in a set of flat ASCII files comprising a model definition. This approach had (and still has) a number of benefits, including that such model definitions are compact and relatively easy to read, understand, and even modify if need be; model definition files get backed up as part of local system backups; models can be put on diskette, into a .zip archive, or FTPed; it also is a software engineering tool to eliminate development bottlenecks. But this incarnation of OOPM is stand-alone software, with no provision for sharing, thus limiting reuse; moreover, this OOPM can be used on a machine only after OOPM software is obtained and installed on that machine.

Subsequent progress on OOPM has continued, including these developments: (1) a new approach to model definition persistence we call *model repository* and (2) making the modeling environment Web-based. The distributed model repository holds model definitions, including class declarations, declarations of attributes and methods, and interfaces. The DMR provides a database management system (DBMS) for model definitions. Models and model components in the DMR are available for browsing, integration, and reuse. Class libraries for modeling collections and geometries for spatial models are available. Pieces of a model may reside on different machines, thus permitting model definitions to be distributed and permitting collaboration within an engineering workgroup on model development. The DMR is more than a DBMS, however, because it transforms information based on multimodeling semantics as data arrives. Results are typically stored in a data field.

Model analysis is an integral part of understanding a model definition. An example that occurs whenever a functional block model (appears is that each block of the FBM must be examined to ascertain whether it is (1) a method of the class containing the FBM, (2) a method of an ADT attribute of the class containing the FBM, or (3) a method of some other class. Each case is handled differently by Translator: as a member method name, a method name qualified with the attribute name, or dynamic binding of a block from the model's context. In addition to the normal mode of receiving model definition(s) from the model author interface, the DMR can also receive model definitions in another way: from text files. These files can be created using a text editor. Historically, such files were originally created by Modeler before the DMR existed. These files now serve as a way to initialize, back up, or load a DMR.

A reuse example involving the DMR is based on the real need to model the snail kite, a bird that is an endangered species and lives in the Everglades. Snail kites eat apple snails, so the snail kite model needs to model the apple snail as the food source. The snail population is heavily dependent on fluctuations in ambient temperature and water depth in the marsh. The snail kite model author is an expert on birds but not on snails. If he or she must write his or her own apple snail model, there will be three drawbacks: (1) Its fidelity may be lower than it would be if it were written by an apple snail expert, (2) the complexity of the snail kite model will be greater if writing an apple snail model is part of the job, and (3) development time will be longer. With this in mind, the snail kite model author goes to the DMR and learns that an apple snail model has already been written. This apple snail model was written by a snail expert, has been tested, and is available. The apple snail model is reused, incorporated into the snail kite model, resulting in a better quality snail kite model, in which complexity is better managed due to the additional abstraction levels, and a shorter development time. Space does not permit us to go into issues such as how the snail kite model author was able to locate the apple snail model, but we have presented this elsewhere [Cubert 1998]. The DMR is presently a C++ creation intended as a proof of concept rather than for production use. Upgrade to industrial strength can be done in the future without altering the architecture, by replacing the C++ DMR with an OO wrapper over a DBMS. No other parts of the system will require changes.

The distributed model repository communicates using connection-based TCP (Transmission Control Protocol) over IP (Internet Protocol) with producers and consumers of model definitions, as an alternative to the local-file-based model definitions previously mentioned. Model authors interact with the model author interface, but persistent model definitions reside within the DMR; similarly, Translator converts model definitions to C++ simulation programs, but model definitions are from the DMR rather than local files.

Benefits include the following: (1) A model defined on machine A can be translated on machine B, (2) a model can be defined and/or translated on a machine with no (or limited) local persistent store, and (3) models reside where they can best be cataloged, indexed, browsed, backed up, and otherwise maintained, without distracting model authors from their primary focus. The DMR also permits model sharing in a way that was not available before. For example, a model defined on machine A can be referenced on machines B and C, so A's model is available to B and C, or they can agree to divide the work and pool their results. This not only (4) increases reuse potential; it also (5) provides an environment to support collaborative development.

Disadvantages include reliance on network connections and consumption of network bandwidth. DMRs may from time to time start and stop, so the OOPM universe may have any number of DMRs. DMRs know about one another, can forward requests to their peers, and can share model information. But a DMR does not, in and of itself, make OOPM Web-based. Fortunately, there is a way for OOPM to be a Web-based modeling and simulation environment. Our litmus test for whether software is Web-based involves the following: (1) that it require no installation of separate software and (2) that it rely on communication conventions of the Web (such as URLs). There are several ways to meet these criteria, combining some or all of the following: Hypertext Markup Language (HTML), JavaScript, Dynamic HTML, Java applets, and browser plugins with or without LiveConnect. For now, we consider browser plugins to satisfy our criteria. The primary OOPM configuration will be Web-based: a browser plugin LiveConnected with Java applets, based on HTML with a sprinkle of JavaScript. DMR is a server-side phenomenon, so in the standard Web-based configuration a DMR will not reside on the client.

28.6 Summary

We contemplate supporting three additional configurations, one Web-based and the other two not Web-based. These are (1) a Web-based runtime-only (Engine and visualization) configuration; (2) a power-user configuration providing a local DMR and/or a local Java-based GUI and/or a Tcl/Tk-based GUI, which operate out of the same consistent plugin top level as the Web-based configurations and which may be more appropriate where network bandwidth and/or security issues are paramount; and (3) a stand-alone configuration of OOPM. The last two configurations are not Web-based because they require OOPM and possibly Tcl/Tk to be installed on the local machine.

The distributed model repository is a substantial step in the right direction. Web-based operation of OOPM will soon be here, and use of DMML as a representation common to all elements of OOPM will tie our architecture together in a way that we hope will have significant benefits for making reuse of object-oriented distributed models practical. We learned that Tcl/Tk neither enforces nor facilitates object-oriented methodology, and we are working on a Java applet–based MAI to improve reusability and extensibility of our code. With our use of VRML, we are confident that the best features of OOPM can be merged with the best features of powerful runtime scenario tools. Dynamic behavior multimodel types now implemented provide breadth, but we are looking at extending further in this direction—for example, petri-nets. We are also looking at immersive technologies for MAI.

28.7 References

[Booch 1994] Booch, Grady. *Object-Oriented Analysis and Design with Applications*, 2nd ed., Reading, MA: Addison-Wesley, 1994.

[Coplien 1992] Coplien, James O. *Advanced C++ Programming Styles and Idioms*. Reading, MA: Addison-Wesley, 1992.

[Cubert 1995] Cubert, Robert M. *The ooSim Object Oriented Simulation Library*. Technical report, University of Florida CISE Simulation Group, December 1995.

[Cubert 1998] Cubert, Robert M., and Paul A. Fishwick. Software architecture for distributed simulation multimodels. *SPIE AeroSense 1998 Conference Proceedings*, Bellingham, WA, April 1998.

[Dahmann 1998] Dahmann, Judith. Department of Defense DMSO high level architecture. *ITEC 1998: International Training and Education Conference*, Palais de Beaulieu, Lausanne, Switzerland, April 1998.

[Fishwick 1992] Fishwick, Paul A. SimPack: Getting started with simulation programming in C and C++. *Proceedings Winter Simulation Conference WSC 1992,* pp. 154–162. Arlington, Virginia, 1992.

[Fishwick 1993] Fishwick, Paul A. A simulation environment for multimodeling. *Discrete Event Dynamic Systems—Theory and Applications* 3:151—171.

[Fishwick 1995] Fishwick, Paul A. *Simulation Model Design and Execution: Building Digital Worlds.* Englewood Cliffs, NJ: Prentice Hall, 1995.

[Fishwick 1996] Fishwick, Paul A., and K. Lee. Two methods for exploiting abstraction in systems. *AI, Simulation and Planning in High Autonomous Systems,* 257—264.

[Fishwick-Zeigler 1992] Fishwick, Paul A., and B.P. Zeigler. A multimodel methodology for qualitative model engineering. *ACM Transactions on Modeling and Computer Simulation* 2(1):52–81.

[Hill 1992] Hill, David R.C. *Object-Oriented Analysis and Simulation.* Reading, MA: Addison-Wesley, 1992.

[Hill-Vigor 1997] Hill, David R.C., and E. Vigor. Simulation and software engineering: Bridging the culture gap with UML. *SCS Object-Oriented Simulation Conference,* pp. 81–87, San Diego, CA, January 1997.

[Johnson 1997] Johnson, Ralph E. Frameworks = (Components + Patterns). *Communications of the ACM,* Theme Issue on Object-Oriented Application Frameworks, M.E. Fayad and D. Schmidt, editors. 40(10):39–42, October 1997.

[Law-Kelton 1991] Law, A.M., and W.D. Kelton. *Simulation Modeling and Analysis.* New York: McGraw-Hill, 1991.

[Lee-Fishwick 1997] Lee, Kangsun, and Paul A. Fishwick. Semi-automated method for dynamic model abstraction. *SPIE Conference Proceedings,* Bellingham, WA, 1997.

[MacDougall 1992] MacDougall, M.H. *Simulating Computer Systems: Techniques and Tools.* Cambridge MA: MIT Press, 1992.

[Riel 1996] Riel, Arthur J. *Object-Oriented Design Heuristics.* Reading, MA: Addison-Wesley, 1996.

[Zeigler 1995] Zeigler, Bernard P., H.S. Song, T.G. Kim, and H. Praehofer. DEVS framework for modeling, simulation, analysis, and design of hybrid systems. In *Hybrid Systems II, Lecture Notes in Computer Science,* pp.529–551, E.P. Antsaklis et al., editors. Berlin, Germany: Springer-Verlag, 1995.

[Zeigler 1997] Zeigler, Bernard P. *Objects and Systems.* Berlin, Germany: Springer-Verlag, 1997.

[Zeigler-Moon 1997] Zeigler, Bernard P., Y. Moon, D. Kim, and G. Ball. The DEVS environment for high-performance modeling and simulation. *IEEE Computational Science and Engineering* 4(3).

CHAPTER 29

Application Frameworks: A Survey

An object-oriented application framework is a semicomplete application that has its own control loop. The framework can be extended into a specific application tailored to the customer's requirements by extending the hooks and hot spots in the framework. This chapter summarizes the topic of frameworks by analyzing the survey results and discussing each topic in detail.

Each section in this chapter discusses a specific aspect of frameworks. *Section 29.1* discusses the framework classification according to the scope and the level of abstraction. *Section 29.2* discusses documentation types used in frameworks. *Section 29.3* compares the number of examples of frameworks in each category and the usage of operating systems, languages, domain areas, selling price ranges, and numbers of derived applications. *Section 29.4* analyzes the framework as a percentage of the final application, along with tools used, average time to learn and develop a framework, and design patterns at work. *Section 29.5* includes some common problems and rules of thumb regarding framework development. Two sidebars are included in this chapter. The first is titled *Object-Oriented Framework Survey Questions* and the second is called *Framework Names, Abbreviations, and Web Sites.*

We conducted a survey of application framework developers, and asked them a series of questions about the frameworks they developed (see the *Object-Oriented Framework Survey Questions* sidebar). In administering the survey, we hoped to document how and in what domains the frameworks are being used.

29.1 Framework Classification

Frameworks are classified either according to their scope of work or to the technique used to extend them [Fayad-Schmidt 1997]. The classification according to scope divides frameworks into system infrastructure frameworks, middleware integration frameworks, and enterprise application frameworks. The classification according to the extension techniques divides them into whitebox frameworks, blackbox frameworks, and graybox frameworks.

29.1.1 Classification According to Scope

[Fayad-Schmidt 1997] classifies application frameworks based on their scope into the three categories discussed in this section.

System Infrastructure Frameworks

This classification is simply the collection of portable and efficient frameworks that support such system infrastructure areas as operating systems, user interfaces, communications, and language processing. They are usually developed and used in-house or as generic applications used by other applications. For example, graphical user interface (GUI) frameworks, Microsoft Foundation Classes (MFC), or MacApp, are used as generic, underlying frameworks for other applications. It is difficult to count the actual number of the derived applications from these frameworks.

Middleware Integration Frameworks

These are designed to enhance software to modularize, reuse, and extend software infrastructure to work seamlessly in a distributed environment. Some examples are the OmniBuilder framework (an open-application generator that builds sophisticated, fully-functional business applications from the Business Model) and object-request brokers (ORBs), such as VisiBroker, Orbit, and DataBroker. It is worth mentioning that a middleware integration framework includes in its underlying layer some kind of system infrastructure framework (see Figure 29.1).

Enterprise Application Frameworks

Enterprise application frameworks address a broad application domain such as banking, telecommunications, or medicine. They represent the cornerstone of domain applications [Fayad-Hamu 1999]. A famous example of an enterprise framework is the IBM SanFrancisco Project, used for applications for the business domain in general. Another example is enterprise resource planning (ERP).

In Figure 29.1 frameworks are classified according to their scope. It is important to mention the relation between enterprise, middleware, and system infrastructure

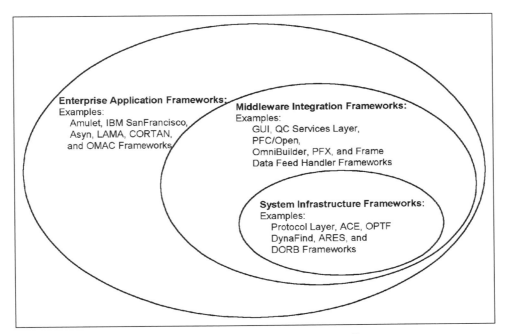

Figure 29.1   Venn diagram of framework classifications according to scope.

frameworks. According to Figure 29.1, a middleware integration framework includes a system infrastructure in its underlying layer. The enterprise framework includes both the middleware integration framework and the system infrastructure framework in the underlying layers.

29.1.2 Classification According to Extending Technique

Application frameworks are classified based on extending techniques, as shown in Figure 29.2. The three categories for achieving extensibility are discussed in the following sections.

Whitebox Framework

In a whitebox framework, extensibility is achieved by using object-oriented features such as inheritance and dynamic binding. Existing functionality is reused and extended by

- Inheriting from the framework base classes
- Overriding predefined hook methods using patterns

Examples of whitebox frameworks include the MacApp and ACE frameworks.

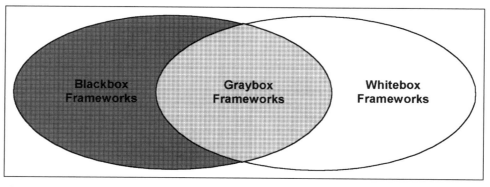

Figure 29.2   Venn diagram of framework classifications according to the extending technique.

Blackbox Framework

In a blackbox framework, extensibility is achieved by defining interfaces for components that can be plugged into the framework using object composition. Existing functionality is extended by:

- Defining components that conform to a particular interface
- Integrating components into the framework using patterns

Examples of blackbox frameworks include G++, the Compound User Interfaces framework [Fayad 1999b], and adaptive object-oriented event-filtering frameworks (see Chapter 22, "Event Filter Framework and Applications").

Graybox Framework

A graybox framework is a mix between the whitebox and the blackbox frameworks. Graybox frameworks allow extensibility by using inheritance and dynamic binding, as well as defining interfaces. Examples of graybox frameworks include GUI and the San-Francisco project.

Before analyzing the data of this survey, we expected the majority of existing application frameworks to be whitebox because they are easier to implement. Instead we found that the majority of existing frameworks, more than half of the survey samples, are graybox. Whitebox frameworks make up about 30 percent, and blackbox frameworks fall below 15 percent of frameworks in use.

This distribution of framework types is a good indication that framework developers are switching to graybox frameworks. Whitebox frameworks expose the framework code to the application developers, which can lead to problems. The use of blackbox frameworks leads to abstractness, lack of flexibility, and a complex dynamic required to update and change applications. In contrast, a good graybox framework design avoids the disadvantages of both whitebox and blackbox frameworks. In other words, the good graybox design has sufficient flexibility and extensibility, as well as the ability to hide unnecessary information from the application developers. Hiding selected code leads to the abstraction of the static parts of the framework and as a result protects the core structure from tampering.

Enterprise frameworks constitute about half of the available samples, while middleware frameworks and system infrastructure frameworks each make up about 20 percent. These results are a good indication of the maturity of frameworks, since they cover diverse enterprise domains such as health care, insurance, finance, and communications. Many business and industry domains rely on frameworks to provide software stability over extended periods of time. For example, it does not make any sense to build a costly application for a bank and rebuild it from scratch after five years to satisfy new needs. By building a flexible framework, the bank's software can grow and change as the company's needs change.

29.2 Framework Documentation

Documentation is an essential part of the software production process. Documentation, in general, is very costly and is a very high risk as well. The ease of use of the framework is tied to the kind and depth of the documentation associated with it. These documents are used as the main knowledge source for the framework in most cases. The main users of framework documentation can be classified into the following two categories:

Framework developers. The documentation is used to modify and enhance the structure as well as the performance of the framework.

Application developers. The documentation is employed to understand and use the framework.

There are several documentation types related to frameworks. Table 29.1 classifies the documentation users and the documentation type associated with each category.

Table 29.1   Framework Documentation

DOCUMENTATION TYPE	FRAMEWORK DEVELOPERS	APPLICATION DEVELOPERS
Example		Yes
Cookbook and recipes		Yes
Design pattern	Yes	
Interface contracts	Yes	Yes
Reference manual		Yes
Framework overview		Yes
Other documentation types	Modeling diagrams	User manual Troubleshooting guide

Some documentation types are used by both framework and application developers. The documentation type could be the same, but the level of detail and the discussed issues are different for each audience. For example, in the framework developing process it is essential to identify the interface contracts for every class, while on the application side, some of these classes are not seen or even used by the application developer at all. Thus, we have to distinguish between the materials used by the framework developers only and the materials used by both the framework developers and the application developer.

29.2.1 Documentation Types

There are several ways for documenting application frameworks [Butler 1999], such as:

Examples. The source code for example applications to extend the current framework. It usually includes a set of several examples, varying gradually in difficulty and coverage of the framework.

Cookbooks and recipes. A recipe is a step-by-step description of how to do to a certain task. A recipe usually includes source code, illustration diagrams, and/or natural language descriptions. A cookbook is a collection of recipes.

Interface contracts. The specification of the obligations and collaborations for every interface in the framework.

Reference manual. In an object-oriented framework, a reference manual for a class usually includes a description of each class (responsibility, role of each data member, and full description of each method in this class). The reference manual can include a description of the global variables, constants, and types.

Framework overview. More than 95 percent of the framework samples have a framework overview. It describes, in general, the purpose of the framework in a way that helps the application developer get a jump start on the learning curve. It defines the domain and scope of the framework. It also helps people other than the application developer become familiar with the purpose of the framework and compare between different frameworks.

Others. Other types of documentation used with frameworks include:

- Design notebooks
- User manual
- Programmer's manual
- Troubleshooting guide
- Object interaction diagrams
- Online class and method references
- Installation guide

From the survey result, it can be seen that the most common documentation type is the *framework overview*. We expected this result because the framework overview is used as the first step in the learning curve of the application developer. The second most commonly used documentation type is the *example*, because it is usually used as a second step in the learning process.

29.3 Framework Comparisons

Operating systems, programming languages, and domain areas are used as comparison parameters of the surveyed application frameworks. The following sections highlight some of these comparisons.

29.3.1 Operating Systems

The survey results show that most frameworks are built for the Microsoft Windows environment since it constitutes the majority of the market. The next most popular operating system is Unix, followed by MAC OS, and OS/2 from IBM. A welcome trend is the development of portable frameworks that work across different platforms using a platform-independent language like Java. Any platform that supports Java Virtual Machine (JVM) can run an application built with a Java framework.

29.3.2 Languages

C++ is still the most common and popular programming language. We found a few examples of Java frameworks. Other popular languages used for implementing frameworks include Smalltalk and VisualBasic, but they constituted less than one-sixth of the survey samples. There are additional programming languages used to implement frameworks, but they constituted a very small fraction (about one or two frameworks for each language).

29.3.3 Domain Areas

Two fields with the largest number of frameworks are business and finance, and telecommunication and networking. There are some frameworks that cover a major portion of the domain area, such as IBM SanFrancisco for business applications. Others cover only a small area, such as CSFramelets, which covers the infrastructure for the client-server application in banking. The majority of the domain areas collected in this survey are detailed in Table 29.2.

Range of Selling Prices

Because of extreme price discrepancies, it is impossible to come up with an estimated price for each of the six categories of frameworks. Twenty percent of the survey frameworks are free, but others sell for up to $5 million. MacApp, LAMA, and Amulet are free of charge. Moderate price frameworks include PrismTech BOF and CORBA services ($200 to $10,000), while the HBOC application framework has a price tag in the

Table 29.2   Framework Domain Areas

NO.	DOMAIN AREA	LIST OF FRAMEWORKS	NO. EXAMPLES
1	General-purpose (domainless)	MaccApp, G++	2
2	General-purpose GUI	GUI, Amulet, Visible Properties and Actions Framework	2
3	Database and data management	FRAMEWARE, PFX (Persistence framework), ROA'D, QC Services Layer framework, Advanced Software Architecture Platform	4
4	Business and finance	Asyn, SanFrancisco, BOOF, PFC/Open Frame, Omni Builder, Rule Parsing, File Parsing, CSFramelets	8
5	Insurance	Asyn, SanFrancisco	2
6	Medical	HBOC application framework, Medical Business Object framework, Advanced Software Architecture Platform, Philips New York Project (under development)	3
7	Education and entertainment	Multimedia framework	1
8	Telecommunication and networking	Adaptive object-oriented event-filtering framework, Advanced Software, Architecture Platform, CORTAN, Protocol Layer framework, ACE, SIGAL, DORB, Javde	9
9	Industrial and manufacturing	OMAC, PrismTech BOF and CORBA services	2
10	Software development	CLOS Meta Object Protocol, G++, OPTF, LAMA	4

millions. Still other frameworks are for internal use only and are not for sale. These internal products are usually used to produce a large-scale framework.

A new trend is framework rentals. Clients can rent the application framework for the development period. When development is complete, they stop paying and can use the generated application free of royalties. Framework renting options are likely to see rapid growth in the future. A typical example of a for-rent framework is the Business Object-Oriented framework(BOOF), such as IBM SanFrancisco Framework.

Number of Derived Applications

There is no upper limit for the number of derived applications since there are no regulations or restrictions on application development. Therefore, we will analyze just the estimated number of derived applications, as suggested by the developers surveyed.

We can divide the frameworks according to the number of derived applications into *popular* and *nonpopular frameworks.* The number of derived applications from a popular framework is quite high. Some are generic or domainless frameworks like GUI and G++ frameworks. The rest of the popular application frameworks are domain specific (not generic), but they cover many application areas. For example, IBM SanFrancisco covers a large number of business areas. IBM SanFrancisco is more than a set of business processes, business components, or business frameworks. It is designed for future evolution and growth, with an architecture that enables reuse within IBM SanFrancisco itself. IBM SanFrancisco has three architected layers: (1) application specific layer called Core Business Processes (CBPs) that are typically high-level commercial business process frameworks, such as General Ledger, Warehouse and Order Management; (2) multiple application layers called Common Business Objects (CBOs) that are primarily commercial objects or mini-framework patterns, for example, customer name and address and currency; and (3) an application independent distributed object-oriented infrastructure called the Foundation layer that supports all applications specific in all industries, and also includes an application infrastructure comprised of a set of fundamental object building blocks that are typically collaborating objects and services. Examples of Foundation content include: entity, dependent, and command objects; a set of utilities that provide session management, synchronization and conflict control; and a set of query, transaction and event/notification services [Gauthier-Truxal 1998]. On the other hand, the number of derived applications from other, nonpopular, frameworks ranges from 3 to 30 applications.

29.4 Frameworks Facts

Framework facts such as the percentage of the framework used in the final application, tools used, average amount of time required to learn and develop a framework, and design patterns at work are discussed in this section.

29.4.1 Framework Percentage to the Final Application

The percentage of the framework used in the final application varies from 10 percent (which is hardly a framework) to 90 percent (which is a comprehensive framework). According to the framework samples in our survey, the average percentage of the framework that makes it into the final application is about 55 percent. This is the minimum percentage, in our opinion.

We believe that at least 75 percent of the framework should be used to be considered a good framework. A framework that covers only 10 percent of the problem domain cannot be considered a satisfactory framework. At 10 percent, we are almost building the application from scratch.

29.4.2 Tools Used

The survey responses indicate that there are no tools currently available specifically for frameworks. There is a great need to create new tools to simplify framework development. For example, these tools should ease the notification of hooks in the framework and the simulation of the control loop.

Some respondents considered the compilers and text editors tools, but since it is mandatory to use both of them in every case we will not discuss them as development tools. Other tools used are *modeling tools* (Rational Rose, Select, UML documentation apps, and so on.), *visual tools* (Visual Café, Visual C++, VisualAge Java, VisualBasic, and so on.), and *database tools* (ORACLE). It is difficult to list all the development tools available, but as we mentioned, there is a great need for framework-oriented tools.

29.4.3 Average Time to Learn and Develop a Framework

One of the factors affecting the ease of use of any framework is the average learning time. The average learning time is measured in *days/person*. Some frameworks take about one day to learn, such as Asyn, Data Feed Handlers, and PFX. Other frameworks take about 90 to 100 days to learn, such as PFC Open/Frame and HBOC application framework. The average learning time is a big factor in estimating the cost of the final application, since management can decide how many hours will be spent in learning a framework. According to the results of our survey, the average learning time is about 16 days.

Two of the development cost parameters are the *person-month* and the *members-per-team*. The framework samples in this survey indicated that the minimum time spent in developing a framework was half a person-month (15 person-days), and the maximum time to develop a framework was 1000 person-months. After excluding these two extremes from the calculation, we found the average time spent in developing a framework was about 21 person-months. This parameter is an indication of the framework size itself. The average team size is 3 members-per-team. When the number of members in a team increases, performance tends to decrease, so 3 members-per-team is a reasonable size.

29.4.4 Design Patterns at Work

Frameworks and design patterns are tied strongly to each other, since a lot of effort can be saved in development by using design patterns. This is not the proper place to show the importance of design patterns, but we need to emphasize their importance to framework developers.

Most design patterns are used in frameworks. There is also a smaller number of more frequently used design patterns in frameworks, such as Strategy, Command, Bridge, Factory, and Singleton. Other design patterns are used, but with less frequency. We would advise novice framework developers to start with the patterns listed previously. On the average, 36 percent of a framework is done using design patterns. This percentage is a good indicator of how much time the design patterns will save in the development process.

Hooks and Hot Spots

Unfortunately, we did not receive enough data regarding hooks and hot spots used in the sample frameworks. Only about 25 percent of the survey responses answered this inquiry. This leads us to believe that the concept of hooks and hot spots is not yet popular in the framework developers' community. The area of hooks and hot spots needs more attention and publicity to popularize it as a concept in the framework arena.

29.5 Problems and Lessons Learned

We know very well that developing frameworks is not an easy task. Teaching proper utilization of frameworks is also very difficult. Sometimes you have to rewrite the framework three or four times, and sometimes more than that to get adequate flexibility and extensibility. But in the end, the framework will be worth the effort spent on it. This section points out some rules of thumb to keep in mind while developing frameworks.

The development of a framework requires one or more domain experts. In some cases the domain expert is part of the design team and not just a point of reference. We have to keep in mind that the framework will be used in real-life applications, so it is important to evaluate the approaches used in any framework. There are many problems associated with framework integration when dealing with third-party libraries or frameworks. There are also general software development problems, such as lack of commonsense discipline (like code reviews), project management discipline (ad hoc configuration management), inconsistent documentation, and lack of consideration for the different needs of different users.

29.5.1 Rules of Thumb and Heuristics for Frameworks

Rules of thumb and frameworks' heuristics are listed in this section.

There is a big difference between the concepts of *frameworks* **and** *classes***.** A framework is a reusable design of all or part of a system that is represented by a set of abstract classes and the way their instances interact. Classes are part of the framework itself [Johnson 1997].

Combining *hot-spot analysis* **and** *design patterns* **provides a powerful tool in the designing process.** Hot spots are the variable aspects of a framework domain, and different applications from the same domain differ from one another with regard to at least one of the hot spots [Fayad 1999a] (see also Chapter 15, "The Bast Framework for Reliable Distributed Computing"). Design patterns describe problems that occur repeatedly in our environment and then describe the core of the solutions to those problems in such a way that you can use the solutions a million times over without ever doing it the same way twice [Gamma 1995].

The framework should have a standard base whenever possible (like CORBA). Using a standard base avoids problems with integration, with communication with other applications, and even with commercializing the framework.

Prototyping is extremely critical (it adds significant flexibility and domain knowledge, but also adds a significant amount of time). In prototyping there is a fine line between gaining knowledge and losing resources (time, money). Thus, prototyping is a critical issue. It can be useful to gain domain knowledge, but it can be dangerous to the project resources. Sometimes the border between the prototype and the project itself is vague, and, accordingly, the process may start by building the prototype and end by building the system itself.

Iteration is a must. Good design and implementation require many iterations. Expect to rewrite the code three to five times. This is normal. The second iteration is always better than the first, and it typical for frameworks to be done more than once. Remember, frameworks are still a new technology.

Framework development needs experienced architects, experienced developers, and experienced engineers. In other words it needs the top people available. The development team must have good experience and skills to minimize the number of iterations and the development time. It is almost impossible to develop a good framework with a team that does not have enough experience.

Good documentation is essential. A framework without any documentation is worthless. Keeping a live document is both difficult and costly. Usually there is more than one documentation type used for frameworks (such as framework overview, example, cookbook & recipes, and interface contracts). In documentation, agree on naming conventions, and use illustrations liberally. All of the documents must include the same naming conventions to allow the documentation user to switch from one documentation type to another without discrepancy.

Educate the team early and agree on a basic methodology. Everyone agrees that an educated development team with high-quality experience reduces the development time and produces a quality product. Thus, it is essential to train the team in the necessary languages, modeling techniques, documentation types, concepts, and methodologies. Also, if the needed methodologies are clear and predefined it helps the development team to start the development instead of negotiating what is appropriate for the project.

Avoid excessive data coupling among framework components. With excessive data coupling, the framework loses its flexibility, and updating any component becomes problematic. The desired framework components should have clean interfaces, be cohesive, and have little data coupling.

Use as many patterns as possible. Using patterns is effective simply because it works better than inventing solutions from scratch and trying to prove that they work.

Choose the correct number of members per development team (to keep things uniform and complete). A large development team can waste time in communication and coordination among different team members. On the other hand, when the number of members per team decreases too much, it can cause an increase in the total number of teams, which can create integration problems.

Spend enough time in the design phase. Do not rush the development phase and race into coding. By skimping on design, the project will overlook many of its core requirements and will have a weak design.

Abstract the functionality and hide the details. Simply use types in your design phase and do not worry about their class implementations. This will ensure that this phase deals only with the design and not the implementation.

Keep it simple. Complexity is automatically added by the size of the structure. Make the design as simple as possible. In time, and with added requirements, the complexity will increase automatically.

Separate generic subdomains from particular subdomains. The generic subdomains can be used in different frameworks, so it is better to separate them and make them like modules, which can be used in implementing other frameworks.

The framework learning curve is very steep. The use of the appropriate documentation type in each phase of the learning curve will help shorten the learning period. The learning process can be divided into three phases:

Phase I, framework overview. In the first phase, general knowledge is needed about the framework and the appropriate applications to be derived from it. The appropriate documentation type to be used is the framework overview. This phase may take as little as a few hours to several days.

Phase II, example and reference manual. The second phase is to learn how the framework can be extended using examples.

Phase III, interface contracts, cookbook and recipes, and design patterns. The third phase deals with the implementation issues in the application and how to extend the existing framework using interface contracts, cookbooks, and recipes.

29.5.2 Commercialization of the Framework

This section provides a list of heuristics for successful framework commercialization.

Make sure your customers or clients agree with your framework approach. The framework appearance for the clients should be considered in the design phase, because nobody wants to build a framework (or other application) that contradicts the client's requirements.

Ensure that the client management understands that this is a long-term investment. Frameworks are a long-term investment. They provide stability for the application over time. Thus, management needs to know the reasons that frameworks are essential for their organization.

Ensure that the client management understands that the framework will become the most reliable part of their system (next to the operating system). Management is looking for reliability and stability. They need to be sure that what they are buying is reliable. A framework provides reliability because it separates the application implementation from the underlying framework implementation.

Provide extensive debug hooks for application developers (they tend to assume that the framework is at fault). Provide extensive debug hooks (as well as other tools and test cases) to test the application. It is usually difficult to tell if the fault is from the derived application or from the framework itself.

The portion of the code needed to complete the application must be small. The needed framework should cover most of the domain area, not just a small portion of it. Clients are looking for a small part of the code to write, not most of it, to get their application running.

Isolate the client from changes within the framework. Clients should not have to worry about changes in the framework. They need to recompile their application with the new framework without errors.

Performance (of execution and of fabrication/maintenance) is an important issue. Clients desire good performance. The performance factors may be different from one client to another. Thus, the framework designers have to consider different aspects of performance to satisfy the differing client needs.

OBJECT-ORIENTED FRAMEWORK SURVEY QUESTIONS

In this survey we hope to gather enough information about object-oriented framework development to provide real-world facts and statistics about frameworks. We believe the analysis of the survey's data will be important to everyone involved in application and enterprise frameworks. This survey consists of 19 questions covering many areas of framework technology. This survey usually takes about 15 to 25 minutes to complete. We promise to send you the survey results as soon as they are available. Please feel free to add your own comments to any question. We hope the survey will answer many questions about the current state of framework technology. We appreciate your help in bringing this survey to life.

1. Framework name _____.

2. My role in this project is _____.

3. Framework classifications:

   First classification:
   ❏ Blackbox (the internal structure is hidden, and the extensions come as ready-made modules)
   ❏ Whitebox (the internal structure is exposed to the application developer)
   ❏ Graybox (a combination of blackbox and whitebox framework)

   Second classification:
   ❏ Enterprise framework (addresses broad application domains, such as telecommunications or banking)
   ❏ Middleware integration framework (used to integrate distributed applications and components)
   ❏ System infrastructure framework (for the development of portable and efficient system infrastructures, such as operating systems)

4. **Framework size:**
   Number of classes _____.
   Number of data points _____.
   Number of function/feature points _____.
   Number of services _____.
   Number of hooks/hot spots _____.
   Number of lines of code _____.

5. **Implementation languages (for example, C++ or Assembly):** _____
   _____.

6. **Operating platform(s):** _____

7. **Domain areas (the domains where this framework is mainly used):**
   _____
   _____
   _____

8. **Who are the customers for this framework (for example, banks or insurance companies)?**
   _____
   _____
   _____

9. **Tools used in development and customization:**
   _____
   _____
   _____
   _____

10. **What is/are the documentation type(s) your framework provides (choose all applicable):**
    ❑ **Cookbooks and recipes**
    ❑ **Example applications**
    ❑ **Design patterns**
    ❑ **Interface contracts (specification of obligations and collaborations)**
    ❑ **Reference manual (class description)**
    ❑ **Framework overview**
    ❑ **Others (please specify)** _____

11. **Range of selling price:** _____

12. **Possible number of applications derived from this framework:** _____
    _____

Continues

OBJECT-ORIENTED FRAMEWORK SURVEY QUESTIONS *(Continued)*

13. What percentage of the framework was used in the final application? _____%

14. What is the average time to learn/develop this framework?

    Learn   **Develop**
    _____ days/person   _____ person-month
                                        _____ members/team

15. Did you use integration to develop/customize this framework?
    ❑ Yes. How many frameworks did you use? _____
    ❑ No.

16. If you used integration, how did you modify the control loop(s)?
    _____
    _____
    _____

17. Please list three difficulties you faced with framework integration:
    _____

18. Which of the following concepts did you use in this framework?
    ❑ Design patterns. How many? _____. What is the most commonly used
       design pattern? _____.
    ❑ Hot spots/hooks. How many? _____.
    ❑ Combinations. How many? _____.

19. If you used design patterns in development/customization, what percentage of your
    work was done using design patterns?
    _____%

20. Please provide three major lessons learned from your experience with framework
    technology:
    _____
    _____
    _____

21. From your experience with frameworks, please provide one to three heuristics:
    _____
    _____
    _____

CONTACT INFORMATION (optional):
Name/title _____.
Company/institution _____.
Street _____.
City _____.

State/country _____ .
Zip code _____ .
Telephone _____ .
Fax _____ .
email _____ .
URL _____ .

FRAMEWORK NAMES, ABBREVIATIONS, AND WEB SITES

ACE: Adaptive Communication Environment.

Adaptive object-oriented event-filtering framework: See Chapter 22 for more detail.

Amulet: A realtime programming system developed to be a general tool for handling time-critical processes (www.cs.uiowa.edu/~jones/amulet/index.html) [also see Chapter 25].

ARES: Abbreviation for "motorway control."

Asyn: (www.asyn.org).

CLOS Metaobject Protocol: The CLOS Metaobject Protocol was the first metaobject protocol designed as such. It provides control over the way CLOS implements objects, including object layout, object initialization, slot access, effective method definition, and generic function invocation (www.parc.xerox.com/spl/projects/mops/existing-mops.html).

BOOF: Business Object Oriented Framework.

CASUS: Computer Animation of Simulation Traces.

CSFramelets: A family of small frameworks for the client server.

Dynafind: Dynamic Finder.

GUI: Graphical User Interface.

HBOC application framework: (www.hboc.com).

IBM SF: IBM SanFrancisco.

Jadve: Java-based distributed graph drawing and viewing system (www.cs.columbia.edu/~wenke/).

MacApp: Macintosh Applications (www.macapp.com).

OMAC: Open Modular Architecture Controller API.

OmniBuilder: OmniBuilder is a tool that manages the full life cycle of the application (www.omnibuilder.com/).

OPTF: Object-Space Program Testing framework.

PFX: Persistence framework.

QC Services Layer framework: (www.quote.com).

SIGAL: Sprint Project.

29.6 Summary

The field of object-oriented application frameworks is not yet mature. It needs standardization in many areas, such as documentation, integration, and terminology. It also needs mature tools oriented to make the framework development cycle easier.

Frameworks can be classified according to their scope (system infrastructure, middleware integration, or enterprise application frameworks) or according to the ways used to extend them and the abstraction of the framework itself (whitebox, graybox, or blackbox). The trend for the future is toward graybox frameworks, since they avoid the drawbacks of both the black- and whitebox frameworks.

It is not worth building a framework if the number of derived applications is fewer than three. Otherwise, it would be much easier to build separate applications for each case and reuse some classes. Finally, there are areas such as hooks and hot spots, as well as framework standardization, that are in dire need of coverage.

29.7 References

[Butler 1999] Butler, Greg, and Pierre Denommee. Documenting Frameworks. Chapter 21 in *Building Application Frameworks: Object-Oriented Foundations of Framework Design,* M.E. Fayad, D. Schmidt, and R. Johnson, editors. New York: John Wiley & Sons, 1999.

[Fayad 1999a] Fayad, Mohamed E., R.E. Johnson, and D.C. Schmidt. *Building Application Frameworks: Object-Oriented Foundations of Framework Design.* New York: John Wiley & Sons, 1999.

[Fayad 1999b] Fayad, Mohamed E., R.E. Johnson, and D.C. Schmidt. *Implementing Application Frameworks: Object-Oriented Frameworks at Work.* New York: John Wiley & Sons, 1999.

[Fayad-Hamu 1999] Fayad, Mohamed E., and David Hamu. Object-oriented enterprise frameworks selection guidelines. Submitted for publication to *IEEE Computer,* 1999.

[Fayad-Schmidt 1997] Fayad, Mohamed E., and Douglas C. Schmidt. Object-oriented application frameworks. *Communications of the ACM* 40(10), October 1997:32–38.

[Gamma 1995] Gamma, Erich, Richard Helm, Ralph Johnson, and John Vlissides. *Design Patterns: Elements of Object-Oriented Software.* Reading, MA: Addison-Wesley, 1995.

[Gauthier-Truxal 1998] Gauthier, Chuck and Dave Truxal. San Francisco Project: Application Development Environment, White paper, www.javasoft.com/javareel/isv/IBM/SanFrancisco/white_paper.html#Header_3, 1998.

[Johnson 1997] Ralph E. Johnson. Frameworks = (Components + Patterns). *Communications of the ACM,* Theme Issue on Object-Oriented Application Frameworks, M.E. Fayad and D. Schmidt, editors. 40(10):39–42, October 1997.

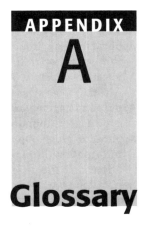

APPENDIX

A

Glossary

The definitions in this glossary are arranged in alphabetical order and were contributed by the authors of this book. A definition may be a single word, such as *component*; a phrase, such as *design patterns*; or an acronym, such as *UML.* Multiple definitions are also included, using enumeration.

The following cross-reference styles are used to show the relationship between definitions and to indicate the chapter in which they are covered:

See refers to a different entry for the definition of a synonym.

See also refers to similar and related definitions.

(#) indicates the chapter in which the term is discussed.

Boldface indicates terms that are defined elsewhere in the glossary.

Ab initio electronic structures. Models of molecules built from first principles of quantum mechanics *(24)*.

Abstract graph object. In Jadve, a graph element (such as a node or an edge) that does not represent application-specific data. In other words, it is a generic graph element. Abstract objects describe only the composition of a graph *(26)*.

Abstract method. A method containing an interface definition but missing an implementation *(27)*.

Adaptor pattern. A pattern documented by Gamma et al., in which an object is wrapped to comply with an independent **interface** *(27)*.

Agent. An element in a managed network. The agent is controlled by a network management system; it executes management requests and informs the management system about significant state changes *(18)*.

API. Application programmer interface, a set of programming functions that provide a well-defined set of services required by an **application** *(8, Sidebar 4)*.

Application. Functionality provided by one or more programs that consist of a collection of interoperating objects *(Sidebar 1)*.

Application directory (AD). A search engine for registering, organizing, and executing **MultiTEL** services *(21)*.

Application engineering. The analysis, design, and assembly of an **application** from the products of **domain engineering** *(10)*.

Application graph object. In Jadve, a graph element that represents application-specific information through its shape, drawing styles, and attributes. The same graph operation can have different semantics with different **application objects** *(26)*.

Application object. A collection of **components** that can be considered a subsystem *(2)*.

Architecture. A conceptual design of interacting **components** *(27)*.

Basis functions. Primitive spatial functions (typically cartesian gaussian functions) whose members are associated with one or more atoms of a molecule for the purpose of approximating solutions to quantum mechanical equations that describe the behavior of electrons in molecules. These equations are most easily solved by expanding the electron wave function or density in terms of a finite set *(24)*.

Behavior. The observable effects and results of performing a requested service *(Sidebar 1)*.

B/L mechanism. Broadcaster/listener communication mechanism *(3, 6)*

Callback. A function that is called in response to some **event**, such as the user clicking on a window button *(8)*.

Capacity requirements planning system. Applications software and databases used for capacity requirements planning. These systems contain information about labor and machine resource availability, planned work, and routings and time standards (machine steps necessary to build products, the amount of time the steps take, and other relevant information) *(9)*.

Chemical system. A molecule or chemical structure that is the subject of study *(24)*.

Chemical system geometry. A physical property—the geometric shape and orientation of a chemical system—that might result from a calculation of ab initio electronic structures or molecular dynamics .

CIM. Computer-integrated manufacturing *(3, 6)*.

CMIS. Common management information service *(Sidebar 4)*.

CNC. Computerized numerically controlled machine *(3, 6)*.

Component. [1] A collection of objects that provide functionality and a specified **interface** *(Sidebar 1)*. [2] A package of functionality comprising any number of actual objects. A component has well-specified functionality with standard interfaces and behaviors *(2)*. [3] A concrete implementation of an area of the system *(27)*. [4] Passive computational entities defined as Interface Definition Languages (IDLs) *(21)*.

Component directory (CD). This tool offers a global infrastructure that enables independently developed software **components** to be published and downloaded from the Internet *(21)*.

Composite pattern. A pattern documented by Gamma, et al., in which an object aggregates several objects while providing a singular view from the perspective of its clients *(27)*.

Compound status. A multiple-fielded value representing the status of an action *(27)*.

Computer-integrated manufacturing. The use of computer software and hardware to monitor and control equipment and machines used for the production of goods *(Sidebar 1)*.

Conformance. A relation defined over types such that type x conforms to type y if any value that satisfies type x also satisfies type y. Adherence to a specified standard or specification in the implementation of a product, process, or service *(Sidebar 1)*.

Connector. Reactive entities that encapsulate a coordination protocol between **components** *(21)*.

Constraint. A relationship that is declared once and then maintained by the system. Constraints are reevaluated whenever any values they depend on change *(25)*.

Control. Another name for a **widget** *(25)*.

Controller. In the **Model/View/Controller** architecture, the part that allows the user to edit the value by manipulating the **view**. In some **architectures**, the view and controller parts of the architecture are combined *(25)*.

CORBA. Common Object Request Broker Architecture *(24, 27)*.

CORBA Event Service. An OMG Services definition of event distribution that decouples the publisher of an **event** from the receipt by the subscriber to that event *(27)*.

C/P mechanism. Caller/provider communication mechanism *(3, 6)*.

CRC. Class responsibility collaborator, an object-oriented design methodology, originated by Kent Beck and Ward Cunningham, which utilizes flash cards to describe the responsibilities of a class and the other classes that it has to collaborate with in order to fulfill those responsibilities *(8)*.

CRP. Capacity requirements planning (processes and techniques), or **capacity requirements planning system** *(9)*.

C³P (common component-connector part). The kernel of the **MultiTEL** middleware platform *(21)*.

Cyclic executive scheduler. An offline scheduler that executes periodic tasks according to the order of their layout in a timeline *(16)*.

Data API layer. A library of application programmer interface functions that access and manipulate standard data representations defined by the common data model of the **Ecce** data-centered software design *(24)*.

Data-centered design model. A system design approach wherein a single, carefully constructed data model is used as the shared basis for tools, methods, and applications that access and manipulate data in a consistent way without regard to a specific data application or analysis process *(24)*. *See also* **Process-centered design model**.

Design pattern. Description of communicating objects and classes that are customized to solve a general design problem in a particular context *(16)*.

Development area. The directory location where programmers make and test early changes to their code *(27)*.

Directed attribute graph. A directed graph where edges and nodes can be annotated with attributes, such as text labels *(26)*.

Distributed memory parallel computers (DMPCs). Computers made of several processors working in parallel and communicating through a high-speed communication network *(14)*.

Distributed message bus. An interprocess communication technique that acts like a post office. Messages are placed in queues that can be read by any appropriate process, even if they run on another computer. The message bus software deals with all the details of **message delivery**, allowing applications that use it to simply open a mailbox, put a message in it or read a message from it, and continue with its work *(8)*.

Distributed object. An object (usually a collection of objects) that is spread among the various processors of a **distributed memory parallel computer (DMPC)**, according to a given **distribution template** *(14)*.

Distributed pattern. A pattern that describes a recurring structure in distributed protocol design and that generates protocols when applied. Distributed patterns are domain-specific, whereas standard **design patterns** generate general-purpose **architecture** that can be applied to any application domain *(15)*.

Distributed shared memory (DSM). Implements the abstraction of a shared memory on top of a distributed memory. It handles issues such as page faults, page caching, cache consistency, and so forth *(14)*.

Distribution template. The definition of the layout of a **distributed object.** A distribution template answers questions such as "on which processor is this item located?" or "what are the items local to this processor?" *(14)*.

Domain. An area of significance to an organization. A domain may have a technical or a business orientation *(10)*.

Domain analysis. The definition of the use cases, boundaries, actors, events, and components of a **domain** *(10)*.

Domain architecture. A model of a **domain** that defines its components, their static and dynamic relationships, and their contracts *(10)*.

Domain engineering. The design and implementation of the products of **domain analysis** *(10)*.

Domain framework. An implementation of a **domain architecture** *(10)*.

Dynamic adaptivity. The ability of a system to reconfigure itself at runtime to optimally meet the dynamic requirements of the system (CPU load, available memory, available bandwidth, and so on) *(17)*.

Dynamic binding. The plugging of **components** and **connectors** belonging to the same distributed application, which is performed inside a **middleware platform** *(21)*.

Earliest deadline first scheduler. An online, preemptive, priority scheduler, which assigns higher priorities to tasks with closer deadlines *(16)*.

Ecce. Extensible Computational Chemistry Environment, an integrated, problem-solving environment for computational chemistry being developed at the Department of Energy's Environmental Molecular Sciences Laboratory. Ecce enables research scientists to easily use computational programs to perform complex molecular modeling and analysis tasks, accessing networked, high-performance computers from their desktop workstations *(24)*.

Electronic structure codes. Computational chemistry codes that construct a mathematical description of the quantum-mechanical electronic wave function of a molecular system *(24)*.

EMSL. The William R. Wiley Environmental Molecular Sciences Laboratory, operated by Battelle for the U.S. Department of Energy in Richland, Washington, USA *(24)*.

ERP. Enterprise requirements planning, such systems generally provide **materials requirements planning** (MRP) and **capacity requirements planning** (CRP) functionality and also support many other business processes, such as payroll and accounting *(9)*.

Event. A message of some importance, sent asynchronously, noting a system state change, such as a new object creation or product movement *(2)*.

Exception. An infrastructure mechanism used to notify a calling client of a service that an unusual condition occurred during the execution of that service *(Sidebar 1)*.

Experiment. Either a set of observations of a natural property or simulations of that property *(24)*.

Explosion. The process whereby demands for products are converted into requirements for subassemblies and raw materials. This takes many factors into account, including inventory, manufacturing lead time, and other characteristics of the products to be manufactured *(9)*.

FMS. Flexible manufacturing system *(3, 6)*.

Formal specification. We have formally specified **MultiTEL** architecture using a formal description technique that allows us to validate existing multimedia services *(21)*.

Framework. [1] A collection of classes or **components** that provide a set of services and functions for a particular **domain** *(Sidebar 1)*. [2] A collection of specifications of interacting software components that comprise a solution for a particular domain *(2)*. [3] An object-oriented class hierarchy plus a built-in model of interaction that defines how the objects derived from the class hierarchy interact with one another *(16)*. [4] An instantiation of an **architecture** allowing components to be designed to interoperate *(27)*.

Garbage collection. The process of returning unused memory automatically to the system for further use without explicit programming intervention *(8)*.

Geometry optimization calculation. A simulation that seeks to identify the geometry of a chemical system with minimum molecular energy with respect to its atomic coordinates *(24)*.

Graph layout. A process that computes the optimal placement (location and size) of each node and edge, as well as the attributes (text labels) of a graph according to graph characteristics (planarity, orientation, and so on) and aesthetic criteria (maximization of the display of symmetries) *(26)*.

GUI. Graphical user interface, currently the most common type of computer **user interface** as utilized by the Apple Macintosh, Microsoft Windows, and Unix X-Window Systems *(8, 27)*.

GUI data model. A portion of Ecce's calculation setup framework, the GUI data model permits the flexible construction of graphical user interfaces (**GUIs**) for capturing general calculation options that can be incorporated into the input files of specific computational codes *(24)*.

Guidelines for the definition of managed objects (GDMO). ITU-T standard (X.722) that defines the formal language in which **managed object classes** are specified *(18)*.

High-performance Fortran. A new dialect of Fortran for programming massively parallel architectures. It is based on the so-called data parallelism model where the set of data involved in a computation is split into partitions, to which processes are associated; this makes it possible to benefit from one of the fundamental aspects of scientific applications, which is the use of repetitive computations on a large data space with extensions *(14)*.

Hook. A term defined by Pree to refer to the variable part of an algorithm *(27)*.

Implosion. A process that considers a desired demand and the availability of materials and capacity, producing a master production schedule that most closely meets the desired demand, taking into account the same factors considered by **explosion** *(9)*.

Instance. In a **prototype-instance object model**, an object created from another object. Initially, an instance has the same **slots** as the **prototype** from which it was made *(25)*.

Interface. The external view of a class, object, or component that emphasizes its abstraction while hiding its structure and internal behavior. A complete interface definition includes its semantics *(Sidebar 1)*.

Interoperability. The ability for two applications or the parts of applications to cooperate by sharing data, invoking services, exchanging events, and publishing service exceptions *(Sidebars 1, 2)*.

Iterator. A class of object that allows a program to traverse a list or network of data structures without explicit knowledge of the internal structure of the data *(8)*.

ITU-T (International Telecommunication Union, Telecommunication Sector). Organization that defines all relevant international standards for telecommunication systems *(18)*.

Java. An object-oriented programming language from Sun Microsystems. Java shares many language features common to most programming languages in use today and has language constructs similar to C and C++. The design and implementation of Jadve relied on Java's distributed, multithreading, portability, and dynamic features *(26)*.

LCF. A script language for the configuration of **MultiTEL** services. The goal of it is the tailoring of generic services *(21)*.

Managed object (MO). Object that represents a logical or physical resource of a network element in a managed network *(18)*.

Managed object class (MOC). Type of logical or physical resources of a network element in managed networks *(18)*.

Management information base (MIB). Repository of all management information available in a network element. The management information is kept as a collection of all **managed objects** of a network element. The MIB represents all logical and physical resources of the network element *(18)*.

Manipulator. An object that performs certain types of management manipulation on an object *(27)*.

Marshal/unmarshal. The process of converting a complex data structure to a data stream or creating a data structure from the contents of a data stream in order to pass the data structure between processes *(8)*.

Materials requirements planning (MRP). Planning the materials required for production using the **explosion** process. According to the *American Production and Inventory Control Society Dictionary*, materials requirements planning is "a set of techniques that uses bills of material data, inventory data, and the master production schedule to calculate requirements for materials. It makes recommendations to release replenishment orders for material. Further, because it is time-phased, it makes recommendations to reschedule open orders when due dates and need dates are not in phase. Time-phased MRP begins with the stocks listed on the MPS and determines the quantity of all components and materials required to fabricate those stocks and the date that the components and material are required. Time-phased MRP is accomplished by exploding the bill of material, adjusting for inventory quantities on hand or on order, and offsetting the net requirements by the appropriate lead times" *(9)*.

Materials requirements planning system. Applications software and databases used for materials requirements planning (MRP systems). These systems contain *bills of material* for each product to be manufactured; inventory data about raw materials, sub-assemblies, and finished products; information about material on order; and master production schedules *(9)*.

Measurement system. A class of systems used to measure the relevant values of a process or product. These systems are different from the better known process control systems in that the measured values are not directly (that is, as part of the same system) used to control the production process that creates the product or process that is measured. A measurement system is used for quality control on parts entering production or on produced products that can then be used to separate acceptable from unacceptable items or to categorize the products in quality categories *(11)*.

MES. Manufacturing execution system, a system to provide work-flow management and integration of manufacturing processes, equipment, and users *(8)*.

Message delivery. An extension of message passing that allows **connectors** to select target **components** by specifying their architectural names, references, or addresses *(21)*.

Metadata. Data about data. It is the definition of the structure of data utilized by a system in terms that can be understood and manipulated by either human operators or computer programs *(8)*.

Middleware platform. Distributed **component** platform that uses component and Internet technologies. It supports the dynamic creation and composition of reusable components *(21)*.

Model. [1] A **callback** package class that implements the subject role of the **Observer pattern** *(27)*. [2] In the **Model/View/Controller** architecture, the model is the part that holds the actual values to be presented to the user *(25)*.

Model/View/Controller. An **architecture** first described for Smalltalk, in which the parts of the software are divided into the **model**, holding the actual data; the **view**, which shows the data; and the **controller**, which allows the data to be manipulated *(25)*.

Molecular dynamics simulation. A time-dependent molecular model where atomic movement comes from solving Newton's laws of motion *(24)*.

MPP. Massively parallel processor *(24)*.

MRP. Materials requirements planning, or **materials requirements planning system** *(9)*.

MultiTEL (multimedia telecommunication services). Designates the **architecture**, the **framework**, and the **middleware platform** of our proposal *(21)*.

NMI. Network management interface *(Sidebar 4)*.

NWCHEM. A suite of distributed-data parallel computational chemistry codes, developed at the Pacific Northwest National Laboratory **(PNNL)** *(24)*.

Object environment. The **components** available to an object *(27)*.

Object services. **Interfaces** for general services that are likely to be used in any program that is based on **distributed objects** *(Sidebar 1)*.

Observer pattern. A pattern documented by Gamma, in which a client object is connected to a publishing subject through an abstract **interface** *(27)*.

OLTP (Online transaction processing system). Systems in which many users or processes typically manipulate a large volume of data and must do so in a way that guarantees the integrity of the data, even when multiple processes try to manipulate the same data at the same time *(8)*.

OMG. Object Management Group *(27)*.

OMT. Object modeling technique, an object-oriented design methodology developed by James Rumbaugh, et al., in the book *Object-Oriented Modeling and Design (8)*.

On-the-fly event. An **event** for which the value is determined at runtime and is usually used to report the completion status of a request *(27)*.

OpenDREAMS. An international project, funded by the European Community, aimed at building a **CORBA**-based platform for the development of supervision and control systems *(13)*.

OSI. Open Systems Interconnection *(Sidebar 4)*.

Pattern. A conceptual solution to a recurring problem *(27)*.

Persistence. The characteristic of data that it will not disappear or change when processes that use it terminate operation *(8)*.

PLC. Programmable logical controllers *(3, 6)*.

PNNL. Pacific Northwest National Laboratory, operated by Battelle for the U.S. Department of Energy *(24)*.

Preprocessor. A compiler step in which macros are expanded to their intended values *(27)*.

Pretty print. Formatted for the programmer to understand *(27)*.

Process-centered design model. A software design approach that considers scientific analysis as three separate data processing activities—preprocessing, solving, and postprocessing—resulting in individual tools that are optimized for specific purposes but not for ease of integrated use *(24)*. *See also* **Data-centered design model**.

Property. In Ecce's data model, the numeric results (typically physical properties) of experiments (observations or simulations) *(24)*.

Protocol object. A **distributed object** that is capable of participating in one or more distributed protocols (not just remote invocation). Its class is sometimes referred to as a *protocol class (15)*.

Prototype. In a **prototype-instance object model**, any object from which other objects are created. In most prototype-instance object systems, any object can serve as a prototype, and there is no special distinction between prototypes and **instances** *(25)*.

Prototype-instance object model. A software **architecture** in which the primary data structure is an object that provides a collection of attribute-value pairs, often called **slots**, where new objects are created by making **instances** of any existing object, which is called the **prototype**. In a prototype-instance object system, there is no concept of a class, since every object can serve as a prototype for other objects, and any instance can override any methods or data values *(25)*.

Rate monotonic scheduler. An online, preemptive, static priority scheduler, which assigns priority to tasks inversely to the task periods *(16)*.

RDBMS. Relation database management system, such as Oracle, Informix, or Sybase. Most commonly these systems utilize **SQL** to manipulate the data they contain *(8)*.

Realtime system. A system in which severe consequences will result if logical as well as timing correctness properties of the system are not satisfied *(16)*.

Reifiable object. An object abstraction that can be readily realized in an implementation (in other words, it can be easily translated to code) *(17)*.

Retained object model. *See* **Structured graphics model**.

Scenario. An account or synopsis of a projected course of action or events to be instantiated with software *(Sidebar 1)*.

SEMATECH. A consortium of major U.S. semiconductor manufacturers organized to further the development of tools and processes required to exploit new technologies used in the semiconductor manufacturing industry *(8)*.

Separation of concerns. The base of the coordination paradigm is to place computation and coordination in different entities. This principle was incorporated in the compositional model of the **MultiTEL** framework *(21)*.

SGMM. Semiconductor generic manufacturing model, an object-oriented model of the semiconductor manufacturing process developed at **SEMATECH** *(8)*.

Singleton pattern. A pattern documented by Gamma, in which a single, global instance of a class is accessed through a dynamically bound **interface** *(27)*.

Slots. In a **prototype-instance object model**, a single data item in an object. Each slot has a name and a value. Slots are similar to member variables or instance variables in other object models *(25)*.

Software architecture. Describes the static organization of software into subsystems interconnected through **interfaces** *(16)*.

SQL. Structure Query Language, a data query and manipulation language first developed by IBM for their System-R, a prototype relational database *(8)*.

Static adaptivity. The ability of a system to be initially configured to optimally meet the static requirements of the system (for example, total memory, total bandwidth, number of CPUs) *(17)*.

Static destructor. The termination of a global object, which happens after the exit from main( ) *(27)*.

Static initializer. The initialization of a global object, which happens before the entry of main( ) *(27)*.

Static value. A C++ construct that creates a global variable scoped within a class and subject to the access restrictions defined by the programmer *(27)*.

Strategy pattern. A pattern documented by Gamma, in which an object is provided a concrete implementation of an abstract **interface** to complete some part of its intended functionality *(27)*.

Structured graphics model. An **architecture** for graphics where each object that is visible on the screen is represented by an object in memory. The system can therefore handle refresh and other operations because it has a representation of the full contents of the screen. Also called a **retained object model** or *display list (25)*.

Stub. A callable implementation that performs the minimal functionality to satisfy the calling client without actually performing the required task *(27)*.

Subject. The role played in the **Observer pattern** that is being observed *(27)*.

Submitted library area. Area in which programmers submit their completed changes for use by other developers *(27)*.

Substitutability. The ability to replace a given **component** from one supplier with a functionally equivalent component from another supplier without impacting other components or clients of the system *(2, Sidebar 1)*.

Supervision and control system. A computer-based system that monitors and controls the behavior of a plant or any industrial process, such as a nuclear reactor or a chemical plant *(13)*.

Telecommunication and multimedia services. Distributed and groupware applications with multimedia data exchange. Examples are video on demand (VoD), business meetings, conferences, remote education, and chats *(21)*.

Template. A term defined by Pree (having nothing to do with the C++ template construct) referring to the concrete part of an algorithm *(27)*.

Template class. A C++ generic programming construct that allows a programmer to define abstract structures and algorithms to the compiler so that later uses of the code result in the compiler instantiating type-specific code based on its actual use *(27)*.

Template method. A pattern documented by Gamma (having nothing to do with the C++ template construct), in which a base class defines the abstract **interface** of a helper method and a derived class implements that interface *(27)*.

Thread. A computer process model that often utilizes fewer resources than a full program process, resulting in better performance and utilization of resources such as memory and CPU cycles *(8)*.

Thread dumb. Design without a multithreaded paradigm in mind *(27)*.

Token. A nondecomposable unit of data, from the perspective of the user of the data *(8)*.

Tokenizer. A class of iterator that can take a stream of data and turn it into tokens, which can then be utilized by programming functions such as parsers and interpreters *(8)*.

Toolkit. In **user interface** software, the collection of **widgets** or **controls** such as menus, scrollbars, and buttons. Usually, a toolkit is not considered a **framework** because it is lower-level and does not provide an object-oriented **architecture** for creating applications *(25)*.

TRIO. A formal specification language, based on an extension of temporal logic, suitable for dealing with realtime systems *(13)*.

User interface. The part of the software of a system that is visible to a human user *(25)*.

USP (user service part). Represents a user inside multimedia services. It performs dynamic composition, that is, the **dynamic binding** of **components** and **connectors** *(21)*.

View. In the **Model/View/Controller** architecture, the part that displays a value on the screen. A view might show the value as a string, or using a **widget** such as a scrollbar, or even as a graphical picture. The user can edit the value of the view using a **controller**. In some **architectures**, the view and controller parts are combined, and both parts together are called the view *(25)*.

Virtual function. A C++ construct that defines a class method implementation to be dynamically resolved to a call at runtime *(27)*.

Visual programming. Specification of application **architecture** by the direct manipulation of visual **components** and **connectors** *(21)*.

Well-known event. A prepublished event value *(27)*.

What-if analysis. An analysis in which a person changes one or more variables (for example, cost of a material) in order to evaluate the impact *(9)*.

Widget. An individual element of a **toolkit** used to enter a value or make a selection. Examples of widgets are scrollbars, buttons, and menus. Also called **controls** *(25)*.

XA. A protocol used to coordinate the work of multiple databases so that all the data in a distributed transaction are stored either correctly or not at all. Most commonly it is used to implement the so-called two-phase commit protocol *(8)*.

X-Windows. A windowing system largely based in the Unix environment *(27)*.

Index of Authors

This author index is arranged in alphabetical order by last name and includes the following information for each author: last name, first name, affiliation, country, primary email, URL, chapters contributed, and a brief biography.

Aarsten, Amund, Ph.D. Dipartimento Automatica e Informatica, Politecnico di Torino, Torino, Italy, email: amund@polito.it, URL: www.polito.it/~amund, Chapter 3, pp. 21–42, and Chapter 6, pp. 85–102.

Amund Aarsten is a developer at the Norwegian Company Economica AS. He specializes in advanced client-server systems and component-based development. He recently completed his Ph.D. thesis on design patterns and distributed systems.

alSafadi, Yasser, Ph.D. Philips Research, Briarcliff Manor, New York, USA, email: yha@philabs.research.philips.com, Sidebar 2, pp. 280–282.

Yasser alSafadi is leading the project on Healthcare Interoperability as a Principal Member of the research staff at Philips Research. He joined Philips in 1995. Before joining Philips, he worked as a Research Associate at the Computer Engineering Research Lab at the University of Arizona. There he received a Ph.D. in Electrical and Computer Engineering with minors in Computer Science and Management Information Systems.

Barghouti, Naser S., Ph.D. Bear Stearns & Co., New York, New York, USA, email: naser@bear.com, Chapter 26, pp. 547–564.

Naser S. Barghouti is a vice president of information services at Bear Stearns & Co. in New York. Prior to that he had been a member of the technical staff at AT&T Bell Laboratories since 1992, after earning his Ph.D. in computer science from Columbia University. He has published dozens of papers on software process management, automation and improvement, rule-based systems, database transactions, data modeling, and middleware. His current research interests are in the areas of software reuse, integration, middleware, and technology management.

Beijderwellen, Peter. Ernst & Young, Utrecht, the Netherlands, email: nlbeijd1@mey.nl, URL: www.mey.nl, Chapter 20, pp. 419–436.

Peter Beijderwellen currently works as a senior consultant at Ernst & Young Consulting in the Netherlands. His main areas of interest and expertise are distributed system architectures and middleware. Before joining Ernst & Young he gained practical experience as a software engineer and systems architect in several international Aerospace & Defense projects at Origin (www.origin-it.com). He graduated with a degree in Computer Science at Delft Technical University in 1988.

Bischofberger, Walter. TakeFive Software AG, Zurich, Switzerland, email: bischofberger@takefive.ch, URL: www.takefive.co.at/ and www.takefive.com, Chapter 23, pp. 495–512.

Walter Bischofberger is chief scientist of TakeFive Software, one of the leading vendors of large-scale source code engineering environments. He is working on concepts and tools for supporting large-scale software development for various programming languages, mainly C++ and Java. He teaches at ETH Zürich.

Bosch, Jan, Ph.D. RISE Research Group, University of Karlskrona/Ronneby, Department of Software Engineering and Computer Science, Ronneby, Sweden, email: Jan.Bosch@ide.hk-r.se, URL: www.ide.hk-r.se/[~bosch,~RISE,~ARCS], Chapter 11, pp. 177–206.

Jan Bosch received a M.Sc. degree from the University of Twente, the Netherlands, in 1991, and a Ph.D. from Lund University, Sweden, in 1995. He is currently a professor of software engineering at the University of Karlskrona/Ronneby, where he heads the Architecture and Composition of Software (ARCS) research group. He is the coeditor of the ECOOP'97 workshop reader, published by Springer-Verlag in the LNCS series, and is the initiator and coordinator of SARIS, a Swedish network on software architecture, involving both academia and industry.

Boyle, William. Brooks Automation Software, Chelmsford, Massachusetts, USA, email: bboyle@brooks.com and bboyle@netway.com, Chapter 8, pp. 121–138.

William Boyle is a principal software engineer at Brooks Automation Software (formerly FASTech Integration, Inc.), with responsibility for the design and development of a distributed transaction processing framework suitable for building large-scale distributed manufacturing systems. He has been engaged in the development of realtime and distributed manufacturing system software since 1982.

Brugali, Davide, Ph.D. Dipartimento Automatica e Informatica, Politecnico di Torino, Torino, Italy, email: brugali@polito.it, URL: www.polito.it/~brugali, Chapter 3, pp. 21–42, and Chapter 6, pp. 85–102.

Davide Brugali is postdoctoral research fellow at the Dept. of Automatica e Informatica of the Politecnico di Torino, Turin, Italy, where he received a Ph.D. in computer science. He received a master's degree in electronics engineering at the Polytechnic of Milan, Italy, in 1994. He was coorganizer of the OOPSLA'97, '98, and '99 Mid-year Workshops on Applied Object Technology for Manufacturing. In 1997, he spent one year at the Robotics Institute of Carnegie Mellon University doing research in the group of Dr. Katia Sycara. His most significant publications can be found in the *Communications of the ACM* and *ACM Computing Surveys.*

Capobianchi, Riccardo. Alcatel, Marcoussis, France, email: Riccardo.Capobianchi @alcatel.fr, URL: www.alcatel.com/, Chapter 13, pp. 231–250.

Riccardo Capobianchi has B.S. and M.S. degrees in electronic engineering and computer science from the Politecnico di Milano, Italy. His master's thesis concerned the development of an intelligent controller for crystal growth experiments on a free-flying platform. In 1992, he joined Alcatel Corporate Research Center in Marcoussis, France, where he managed several projects, including the Esprit IMPRESS, OpenDREAMS, and VENN. His areas of expertise include distributed architectures and middleware, object-oriented modeling and frameworks, advanced human-computer interfaces, multimedia and virtual reality, database systems, design methodologies, documentation management systems, parallel languages, and knowledge representation techniques.

Carcagno, Denis. SSD/Network Management Product Line, Alcatel CIT, Marcoussis, France, email: Denis.Carcagno@alcatel.fr, Chapter 13, pp. 231–250.

Denis Carcagno obtained his degrees in computer science at Paris VI University. He worked for Dassault Aviation laboratories, Odyssey Research Associates in Montreal, Canada, and Alcatel Alsthom Recherche, Alcatel. Since 1997, he has organized and is now heading a software development unit in charge of building new-generation network management products for the Alcatel Switching Systems Division.

Chan, Sally, M. The Boeing Company, Seattle, Washington, USA, email: sally.m .chan@boeing.com, Chapter 10, pp. 159–176.

Sally Chan is an associate technical fellow in the Information Systems division of The Boeing Company. Her areas of expertise are knowledge-based systems, case-based reasoning technology, and object-oriented domain engineering. She has more than 16 years of industrial experience in manufacturing. She has supported projects in manufacturing systems and generative numerical control systems at Boeing; computer-integrated manufacturing (CIM) at McDonnell Douglas; and CAD/CAM at IBM. She has an M.A. in computer-aided design and a B.A. in graphics design from UCLA, and a certificate in software product management from the University of Washington.

Chen, Sao-Jie, Ph.D. Department of Electrical Engineering, National Taiwan University, Taipei, Taiwan, R.O.C., email: csj@cc.ee.ntu.edu.tw, Chapter 16, pp. 327–338.

Sao-Jie Chen received B.S. and M.S. degrees in electrical engineering from the National Taiwan University, Taipei, Taiwan, R.O.C., in 1977 and 1982, respectively, and a Ph.D. in electrical engineering from Southern Methodist University,

Dallas, Texas, in 1988. He is a full professor in the Department of Electrical Engineering, National Taiwan University. His current research interests include VLSI circuit design and physical design, object-oriented software engineering, and multiprocessor architecture design and simulation.

Chin, Goodwin R., Ph.D. System Software Associates, San Francisco, CA, USA, email: Gchinatssa@aol.com, Chapter 9, pp. 139–158.

Goodwin Chin received a Ph.D. in electrical engineering and computer science from Stanford University in 1992. At the IBM T.J. Watson Research Center he worked on the development of object-oriented frameworks in the domains of technology computer-aided design and manufacturing logistics. Currently he is the technical services manager for System Software Associates and is responsible for implementations of the BPCS Enterprise Resource Planning system.

Coen-Porisini, Alberto, Ph.D. Dipartimento di Elettronica e Informazione, Politecnico di Milano, Italy, email: coen@elet.polimi.it, URL: www.elet.polimi.it/people/coen, Chapter 13, pp. 231–250.

Alberto Coen-Porisini received a Laurea degree in electrical engineering and a Ph.D. in computer science from the Politecnico di Milano, Italy, in 1987 and 1992, respectively. He has been an associate professor at the University of Lecce since November 1998. His main research interests are in software engineering, with particular reference to formal specification languages and object-oriented systems.

Cubert, Robert M. Department of Computer and Information Science and Engineering, University of Florida, Gainesville, Florida, USA, email: rmc@cise.ufl.edu, URL: www.cise.ufl.edu/~rmc, Chapter 28, pp. 591–614.

Robert M. Cubert is a Ph.D. candidate in Computer and Information Science and Engineering (CISE) at the University of Florida with a research interest in making practical the Web-based reuse of simulation models. He holds B.S. degrees in electrical engineering from the Massachusetts Institute of Technology and in zoology from the University of Oklahoma, and an M.S. in computer science from the University of Oklahoma. He spent three years on the computer science faculty at California State University, Sacramento, and has a decade of industry experience in software for realtime control systems and data communications.

Dee, Chris. Logica UK, Cambridge, United Kingdom, email: chrisd@logcam.co.uk, URL: www.logica.com, Chapter 20, pp. 419–436.

Chris Dee currently works as a senior consultant at Logica. He has considerable experience in the development of knowledge-based systems for industry and in the application of object-oriented techniques and software development. His interests include agent- and component-based architectures and planning and scheduling technology. Chris graduated with degrees in Math and Computer Science from the University of Birmingham in 1989.

Dietrich, Brenda L., Ph.D. IBM, T.J. Watson Research Center, Yorktown Heights, New York, USA, email: dietric@watson.ibm.com, Chapter 9, pp. 139–158.

Brenda Dietrich joined the IBM Research Division in 1984, after completing studies for her Ph.D. in operations research and industrial engineering at Cornell.

She has done research in manufacturing modeling and scheduling, inventory management, transportation logistics, mathematical programming, and combinatorial optimization. She is a member of the IBM Academy of Technology and is currently the senior manager of the Optimization Center, where she manages both the optimization research and the application of optimization to supply chain and transportation.

Dietrich, Walter C., Jr. IBM; T.J. Watson Research Center, Yorktown Heights, New York , USA, email: wally@watson.ibm.com, Chapter 9, pp. 139–158.

Wally Dietrich is a research staff manager at the IBM T.J. Watson Research Center. He received a B.S. in math sciences from the University of North Carolina–Chapel Hill in 1979 and an M.S. in computer science from Cornell in 1983. He has done research in object-oriented programming languages, software reengineering using objects, computer-aided design frameworks, object-oriented frameworks, and pattern matching. Most of his projects have involved multidisciplinary teams combining fields such as computer science, electrical engineering, and operations research.

Doscher, David. IBM, Austin, Texas, USA, email: doscher@ibm.net, Chapter 2, pp. 7–20.

David Doscher is an IBM Advisory Level software engineer and was an IBM assignee to Sematech from 1996 to 1998, working on the computer-integrated manufacturing (CIM) framework. While at Sematech, he was team leader of the CIM Framework Architecture Team and editor of the 1.5 and 2.0 version of the CIM Framework Specification, as well as the 1.0 version of the CIM Framework Architecture Guide. Prior to his time with Sematech, he worked on various IBM product development projects, including manufacturing execution systems (MESs). He is a member of the Association for Computing Machinery (ACM) and Institute of Electrical and Electronics Engineers (IEEE).

Ervolina, Thomas Robert, Ph.D. IBM; T.J. Watson Research Center, Yorktown Heights, New York, USA, email: ervolina@us.ibm.com, Chapter 9, pp. 139–158.

Thomas Ervolina is a research staff member at the IBM T.J. Watson Research Center in the Enterprise Solutions Research department. He received a B.S. degree in mathematics from the State University of New York at Stony Brook in 1982, and M.S. and Ph.D. degrees in operations research from Columbia University in 1983 and 1989, respectively. While at IBM Research, he participated in the development of an application framework for manufacturing logistics. In addition, he has developed optimization software for supply chain management using the framework.

Fasano, J.P. IBM, T.J. Watson Research Center, Yorktown Heights, New York, USA, email: jpfasano@us.ibm.com, Chapter 9, pp. 139–158.

J.P. Fasano joined IBM in 1979 and has worked on a large variety of software projects, including early Intel-based operating systems, performance-enabling mainframe vector applications, compiler development, advanced planning and scheduling solutions in the manufacturing industry (www.research.ibm.com/pdtr/prm.html), and math programming solutions (ism.boulder.ibm.com/es/oslv2/startme.htm). He is currently the development manager of Optimization

Solutions. He has a B.S. in electrical engineering, an M.S. in computer science, and an M.S. in operations research from Rensselaer Polytechnic Institute.

Fayad, Mohamed, E., Ph.D. Department of Computer Science and Engineering, University of Nebraska, Lincoln, USA, email: fayadm@acm.org, URL: www.cse .unl.edu/~fayad, lead book editor of this book, front matter and back matter, book parts, Chapter 1 (pp. 1–6), Chapter 22 (pp. 469–494), Chapter 29 (615–632), and the book Web site materials. Updates, news, question-and-answer sessions, and comments for the authors can be found on www.cse.unl.edu/~fayad and the Wiley Web page for this book www.wiley.com/compbooks/fayad.

Mohamed Fayad is an associate professor of computer science and engineering at the University of Nebraska, Lincoln. He was an associate professor at computer science, University of Nevada from 1995–1999. He has more than 15 years of industrial experience, and has been actively involved in more than 60 object-oriented projects for several companies He has been the guest editor of five theme issues: *CACM's OO Experiences* (October 1995), *IEEE Computer's Managing OO Software Development Projects* (September 1996), *CACM's Software Patterns* (October 1996), *CACM's OO Application Frameworks* (October 1997), and *ACM Computing Surveys—Application Frameworks* (June 1999). He has published articles in *IEEE Software, IEEE Computer, JOOP, ACM Computing Surveys,* and *CACM.* He is a distinguished speaker and has given lectures, tutorials, and seminars at national and international conferences, universities, and companies. Dr. Fayad is a senior member of the Institute of Electrical and Electronics Engineers (IEEE), a senior member of the IEEE Computer Society, a member of the Association for Computing Machinery (ACM), and he serves on several conference program committees, such as TOOLS USA '96 and Hong Kong QSD '96. In addition, he is an IEEE Distinguished Speaker; an associate editor, an editorial advisor, and a columnist for *Communications of the ACM IEEE Software,* Al-Ahram (the Egyptian Newspaper); editor-in-chief of the IEEE Computer Society Press—Computer Science and Engineering Practice Press (1995–1997); and an international advisor for several universities. He received an M.S. and a Ph.D. in computer science from the University of Minnesota at Minneapolis; his research topic was entitled "Object-Oriented Software Engineering: Problems & Perspectives." He is the lead author of *Transition to Object-Oriented Software Development* (John Wiley & Sons, 1998) and lead editor of this three-volume work on object-oriented application frameworks (John Wiley & Sons, 1999).

Fishwick, Paul A., Ph.D. Department of Computer and Information Science and Engineering, University of Florida, Gainesville, Florida, USA, email: fishwick@cise .ufl.edu, URL: www.cise.ufl.edu/~fishwick, Chapter 28, pp. 591–614.

Paul A. Fishwick is a professor in the Department of Computer and Information Sciences at the University of Florida. He received a B.S. in mathematics from the Pennsylvania State University, an M.S. in applied science from the College of William and Mary, and a Ph.D. in computer and information science from the University of Pennsylvania in 1986. He also has six years of industrial/government production and research experience. He founded the comp.simulation Internet news group (*Simulation Digest*) in 1987. He is on the editorial boards of several journals, including the *ACM Transactions on Modeling and Computer Simu-*

lation, IEEE Transactions on Systems, Man and Cybernetics, The Transactions of the Society for Computer Simulation, International Journal of Computer Simulation, and the *Journal of Systems Engineering.*

Fuentes, Lidia, Ph.D. Depto. de Lenguajes y Ciencias de la Computación, E.T.S.I en Informática, Universidad de Málaga, Spain, email: lff@lcc.uma.es, URL: www.lcc .uma.es/personal/fuentes/fuentes-en.html, Chapter 21, pp. 437–468.

Lidia Fuentes received her M.Sc. degree in computer science from the University of Málaga, Spain, in 1992, and her Ph.D. in 1998. Her Ph.D. thesis was on frameworks, software architectures, and multimedia services. She is an assistant professor in the Department of Computer Science of the University of Málaga. Her research interests deal with the practical applications of software architecture, in particular, composition and frameworks to intranets. She also works on multimedia programming in distributed systems.

Garbinato, Benoît, Ph.D. EPFL IN-Ecublens, Lausanne, Switzerland, email: Benoit .Garbinato@epfl.ch, URL: lsewww.epfl.ch/~garbinat, Chapter 15, pp. 283–326.

Benoît Garbinato has an M.S. (1993) and a Ph.D. in computer science from the Swiss Federal Institute of Technology of Lausanne (EPFL). His Ph.D. thesis was entitled "Protocol Objects and Patterns for Structuring Reliable Distributed Systems." In January 1999, he joined Ubilab, the UBS Information Technology Laboratory.

Gracio, Deborah K. Environmental Molecular Sciences Laboratory, Pacific Northwest National Laboratory, Richland, Washington, USA, email: gracio@pnl.gov, Chapter 24, pp. 513–528.

Deborah K. Gracio joined Pacific Northwest National Laboratory in 1990. She is a program manager for the Extensible Computational Chemistry Environment (Ecce). She was awarded a Certificate of Accomplishment by the Department of Energy in 1994 for her work on the Atmospheric Radiation Measurement Program, a program focused on the advancement of understanding of the effects of clouds on the atmosphere. She received her M.S. degree in electrical engineering from Washington State University in 1995. She currently serves on the advisory council for the School of Electrical Engineering and Computer Science at Washington State University.

Guerraoui, Rachid, Ph.D. EPFL IN-Ecublens, Lausanne, Switzerland, email: Rachid .Guerraoui@epfl.ch, URL: lsewww.epfl.ch/~rachid, Chapter 15, pp. 283–326.

Rachid Guerraoui obtained an M.S. in computer science from the University of Paris and an M.S. in electrical engineering from Ecole Superieure d'Informatique, Electronique et Automatique (Paris), both in 1989. He then worked for the French Atomic Agency in Saclay and obtained a Ph.D in computer science from the University of Orsay (Paris) in 1992. Since then, he has been affiliated with the Computer Science Department of the Swiss Federal Institute of Technology in Lausanne (EPFL), where he holds a position of assistant professor. Rachid's research interests are in the areas of object-oriented programming and distributed systems.

Hodges, Bob. Texas Instruments, Austin, Texas, USA, email: bhodges@ti.com, Chapter 2, pp. 7–20.

Bob Hodges is a senior member of the Technical Staff at Texas Instruments and a TI assignee to International SEMATECH. At SEMATECH, he contributed to the final revision of the SEMATECH computer-integrated (CIM) framework and the transition of the CIM framework into industry standards adoption processes in the SEMI International Standards program and the Object Management Group. Bob founded and chaired TI's object technology center and represented TI in industry consortia and standards bodies pioneering the application of object technology to business problems.

Hu, James. Entera, Inc., St. Louis, Missouri, USA, email: hu@cs.wustl.edu, URL: www.cs.wustl.edu/~hu, Chapter 17, pp. 339–382.

James Hu is principal engineer at Entera, Inc., and a doctoral candidate in the Department of Computer Science at Washington University in St. Louis. His research activities have included the development of a formal design methodology for distributed components, performance analysis of HTTP servers, and the design and development of a high-performance adaptive Web system framework. He dual majored in mathematics and computer science at Kansas State University, Manhattan, Kansas, in 1992, and received an M.S. degree in computer science from Washington University in 1995.

Hu, Jingkun. Philips Research, Philips Eletronics North America Corp., Briarcliff Manor, New York, USA, email: jhu@philabs.research.philips.com, Chapter 22, pp. 469–490.

Jingkun Hu is a member of the research staff in the software systems and architecture department at Philips Research, Philips Eletronics North America Corp. He received a master's degree in computer science from the University of Nevada in 1998.

Jezequel, Jean-Marc, Ph.D. IRISA/CNRS, Rennes, France, email: jezequel@irisa.fr, URL: www.irisa.fr/prive/jezequel, Chapter 14, pp. 251–282.

Jean-Marc Jezequel has an engineering degree in telecommunications from the ENSTB in 1986, and a Ph.D. degree in computer science from the University of Rennes, France, in 1989. He is a research manager in the Irisa Lab for the Centre National de la Recherche Scientifique. His research interests include software engineering and object-oriented technology for telecommunications and distributed computers. He is the author of the book, *Object Oriented Software Engineering with Eiffel* (Addison-Wesley, 1996).

Johnson, Ralph E., Ph.D. Department of Computer Science, University of Illinois at Urbana-Champaign, USA, email: johnson@cs.uiuc.edu, URL: www.cs.uiuc.edu/users/~johnson, a coeditor of this book.

Ralph E. Johnson is on the faculty of the Department of Computer Science at the University of Illinois. He is the leader of the UIUC patterns/Smalltalk group and the coordinator of the senior projects program for the department. His professional interests cover nearly all things object oriented, especially frameworks, patterns, business objects, Smalltalk, common object model (COM), and refactoring. He has been to every OOPSLA. He received his Ph.D. and M.S. from Cornell and his B.A. from Knox College. He is a member of the Association for Computing Machinery (ACM) and the IEEE Computer Society. He is a coauthor of *Design*

Patterns: Elements of Object-Oriented Software (Addison-Wesley, 1996). He is also a coeditor of this three-volume work on object-oriented application frameworks (John Wiley & Sons, 1999).

Jones, Donald R., Ph.D. Environmental Molecular Science Laboratory, Pacific Northwest National Laboratory, Richland, Washington, USA, email: dr.jones@pnl.gov, Chapter 24, pp. 513–528.

Donald R. Jones has been a staff scientist at Pacific Northwest National Laboratory since 1989. Currently, he is a technical group leader for the Molecular Science Compute Facility (MSCF) Scientific Consulting group and manager of the EMSL MSCF Graphics and Visualization Laboratory. He also holds an adjunct faculty position at Washington State University—Tri-Cities. He received a Ph.D. in engineering from Brigham Young University in 1985. He has been an invited speaker at numerous symposia and conferences.

Keller, Rudolf K., Ph.D. Département d'informatique et de recherche opérationnelle, Université de Montréal, Canada, email: keller@iro.umontreal.ca, Sidebar 4, pp. 489–490.

Rudolf K. Keller is an associate professor in the software engineering group at the Département d'informatique et de recherche opérationnelle, Université de Montréal, Canada.

Keller, Thomas L. ThemeMedia, Inc., Redmond, Washington, USA, Chapter 24, pp. 513–528.

Kocher, Hartmut, Ph.D. Cortex Brainware GmbH Germany, email: hwk@cortex-brainware.de, URL: www.cortex-brainware.com, Chapter 18, pp. 383–396.

Hartmut Kocher received a Ph.D. in electronic engineering from the University of Stuttgart in 1994. From 1993 to 1998, he worked as a senior technical consultant for Rational Software Germany, where he worked as a software architect for several customers. He teaches courses at the University of Stuttgart on management of object-oriented projects, software architecture, and the UML, and has published numerous papers on these subjects.

Lammers, Terence L., Ph.D. The Boeing Company, Seattle, Washington, USA, email: terence.l.lammers@boeing.com, Chapter 10, pp. 159–176.

Terry Lammers is a senior principal engineer in the Information Systems division of The Boeing Company. His areas of expertise are object-oriented technology, object-oriented domain engineering, distributed object architectures and applications, object-oriented software engineering, and application development. He serves as both an application project manager and lead software engineer. He holds a B.S. in computer science from the University of Montana, an M.S. in computer science from Montana State University, and Ph.D. in Slavic linguistics from Indiana University.

Lee, Wenke. Computer Science Department, Columbia University, New York, New York, USA, email: wenke@cs.columbia.edu, URL: www.cs.columbia.edu/~wenke, Chapter 26, pp. 547–564.

Wenke Lee is a Ph.D. candidate in computer science at Columbia University. Prior to that, he was a senior software engineer at Intergraph Corporation from 1990 to 1994. His current research interests include data mining, intrusion detection, objected-oriented databases, and work-flow modeling and management.

Liver, Beat, Ph.D. IBM Research Division Zürich Research Laboratory, Switzerland, email: bli@zurich.ibm.com, URL: www.zurich.ibm.com/~bli, Chapter 19, pp. 397–418.

Beat Liver received a diploma in Informatics from the Swiss Federal Institute of Technology (ETH) in Zürich in 1989. He completed his Ph.D. in artificial intelligence and software engineering in the Computer Science Department of the Swiss Federal Institute of Technology in Lausanne (EPFL) in 1996, on a novel, generic software-component model (called Zweckdarstellung and ZD, pronounced "Zeddy"). He joined the IBM Zürich Research Laboratory, where he is developing network management solutions.

Lougee-Heimer, Robin, Ph.D. IBM; T.J. Watson Research Center, Yorktown Heights, New York, USA, email: rlh@watson.ibm.com, Chapter 9, pp. 139–158.

Robin Lougee-Heimer works in the Mathematical Sciences Department of IBM's Research Division, where she supports IBM manufacturing and conducts research in the areas of mathematical programming and combinatorial optimization. She has been with IBM Research since earning her Ph. D. degree in mathematical sciences from Clemson University in 1993. Her contributions to IBM and its customers center on developing optimization-based decision support tools to address manufacturing resource allocation problems. Currently, she is investigating new polyhedral approaches to solve integer programming problems that arise in manufacturing applications.

Mandrioli, Dino, Ph.D. Dipartimento di Elettronica e Informazione, Politecnico di Milano, Italy, email: mandriol@elet.polimi.it, URL: www.elet.polimi.it/people/mandriol, Chapter 13, pp. 231–250.

Dino Mandrioli graduated in electrical engineering from the Politecnico di Milano in 1972 and in mathematics from the Università Statale di Milano in 1976. He is a professor of computer science at the Politecnico di Milano. His research interests include theoretical computer science and software engineering, with particular reference to specification languages and environments, programming languages, and realtime systems. He has published more than 70 scientific papers in major journals of the field, such as *Journal of the ACM; SIAM Journal on Computing, Information and Control; ACM-Transactions on Programming Languages and Systems (TOPLAS); ACM Transactions on Software Engineering and Methodology (TOSEM); ACM-Transactions on Computer Systerms (TOCS); and IEEE Transactions on Software Engineering (TSE).* He is also a coauthor of several books, including *Formal Methods for Real-Time Computing* (John Wiley & Sons, 1996), *Fundamentals of Software Engineering* (Prentice Hall, 1991), and *The Art and Craft of Computing* (Addison-Wesley, 1997).

Mätzel, Kai-Uwe. Object Technology International Inc., Zürich, Switzerland, email: kai-uwe_maetzel@oti.com or maetzel@acm.org, URL: www.oti.com, Chapter 23, pp. 495–512.

Kai-Uwe Mätzel is senior software engineer at Object Technology International Inc. (OTI). He worked as a research scientist at Ubilab, the former information technology research lab of Union Bank of Switzerland. His work focuses on component systems and adaptive software architectures. He teaches at ETH Zürich and University of Zürich.

McDaniel, Richard. Computer Science Department, Carnegie Mellon University, Pittsburgh, Pennsylvania, USA, email: richm@cs.cmu.edu, URL: www.cs.cmu .edu/~richm, Chapter 25, pp. 529–546.

Richard McDaniel is a Ph.D. candidate in computer science at Carnegie Mellon University. He worked as an intern for the Object Linking and Embedding (OLE) group at Microsoft for three years, where he prototyped advanced OLE 2.0 interfaces such as inplace editing. His research interests include programming environments, visual languages, programming by demonstration, and user interfaces.

Mehta, Uday. Alta Software, Inc., Hinsdale, Illinois, USA, email: umehta@altasoft .com, URL: www.altasoft.com, Chapter 7, pp. 105–120.

Menga, Giuseppe, Ph.D. Dipartimento Automatica e Informatica, Politecnico di Torino, Italy, email: menga@polito.it, URL: cimserver.polito.it/, Chapter 3, pp. 21–42, and Chapter 6, pp. 85–102.

Giuseppe Menga has been a professor and has held the chair of Automatic Controls at the Polytechnic of Turin since 1981. For the past 10 years, his academic and professional activity has been focused on modeling and control of computer-integrated manufacturing systems, and he has pioneered the use of object-oriented technology in this field since 1985. His most significant publications can be found in the *IEEE Transactions on Automatic Control,* the *IEEE Transactions on Robotics and Automation, Communications of the ACM,* and the *Journal of Object-Oriented Programming.* He was the general chairman of the 1992 IEEE Robotics and Automation International Conference held in Nice, France.

Messmer, Bruno, Ph.D. Swisscom AG, Bern, Switzerland, email: Bruno.Messmer @swisscom.ch, Chapter 19, pp. 397–418.

Bruno T. Messmer is an artificial intelligence and software engineering expert working for the Corporate Information and Technology Unit of Swisscom. Before joining Swisscom in 1996, he received a doctoral degree from the University of Berne for his work in the area of pattern recognition and graph matching. Currently, he is working in the area of voice-controlled telephone services and intelligent agents and also on problems concerning the planning and optimization of GSM, ATM, and IP networks. He has an ongoing interest in object-oriented technologies, Java and C++, Internet applications, and, in general, the application of AI techniques to the telecommunication domain.

Miller, Rob. Computer Science Department, Carnegie Mellon University, Pittsburgh, Pennsylvania, USA, email: rcm@cs.cmu.edu, URL: www.cs.cmu.edu/ ~rcm/, Chapter 25, pp. 529–546.

Rob Miller is a Ph.D. candidate in computer science at Carnegie Mellon University, where his research interests are end-user programming, user interface software, World Wide Web automation, and structured text processing. In 1995 he earned a B.S. and an M.Eng. in electrical engineering and computer science from the Massachusetts Institute of Technology.

Morzenti, Angelo, Ph.D. Dipartimento di Elettronica e Informazione, Politecnico di Milano, Italy, email: morzenti@elet.polimi.it, URL: www.elet.polimi.it/people/morzenti, Chapter 13, pp. 231–250.

Angelo Morzenti graduated in electrical engineering in 1985 from Politecnico di Milano, where he also gained a Ph.D. in computer science in 1989. He became an assistant professor in 1990 and has been an associate professor since 1998 at Politecnico di Milano. His research interests are centered on software engineering, with a focus on languages, methods, and tools for specification and analysis of critical systems. He has published several papers on these subjects at international conferences and in journals.

Myers, Brad A., Ph.D. Human Computer Interaction Institute, School of Computer Science, Carnegie Mellon University, Pittsburgh, PA, USA, email: bam@cs.cmu.edu, URL: www.cs.cmu.edu/~bam, Chapter 25, pp. 529—546.

Brad A. Myers is a senior research scientist at the Human-Computer Interaction Institute. He is the principal investigator for various projects including the User Interface Software project, the Demonstrational Interfaces project, the Natural Programming project, and the Pebbles PalmPilot Project. He is the author or editor of more than 180 publications, including the books, *Creating User Interfaces by Demonstration* and *Languages for Developing User Interfaces.* He received a Ph.D. in computer science at the University of Toronto, where he developed the Peridot UIMS. He received M.S. and B.Sc. degrees from the Massachusetts Institute of Technology, during which time he was a research intern at Xerox PARC. From 1980 until 1983, he worked at PERQ Systems Corporation.

Pacherie, Jean-Lin, Ph.D. IRISA/CNRS, Rennes, France, email: jezequel@irisa.fr, URL: www.irisa.fr/prive/jezequel, Chapter 14, pp. 251–282.

Jean-Lin Pacherie received his DEA (master of science) in computer science and applied mathematics from the National Polytechnic Institute of Grenoble (INPG, France), in 1994. He received a Ph.D. in computer science from the University of Rennes, France, in 1997. His research interests include design patterns, software library design, and distributed programming.

Poole, Elizabeth J. IBM; T.J. Watson Research Center, Yorktown Heights, New York, USA, email: ejp@us.ibm.com, Chapter 9, pp. 139–158.

Elizabeth Poole joined IBM in 1986, to port internal accounting systems to a newer version of APL while completing her undergraduate double major in computer science and graphic design. The combination of the two programs and her continuing work in the field of human-computer interaction have led her to contribute to the development of many of IBM's commercial office software offerings. She has been developing user interfaces for advanced planning, scheduling and supply chain solutions since 1994.

Schabernack, Joerg. Alcatel Stuttgart, Germany, email: Joerg.Schabernack@ks.sel.alcatel.de, Chapter 18, pp. 385–396.

Joerg Schabernack has a master's degree in computer science from Koblenz University. In 1993 he joined the Transmission Systems Division of Alcatel Germany.

Schmid, Hans Albrecht, Ph.D. Fachbereich Informatik, Fachhochschule Konstanz, Germany, email: schmidha@fh-konstanz.de, Chapter 4, pp. 43–66, and Chapter 5, pp. 67–84.

Hans Albrecht Schmid has an M.Sc. in electrical engineering from the University of Stuttgart, an M.Sc. in computer science from the Institut Nationale Polytechnique de Grenoble (1973), and a Ph.D. in computer science from the University of Karlsruhe. He has been visiting assistant professor in the Department of Computer Science at the University of Toronto. He was head of the research group on database management systems in the Department of Computer Science at the University of Stuttgart. From 1977 to 1987, he held different technical lead and management positions with the IBM development laboratory in Boeblingen. Since 1987, he has been a professor of computer science at the University for Applied Research in Konstanz. His current areas of interest include design patterns, frameworks, manufacturing cells and automation, and Internet client-server applications.

Schmidt, Douglas C., Ph.D. Department of Computer Science, Washington University, St. Louis, MO, USA, email: schmidt@cs.wustl.edu, URL: www.cs.wustl.edu/~schmidt, Chapter 17, pp. 339–382.

Douglas Schmidt is an associate professor in the Department of Computer Science and in the Department of Radiology at Washington University in St. Louis, Missouri. His research focuses on design patterns, implementation, and experimental analysis of object-oriented techniques that facilitate the development of high-performance, realtime distributed object computing systems on parallel processing platforms running over high-speed asynchronous transfer mode (ATM) networks. He received B.S. and M.A. degrees in sociology from the College of William and Mary in Williamsburg, Virginia, and an M.S. and a Ph.D. in computer science from the University of California, Irvine (UCI) in 1984, 1986, 1990, and 1994, respectively. He is a member of the USENIX, Institute of Electrical and Electronics Engineers (IEEE), and Association for Computing Machinery (ACM). He is also a coeditor of this three-volume work on object-oriented application frameworks (JohnWiley & Sons, 1999).

Schuchardt, Karen L. Environmental Molecular Sciences Laboratory, Pacific Northwest National Laboratory, Richland, Washington, USA, email: karen.schuchardt@pnl.gov, Chapter 24, pp. 513–528.

Karen Schuchardt is a senior research scientist at the Pacific Northwest National Laboratory. She has been a technical lead on the Extensible Computational Chemistry Environment (Ecce) project for the past four years. She received her B.S. in computer science from the University of Wisconsin—Madison in 1984. Her interests are software engineering, systems analysis and requirements definition, systems architecture, graphical user interfaces, and object databases.

See, Win-Bin. National Taiwan University, Tai-Chung, Taiwan, R.O.C., email: wbsee@ms6.hinet.net, Chapter 16, pp. 327–338.

Win-Bin See received a B.S. in electronics engineering from the Feng-Chia University, Taichung, Taiwan, in 1980, and an M.S. in electrical engineering from the

National Cheng-Kung University, Tainan, Taiwan, in 1984. He worked as a software engineer at Aerospace Industrial Development Corporation (AIDC), Taichung, Taiwan. He is a Ph.D. candidate at National Taiwan University, Taipei, Taiwan.

Spilling, Per, ObjectWare AS, Oslo, Norway, email: per.spilling@objectware.no, URL: www.objectware.no, Chapter 20, pp. 419–436.

Per Spilling has been involved with object technology since 1989 when he was introduced to C++ by Guido van Rossum (creator of Python) at CWI in the Netherlands. He stayed at CWI for more than 6 years doing R&D work on HCI, application frameworks, and helping to develop a language for coordinating parallel processes. In 1994 he joined Origin (www.origin-it.com) where he, among others, worked on several international Aerospace & Defense projects. Since 1998 he has worked as a software architect and consultant at Objectware in Oslo, Norway. His main areas of interest and expertise are object-oriented software engineering, patterns, software process improvement, distributed system architectures, and middleware. He graduated in 1987 with a degree in mechanical engineering from the Norwegian Institute of Technology, Trondheim.

Stafford, James C. RABA Technologies, Inc., Columbia, Maryland, USA, email: jim.stafford@raba.com, URL: www.raba.com/~jcstaff, Chapter 27, pp. 565–590.

James C. Stafford is chief scientist of object-oriented technologies at RABA Technologies, Inc. He also teaches OOP/C++ at The Johns Hopkins University. He has been involved in object-oriented (OO) development since 1991. He has a bachelors of arts degree in physics from Gettysburg College and a master of science in computer science from The Johns Hopkins University.

Tang, Jung-Mu. IBM; T.J. Watson Research Center, Yorktown Heights, New York, USA, email: jmt@watson.ibm.com, Chapter 9, pp. 139–158.

Jung-Mu Tang received a B.S. degree from National Taiwan University, Taiwan, R.O.C., in 1975, and an M.S. degree in civil engineering from the University of California at Berkeley in 1978. Since then, she has worked for several engineering consulting firms on projects related to the analysis and evaluation of transportation systems and nuclear power plants. In 1983, she joined IBM T.J. Watson Research Center and has worked on projects related to solid modeling systems, the 2-D automatic finite element mesh generator, the Production Resource Manager (PRM) framework, and Lotus/Notes-based applications.

Taylor, Hugh L., Ph.D. WRQ, Inc., Seattle, Washington, USA, email: hught@wrq.com, Chapter 24, pp. 513–528.

Hugh L. Taylor has an A.B. in chemistry from the University of Chicago and a Ph.D. in theoretical chemistry from the University of Utah. He joined the PNNL staff as domain specialist and as a developer for the Extensible Computational Chemistry Environment. He is now a software developer at WRQ, Inc., in Seattle, specializing in security issues. His interests include problem-solving environments, high-performance scientific computation, and the design of distributed object systems.

Tessier, Jean. AT&T Labs, Menlo Park, California, USA, email: Jean.Tessier@att.com, Sidebar 4, pp. 489-490.

Jean Tessier is a software engineer at AT&T Labs in Menlo Park, California. The research presented in this volume was conducted when he was a master's student (1992–1995) at the Département d'informatique et de recherche opérationnelle, Université de Montréal, Canada. He is now working on distributed object systems and prototyping of telecommunication services for the Internet.

Troya, José M., Ph.D. Depto. de Lenguajes y Ciencias de la Computación, E.T.S.I en Informática, Universidad de Málaga, Spain, email: troya@lcc.uma.es, URL: www.lcc.uma.es/personal/troya/troya.html, Chapter 21, pp. 437–467.

José M. Troya received his M.Sc. and Ph.D. degrees from the Universidad Complutense of Madrid, Spain, in 1975 and 1980, respectively. He is a professor and head of the Department of Computer Science at the University of Málaga. His current research interests are coordination languages, software architectures, compositional frameworks, and heterogeneous distributed systems. His most significant publications can be found in international journals such as *Computer Journal, Computer Languages, Computing, Parallel Computing,* and the *Journal of Evolutionary Computation.*

Tsai, Wei-Tek, Ph.D. Department of Computer Science and Engineering, University of Minnesota, Minneapolis, Minnesota, USA, email: tsai@cs.umn.edu, URL: www.cs.umn.edu/~tsai, Sidebar 3, pp. 379–381.

Wei-Tek Tsai is currently professor of computer science at the University of Minnesota, Minneapolis, Minnesota. He earned his S.B. in computer science and engineering from the Massachusetts Institute of Technology at Cambridge, and his M.A., M.S., and Ph.D. in computer science from the University of California at Berkeley. His current interest is in Internet programming and software engineering. He is on the editorial board of the Institute of Electrical and Electronics Engineers (IEEE) Computer Society Press, the *Journal of Software Maintenance,* the *Journal of Software Engineering and Knowledge Engineering,* and the *Journal of AI Tools.* He was the program chair of the IEEE International Conference on Computer Software and Application in 1997.

Vijayananda, Kateel, Ph.D. Swisscom AG, Bern, Switzerland, email: vijay@uniplus.ch, Chapter 19, pp. 397–418.

Kateel Vijayananda received a B.S in computer science from BITS, Pilani, India, in 1988; an M.S in computer science from IIT Madras, India, in 1990; an M.S in computer science from the University of Maryland at College Park, Maryland, USA, in 1994; and a Ph.D. in computer science from EPFL, Lausanne, Switzerland, in 1996. His Ph.D. thesis is related to diagnosis of faults in communication protocols. He is working at Data & Multimedia, Swisscom AG as a network engineer involved in developing network services. His current areas of interest include network planning, resource allocation, and diagnosis of faults in communication networks to ensure better quality of service.

Wang, Robert H., Ph.D. Siebel Systems, Inc., San Mateo, California, USA, email: rwang@siebel.com, URL: www.siebel.com, Chapter 9, pp. 139–158.

Robert H. Wang is a senior software engineer in the Sales Enterprise Application Development Group at Siebel Systems, Inc., in San Mateo, California. He was a research staff member at IBM Research, Yorktown Heights, New York. As a lead designer and the project manager, he was a member of the team that developed an object-oriented integration framework for shipment planning. He received his B.S., M.S., and Ph.D. degrees in electrical engineering and computer sciences from the University of California at Berkeley in 1989, 1991, and 1995, respectively. His doctoral thesis was on the integration of solid modeling operations in 3-D integrated circuit topography simulators.

Wegner, Peter, Ph.D. Computing Surveys Editor-in-Chief, Department of Computer Science, Brown University, Providence, Rhode Island, USA, email: pw@cs.brown .edu, Chapter 12, pp. 211–230.

Peter Wegner is a professor of computer science at Brown University and editor-in-chief of *Computing Surveys* and of *The Brown Faculty Bulletin*. His current research interests are interaction, compound and active document systems (such as OpenDoc, JavaBeans and ActiveX), object-oriented programming, and programming languages.

Whelan, Pete, Ph.D. Motorola Semiconductor Products Sector, Austin, Texas, USA, email: rzgf30@email.sps.mot.com, Sidebar 1, pp. 100–102.

Pete Whelan manages a manufacturing systems architecture group in the Motorola Semiconductor Product Sector's Information Technology organization. Prior to his current role, he worked for three years as a Motorola assignee to SEMATECH, where he managed a program to develop the computer-integrated manufacturing (CIM) framework, a component-based manufacturing system application architecture. Before joining SPS, he was a member of Motorola's Corporate Manufacturing Research Center. He earned his Ph.D. in mechanical engineering and a certificate in computer-integrated manufacturing systems from the Georgia Institute of Technology.

Wittrock, Robert J., Ph.D. IBM, T.J. Watson Research Center, Yorktown Heights, New York, USA, email: bobw@watson.ibm.com, Chapter 9, pp. 139–158.

Robert Wittrock is a research staff member in the Mathematical Sciences Department at the IBM T.J. Watson Research Center. He received his Ph.D. in operations research from Stanford University in 1983. He conducts research and develops software in the area of applied optimization.

Wong, Danny C. IBM; T.J. Watson Research Center, Yorktown Heights, New York, USA, Chapter 9, pp. 139–158.

Danny C. Wong is an advisory engineer at the IBM T.J. Watson Research Center in Yorktown Heights, New York. His current focus is on developing object-oriented software in the areas of pervasive computing and enterprise integration systems. He received his master's degree in electrical engineering from the University of Virginia.

Yang, DerShung, Ph.D. Alta Software, Inc, Buffalo Grove, Illinois, USA, email: dyang@altasoft.com, URL: www.altasoft.com, Chapter 7, pp. 105–120.

DerShung Yang is a Technical Project Manager at Alta Software, Inc., a consulting firm specializing in enterprise-wide E-business applications. For the past four years, Dr. Yang has led two successful large-scale, long-term projects using object-oriented technologies. His team's services are currently retained by a premier on-line service provider in the classified advertising marketplace to develop their web sites. Dr. Yang's primary interest is applying distributed object-oriented technologies to the development of commercial web sites and Internet applications. Dr. Yang holds a Ph.D. in Computer Science from the University of Illinois at Urbana-Champaign, where he specialized in Artificial Intelligence.

Yassin, Amr F. Department of Computer Science, University of Nevada, Reno, Nevada, USA, email: yassin@cs.unr.edu, URL: www.cs.unr.edu/~yassin, Chapter 29, pp. 615–632.

Amr F. Yassin has a Masters Degree in Computer Science from the University of Nevada, Reno, USA, in 1999; he got his B.Sc. in Communication and Electronics from Ain Shams University, Cairo, Egypt, with an Honors Degree in 1994. Amr is currently working as a Teaching Assistant in the computer science department at University of Nevada. He has also worked as a customer support engineer for IBM, Cairo. Amr was nominated as an Outstanding Teaching Assistant at the University of Nevada, Reno for the spring of 1999.

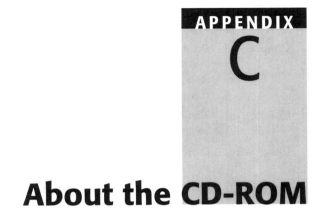

APPENDIX

C

About the CD-ROM

The CD-ROM contains close to 700 MB of materials related to thirteen chapters, a sidebar, and an invited framework called EFLIB. The CD-ROM includes:

- Design patterns implementations
- Case studies
- Sample models
- Framework code
- Demos
- Manuals and documentation

Each of the chapters that are included on the CD-ROM have a readme file that describes the contents specific to its chapter, how to navigate through the CD contents, how to use the software contained on the CD-ROM, and how to get technical support.

Additional information regarding individual framework projects can be found at the contributors' URLs included in the readme file for each chapter. Updates, if any, to the CD materials will be available on the companion Web site at www.wiley.com/compbooks/frameworks.

CD-ROM Table of Contents

Chapter 6   **A Case Study for Flexible Manufacturing Systems**
Davide Brugali, Giuseppe Menga, Amund Aarsten

Chapter 8   **Distributed Manufacturing Execution Systems Framework**
William Boyle

Chapter 9   **Production Resource Manager (PRM) Framework**
Walter C. Dietrich, Jr., Goodwin R. Chin, Brenda L. Dietrich, Thomas
Robert Ervolina, J.P. Fasano, Robin Lougee-Heimer, Elizabeth J. Poole,
Jung-Mu Tang, Robert H. Wang, Robert J. Wittrock, Danny C. Wong

Chapter 15   **The BAST Framework for Reliable Distributed Computing**
Benoit Garbinato and Rachid Guerraoui

Chapter 16   **Object-Oriented Realtime System Framework**
Win-Bin See and Sao-Jie Chen

Chapter 17   **JAWS: A Framework for High-Performance Web Servers**
James Hu and Douglas Schmidt

Chapter 21   **MultiTel: Multimedia Telecommunication Service Framework**
Lidia Fuentes and Jose M. Troya

Chapter 22   **Event Filter Framework and Applications**
Mohamed Fayad and Jingkun Hu

Chapter 25   **The Amulet Protoype-Instance Framework**
Brad A. Myers, Richard G. McDaniel, Robert C. Miller

Sidebar 4   **Layla: Network Management Interfaces Framework**
Rudolf K. Keller and Jean Tessier

Invited Frameworks

Blueprint

Grant Larsen and Jon Hopkins

Framework Studio catalogs, searches, retrieves, and applies reusable frameworks and patterns. UML models, code, and related artifacts can be stored in the UML repository for any given pattern or framework. Framework Studio's repository comes laden with the Gamma and Buschmann design patterns ready to go. Framework Studio integrates with Rational Rose and Microsoft Visual Studio to capture content, models, and code. This allows you to take control of your reuse initiatives within your projects by sharing the Framework Studio repositories. Reusing the frameworks and patterns you capture—or the ones already in the repository—you can inject the models into Rational Rose to augment and speed your development efforts.

A Framework Recipe

Steven R. Jones

The goal of this CD content is to describe a proven technique that software architects can use in creating the foundation of an application architecture. The technique is presented as a recipe that includes seven individual patterns as the raw ingredients, and a series of steps or guidelines for combining the patterns to create a flexible application framework. Architects can use the recipe to gain insight into a subset of the challenges of building robust technology solutions. These architectures are crucial to the successful adoption of new technologies that are ultimately used to support the ongoing business of an organization. The main contributions of this work are a self-contained pattern system that builds upon the growing catalog of design patterns available to software developers and which is open to extension and customization. The technical innovations of this work are that framework-based development is encouraged as a means to resolve the various issues surrounding application architecture design. Both inheritance-based and delegation-based framework approaches are provided in the recipe's solutions. A pattern approach to describing frameworks was made popular by Ralph Johnson. This work continues in that vein. For more information on this framework, refer to Chapter 10 of *Building Application Frameworks* (John Wiley & Sons, 1999).

Managing Class Dependencies

Andreas Rüping

The goal of this CD content is to show how to classify and to describe techniques for managing class dependencies in frameworks. Class dependencies occur when different hot spots within a framework are not independent of each other, such that the flexibility offered by one hot spot reduces the flexibility offered by others. The classification introduces four categories of techniques for managing class dependencies: closely coupled classes, consistent object creation, data-driven classes, and meta-level configuration. Several techniques from each category are presented and their advantages and disadvantages are discussed. A framework for interactive and animated presentations on the Web is presented as a case study. For more information on this framework, refer to Chapter 14 of *Building Application Frameworks* (John Wiley & Sons, 1999).

Index

Page references followed by *t* indicate material in tables.

A

1641SX Digital Cross-Connect (Alcatel), 385, 386
ABCL/1, 253
abort spheres, 235
Abstract Factory pattern
  Beyond-Sniff environment, 597
  measurement systems framework, 187
abstract interfaces, 11
Acceptor pattern, JAWS framework, 346, 348
access constraints database, 445
accessors, 266
ACE framework, 317
  JAWS framework development, 340
  as whitebox framework, 617
action component, event-filtering framework, 471
Actions Triggered by Events pattern (G++), 29–30

Active Object pattern, JAWS framework, 342, 347, 350–351, 352
active objects, 28–29, 89
ActiveX controls, 220–221
actuator, measurement systems framework, 188–189, 191
Adapter pattern
  Beyond-Sniff environment, 597
  event-filtering framework, 471, 477
  JAWS framework, 347, 352
  object environment framework, 576
  OORTSF framework, 332
  OSEFA framework, 58–59, 60
adaptive object-oriented event-filtering frameworks, as blackbox frameworks, 618
aggregation relationship, 328, 596, 598
agile manufacturing execution systems (MESs), 5, 8

airborne vehicle flight-path control realtime application, using OORTSF, 334–336
air traffic control systems, 283
alarm package, object environment framework, 566, 579–582
Alcatel 1641SX Digital Cross-Connect, 385, 386
algorithm framework, NETPLAN framework, 410–414
AMD, in SEMATECH, 7
Amulet framework, 529–530
  applications, 542–543
  command objects, 540–542
  constraints, 534–536
  debugging tools, 543
  design, 530–542
  future work, 544
  Gem interface, 531
  interactors, 538–540
  object system, 531–534
  Opal output model, 537

Amulet framework *(Continued)*
related work, 544
widgets, 540
analysis patterns, 625. *See also* specific analysis patterns
object-oriented domain engineering, 160
Andover Working Group, Health Level 7 implementation, 280–281
Anonymous Publish-Subscribe pattern, FIONA framework, 423–424, 429–430
applets, 223
application controllers, 399
application entries, debug logs, 572
application events package, object environment framework, 566, 587–589
Application framework, PRM framework, 145, 147–148
application frameworks. *See also* specific frameworks
abbreviations, 631
callable and calling, 10
classes contrasted, 625
classification by extending technique, 617–619
classification by scope, 2, 616–617
commercialization, 627–628
defined, 1, 211, 340
development, 625–627
documentation, 619–621
five-module framework, 379–381
heuristics for, 487, 625–627
learning curve, 342, 624, 627

lessons learned, 625–628
names, abbreviations, and Web sites, 631
need for standardization, 632
percentage used in final application, 623
renting options, 622
and reuse, 329
rules of thumb for, 625–627
selling prices, 621–623
shortcomings, 101
survey questions, 628–631
survey results, 615–628
tools for developing, 624
with web servers, 342–345
Web sites, 631
application objects, SEMATECH CIM framework, 11, 13, 15
application programmer, view of Bast framework, 285–286, 294–296
application programming interfaces (APIs), 489
architectural design style, 329
architectural framework, 329
architectural platform, 329
architectural style, 329
architectures
COTS-centric, 433
five-module, 379–381
hierarchical decentralized, 24
three-layer, 379, 380
artificial intelligence, 227, 419
ASIST, 469
association relation, 596
Asynchronous Completion Token pattern, JAWS framework, 347

asynchronous distributed systems, 289
asynchronous I/O strategy, 347, 357
atomic broadcasts, 295
atomic commitment problem, 307
atomic commit service, Bast framework, 294, 307–310
atomic group service, Bast framework, 294
atomicity property, 289
attribute-value pairs, 533
automatic guided vehicle system, 23
automatic manufacture of usable and learnable editors and toolkits. *See* Amulet framework
automation, 177
availability, FACTORY-works, 122
Avoca, 290

B
BASEstar Open, 88
Bast framework, 287–288
application programmer's view of, 285–286, 294–296
atomic commit service, 294, 307–310
atomic group service, 294
communication service, 293, 314
distributed agreement service, 293–294, 314–315
DTM agreement pattern application, 293, 305–313
failure detection service, 293, 314
implementation issues, 313–318
in-depth view, 296–302

overview, 291–294
performance, 318–321
possible optimizations, 321–323
protocol composition and tuning, 302–305
protocol programmer's view of, 285–286, 296–302
reliability approaches, 284–286
reliable multicast example, 300–301
Strategy pattern, 298–302
using, 294–296
beer can measurement system, 193–199
Bento, 217
Beyond-Sniff environment, 495–497
architecture, 498–503
Boar case study, 508–509
compatibility restrictions, 503*t*
component structure view, 500–501
component view, 499–500
framework reuse view, 502
framework structure view, 501–502
iterative development support, 505–508
lessons learned, 509–510
Tool Integration framework, 503–505
Beyond-Sniff ISVs, 496
bill of capacity, 141
bill of material, 141
Binary Object Storage Service (BOSS), 321
binding, 617
blackbox frameworks, 85, 618
domain-specific, 44–45
blackbox reusability, 317–318

blocking objects, 28, 31–32, 89
block synchronous parallel (BSP) model, 253
Boar case study, Beyond-Sniff, 508–509
Booch method, 595
Bridge pattern, 152, 509, 624
Beyond-Sniff environment, 597
broadcaster/listener mechanism, 26, 27, 90
Broker pattern, Beyond-Sniff environment, 597
Builder pattern
event-filtering framework, 471, 475
TMN framework, 389
business frameworks, 622*t*
business logic layer, 379, 380
business meetings, 437

C

C++, 621
Amulet framework, 530
FACTORYworks framework, 122, 125
FIONA framework, 422, 434
High Performance, 276
measurement systems framework, 178
object environment framework, 567, 574
OOPM framework, 594, 606, 609, 611
OSEFA framework, 44
Cached Virtual Filesystem component, JAWS framework, 347, 362–363
caching, 362–363, 373
Calculation Processing framework, Ecce framework, 519, 521–523

Calculation Setup framework, Ecce framework, 519, 523–524
callable frameworks, 10
callback package, object environment framework, 566, 574–579
callback procedures, 541
caller/provider mechanism, 26, 27, 90
calling frameworks, 10
Capacitated MRP Application, 156–157
cardinality, 597
case modeling, 108–109
CASE tools, with G++, 41
CEF (Concurrent Engineering Framework), 105–106
architectural design, 113–117
Change Manager class, 115
Command class, 114–115
customization process, 106–109
Data Manager class, 115
dynamic domain modeling, 109–113
lessons learned, 117–118
Lock Manager class, 116–117
Security Manager class, 116
CELLworks, 128, 137
change propagation, CEF, 111–113
chats, 437
Chava example, Jadve framework, 558–559
Chemistry Data Model framework, Ecce framework, 519, 520–521
Choice Interactor, Amulet, 538–539
Choices, 290

CIM frameworks. *See* computer-integrated manufacturing (CIM) frameworks; SEMA-TECH CIM framework

C³I systems (command, control, communications, and intelligence), 419. *See also* FIONA framework

classes, 327, 625

Classifier Visualizer example, Jadve framework, 559–560

class libraries, 10
  defined, 340
  FACTORYworks, 130–137

clients, considering needs of in framework commercialization, 627–628

Client/Server/Service pattern (G++), 32–34

Clinical Context Object Work Group, 282

CMRP application, PRM framework, 156–157

CNCs. *See* computerized numerical controls

code, keeping portion needed to complete application small, 628

collaborative work environments, 1

command, control, communications, and intelligence (C³I) systems, 419. *See also* FIONA framework

command objects, Amulet framework, 540–542

Command pattern, 624
  FIONA framework, 424, 430–431
  OSEFA framework, 57

commercialization, 627–628

commit spheres, 235

Common Business Objects, IBM San Francisco Project, 623

common gateway interfaces (CGIs), 359

Common Management Information Service (CMIS), Layla application, 489

Common Object Request Broker Architecture. *See* CORBA

communications application frameworks, 619

communication service, Bast framework, 293, 314

COM/OLE/ActiveX, 211, 212
  compound active documents, 219–221

compilers, 624
  semiautomatic parallelizing, 251

complexity, 342, 627

component entries, debug logs, 572

components
  data coupling between, 626
  defined, 211, 340
  and reuse, 565
  SEMATECH CIM framework, 12

composite event, 470

Composite pattern
  FIONA framework, 424
  measurement systems framework, 182, 186

compositional modeling, 398

composition relation, 596

compound active documents, 211
  COM/OLE/ActiveX, 219–221
  CORBA, 212–216
  event models, 224–226

framework specification by constraints on component behavior, 228–230
  interaction modes, 226–228
  Java and JavaBeans, 221–226
  OpenDoc, 216–219

compound status package, object environment framework, 566, 567–570

Compound User Interfaces framework, as blackbox framework, 618

computer-integrated manufacturing (CIM) frameworks, 1, 5–6, 103–104. *See also* specific frameworks
  framework reuse over different subdomains, 67–83

computerized numerical controls (CNCs), 23
  OSEFA control, 46–63

computer mapping, 547

computer-supported collaborative work, 437

computer-supported cooperative work, 544

concrete interfaces, 11

Concurrency Strategy framework, JAWS framework, 347, 352–356

concurrent engineering, 105

Concurrent Engineering Framework. *See* CEF

Conduits+ framework, 290, 317, 318

conferences, 437

configuration package, object environment framework, 566, 582–584

constraint-based specifications, 229
constraint solvers, Amulet framework, 534–536
Consul, 291
containment relation, 596
containment tree, 389
controller framework, NETPLAN framework, 406–408
control relationship, 441
controls, 220
cookbooks, 619t, 620, 627
CORBA (Common Object Request Broker Architecture), 212, 626
  as architectural platform, 329
  CEF integration, 115
  FIONA integration, 424–425
  with GUI software, 424–425
  object environment framework integration, 567
  OORTSF integration, 336
  software architecture, 212–216
  and supervision and control systems, 231–247
CORBADomains, 234
CORBAFacilities, 234
  SEMATECH CIM framework, 13, 15
CORBAmed, 281–282
CORBA Object Services, 214
CORBA/OpenDREAMS services, 235–247
CORBAServices, 233–234
  SEMATECH CIM framework, 13, 15
CORBA System Services, 215
Core Business Processes, IBM San Francisco Project, 623

Core framework, PRM framework, 144–145, 146–147
cost
  application frameworks, 621–623
  OSEFA framework, 64–65
COTS-centric architectures, 433
CSFramelets, 621
C++ Standard Template Library, 345
customization
  CEF, 106–109
  Jadve framework, 549
cyclic executive, 335
cyclic scheduler (CYS), 330

D
database frameworks, 622t
database tools, 624
DataBroker, as middleware integration framework, 616
data-centered software design, 515–516
Data Collection System, PM&D domain case study, 167
data coupling, avoiding excessive, 626
Data Interface framework, PRM framework, 144, 151–154
data visualization, 547. See also Jadve framework
debugging, Amulet framework, 543
debug hooks, 628
debug logging package, object environment framework, 566, 570–574
decision-support systems
  FIONA framework, 420
  healthcare applications, 280

manufacturing logistics, 139–142
decomposition, 287
design, 627
  importance of iteration to, 626
design notebook, 620
design patterns, 487. See also specific design patterns
  hot-spot subsystems, 45
  Layla, 489
  object-oriented domain engineering, 160
  and pattern languages, 86–87
  and reuse, 22, 328–329
  survey results, 624–625, 627
  with web servers, 342–345
development team, 626
dictionaries, prototype design objects, 111
Digital, in SEMATECH, 7
directed attributed graphs, 547
Discrete Event System Specifications (DEVS) system, 595
display list, 537
distinguished name, 389
distributed agreement service, Bast framework, 293–294, 314–315
distributed algorithm tuning, 304–305
Distributed Interactive Web-Site (DIWB) builder, 381
distributed memory parallel computers (DMPCs), 251–252
distributed model repository (DMR), 593–594, 610–612
Distributed Multimodeling Language (DMML), 594

distributed objects, 286
distributed patterns, 302
distributed programming
    environments,
    289–291
distributed systems, 283
distributed systems
    frameworks, 1, 2,
    207–209. *See also* spe-
    cific frameworks
Distributed Transaction
    Processing Frame-
    work (DTPF),
    123–124
Distribution of Control
    Modules pattern
    (G++), 38–39
documentation, 619–621
  design patterns for, 22,
    86
  need for, 626
documents, 211
domain engineering, 159
domain experts, 625
  and knowledge engi-
    neering, 106
domain interfaces,
    SEMATECH CIM
    framework, 15
domain modeling, 108,
    109–113
domain-specific blackbox
    frameworks, 44–45
domain use cases, 162
dot, 548
dotty, 560
DTM agreement pattern,
    305–313
dumb machines, 69
dynamic behavior model-
    ing, object-oriented
    physical multi-
    modeling, 595–598,
    602–606
dynamic binding, 617
dynamic domain model-
    ing, 108, 109–113
dynamic multimodels,
    602–606

Dynamic Terminating
    Multicast (DTM),
    293
  DTM agreement pattern
    application, 305–313

E
earliest deadline first
    (EDF) scheduler, 330
early consensus algo-
    rithm, 304
Ecce. *See* Extensible Com-
    putational Chemistry
    Environment
EDGE, 560
education frameworks,
    622*t*
Eiffel, 252, 271
Eiffel Parallel Execution
    Environment frame-
    work. *See* EPEE
    framework
e-mail filter application,
    480–481
Encore! Group, 8
Engine, object-oriented
    physical multimodel-
    ing framework, 593,
    594, 607, 609–612
enterprise application
    frameworks, 2,
    616–617
  percentage of overall
    frameworks, 619
Enterprise Communicator
    (EC), 280–281
enterprise resource plan-
    ning (ERP), 616
Enterprise Shortfall
    Implosion Tool
    (ESIT), 142
entertainment frame-
    works, 622*t*
Environmental Molecular
    Sciences Laboratory,
    513
environment frameworks,
    491–493. *See also* spe-
    cific frameworks

EPEE (Eiffel Parallel Exe-
    cution Environment)
    framework, 252–254
basic communication
    and data-sharing
    components, 254–255
distribution manage-
    ment components,
    255–258
Operator pattern, 259–265
Paladin design princi-
    ples, 265–267
Paladin distributed
    matrix implementa-
    tion, 267–269
Paladin for application
    writing, 272–275
parallelization tech-
    niques, 270–271
parallel linear algebra
    library, 265–272
parallel operators,
    258–259, 264–265
performance issues,
    271–272
related work, 275–276
ET++ framework, 496, 497
event definition construc-
    tor component, event-
    filtering framework,
    470
Event Dispatcher compo-
    nent, JAWS frame-
    work, 346–347
event filtering, 469
event-filtering framework
  action component, 471
  design, 471–474
  development heuristics,
    487
  e-mail filter application,
    480–481
  event definition con-
    structor component,
    470
  filter iterator component,
    470–471
  implementation, 474–479
  lessons learned, 483–486

network management
application, 483
subscription component,
470
Web filter application,
481–483
event models, 224–226
Everglades ecosystem
model example,
594–612
example (documentation
type), 619*t*, 620, 621,
627
explode and net iterative
logic, 140
explode step, 141
Extended Command pat-
tern, FIONA frame-
work, 424
extensibility
FACTORYworks, 122
Jadve framework, 549
Extensible Computational
Chemistry Environ-
ment (Ecce), 513–514
architecture, 518–519
Calculation Processing
framework, 519,
521–523
Calculation Setup frame-
work, 519, 523–524
Chemistry Data Model
framework, 519,
520–521
computational chemistry
domain, 517–518
data-centered design,
515–516
design objectives, 514–515
future work, 526
lessons learned, 525–526
Property Analysis frame-
work, 519, 524–525

F
Façade pattern, 329, 509
Beyond-Sniff environ-
ment, 597
EPEE framework, 254

Fachhochschule Konstanz
manufacturing cell,
47
Factory pattern, 624
FACTORYworks, 121–122
application core classes,
136–137
application-enabling ser-
vices, 128–129
application services,
124–128
architecture, 122–129
class libraries, 130–137
distribution classes,
130–131
equipment integration
services, 128
framework implementa-
tion, 129–137
future work, 137
persistence classes,
132–136
presentation classes,
131–132
utility classes, 130
failure detection service,
Bast framework, 293,
314
FASTech Integration, 121
fault tolerance, 284. *See
also* Bast framework
feature-oriented domain
analysis (FODA), 166
field buses, 88, 231
file caching, 362–363, 373
filter composer, 470
filtering expression operators, 470
filter iterator component,
event-filtering frame-
work, 470–471
finance application frameworks, 619
finance frameworks, 622*t*
FIONA framework, 419,
423–424
Anonymous Publish-
Subscribe pattern,
423–424, 429–430

applet framework,
431–433
Command pattern,
430–431
CORBA with, 424–425
GRACE system architec-
ture, 421–423
lessons learned, 433–434
Storable pattern, 423,
425–429
five-module framework,
379–381
flexibility, SEMATECH
CIM framework, 8–9
flexible coupling, 507–508
flexible manufacturing
systems, 23, 88–89
G++ framework applica-
tion, 93–97
G++ pattern examples,
23–41
flight-path control real-
time application,
using OORTSF,
334–336
flow-centered manufac-
turing subdomains,
68, 69
Fortran, High Perfor-
mance, 251
Foundation layer, IBM San
Francisco Project, 623
framework domain, 44
framework life span, 86
framework overview,
619*t*, 620–621, 627
frameworks, 44, 625. *See
also* application
frameworks
defined, 211, 340
frozen spots, 43, 44, 71
manufacturing subdo-
main with, 45–49
function overloading, 272

G
garbage collection, EPEE
framework, 271
GARF, 290

gather-write, 373
Gaussian –9x code, 525
Gem interface, Amulet framework, 531
generalization relationship, 327–328, 596
 as most important step in framework development, 487
general-purpose frameworks, 622*t*
Geographical Information Systems (GISs), 547
geometry modeling, object-oriented physical multimodeling, 595–598, 600–602, 603
Gesture Interactor, Amulet, 538–539
G++ framework, 21–23, 89–93, 232
 as blackbox framework, 618
 flexible manufacturing system application, 93–97
Gilt interface builder, Amulet, 540
Gina, 544
G++ pattern language, 21
 Actions Triggered by Events pattern, 29–30
 application domain, 87–89
 Client/Server/Service pattern, 32–34
 Distribution of Control Modules pattern, 38–39
 Hierarchy of Control Layers pattern, 24–25
 Implementation of Control Modules pattern, 34–35
 Interface to Control Modules pattern, 35–37

Objects and Concurrency pattern, 27–29
 Prototype and Reality pattern, 37–38
 Remote Control pattern, 39–41
 Services Waiting for a Condition pattern, 31–32
 structure, 23–24
 Visibility and Communication between Control Modules pattern, 25–27
GRACE system architecture, 421–423
granularity levels, 28
graph-based data visualization, 547–548. *See also* Jadve framework
graphical user interface (GUI) frameworks
 CORBA with, 424–425
 customization with CEF, 107–108
 general-purpose, 622*t*
 as graybox frameworks, 618
 as system infrastructure frameworks, 616
graybox frameworks, 618–619
Gremlin, 508
group-based distributed programming environments, 290
group communication model, 286
group membership, 289, 290
groupware toolkits, 290
Guide for CIM Framework Technical Architecture, 18
Guidelines for the Definition of Managed Objects (GDMO), 386, 508

H
Hardware Variability Control System, PM&D domain case study, 168–169
healthcare application frameworks, 280–282, 619, 622*t*
Health Level 7 standard, 280–281
heuristics, for application frameworks, 487, 625–627
Hewlett-Packard, in SEMATECH, 7
hierarchical decentralized architecture, 24
Hierarchy of Control Layers pattern (G++), 24–25
high-level reuse techniques, 328–330
High Performance C++, 276
High Performance Fortran, 251
hinted caching, 362–363
hooks, 574, 625
Hooks pattern, FIONA framework, 424
Horus, 290–291
HotDraw, 560–561
HotJava, 223
hot spot diagram, 51
hot spots, 625
 defined, 43, 44–45
 OSEFA framework, 51–60, 71
hot-spot subsystem, 45
HTML. *See* Hypertext Markup Language
human-computer interface, 419
 OOPM, 593
Hypertext Markup Language (HTML), 339
 JAWS implementation, 345, 359–360, 372–375

NETPLAN framework, 404, 410–415
TCP/IP delay behavior over ISDN, 404

I
IBM
implosion technology experience, 142–143
in SEMATECH, 7
IBM San Francisco Project, 621, 623
as enterprise application framework, 616
as graybox framework, 618
as rentable framework, 622
Ident lookups, 374
ILOG Views, for NETPLAN framework development, 403
implementation, 627
importance of iteration to, 626
Implementation of Control Modules pattern (G++), 34–35
implosion, 142–143
The Implosion Application (TIA), 155–156
Improvise system, 547
Jadve framework example, 557–558
industrial frameworks, 622t
inheritance, 10, 617
prototype-based object systems, 110–111
and reliable distributed computing, 316
structural, 531
virtual, 402
installation guide, 620
Instance Type pattern, 111
insurance application frameworks, 619, 622t
Intel, in SEMATECH, 7
intelligent stations, 69

interactive interfaces, 225–226
interactive tools, 544
interactors, Amulet framework, 538–540
interface contracts, 619t, 620, 627
Interface Definition Language (IDL), 233
need for pre- and postcondition support, 101
SEMATECH CIM framework, 11, 17
interface framework, NETPLAN framework, 408–410
Interface pattern, event-filtering framework, 471
interfaces, 222
generating with TRIO, 246
SEMATECH CIM framework, 11–12
thread dumb, 567
Interface to Control Modules pattern (G++), 35–37
Internet, 469
and reliable computing, 283
interoperability
and CORBA, 212
and Paladin class organization, 272
SEMATECH CIM framework, 9
Interpreter pattern, event-filtering framework, 471, 473, 477
InterViews, 544
intranets, 438
introspection, 226
inversion of control, 344, 345
I/O Strategy framework, JAWS framework, 347, 356–358

ISDN, TCP/IP delay behavior over, 404
Isis, 290
ISO-9000, 177
isolation property, 289
iteration, importance in framework development, 487, 626
Iterator pattern
EPEE framework, 259
event-filtering framework, 471, 474

J
Jadve API, 555–556
Jadve client, 554
Jadve framework, 548
Chava example, 558–559
Classifier Visualizer example, 559–560
design goals, 549
future work, 561
graph objects, 551–553
graph representation, presentation, and layout, 550
Improvise example, 557–558
Jadve API, 555–556
Jadve client, 554
Jadve server, 555
multiuser collaboration support, 550–551
related work, 560–561
Jadve server, 555
Java, 212, 621
Bast framework test, 318, 321
compound active documents, 221–222
Jadve framework, 548, 549
lack of multiple inheritance, 317
MultiTEL framework, 450–457
Serialize mechanism, 426

Java AWT toolkit, 484
JavaBeans, 211, 212
    compound active docu-
        ments, 223–226
JavaBeans GUI Bean
    Box bean builder
    tool, 595
Java Generic Library, 484
Java.lang.net, 342
Java Virtual Machines,
    621
JAWS Adaptive Web
    Server (JAWS) frame-
    work, 340, 363–365
    benchmarking testbed,
        365–370
    Cached Virtual Filesys-
        tem component, 347,
        362–363
    Concurrency Strategy
        framework, 347,
        352–356
    Event Dispatcher com-
        ponent, 346–347
    I/O Strategy framework,
        347, 356–358
    overview, 345–347
    Protocol Handler frame-
        work, 347
    Protocol Pipeline frame-
        work, 347, 358–362
    strategic patterns,
        348–351
    tactical patterns, 351–352
    Tilde Expander compo-
        nent, 347
Joint Integrated Avionics
    Working Group
    object-oriented
    domain analysis
    (JODA), 166
Junkfilter, 469

K
knowledge discovery and
    data mining (KDD),
    559
knowledge engineering,
    106

L
Language of Temporal
    Ordering Specifica-
    tion (LOTOS), 439
Lapack.h++, 275
latency degree, 304
Layla, 489–490
learning curve, 342, 624,
    627
least frequently used
    (LFU) caching, 362
least recently used (LRU)
    caching, 362
legacy system integration,
    SEMATECH CIM
    framework, 9
libraries. *See* class libraries
lifetime test, 597
lightweight concurrency,
    371–372
line-centered manufactur-
    ing subdomains, 69
listening membranes, 224
listen queue, 374–375
local area networks
    (LANs), 231
location transparency, 39
    and partial failures, 283
logging, 374
LOTOS (Language of
    Temporal Ordering
    Specification), 439
Lucent, in SEMATECH, 7

M
MacApp framework, 544
    as system infrastructure
        framework, 616
    as whitebox framework,
        617
Mac OS operating system,
    621
main event loop, 424
managed object classes,
    386
managed object data
    classes, 392
managed objects,
    385–386

management information
    base (MIB), 385
management information
    base (MIB) frame-
    work, TMN, 387–395
manufacturing cell con-
    trol. *See* OSEFA
    framework
manufacturing execution
    systems (MESs), 5, 8,
    121
    as online transaction
        processing, 129
manufacturing frame-
    works, 622*t*
manufacturing informa-
    tion systems, 151
manufacturing logistics
    decision support,
    139–142
manufacturing subdo-
    mains, 68–71
Manufacturing Virtual
    Enterprise (MVE)
    architecture, 232
marshaling, 131
master production sched-
    ule, 140–141
material flow and part
    processing, 54
material requirements
    planning, 140–141
measurement systems
    framework, 177–178
    actuator, 188–189, 191
    beer can example,
        193–199
    calculation strategy, 184
    calibration strategy,
        186–187
    design, 181–189
    evaluation, 199–204
    item factory, 187–188
    lessons learned, 199–204
    measurement item, 185
    measurement process,
        181–182
    measurement value, 186
    realtime aspects, 189

related work, 204
requirements, 178–181
sensor, 182–183, 190–191
simulation, 189–193
update strategy, 183–184
Mediator pattern
   Beyond-Sniff environment, 597
   OSEFA framework, 55
members-per-team, for
      framework development, 624
Memento pattern, JAWS
      framework, 347
message-oriented middleware (MOM), FACTORYworks, 123
metal part-processing
      manufacturing, 68
Method pattern, FIONA
      framework, 424
Microelectronics Manufacturing Science and
      Technology project, 8
Micron Millennia PRO2
      plus workstation,
      JAWS test with,
      365–366
Microsoft Foundation
      Classes (MFCs), as
      system infrastructure
      framework, 616
Microsoft Health User's
      Group (MS-HUG),
      281
middleware integration
      frameworks, 2, 616
   percentage of overall
      frameworks, 619
middleware programmer,
      285
mixin classes, 317
mobile object store (MOS),
      593–594
MO data classes, 392
Modeler, object-oriented
      physical multimodeling framework,
      593–594, 600–609

modeling, 594–595. *See also*
      object-oriented physical multimodeling
   closed under coupling,
      599
   metamodel for, 592
   multimodeling, 593
modeling tools, 624
Model/View/Controller
      pattern, 406, 538
modular operating systems, 290
molecular dynamics simulation, 521
Morpheus, 290
Motorola, in SEMATECH,
      7
Move-Grow Interactor,
      Amulet, 538–539
MPC++, 276
multimedia collaborative
      work environments, 1
multimedia telecommunication services, 437.
      See also MultiTEL
      framework
multimodeling, 593, 599.
      See also object-oriented physical multimodeling
multimodel units, 598–599
multiple dispatching, 272
MultiTEL framework,
      438–439
   application directory,
      439, 458–459, 463–465
   component base classes,
      451–452
   component directory,
      458, 459–463
   component-oriented
      model, 439–443
   components, 440–443
   compositional architecture, 443–450
   connector base classes,
      452–454
   connectors, 440–443
   deployment, 459–465

formal specification tool,
      439, 462–463
   implementation, 450–457
   middleware platform,
      457–459
   multimedia subsystem,
      446–447
   network subsystem,
      447–448
   remote communications,
      459
   service subsystem,
      444–446
   video on demand service, 448–450
   visual builder tool, 439,
      461–462
mutual exclusion, 330

N
Nagle's algorithm, 375
name test, 597
National Institute for Standards and Technology
      (NIST), CIM Framework projects, 18
National Semiconductor,
      in SEMATECH, 7
Net.h++, 342
NETPLAN framework,
      398
   algorithm framework,
      410–414
   controller framework,
      406–408
   delay behavior of
      TCP/IP over ISDN,
      404
   example application,
      414–415, 416
   implementation considerations, 402–403
   interface framework,
      408–410
   lessons learned, 415–416
   network model, 405–406
   overview, 399–402
   platform considerations,
      402–403

netting step, 141
networking and telecommunications application frameworks, 1, 2, 383–384, 622t. *See also* specific frameworks
network management interfaces, 489
network management systems, 385–387
event-filtering framework application, 483
New Points Interactor, Amulet, 538–539
NWChem suite, 517, 525

O
(object) Adapter pattern, with OSEFA framework, 60
object environment framework, 565–567
alarm package, 566, 579–582
application events package, 566, 587–589
callback package, 566, 574–579
compound status package, 566, 567–570
configuration package, 566, 582–584
debug logging package, 566, 570–574
timer package, 566, 584–587
object instances, 327
object interaction diagrams, 620
Object Linking and Embedding (OLE), 220
Object Management Architecture (OMA), SEMATECH CIM framework, 11

Object Management Group (OMG). *See also* CORBA
Domain Technology Committee, 10
Manufacturing Domain Task Force, 18
Object Modeling Technique (OMT), 227, 327–328, 595
with Bast framework, 292
with NETPLAN framework, 399
object-oriented analysis and design (OOA&D), 595
object-oriented application frameworks, 1, 615
object-oriented database management systems (OODBMSs), with Ecce framework, 513
object-oriented domain analysis (OODA), 159–163
object-oriented domain design (OODD), 159–160, 163–165
object-oriented domain engineering delivery (OODED), 159–160, 165
object-oriented domain engineering (OODE) method, 159–160
advantages, 166–167
future work, 175
object-oriented domain analysis phase, 159–163
object-oriented domain design phase, 159–160, 163–165
object-oriented domain engineering delivery phase, 159–160, 165

Process Monitoring and Diagnosis domain case study, 167–175
relationship to other methods, 166–167
object-oriented frameworks, 516–517
object-oriented physical multimodeling (OOPM), 591–594
conceptual models, 600–609
distributed model repository, 593–594, 610–612
dynamic behavior modeling, 595–598, 602–606
elements of, 593
Engine, 593, 594, 607, 609–612
future work, 612
geometry modeling, 595–598, 600–602, 603
Modeler, 593–594, 600–609
model refinement, 598–600
nonvisual elements, 593, 609–612
overview, 594–595
Scenario, 593, 594, 607–609
Translator, 593, 594, 609
visual elements, 593, 600–609
object-oriented realtime system framework (OORTSF), 327–328
application systems development, 334–336
class hierarchy, 330–332
extending, 336
high-level reuse techniques, 328–330
object collaboration scenario, 332–334

object-oriented technology, 159
Object Request Brokers (ORBs)
  FACTORYworks, 123
  as middleware integration framework, 616
  OORTSF integration, 336
  SEMATECH CIM framework, 13–15
objects, 566
  defined, 211
  distributed, 286
  marshaling and unmarshaling, 131
Objects and Concurrency pattern (G++), 27–29
observation node, 255
Observer pattern, 329, 345
  Beyond-Sniff environment, 597
  PRM framework, 149
OmniBuilder framework, as middleware integration framework, 616
One Shot Interactor, Amulet, 538–539
online class and method references, 620
OOPM. *See* object-oriented physical multimodeling
OORTSF. *See* object-oriented realtime system framework
ooSim, 609
Opal output model, Amulet framework, 537
OpenDoc, 211, 212
  compound active documents, 216–219
OpenDREAMS Espirit project, 232
  architecture and methodology, 233–234
OpenStep, 381

operating systems, 621
  modular, 290
  specialized web server features, 672–673
Operator pattern, with EPEE framework, 259–265
operators, 258, 266
ORACLE, 624
Orbit, as middleware integration framework, 616
Orbix filters, 424–425
order schedules, 155
organization domain modeling (ODM), 166
OSEFA framework, 43–44
  application creation, 43–4461–63
  concrete machine and device layer, 60–61
  domain object layer, 57–59
  domain-specific blackbox frameworks, 44–45
  framework reuse over different subdomains, 69–83
  frozen spots, 43, 45–49
  hot spots, 43, 44–45, 51–60
  interactive configurator, 43–44, 63
  layered framework architecture, 52–53
  lessons learned, 63–65
  manufacturing subdomain with frozen spots, 45–49
  processing command hot spot, 56–57
  processing control layer, 53–56
  standardized machine and device layer, 59–60
  variability of cell configuration, 49–50
OS/2 operating system, 621

P
packages, 111
Paladin, 252
  application writing with, 272–275
  design principle, 265–267
  distributed matrix implementation, 267–269
parallel linear algebra library, 265–272
parallel operators, 258–259, 264–265
PARAMAT, 251
partial failures, 283
pattern languages, 21–22, 85–87
patterns, 626. *See also* analysis patterns; design patterns; specific patterns
  defined, 340
  distributed, 302
  and reuse, 21–22, 565
  with web servers, 342–345
performance, 628
persistence, FACTORYworks, 132–136
person-month, for framework development, 624
physical multimodeling, object-oriented. *See* object-oriented physical multimodeling
Pipes and Filters pattern, JAWS framework, 347
polymorphic matrix, 274
polymorphism, 10
  NETPLAN framework, 402
  OOPM framework, 604
POOL-T, 253
portability, Jadve framework, 549

portable common tool environment (PCTE), 561
presentation layer, 379, 380
primitive event, 470
PRM (Production Resource Manager) framework, 139–140
  Application framework, 145, 147–148
  architecture, 143–146
  CMRP application, 156–157
  Core framework, 144–145, 146–147
  Data Interface framework, 144, 151–154
  design objectives, 140–143
  domain background, 140–143
  Implosion application, 155–156
  Scenario framework, 144–151
  Schedule framework, 147–148
  subscription mechanism, 149–150
  User Interface framework, 145–146, 154–155
Proactor pattern, JAWS framework, 347, 349–350, 357
problem/solution pairs, 289
procedural abstraction, 535
process-centered software design, 515
process controls, 283
process-per-request server, 359
production automation, 177
production data administration, 69–71

Production Resource Manager framework. *See* PRM framework
programmable logic controllers, 23, 40
  OSEFA control, 46
programmer's manual, 620
programming languages, 621
Property Analysis framework, Ecce framework, 519, 524–525
protocol-based distributed programming environments, 290–291
protocol classes, 292
protocol composition, 302–304
Protocol Handler framework, JAWS framework, 347
protocol objects, 292
Protocol Pipeline framework, JAWS framework, 347, 358–362
protocol programmer, view of Bast framework, 285–286, 296–302
protocol tuning, 304–305
Prototype and Reality pattern (G++), 37–38
prototype-based object systems, 109–113
Prototype pattern, measurement systems framework, 187
prototyping, 626
Provisional Specification for CIM Framework Domain Architecture, 18
Proxy pattern, 336
public switched telephone networks, 283

Q
quality control, 177

R
rate monotonic scheduler (RMS), 330
Rational Rose, 624
reactive I/O strategy, 347, 357
Reactor pattern, JAWS framework, 342, 348–349, 352, 357, 358
realtime systems, 327. *See also* object-oriented realtime system framework
recipes, 619*t*, 620, 627
recomposition, 287
reference manuals, 619*t*, 620, 627
regular operation, 260
relations, 596–597
reliability, 284–286, 627. *See also* Bast framework
  decomposition and recomposition, 287–288
  FACTORYworks, 122
reliable distributed programming, 288–291
reliable multicast, Bast framework example, 300–301
reliable total order multicast problem, 310
Remote Control pattern (G++), 39–41
remote education, 437
remote graph drawing, 548
Rendezvous, 544
renting, application frameworks, 622
replicated objects, 295
request lifecycle, 373
restricted intelligence stations, 69
  and OSEFA, 45–46

reuse, 1
  Beyond-Sniff environment, 502
  CIM frameworks over different subdomains, 67–83
  and object environments, 565
  object-oriented realtime system framework, 328–330
  and patterns, 21–22
  SEMATECH CIM framework, 9–10
reverse DNS lookups, 374
Rivet Monitoring System, PM&D domain case study, 167–168
Rockwell, in SEMATECH, 7
RTP6.1 research program, 419–421
rules of thumb, for application frameworks, 625–627

S

San Francisco Project. *See* IBM San Francisco Project
scalability, FACTORYworks, 122
ScaLAPACK, 275
Scenario framework
  object-oriented physical multimodeling framework, 593, 594, 607–609
  PRM framework, 144–151
Schedule framework, PRM framework, 147–148
schema evolution, 106–107, 118
Select, 624
selection schedules, 155

semantic data representation mechanisms (SDRMs), 510
SEMATECH, 7
Semiconductor Generic Manufacturing Model, 121
SEMATECH CIM framework, 7–10, 232
  documentation, 16–17
  future work, 18
  infrastructure support, 14–15
  lessons learned, 17–18, 100–102
  structure, 11–13
SEMATECH CIM Framework Architecture Guide, 16
SEMATECH CIM Framework Specification, 16
SEMATECH Technology Transfer documents, 16
semiautomatic parallelizing compilers, 251
Semiconductor Equipment and Materials International (SEMI) Task Force, 18, 102
Semiconductor Generic Manufacturing Model, 121
sensor, measurement systems framework, 182–183, 190–191
sequential objects, 28, 89
Serialize mechanism (Java), 426
Service Configurator pattern, JAWS framework, 347, 351
Services Waiting for a Condition pattern (G++), 31–32
sessions, 353
SimPack, 609

simulation, 594–595. *See also* object-oriented physical multimodeling
  measurement systems framework, 189–193
  metamodel for, 592
single-threaded concurrency model, 347, 354–355
Singleton pattern, 624
  JAWS framework, 347, 352
situation objects, 238
1641SX Digital Cross-Connect (Alcatel), 385, 386
SketchPad, 544
Smalltalk, 621
  Bast framework test, 318–320
  FACTORYworks prototype, 122
  lack of multiple inheritance, 317
  measurement systems framework, 178, 201
smart pointers, 133
Sniff environment, 495, 497–498. *See also* Beyond-Sniff environment
snowplows, 565
socket send buffers, 375
software architecture, and reuse, 329
software development frameworks, 622t
software engineering, 227
software reuse. *See* reuse
specialization relation, 596
stability, 627
State pattern, JAWS framework, 347, 352
Storable pattern, FIONA framework, 423, 425–429
storage adaptors, 135

store-centered manufacturing subdomains, 68, 69
Strategy pattern, 509, 624
Bast framework, 298–302
callback link to Hook, 575
CEF, 116
JAWS framework, 347, 351–352
measurement systems framework, 183, 201–202
OSEFA framework, 54–55
PRM framework, 148
TMN framework, 394
street sweepers, 565
structural graphics model, 537
structural inheritance, 531
structured caching, 363
subscription component, event-filtering framework, 470
subscription mechanism, PRM framework, 149–150
substitutability, SEMATECH CIM framework, 9
supercomputing, 251. *See also* EPEE framework
SuperPOSEIDON project, 8
supervision and control systems, 231
CORBA/OpenDREAMS services, 235–247
future work, 247–248
OpenDREAMS architecture and methodology, 233–234
TRIO-based development method, 239–247
synchronization, 330
synchronous I/O strategy, 347, 356–357

synthesis domain engineering method, 166
system development environment frameworks, 2
system infrastructure frameworks, 2, 616
percentage of overall frameworks, 619
system layer, 379, 380
system programmer, 285

T
Taligent Application Environment, 232
Tcl/Tk, for OOPM framework, 602, 608, 612
TCP/IP over ISDN, delay behavior, 404
Telecommunication Intelligent Network Architecture (TINA), 437
Telecommunication Management Network (TMN), 385, 508
MIB framework, 387–395
telecommunication networks, 397–398
Template pattern, FIONA framework, 424
Texas Instruments, in SEMATECH, 7
Text Edit Interactor, Amulet, 538–539
text editor tools, 624
The Implosion Application (TIA), 155–156
ThingLab, 544
thread dumb interfaces, 567
threaded applications, 584
thread-per-request concurrency model, 347, 353
thread-per-session concurrency model, 347, 353–354
thread pool concurrency model, 347, 354

three-layer architecture, 379, 380
Tilde Expander component, JAWS framework, 347
timer package, object environment framework, 566, 584–587
Tool Integration framework, Beyond-Sniff, 503–505
tools, for developing frameworks, 624
total order multicast, 310–313
transaction-based distributed programming environments, 289–290
transactions, 286
FACTORYworks, 129, 135–136
Translator, object-oriented physical multimodeling framework, 593, 594, 609
Translator Target Language, 594, 609
TransmitFile function, 372–373
triggers
measurement systems framework, 189
object-oriented domain engineering method, 160
TRIO, 239
TRIO/OpenDREAMS method, 239–247
troubleshooting guide, 620

U
UML documentation applications, 624
Unified Modeling Language (UML), 595
OODE method, 167
TMN MIB framework, 388

Unix operating system, 621
unmarshaling, 131
unreliable failure detectors, 289
usage relation, 596
USA-NBS reference model, 25, 87
use relationship, 441
User Interface framework, PRM framework, 145–146, 154–155
user interfaces, 1
user manual, 620

V
validity condition, 306–307
video on demand, 437
   using MultiTEL, 448–450
virtual inheritance, 402
virtual reality, 227
Virtual Reality Modeling Language (VRML), for OOPM framework, 602, 608, 612
Visibility and Communication between Control Modules pattern (G++), 25–27

VisiBroker, as middleware integration framework, 616
VisualAge Java, 624
VisualBasic, 621, 624
Visual C++, 624
Visual Café, 624
visual interfaces, 225
visual metaphors, use in OOPM, 592–593
visual tools, 624

W
Web. *See* World Wide Web
Web browsers, 339
WebFilter, 469
WebObjects, 381
Web servers, 339, 438. *See also* JAWS Adaptive Web Server framework
   patterns and frameworks with, 342–345
   pitfalls of software development, 341–342
   summary of optimization techniques, 370–375

WebSTONE v2.0, JAWS test with, 365–366
whitebox frameworks, 85, 617
whitebox reusability, 317–318
wide area networks (WANs), 231
wide area picture (WAP) database, 420
widgets, Amulet, 530, 540
Windows operating system, 621
WORKS project, 8
World Wide Web, 339. *See also* Web servers
   Web-based OOPM, 612
   Web filter application, 481–483
   Web sites with information on frameworks, 631

X
x-Kernel, 290